Lecture Notes in Artificial In

Edited by J. G. Carbonell and J. Siekma

Subseries of Lecture Notes in Computer Science

Yasubumi Sakakibara   Satoshi Kobayashi
Kengo Sato   Tetsuro Nishino
Etsuji Tomita (Eds.)

Grammatical Inference: Algorithms and Applications

8th International Colloquium, ICGI 2006
Tokyo, Japan, September 20-22, 2006
Proceedings

 Springer

Series Editors

Jaime G. Carbonell, Carnegie Mellon University, Pittsburgh, PA, USA
Jörg Siekmann, University of Saarland, Saarbrücken, Germany

Volume Editors

Yasubumi Sakakibara
Keio University, Yokohama, Japan
E-mail: yasu@bio.keio.ac.jp

Satoshi Kobayashi
University of Electro-Communications, Tokyo, Japan
E-mail: satoshi@cs.uec.ac.jp

Kengo Sato
National Institute of Advanced Industrial Science and Technology, Tokyo, Japan
E-mail: sato-kengo@aist.go.jp

Tetsuro Nishino
University of Electro-Communications, Tokyo, Japan
E-mail: nishino@ice.uec.ac.jp

Etsuji Tomita
University of Electro-Communications, Tokyo, Japan
E-mail: tomita@ice.uec.ac.jp

Library of Congress Control Number: 2006932583

CR Subject Classification (1998): I.2, F.4, F.3

LNCS Sublibrary: SL 7 – Artificial Intelligence

ISSN   0302-9743
ISBN-10   3-540-45264-8 Springer Berlin Heidelberg New York
ISBN-13   978-3-540-45264-5 Springer Berlin Heidelberg New York

Springer is a part of Springer Science+Business Media

springer.com

© Springer-Verlag Berlin Heidelberg 2006
Printed in Germany

Typesetting: Camera-ready by author, data conversion by Scientific Publishing Services, Chennai, India
Printed on acid-free paper   SPIN: 11872436   06/3142   5 4 3 2 1 0

Preface

The 8th International Colloquium on Grammatical Inference (ICGI 2006) was held at the University of Electro-Communications (UEC), Tokyo, Japan on September 20-22, 2006. ICGI 2006 was the eighth in a series of successful biennial international conferences in the area of grammatical inference. Previous meetings were held in Essex, UK; Alicante, Spain; Montpellier, France; Ames, Iowa, USA; Lisbon, Portugal; Amsterdam, Netherlands; Athens, Greece. ICGI 2006 was the first conference in this series to be held in Asia. This series of conferences seeks to provide a forum for presentation and discussion of original research papers on all aspects of grammatical inference.

Grammatical inference, the study of learning grammars from data, is an established research field in artificial intelligence, dating back to the 1960s and has been extensively addressed by researchers in automata theory, language acquisition, computational linguistics, machine learning, pattern recognition, computational learning theory and neural networks. ICGI 2006 successively emphasized on the multi-disciplinary nature of the research field and the diverse domains in which grammatical inference is being applied, such as natural language acquisition, computational biology, structural pattern recognition, information retrieval, Web mining, text processing, data compression and adaptive intelligent agents.

We received 44 high-quality papers from 14 countries around the world. The papers were reviewed by three reviewers. Based on the positive comments of the reviewers, 25 full papers were accepted. In addition, we decided to accept 8 short papers for poster presentation. Short papers appear as two-page extended abstracts in a separate section of this volume. The topics of the accepted papers vary from theoretical results of learning algorithms to innovative applications of grammatical inference, and from learning several interesting classes of formal grammars to applications to natural language processing.

In parallel to the submission and reviewing of research papers, a machine translation competition, named Tenjinno, took place. In a separate paper in this volume, the organizers of the competition report on the peculiarities of such an endeavor and some interesting theoretical findings to which they have been led. Last but not least, we were honored by the contributions of our two invited speakers, Yuji Matsumoto, from Nara Institute of Science and Technology, Japan, and Jean-Philippe Vert, from Ecole des Mines de Paris, France. Both invited speakers provided interesting talks on the topics of natural language processing and bioinformatics, and we hope both talks invoked potential applications of grammatical inference.

The editors would like to acknowledge the contribution of the conference's Program Committee and the Additional Reviewers in reviewing the submitted papers and thank the Organizing Committee for their invaluable help in organizing the conference. Particularly, we would like to thank Colin de la Higuera, Menno van Zaannen, Bradford Starkie, and Dominique Estival for their additional voluntary service to the grammatical inference community, through this conference. We would also like to acknowledge the use of the Cyberchair software, from Borbala online conference services, in the submission and reviewing process. Finally, we are grateful for the generous support and sponsorship of the conference by the University of Electro-Communications, the PASCAL, Inoue foundation for Science, SIG Mathematical Modeling and Problem Solving in Information Processing Society of Japan and New Horizons in Computing (NHC) (Scientific Research on Priority Areas, supported by MEXT, Japan).

September 2006

Yasubumi Sakakibara
Satoshi Kobayashi
Kengo Sato
Tetsuro Nishino
Etsuji Tomita

Organization

Conference Chair

Etsuji Tomita   University of Electro-Communications, Japan

Technical Program Committee Co-chairs

Yasubumi Sakakibara   Keio University, Japan
Satoshi Kobayashi   University of Electro-Communications, Japan

Technical Program Committee

Naoki Abe	IBM Thomas J. Watson Research Center, USA
Pieter Adriaans	Perot Systems Corporation/University of Amsterdam, Netherlands
Dana Angluin	Yale University, USA
Hiroki Arimura	Hokkaido University, Japan
Mitra Basu	City University of New York, USA
François Coste	Symbiose, INRIA/IRISA, France
Pierre Dupont	University of Louvain, Belgium
Henning Fernau	University of Hertfordshire, UK
Colin de la Higuera	EURISE, Univ. de St. Etienne, France
Vasant Honavar	Iowa State University, USA
Chih-Jen Lin	National Taiwan University, Taiwan
Laurent Miclet	ENSSAT, Lannion, France
Gopalakrishnaswamy Nagaraja	Indian Institute of Technology, India
Katsuhiko Nakamura	Tokyo Denki University, Japan
Jacques Nicolas	IRISA, France
Tim Oates	University of Maryland Baltimore County, USA
Arlindo Oliveira	Lisbon Technical University, Portugal
Jose Oncina Carratala	Universidad de Alicante, Spain
Georgios Paliouras	Inst. of Informatics and Telecommunications, NCSR , Greece
Rajesh Parekh	Yahoo!, USA
Kengo Sato	CBRC, NAIST, Japan
Giora Slutzki	Iowa State University, USA
Bradford Starkie	Starkie Enterprise, Australia
Eiji Takimoto	Tohoku University, Japan
Menno van Zaanen	Universiteit van Amsterdam, Netherlands
Enrique Vidal	Universidad Politecnica de Valencia, Spain
Osamu Watanabe	Tokyo Institute of Technology, Japan
Thomas Zeugmann	Hokkaido University, Japan

Additional Reviewers

T. Armstrong	J.-C. Janodet	J. Poland
L. Becerra-Bonache	H.-U. Krieger	J. M. Vilar
M. Bugalho	J. A. Laxminarayana	
D. Eisenstat	A. Martins	

Organizing Committee Chair

Tetsuro Nishino   University of Electro-Communications, Japan

Organizing Committee

Colin de la Higuera   EURISE, Univ. de St. Etienne, France
Kazuhiro Hotta   University of Electro-Communications, Japan
Satoshi Kobayashi   University of Electro-Communications, Japan
Yoichi Motomura   National Institute of Advanced Industrial
                          Science and Technology, Japan
Katsuhiko Nakamura   Tokyo Denki University, Japan
Seiya Okubo   University of Electro-Communications, Japan
Yasuhiro Tajima   Tokyo University of Agriculture and
                          Technology, Japan
Haruhisa Takahashi   University of Electro-Communications, Japan
Jun Tarui   University of Electro-Communications, Japan
Mitsuo Wakatsuki   University of Electro-Communications, Japan

Sponsoring Institutions

University of Electro-Communications   UEC Tokyo

PASCAL Network

Inoue Foundation for Science

SIG Mathematical Modeling and Problem Solving in Information Processing Society of Japan

New Horizons in Computing (NHC) (Scientific Research on Priority Areas, supported by MEXT, Japan)

Table of Contents

Poster Papers

Parsing Without Grammar Rules

Yuji Matsumoto

Graduate School of Information Science
Nara Institute of Science and Technology
Takayama, Ikoma, Nara 630-0192 Japan
matsu@is.naist.jp

Abstract. In this article, we present and contrast recent statistical approaches to word dependency parsing and lexicalized formalisms for grammar and semantics. We then consider the possibility of integrating those two extreme ideas, which leads to fully lexicalized parsing without any syntactic grammar rules.

Keywords: dependency parsing, lexicalized grammar, lexical semantics.

1 Introduction

Traditional syntactic analysis of natural languages mainly assumes a set of phrase structure grammar rules possibly with some syntactic information in the lexicon such as case frames. Then, parsing is done with phrase structure parsing algorithms such as Chart Parsing or CKY Parsing algorithms. In contrast, recent grammar formalisms, such as HPSG (Head-driven Phrase Structure Grammar)[15] and LTAG (Lexicalized Tree Adjoining Grammar)[14], originating from phrase structure-style grammars, are extremely lexicalized (termed radical lexicalism), and now have only a few grammar rules (or grammar schemes). In such systems, most of syntactic information is stored in lexical entries. On the other hand, lexical semantic theories such as LCS (Lexical Conceptual Structure)[6] and GL (Generative Lexicon)[13] propose to assume very rich semantic information in lexical entries in a language, and give a systematic explanation of syntactic ambiguities or syntactic alternation that are dealt with in traditional phrase structure-based analysis by describing multiple frames corresponding to each of possilbe syntactic constructions. Furthermore, constructions that are not assumed in the case frames of a word may appear in real language use. Construction grammar approaches to language[5][12] aim to explain such phenomena.

Recent trend of natural language parsing moved to corpus-based research, where a large scale parsed corpus is used to estimate statistical properties of language constructions. Early research in this direction[1][3] used to use phrase structure trees in their analysis as they base their syntactic structure on Penn Treebank[8]. More recently, word dependency parsing is getting larger attention [9][11][16] because of its simplicity and easiness in adaptability to various languages (e.g., this year's CoNLL shared task was multi-lingual dependency parsing[1]).

---

[1] http://nextens.uvt.nl/~conll/

Y. Sakakibara et al. (Eds.): ICGI 2006, LNAI 4201, pp. 1–6, 2006.

In this paper, we introduce those recent trends in lexicalism in both parsing domain and grammar formalisms, and discuss possible integration of these two extreme ideas.

2   Word Dependency Parsing

There is a traditional syntactic analysis for Japanese sentences, named bunsetsu dependency analysis. A bunsetsu means a base Japanese phrase consisting of content words followed by functional words/functional inflection form. The syntactic structure of a Japanese sentence can be represented by dependency relation between bunsetsu's. Only the conditions of this dependency are quite simple that dependency trees must be connected, single headed, acyclic and projective (no-crossing). An interesting characteristics of Japanese dependency structure is that any bunsetsu (except the right most one) modifies one of the bunsetsu's on its right side because Japanese is a head-final language. This makes it easy to construct a bunsetsu dependency parsing in a very simple way, and we proposed a Japanese deterministic dependency parser[7] based on Support Vector Machines.

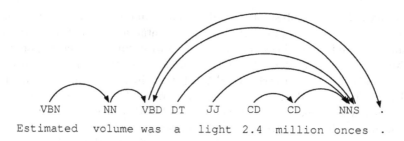

Fig. 1. An example of English projective dependency tree

We then extended this idea into a Shift-Reduce style depterministic parsing, and applied it to English and Chinese parsing[2][16]. Fig. 1 shows an example of English word dependency tree. The examples shown in this paper are unlabeled trees, while some dependency trees assume their edges to be labeled with something like SUBJ, OBJ, etc. In our approach, dependency relationship (left-direction, right-direction, or none) between two adjacent nodes (words) is deterministically decided as a classification task learned by Support Vector Machines, and the parsing is done from bottom to top. Because of robust learning ability of SVMs, the current parser can achieve more than 90% accuracy in practical English sentence analysis (for sentences in Penn Treebank). Nivre et al[11] took a similar approach to dependency tree analysis.

This year's CoNLL (Conference on Natural Language Learning) shared task was Multi-lingual Dependency Parsing, and the target was to built a corpus-based language independent dependecy parser and to test it with thirteen languages provided by the conference organizer. In many of languages there are non-projective sentences, in which some dependency relations cross each other (Fig. 2 shows one of such examples). This kind of sentences cannot be formulated by phrase structure grammars and are difficult to parse with the parsing algorithms originally designed for phrase structure grammars.

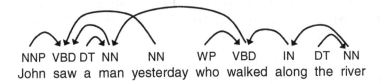

Fig. 2. An example of English non-projective dependency tree

Recent McDonald et al's work[10] showed that non-projected dependency analysis is easily formulated as a search problem for the maximum cost spanning tree.

Since resolution of syntactic ambiguity has been the most difficult problem in parsing natural language sentences, the advantage of those corpus-based or statistical approaches is its ability of disambiguation, that is, they produce the most plausible parse tree considering all the dependency relation appeared in the training corpus.

3   Lexicalized Grammars and Lexical Semantic Thoeries

3.1   Lexicalized Grammars and Dependency Parsing

As we explained in Introduction, recent lexicalized grammar formalisms put most of the grammatical information to the lexicon. In HPSG, each predicate (a verb, an adjective or an auxiliary verb) has argument structure that describes information of its complements. There are only a few grammar schemes such as head complement rule, head adjunct rule, head specifier rule, and so on, all of which can be specified as a binary tree where either one of them plays a role of syntactic head. In LTAG, every lexical entry is associated with a tree that shows its syntactic property. There are only two grammar rules or attachment rules, substitution and adjoining. The application of these rules can be depicted as a derivation tree, where one tree structure is attached to another with either of two attachment rules. In both of HPSG and LTAG, basic operations can be defined as a binary construction of a tree, which seems to have close relationship with word dependency structure. Although there may be some discrepancy between the binary relations in different systems, dependency parsing will give a good control information in syntactic parsing based on lexicalized grammar formalisms.

3.2   Lexical Semantics and Dependency Parsing

While lexical semantics theories such as Lexical Conceptual Structure[6] and Generative Lexicon[13] do not specify syntactic structure of a language, they define semantic relationship between a word and other constituents in a sentence and indirectly assume syntactic construction of a sentence. In LCS, for example, verbs are categorized according to their inner structure, which is described by a small number of primitive predicates such as ACT, GO, BECOME, etc. Though there are lots of derivative versions of LCS and they employ different sets of primitives and different way of describing the semantic structure, action verbs, state-change verbs, causative verbs and creation verbs are described in something like the following forms:

- Action verbs: [x ACT on y]
- State-change verbs: [BECOME [y BE at z]]
- Causative verbs: [[x ACT (on y)] CAUSE [BECOME [y BE at z]]]
- Creation verbs: [[x ACT (on y′)] CAUSE [BECOME [y BE at z]]]

In those representation, upper case terms, ACT, BECOME, BE and CAUSE stand for event types of action, state change, state and causality relation between two events. Lower case alphabets such as x, y and z stand for arguments of the verb, which are mapped to syntactic constituents such as a subject and an object in a systematic manner named linking rules[4]. The more interesting is that specific types of adjuncts (prepositional phrases or adverbs) select some specific event in the structure. For example, those adjuncts that represent "manner" or "tools" attach to ACTION event, those that represent "cause" attach to BECOME event and those that represent "results" or "state" attach to STATE event. By having such information in lexical entries, integration of dependency parsing and construction of semantic structure should work in a complementary manner, and make it possible to achieve more accurate dependency parsing as well as systematic explanation of dependency relations.

In contrast with LCS, Generative Lexicon and Construction Grammar[5] propose generative or self-extending functions in their formalisms. Let us consider the following examples:

1. He began the book.
2. He sneezed a handkerchief off the table.

In the former example, "begin" is assumed to take an event noun for its object (such as "to read a book" or "reading a book"), and the sentence is analyzed as ungrammatical if the case frame of the verb strictly selects its complements. Generative Lexicon proposes three generative operations that dynamically modifies lexical structure so as to obtain appropriate interpretation of sentences. In this example, "a book" is coerced to change its structure into an eventive noun with the help of its inner structure called Qualia Structure, which contains Telic and Agentive structures that describe how a book is used and how a book is produced. The latter example itself looks ungrammatical since "sneeze" is an intransitive verb and does not usually take an object. However, this kind of productive use is often seen in real language. Construction Grammar treats such productive use of language and introduces an idea that construction gives some additional semantics to a sentence.

Those kind of seemingly ungrammatical constructions are hardly manageable by strictly constaint-based grammar formalisms. In contrast, statistical dependency parsing is quite robust in analyzing such sentences since statistically those constructions form typical syntactic structures. So, also in this case, using statistical dependency parsing as the control mechanism and using lexical semantic structure for explaining semantic relationship between two attached constituents will achieve both syntactically and semantically robust sentence analysis.

4   Final Remarks

Although we proposed integration of statistical word dependency parsing and lexicalized formalisms of grammar and semantics, this is at the planning stage. We have achieved very good performance in word dependency parsing, but still we have lots of phenomena to be solved properly. Our colleagues are now developing a LCS lexicon of Japanese verbs, and this will make it possible to conduct a large scale integiration of statistical dependency parsing and a lexical semantics theory.

References

1. Charniak, E., "A Maximum-Entropy-Inspired Parser," 1st Meeting of the North American Chapter of the Association for Computational Linguistics, pp.132-139, 2000.
2. Cheng, Y., Asahara, M., Matsumoto, Y., "Deterministic Dependency Structure Analyzer for Chinese," The First International Joint Conference on Natural Language Processing, pp.135-140, 2004.
3. Collins, M., "Three Generative, Lexicalised Models for Statistical Parsing," 35th Annual Meeting of the Association for Computational Linguistics and 8th Conference of the European Chapter of the Association for Computational Linguistics, pp.16-23, 1997.
4. Davis, A.R.(ed.): Linking by Types in the Heirarchical Lexicon, CSLI Publications, 2001.
5. Goldberg, A.E.: Constructions: A Construction Grammar Approach to Argument Structure, The University Chicago Press, 1995.
6. Jackendoff, R.: Semantic Structures, Current Studies in Linguistics 18, The MIT Press, 1990.
7. Kudo, T., Matsumoto, Y., "Japanese Dependency Analysis using Cascaded Chunking," 6th Conference on Natural Language Learning, pp.63-69, 2002.
8. Marcus, M.P., Santorini, B., Marcinkiewicz, M.A., "Building a Large Annotated Corpus of English:The Penn Treebank," Computational Linguistics, Vol.19, No.2, pp.313-330, 1993.
9. McDonald, R.,Crammer, K., Pereira, F., "Online Large-Margin Training of Dependency Parsers," 43rd Annual Meeting of the Association for Computational Linguistics: Proceedings of the Conference, pp.91-98, 2005.
10. McDonald, R., Pereira, F., Hajic, J., "Non-Projective Dependency Parsing using Spanning Tree Algorithms," HLT-EMNLP, 2005.

11. Nivre, J., Scholz, M., "Deterministic Dependency Parsing of English Text," 20th International Conference on Computational Linguistics, pp.64-70, 2004.
12. Östman, J-O., Fried, M: Construction Grammars: Cognitive Grounding and Theoretical Extensions, John Benjamins Publishing Company, 2005.
13. Pustejovsky, J.: The Generative Lexicon, The MIT Press, 1995.
14. Rambow, O.(eds.): Tree Adjoining Grammars: Formalisms, Linguistic Analysis and Processing, CSLI Lecture Notes, No.107, CSLI Publications, 2000.
15. Sag, I.A., Wasow, T., Bender, E.M.(eds.): Syntactic Theory: A Formal Introduction, CSLI Lecture Notes, No.152, CSLI Publications, 2003.
16. Yamada, H., Matsumoto, Y., "Statistical Dependency Analysis with Support Vector Machines," 8th International Workshop on Parsing Technologies, pp.195-206, 2003.

Classification of Biological Sequences with Kernel Methods

Jean-Philippe Vert

Centre for Computational Biology, Ecole des Mines de Paris
35 rue Saint-Honoré, 77300 Fontainebleau, France
Jean-Philippe.Vert@ensmp.fr

Abstract. We survey the foundations of kernel methods and the recent developments of kernels for variable-length strings, in the context of biological sequence analysis.

1   Introduction

The various genome sequencing projects have produced and continue to produce at a fast rate huge amounts of sequence data, including genomes, genes, and proteins sequences. The urgent need for methods to automatically process, segment, annotate and classify these various biological sequences has triggered the fast development of numerous algorithms for strings. In this context, support vector machines and kernel methods are increasingly popular machine learning algorithms for biological sequence processing [1]. These methods provide a coherent mathematical and computational framework to embed strings in Hilbert spaces and apply powerful statistical analysis in the resulting Hilbert spaces. The embedding is performed only implicitly, thanks to the use of a so-called kernel function for variable-length strings, and once the embedding is done the algorithms used for tasks such as supervised classification or regression are generic. The last decade has witnessed the development of a number of ingenious solutions to the problem of embedding biological sequences in a Hilbert space through kernel functions, which we review in this paper. Although the focus is on biological sequences, interesting developments have also occurred and continue to emerge for the processing of strings in different contexts (e.g., [2]) and more generally for analysis of structured data (e.g., [3]).

2   Kernels and Kernel Methods

In this section we review basic material about positive definite kernels and kernel methods. The interested reader is referred to [4,5] and references therein for further details.

2.1   Positive Definite Kernels

Kernel methods [4] encompass a variety of algorithms for data analysis and machine learning, including the popular support vector machine (SVM) [6], that

Y. Sakakibara et al. (Eds.): ICGI 2006, LNAI 4201, pp. 7–18, 2006.

share in common the use of positive definite (p.d.) kernel to represent data. Formally, a p.d. kernel K over a space of data $\mathcal{X}$ (e.g., the set of finite-length strings over an alphabet) is a function $K : \mathcal{X} \times \mathcal{X} \to \mathbb{R}$ that is symmetric (i.e., $K(x, y) = K(y, x)$ for any $x, y \in \mathcal{X}$) and positive definite in the sense that for any $n \in \mathbb{N}$, any $(a_1, \ldots, a_n) \in \mathbb{R}^n$ and any $(x_1, \ldots, x_n) \in \mathcal{X}^n$, the following holds:

$$\sum_{i,j=1}^{n} a_i a_j K(x_i, x_j) \geq 0.$$

The simplest p.d. kernel over finite dimensional vectors ($\mathcal{X} = \mathbb{R}^n$) is the Euclidean inner product $K(x, y) = x^\top y$. More generally, Aronszajn proved in the 1950's that, without any assumption of the set $\mathcal{X}$, any p.d. kernel can be seen as an inner product after some embedding of $\mathcal{X}$ into a Hilbert space:

Theorem 1 (Aronszajn, 1950). *K is a p.d. kernel on the set $\mathcal{X}$ if and only if there exists a Hilbert space $\mathcal{H}$ and a mapping*

$$\Phi : \mathcal{X} \mapsto \mathcal{H} \, ,$$

such that, for any x, x' in $\mathcal{X}$:

$$K(x, x') = \Phi(x)^\top \Phi(x') \, .$$

Together with this characterization of kernels as inner product came the construction of a Hilbert space of functions associated with each p.d. kernel, called the reproducing kernel Hilbert space (RKHS). The RKHS $\mathcal{H}$ associated with a kernel K contains all functions of the form $f(x) = \sum_{i=1}^{n} \alpha_i K(x_i, x)$ and their pointwise limits, where n ranges over $\mathbb{N}$, the x_i's are elements of $\mathcal{X}$ and the α_i's a real numbers. The norm of such a function in the RKHS is given by:

$$\|f\|_{RKHS}^2 = \sum_{i=1}^{n} \sum_{j=1}^{n} \alpha_i \alpha_j K(x_i, x_j). \tag{1}$$

As an example, in the case $\mathcal{X} = \mathbb{R}^n$, the RKHS of the linear kernel $K(x, x') = x^\top x'$ is the set of linear functions $f_w(x) = w^\top x$, where $w \in \mathbb{R}^n$, and norm of a linear function satisfies $\|f_w\|_{RKHS} = \|w\|$.

To summarize, the construction of a p.d. kernel K over any data space $\mathcal{X}$ is equivalent to:

- Implicitly embedding $\mathcal{X}$ into a Hilbert space, the distance between two points $x, x' \in \mathcal{X}$ in the embedding being given by:

$$d_K(x, x') = \sqrt{K(x, x) + K(x', x') - 2K(x, x')} \, .$$

- Defining a Hilbert space of functions $f : \mathcal{X} \to \mathbb{R}$ where the norm of a function $f(x) = \sum_{i=1}^{n} \alpha_i K(x_i, x)$ is given by (1).

2.2 Kernel Methods

For simplicity we restrict ourselves to kernel methods for regression and pattern recognition, although other applications (e.g., dimensionality reduction or novelty detection) have been studied too [4]. We assume that the goal is to find a function $f : \mathcal{X} \to \mathbb{R}$ that assigns real number $y \in \mathbb{R}$ to any object $x \in \mathcal{X}$, given a training set of pairs (x_i, y_i), $i = 1, \ldots, n$ of object with known values. This framework encompasses many applications, e.g., predicting whether a biological sequence x belongs to a particular function family ($y = 1$) or not ($y = -1$), given a training set of sequences known to belong or not to the family. The classical approach to solve such a problem with kernel methods is to define a loss function $L : \mathbb{R} \times \mathbb{R} \to \mathbb{R}$, a p.d. kernel $K : \mathcal{X} \times \mathcal{X} \to \mathbb{R}$, and to solve the following optimization problem in the RKHS $\mathcal{H}$ associated with K:

$$\min_{f \in \mathcal{H}} \frac{1}{n} \sum_{i=1}^{n} L(y_i, f(x_i)) + \lambda \|f\|_{RKHS}^2 , \qquad (2)$$

where λ is a parameter of the algorithm. The objective function to be minimized over $\mathcal{H}$ is a sum of two terms. The first term measures the fitness of the function f to the data (as the average L-loss between y_i and $f(x_i)$ over the training set), while the second favors functions f with small RKHS norm. As we will see in the next section, having a small RKHS norm is related to being smooth over $\mathcal{X}$, so the objective of the minimization problem is to find a smooth function that fits the data, and λ controls the trade-off between these two requirements. Various choices of loss function L give rise to well-known algorithms, such as support vector machines ($L(y, y') = \max(0, 1 - yy')$), kernel logistic regression ($L(y, y') = \log(1 + \exp(-yy'))$) or kernel ridge regression ($L(y, y') = (y - y')^2$). While the minimization of (2) is primarily motivated by statistical considerations about the possibility to infer a function from a finite number of observations [6], this optimization problem over a potentially infinite-dimensional function space also has the very good practical property that it can usually be solved efficiently. Indeed it always boils down to a finite-dimensional optimization problem of dimension at most n, the number of training points, thanks to a theorem known as the representer theorem, initially proved in the context of splines [7].

2.3 On the Choice of Kernels

A crucial property of kernel methods is their ability to process virtually any types of data as long as a p.d. kernel can be defined over the set of data considered. The construction of a kernel for a specific type of data (e.g., strings) and a specific application (e.g., prediction of functional classes for protein sequences) can be thought of as a modeling phase, where prior knowledge can help define some form of optimal embedding of the data into a Hilbert space; the power of modern statistical algorithms such as SVM comes then at no additional cost. Following this strategy a number of p.d. kernels for various types of data have flourished in the last decade, often trying to incorporate prior knowledge in the kernel.

Choosing a kernel for a particular application can be seen as defining (virtually) an embedding of the space of data $\mathcal{X}$ into a Hilbert space (by Theorem 1), or as defining a Hilbert space of function over $\mathcal{X}$ (its RKHS). Both views are related by the following simple inequality valid for any function f in the RKHS of the kernel K and any data x and x':

$$|f(x) - f(x')| \leq ||f||_{RKHS} \times d_K(x, x').$$

Intuitively, this shows that if f has a small norm in the RKHS, then it varies slowly between points close to each other with respect to the geometry defined by the embedding. By (2) we know that kernel methods therefore look in priority for smooth function with respect to norm in the embedding. When no obvious vector embedding of the data is available (e.g., for strings), this provides a useful alternative guidelines for kernel design: define a kernel such that the function to be inferred varies smoothly with respect to the distance defined by the kernel.

3 Kernels for Biological Sequences

Many problems in computational biology involve sequences of variable lengths. For example, the automatic functional or structural annotation of genes found in sequenced genomes requires the processing of amino-acid sequences with no fixed length. Learning from variable-length sequences is a challenging problem for most classical statistical procedures, because there is no natural way to transform a variable-length string into a vector. For kernel methods, this issue boils down to the problem of defining kernels for variable-length strings, a topic that has deserved a lot of attention in the last few years and has given rise to a variety of ingenious solutions summarized in this section.

3.1 Explicit Vector Embedding

The most common approach to make a kernel for strings, as for many other types of data, is to design explicitly a set of numerical features that can be extracted from strings, and then to form a kernel as a dot product between the resulting feature vectors. As an example, [8] represent a sequence by the vector of counts of occurrences of all possible k-mers in the sequence, for a given integer k, effectively resulting in a vector of dimension a^k, where a is the size of the alphabet. As an example, the sequence $AACGTCACGAA$ over the alphabet (A, C, G, T) is represented by the 16-dimensional vector $(2, 2, 0, 0, 1, 0, 2, 0, 1, 0, 0, 1, 0, 1, 0, 0)$ for $k = 2$, where the dimensions are the counts of occurrences of each 2-mer $AA, AC, ..., TG, TT$ lexicographically ordered. The resulting spectrum kernel between this sequence and the sequence $ACGAAA$, defined as the linear product between the two 16-dimensional representation vectors, is equal to 9. It should be noted that although the number of possible k-mers easily reaches the order of several thousands as soon as k is equal to 3 or 4, classification of sequences by SVM in this high-dimensional space results in fairly good results. A major advantage of the spectrum kernel is its fast computation; indeed, the set of k-mers appearing in a given sequence can be indexed in linear time in a trie structure, and the inner product between two vectors is linear with respect to the non-zero coordinates, i.e., at most linear in the total lengths of the sequences. Several variants to the basic spectrum kernel have also been proposed, including for example kernels based on counts of k-mers appearing with up to m mismatches in the sequences [9].

Another natural approach to vector representation for variable-length strings is to replace each letter by one or several numerical features, such as physico-chemical properties of amino-acids, and then to extract features from the resulting variable-length numerical time series using classical signal processing techniques such as Fourier transforms [10] or autocorrelation analysis [11]. For example, if $h_1, \ldots, h_n$ denote n numerical features associated to the successive letters of a sequence of length n, then the autocorrelation function r_j for a given $j > 0$ is defined by

$$r_j = \frac{1}{n-j} \sum_{i=1}^{n-j} h_i h_{i+j}.$$

One can them keep a fixed numbers of these coefficients, for example $r_1, \ldots, r_J$, and create a J-dimensional vector to represent each sequence.

Finally, another popular approach to design features and therefore kernels for biological sequences is to "project" them onto a fixed dictionary of sequences or motifs, using classical similarity measures, and to use the resulting vector of similarities as feature vector. For example, [12] represent each sequence by a 10,000-dimensional vector indicating the presence of 10,000 motifs of the BLOCKS database; similarly, [13] use a vector that indicates the presence or absence of about 500,000 motifs in the eMOTIF database, requiring the use of a trie structure to compute efficiently the kernel without explicitly storing the 500,000 features; and [14] represent each sequence by a vector of sequence similarities with a fixed set of sequences.

3.2 Using Stochastic Models

A completely different approach for kernel design is to derive them from probabilistic models. Indeed, before the interest on string kernels grew, a number of ingenious probabilistic models had been defined to represent biological sequences or families of sequences, including for example Markov and hidden Markov models for protein sequences, or stochastic context-free grammars for RNA sequences [15]. Several authors have therefore explored the possibility to use such models to make kernels, starting with the seminal work of [16] that introduced the *Fisher kernel*. The Fisher kernel is a general method to extract a fixed number of features from any data x for which a parametric probabilistic model P_θ is defined. Here, θ represents a continuous d-dimensional vector of parameters for the probabilistic model, such as transition and emission probabilities for a hidden Markov model, and each P_θ is a probability distribution. Once a particular parameter θ_0 is chosen to fit a given set of objects, for example by maximum likelihood, then a d-dimensional feature vector for each individual object x can be extracted by taking the gradient in the parameter space of the log-likelihood of the point:

$$\phi(x) = \nabla_\theta \log P_\theta(x).$$

The intuitive interpretation of this feature vector, usually referred to as the Fisher score in statistics, is that it represents how changes in the d parameters affect the likelihood of the point x. In other word, one feature is extracted for each parameter of the model; the particularities of the data point are seen from the eyes of the parameters of the probabilistic model. The Fisher kernel is then obtained as the dot product of these d-dimensional vectors, eventually multiplied by the inverse of the Fisher information matrix to render it independent of the parametrization of the model.

A second line of thoughts to make a kernel out of a parametric probabilistic model is to use the concept of mutual information kernels [17], that is, kernels of the form:

$$K(x, x') = \int P_\theta(x) P_\theta(x') d\mu(\theta),$$

where $d\mu$ is a prior distribution on the parameter space. Here, the features correspond to the likelihoods of the objects under all distributions of the probabilistic model; objects are considered similar when they have large likelihoods under similar distributions. An important difference with the kernels seen so far is that here, no explicit extraction of finite-dimensional vectors can be performed. Hence for practical applications one must chose probabilistic models that allow the computation of the integral above. This was carried by [18] who present a family of variable-length Markov models for strings and an algorithm to perform the integral over parameters and models in the same time, resulting in a string kernel with linear complexity in time and memory with respect to the total length of the sequences. A further extension to this approach to the more general and abstract setting of kernels for finite measures was proposed in [19], paving the way to further developments of kernels for complex objects.

Alternatively, many probabilistic models for biological sequences, such as hidden Markov models, involve a hidden variable that is marginalized over to obtain the probability of a sequence, i.e., can be written as

$$P(x) = \sum_h P(x, h).$$

For such distributions, [20] introduced the notion of *marginalized kernel*, obtained by marginalizing a kernel for the complete variable over the hidden variable. More precisely, assuming that a kernel for objects of the form (x, h) is defined, the marginalized kernel for observed objects x is given by

$$K(x, x') = \sum_{h, h'} K\left((x, h), (x', h')\right) P(h|x) P(h'|x').$$

In order to motivate this definition with a simple example, let us consider a hidden Markov model with two possible hidden states, to model sequences with two possible regimes, such as introns/exons in eukaryotic genes. In that case the hidden variable corresponding to a sequence x of length n is a binary sequence h of length n describing the states along the sequence. For two sequences x and x', if the correct hidden states h and h' were known, such as the correct decomposition into introns and exons, then it would make sense to define a kernel $K\left((x,h),(x',h')\right)$ taking into account the specific decomposition of the sequences into two regimes; for example, the kernel for complete data could be a spectrum kernel restricted to the exons, i.e., to positions with a particular state. Because the actual hidden states are not known in practice, the marginalization over the hidden state of this kernel using an adequate probabilistic model can be interpreted as an attempt to apply the kernel for complete data by guessing the hidden variables. As for the covariance kernel, marginalized kernels can often not be expressed as inner products between feature vectors, and require computational tricks to be computed. Several beautiful examples of such kernels for various probabilistic models have been worked out, including hidden Markov models for sequences [20,21], stochastic context-free grammars for RNA sequences [22], or random walk models on graphs for molecular structures [23].

3.3   Using Sequence Convolution and Alignment

Following a different line of thought, [24] introduced the concept of *convolution kernels* for objects that can be decomposed into subparts, such as sequences or trees. For example, the concatenation of two strings x_1 and x_2 results in another string $x = x_1 x_2$. If two initial string kernels K_1 and K_2 are chosen, then a new string kernel is obtained by convolution of the initial kernels following the equation:

$$K(x,x') = \sum_{x=x_1 x_2, x'=x_1' x_2'} K_1(x_1, x_1') K_2(x_2, x_2').$$

Here the sum is over all possible decompositions of x and x' into two concatenated subsequences. The rational behind this approach is that it allows the combination of different kernels adapted to different parts of the sequences, such as introns/exons or gaps/aligned residues in alignment, without knowing the exact segmentation of the sequences. Besides proving that the convolution of two kernels is a valid kernel, [24] gives several examples of convolution kernels relevant for biological sequences; for example, he shows that the joint probability $P(x,x')$ of two sequences under a pair HMM model is a valid kernel, under mild assumptions. This work is extended by [25,26] where a valid convolution kernel based on the alignment of two sequences is proposed. This kernel, named *local alignment kernel*, is a close relative of the widely used Smith-Waterman local alignment score [27]. It can be implemented with a complexity of the order of $|x| \times |x'|$, where $|x|$ is the length of sequence x, using for example the weighted finite-state transducer shown in Figure 1. We note that similar attempts to construct kernels using alignments were proposed in the field of language processing with the concept of dynamic time-warping kernels [28], that however lack positive definitiveness.

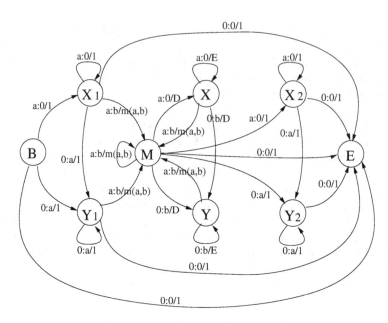

Fig. 1. A weighted finite-state transducer to compute the local alignment kernel. (from [25])

4   Application

These kernels for variable-length sequences have been widely applied, often in combination with SVM, to various classification tasks in computational biology. Examples including the prediction of protein structural or functional classes from their primary sequence [29,16,25,30,31], the prediction of the subcellular localization of proteins [32,33,34], the classification of transfer RNA [22] and non-coding RNA [35], the prediction of pseudo-exons and alternatively spliced exons [36,37], the separation of mixed plant-pathogen EST collections [38], the classification of mammalian viral genomes [39], or the prediction of ribosomal proteins [40].

In order to illustrate the influence of the kernel choice let us consider a benchmark experiment designed by [16] for remote homology detection. This benchmark is a series of 54 binary classification problems, where each problem amounts to recognize the super-family of a family of protein sequences. Two proteins are in the same super-family if they descend from a common ancestor protein and have kept a similar structure and function. The difficulty of the benchmark is that the sequences used to train a model for a given super-family are only remote homologs to the sequences tested, i.e., they share very little sequence similarity at first sight (although they share by definition a similar 3D structure). The performance on each binary classification problem is assessed in terms of the ROC50 curve of true positives as a function of false positives, up to the first 50 false positives, when the classification threshold is varied, and more precisely in terms of area under the ROC50 curve that varies between 0 (no true positive in the first 50 positive predicted) and 1 (perfect classification). Figure 2 shows the performance of a support vector machine with four different kernels: the Fisher kernel [16], mismatch kernel [9], pairwise kernel [14] and local alignment kernel [25,26]. We observe significant differences between the performances of the different kernels, highlighting the influence of the kernel in the final performance of the algorithm. In this particular case, the most relevant biological prior knowledge about the problem that can be used is that, by definition, proteins belong to the same superfamily if they are evolutionary related. Not surprisingly, the best performing kernel is the local alignment kernel that attempts to define an embedding where distances between sequences approximate their evolutionary distances.

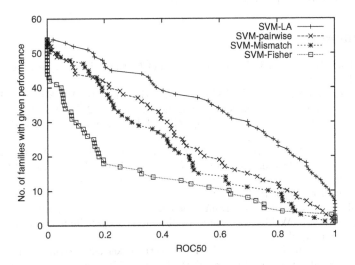

Fig. 2. Performance of support vector machines with four different kernels on the remote homology benchmark (from [25])

5   Conclusion

This short review of kernels developed for the purpose of biological sequence classification, besides highlighting the dynamism of research in kernel methods resulting from practical needs in computational biology, naturally raises the practical question of which kernel to use for a given application. Although no clear answer has emerged yet, some lessons can be learned from early studies. First, there is certainly no kernel universally better than others, and the choice of kernel should depend on the targeted application. Intuitively, a kernel for a classification task is likely to work well if it is based on features relevant to the task; for example, a kernel based on sequence alignments, such as the local alignment kernel, gives excellent results on remote homology detection problems, while a kernel based on the global content of sequences in short subsequences, such as the spectrum kernel, works well for the prediction of subcellular localization. Although some methods for systematic selection and combination of kernels are starting to emerge [41], empirical evaluation of different kernels on a given problem seems to be the most common way to chose a kernel. Another important point to notice, besides the classification accuracy obtained with a kernel, is its computational cost. Indeed, practical applications often involve datasets of thousands or tenth of thousands of sequences, and the computational cost of a method can become a critical factor in this context, in particular in an online setting. The kernels presented above differ a lot in their computational cost, ranging from fast linear-time kernels like the spectrum kernel, to slower kernels like the quadratic-time local alignment kernel. The final choice of kernel for a given application often results from a trade-off between classification performance and computational burden.

References

1. Schölkopf, B., Tsuda, K., Vert, J.P.: Kernel Methods in Computational Biology. MIT Press (2004)
2. Lodhi, H., Saunders, C., Shawe-Taylor, J., Cristianini, N., Watkins, C.: Text classification using string kernels. J. Mach. Learn. Res. **2** (2002) 419–444
3. Gärtner, T., Lloyd, J., Flach, P.: Kernels and distances for structured data. Mach. Learn. **57**(3) (2004) 205–232
4. Schölkopf, B., Smola, A.J.: Learning with Kernels: Support Vector Machines, Regularization, Optimization, and Beyond. MIT Press, Cambridge, MA (2002)
5. Shawe-Taylor, J., Cristianini, N.: Kernel Methods for Pattern Analysis. Cambridge University Press (2004)
6. Vapnik, V.N.: Statistical Learning Theory. Wiley, New-York (1998)
7. Kimeldorf, G.S., Wahba, G.: Some results on Tchebycheffian spline functions. J. Math. Anal. Appl. **33** (1971) 82–95
8. Leslie, C., Eskin, E., Noble, W.: The spectrum kernel: a string kernel for SVM protein classification. In Altman, R.B., Dunker, A.K., Hunter, L., Lauerdale, K., Klein, T.E., eds.: Proceedings of the Pacific Symposium on Biocomputing 2002, World Scientific (2002) 564–575
9. Leslie, C.S., Eskin, E., Cohen, A., Weston, J., Noble, W.S.: Mismatch string kernels for discriminative protein classification. Bioinformatics **20**(4) (2004) 467–476
10. Wang, M., Yang, J., Liu, G.P., Xu, Z.J., Chou, K.C.: Weighted-support vector machines for predicting membrane protein types based on pseudo-amino acid composition. Protein Eng. Des. Sel. **17**(6) (2004) 509–516
11. Zhang, S.W., Pan, Q., Zhang, H.C., Zhang, Y.L., Wang, H.Y.: Classification of protein quaternary structure with support vector machine. Bioinformatics **19**(18) (2003) 2390–2396
12. Logan, B., Moreno, P., Suzek, B., Weng, Z., Kasif, S.: A Study of Remote Homology Detection. Technical Report CRL 2001/05, Compaq Cambridge Research laboratory (2001)
13. Ben-Hur, A., Brutlag, D.: Remote homology detection: a motif based approach. Bioinformatics **19**(Suppl. 1) (2003) i26–i33
14. Liao, L., Noble, W.: Combining Pairwise Sequence Similarity and Support Vector Machines for Detecting Remote Protein Evolutionary and Structural Relationships. J. Comput. Biol. **10**(6) (2003) 857–868

15. Durbin, R., Eddy, S., Krogh, A., Mitchison, G.: Biological Sequence Analysis: Probabilistic Models of Proteins and Nucleic Acids. Cambridge University Press (1998)
16. Jaakkola, T., Diekhans, M., Haussler, D.: A Discriminative Framework for Detecting Remote Protein Homologies. J. Comput. Biol. **7**(1,2) (2000) 95–114
17. Seeger, M.: Covariance Kernels from Bayesian Generative Models. In: Adv. Neural Inform. Process. Syst. Volume 14. (2002) 905–912
18. Cuturi, M., Vert, J.P.: The context-tree kernel for strings. Neural Network. **18**(4) (2005) 1111–1123
19. Cuturi, M., Vert, J.P.: Semigroup kernels on finite sets. In Saul, L.K., Weiss, Y., Bottou, L., eds.: Adv. Neural Inform. Process. Syst. Volume 17., MIT Press, Cambridge, MA (2005) 329–336
20. Tsuda, K., Kin, T., Asai, K.: Marginalized Kernels for Biological Sequences. Bioinformatics **18** (2002) S268–S275
21. Vert, J.P., Thurman, R., Noble, W.S.: Kernels for gene regulatory regions. In: Adv. Neural. Inform. Process Syst. (2006)
22. Kin, T., Tsuda, K., Asai, K.: Marginalized kernels for RNA sequence data analysis. In Lathtop, R., Nakai, K., Miyano, S., Takagi, T., Kanehisa, M., eds.: Genome Informatics 2002, Universal Academic Press (2002) 112–122
23. Kashima, H., Tsuda, K., Inokuchi, A.: Kernels for graphs. In Schölkopf, B., Tsuda, K., Vert, J., eds.: Kernel Methods in Computational Biology. MIT Press (2004) 155–170
24. Haussler, D.: Convolution Kernels on Discrete Structures. Technical Report UCSC-CRL-99-10, UC Santa Cruz (1999)
25. Vert, J.P., Saigo, H., Akutsu, T.: Local alignment kernels for biological sequences. In Schölkopf, B., Tsuda, K., Vert, J., eds.: Kernel Methods in Computational Biology. MIT Press (2004) 131–154
26. Saigo, H., Vert, J.P., Ueda, N., Akutsu, T.: Protein homology detection using string alignment kernels. Bioinformatics **20**(11) (2004) 1682–1689
27. Smith, T., Waterman, M.: Identification of common molecular subsequences. J. Mol. Biol. **147** (1981) 195–197
28. Shimodaira, H., Noma, K.I., Nakai, M., Sagayama, S.: Dynamic time-alignment kernel in support vector machine. In: Adv. Neural. Inform. Process Syst. (2001) 921–928
29. Ding, C., Dubchak, I.: Multi-class protein fold recognition using support vector machines and neural networks. Bioinformatics **17** (2001) 349–358
30. Karchin, R., Karplus, K., Haussler, D.: Classifying G-protein coupled receptors with support vector machines. Bioinformatics **18** (2002) 147–159
31. Cai, C., Wang, W., Sun, L., Chen, Y.: Protein function classification via support vector machine approach. Math. Biosci. **185**(2) (2003) 111–122
32. Hua, S., Sun, Z.: Support vector machine approach for protein subcellular localization prediction. Bioinformatics **17**(8) (2001) 721–728
33. Park, K.J., Kanehisa, M.: Prediction of protein subcellular locations by support vector machines using compositions of amino acids and amino acid pairs. Bioinformatics **19**(13) (2003) 1656–1663
34. Matsuda, A., Vert, J.P., Saigo, H., Ueda, N., Toh, H., Akutsu, T.: A novel representation of protein sequences for prediction of subcellular location using support vector machines. Protein Sci. **14**(11) (2005) 2804–2813
35. Karklin, Y., Meraz, R.F., Holbrook, S.R.: Classification of non-coding RNA using graph representations of secondary structure. Pac. Symp. Biocomput. (2005) 4–15

36. Zhang, X.H.F., Heller, K.A., Hefter, I., Leslie, C.S., Chasin, L.A.: Sequence Information for the Splicing of Human Pre-mRNA Identified by Support Vector Machine Classification. Genome Res. **13**(12) (2003) 2637–2650

37. Dror, G., Sorek, R., Shamir, R.: Accurate identification of alternatively spliced exons using support vector machine. Bioinformatics **21**(7) (2005) 897–901

38. Friedel, C.C., Jahn, K.H.V., Sommer, S., Rudd, S., Mewes, H.W., Tetko, I.V.: Support vector machines for separation of mixed plant-pathogen EST collections based on codon usage. Bioinformatics **21** (2005) 1383–1388

39. Rose, J.R., Turkett, W. H., J., Oroian, I.C., Laegreid, W.W., Keele, J.: Correlation of amino acid preference and mammalian viral genome type. Bioinformatics (2005)

40. Lin, K., Kuang, Y., Joseph, J.S., Kolatkar, P.R.: Conserved codon composition of ribosomal protein coding genes in Escherichia coli, Mycobacterium tuberculosis and Saccharomyces cerevisiae: lessons from supervised machine learning in functional genomics. Nucl. Acids Res. **30**(11) (2002) 2599–2607

41. Lanckriet, G., Cristianini, N., Bartlett, P., El Ghaoui, L., Jordan, M.: Learning the Kernel Matrix with Semidefinite Programming. J. Mach. Learn. Res. **5** (2004) 27–72

Identification in the Limit of Systematic-Noisy Languages*

Frédéric Tantini, Colin de la Higuera, and Jean-Christophe Janodet

EURISE, Université de Saint-Etienne, 23 rue du Docteur Paul Michelon,
42023 Saint-Etienne
{frederic.tantini, cdlh, janodet}@univ-st-etienne.fr

Abstract. To study the problem of learning from noisy data, the common approach is to use a statistical model of noise. The influence of the noise is then considered according to pragmatic or statistical criteria, by using a paradigm taking into account a distribution of the data. In this article, we study the noise as a nonstatistical phenomenon, by defining the concept of systematic noise. We establish various ways of learning (in the limit) from noisy data. The first is based on a technique of reduction between problems and consists in learning from the data which one knows noisy, then in denoising the learned function. The second consists in denoising on the fly the training examples, thus to identify *in the limit* good examples, and then to learn from noncorrupted data. We give in both cases sufficient conditions so that learning is possible and we show through various examples (coming in particular from the field of the grammatical inference) that our techniques are complementary.

Keywords: Identification in the limit, languages, noise, pretopology.

1 Introduction

Grammatical inference [1,2] is a field that provides a lot of algorithms to learn from sequential or structured data: words, trees, ... Among the advantages of these techniques, we can underline the comprehensibility of the learned models, solid theories which allow in particular to avoid working with nonexplicit bias, the power of the functions which define the concepts (automata and grammars), the fact that the training data can be analysed in their globality and not by taking into account only pieces of information, *etc.* But these qualities have a counterpart: they are not (or hardly) noise resistant [3,4].

Noise appears in the data for several reasons. It can be due to the fact that the bias is inadapted: if we try to learn a regular language from data that comes from a context-free language, we can expect problems. It can also be due to poor experimental conditions or to the fact that cleaning the data is either too difficult or too expensive. This can occur in voice recognition, or when we wish to learn from manually-built HTML files.

---

* This work was supported in part by the IST Programme of the European Community, under the PASCAL Network of Excellence, IST-2002-506778. This publication only reflects the authors' views.

Y. Sakakibara et al. (Eds.): ICGI 2006, LNAI 4201, pp. 19–31, 2006.

The management of noise is a crucial and recurring problem in machine learning in general. Concerning grammatical inference, we can quote the following lines of research. Very theoretical works were undertaken, either within the framework of inductive inference [5,6] and following the track of old results [7], or in that of approximate learning [8,9]. Other works tried to use well-founded ideas in existing algorithms to make them more robust to noise [10,11]. In addition, nondeterministic automata are probably more resistant to the noise than the deterministic ones [12]. More pragmatic works were undertaken to use techniques of grammatical inference on naturally noisy time series [13]. We can also note studies on approximated learning of languages, which are based on the *rough sets* theory and brings algorithms intrinsically more resistant to noisy data [14]. The paradigm of learning by analogy was also the subject of a study under the angle of its resistance to noisy data [15]. Lastly, a traditional approach is that of learning stochastic automata. This approach aims at avoiding the problem by imposing a different bias: the data come from a distribution, itself represented by a stochastic automaton [16]. The question is then not that of learning a language but a distribution. Results in this direction are both theoretical [17,18] and algorithmic [19].

Let us note that in most of the theoretical approaches, the treatment of noise is statistical. In this work, we explore the case of a *systematic* noise based on the edit distance; we study the properties of this kind of noise in the context of the identification in the limit [20,21].

In this setting we propose various ways of learning (in the limit) from noisy data. The first one is based on a technique of reduction between problems and consists in learning from the data, knowing that it is noisy, then in denoising the learned function. The second one consists in denoising on the fly the learning examples, thus in identifying *in the limit* good examples, and in learning from noncorrupted examples. In this second approach, we show that it is possible (and sometimes recommended) to add additional noise to boost the training.

We give for these two outlines sufficient conditions for the learning and we show through various examples (and in particular examples coming from the field of grammatical inference) that the techniques are complementary. The definitions we tailor are general, and we use them within the framework of the systematically noisy texts, but we believe they might be used in a broader way.

2   Preliminaries

An *alphabet* Σ is a non-empty finite set of symbols called *letters*. A *word* w is a finite sequence $w = a_1 a_2 \ldots a_n$ of letters. Let $|w|$ denote the length of w. In the following, letters will be indicated by $a, b, c, \ldots$, words by $u, v, \ldots, z$ and the empty word by λ. Let Σ^* be the set of all finite words over alphabet Σ. We call language any subset $L \subseteq \Sigma^*$.

The identification in the limit paradigm has been introduced by Gold [20]. We give it here in the formalism of [22] which allows to study reductions between identification problems (section 4). Let $\mathcal{L}$ be a class of languages and $\mathcal{R}(\mathcal{L})$ a class of representations for $\mathcal{L}$ (*e.g.* the class of regular languages and that of deterministic automata). Let $\mathbb{L}_{\mathcal{L}} : \mathcal{R}(\mathcal{L}) \to \mathcal{L}$ be the function that for every representation returns the corresponding language. This function is surjective: every language can be represented. But it does not have to be injective. Indeed, two different functions can represent the same language. We suppose that the following word problem is decidable: "given $w \in \Sigma^*$ and $G \in \mathcal{R}(\mathcal{L})$, $w \in \mathbb{L}_{\mathcal{L}}(G)$?".

Definition 1 (Presentation). *A presentation of $L \in \mathcal{L}$ is a function $f : \mathbb{N} \to X$ where X is a set. Let **Pres**$(\mathcal{L})$ be the set of all presentations. Since a presentation denotes a language of $\mathcal{L}$, there exists a function yield : **Pres**$(\mathcal{L}) \to \mathcal{L}$. I.e., if $L = yield(f)$ then f is a presentation of L, or $f \in$ **Pres**(L). Let f_n denote the set $\{f(j) : j < n\}$.*

With this definition, the notion of presentations is very large: they are sequences of information of any type that inform us on the language. Indeed, X can be Σ^* in the case of positive examples only. If in addition, $yield(f) = f(\mathbb{N})$, then such presentations are called *texts*. In the case of an *informant*, which is a presentation with both negative and positive examples, $X = \Sigma^* \times \{0, 1\}$.

If two languages share one presentation,then they cannot be distinguished, so $\mathcal{L}$ will not be learnable from **Pres**$(\mathcal{L})$. Therefore, we will suppose that if two presentations f and g are such that $f(\mathbb{N}) = g(\mathbb{N})$, then $yield(f) = yield(g)$.

A *learning algorithm* **alg** is a program taking as input the first n elements of a presentation and returning a representation:

$$\mathbf{alg} : \bigcup_{f \in \mathbf{Pres}(\mathcal{L}), i \in \mathbb{N}} \{f_i\} \to \mathcal{R}(\mathcal{L})$$

The next definition is adapted from [21]:

Definition 2. *We say that $\mathcal{L}$ is learnable in the limit from **Pres**$(\mathcal{L})$ in terms of $\mathcal{R}(\mathcal{L})$ if there exists a learning algorithm **alg** such that for any $L \in \mathcal{L}$ and for any presentation $f \in$ **Pres**(L), there exists a rank n such that for all $m \geq n$, $\mathbb{L}_{\mathcal{L}}(\mathbf{alg}(f_m)) = L$.*

Usual classes of languages (defined by automata, grammars, . . .) are not appropriate in the case of noise. The essential problem is that in a quasi systematic way, the modification of a symbol in a word swaps it from the language to its complementary. To use an image coming from a field in which the noise was better analysed, it is like if, by drawing on a screen the words of a language, no shape was perceptible: all the languages would look like uniform grey. We thus introduce distance and simple topological objects, the balls, which do not present this problem.

The edit distance between two words was defined by Levenshtein in 1965 [23]. It consists in counting the minimal number of symbol operations needed to rewrite the former into the latter, where the operations are the insertion, the substitution and the deletion. More formally, let w and w' be two words in Σ^*, we rewrite w into w' in one step if one of the following condition is true:

- $w = uav, w' = uv$ and $u, v \in \Sigma^*, a \in \Sigma$ (deletion),
- $w = uv, w' = uav$ and $u, v \in \Sigma^*, a \in \Sigma$ (insertion),
- $w = uav, w' = ubv$ and $u, v \in \Sigma^*, a, b \in \Sigma$ (substitution).

We consider the reflexive and transitive closure of this relation and we note $w \xrightarrow{k} w'$ iff w can be rewritten into w' by means of k operations. Then the Levenshtein distance between w and w', noted $d_{edit}(w, w')$, is the smallest k such that $w \xrightarrow{k} w'$. For instance, $d_{edit}(abaa, aab) = 2$ since $abaa \rightarrow aaa \rightarrow aab$.

Notice that the edit distance between two words is computed by dynamic programming [24]. Moreover several variants have been studied and the distance has been adapted to the case of circular words and trees. The weight of the edit operations can also differ from 1. We have chosen in this work to study only the standard case.

Definition 3 (Balls). *The ball of centre $u \in \Sigma^*$ and radius $r \in \mathbb{N}$ is defined by $B_r(u) = \{w \in \Sigma^* : d(w, u) \leq r\}$. A representation of the ball $B_r(u)$ will then be the couple (u, r). Let $\mathcal{B}_\Sigma$ denote the set of all the balls: $\mathcal{B}_\Sigma = \{B_k(u) : k \in \mathbb{N}, u \in \Sigma^*\}$.*

Note that if the alphabet Σ contains only one letter, the same ball can be represented in several ways ($B_2(a) = B_3(\lambda)$), but this characteristic is not a problem: many classes of representations have this property (automata, grammars).

3   Identification in the Limit from Noisy Data

In this paper, we propose a model of noise that we call *systematic*: noise will be added to a data in all the possible ways up to a certain distance. This idea can be illustrated by considering spots of painting on a paper sheet: putting an object on the sheet makes the points become blurs.

Definition 4 (Noise of a language). *Let L be a language on Σ^*. The k-noise of L is $N_k(L) = \{w : \exists x \in L, d(x, w) \leq k\}$.*

Let us first notice that once noise is added, if two languages of the class are not distinguishable one from the other, then the class itself is not resistant to systematic noise. In particular, this is the case of the class of rational languages, and in a broader way for any class defined by rewriting systems. The possibility to represent in these classes *parity functions* is susceptible to convince us of the low resistance to the noise of these languages [4]. This justifies our interest in classes of languages defined differently than through grammars.

It is reasonable to study systematic noise in the paradigm of the identification in the limit, due to the absence of distribution on the data. To this purpose, we introduce the following new notion of presentation:

Definition 5 (Noisy presentation). *A noisy presentation is a presentation $f : \mathbb{N} \rightarrow X$ for which there exists an (unknown) function isnoise $: X \rightarrow \{0, 1\}$ that is able to distinguish noisy elements and pure ones.*

This definition allows to model a variety of situations, for instance:

Definition 6 (*k*-**noisy presentation**). *Let L be a language. A k-noisy presentation of L is a presentation of $N_k(L)$. The function isnoise is then equal to 0 on the elements of L and to 1 on those of $N_k(L) \setminus L$.*

We now tackle the problem of learning in presence of noisy data. Two solutions seem relevant as shown by the following diagram:

$$
\begin{array}{ccc}
\mathbf{Pres}(\mathcal{L}) & \longrightarrow & \mathcal{L}' \\
\downarrow & & \downarrow \\
\overline{\mathbf{Pres}}(\mathcal{L}) & \longrightarrow & \mathcal{L}
\end{array}
$$

In this diagram the problem is to learn a language $\mathcal{L}$ from a noisy presentation of $\mathbf{Pres}(\mathcal{L})$. First, we can try to learn instead a language from another class which would incorporate the noise (the class $\mathcal{L}'$) and then try to deduce the original language. On the other hand, we can try to denoise the data in order to obtain a nonnoisy presentation in $\overline{\mathbf{Pres}}(\mathcal{L})$ and then learn from this one. In this second strategy, it is thus the function isnoise that we want to identify.

4 Reduction

A technique implemented in many fields of computer science and mathematics is that of *reductions*. They make are used to obtain negative results (such problem is at least as difficult as such other, known as being too hard) but also to use algorithms that are valid in a case for another case. Here, we consider the latter technique: following the arguments of [22], we show that the balls are identifiable from noisy data. Beyond this result, we think that the reductions are an effective way to learn from noisy data.

We recall that a situation of identification is defined by the class of languages, that of the representations and the type of allowed presentations. Let $\mathcal{L}$ and $\mathcal{L}'$ be the two classes of languages represented respectively by $R(\mathcal{L})$ and $R(\mathcal{L}')$. We denote by $\mathbb{L}_{\mathcal{L}}$ (*resp.* $\mathbb{L}_{\mathcal{L}'}$) the surjective mapping $R(\mathcal{L}) \to \mathcal{L}$ (*resp.* $\mathbb{L}_{\mathcal{L}'} : R(\mathcal{L}') \to \mathcal{L}'$).

Given a surjective mapping $\phi : \mathcal{L} \to \mathcal{L}'$, we denote by ψ a surjective mapping $R(\mathcal{L}) \to R(\mathcal{L}')$ for which the diagram commutes ($\phi \circ \mathbb{L}_{\mathcal{L}} = \mathbb{L}_{\mathcal{L}'} \circ \psi$):

$$
\begin{array}{ccc}
R(\mathcal{L}) & \xrightarrow{\ \psi\ } & R(\mathcal{L}') \\
\mathbb{L}_{\mathcal{L}} \downarrow & & \downarrow \mathbb{L}_{\mathcal{L}'} \\
\mathcal{L} & \xrightarrow{\ \phi\ } & \mathcal{L}'
\end{array}
$$

Given a surjective mapping $\phi : \mathcal{L} \to \mathcal{L}'$, we denote ξ a surjective mapping $\mathbf{Pres}(\mathcal{L}) \to \mathbf{Pres}(\mathcal{L}')$ for which the following diagram commutes ($\phi \circ yield_{\mathcal{L}} = yield_{\mathcal{L}'} \circ \xi$):

$$\mathcal{L} \xrightarrow{\phi} \mathcal{L}'$$

$$yield_{\mathcal{L}} \uparrow \qquad\qquad \uparrow yield_{\mathcal{L}'}$$

$$\mathbf{Pres}(\mathcal{L}) \xrightarrow{\xi} \mathbf{Pres}(\mathcal{L}')$$

As a presentation may not be a computable function, describing the computation aspects of function ξ is as follows:

Definition 7. *Let $\mathcal{L}$ be a class of languages represented in $R(\mathcal{L})$ with presentations in $\mathbf{Pres}(\mathcal{L}) : \mathbb{N} \to X$ and let $\mathcal{L}'$ be a class of languages represented in $R(\mathcal{L}')$ with presentations in $\mathbf{Pres}(\mathcal{L}') : \mathbb{N} \to Y$. A reduction between presentations $\xi : \mathbf{Pres}(\mathcal{L}) \to \mathbf{Pres}(\mathcal{L}')$ such that $\xi(\boldsymbol{f}) = \boldsymbol{g}$ is computable if and only if there exists a computable function $\overline{\xi} : X \to 2^Y$ such that $\bigcup_{i \in \mathbb{N}} \overline{\xi}(\boldsymbol{f}(i)) = \boldsymbol{g}(\mathbb{N})$.*

$\overline{\xi}$ is the description of the function ξ in all its points. We suppose here that $\forall i \in \mathbb{N}$, $\overline{\xi}(\boldsymbol{f}(i))$ is a finite set.

By combining the two previous diagrams we obtain:

$$R(\mathcal{L}) \xrightarrow{\psi} R(\mathcal{L}')$$

$$\mathbb{L}_{\mathcal{L}} \downarrow \qquad\qquad \downarrow \mathbb{L}_{\mathcal{L}'}$$

$$\mathcal{L} \xrightarrow{\phi} \mathcal{L}'$$

$$yield_{\mathcal{L}} \uparrow \qquad\qquad \uparrow yield_{\mathcal{L}'}$$

$$\mathbf{Pres}(\mathcal{L}) \xrightarrow{\xi,\overline{\xi}} \mathbf{Pres}(\mathcal{L}')$$

Theorem 1. *If (i) $\mathcal{L}'$ is learnable in terms of $R(\mathcal{L}')$ from $\mathbf{Pres}(\mathcal{L}')$, (ii) there exists a computable function $\chi : R(\mathcal{L}') \to R(\mathcal{L})$ and a computable function $\psi : R(\mathcal{L}) \to R(\mathcal{L}')$ such that $\psi \circ \chi = Id$ and (iii) ξ is a computable reduction, then $\mathcal{L}$ is learnable in terms of $R(\mathcal{L})$ from $\mathbf{Pres}(\mathcal{L})$.*

$$R(\mathcal{L}) \xleftarrow{\chi} R(\mathcal{L}')$$

$$\mathbb{L}_{\mathcal{L}} \downarrow \qquad\qquad \downarrow \mathbb{L}_{\mathcal{L}'}$$

$$\mathcal{L} \xrightarrow{\phi} \mathcal{L}'$$

$$yield_{\mathcal{L}} \uparrow \qquad\qquad \uparrow yield_{\mathcal{L}'}$$

$$\mathbf{Pres}(\mathcal{L}) \xrightarrow{\xi,\overline{\xi}} \mathbf{Pres}(\mathcal{L}')$$

Proof. Let **alg2** be a learning algorithm that identifies $\mathcal{L}'$. Consider algorithm **alg1** below, that takes a presentation $\boldsymbol{f}$ by its n first items $(\boldsymbol{f}_n)$ and then executes:

$$g_m \longleftarrow \overline{\xi}(\boldsymbol{f}_n)$$
$$G_{\mathcal{L}'} \longleftarrow \mathbf{alg2}(g_m)$$
$$G_{\mathcal{L}} \longleftarrow \chi(G_{\mathcal{L}'})$$
$$\text{return } G_{\mathcal{L}}$$

$G_{\mathcal{L}}$ and $G_{\mathcal{L}'}$ are grammars of $R(\mathcal{L})$ and $R(\mathcal{L}')$. As ξ is computable, g_m can effectively be built.

As a consequence of Theo. 1, we can prove known results like the identification of even linear grammars [25], by reduction from deterministic finite automata. In the context of noisy data, we get:

Theorem 2. $\mathcal{B}_\Sigma$ *is learnable in the limit from k-noisy text.*

We first establish that the k-noise of a ball is a ball:

Lemma 1. $N_k(B_{k'}(u)) = B_{k+k'}(u)$

Proof. ($\subseteq$) Let $x \in N_k(B_{k'}(u))$. Then $\exists y \in B_{k'}(u) : d(y,x) \leq k$, so $d(u,y) \leq k' \wedge d(y,x) \leq k$, therefore $d(u,x) \leq k' + k$.
($\supseteq$) Let $x \in B_{k+k'}(u)$ so $d(u,x) \leq k + k'$. Let $d(u,x) > k'$. The fact that $k' < d(u,x) \leq k + k'$ means that u can be changed in x by the mean of $k + k'$ operations of edition. Let y be the word obtained after the first k' operations. Then $d(u,y) = k'$ and $d(y,x) \leq k$; thus $y \in B_{k'}(u)$ and $x \in N_k(B_{k'}(u))$.

We also get the following result:

Lemma 2. $\mathcal{B}_\Sigma$ *is identifiable in the limit from text.*

Proof. By saturation, when all the points have appeared, the ball can be computed. If only some points are given, the problem is NP-hard [26], but, with all the points, it is easy: let B_{max} be the set of the longuest words. The centre u is the only word such that $a^k u$ and $b^k u$ are in B_{max}, where k is the greatest integer such that a^k and b^k are left factors of B_{max}. The ball is then $B_k(u)$.

From Lemmas 1 and 2 we deduce:

Proof (of Theo. 2). Taking $\chi=$*if the radius of the ball is at least k, then deduct k from the radius, if not identity*, we obtain the following diagram:

$$
\begin{array}{ccc}
\mathcal{B}_\Sigma & \xleftarrow{\quad \chi \quad} & \mathcal{B}_\Sigma \\
{\scriptstyle \mathbb{L}_{\mathcal{L}}} \downarrow & & \downarrow {\scriptstyle \mathbb{L}_{\mathcal{L}'}} \\
\mathcal{B}_\Sigma & \xrightarrow{\quad Id \quad} & \mathcal{B}_\Sigma \\
{\scriptstyle yield_{\mathcal{L}}} \uparrow & & \uparrow {\scriptstyle yield_{\mathcal{L}'}} \\
k\text{-noisy text} & \xrightarrow{Id,\overline{Id}} & \text{Text}
\end{array}
$$

So we deduce the result from Theo. 1.

5 Denoising in the Limit

Another way to learn from noisy data is to denoise the data on the fly, then to learn the language from these pure data. In order to denoise the data, we will see that it can even be useful to add more noise as a preliminary. The data processing sequence is then the following one:

$$\mathbf{Pres}(\mathcal{L}) \xrightarrow{\text{add noise}} \overline{\mathbf{Pres}}(\mathcal{L}) \xrightarrow{\text{remove noise}} \overline{\overline{\mathbf{Pres}}}(\mathcal{L})$$

where $\mathbf{Pres}(\mathcal{L})$ and $\overline{\mathbf{Pres}}(\mathcal{L})$ are noisy presentations and $\overline{\overline{\mathbf{Pres}}}(\mathcal{L})$ is a presentation of pure data. Once the presentation is denoised, we can then learn in the limit a language L' and use it to deduce the language L which interests us. Note that if we *strictly* denoise a presentation, *i.e.* if we remove all the noise and only the noise, we will then obtain directly $L' = L$.

Definition 8 (Denoisable in the limit). *Let $\mathbf{Pres}(\mathcal{L})$ be a class of k-noisy presentations. If there exists an algorithm $\theta : X \times \bigcup_{f \in \mathbf{Pres}\,\mathcal{L}, i \in \mathbb{N}} \{f_i\} \to \{0, 1\}$ such that : $\forall x \in X, \forall f \in \mathbf{Pres}(L), \exists n_x$ such that $\forall m \geq n_x\ \theta(x, f_m) = \theta(x, f_{n_x}) = \text{isnoise}(x) = \text{ if } x \in N_k(L) \setminus L \text{ then } 1 \text{ else } 0$, then we say that the presentations of $\mathbf{Pres}(\mathcal{L})$ are denoisable in the limit.*

Note that the identification of the noise is not monotonic: we can have identified some data as pure and cannot guess for others. Moreover, denoising in the limit is not identification in the limit: the function isnoise is learned point-to-point but never in its globality.

In the following, we consider only learning from k-*noisy text*. In this case, $\theta_k(x, f_m) = 1$ indicates the fact that at the rank m the algorithm estimates that x is a noisy piece of data and therefore is not in L.

To denoise the data, we must thus know if the data belong to the target language or not, *i.e.* we must be able to decide if a data is noise. For that, we will need to know the relations of proximity of the data compared one to the other, and in particular compared to those which belong indeed to the language. This concept of "neighbourhood" naturally leads to topology.

However, for our problem, traditional topology with its numerous axioms is too constraining. We thus will use pretopologic spaces which aim at defining "topologies with less axioms". For sake of clarity, we point out the definitions of the pretopologies and their properties in appendix.

Let I_k and E_k define the function allowing the deletion and the addition of noise: $I_k(L) = \{w \in \Sigma^* : N_k(\{w\}) \subseteq L\}$ and $E_k(L) = \{w \in \Sigma^* : N_k(\{w\}) \cap L \neq \emptyset\}$

Definition 9. *A language L is said to be closed for the pretopologic space $\mathbb{E}_j = (\Sigma^*, E_k \circ I_k, I_k \circ E_k)$ if and only if $I_j(E_j(L)) = L$ and a language class is closed if all its elements are closed.*

We can show that:

$$L \text{ closed} \Rightarrow (\forall x \in \Sigma^* N_k(x) \subseteq E_k(L) \Rightarrow x \in L) \tag{1}$$

The function I_k enables us to implement a way to denoise data:

Theorem 3. *Let k be the level of noise and $\mathbb{E}_k$ be a pretopologic space. If $\mathcal{L}$ is closed (for $\mathbb{E}_k$) then $\mathbf{Pres}(\mathcal{L})$ is k-denoisable in the limit.*

Proof. We consider the following algorithm θ_k: let f be a k-noisy presentation of a language L and $x \in N_k(L)$; $\theta_k(x, f_p) = 0$ if $x \in I_k(f_p)$ and 1 if $B_k(x) \not\subseteq f_p$.

Let f be a k-noisy presentation of a language L and $x \in N_k(L)$. If isnoise$(x) = 0$ then $x \in L$ thus $B_k(x) \subseteq N_k(L)$ and as $f(\mathbb{N}) = N_k(L)$, there is a rank n_x such that $B_k(x) \subseteq f_{n_x}$ and thus $x \in I_k(B_k(x)) \subseteq I_k(f_{n_x})$. Consequently $\theta_k(X, f_{n_x}) = 0 = $ isnoise(x). Conversely, if isnoise$(x) = 1$, then $x \notin L$ and as L is closed for $\mathbb{E}_k$ then $B_k(x) \not\subseteq N_k(L)$ (cf equation 1) and thus $\forall p \in \mathbb{N}, B_k(x) \not\subseteq f_p$. Consequently, $\forall p \in \mathbb{N}, \theta(x, f_p) = 1 = $ isnoise(x).

Example 1. Let $\overline{\mathcal{B}_\Sigma}$ be the set defined by $\overline{\mathcal{B}_\Sigma} = \left\{ \overline{B_k(u)} : k \in \mathbb{N}, u \in \Sigma^* \right\}$ where $\overline{B_k(u)} = \Sigma^* \setminus B_k(u)$. Presentations of $\overline{\mathcal{B}_\Sigma}$ are denoisable in the limit. Indeed, we can show that balls are open and that the complementary of an open set is a closed set, thus the class $\overline{\mathcal{B}_\Sigma}$ is closed.

To add noise, however, can seem strange; nevertheless, it makes it possible to obtain the following result:

Theorem 4. *Let k be the level of noise and $\mathbb{E}_j$ be a pretopologic space. If $\mathcal{L}$ is closed and if $j \geq k$ then $\mathcal{L}$ is k-denoisable in the limit.*

Proof. Consider the algorithm $\theta_k(x, f_p) = 0$ if $x \in I_k(E_{j-k}(f_p))$ and 1 if not. Then take again the proof of Theo. 3. More intuitively, let f be a k-noisy presentation of L. For all p we define $g_p = E_{j-k}(f_p)$. As f is a presentation of $N_k(L)$, g is a presentation of $N_j(L)$. Moreover L is closed for $\mathbb{E}_j$ thus according to Theo. 3, g is j-denoisable in the limit and thus f is k-denoisable in the limit

However, the addition of noise will not allow the identification of new classes which were not learnable without noise.

6   Experiments and Concluding Remarks

In order to show that indeed, adding noise can accelerate the learning process by validating non noisy data earlier, we have made the following experiments: For different balls centred in λ (radius r) of sizes 3, 7, 15 and 31 because of using an alphabet of size 2, two levels of noise ($k = 1$ and $k = 2$), and 4 levels of added noise (j), we have generated strings from $B_{r+k}(\lambda)$, and counted how many of these strings remained after denoising through considering a level of added noise j. The number $|f|$ of generated strings in each case varies with the size of the ball. The experiments were repeated in each case one thousand times and the results are presented in Table 1. Clearly, in all cases, adding noise allows to validate the data earlier.

Lastly, the majority of the languages are naturally not totally denoisable in the limit. Nevertheless, it is possible to *deduce* the class $\mathcal{L}$ from a class of language $\mathcal{L}'$ by combining addition and deletion of noise.

Table 1. Addition of noise can be useful

			k=1					k=2		
r	$|B_r(\lambda)|$	$|f|$	j=0	j=1	j=2	j=3	$|f|$	j=0	j=1	j=2	j=3
1	3	6	0.183	1.774	1.876	1.876	12	0.004	1.338	1.761	1.765
2	7	14	0.278	4.711	5.462	5.473	28	0.026	3.818	5.126	5.330
3	15	30	0.420	11.017	12.929	13.157	60	0.030	9.112	12.453	13.000
4	31	62	0.422	21.755	29.213	29.592	124	0.041	22.831	27.690	29.244

Example 2. Let $\mathcal{B}_\Sigma$ be the class of balls. We recall that this class is not closed. Let $L = B_r(u)$. Then $I_{j+k}(E_j(N_k(L))) = I_{j+k}(E_{j+k}(L))$ which contains an approximation of L, *i.e.*, L plus possibly some words (for example $bbbaaa \in I_1(E_1(B_4(aabb)))$ but $bbbaaa \notin B_4(aabb)$). However in $I_{j+k}(E_{j+k}(L))$, there exists a couple $(a^n v, b^n v)$ which are respectively the smallest and the greatest word of the longest words of L. These words enable us to deduce $r = n$ and $u = v$, thus to identify $L = B_r(u)$. Consequently, there is an algorithm allowing to identify indirectly $\mathcal{B}_\Sigma$ after an approximate denoising of the data.

To conclude, we introduced two techniques allowing to learn languages in presence of systematic noise. One of them is based on a theorem of reduction. The other uses the idea of the on the fly denoising of the data (denoising whose correction is obtained only in the limit). We also established the fact that this process could advantageously be accompanied by an over-noising of the data in order to accelerate the identification.

Several problems remain open: we did not tackle the questions of complexity. It is obvious, for example, that the over-noising should not be explicit since it is too expensive. Techniques simulating it must be introduced. The systematic noise is also a strong assumption: a more realistic model could be based on the fact that only a part (the majority?) of the noisy examples appears in the presentation. In the same way, we chose here to use a strict denoising: as long as all the elements of the noise of x did not appear, x is regarded as noise. Other strategies are possible and deserve to be analysed. Finally, balls are a first candidate of topologically robust languages. But other classes of languages, defined by topological properties, can be richer and maintain the necessary robustness.

Acknowledgement

Several ideas related in particular to the systematic noise and the balls were discussed in June 2004 with Rémi Eyraud and Jose Oncina during its stay in Saint-Etienne as an invited professor.

References

1. Sakakibara, Y.: Recent advances of grammatical inference. Theoretical Computer Science **185** (1997) 15–45
2. de la Higuera, C.: A bibliographical study of grammatical inference. Pattern Recognition **38** (2005) 1332–1348

3. Lang, K.J., Pearlmutter, B.A., Price, R.A.: Results of the abbadingo one DFA learning competition and a new evidence-driven state merging algorithm. LNCS **1433** (1998) 1–12

4. de la Higuera, C.: Data complexity in Grammatical Inference. Number ISBN: 1-84628-171-7 in Advanced Information and Knowledge Processing. In: Data complexity in Pattern Recognition. Springer Verlag (2006)

5. Case, J., Jain, S., Sharma, A.: Synthesizing noise-tolerant language learners. Theoretical Computer Science **261** (2001) 31–56

6. Stephan, F.: Noisy inference and oracles. Theoretical Computer Science **185** (1997) 129–157

7. Wharton, R.M.: Approximate language identification. Information and Control **26** (1974) 236–255

8. Kearns, M., Valiant, L.: Cryptographic limitations on learning boolean formulae and finite automata. In: 21st ACM Symposium on Theory of Computing. (1989) 433–444

9. Kearns, M.: Efficient noise-tolerant learning from statistical queries. In: Proceedings of the Twenty-Fifth Annual ACM Symposium on Theory of Computing. (1993) 392–401

10. Sebban, M., Janodet, J.C.: On state merging in grammatical inference: a statistical approach for dealing with noisy data. In: Proceedings of ICML. (2003)

11. Habrard, A., Bernard, M., Sebban, M.: Improvement of the state merging rule on noisy data in probabilistic grammatical inference. In Lavrac, N., Gramberger, D., Blockeel, H., Todorovski, L., eds.: 10th European Conference on Machine Learning. Number 2837 in LNAI, Springer-Verlag (2003) 169–1180

12. Coste, F., Fredouille, D.: Unambiguous automata inference by means of state-merging methods. In: Proceedings of ECML (LNAI 2837). (2003) 60–71

13. Giles, C.L., Lawrence, S., Tsoi, A.: Noisy time series prediction using recurrent neural networks and grammatical inference. Machine Learning Journal **44** (2001) 161–183

14. Yokomori, T., Kobayashi, S.: Inductive learning of regular sets from examples: a rough set approach. In: Proc. of International Workshop on Rough Sets and Soft Computing. (1994)

15. Miclet, L., Bayoudh, S., Delhay, A.: Définitions et premières expériences en apprentissage par analogie dans les séquences. In Denis, F., ed.: CAP, PUG (2005) 31–48

16. Vidal, E., Thollard, F., de la Higuera, C., Casacuberta, F., Carrasco, R.C.: Probabilistic finite state automata – part I and II. Pattern Analysis and Machine Intelligence **27** (2005) 1013–1039

17. Abe, N., Warmuth, M.: On the computational complexity of approximating distributions by probabilistic automata. Machine Learning Journal **9** (1992) 205–260

18. Thollard, F., Clark, A.: Pac-learnability of probabilistic deterministic finite state automata. Journal of Machine Learning Research (2004) 473–497

19. Carrasco, R.C., Oncina, J.: Learning stochastic regular grammars by means of a state merging method. In: Proceedings of ICGI (LNAI 862). (1994) 139–150

20. Gold, M.: Language identification in the limit. Information and Control **10** (1967) 447–474

21. Gold, E.M.: Complexity of automaton identification from given data. Information and Control **37** (1978) 302–320

22. de la Higuera, C.: Complexity and reduction issues in grammatical inference. Technical Report ISSN 0946-3852, Universität Tübingen (2005)

23. Levenshtein, V.I.: Binary codes capable of correcting deletions, insertions, and reversals. Cybernetics and Control Theory **10** (1965) 707–710 Original in *Doklady Akademii Nauk SSSR* 163(4): 845–848 (1965).
24. Wagner, R., Fisher, M.: The string-to-string correction problem. Journal of the ACM **21** (1974) 168–178
25. Takada, Y.: Grammatical inference for even linear languages based on control sets. Information Processing Letters **28** (1988) 193–199
26. de la Higuera, C., Casacuberta, F.: Topology of strings: median string is NP-complete. Theoretical Computer Science **230** (2000) 39–48
27. Belmandt, Z.: Manuel de prétopologie et ses applications. Herms (1993)
28. Pawlak, Z.: Theory of rough sets: A new methodology for knowledge discovery (abstract). In: ICCI. (1990) 11
29. Kobayashi, S., Yokomori, T.: On approximately identifying concept classes in the limit. In: ALT. (1995) 298–312

Appendix

We recall here some definitions of pretopology [27], then we define a pretopologic space adapted to the study of Σ^* and we study its properties within the framework of denoising in the limit.

Definition 10 (c-duality). *We note c the* complementary*: let U be a set, $\forall A \in \mathcal{P}(U), c(A) = U \setminus A = \bar{A}$. Two applications e and i from $\mathcal{P}(U)$ to $\mathcal{P}(U)$ are c-duals if and only if $i = c \circ e \circ c$ or $e = c \circ i \circ c$.*

Definition 11 (Pretopologic space). *(U, i, e) defines a* pretopologic space*, if and only if: (i) i are e c-duals, (ii) $i(U) = U$, (iii) $\forall L \in \mathcal{P}(U), i(L) \subset L$.*

The concept of topology is thus a particular case of pretopology. It is a pretopologic space such as $\forall A, B \in \mathcal{P}(U), e(A \cup B) = e(A) \cup e(B)$ and $e(e(A)) = e(A)$. With the tools of the pretopology, we can model processes of extension $L = e^0(L) \subset e(L) \subset e[e(L)] \subset \ldots \subset e^n(L) \subset \ldots \subset U$ and erosion $L = i^0(L) \supset i(L) \supset i[i(L)] \supset \ldots \supset i^n(L) \supset \ldots \supset \emptyset$, what is not the case in topology because of the idempotence of the applications e and i.

Definition 12 (Closed and open sets). *Let (U, i, e) be a pretopologic space. K is a* closed set *of U if and only if $e(K) = K$ and L is an* open set *of U if and only if $i(L) = L$. A class of languages $\mathcal{L}$ is* closed *if and only if $\forall L \in \mathcal{L}$, L is a closed set and is* open *if and only if $\forall L \in \mathcal{L}$, L is an open set.*

Below, we define functions i and e thanks to which we will build the pretopologic spaces adapted to our study. We recall that the distance used (and in particular for the function of noise N) is the edit distance.

Definition 13 (Interior and exterior). *We call the* k-interior *of L the function defined by $I_k(L) = \{w \in \Sigma^* : N_k(\{w\}) \subseteq L\}$ and the* k-exterior *of L the function defined by $E_k(L) = \{w \in \Sigma^* : N_k(\{w\}) \cap L \neq \emptyset\}$.*

These concepts are similar to those of *lower and upper approximation* of a set in the framework of *Rough Sets* [28,29]

A first naive idea would consist in choosing $i = I_k$ and $e = E_k$ as functions of interior and exterior. However, defined as this, the extension and erosion are too important to find interesting closed and open sets. We will then take $i = E_k \circ I_k$ and $e = I_k \circ E_k$. We now show that these two functions fulfil the properties.

Lemma 3. $I_k \circ E_k$ and $E_k \circ I_k$ are c-duals in Σ^*, i.e., $\forall L \in \mathcal{P}(\Sigma^*), I_k(E_k(L)) = \overline{E_k(I_k(\overline{L}))}$.

Proof. I_k and E_k are c-duals: $I_k(\overline{L}) = \{w \in \Sigma^* : N_k(\{w\}) \subseteq \overline{L}\} = \{w \in \Sigma^* : N_k(\{w\}) \cap L = \emptyset\} = \overline{E_k(L)}$. So $E_k(I_k(\overline{L})) = I_k(\overline{I_k(\overline{L})}) = \overline{I_k(E_k(L))}$.

Theorem 5. $\mathbb{E}_k = (\Sigma^*, E_k \circ I_k, I_k \circ E_k)$ defines a pretopologic space, and then verifies: (i) $I_k \circ E_k$ and $E_k \circ I_k$ are c-duals, (ii) $E_k(I_k(U)) = U$ and (iii) $\forall L \in \mathcal{P}(U), I_k(E_k(L)) \subset L$

Proof. (i) By Lemma 3. (ii) straightforward. (iii) If $x \in E_k(I_k(L))$ then $N_k(\{x\}) \cap I_k(L) \neq \emptyset$, so $\exists y \in I_k(L) : d(x, y) \leq k$. Since $(d(x, y) \leq k \Rightarrow x \in N_k(\{y\}))$ and $(y \in I_k(L) \Rightarrow N_k(\{y\}) \subseteq L)$, we deduce $x \in L$ and $E_k(I_k(L)) \subseteq L$.

The function E_k, *respectively* I_k, allows to add noise to L, *respectively* to remove some noise. We can then use them within our framework of denoising in the limit. Note that $E_k \neq I_k^{-1}$ since $E_1(B_1(aa)) = B_2(aa)$ but $I_1(B_2(aa)) = B_1(aa) \cup \{\lambda, b\}$

Ten Open Problems in Grammatical Inference[*]

Colin de la Higuera

Laboratoire Hubert Curien, UMR CNRS 5516
Université Jean Monnet Saint-Etienne, France
cdlh@univ-st-etienne.fr
http://eurise.univ-st-etienne.fr/~cdlh

Abstract. We propose 10 different open problems in the field of grammatical inference. In all cases, problems are theoretically oriented but correspond to practical questions. They cover the areas of polynomial learning models, learning from ordered alphabets, learning deterministic POMDPs, learning negotiation processes, learning from context-free background knowledge.

1 Introduction

Results in grammatical inference can usually be of use in several different domains. For instance progress in learning stochastic finite state machines and grammars has occurred because of efforts for computational biology [1,2], or speech recognition [3], or even document representation [4]. Another example is that of learning transducers where research has taken place in very different fields like wrapper induction [5,6] or automatic translation [7]. In order for these fields to cross fertilise it can be useful to use theory as a common language. In the theoretical world it is possible to pose problems, and then to try to solve them.

This paper addresses only the first issue. After discussions with practitionneers and synthesis of the questions that correspond to bottlenecks for the use of grammatical inference, we visit here several problems. Each one has its motivations, is given with the main definitions, and the corresponding references. Even if the goal was to make the problems as unambiguous as possible, some require additional definitions (as part of the problem!) before attempting to solve them.

The paper is organised as follows: after giving in section 2 some basic notations, we study the question of polynomial learning (section 3). A number of key definitions have been proposed over the years and hardly no work has been done in order to compare these. We then consider the case where the alphabet is an ordered set. To deal in section 4 with these we introduce ordered automata, and suggest that their learnability could be an interesting question. A small problem of learning regular languages from a context-free background knowledge is

---

[*] This work was supported in part by the IST Programme of the European Community, under the PASCAL Network of Excellence, IST-2002-506778. This publication only reflects the authors' views.

Y. Sakakibara et al. (Eds.): ICGI 2006, LNAI 4201, pp. 32–44, 2006.

proposed in section 5. Solving the question of testing equivalence of regular distributions would enable to better learn stochastic finite state automata. The problem is presented in section 6.

Another line of research is that of active learning. There are in this context 3 problems. The first question is related with the fact that over the past few years the Oracle learning model defined by Angluin has ceased to be a theoretical model (section 7). Today it is of interest to consider Oracles that may make errors, or contradict themselves. How do we learn languages with these unreliable Oracles? The second (section 8) is concerned with learning Partially Observable Markov Decision Processes (POMDPs). These intervene in reinforcement learning and the question of their learnability has hardly been addressed (and certainly not from an inductive inference point of view). A last question is that of negotiation (section 9): two agents have to identify the common language by using their own language to interrogate the other agent, and thus giving away information about their language. How do we learn?

2   Notations and Definitions

Strings. A *string* w over Σ is a finite sequence $w = a_1 a_2 \ldots a_n$ of letters. Let $|w|$ denote the length of w. Letters of Σ will be indicated by $a, b, c, \ldots$, strings over Σ by $u, v, \ldots, z$, and the empty string by λ.

Let $\Sigma^\star$ be the set of all finite strings over alphabet Σ.

Languages. A language is any set of strings, so therefore a subset of $\Sigma^\star$. Operations over languages include: set operations (union, intersection, complement); product $L_1 \cdot L_2 = \{uv : u \in L_1, v \in L_2\}$; powerset $L^0 = \{\lambda\}$ $L^{n+1} = L^n \cdot L$; and star $L^* = \cup_{i \in \mathbb{N}} L^i$. We denote by $\mathcal{L}$ or $\mathcal{A}$ a class of languages.

Automata and Regular Languages. A deterministic finite automaton (DFA) is a quintuple $A = \langle Q, \Sigma, \delta, F, q_0 \rangle$ where Σ is an alphabet, Q is a finite set of states, $q_0 \in Q$ is the initial state, $\delta : Q \times \Sigma \to Q$ is a transition function, and $F \subseteq Q$ is a set of marked states, called the final states.

It is usual to recursively extend δ to Σ^*: $\delta(q, \lambda) = q$ and $\delta(q, a.w) = \delta(\delta(q, a), w)$ for all $q \in Q, a \in \Sigma, w \in \Sigma^*$. Let $\mathbb{L}(A)$ denote the language recognized by automaton A: $\mathbb{L}(A) = \{w \in \Sigma^* \mid \delta(q_0, w) \in F\}$.

Other mechanism to define, generate or recognise languages are non deterministic finite state automata, context-free grammars, regular expression,... and are described in textbooks, for instance [8].

Identification in the Limit. Let $\mathcal{A}$ be a class of languages. A presentation is an element of $Pres(\mathcal{A})$ which is a set of functions $\mathbb{N} \to X$ with X a set. In some way these presentations *denote* languages from $\mathcal{A}$, *i.e.* there exists a function *yield* : $Pres(\mathcal{A}) \to \mathcal{A}$. If $L = yield(f)$ then we will say that f is a presentation of L.

With this definition one should not think of presentations as text or informant, but in a broader sense as a sequence of informations of any type that hopefully inform us on the language we are to learn.

Typical presentations could be Text, Informant, Prefixes,... Here are some examples of possible presentations:

- Text=$\{f : \mathbb{N} \to \Sigma^* \cup \{\#\} : f(\mathbb{N}) = L$ or $\{\#\}$ where $L \subset \Sigma^*\}$.
- Informant=$\{f : \mathbb{N} \to \Sigma^* \times \{0,1\} : f(\mathbb{N}) = L \times \{1\} \cup \overline{L} \times \{0\}\}$.

Definition 1. *Let $\mathcal{A}$ be a class of languages and $Pres(\mathcal{A})$ be a type of presentations for $\mathcal{A}$, with associated function yield. The setting is said to be* valid *when given 2 presentations f and g, if their range is equal (i.e. if $f(\mathbb{N}) = g(\mathbb{N})$) then $yield(f) = yield(g)$.*

If a setting is not valid, $\mathcal{A}$ is not going to be learnable from $Pres(\mathcal{A})$. Practically, to a language class $\mathcal{A}$ is associated a representation class $R(\mathcal{A})$. The association is done through a *naming* function $\mathbb{L}_{\mathcal{A}}$ which associates to a representation (also called a *grammar*) G a language $L = \mathbb{L}_{\mathcal{A}}(G)$. Two grammars G_1 and G_2 are equivalent when $\mathbb{L}_{\mathcal{A}}(G_1) = \mathbb{L}_{\mathcal{A}}(G_2)$.

Given a presentation f we denote by f_n the set $\{f(j) : j \le n\}$. Given a presentation f we denote by $f(n) \vDash G$ (conversely $f(n) \nvDash G$) when $f(n)$ is consistent with $\mathbb{L}_{\mathcal{A}}(G)$.

A *learning algorithm* **a** is a program that takes the first n elements of a presentation and returns a representation as output. $\mathbf{a} : \bigcup_{i \in \mathbb{N}} \{f_i\} \to R(\mathcal{A})$. The following definition is directly adapted from [9]:

Definition 2. *We say that $\mathcal{A}$ is* learnable *from $Pres(\mathcal{A})$ in terms of $R(\mathcal{A})$ if there exists a learning algorithm **a** such that for all $L \in \mathcal{A}$ and for any presentation f of L (belonging to $Pres(\mathcal{A})$), there exists a rank n such that for all $m \ge n$, $\mathbb{L}_{\mathcal{A}}(\mathbf{a}(f_m)) = L$.*

In order to be able to study complexity we define sizes as follows:

- $|G|$ is the size of a grammar (number of bits);
- $|f_n| = n + 1$ is the number of items in the first elements of a presentation;
- $\|f_n\|$ is the number of symbols in in the first $n+1$ elements of a presentation (number of bits);
- $|L| = \min\{|G| : \mathbb{L}(G) = L\}$. The "size" of a language is the size of the smallest grammar of the considered class that can generate it;

3   About Polynomial Identification in the Limit

The question of polynomial learning has been of interest for some time. A first discussion has taken place in [10], with further ideas in [11] and [12]. Original ideas concerning these questions (with a notion of *stochastically polynomial* learning) can be found in [13].

Nevertheless there is no general agreement between the authors in the field about which definitions should be used, neither (with the exception of [14]) have definitions been compared.

Definitions. The following are some of the definitions of (some type of) polynomial identification in the limit:

The first definition just states that to produce its next hypothesis the algorithm only requires polynomial time. This definition alone is insufficient as shown in [10].

Definition 3 (Polynomial update time). *An algorithm a is said to have* polynomial update time *if there is a polynomial $p()$ such that, for every presentation f and every integer n, constructing $H_n = a(f_n)$ requires $p(\|f_n\|)$ time.*

Another definition that has allowed more results is given by [11]:

Definition 4 (Polynomial characteristic sets). *An algorithm a admits* polynomial characteristic sets *if there exists a polynomial $p()$ such that $\forall G \in R(\mathcal{A})$ $\exists W \subset X : \|W\| \leq p(|G|) \wedge W \subset f_n \implies \mathbb{L}_\mathcal{A}(a(f_n)) = \mathbb{L}_\mathcal{A}(G)$.*

A notion that has been used in various papers was introduced in [10]:

Definition 5 (Implicit prediction errors). *Given a learning algorithm a and a presentation f, we say that a makes an* implicit prediction error *at time n if $f(n) \nvDash a(f_{n-1})$.*

Let f be a presentation for L, algorithm a is said to make a polynomial number of implicit prediction errors *if there is a polynomial $p()$ such that, for each language L and each presentation f for L, $|\{k \in \mathbb{N} : f(k+1) \nvDash a(f_k)\}| \leq p(|L|)$.*

A nice alternative to counting the number of errors is that of counting the number of changes of hypothesis one makes. On its own, this is meaningless (why change?), but if combined with identification in the limit the definition makes sense:

Definition 6 (Polynomial mind changes). *Given a learning algorithm a and a presentation f, we say that a* changes its mind *at time n if $a(f_n) \neq a(f_{n-1})$.*

Let f be a presentation for L, algorithm a is said to make a polynomial number of mind changes *if there is a polynomial $p()$ such that, for each language L and each presentation f for L, $|\{k \in \mathbb{N} : a(f_k) \neq a(f_{k+1})\}| \leq p(|L|)$.*

Combining ideas, one gets:

Definition 7 (Yokomori [12]). *An algorithm a identifies a class $\mathcal{A}$ in the limit in* IPE *polynomial time if:*

- *a identifies $\mathcal{A}$ in the limit;*
- *a has polynomial update time;*
- *a makes a polynomial number of implicit prediction errors.*

Note that the first condition is not implied by the two other; in a similar way Pitt [10] introduced a definition where instead of requiring a polynomial number of implicit prediction errors, what is counted is the number of mind changes. Here also, the first condition is not implied by the two other. Generally speaking there are a number of problems related with deciding which definition applies best to which learning setting (text, informant,...). A comparison between these definitions would also be of use: is one definition more general than another? Further, can a polynomial algorithm for one setting be transformed into a polynomial algorithm in another?

If all these questions are interesting, we extract just one that has been puzzling researchers for some time:

Problem 1. *Definition 4 of characteristic sets uses as size of the characteristic sets a measure related to the number of bits needed to encode. Other authors (for instance [6]) propose to use the number of strings. Is this fair? Are there classes of grammars that are not learnable in this context?*

Discussion. A clear picture of what polynomial learning means in the identification in the limit setting would help enormously the field. There are today several "schools" each with their definitions. That makes theoretical results difficult to compare.

4 Ordered Alphabets

We propose to consider the case where the alphabet is ranked, *i.e.* there is a partial order over the symbols in the alphabet. The situation arises in a number of settings:

- either when the alphabet is naturally ordered as in the case of music [15];
- if the original data is numeric, the normal discretisation loses the proximity/topological characteristics that should help and that are contained in the data [16];
- sometimes the alphabet can consist in subsets of strings in which case we can also have a relation which may be a generalisation or subsumption [17].

Definitions. We introduce k-edge deterministic finite state automata.

A ranked alphabet $\langle \Sigma, \leq \rangle$ is an alphabet Σ with a relation $\leq_\Sigma$ which is a partial order (reflexive, antisymmetric and transitive) over Σ.

Example 1. Here are two possible relations:

- $\langle \Sigma, \leq \rangle$ where $\Sigma = \{0, 1, 2, 3\}$ and $0 \leq 1 \leq 2 \leq 3$. This is the case in music or working with numerical data
- $\langle \Sigma, \leq \rangle$ where $\Sigma = \{00, 01, 10, 11\}$ and $00 \leq 01 \leq 11$ and $00 \leq 10 \leq 11$. This means that the automaton may not need to be based on a total order.

Definition 8 (k-edge deterministic finite state automaton). *A k-edge deterministic finite state automaton (k-edge DFA) A is a tuple $\langle \Sigma, Q, q_0, F, \delta \rangle$ where Σ is a finite alphabet, Q is a finite set of states, $q_0 \in Q$ is the initial state, $F \subseteq Q$ is the set of final states, $\delta : Q \times \Sigma \times \Sigma \to Q$ is the transition function verifying: $\forall q \in Q, |\{x, y : \delta(q, x, y) \text{ is defined}\}| \leq k$, and if $\delta(q, a_1, b_1) \neq \delta(q, a_2, b_2)$ then $\{z : a_1 \leq z \leq b_1\} \cap \{z : a_2 \leq z \leq b_2\} = \emptyset$.*

A string x belongs to L if there is a sequence of states $q_0, q_1, ... q_{|x|}$ with $\delta(q_i, a_i, b_i) = q_{i+1}$ and $a_i \leq x_i \leq b_i$. And of course $q_{|x|}$ has to be final.

The extension of δ is as usual: the transition function δ is classically extended to sequences by: $\forall q \in Q$, $\forall w \in \Sigma^*$, $\forall a \in \Sigma$, $\delta(q, aw) = \delta(\delta(q, a), w)$. The language recognised by A, $\mathbb{L}(A)$ is $\{w \in \Sigma^* : \delta(q_0, w) \in F\}$.

Example 2. We represent in Figure 1 a 2-edge automaton. Notice that the same language can also be represented by a 3-edge automaton, but not by a 1-edge automaton. Here, $102 \in L$,

Clearly any k-edge DFA is also a DFA but the converse is not true. Moreover some regular languages cannot be represented by k-edge DFA, for any k. Also, the case where k is the size of the alphabet is of no new interest at all, as it corresponds to normal DFA.

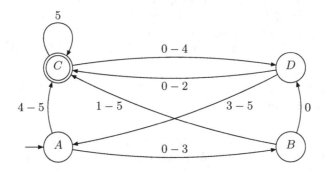

Fig. 1. A 2-edge DFA

Definition 9. *A sample $\langle X+, X- \rangle$ is k-acceptable if there is a k-edge DFA consistent with the data.*

Problem 2. *Given a sample $\langle X+, X- \rangle$, can we decide in polynomial time if a sample is k-acceptable?*

Problem 3. *Learn k-edge DFA from an informant, as in definition 4.*

Discussion. We have proposed a way to use ranked alphabets in automata. Other ideas may be possible but we believe our formalism to be interesting because it is simple, it can take into account the fact the partial order may not be total; it can adapt very easily to continuous variables (even if in that case the language theory flavour will be lost); by having the intervals overlap it is possible to have various degrees of non-determinism.

There are some accessory problems more in the line of general formal language theory: do we have a pumping lemma? what are the closure properties?

5   Learning Regular Parts of Context-Free Languages

In [18] was introduced the notion of learning with background knowledge. It is also well known that learning context-free grammars is much harder than learning DFA. The question would be to know if we could learn the intersection of a regular language L_1 and a context-free language L_2, given examples and counter-examples (of L_1) only from L_2.

Definitions. Let $CF(\Sigma)$ be the class of all context-free languages over some alphabet Σ and let $REG(\Sigma)$ be the class of all regular languages over Σ.

Let C_1 and C_2 be two language classes. Let $L = L_1 \cap L_2$, with $L_1 \in C_1$ and $L_2 \in C_2$. A presentation of L with respect to L_2 is a function $f : \mathbb{N} \to \Sigma^* \times \{0, 1\}$: $f(\mathbb{N}) = L \times \{1\} \cup L_2 \setminus L_1 \times \{0\}$.

Definition 10 (Polynomial learning with help). *An algorithm **a** learns C_1 from C_2-knowledge if there exists a polynomial $p()$ and given any language $L = L_1 \cap L_2$, with $L_1 \in C_1$ and $L_2 \in C_2$, if G is the smallest grammar such that $\mathbb{L}(G) \cap L_2 = L$, and $\mathbb{L}(G) \in C_1$ then $\exists W \subset X : \|W\| \le p(|G|) \wedge W \subset f_n \implies \mathbb{L}(\mathbf{a}(f_n)) \cap L_2 = L$.*

Problem 4. *Find an algorithm that learns $REG(\Sigma)$ from $CF(\Sigma)$-knowledge in the sense of definition 10.*

Discussion. The problem may seem easy but the problem is that the characteristic sets may be inaccessible because outside language L_1. It should be noticed that attempting to learn directly language L is going to be impossible (take $L_2 = L_1$).

6   Testing Equivalence of Regular Deterministic Distributions

Learning stochastic languages is an important topic in grammatical inference. A number of algorithms have been proposed, with partial results: distributions defined by stochastic deterministic finite automata can be identified in the limit whith probability one. The algorithms are polynomial but obviously do not work from only polynomial amount of data. The question of learning such automata from only a reasonable quantity of data thus still remains open. One step towards an answer consist in being able (or not) to decide the equivalence between distributions given finite samples.

Definitions. A *stochastic language* $\mathcal{D}$ is a probability distribution over Σ^*.

The probability of a string $x \in \Sigma^*$ under the distribution $\mathcal{D}$ is denoted as $\Pr_{\mathcal{D}}(x)$ and must verify $\sum_{x \in \Sigma^*} \Pr_{\mathcal{D}}(x) = 1$. If the distribution is modelled by some syntactic machine A, the probability of x according to the probability distribution defined by A is denoted $\Pr_A(x)$. The distribution modelled by a machine A will be denoted $\mathcal{D}_A$ and simplified to $\mathcal{D}$ if the context is non ambiguous.

Two distributions $\mathcal{D}$ and $\mathcal{D}'$ are equal (denoted by $\mathcal{D} = \mathcal{D}'$) if $\forall w \in \Sigma^\star$: $\mathrm{Pr}_{\mathcal{D}}(w) = \mathrm{Pr}_{\mathcal{D}'}(w)$. Alternatively one can define distances between distributions; a survey can be found in [19].

Problem 5. *Find an algorithm (or prove that it does not exist) that, given 2 samples extracted from* SDFA *A and B, will tell us with high probability if A and B are equivalent (or close). Formally, if d is some distance between distributions:*

given $\epsilon, \delta > 0$, find an algorithm that given 2 samples extracted from SDFA *A and B, will tell us if $d(\mathcal{D}_A, \mathcal{D}_B) < \epsilon$ with probability at least $1 - \delta$.*

Discussion. To tighten the definition it would be necessary to use a *sampling query* allowing to sample (in $\mathcal{O}(1)$) $\mathcal{D}_A$ and $\mathcal{D}_B$. The number of examples should, like the algorithm, be polynomial in the sizes of the automata, $\frac{1}{\epsilon}$ and $\frac{1}{\delta}$. If the hardness of the equivalence problem is closely linked with that of identifying in the limit [11], the related problem in the context of stochastic learning is the one above. The above problem is what most SDFA learning algorithms try to solve, through comparing prefixes in the case of [20], or looking for some important string [21].

Solving this problem in a better way would allow to derive a test for the compatibility between 2 states in typical state merging algorithms. On the other hand, a negative answer to the above question would give us the clue towards proving the non learnability of SDFA. Alternatively, partial results over special classes of SDFA would also be helpful.

7   Queries

Learning with queries was introduced by Angluin [22] in order to study the non learnability of languages. The first results were therefore essentially negative [23], until a first algorithm ($L*$) was proposed [24] which could learn deterministic finite automata from membership queries (does this string belong to the target?) and equivalence queries (is this a representation of the language? If not, please provide me with a counter-example). This combination of queries (called a *minimum adequate teacher*) has been studied in [25] where the possibility of trading off some equivalence queries for some membership queries is explained. A survey paper is [26].

But these studies are based on the general idea that the Oracle is some perfect abstract machine. Indeed, Angluin [24] actually proposed techniques to implement the Oracle. *A contrario*, we believe that one should think of an Oracle as something quite different from that. Here are some arguments in favour of this point:

- Learning neural networks [16] that simulate automata. In that case, an issue is that of extracting an automaton from a neural network. A way to do this is to use the black box/neural network as an Oracle.
- Testing hardware [27]: the physical system or chip to be tested is the Oracle.
- System SQUIRREL [6] is used for wrapper induction. The system will interrogate the (human) user who will mark web pages.
- Today the World wide web can be seen as an Oracle. The knowledge is there, you cannot expect it to be sampled for you, nor to be able to use it all.

Definitions. In a standard query learning algorithm, the learner interacts with an *oracle* (also called *minimally adequate teacher*), who knows the *target language* (a regular language L over a known alphabet) and is assumed to answer correctly. The teacher has to answer two types of queries: *membership queries* - the teacher's answer is *yes* or *no*, depending if the submitted string belongs or not to the language and *equivalence queries* - the learner produces a DFA A and asks whether $\mathcal{L}(A) = L$; the teacher answers *yes* if they accept the same language or *no* otherwise. If the answer is no, a string s in the symmetric difference of $\mathbb{L}(A)$ and L is returned. This returned string is called *counterexample*.

Definition 11. *Let $\epsilon > 0$. An ϵ-correct membership query is made by giving the Oracle a string. Then the Oracle answers correctly with probability 1-ϵ, unless it has already been submitted that query, in which case it replies consistently.*

Problem 6. *Are DFA learnable from ϵ-correct membership queries and equivalence queries?*

Discussion. Equivalence queries should probably not be exact either. Being able to learn with such queries would allow to consider active learning in settings where it is unrealistic to believe that answers are going to be correct, *e.g.* from the Web.

8   Partially Observable Markov Decision Processes

Partialy Observable Markov Decision Processes are an extension of Markov Decision Processes, these being related to Hidden Markov Models. We consider here the case where the outputs at the states are some sort of reward function. They are important models in the setting of reinforcement learning, and inferring POMDPs is still a relatively untouched problem. The relationship with multiplicity automata has been shown in [28], and algorithm to learn these have also been studied [29].

Definitions. A POMDP is defined by a set of states Q, an input alphabet Σ, an initial state q_0 and 2 functions:

- A probabilistic transition function $\delta : Q \times \Sigma \times Q \to \mathbb{R}^+$ with $\forall q \in Q$, $\sum_{q \in Q, a \in \Sigma} \delta(q, a, q') = 1$.
- A probabilistic reward function $r : Q \to \mathbb{R}$

A POMDP is deterministic if function δ is deterministic, *i.e.* if $\forall q \in Q, \forall a \in \Sigma, \exists q' \in Q$ such that $\delta(q, a, q') = 1$.

Example 3. Figure 2 represents a deterministic POMDP. Notice that the output function may be much more complex. A possible outcome of taking the decisions $b \cdot b \cdot a$ could be 30, which would have occurred with probability $0.6 \cdot 0.3 \cdot 0.3 \cdot 0.1 + 0.6 \cdot 0.3 \cdot 0.7 \cdot 0.9 + 0.6 \cdot 0.7 \cdot 0.3 \cdot 0.9 + 0.4 \cdot 0.3 \cdot 0.3 \cdot 0.9 = 0.3132$

Problem 7. *Study the learnability of deterministic POMDPs.*

Problem 8. *Study the learnability of ordinary POMDPs.*

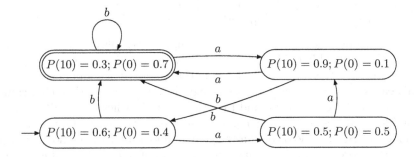

Fig. 2. A deterministic POMDP

Discussion. There are several issues in the study of the learnability of POMPDs. Identification in the limit with probability 1 is an issue. But using convergence criteria from reinforcement learning (such as *regret*) is probably a better idea. The problem should also be related with strategy learning, as in [30].

9   Negotiation

Consider the situation where two adversaries have to negotiate something. The goal of each is to learn the model of the opponent while giving away as little information as possible. The situation can be modelled as follow:

Let L_1 be the language of adversary 1 and L_2 be the language of adversary 2. We suppose here that the languages are regular and can be represented by deterministic finite automata with respectively n_1 and n_2 states. The goal for each is to learn the common language, *i.e.* language $L_1 \cap L_2$.

It is well known that language $L_1 \cap L_2$ is also a regular language which can be represented by the product automaton. So there is an automaton of at most $n_1 * n_2$ states recognising $L_1 \cap L_2$.

The rule is that each adversary can only query the opponent by asking questions from his own language. This means that when player 1 names string w, then $w \in L_1$. In turn, the adversary will answer if, or not, string w belongs to the language.

Definitions. The goal of each adversary is to identify language $L_1 \cap L_2$. This means that the protocol goes as follows:

- Player 1 announces some string w from L_1. Player 2 answers YES if this string belongs to L_2, NO otherwise.
- From this answer player 1 may update his hypothesis H_1 of language $L_1 \cap L_2$.
- From the information $w \in L_1$, player 2 may update his hypothesis H_2 of language $L_1 \cap L_2$
- Player 2 announces some string w from L_2.
- ...

We argue that for the problem to be well posed, one should be careful to avoid passive strategies, and count appropriately.

1. If L_1 is empty then the game is over straight away: player 1 has, as unique hypothesis possible for $L_1 \cap L_2$, the empty set which is correct.
2. The strategy "I shall wait and say nothing and let the opponent uncover his cards" is not always a good strategy: it is well known that DFA cannot be identified from text [9]: and take the situation where $L_1 = \Sigma^*$, then the problem reduces to learning L_2, and using positive information only is not sufficient. But this holds only if the goal is to identify the common language!
3. It is therefore essential to count errors made, but only if the goal is reached. A draw should be counted as a loss for both players. In a sense the issue is similar to that of definition 7.

We propose the following definitions of successful learning: to make things simpler, we shall only consider here deterministic (non randomised) learners, in which case a game is defined by a pair $\langle L_1, L_2 \rangle$, and the outcome of each game is unique for each pair of players A and B. We call $errors(X)$ the set of errors made by player X: an error is made when the string proposed by player X receives a negative answer from the other player.

Definition 12. *Given a game $\langle L_1, L_2 \rangle$ and 2 players A and B, A wins if A identifies $L_1 \cap L_2$ in the limit and if either B identifies $L_1 \cap L_2$ in the limit and $|errors(A)| < |errors(B)|$ or if B does not identify $L_1 \cap L_2$ in the limit.*

Problem 9. *Study the general problem. What is a good strategy? Can identification be avoided? Are there any "no win" situations? Are there strategies that are so close one to the other (corresponding to what Angluin called "lock automata") that through only membership queries, learning is going to take too long?*

Problem 10. *Using definition 12, find a winning algorithm, in the case where $n_1 = n_2$.*

Discussion. Being a good learning algorithm can be defined in alternative ways. One can want to be uniformly better than an adversary, than all the adversaries...

An intriguing question is: what happens if both opponents "agree" on a stalemate position, *i.e.* are satisfied with an identical language L which in fact is a subset of the target?

And, in a similar line to [30] one may considerlearning the strategy of the adversary; if we notice the adversary is daring/cautious, do we have anything better to do?

Acknowledgements

Thanks to Jose Oncina for different discussions that led to several definitions and problems from sections 4 and 6. Work with Henning Fernau on polynomial learning is where the ideas in section 3 come from. Philippe Jaillon gave me the initial ideas for the negotiation problem in section 9. Discussions with Cristina Bibire and Leonor Becerra led to seeing the importance of the questions from section 7. I have also worked with Franck Thollard on learning stochastic deterministic finite state automata (section 6). It is also clear that had other specialists in grammatical inference given their problems, an alltogether different list would have been compiled. I therefore apologize to those who will not find their favourite problem here, or who believe that the really important are elsewhere.

References

1. Sakakibara, Y., Brown, M., Hughley, R., Mian, I., Sjolander, K., Underwood, R., Haussler, D.: Stochastic context-free grammars for tRNA modeling. Nuclear Acids Res. **22** (1994) 5112–5120
2. Abe, N., Mamitsuka, H.: Predicting protein secondary structure using stochastic tree grammars. Machine Learning Journal **29** (1997) 275–301
3. Kashyap, R.L.: Syntactic decision rules for recognition of spoken words and phrases using stochastic automaton. IEEE Trans. on Pattern Analysis and machine Intelligence **1** (1979) 154–163
4. Young-Lai, M., Tompa, F.W.: Stochastic grammatical inference of text database structure. Machine Learning Journal **40** (2000) 111–137
5. Chidlovskii, B., Ragetli, J., de Rijke, M.: Wrapper generation via grammar induction. In: Machine Learning: ECML 2000, 11th European Conference on Machine Learning. Volume 1810., Springer-Verlag (2000) 96–108
6. Carme, J., Gilleron, R., Lemay, A., Niehren, J.: Interactive learning of node selecting tree transducer. In: IJCAI Workshop on Grammatical Inference. (2005) Submitted to a Journal.
7. Amengual, J.C., Benedí, J.M., Casacuberta, F., Castaño, A., Castellanos, A., Jiménez, V.M., Llorens, D., Marzal, A., Pastor, M., Prat, F., Vidal, E., Vilar, J.M.: The EuTrans-I speech translation system. Machine Translation **15** (2001) 75–103
8. Harrison, M.H.: Introduction to Formal Language Theory. Addison-Wesley Publishing Company, Inc., Reading, MA (1978)
9. Gold, E.M.: Language identification in the limit. Information and Control **10** (1967) 447–474
10. Pitt, L.: Inductive inference, DFA's, and computational complexity. In: Analogical and Inductive Inference. Number 397 in LNAI. Springer-Verlag, Berlin, Heidelberg (1989) 18–44
11. de la Higuera, C.: Characteristic sets for polynomial grammatical inference. Machine Learning Journal **27** (1997) 125–138
12. Yokomori, T.: Polynomial-time identification of very simple grammars from positive data. Theoretical Computer Science **1** (2003) 179–206
13. Zeugmann, T.: Can learning in the limit be done efficiently? In Gavaldà, R., Jantke, K., Takimoto, E., eds.: ALT. Number 2842 in LNCS, Berlin, Heidelberg, Springer-Verlag (2003) 17–38
14. Parekh, R.J., Honavar, V.: On the relationship between models for learning in helpful environments. In de Oliveira, A., ed.: Grammatical Inference: Algorithms and Applications, Proceedings of ICGI '00. Volume 1891 of LNAI., Berlin, Heidelberg, Springer-Verlag (2000) 207–220

15. Cruz, P., Vidal, E.: Learning regular grammars to model musical style: Comparing different coding schemes. [31] 211–222

16. Giles, C.L., Lawrence, S., Tsoi, A.: Noisy time series prediction using recurrent neural networks and grammatical inference. Machine Learning Journal **44** (2001) 161–183

17. Dupont, P., Chase, L.: Using symbol clustering to improve probabilistic automaton inference. [31] 232–243

18. Kermorvant, C., de la Higuera, C.: Learning languages with help. In Adriaans, P., Fernau, H., van Zaannen, M., eds.: Grammatical Inference: Algorithms and Applications, Proceedings of ICGI '02. Volume 2484 of LNAI., Berlin, Heidelberg, Springer-Verlag (2002) 161–173

19. Vidal, E., Thollard, F., de la Higuera, C., Casacuberta, F., Carrasco, R.C.: Probabilistic finite state automata – part I and II. Pattern Analysis and Machine Intelligence **27** (2005) 1013–1039

20. Carrasco, R.C., Oncina, J.: Learning stochastic regular grammars by means of a state merging method. In Carrasco, R.C., Oncina, J., eds.: Grammatical Inference and Applications, Proceedings of ICGI '94. Number 862 in LNAI, Berlin, Heidelberg, Springer-Verlag (1994) 139–150

21. Ron, D., Singer, Y., Tishby, N.: On the learnability and usage of acyclic probabilistic finite automata. In: Proceedings of COLT 1995. (1995) 31–40

22. Angluin, D.: Queries and concept learning. Machine Learning Journal **2** (1987) 319–342

23. Angluin, D.: A note on the number of queries needed to identify regular languages. Information and Control **51** (1981) 76–87

24. Angluin, D.: Learning regular sets from queries and counterexamples. Information and Control **39** (1987) 337–350

25. Balcazar, J.L., Diaz, J., Gavaldà, R., Watanabe, O.: The query complexity of learning DFA. New Generation Computing **12** (1994) 337–358

26. Angluin, D.: Queries revisited. In Abe, N., Khardon, R., Zeugmann, T., eds.: Proceedings of ALT 2001. Number 2225 in LNCS, Berlin, Heidelberg, Springer-Verlag (2001) 12–31

27. Hagerer, A., Hungar, H., Niese, O., Steffen, B.: Model generation by moderated regular extrapolation. In R. Kutsche, H.W., ed.: Proc. of the 5th Int. Conference on Fundamental Approaches to Software Engineering (FASE '02). Volume 2306 of LNCS., Heidelberg, Germany, Springer-Verlag (2002) 80–95

28. Eyal Even-Dar, S.K., Mansour, Y.: Planning in pomdps using multiplicity automata. In: Proceedings of 21st Conference on Uncertainty in Artificial Intelligence (UAI). (2005) 185–192

29. Beimel, A., Bergadano, F., Bshouty, N.H., Kushilevitz, E., Varricchio, S.: Learning functions represented as multiplicity automata. J. ACM **47** (2000) 506–530

30. Carmel, D., Markovitch, S.: Exploration strategies for model-based learning in multiagent systems. Autonomous Agents and Multi-agent Systems **2** (1999) 141–172

31. Honavar, V., Slutski, G., eds.: Grammatical Inference, Proceedings of ICGI '98. In Honavar, V., Slutski, G., eds.: Grammatical Inference, Proceedings of ICGI '98. Number 1433 in LNAI, Berlin, Heidelberg, Springer-Verlag (1998)

Polynomial-Time Identification of an Extension of Very Simple Grammars from Positive Data

Ryo Yoshinaka

University of Tokyo,
National Institute of Informatics
ry@iii.u-tokyo.ac.jp

Abstract. The class of very simple grammars is known to be polynomial-time identifiable in the limit from positive data. This paper introduces an extension of very simple grammars called *right-unique simple grammars*, and presents an algorithm that identifies right-unique simple grammars in the limit from positive data. The learning algorithm possesses the following three properties. It computes a conjecture in polynomial time in the size of the input data if we regard the cardinality of the alphabet as a constant. It always outputs a grammar which is consistent with the input data. It never changes the conjecture unless the newly provided example contradicts the previous conjecture. The algorithm has a sub-algorithm that solves the inclusion problem for a superclass of right-unique simple grammars, which is also presented in this paper.

1 Introduction

Since Gold [1] proposed a mathematical model of language acquisition, diverse types of learning schemes and learnable classes of languages have been proposed and investigated. It is desirable to find a rich class of languages that is efficiently learnable from limited information. These three desiderata, i.e., richness of the language class, efficiency of the learning algorithm, and limitation on input, have no well established definitions. In this paper, we focus on "polynomial-time identification of context-free grammars in the limit from positive data".

While there are several definitions of "polynomial-time identification", this paper uses the term to mean that the learning algorithm should output its conjectures in polynomial time in the sizes of the input data and the target grammar, and should be *consistent* and *conservative*. A learning algorithm is said to be consistent if it always outputs a grammar whose language includes the input positive data. A learning algorithm is conservative if the algorithm changes its conjecture only when the previous output contradicts the newly given example of the language. Under these conditions, there are few "rich" classes of context-free languages known to be polynomial-time identifiable in the limit from positive data if we demand rich classes to contain infinitely many nonregular languages.

In this circumstance, it is worthwhile mentioning the results obtained by Yokomori [2] and Wakatsuki, Teraguchi, and Tomita [3]. They have presented

Y. Sakakibara et al. (Eds.): ICGI 2006, LNAI 4201, pp. 45–58, 2006.

algorithms that identify *very simple grammars (VSGs)* and *Szilard strict deterministic restricted one-counter automata* in the limit from positive data only, respectively. Indeed, both classes of context-free languages contain infinitely many nonregular languages and their algorithms run in polynomial-time in the above sense.

In this paper, we introduce a new subclass of context-free grammars, called *right-unique simple grammars (RSGs)*. The class of RSGs is intermediate between the classes of simple grammars and of VSGs. Besides the class of the languages generated by RSGs is incomparable to the class of the languages accepted by Szilard strict deterministic restricted one-counter automata. We show that the class of RSGs is polynomial-time identifiable in the limit from positive data. The strategy we use to identify RSGs is similar to those used by Yokomori and Wakatsuki et al. except for the method to avoid over-generalization.

For two VSGs G_1 and G_2, there is a simple criterion to pick one of these grammars whose language does not properly include the other's. However, this does not work for RSGs. To avoid conjecturing grammars that are too general, we propose a key algorithm that decides the inclusion of *length-uniform simple grammars (LSGs)*, which form a superclass of RSGs. Although there are algorithms that solve the inclusion problems for some superclasses of RSGs (Linna [4], Greibach and Friedman [5]), they are not sufficiently efficient to make our learning algorithm run in polynomial time.

In Section 3, after giving the formal definitions of an RSG and an LSG, we present some of their basic mathematical properties. In Section 4, we describe an algorithm that decides whether $L(G) \subseteq L(G')$ for a context-free grammar G and an LSG G'. The main result of this paper, a learning algorithm for RSGs, is presented in Section 5.

An application of our learning algorithm is presented by Shibata, Yoshinaka, and Chikayama [6].

2   Preliminaries

$\mathbb{Z}$ and $\mathbb{N}$ denote the set of integers and the set of nonnegative integers, respectively. ε is the empty sequence and $\varnothing$ is the empty set. $|X|$ denotes the length of a sequence X or the cardinality of a set X depending on the context. For a set X, X^* denotes the set of finite (possibly empty) sequences of elements of X and $X^+ = X^* - \{\varepsilon\}$.

Definition 1. A *context-free grammar (CFG)* is $G = \langle N, \Sigma, P, S \rangle$, where N is a finite set of *nonterminal symbols*, Σ a finite set of *terminal symbols*, $P \subseteq N \times (N \cup \Sigma)^*$ a finite set of *productions*, and $S \in N$ the *start symbol*. $\Rightarrow_G$ denotes the one step derivation, $\Rightarrow_G^n$ the n step derivation, and $\Rightarrow_G^*$ the reflexive and transitive closure of $\Rightarrow_G$. The subscript G of $\Rightarrow_G$ is omitted if it is understood from the context. *The language $L(G)$ generated by G* is the set $L(G, S)$, where $L(G, \zeta) = \{ w \in \Sigma^* \mid \zeta \overset{*}{\Rightarrow} w \}$ for $\zeta \in (N \cup \Sigma)^*$. A CFG G is *reduced* iff for every $A \in N$, there are $x, y, z \in \Sigma^*$ such that $S \overset{*}{\Rightarrow} xAz \overset{*}{\Rightarrow} xyz$. The description size of a CFG G is defined as $\|G\| = \sum_{A \to \zeta \in P} |A\zeta|$. The *thickness of a nonterminal* $A \in N$ is defined as $\tau(G, A) = \min\{ |w| \mid w \in L(G, A) \}$ and the *maximum thickness of a CFG G* is defined as $\tau_G = \max\{ \tau(G, A) \mid A \in N \}$. The size of a finite language L is $\|L\| = \sum_{w \in L} |w|$.

We assume that given grammars are all reduced in this paper. We use early lower Italic letters for terminal symbols, late lower Italic letters for sequences of terminal symbols, early upper Italic letters for nonterminal symbols, and early lower Greek letters for sequences of nonterminal symbols.

Definition 2. For an infinite sequence R of strings, $R(n)$ denotes the n-th string of R and $R_n = \{ R(1), \ldots, R(n) \}$ $(n \geq 1)$. R is said to be a *positive presentation of a language L* if $L = \{ R(n) \mid n \geq 1 \}$. Let $\mathcal{G}$ be a class of some finite representations of languages. We denote the language represented by $G \in \mathcal{G}$ by $L(G)$. A *learning algorithm $\mathcal{A}$ on $\mathcal{G}$* is an algorithm which takes a positive presentation R as an input, and outputs some infinite sequence $G_1, G_2, \ldots$ of representations in $\mathcal{G}$, i.e., $\mathcal{A}$ infinitely repeats the cycle where $\mathcal{A}$ receives the string $R(n)$ and outputs a representation G_n in $\mathcal{G}$ for $n = 1, 2, \ldots$. We denote the n-th output of $\mathcal{A}$ on a positive presentation R by $\mathcal{A}(R, n)$. A learning algorithm $\mathcal{A}$ *converges to G on a positive presentation R* if there is an integer $n_0 \in \mathbb{N}$ such that for all $n \geq n_0$, $\mathcal{A}(R, n) = G$. $\mathcal{A}$ *identifies a language L in the limit from positive data* if for every positive presentation R of L, there is $G \in \mathcal{G}$ such that $L(G) = L$ and $\mathcal{A}$ converges to G on R. A class $\mathcal{L}$ of languages is *identifiable in the limit from positive data* if there is a learning algorithm $\mathcal{A}$ that identifies every $L \in \mathcal{L}$ in the limit from positive data.

Suppose that a learning algorithm $\mathcal{A}$ identifies a class $\mathcal{L}$ of languages in the limit from positive data. $\mathcal{A}$ is said to be *consistent* if $R_n \subseteq L(\mathcal{A}(R, n))$ for every positive presentation R of a language in $\mathcal{L}$. $\mathcal{A}$ is *conservative* if $R(n + 1) \in L(\mathcal{A}(R, n))$ implies $\mathcal{A}(R, n) = \mathcal{A}(R, n + 1)$ for every positive presentation R of a language in $\mathcal{L}$.

3   Length-Uniform Simple Grammars and Right-Unique Simple Grammars

Definition 3. A CFG G in Greibach normal form is called a *simple grammar* iff $A \to a\alpha$, $A \to a\beta \in P$ implies $\alpha = \beta$. The language generated by a simple grammar is a *simple language*.

A simple grammar G is called a *very simple grammar (VSG)*, *right-unique simple grammar (RSG)*, *length-uniform simple grammar (LSG)* respectively iff $A \to a\alpha$, $B \to a\beta \in P$ implies

[VSG] $A = B$ and $\alpha = \beta$,
[RSG] $\alpha = \beta$,
[LSG] $|\alpha| = |\beta|$.

The languages generated by a VSG, an RSG, and an LSG are a *very simple language (VSL)*, a *right-unique simple language (RSL)*, and a *length-uniform simple language (LSL)*, respectively.

Example 1. Let us define an RSG $G = \langle N, \Sigma, P, F \rangle$ by

$$N = \{S, T, V\}, \quad \Sigma = \{\neg, \vee, \exists, p, q, f, g, a, b, x, y\},$$
$$P = \{S \to \neg S \mid \vee SS \mid \exists VS \mid pT \mid qTT, T \to fT \mid gTT \mid a \mid b \mid x \mid y, V \to x \mid y\}.$$

G generates the set of formulae of first-order logic in Polish notation. $L(G)$ is not a VSL.

Theorem 1. *Let $\mathcal{L}_{\text{finite}}$, $\mathcal{L}_{\text{regular}}$, $\mathcal{L}_{\text{vs}}$, $\mathcal{L}_{\text{rs}}$, and $\mathcal{L}_{\text{ls}}$, be the classes of finite languages, regular languages, VSLs, RSLs, and LSLs respectively. Then,*

$$\mathcal{L}_{\text{finite}}\$ \not\subseteq \mathcal{L}_{\text{rs}}, \quad \mathcal{L}_{\text{regular}}\$ \subsetneq \mathcal{L}_{\text{ls}}, \quad \mathcal{L}_{\text{vs}} \subsetneq \mathcal{L}_{\text{rs}} \subsetneq \mathcal{L}_{\text{ls}}$$

where $\mathcal{L}\$ = \{ L\$ \mid L \in \mathcal{L} \}$.

By the super-finiteness (Gold [1]) of the class of regular languages, the class of LSLs is not identifiable in the limit from positive data. Angluin [7] has shown that the class of k-reversible languages is polynomial-time identifiable in the limit from positive data for any natural number k. A regular language L is said to be *k-reversible* iff $\{x_1 y z_1, x_1 y z_2, x_2 y z_1\} \subseteq L$ and $|y| = k$ imply $x_2 y z_2 \in L$. Yokomori [2] has shown that if L is a regular and very simple language then L is zero-reversible. In contrast, there is a regular language L generated by an RSG which is not k-reversible for any k, e.g., a regular language $L = \{ ac^n de, ac^n df, bc^n de \mid n \geq 0 \}$ is generated by an RSG whose productions are $S \to aCF$, $S \to bCE$, $C \to cC$, $C \to d$, $E \to e$, $F \to e$, $F \to f$.

The following function $\sharp_G$ plays a key role throughout this paper.

Definition 4. For an alphabet Σ, a function $\sharp$ from Σ^* to $\mathbb{Z}$ is called a *shape* iff

- $\sharp(xy) = \sharp(x) + \sharp(y)$ for all $x, y \in \Sigma^*$ (homomorphism),
- $\sharp(a) \geq -1$ for all $a \in \Sigma$.

The shape of an LSG $G = \langle N, \Sigma, P, S \rangle$ denoted by $\sharp_G$ is the shape such that

$$\sharp_G(a) = |\alpha| - 1 \quad \text{if } A \to a\alpha \in P.$$

A function $\flat_G$ from Σ^* to $\mathbb{N}$ is defined as

$$\flat_G(x) = \begin{cases} 0 & \text{if } x = \varepsilon, \\ \max\{ 1 - \sharp_G(x') \mid x' \text{ is a proper prefix of } x \} & \text{if } x \in \Sigma^+. \end{cases}$$

Since the empty string ε is a proper prefix of any non-empty string, $\flat_G(x) \geq 1$ for every $x \in \Sigma^+$.

Lemma 1. *Let $G = \langle N, \Sigma, P, S \rangle$ be an LSG. For every derivation $\alpha \Rightarrow_G^* x\beta$ where $\alpha, \beta \in N^*$ and $x \in \Sigma^*$, all of the following hold:*

1. $\natural_G(x) = |\beta| - |\alpha|$,
2. $|\alpha| \geq \flat_G(x)$,
3. $\alpha' \Rightarrow^*_G x\beta'$ where $|\alpha'| = \flat_G(x)$, $\alpha = \alpha'\gamma$, $\beta = \beta'\gamma$.

In particular, we have $\natural_G(w) = -1$ and $\flat_G(w) = 1$ for $w \in L(G)$.

Example 2. Let a VSG G have the productions $S \rightarrow aSS$, $S \rightarrow bS$, $S \rightarrow c$. We have $\natural_G(a) = 1$, $\natural_G(b) = 0$, $\natural_G(c) = -1$. For $w = accbaa \in \Sigma^*$, we have $\natural_G(w) = 1$ and $\flat_G(w) = 1 - \natural_G(acc) = 2$. Thus, $S^m \stackrel{*}{\Rightarrow} wS^n$ implies $m \geq 2$ and $n = m + 1$, as the following derivations illustrate:

$$S \Rightarrow aSS \Rightarrow acS \Rightarrow acc,$$
$$SS \Rightarrow aSSS \Rightarrow acSS \Rightarrow accS \Rightarrow accbS \Rightarrow accbaSS \Rightarrow accbaaSSS.$$

Definition 5 (compatible shape). We say that a shape $\natural$ is *compatible with* a language L iff $\natural(w) = -1$ and $\flat(w) = 1$ for all $w \in L$, where $\flat$ is defined from $\natural$ as $\flat_G$ is defined from $\natural_G$ in Definition 4.

Lemma 2. *Let L be a language and $\natural$ a shape. There is an LSG (RSG, VSG) G such that $L \subseteq L(G)$ and $\natural_G = \natural$ iff $\natural$ is compatible with L.*

The above inclusion relation $L \subseteq L(G)$ cannot be replaced with the equivalence relation; e.g., the simple language $L = \{abc, acb\}$, which is not an LSL, has a compatible shape.

Proposition 1. *The problem that decides whether a finite language on an alphabet has a compatible shape is NP-complete (an alphabet is a part of an instance).*

The following lemma is trivial but will be conveniently referred to.

Lemma 3. *Let L be a language over Σ such that every element of Σ appears in L. If a shape $\natural$ is compatible with L, then $\natural(a) < \min\{ |y| \mid xay \in L \}$ for all $a \in \Sigma$. Hence L has a finite number of compatible shapes on Σ.*

4   Inclusion Problem for LSGs

This section presents an algorithm which decides whether $L(G) \subseteq L(G')$ for a CFG G and an LSG G'. We fix a CFG as $G = \langle N, \Sigma, P, S \rangle$ and an LSG as $G' = \langle N', \Sigma, P', S' \rangle$ throughout this section. If (and only if) $L(G) \not\subseteq L(G')$, at least one of the following cases occurs:

C1. $S \Rightarrow^*_G x$ and $S' \Rightarrow^*_{G'} xy$ for some $x \in \Sigma^*$ and $y \in \Sigma^+$.
C2. $S \Rightarrow^*_G xy$ and $S' \Rightarrow^*_{G'} x$ for some $x \in \Sigma^*$ and $y \in \Sigma^+$.
C3. $S \Rightarrow^*_G xa\zeta$ and $S' \Rightarrow^*_{G'} xA'\gamma$ (left most derivations) for some $x \in \Sigma^*$ and $a \in \Sigma$, but G' does not have a production $A' \rightarrow a\beta$ for any β.

If $\natural_{G'}$ is compatible with $L(G)$, (C1) and (C2) never occur. This is because, for every $x \in \Sigma^*$ and $y \in \Sigma^+$, we have $\flat_{G'}(xy) \geq 1 - \natural_{G'}(x)$ by the definition of $\flat_{G'}$, and thus, the equations $\flat_{G'}(xy) = 1$ and $\natural_{G'}(x) = -1$ contradict each other. Our algorithm first checks whether $\natural_{G'}$ is compatible with $L(G)$. If we conclude that $\natural_{G'}$ is compatible with $L(G)$, then it is enough to check whether (C3) occurs or not. The compatibility of $\natural_{G'}$ with $L(G)$ is just a necessary condition for $L(G) \subseteq L(G')$, nevertheless the compatibility checking algorithm produces important values to decide whether (C3) occurs.

4.1 Checking the Compatibility of the Shape

Lemma 4. *If $\natural_{G'}$ is compatible with $L(G)$, then for every $A \in N$, there are integers n_A and m_A such that $\natural_{G'}(y) = n_A$ and $\flat_{G'}(y) \leq m_A$ for all $y \in L(G, A)$.*

The above lemma ensures that the following definition is well defined.

Definition 6. *If $\natural_{G'}$ is compatible with $L(G)$, then $\natural_{G'}$ and $\flat_{G'}$ are extended (mapping from $(\Sigma \cup N)^*$ to $\mathbb{Z}$) as follows:*

$$\tilde{\natural}_{G'}(\zeta) = \natural_{G'}(x) \text{ for } \zeta \in (\Sigma \cup N)^* \text{ and } x \in L(G, \zeta),$$
$$\tilde{\flat}_{G'}(\zeta) = \max\{\flat_{G'}(x) \mid x \in L(G, \zeta)\} \text{ for } \zeta \in (\Sigma \cup N)^*.$$

If $\natural_{G'}$ is compatible with $L(G)$, we have $\tilde{\natural}_{G'}(S) = -1$ and $\tilde{\flat}_{G'}(S) = 1$.

Example 3. Let G have the productions $S \rightarrow ABBC$, $A \rightarrow a$, $B \rightarrow Bc \mid b$, $C \rightarrow b$, and let $\natural_{G'}$ be such that $\natural_{G'}(a) = 2$, $\natural_{G'}(b) = -1$, $\natural_{G'}(c) = 0$. Then $\natural_{G'}$ is compatible with $L(G)$, $\tilde{\natural}_{G'}(S) = -1$, $\tilde{\natural}_{G'}(A) = 2$, $\tilde{\natural}_{G'}(B) = \tilde{\natural}_{G'}(C) = -1$, $\tilde{\flat}_{G'}(S) = \tilde{\flat}(A) = 1$, $\tilde{\flat}_{G'}(B) = 2$, $\tilde{\flat}_{G'}(C) = 1$. If G' consists of the productions $S' \rightarrow aS'S'S'$, $S' \rightarrow b$, $S' \rightarrow cS'$, then for any $X \in \{S, A, B, C\}$ and any $w \in L(G, X)$, we have $S'^{\tilde{\flat}(X)} \Rightarrow^*_{G'} wS'^{\tilde{\flat}(X)+\tilde{\natural}(X)}$.

Lemma 5. *If $\natural_{G'}$ is not compatible with $L(G)$, the algorithm in Figure 1 outputs "INCOMPATIBLE". Conversely, if $\natural_{G'}$ is compatible with $L(G)$, then the algorithm correctly computes $\tilde{\natural}$ and $\tilde{\flat}$ such that $\tilde{\natural}(A) = \tilde{\natural}_{G'}(A)$ and $\tilde{\flat}(A) = \tilde{\flat}_{G'}(A)$ for all $A \in N$, and goes into Stage 2.*

4.2 Comparison Forest

Suppose that Stage 1 of the algorithm in Figure 1 ensures that $\natural_{G'}$ is compatible with $L(G)$. Hereafter, we abbreviate $\tilde{\natural}_{G'}$ and $\tilde{\flat}_{G'}$ to $\natural$ and $\flat$ respectively. To decide whether $L(G) \subseteq L(G')$ or not, Stage 2 of the algorithm constructs a collection of trees, called *the comparison forest* $\mathcal{F}$[1]. For each nonterminal $A \in N$ of G, let T_A be the prefix tree (trie) of the set $\{\zeta \mid A \rightarrow \zeta \in P\}$. $\mathcal{F}$ gives a label to each

---

[1] Our algorithm is based on the algorithm for the inclusion problem for VSGs proposed by Wakatsuki and Tomita [8]. One can construct one large comparison tree by combining trees of the comparison forest, like Wakatsuki and Tomita's algorithm.

Input: a CFG $G = \langle N, \Sigma, P, S \rangle$ and an LSG $G' = \langle N', \Sigma, P', S' \rangle$;
Output: whether $L(G) \subseteq L(G')$?
Begin Algorithm
  let $\tilde{\#}(a) := \#_{G'}(a)$ for all $a \in \Sigma$;
  $(\tilde{\#}(X_1 \ldots X_m) = \sum_{i=1}^{m} \tilde{\#}(X_i)$ for $X_1, \ldots, X_m \in N \cup \Sigma$ if all $\tilde{\#}(X_i)$ are defined)

  — *Stage 1. Check the Compatibility* —
  — *Stage 1.1. Compute $\tilde{\#}(N)$* —
  let every production in G be *unmarked*;
  while there remains an *unmarked* production **do**
    take some *unmarked* production $A \to \zeta \in P$ such that $\tilde{\#}(\zeta)$ is defined;
    if $\tilde{\#}(A)$ is not defined yet **then** define $\tilde{\#}(A) := \tilde{\#}(\zeta)$;
      elseif $\tilde{\#}(A) \neq \tilde{\#}(\zeta)$ **then** output "INCOMPATIBLE" and **halt**;
    fi
    mark the production $A \to \zeta$;
    if $\tilde{\#}(S)$ is defined and $\tilde{\#}(S) \neq -1$ **then** output "INCOMPATIBLE" and **halt**; **fi**
  od
  — *Stage 1.2. Compute $\tilde{b}(N)$* —
  let $\bar{b}(A) := 0$ for all $A \in N$ and $\bar{b}(a) := 1$ for all $a \in \Sigma$;
  until $\bar{b}$ cannot be updated **do**
    for each nonterminal $A \in N$ **do**
      let $\bar{b}(A) := \max\{ -\tilde{\#}(X_1 \ldots X_{k-1}) + \bar{b}(X_k) \mid A \to X_1 \ldots X_m \in P, 1 \leq k \leq m \}$;
    od
    if $\bar{b}(S) > 1$ **then** output "INCOMPATIBLE" and **halt**; **fi**
  od

  — *Stage 2. Construct the Comparison Forest $\mathcal{F}$* —
  let $\mathcal{F}(A \twoheadrightarrow \zeta) := \varnothing$ for all $A \twoheadrightarrow \zeta \in \text{dom}(\mathcal{F})$;
  let $\mathcal{F}(S \twoheadrightarrow \varepsilon) := \{[S'_{(1)} \lhd S'_{(1)}]\}$;
  until none of the following if-clauses is satisfied **do**
    — Case 1 —
    if there is $A \twoheadrightarrow \zeta a \in \text{dom}(\mathcal{F})$ with $a \in \Sigma$ such that
        $[B'_{(1)} \lhd A'_{(i)}] \in \mathcal{F}(A \twoheadrightarrow \zeta)$ but $B' \to a\beta \notin P'$ for any β
      then output "$L(G) \not\subseteq L(G')$" and **halt**;
    fi
    — Case 2 —
    if there are $A \twoheadrightarrow \zeta B \in \text{dom}(\mathcal{F})$ with $B \in N, B' \in N', j \in \{1, \ldots, \bar{b}(B)\}$ s.t.
        $[B'_{(j)} \lhd A'_{(i)}] \in \mathcal{F}(A \twoheadrightarrow \zeta)$ and $[B'_{(j)} \lhd B'_{(j)}] \notin \mathcal{F}(B \twoheadrightarrow \varepsilon)$ for some A' and i,
      then add $[B'_{(j)} \lhd B'_{(j)}]$ to $\mathcal{F}(B \twoheadrightarrow \varepsilon)$;
    fi
    — Case 3 —
    if there is $A \twoheadrightarrow \zeta X \in \text{dom}(\mathcal{F})$ with $X \in N \cup \Sigma$ such that
        there is $[B'_{(j)} \lhd A'_{(i)}] \in \text{Derive}(\mathcal{F}(A \twoheadrightarrow \zeta), X) - \mathcal{F}(A \twoheadrightarrow \zeta X)$
      then add $[B'_{(j)} \lhd A'_{(i)}]$ to $\mathcal{F}(A \twoheadrightarrow \zeta X)$;
    fi
  od
  output "$L(G) \subseteq L(G')$" and **halt**;
End Algorithm

Fig. 1. Algorithm that decides whether $L(G) \subseteq L(G')$

node in T_A for $A \in N$. Formally speaking, the comparison forest is a function $\mathcal{F}$ whose domain is

$$\mathrm{dom}(\mathcal{F}) = \{\, A \rightharpoonup \zeta \mid A \to \zeta\eta \in P \,\}.$$

Each element of $\mathrm{dom}(\mathcal{F})$ is called a *node*. The node $A \rightharpoonup \varepsilon$ is *the root node* of T_A, and a node $A \rightharpoonup \zeta$ is called a *final node* of T_A if $A \to \zeta \in P$. Note that although all the leaf nodes are final nodes, a final node is not necessarily a leaf node. The *label* $\mathcal{F}(A \rightharpoonup \zeta)$ of a node $A \rightharpoonup \zeta$ is a set such that

$$\mathcal{F}(A \rightharpoonup \zeta) \subseteq N' \times \{1, \dots, \flat(A) + \sharp(\zeta)\} \times N' \times \{1, \dots, \flat(A)\}.$$

Hereinafter, we represent an element $\langle B', j, A', i \rangle$ of $N' \times \mathbb{N} \times N' \times \mathbb{N}$ as $[B'_{(j)} \lhd A'_{(i)}]$. At the beginning, the algorithm initializes the value $\mathcal{F}(A \rightharpoonup \zeta)$ to $\varnothing$ for every $A \rightharpoonup \zeta \in \mathrm{dom}(\mathcal{F})$ other than $\mathcal{F}(S \rightharpoonup \varepsilon) = \{[S'_{(1)} \lhd S'_{(1)}]\}$. The algorithm adds to the labels on nodes new elements that satisfy the following statements S-I and S-II. In our setting, every element of the label $\mathcal{F}(A \rightharpoonup \varepsilon)$ of the root node of T_A has the form $[A'_{(i)} \lhd A'_{(i)}]$.

S-I. *If* $[A'_{(i)} \lhd A'_{(i)}] \in \mathcal{F}(A \rightharpoonup \varepsilon)$, *then there are* $x \in \Sigma^*$ *and* $\alpha_1 \in N'^*$ *with* $|\alpha_1| = i - 1$ *such that*

$$S \overset{*}{\underset{G}{\Rightarrow}} xA\theta,$$

$$S' \overset{*}{\underset{G'}{\Rightarrow}} x\alpha_1 A'\alpha_2,$$

for some $\theta \in (N \cup \Sigma)^*$ *and* $\alpha_2 \in N^*$.

S-II. *If* $[B'_{(j)} \lhd A'_{(i)}] \in \mathcal{F}(A \rightharpoonup \zeta)$ *for* $\zeta \in (N \cup \Sigma)^+$, *then there are* $x \in \Sigma^*$, $y \in L(G, \zeta)$, $\alpha_1 \in N'^*$ *with* $|\alpha_1| = i - 1$, $\beta_1 \in N'^*$ *with* $|\beta_1| = j - 1$ *such that*

$$S \overset{*}{\underset{G}{\Rightarrow}} xA\theta \Rightarrow x\zeta\eta\theta \overset{*}{\Rightarrow} xy\eta\theta,$$

$$S' \overset{*}{\underset{G'}{\Rightarrow}} x\alpha_1 A'\alpha_2 \overset{*}{\Rightarrow} xy\beta_1 B'\beta_2,$$

where the occurrence of B' *is a descendant of the occurrence of* A' *(including the case where* B' *is* A' *itself and* A' *does not contribute to the derivation of* y*) in the derivation tree of* $\alpha_1 A'\alpha_2 \Rightarrow^*_{G'} y\beta_1 B'\beta_2$. *That is, either*

$$\begin{cases} \alpha_1 \Rightarrow^*_{G'} y_1, \ A' \Rightarrow^*_{G'} y_2\beta_1 B'\beta'_2, \text{ where } \beta'_2\alpha_2 = \beta_2, \ y = y_1 y_2, \text{ or} \\ \alpha_1 \Rightarrow^*_{G'} y\beta_1, \ A' = B', \ \alpha_2 = \beta_2. \end{cases}$$

If $[B'_{(j)} \lhd A'_{(i)}] \in \mathcal{F}(A \rightharpoonup \zeta)$, then $[A'_{(i)} \lhd A'_{(i)}] \in \mathcal{F}(A \rightharpoonup \varepsilon)$ holds. When it occurs that for some $A \rightharpoonup \zeta a \in \mathrm{dom}(\mathcal{F})$ and $a \in \Sigma$, $[B'_{(1)} \lhd A'_{(i)}] \in \mathcal{F}(A \rightharpoonup \zeta)$ but $B' \to a\beta \notin P'$ for any β, we conclude $L(G) \not\subseteq L(G')$ due to S-II. If it does not happen until when the forest becomes unable to be updated, then we conclude that $L(G) \subseteq L(G')$. In the completed comparison forest, the following statement holds:

S-III. *for every* $A \to \zeta \in \text{dom}(\mathcal{F})$, $y \in L(G, \zeta)$, $[A'_{1(1)} \lhd A'_{1(1)}], \ldots, [A'_{b(A)(b(A))} \lhd A'_{b(A)(b(A))}] \in \mathcal{F}(A \to \varepsilon)$, *there are* $B'_1, \ldots, B'_{b(A)+\sharp(\zeta)} \in N'$ *such that*

$$A'_1 \ldots A'_{b(A)} \overset{*}{\underset{G'}{\Rightarrow}} y B'_1 \ldots B'_{b(A)+\sharp(\zeta)}$$

and

$$\begin{cases} [B'_{j(j)} \lhd A'_{b(y)(b(y))}] \in \mathcal{F}(A \to \zeta) & \text{if } 1 \le j \le b(y) + \sharp(y), \\ [B'_{j(j)} \lhd A'_{j-\sharp(y)(j-\sharp(y))}] \in \mathcal{F}(A \to \zeta), \ A'_{j-\sharp(y)} = B'_j & \text{if } j > b(y) + \sharp(y). \end{cases}$$

The right part $A'_{(i)}$ of $[B'_{(j)} \lhd A'_{(i)}]$ plays an important role in updating the forest correctly. The definitions and notations used in our algorithm are given as follows:

Definition 7. Let $\Gamma, \Delta \subseteq N' \times \mathbb{N} \times N' \times \mathbb{N}$, $A \in N$, $a \in \Sigma$.

$$\Gamma^{\le k} = \{ [B'_{(j)} \lhd A'_{(i)}] \in \Gamma \mid j \le k \},$$
$$\Gamma^{>k} = \{ [B'_{(j)} \lhd A'_{(i)}] \in \Gamma \mid j > k \},$$
$$\Gamma^{+k} = \{ [B'_{(j+k)} \lhd A'_{(i)}] \mid [B'_{(j)} \lhd A'_{(i)}] \in \Gamma \},$$
$$\Gamma * \Delta = \{ [C'_{(k)} \lhd A'_{(i)}] \mid [C'_{(k)} \lhd B'_{(j)}] \in \Gamma \text{ and } [B'_{(j)} \lhd A'_{(i)}] \in \Delta \},$$
$$\text{Final}(A) = \bigcup \{ \mathcal{F}(A \to \zeta) \mid A \to \zeta \in P \},$$
$$\text{Derive}(\Gamma, a) = \{ [C'_{j(j)} \lhd A'_{(i)}] \mid B' \to aC'_1 \ldots C'_{1+\sharp(a)} \in P'$$
$$\text{and } [B'_{(1)} \lhd A'_{(i)}] \in \Gamma^{\le 1} \} \cup (\Gamma^{>1})^{+\sharp(a)},$$
$$\text{Derive}(\Gamma, A) = (\text{Final}(A) * \Gamma^{\le b(A)}) \cup (\Gamma^{>b(A)})^{+\sharp(A)}.$$

Example 4. Let a CFG G have the productions

$$S \to aEb \mid cEd, \quad E \to e$$

and an LSG G' have the productions

$$S' \to aA' \mid cC', \quad A' \to eB', \quad B' \to b \mid d, \quad C' \to eD', \quad D' \to b.$$

After the algorithm computes $\sharp(S) = -1$, $\sharp(E) = 0$, $b(S) = 1$, $b(E) = 1$ ($\sharp_{G'}$ is compatible with $L(G)$), it starts constructing the comparison forest. Figure 2 shows the comparison forest under construction. At the beginning, all the nodes in the forest are labeled with $\varnothing$ except $\mathcal{F}(S \to \varepsilon) = \{ [S'_{(1)} \lhd S'_{(1)}] \}$. To the derivation $S \Rightarrow_G aEb$ in G, G' has the corresponding derivation $S' \Rightarrow_{G'} aA'$, so we put $[A'_{(1)} \lhd S'_{(1)}]$ into $\mathcal{F}(S \to a)$ (by Case 3 in the algorithm). Indeed the added element satisfies the statement S-II. At the same time, $[A'_{(1)} \lhd A'_{(1)}]$ is put into $\mathcal{F}(E \to \varepsilon)$ (Case 2, S-I). By $E \Rightarrow_G e$ and $A' \Rightarrow_{G'} eB'$, we put $[B'_{(1)} \lhd A'_{(1)}]$ into $\mathcal{F}(E \to e)$ (Case 3, S-II). Recall that the node $E \to e$ is a final node of T_E. The fact that $[B'_{(1)} \lhd A'_{(1)}]$ is in a final node of T_E (i.e., $[B'_{(1)} \lhd A'_{(1)}] \in \text{Final}(E)$)

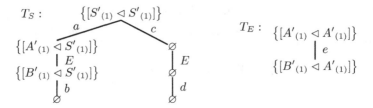

Fig. 2. The comparison forest under construction

expresses the fact that for some $y \in L(G, E)$ (you can forget what y actually is), $A' \Rightarrow^*_{G'} yB'$ where B' is a descendant of A' in the derivation tree. Therefore, for the derivation $S \Rightarrow_G aEb \stackrel{*}{\Rightarrow} ayb$, we have $S' \Rightarrow_{G'} aA' \stackrel{*}{\Rightarrow} ayB'$. In this derivation, we know that B' is a descendant of A' by $[B'_{(1)} \lhd A'_{(1)}] \in \mathrm{Final}(E)$, and that A' is a descendant of S' by $[A'_{(1)} \lhd S'_{(1)}] \in \mathcal{F}(S \rightharpoonup a)$. Therefore B' is a descendant of S' and thus we put $[B'_{(1)} \lhd S'_{(1)}]$ into $\mathcal{F}(S \rightharpoonup aE)$ (Case 3, S-II). The label of the node $S \rightharpoonup aEb$ is always the empty set by $\flat(S) + \sharp(aEb) = 0$. Since $B' \rightarrow b \in P'$, we have no evidence for $L(G) \not\subseteq L(G')$ at this point, where the comparison forest has the form shown in Figure 2.

Similarly, we add $[C'_{(1)} \lhd S'_{(1)}]$ to $\mathcal{F}(S \rightharpoonup c)$, $[C'_{(1)} \lhd C'_{(1)}]$ to $\mathcal{F}(E \rightharpoonup \varepsilon)$, $[D'_{(1)} \lhd C'_{(1)}]$ to $\mathcal{F}(E \rightharpoonup e)$, $[D'_{(1)} \lhd S'_{(1)}]$ to $\mathcal{F}(S \rightharpoonup cE)$. Here, the node $S \rightharpoonup cE$ has the child $S \rightharpoonup cEd$ and $[D'_{(1)} \lhd S'_{(1)}] \in \mathcal{F}(S \rightharpoonup cE)$, but we have no production of the form $D' \rightarrow d\beta$ in G' for any β. Thus the algorithm concludes "$L(G) \not\subseteq L(G')$" by Case 1 in the algorithm. Indeed $ced \in L(G) - L(G')$. If G' had the production $D' \rightarrow d$ in R', the algorithm would conclude "$L(G) \subseteq L(G')$", because we cannot update the comparison forest any longer.

Lemma 6. *The algorithm in Figure 1 always terminates. $L(G) \subseteq L(G')$ iff the algorithm in Figure 1 outputs "$L(G) \subseteq L(G')$".*

Proof. Since $\mathcal{F}(A \rightharpoonup \zeta)$ is increased monotonically and it has the upper bound $N' \times \{1, \dots, \flat(A) + \sharp(\zeta)\} \times N' \times \{1, \dots, \flat(A)\}$, the algorithm eventually terminates. Suppose that $L(G) \subseteq L(G')$. We can check that whenever a new element is added to the label of a node in the comparison forest, it satisfies the statements S-I and S-II. This ensures that the algorithm never outputs "$L(G) \not\subseteq L(G')$". Conversely, suppose that the algorithm outputs "$L(G) \subseteq L(G')$". We can check S-III by induction on $n + |y|$ for $A \Rightarrow_G \zeta\eta \Rightarrow^n y\eta$.

4.3   Time Complexity

Let $\rho_G = \max\{|\zeta| \mid A \rightarrow \zeta \in P\}$. While $\tau_G \leq \rho_G^{|N|-1}$ holds, the maximum thickness τ_G of G cannot be bounded by a polynomial in the size of G.

Lemma 7. *If the algorithm in Figure 1 goes into Stage 1.2, then $-\tau(G, X) \leq \bar{\sharp}(X) < |N|\rho_G\tau_G$ for every $X \in N \cup \Sigma$, where $\tau(G, a)$ is regarded as 1 for $a \in \Sigma$. If the algorithm goes into Stage 2, then $\bar{\flat}(A) \leq |N|^2\rho_G^2\tau_G$ for any $A \in N$.*

Proof. It is trivial that $-\tau(G, X) \leq \ddot{\sharp}(X)$ holds for all $X \in N \cup \Sigma$, since $-|w| \leq \sharp(w)$ for all $w \in \Sigma^*$. Let $d(X) = \min\{ n \mid S \Rightarrow_G^n \zeta X \eta$ for some $\zeta, \eta \in (N \cup \Sigma)^* \}$ for $X \in N \cup \Sigma$. Both claims $\ddot{\sharp}(X) < d(X)\rho_G \tau_G$ and $\flat(X) \leq d(X)|N|\rho_G^2 \tau_G + 1$ can be shown by induction on $d(X)$ respectively. By $d(A) < |N|$ for all $A \in N$ and $\flat(a) = 1$ for all $a \in \Sigma$, we obtain the conclusion.

Clearly Stage 1.1 of the algorithm runs in polynomial time in $\|G\|$. If $\sharp_{G'}$ is compatible with $L(G)$, then Stage 1.2 runs in polynomial time in $\|G\|$ and τ_G by Lemma 7, since $\flat(A)$ increases monotonically in the algorithm. This is true also when $\sharp_{G'}$ is not compatible with $L(G)$. For the comparison forest, $\text{dom}(\mathcal{F}) \leq \|G\|$ and $|\mathcal{F}(A \rightharpoonup \zeta)| \leq |N'|(\flat(A) + \sharp(\zeta))|N'|\flat(A)$ hold. Since $\mathcal{F}$ is extended monotonically, Stage 2 runs in polynomial time in $\|G\|$, $|N'|$, and the maximums of $\flat(X)$, $\sharp(X)$ for $X \in N \cup \Sigma$.

Theorem 2. *For an LSG G' and a CFG G, the question whether $L(G) \subseteq L(G')$ is decidable in $p(\tau_G\|G\|\|G'\|)$ steps for a polynomial p.*

Notice that it is undecidable whether $L(G') \subseteq L(G)$ for a CFG G and a VSG G'. This is because we can construct a VSG G' with $L(G') = \Sigma^*\$$ and it is well known that whether $L(G) = \Sigma^*\$$ or not for a CFG G is undecidable.

5 Learning Algorithm for RSGs

Our learning algorithm for RSGs outputs RSGs in the following *normal form*.

Definition 8. For a shape $\sharp$, let $N_\sharp = \{S_0\} \cup \{ [a, k] \mid a \in \Sigma, 0 \leq k \leq \sharp(a) \}$. An RSG G is *normal* iff the set of nonterminals is $N_{\sharp_G}$ and every production has the form

$$A \rightarrow a[a, 0] \ldots [a, \sharp_G(a)] \qquad (*)$$

for some $A \in N_{\sharp_G}$.

Indeed, every RSG G can be converted into a normal RSG $G' = \langle N_{\sharp_G}, \Sigma, P', S_0 \rangle$ such that $L(G') = L(G)$ and $\sharp_{G'} = \sharp_G$. For instance, an RSG G consisting of the productions $S \rightarrow aSA$, $S \rightarrow bA$, $A \rightarrow c$ is converted into G' with the productions

$$S_0 \rightarrow a[a, 0][a, 1], \quad [a, 0] \rightarrow a[a, 0][a, 1], \quad S_0 \rightarrow b[b, 0], \quad [a, 0] \rightarrow b[b, 0],$$
$$[a, 1] \rightarrow c, \quad [b, 0] \rightarrow c.$$

The difference between two normal RSGs with the same shape $\sharp$ is in which nonterminals in $N_\sharp$ appear as A in productions of the form $(*)$ for each $a \in \Sigma$. Thus, there are at most $2^{|N_\sharp||\Sigma|}$ RSGs in the normal form with a fixed shape $\sharp$. This and Lemma 3 entail that for any language L over Σ, finitely many RSLs on Σ exist that include L (if every element of Σ appears in L). This property is known as *finite thickness*. Angluin [9] has shown that a class of languages that has finite thickness is identifiable in the limit from positive data.

Our strategy to identify RSLs is similar to the strategies by Yokomori [2] and Wakatsuki et al. [3] except for the method to avoid generating a too general

```
Input: a positive presentation R;
Output: an infinite sequence of RSGs;
Begin Algorithm
   let G_0 = ⟨{S_0}, ∅, ∅, S_0⟩;
   for n = 1, 2, ..., do
      take the next string R(n);
      if R(n) ∉ L(G_0) then
         enumerate all the shapes ♮_1, ..., ♮_m compatible with R_n;
         if m = 0 then output "It's NOT an RSG" and halt; fi
         for i = 1 to m do
            construct the minimum G_i with ♮_{G_i} = ♮_i and R_n ⊆ L(G_i);
         od
         redefine G_0 := G_1;
         for i = 2 to m do
            if G_i ⊊ G_0 then redefine G_0 := G_i; fi
         od
      fi
      output G_0;
   od
End Algorithm
```

Fig. 3. Learning algorithm for RSGs

grammar. Let R be a positive presentation of the target RSL L_* over Σ, $\Sigma_n = \{ a \in \Sigma \mid \text{there is } k \le n \text{ such that } R(k) \text{ contains } a \}$, and $\mathcal{S}_n = \{ \sharp \mid \sharp \text{ is a shape}$ on Σ_n compatible with $R_n \}$. Our learning algorithm in Figure 3 runs as follows.

First, we enumerate all the elements of $\mathcal{S}_n$. By Lemma 3, we have $|\mathcal{S}_n| \le \|R_n\|^{|\Sigma_n|}$ and this enumeration needs at most $O(\|R_n\|^{|\Sigma_n|})$ steps.

Secondly, for each shape $\sharp \in \mathcal{S}_n$, we construct the minimum RSG G in the normal form such that $\sharp_G = \sharp$ and $R_n \subseteq L(G)$ as follows. Initially we let $G = \langle N_\sharp, \Sigma_n, P_0, S_0 \rangle$ have no productions ($P_0 = \varnothing$). We repeat the following procedure until we have $S_0 \overset{*}{\Rightarrow} w$ for each $w \in R_n$:

– if $S_0 \overset{*}{\Rightarrow} xA\alpha$ for $xay = w$, add the production $A \to a[a, 0] \ldots [a, \sharp(a)]$ to G.

Clearly this is done in $O(\|R_n\|)$ steps, and $\|G\| \le 3\|R_n\|$ and $\tau_G \le \|R_n\|$ hold.

Let $\mathcal{G}_n$ be the set of RSGs obtained by the previous step ($|\mathcal{G}_n| = |\mathcal{S}_n|$). Third, we pick a minimal RSG among RSGs in $\mathcal{G}_n$. By Theorem 2, we can decide the inclusion of two RSGs in $p(\|R_n\|)$ steps for a polynomial p. Thus, the third step needs at most $O(p(\|R_n\|)|\mathcal{G}_n|) \le O(p(\|R_n\|)\|R_n\|^{|\Sigma_n|})$ steps.

Example 5. For $R_1 = \{abbc\}$, there are two compatible shapes $\sharp_1$ and $\sharp_2$:

$$\sharp_1 = \{ a \mapsto 0, \ b \mapsto 0, \ c \mapsto -1 \}, \qquad \sharp_2 = \{ a \mapsto 2, \ b \mapsto -1, \ c \mapsto -1 \},$$

The minimum consistent RSGs G_1 and G_2 constructed on $\sharp_1$ and $\sharp_2$, respectively, have the following productions:

$$G_1 : S_0 \to a[a, 0], \ [a, 0] \to b[b, 0], \ [b, 0] \to b[b, 0], \ [b, 0] \to c,$$
$$G_2 : S_0 \to a[a, 0][a, 1][a, 2], \ [a, 0] \to b, \ [a, 1] \to b, \ [a, 2] \to c.$$

We have $L(G_2) = R_1 \subsetneq L(G_1) = \{\, ab^n c \mid n \geq 1 \,\}$. The algorithm outputs G_2.

Theorem 3. *The algorithm in Figure 3 identifies the class of RSLs in the limit from positive data. It computes each conjecture in polynomial time in the input size if we regard $|\Sigma|$ as a constant. Moreover, it is consistent and conservative.*

Proposition 1 implies that there is no consistent learning algorithm for RSGs (VSGs, Szilard strict deterministic restricted one-counter automata) that updates its conjecture in polynomial time in both $\|R_n\|$ and $|\Sigma|$ unless P = NP.

6   Future Work

The function *shape* plays a very important role in deciding the inclusion of a CFG and an LSG and in enumerating RSGs consistent with a given finite language. One may expect that our technique is applicable to some other class of grammars which have shapes. One possibility may be deterministic pushdown automata (DPDAs) obtained by adding states to RSGs; we call them *right-unique DPDAs*. An ε-free DPDA that accepts input by empty stack is called right-unique iff

- $\langle q_1, A \rangle \xrightarrow{a} \langle q_2, \alpha \rangle$ and $\langle q_1', A' \rangle \xrightarrow{a} \langle q_2', \alpha' \rangle$ imply $q_2 = q_2'$ and $\alpha = \alpha'$,

where $\langle q_1, A \rangle \xrightarrow{a} \langle q_2, \alpha \rangle$ is read as "when the automaton in the state q_1 with the stack symbol A on the top of the stack reads the input letter a, it goes into the state q_2 and replaces A by α". Right-unique DPDAs include all RSGs, VSGs, and Szilard strict deterministic restricted one-counter automata (if we identify a simple grammar with a simple DPDA). Since the class of right-unique DPDAs has finite thickness, it is identifiable in the limit from positive data. The author conjectures that there is an efficient algorithm solving the inclusion problem for right-unique DPDAs that enables polynomial-time identification of right-unique DPDAs.

References

1. Gold, E.M.: Language identification in the limit. Information and Control **10**(5) (1967) 447–474
2. Yokomori, T.: Polynomial-time identification of very simple grammars from positive data. Theoretical Computer Science **298** (2003) 179–206
3. Wakatsuki, M., Teraguchi, K., Tomita, E.: Polynomial time identification of strict deterministic restricted one-counter automata in some class from positive data. In: Proceedings of the 7th International Colloquium on Grammatical Inference. Volume 3264 of Lecture Notes in Computer Science. (2004) 260–272
4. Linna, M.: Two decidability results for deterministic pushdown automata. Journal of Computer and System Science **18** (1979) 92–107
5. Greibach, S.A., Friedman, E.P.: Superdeterministic PDAs: A subcase with a decidable inclusion problem. Journal of the Association for Computing Machinery **27**(4) (1980) 675–700

6. Shibata, T., Yoshinaka, R., Chikayama, T.: Probabilistic generalization of simple grammars and its application to reinforcement learning. In: Proceedings of the 17th International Conference on Algorithmic Learning Theory. Lecture Notes in Artificial Intelligence, Barcelona (2006) to appear.
7. Angluin, D.: Inference of reversible languages. Journal of the Association for Computing Machinery **29**(3) (1982) 741–765
8. Wakatsuki, M., Tomita, E.: A fast algorithm for checking the inclusion for very simple deterministic pushdown automata. IEICE transactions on information and systems **E76-D**(10) (1993) 1224–1233
9. Angluin, D.: Inductive inference of formal languages from positive data. Information and Control **45**(2) (1980) 117–135

PAC-Learning Unambiguous NTS Languages

Alexander Clark

Department of Computer Science, Royal Holloway University of London,
Egham, Surrey, TW20 0EX

Abstract. Non-terminally separated (NTS) languages are a subclass of
deterministic context free languages where there is a stable relationship
between the substrings of the language and the non-terminals of the
grammar. We show that when the distribution of samples is generated by
a PCFG, based on the same grammar as the target language, the class of
unambiguous NTS languages is PAC-learnable from positive data alone,
with polynomial bounds on data and computation.

1 Introduction

A long term research goal in grammatical inference is to find a class of languages
which includes the natural languages, and is efficiently learnable from positive
data. One of the earliest approaches in grammatical inference, though envisioned
as a discovery procedure for linguists, rather than a model of first language
acquisition is the distributional learning approach of [Har54]. This approach can
form the basis for efficient algorithms for large scale context free grammatical
inference, [Cla06], but the precise theoretical justification is still unclear. Given
that it is possible to construct acyclic deterministic finite state automata that
are hard to learn from positive examples, it is important to identify precisely
what the language theoretic properties that allow learning to proceed are.

In this paper, we take a significant step towards this goal: we combine [CT04a]
and [CE05] to prove a PAC-learnability result in a partially distribution-free setting of a class of context-free grammars from positive examples, without membership queries, structural information or any other side information except for
some parameters we use to stratify the class. [CT04a] argues that for many problems, including natural language, there is a natural distribution or set of distributions, and that therefore the requirement in the standard PAC-framework for
distribution-free learnability is too strict. They therefore argue that an appropriate modification is to consider a suitable set of distributions modelled by a
related family of probabilistic automata (since they study finite automata).

[CE05], on the other hand, which shows the learnability of a class of "substitutable languages" is incomplete in a number of respects. Firstly, though it
demonstrates polynomial identification in the limit, this is not enough to guarantee efficient learnability in practice, and secondly the class of substitutable
languages is very small. For example, the language $\{a^n b^n | n > 0\}$ is not a sub-
stitutable language.

In this paper we consider context free grammars; given that distribution free
learning is too difficult, we assume the data is generated by a PCFG, so that

Y. Sakakibara et al. (Eds.): ICGI 2006, LNAI 4201, pp. 59–71, 2006.

the distribution will be reasonable helpful, but without trivialising the results through possible collusion. Under this circumstance, we can then use statistical properties of the distribution to determine whether two substrings are congruent. The whole class of CFGs is too ambitious a goal to strive for; in this paper we use the class of non-terminally separated (NTS) languages [BS85, Sen85].

We attempt to stratify the learnability of this by adding a number of parameters that affect the complexity of learning. We use separate parameters wherever possible to get maximum discrimination over this class of languages; as a result some of the bounds may appear complicated, but they could be radically simplified by combining bounds.

The relevance of this approach to natural language needs some explanation. Natural languages are close to being NTS. The origin of the name is from non-terminally separated, and indeed if we take a natural language such as English, then given two non-terminals such as noun phrase and verb phrase, the sets of strings that can be generated by each of these are almost disjoint. Of course, lexical ambiguity is a problem, since a word like *share* can be both a noun and a verb, but working with a suitably disambiguated representation, to a large extent, natural languages are NTS. The underlying distributions we use are those of PCFGs. This seems well motivated since the current state of the art in language modelling uses just this sort of model [Cha01, JC00]. Thus the approach we take here, starting from a linguist's idea, is well motivated both in terms of learnability, (the constraints on the distribution) and in terms of the class of languages we consider. There are a number of limitations to the work presented here which we will discuss in the conclusion.

2   Notation and Definitions

An *alphabet* Σ is a finite nonempty set of symbols called *letters*. A *string* w over Σ is a finite sequence $w = a_1 a_2 \ldots a_n$ of letters. Let $|w|$ denote the length of w. In the following, letters will be indicated by $a, b, c, \ldots$, strings by $u, v, \ldots, z$, and the empty string by λ. Let Σ^* be the set of all strings, the free monoid generated by Σ. By a language we mean any subset $L \subseteq \Sigma^*$. u is a substring of v, written $u \sqsubseteq v$ if there are $l, r \in \Sigma^*$ such that $lur = v$. The set of all substrings of a language L is denoted

$$Sub(L) = \{u \in \Sigma^+ : \exists w \in L \text{ such that } u \sqsubseteq w\} \tag{1}$$

(notice that the empty word does not belong to $Sub(L)$). We will define the number of contiguous occurrences of a substring u in w by $|w|_u = \sum_{l,r \in \Sigma^* : lur = w} 1$, so for example $|abab|_{ab} = 2$.

2.1   Grammars

A grammar is a quadruple $G = \langle V, \Sigma, P, I \rangle$ where Σ is a finite alphabet of *terminal symbols*, V is a finite alphabet of *non-terminals*, P is a finite set of *production rules*, and $I \subseteq V$ is a set of start (initial, or sentence) symbols. If

$P \subseteq V \times (\Sigma \cup V)^+$ then the grammar is said to be context-free (CF), and we will write the productions as $N \to w$. We will write $uNv \Rightarrow uwv$ when $N \to w \in P$. $\stackrel{*}{\Rightarrow}$ is the reflexive and transitive closure of $\Rightarrow$. The language defined by G is $L(G) = \{w \in \Sigma^* | \exists S \in I \text{ s.t. } S \stackrel{*}{\Rightarrow} w\}$.

Given a set $L \subseteq \Sigma^*$ we define the syntactic congruence of L to be the relation $u \equiv_L v$ iff $\forall l, r \in \Sigma^*, lur \in L$ iff $lvr \in L$. This is an equivalence relation and indeed a monoid congruence since $u \equiv_L v$ implies $lur \equiv_L lvr$ for all $l, r \in \Sigma^*$.

2.2   NTS Languages

In this paper we are interested in the class of NTS languages.

Definition 1. *A grammar $G = \langle \Sigma, V, P, A \rangle$ is non-terminally separated (NTS) iff whenever $N \in V$ such that $N \stackrel{*}{\Rightarrow} \alpha\beta\gamma$ and $M \stackrel{*}{\Rightarrow} \beta$ then $N \stackrel{*}{\Rightarrow} \alpha M \gamma$.*

A language L is NTS if it can be described by an NTS grammar. Space does not permit a full exposition of the properties of this class but we note first that the class of NTS languages properly includes all regular languages, and that there are efficient polynomial algorithms for deciding the NTS property.

NTS languages are deterministic and thus not inherently ambiguous. We shall restrict ourselves here to unambiguous grammars – i.e. those grammars such that every string in the language has only one (rightmost) derivation. Surprisingly, this restriction does reduce the class of languages significantly, i.e. there are NTS languages which cannot be described by an unambiguous NTS grammar. Consider the language $L = \{a^n | n > 0\}$. This is a NTS language, and it is easy to see that the grammar must contain at least the productions $S \to a$ and $S \to SS$ (since $S \stackrel{*}{\Rightarrow} aa$ and $S \stackrel{*}{\Rightarrow} a$). Therefore, this is ambiguous since aaa will have at least two rightmost derivations. $S \Rightarrow SS \Rightarrow Sa \Rightarrow SSa \Rightarrow Saa \Rightarrow aaa$ and $S \Rightarrow SS \Rightarrow SSS \Rightarrow SSa \Rightarrow Saa \Rightarrow aaa$.

We will also make some other assumptions about the form of the grammar, that do not affect the class of languages defined. In particular we assume that there are no redundant non-terminals in the grammar, i.e. that for all $N \in V \exists u \in \Sigma^* N \stackrel{*}{\Rightarrow} u$ and $\exists S \in I, l, r \in \Sigma^* S \stackrel{*}{\Rightarrow} lNr$. We will also assume that there are no duplicate non-terminals – i.e. no non-terminals that generate the same strings.

2.3   Distributions

A distribution D over Σ^* is a function $P_D : \Sigma^* \to [0, 1]$ such that $\sum_{u \in \Sigma^*} P_D(u) = 1$. We will write $supp(D) = \{w \in \Sigma^* | P_D(w) > 0\}$. For a language $L \subseteq \Sigma^*$ we will write $P_D(L) = \sum_{w \in L} P_D(w)$.

The L_∞ norm of a function F over a countable set X is defined as

$$L_\infty(F) = \max_{x \in X} |F(x)|$$

Note that this defines a metric ($L_\infty(F_1 - F_2) = 0$ implies $F_1 = F_2$), and it satisfies the triangle inequality.

We define $E_D[u] = \sum_{l,r \in \Sigma^*} P_D(lur)$, the expected number of times the substring will occur (not the probability since it can be greater than 1). We define the probability that we observe one or more us to be $O_D(u) = P_D(\{w \in \Sigma^* : u \sqsubseteq w\})$

A context distribution C is a function from $\Sigma^* \times \Sigma^* \to [0,1]$ such that $\sum_{l \in \Sigma^*} \sum_{r \in \Sigma^*} C(l,r) = 1$.

The context distribution of a string u, where $u \in Sub(L)$, is written as C_u^D and is defined as

$$C_u^D(l,r) = \frac{P_D(lur)}{E_D(u)} \tag{2}$$

We will normally suppress the distribution when it is unambiguous. Given a multiset M of elements of $\Sigma^* \times \Sigma^*$, we will write $\hat{M}$ for the empirical distribution.

We define a notion of probabilistic congruence analogous to that of syntactic congruence.

Definition 2. *Given two strings $u, v \in \Sigma^*$ and a distribution D over Σ^*, u and v are probabilistically congruent with respect to a distribution D, written $u \cong_D v$ if and only if $C_u^D = C_v^D$*

2.4   PCFGs

We will concern ourselves with distributions generated by probabilistic context free grammars. A PCFG is a CFG $G = \langle \Sigma, V, P, I \rangle$ together with two functions, an initial symbol probability function, $\iota : I \to (0,1]$ and a production probability function $\pi : P \to (0,1]$ that satisfy the following constraints, $\sum_{S \in I} \iota(S) = 1$ and for all $N \in V$ $\sum_{N \to \alpha \in P} \pi(N \to \alpha) = 1$. For any rightmost derivation we can attach a probability which is the product of the $\pi(N \to \alpha)$ of all productions used in the derivation, and the probability of a string is then the product of the $\iota(S)$ for the start symbol used, and the probability of the derivation: $P_D(u) = \iota(S)P(S \xRightarrow{*}_G u)$ if $S \xRightarrow{*}_G u$. (We assume here that it is unambiguous and NTS). If a PCFG is such that $\sum_{w \in \Sigma^*} P(w) = 1$ then this is a consistent PCFG, and it defines a distribution, whose support is $L(G)$.

3   Learnability and Parameters

Given an unambiguous NTS grammar G defining a language $L(G)$, and assuming that D a distribution is defined by a PCFG based on the same grammar, we can establish the following result.

Lemma 1. *if $N \xRightarrow{*}_G u$ and $N \xRightarrow{*}_G v$ then $u \cong_D v$.*

Proof Since G is NTS, $u \equiv_L v$. Consider any $l, r \in \Sigma^*$ such that $lur \in L$. Let $p_u = P(N \xRightarrow{*}_G u)$ and $p_v = P(N \xRightarrow{*}_G v)$ For any l, r such that $S \xRightarrow{*}_G lNr$, let $p_{l,r} = \iota(S)P(S \xRightarrow{*}_G lNr)$. By PCFG assumptions, $P(S \xRightarrow{*} lur) = p_{l,r}p_u$ and $P(S \xRightarrow{*} lvr) = p_{l,r}p_v$; therefore $u \cong_D v$.

Given the well-known results on learning acyclic PDFAs [KMR+94], it is necessary to add some criterion for distinguishability of states. We modify the definition of [RST98] to handle PCFGs as follows:

Definition 3. *A PCFG is μ_1-distinguishable iff for every non-terminal N there is a string u such that $P(N \overset{*}{\Rightarrow} u) > \mu_1$.*

Note that since NTS grammars are non-terminally separated, this is sufficient for them to be distinguishable in the sense of [RST98].

We also need to add some restrictions not on the distribution of strings generated by the nonterminals but also on the context distributions. Since we will be using context distributions to identify the relation of syntactic congruence, we will require the context distributions to be reasonably far apart in the L_∞ norm. Clearly, given that there will be an infinite number of congruence classes, we cannot require an absolute lower bound on the distance between context distributions. Even for regular languages, the number of congruence classes can be exponentially large, though finite. So we will have two further requirements on our distribution.

Definition 4. *A PCFG is ν-separable for some $\nu > 0$ if for every pair of strings u, v in $Sub(L(G))$ such that $u \not\equiv v$, it is the case that $L_\infty(C_u - C_v) \geq \nu \min(L_\infty(C_u), L_\infty(C_v))$*

Note that according to this definition, if a language is substitutable [CE05], then it is ν-separable with $\nu = 1$.

Additionally we require a certain degree of concentration in the contexts. It is easy to construct examples where the L_∞ norms of the context distributions are exponentially small, in which case we will need exponentially large amounts of data to be able to reliable determine when two strings are congruent or not using the separability property. Accordingly we add the following definition.

Definition 5. *A PCFG is μ_2-reachable, if for every non-terminal $N \in V$ there is a string u such that $N \overset{*}{\Rightarrow}_G u$ and $L_\infty(C_u) > \mu_2$.*

Clearly every PCFG is μ_2-reachable for some μ_2. This implies that there are strings l, r such that $P(lur) > \mu_2 P(N \overset{*}{\Rightarrow}_G u)$. Formulating the bound in terms of the norm of the context distribution is slightly stronger, since there might be more than one occurrence of u in lur. Alternatively we could combine this with distinguishability: if a PCFG is both μ_1-distinguishable and μ_2-reachable, then we know that for every non terminal N there are strings l, u, r such that $\iota(S)P(S \overset{*}{\Rightarrow}_G lNr \overset{*}{\Rightarrow}_G lur) > \mu_1\mu_2$, and so we could simply have a single bound corresponding to $\mu_1\mu_2$. While this is more compact, it is conceptually cleaner to separate the two bounds and treat them independently – this gives a more accurate representation of the functional dependence of the sample complexity on these parameters.

Intuitively we require that we do not have any strings that are very frequent but such that all of the strings that they occur in have exponentially small probability.

4 Algorithm

We now define the algorithm **PACCFG**. Our primary concern here is not with the algorithmic aspects of this, so we will present this using naive, but polynomial, procedures. When implementing this, we would obviously use more efficient data structures. We will start by defining it informally.

We are given a sequence of positive strings $S = w_1, \ldots w_N$. First of all we collect all the frequent substrings, those strings that occur in more than a certain threshold m_0 of these strings. For each of these frequent strings, we collect a multiset of contexts, as follows: for a string u, we consider each data point w_i such that $u \sqsubseteq w_i$, calculate $|w_i|_u$, and then collect all of the contexts from this string. Thus if we have $u = a$ and $w_i = axayaz$, then we add these three contexts $(\lambda, xayaz), (ax, yaz), (axay, z)$. This procedure will give at least m_0 samples from the context distribution, but these will not in general be independent; nonetheless we can be sure that we will have a good estimate with high probability, i.e. that $L_\infty(\hat{C}_u, C_u)$ is small. We then form the set of all those frequent strings u that have $L_\infty(\hat{C}_u) > \mu_2/2$. We then construct a graph, where each node corresponds to one of these frequent substrings, and there is an arc between two distinct nodes, if and only if the two context distributions are similar. The test we use returns true if

$$L_\infty(\hat{C}(u) - \hat{C(v)}) \leq 2\mu_3 \tag{3}$$

We design this similarity test so that we can be sure, knowing the separability of the distribution, that it will pass only if these two substrings are probabilistically congruent and thus syntactically congruent. Given this graph, we then identify the components (i.e. the maximal connected subgraphs). All of the substrings in a given component will be syntactically congruent. We will write below $[u]$ for the component that contains the string u. We then construct a grammar from this, using the procedure in [CE05].

For every component we have a corresponding non-terminal. The set of initial symbols, will be the set of components that contain one of the sentential strings $w_1, \ldots w_n$. The set of productions is defined as follows. For every letter $a \in \Sigma$ that is in U, we add a production $[a] \to a$. For every string of length greater than one, $u \in U$, we add every production of the form $[u] = [v][w]$ where $u = vw, |v| > 0, |w| > 0$; there will be $|u| - 1$ such productions for every string. Note that if $u \in U$ and v is a substring of u then v must occur at least as many times as u and thus $v \in U$ as well.

More formally we define the algorithm in Algorithm 1.

Proposition 1. PACCFG *runs in time polynomial in the total length of strings in the input data.*

Proof (sketch) The number of substrings is polynomial, all of the computations can be performed using standard algorithms that are polynomial in the number of substrings.

4.1 Bounds

We now define the various bounds that are used in the algorithm and its analysis. We start by defining the various parameters. One of the problems with CFGs is

Algorithm 1. PACCFG algorithm

Data: A sequence of strings $W = w_1, w_2 \ldots, w_n$, parameters m_0, ν, μ_2, alphabet Σ

Result: A context free grammar $\hat{G}$

Find all substrings that occur at least m_0 times

$U = \{u \in \Sigma^+ : |\{w_i|u \sqsubseteq w_i\}| \geq m_0\}$;

foreach $u \in U$ **do**

   $C_u = \{\}$ empty list ;

   foreach $w_i \in W$ **do**

      if $u \sqsubseteq w_i$ **then**

         foreach l, r *such that* $lur = w_i$ **do**

            | Append (l, r) to C_u ;

         end

      end

   end

end

$U_c = \{u \in U | L_\infty(\hat{C}_u) > \mu_2/2\}$;

$E = \{(u_i, u_j) \in U_c : L_\infty(\hat{C}(u_i) - \hat{C}(u_j)) < 2\mu_3\}.$;

Construct a graph $SG = (U, E)$;

Compute $\hat{V} = \{V_1, \ldots\}$ be the set of components of the graph SG;

Compute the set of productions

$\hat{P} = \{[a] \to a | a \in \Sigma\} \cup \{[w] \to [u][v] | w \in U, w = uv\}$;

Select the initial symbols : $\hat{I} = \{N \in \hat{V} | w_i \in \hat{N}\}.$;

output $\hat{G} = \langle \Sigma, \hat{V}, \hat{P}, \hat{I} \rangle$;

---

that the strings can be exponentially large, even if we observe a low expected length in the sample, the true expectation could still be exponentially large because there might be a very rare nonterminal that generates very long strings. We need to have a loose bound on the expected number of substrings, so that we can bound the number of possible context distributions we need to estimate: this only appears in a logarithmic bound so it is not very significant. Thus we require the following upper bound L where

$$\sum_{w \in \Sigma^*} \frac{1}{2}|w|\,(|w| + 1)\,P_D(w) \leq L \tag{4}$$

We have precision and confidence parameters, ϵ and δ, alphabet size $|\Sigma|$, an upper bound on the number of non-terminals of the grammar, n, and on the number of productions p. We will assume an upper bound on the length of the right hand sides of the productions of l. We also require that the distribution is μ_1-distinguishable, μ_2-reachable and ν-separable. Given these constraints we define the following quantities.

$$\epsilon_2 = \frac{\epsilon}{p + n} \tag{5}$$

$$\mu_3 = \frac{\nu\mu_2}{16} \tag{6}$$

$$M = \frac{2}{\mu_1^l \epsilon_2} \qquad (7)$$

$$\delta_1 = \delta/4 \qquad (8)$$

$$\delta_2 = \frac{\delta_1^2}{LM} \qquad (9)$$

$$(10)$$

The threshold for the counts of substrings is m_0:

$$m_0 = \max\left(\frac{1}{2\mu_3^2}\log\frac{8}{\mu_3\delta_2}, \frac{1}{\mu_3}\log\frac{128}{\delta_2\mu_3}, 4\log\frac{p}{\delta_1}\right) \qquad (11)$$

The total number of strings we require, the sample complexity is N:

$$N = m_0 M \qquad (12)$$

Given these quantities, we will now state and prove a series of propositions showing that with high probability, the samples we draw will have the right properties. We assume that the data is being generated by a PCFG with the properties discussed above. We draw N strings $w_1, \ldots, w_N$.

Proposition 2. *With probability greater than $1 - \delta_1$,*

$$\sum_{i=1}^{N} \frac{1}{2}|w_i|(|w_i| + 1) \le NL\delta_1^{-1} \qquad (13)$$

Proof By the definition of L the expectation of the left hand side is less than NL. Using the Markov inequality establishes the result.

Therefore we can see that the total number of strings with counts above m_0 will be at most $NL\delta_1^{-1}m_0^{-1} = ML\delta_1^{-1}$. We will divide the productions into two sets, a set of frequent productions, that we expect to observe a significant number of, and a set of infrequent productions, that will constitute a source of errors. For every production $N \to \alpha$ in the set of productions P, we define the set of strings that use that production

$$W(N \to \alpha) = \{w \in \Sigma^* : \exists S \in I, \exists \beta, \gamma \in (V \cup \Sigma)^* \text{ s.t. } S \overset{*}{\Rightarrow}_G \beta N\gamma \Rightarrow \beta\alpha\gamma \overset{*}{\Rightarrow} w\}$$

A production is ϵ_2-frequent if $P_D(W(N \to \alpha)) > \epsilon_2$.

Proposition 3. *For every ϵ_2-frequent production $N \to \alpha$ in P, with probability at least $1 - \delta_1$, there will be a string u such that $\alpha \overset{*}{\Rightarrow} u$, and that u occurs in at least m_0 strings.*

Proof There must be a string u such that $\alpha \overset{*}{\Rightarrow} u$ and $P(\alpha \overset{*}{\Rightarrow} u) > \mu_1^l$, by the distinguishability, and the fact that $|\alpha| \le l$. Therefore $O_D(u) \ge \epsilon_2\mu_1^l$. We have that $N > 2m_0\epsilon_2^{-1}\mu_1^{-l}$ therefore given N samples we would expect for any given production, using Chernoff bounds, the probability of seeing less than m_0

occurrences to be less than $e^{-N\epsilon_2\mu_1^l/8}$. Since there are at most p productions we will require

$$e^{-N\epsilon_2/8} < e^{-m_0/4} < \frac{\delta_1}{p} \tag{14}$$

which is satisfied by $m_0 > 4\log\frac{p}{\delta_1}$.

For every initial symbol $S \in I$, we define $I(S) = \{w : S \overset{*}{\Rightarrow} w\}$. An initial symbol is ϵ_2-frequent iff $P_D(I(S)) > \epsilon_2$.

Proposition 4. *For every ϵ_2-frequent initial symbol S, with probability at least $1 - \delta_1$ there will be a string u such that u occurs at least m_0 times in the sample and $S \overset{*}{\Rightarrow} u$.*

Proof Since it is ϵ_2-frequent we know that $\iota(S) > \epsilon_2$. Since the PCFG is μ_1-distinguishable we know that there must be a string u such that $P(S \overset{*}{\Rightarrow}_G u) > \mu_1$, therefore there must be a string with $P_D(u) > \mu_1\epsilon_2$. Since $N > 2m_0\mu_1^{-1}\epsilon_2^{-1}$, using Chernoff bounds we expect for a given symbol S, the probability of not seeing this string to be less than $e^{-N\mu_1\epsilon_2/8}$. Since there are at most n initial symbols, we will require

$$e^{-N\epsilon_2\mu_1/8} < \frac{\delta_1}{n} \tag{15}$$

which is satisfied by $m_0 > 4\log\frac{n}{\delta_1}$, which is a weaker bound.

Proposition 5. *Assuming that the bound above holds, with probability at least $1 - \delta_1$, for every substring u with count greater than m_0, $L_\infty(\hat{C}_u, C_u) < \mu_3$.*

Proof The following lemma can be proved, using techniques similar to those in [CT04b]. The important difference is that even though the strings may be drawn from the distribution independently, the draws from the context dstribution will not be independent, since the same substring may occur more than once in a single string, and thus there will be dependencies. Fortunately, the Bernouilli indicator variables associated with each context are negatively associated [DR98] and thus we can still apply Chernoff/Hoeffding bounds.

Lemma 2. *For any context distribution D, for any $\epsilon' > 0$ and any $\delta' > 0$, given N' samples drawn from D, which are negatively associated [DR98], where*

$$N' > \max\left(\frac{1}{2\epsilon'^2}\log\frac{8}{\epsilon'\delta'}, \frac{1}{\epsilon'}\log\frac{128}{\delta'\epsilon'}\right) \tag{16}$$

the empirical distribution $\hat{S}$ of the samples will satisfy $L_\infty(\hat{S} - D) < \epsilon'$, with probability at least $1 - \delta'$.

Using the assignments $\delta' = \delta_2$ and $\epsilon' = \mu_3$, establishes the result, given the bound on the number of substrings given above.

If all of these properties hold, then we say that the sample is m_0, μ_3-good.

We now come to the most important step; this lemma establishes that the comparison of the context distributions will give the right answer.

Proposition 6. *If the sample is m_0, μ_3-good, then whenever we have two strings u, v whose counts are at least m_0, and such that $L_\infty(\hat{C}_u) > \mu_2/2$ and $L_\infty(\hat{C}_v) > \mu_2/2$ then $L_\infty(\hat{C}_u, \hat{C}_v) < 2\mu_3$ if and only if $u \equiv_L v$.*

Proof Since $L_\infty(\hat{C}_v) > \mu_2/2$, and the sample is good, we know that $L_\infty(C_v) > \mu_2/4$. (and similarly for v). Suppose u and v are not congruent, then since the distribution is ν-separable, we know that $L_\infty(C_u, C_v) \geq \nu\mu_2/4 = 4\mu_3$. Since the sample is good, we know that $L_\infty(\hat{C}_u, C_u) < \mu_3$ and $L_\infty(\hat{C}_v, C_v) < \mu_3$. Therefore by the triangle inequality $L_\infty(\hat{C}_u, \hat{C}_v) > 2\mu_3$. Conversely if they are congruent, then $C_u = C_v$, and by the triangle inquality $L_\infty(\hat{C}_u, \hat{C}_v) < 2\mu_3$.

Proposition 7. *If the number of samples exceeds N then the sample is good with probability at least $1 - \delta$.*

Proof With probability at most δ_1 the strings are too long, with probability at most δ_1 some frequent production does not occur at least m_0 times. With probability at most δ_1 the sample is m_0, μ_3-good. Therefore the total probability this not being the case is less than δ.   QED

5   Proof

Having established these proposition we can now prove the correctness of the algorithm. We now work under the assumption that the sample is good and show that in this situation the algorithm produces a hypothesis with small error.

First of all, we show that the hypothesized language will be a subset of the target language. Here the proof is very similar to [CE05]. For a string of terminal and non terminal symbols $\alpha \in (V \cup \Sigma)^+$, we can define $w(\alpha)$ to be the set of strings of Σ^* formed by replacing every element of $N \in V$ with one of the strings w in the component corresponding to N. So if $N_1 = \{u_1, u_2\}$ and $N_2 = \{v_1, v_2 v_3\}$ and $\alpha = aN_1bN_2$, then $w(\alpha) = \{au_1bv_1, au_1bv_2, au_1bv_3, au_2bv_1, au_2bv_2, au_2bv_2\}$. If $\alpha \in \Sigma^*$ then $w(\alpha) = \{\alpha\}$, and if $\alpha = N \in \hat{V}$ then $w(N)$ is precisely the set of substrings in that component of the substitution graph.

Lemma 3. *For every α, $u \in w(\alpha)$ and $v \in w(\alpha)$ implies that $u \equiv_L v$.*

Proof If u and v are in the same component, then they are congruent. Since syntactic congruence is a monoid congruence the result holds, by induction on the length of α.

Lemma 4. *For all $v \in \Sigma^*$, for all $\alpha \in (V \cup \Sigma)^*$, $\alpha \overset{*}{\Rightarrow}_{\hat{G}} \beta$ and $u \in w(\alpha), v \in w(\beta)$ implies $u \equiv_L v$*

Proof By induction on the length of the derivation $\alpha \overset{*}{\Rightarrow}_{\hat{G}} \beta$. Suppose we have a derivation of length 0, i.e. $\alpha = \beta$, then the previous lemma establishes the result. Otherwise suppose it is true for all derivations of length at most k. Suppose we have a derivation $\alpha \Rightarrow_{\hat{G}} \alpha' \overset{*}{\Rightarrow}_{\hat{G}} \beta$, and suppose $u \in w(\alpha)$ and $v \in w(\beta)$.

There are two possibilities. Suppose the production used in the derivational step $\alpha \Rightarrow_{\hat{G}} \alpha'$ is of the form $N \to QR$, where $N, Q, R \in \hat{V}$. Then $\alpha = \beta N \gamma$, and $\alpha' = \beta QR\gamma$ for some β, γ. Since $u \in w(\alpha)$, we must have $u = u_{\beta} u_N u_{\gamma}$, $u_{\beta} \in w(\beta), u_{\gamma} \in w(\gamma)$. Pick an element of $u_Q \in w(Q)$, and $u_R \in w(R)$. Clearly $u' = u_{\beta} u_Q u_R u_{\gamma} \in w(\alpha')$, and therefore by the inductive hypothesis $u' \equiv_L v$. Since there is a production $N \to QR$ in the grammar $\hat{G}$, it must be the case that u_N was in the same component as $u_Q u_R$. Therefore $u_N \equiv_L u_Q u_R$, which implies $u \equiv_L u'$, which establishes that $u \equiv_L v$. Alternatively suppose the production used is of the form $N \to a$. As before we have $u' = u_{\beta} a u_{\gamma}$. By the inductive hypothesis $u' \equiv_L v$, and by the construction of the grammar we have $a \in w(N)$ therefore $u \equiv_L v$.   QED

Lemma 5. $L(\hat{G}) \subseteq L(G)$

Since $w(u) = \{u\}$, it immediately follows from the previous lemma that if $\alpha \overset{*}{\Rightarrow}_{\hat{G}} u$ and $\alpha \overset{*}{\Rightarrow}_G v$, then $u \equiv_L v$. Suppose we have some $u \in L(\hat{G})$, then $\exists S \in \hat{I}$ such that $S \overset{*}{\Rightarrow}_{\hat{G}} u$. Since $S \in \hat{I}$ there must have been a string $v \in L(G)$ which occurred frequently and is thus in $w(S)$. Therefore $v \equiv_L u$, which means that $u \in L(G)$.   QED

Now we prove that the error will be small.

Lemma 6. $P_D(L(G) - L(\hat{G})) < \epsilon$

First of all we define the error set to be

$$L_{error} = \left(\bigcup_{N \to \alpha \in P : P_D(W(N \to \alpha)) < \epsilon_2} W(N \to \alpha) \right) \cup \bigcup_{S \in I : P_D(I(S)) < \epsilon_2} I(S) \quad (17)$$

We can define a partial mapping ϕ from the non-terminals in G to those in $\hat{G}$, (from $V \to \hat{V}$). If $N \in V$, then since it is μ_1-distinguishable we will have at least one frequent string u_N, since it is μ_2-reachable, the context distribution will have sufficently large norm, therefore there will be at least one non-terminal $[u_N]$ in $\hat{G}$. Every string $u \in U$ such that $N \overset{*}{\Rightarrow} u$, will be congruent to u_N and thus, since the sample is good, it will be in the same component. Therefore there is a unique non terminal in $\hat{V}$ corresponding to N, and thus ϕ is well defined. Define $\phi(a) = a$ for every letter $a \in \Sigma$ and then extend it to $(V_G \cup \Sigma)^+$. For every ϵ_2-frequent production $N \to \alpha$, we will also have a frequent string u such that $\alpha \overset{*}{\Rightarrow}_G u$. Write $\alpha = \alpha_1 \ldots \alpha_k$ where $k = |\alpha|, \alpha_i \in \Sigma \cup V$ and let $u = u_1, \ldots u_n$ where $\alpha_i \overset{*}{\Rightarrow} u_i$. By the construction of the set of productions we will have productions $[u] \to [u_1][u_2 \ldots u_n]$, $[u_2 \ldots u_n] \to [u_2][u_3 \ldots u_n]$ up to $[u_{n-1} u_n] \to [u_{n-1}][u_n]$. Since for all of these productions $[u_i] = \phi(\alpha_i)$ we have that $\phi(N) \overset{*}{\Rightarrow}_{\hat{G}} \phi(\alpha)$. Similarly since the sample is good we will have that the non-terminal symbol S will be in the initial set, if it is frequent. Thus if $u \in L - L_{error}$, there will be a derivation $S \Rightarrow_G \alpha_1 \Rightarrow_G \cdots \Rightarrow_G \alpha_k \Rightarrow_G u$, for some $S \in I$; since u is not in L_{error} all of the productions will be frequent and therefore there will be a derivation $\phi(S) \Rightarrow_{\hat{G}} \phi(\alpha_1) \Rightarrow_{\hat{G}} \dots \phi(\alpha_k) \Rightarrow_{\hat{G}} u$, and thus $u \in L(\hat{G})$. Therefore $L(G) - L(\hat{G}) \subseteq L_{error}$, and since $P_D(L_{error}) < (p + n)\epsilon_2 = \epsilon$ we have the result. QED

Theorem 1. *If the sample is μ_3 good then* **PACCFG** *will generate a hypothesis grammar which is a subset of the target language and with error less than ϵ.*

6 Discussion

There are no directly comparable results for PAC-learning context free grammars. [Adr99] uses simple distributions in the Kolmogorov sense and membership queries to prove a learnability result for a class of rigid categorial grammars, but the proof is incomplete.

The results here are still incomplete – we are still in some sense hiding a language theoretic property in terms of a distributional property. The same problem occurs with the learning of DFAs in [RST98] – essentially we have some automata which will generally have exponentially small distinguishability. The best way of viewing this is that we have a parameter that measures the difficulty of learning some languages – the difficulty is affected both by the language and the distribution. This approach is worse, because while every PDFA is μ-distinguishable for some μ, it appears not to be necessarily the case that there will always be a polynomial that will bound the separability, though we have not yet managed to construct a counter-example.

Putting the bounds together and ignoring log factors we have, for a grammar $G = \langle \Sigma, V, P, I \rangle$ the sample complexity of $\mathcal{O}\left(\frac{|V|+|P|}{\epsilon \mu_1^l \mu_2^2 \nu^2}\right)$. The presence of the term μ_1^l is worrying. It is not always the case that one can convert an NTS grammar to a CNF grammar while preserving the NTS property. Thus l could in principle be large. However, a very slight strengthening of the NTS property, requiring the reduction system to be weakly confluent on $Sub(L)$ allows this reduction to take place, and thus allows l to be at most 2. Thus the sample complexity is not excessively high, and establish that polynomial learnability of interesting context free languages is an achievable goal.

This is a step towards a long term research goal of grammatical inference – finding a simple class of languages/distributions, defined in domain-general terms, that is provably learnable, in some practical sense, and includes observed natural languages. The class we present here is too limited in a number of respects; most importantly, the requirement that the grammars are unambiguous is too sharp, and we hope to remove this in future work. Additionally, just as our definition of separability allows a certain amount of overlap between the contexts of non congruent substrings, it might be possible to go beyond NTS languages, by allowing a limited amount of overlap between the strings generated by distinct non-terminals.

Acknowledgments

I would like to thank Remi Eyraud and Franck Thollard for collaborating on previous work that has led into this paper. This work was partly supported by the PASCAL network of excellence in machine learning.

References

[Adr99]   Pieter Adriaans. Learning shallow context-free languages under simple distributions. Technical Report ILLC Report PP-1999-13, Institute for Logic, Language and Computation, Amsterdam, 1999.

[BS85]   L Boasson and S Senizergues. NTS languages are deterministic and congruential. *J. Comput. Syst. Sci.*, 31(3):332–342, 1985.

[CE05]   Alexander Clark and Remi Eyraud. Identification in the limit of substitutable context free languages. In Sanjay Jain, Hans Ulrich Simon, and Etsuji Tomita, editors, *Proceedings of The 16th International Conference on Algorithmic Learning Theory*, pages 283–296. Springer-Verlag, 2005.

[Cha01]   Eugene Charniak. Immediate head parsing for language models. In *Proceedings of the 39th annual meeting of the ACL*, pages 116–123, Toulouse, France, 2001.

[Cla06]   Alexander Clark. Learning deterministic context free grammars in the Omphalos competition. *Machine Learning*, 2006. to appear.

[CT04a]   Alexander Clark and Franck Thollard. PAC-learnability of probabilistic deterministic finite state automata. *Journal of Machine Learning Research*, 5:473–497, May 2004.

[CT04b]   Alexander Clark and Franck Thollard. Partially distribution-free learning of regular languages from positive samples. In *Proceedings of COLING*, Geneva, Switzerland, 2004.

[DR98]   Devdatt P. Dubhashi and Desh Ranjan. Balls and bins: A study in negative dependence. *Random Structures and Algorithms*, 13(2):99–124, 1998.

[Har54]   Zellig Harris. Distributional structure. *Word*, 10(2-3):146–62, 1954.

[JC00]   F. Jelinek and C. Chelba. Structured language modeling for speech recognition. *Computer, Speech and Language*, 14(4), 283-332 2000.

[KMR+94]   M.J. Kearns, Y. Mansour, D. Ron, R. Rubinfeld, R.E. Schapire, and L. Sellie. On the learnability of discrete distributions. In *Proc. of the 25th Annual ACM Symposium on Theory of Computing*, pages 273–282, 1994.

[RST98]   D. Ron, Y. Singer, and N. Tishby. On the learnability and usage of acyclic probabilistic finite automata. *J. Comput. Syst. Sci.*, 56(2):133–152, 1998.

[Sen85]   G Senizergues. The equivalence and inclusion problems for NTS languages. *J. Comput. Syst. Sci.*, 31(3):303–331, 1985.

Incremental Learning of Context Free Grammars by Bridging Rule Generation and Search for Semi-optimum Rule Sets

Katsuhiko Nakamura

College of Science and Engineering, Tokyo Denki University,
Hatoyama-machi, Saitama-ken, 350-0394 Japan
nakamura@k.dendai.ac.jp

Abstract. This paper describes novel methods of learning general context free grammars from sample strings, which are implemented in *Synapse* system. Main features of the system are incremental learning, rule generation based on bottom-up parsing of positive samples, and search for rule sets. From the results of parsing, a rule generation process, called "bridging," synthesizes the production rules that make up any lacking parts of an incomplete derivation tree for each positive string. To solve the fundamental problem of complexity for learning CFG, we employ methods of searching for non-minimum, semi-optimum sets of rules as well as incremental learning based on related grammars. One of the methods is search strategy called "serial search," which finds additional rules for each positive sample and not to find the minimum rule set for all positive samples as in global search. The other methods are not to minimize nonterminal symbols in rule generation and to restrict the form of generated rules. The paper shows experimental results and compares various synthesis methods.

Keywords: grammatical inference, CFL, bottom-up parsing, iterative deepening, Synapse.

1 Introduction

In this paper, we discuss novel methods of learning general context free grammars (CFGs) from sample strings, which are implemented in *Synapse* system. We employ a covering-based, or top-down, approach [2]: the learning system gradually covers all the positive samples, beginning with the empty set or a small set of initial rules. It iteratively synthesizes the rules until the rule set derives all positive sample strings but no negative sample string. The covering approach is also employed by Sakakibara et. al. [14], whereas many other grammatical inference systems for CFGs, including GRIDS [5] and Emile [16], are classified into generalization based approach, in which the systems generate the rules by analyzing the samples, and generalizing and abstracting the generated rules.

The main features of Synapse are incremental learning, rule generation based on bottom-up parsing, and search for rule sets. The rule generation in Synapse

Y. Sakakibara et al. (Eds.): ICGI 2006, LNAI 4201, pp. 72–83, 2006.

is based on bottom-up parsing for positive sample strings. The previous version of Synapse uses inductive CYK algorithm [6,8] for generating the rules, which is based on CYK (Cocke, Younger and Kasami) algorithm for the bottom-up parsing. In the new version, a novel process, called *bridging*, generates the production rules that bridge, or make up, any lacking parts of an incomplete derivation tree of the result of parsing a positive string.

The system searches for a set of rules that satisfies the samples. To obtain the minimum sets of rules, we use iterative deepening in the search. In the new version of Synapse, we employ a novel search strategy called *serial search* in addition to *global search*, in which the system searches for the minimum set of rules satisfying given sets of positive and negative samples by iterative deepening and backtracking. In serial search, the system searches for the minimum set of rules for each positive sample, and generally does not backtrack to the choice points for the previous positive samples.

We use incremental learning in two ways. First, for learning a grammar from its sample strings, the positive samples are given to the rule generation process in the order of their lengths. This process continues until the system finds a set of rules that derives all the positive samples, but none of negative samples. Second, the main use of incremental learning is to synthesize a grammar by adding rules to previously learned grammars of either similar languages or a subset of the target language.

The most serious problem in learning CFG is the degree of computational complexity. Among previous theoretical works on grammatical inference, several papers show that CFGs, and more restricted grammars, are not learnable in polynomial time [1,11]. Many works [12,3] on learning CFG restrict the grammar to subclasses of CFG and/or add some structural information to the samples for polynomial-time learning.

As we reported in [8], learning general CFG by searching for the minimum rule sets generally requires time exponential to the size of rule sets. In an attempt to solving this fundamental problem, we employ methods to search for non-minimum, semi-optimum sets of rules as well as incremental learning based on related grammars. The serial search is one method of searching for the semi-optimum rule sets. Other methods include using non-minimum nonterminal symbols in the rule generation and restricting the form of generated rules. These methods generally increase the efficiency of searching for rule sets at the cost that the rule sets may not be minimum.

2   Context Free Grammars and Normal Forms

A *context free grammar* (CFG) is a system $G = (N, T, P, S)$, where N, T and P are finite sets of nonterminal symbols, terminal symbols and production rules (or simply rules), respectively, and $S \in N$ is the starting symbol. The rules are of the form $A \rightarrow u$ with $A \in N, u \in (N \cup T)^+$. We represent nonterminal symbols by uppercase characters, terminal symbol by lower case characters $a, b, c, \cdots$, and any symbols in $N \cup T$ by Greek characters.

The set P of rules *derives* a string v from a string u, if there is a sequence $u = w_1, w_2, \cdots, w_n = v$ of strings over $(N \cup T)^+$, called *left derivation*, such that the leftmost nonterminal symbol B in w_i is replaced by u in w_{i+1} if and only if $B \rightarrow u \in P$, for each $i, 1 \leq i \leq n - 1$. The *language* $L(G)$ of a CFG G is the set of strings over Σ^+ derived from the starting symbol S. A CFG G is *ambiguous*, if there are two or more left derivations for a string $w \in L(G)$.

It is known that rules of CFGs can be restricted to Chomsky normal form (CNF) of the form either $A \rightarrow BC$ or $A \rightarrow a$. The previous version of Synapse [6,8] synthesizes *revised* CNF of the form $A \rightarrow \beta\gamma$. By using this form, we can generally simplify grammatical inference by omitting rules of the form $A \rightarrow a$, when the number of terminal symbols is not large. The improved version of Synapse synthesizes CFGs in *extended Chomsky normal form* (*extended* CNF) of the form, $A \rightarrow \beta$ and $A \rightarrow \beta\gamma$, $(\beta, \gamma \in N \cup T)$. Note that CNF is a special case of the extended CNF. A feature of extended CNF is that we can make grammars of this form simpler than those of Chomsky normal form.

3   Rule Generation Based on Bottom-Up Parsing

Fig. 1 shows the rule generation procedure, which receives a string $a_1 \cdots a_n$ and a set of rules from the top-level search procedure by global variable P, and returns a set of rules of extended CNF that derives the string from the starting symbol S. The procedure is nondeterministic in the sense that its subprocedure contains choice points, and that end terminals are labeled either "Success" or "Failure." In practical computation, whenever a process terminates at "Failure" terminal, the control backtracks to the previous choice points.

3.1   Parsing by Inverse Derivation and Rule Generation

The rule generation procedure includes parsing algorithm for parsing an input string $a_1 \cdots a_n$ using the rules in the set P. If the parsing does not succeed, the bridging process generates rules in extended CNF, which bridge any lacking parts of the incomplete derivation tree. We call the parsing method *inverse derivation*, since the production rules are inversely applied to the input strings in the parsing process. Experimental results show that the parsing time is almost equivalent to that of CYK algorithm for ambiguous, complex grammars, but faster for simpler grammars.

In the procedure, the input string $a_1 a_2 \cdots a_n$ is represented by a set $\{a_1(0, 1), a_2(1, 2), \cdots, a_n(n-1, n)\}$ of terms, and the resulting derivation tree by a set D of terms of the form $Q(i, j)$, each of which represents that the set of rules derives $a_i \cdots a_j$ from Q. For the ambiguity check, each time a new term $Q(i, j)$ is generated, this term is tested whether it has been generated before.

Subprocedure $Bridge(A, i, k)$ generates additional rules that bridge lacking parts in the incomplete derivation tree represented by the set of terms in D. It consists of nondeterministically chosen seven operations. In operations 5 and 6, nonterminal symbols R and Q are also nondeterministically chosen from either

Procedure *RuleGeneration*($a_1a_2 \cdots a_n$: string, K : integer) (Comment: K is
a limit of the number of rules. Global variable P holds a set of rules.)
Step 1 (Initialize variables.)
  $D \leftarrow \emptyset$. (D is a set of terms of the form $\beta(i,j)$.)
  $k \leftarrow |P|$. (k holds the initial number of rules in P.)
Step 2: iParsing by inverse derivationj
  For each $i, 1 \leq i \leq n$, call *Derive*($a_i, i-1, i$) in order.
  If $S(0,n) \in D$ then terminate (Success). Otherwise, go to Step 3.
Step 3: (Bridging rule generation)
  If $|P| \geq K$ and $|P| - k \geq R_{\max}$ then terminate (Failure). ($R_{\max}$ is a constant
  limit for the number of rules generated for one sample.)
  Call procedure *Bridge*($S, 0, n$). (where, S is the starting symbol.)
  Terminate (Success). (Return the set P of rules).

Procedure *Derive*(β : symbol, i, j :integer)
  1. Add $\beta(j,k)$ to D. If $A \to \beta \in P$ then add also $A(j,k)$ to D.
     In the case of synthesizing an unambiguous grammar, whenever ambiguity
     is detected, terminate (Failure).
  2. If $A \to \alpha\beta \in P$ and $\alpha(i,j) \in D$ then add $A(i,k)$ to D, and call
     Derive(A, i, j).

Procedure *Bridge*(A : nonterminal symbol, i, k : integer)
  Nondetermistically chose one of the following operations.
  1. If $\beta(i,k) \in D$, add rule $A \to \beta$ to P.
  2. If $\beta(i,j) \in D$ and $\gamma(j,k) \in D$, add rule $A \to \beta\gamma$ to P.
  3. If $A \to Q \in P$, call *Bridge*(Q, i, k).
  4. If $A \to QR \in P$ and $Q(i,j) \in D$ (or $R(j,k) \in D$), call *Bridge*(R, i, k)ior
     Bridge(Q, i, j), respectively).
  5. If $Q(i,j) \in D$ (or $R(j,k) \in D$), add rule $A \to QR$ to P and call
     Bridge(R, j, k) (or *Bridge*(Q, i, j), respectivelyj.
  6. For each j, $i+2 \leq j \leq k-2$, if $A \to QR \in P$, call *Bridge*(Q, i, j) and call
     Bridge(R, j, k).
  7. For each j, $i+2 \leq j \leq k-2$, add rule $A \to QR$ to P and call *Bridge*(Q, i, j)
     and *Bridge*(R, j, k).

Fig. 1. Procedure for Rule Generation by Bridging

previously used symbols or new symbols. The method of this determination is
related to the restrictions on using nonterminal symbols discussed in Section 5.1.

3.2   Generating CNF Rules

The rule generation procedure produces mainly revised CNF rules, and does
not generate the rules of the form $A \to a$ other than $S \to a$ with the starting symbol S. This is a problem for learning grammars for natural languages,
since grammars with a large number of terminal symbols need a large number of revised CNF rules. To extend the procedure to synthesize CNF rules,
we change rule generation operations (2) and (5) of *Bridge* in Figs. 1 and 2 as
follows.

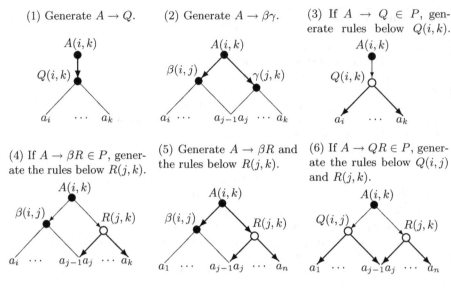

(1) Generate $A \to Q$.

(2) Generate $A \to \beta\gamma$.

(3) If $A \to Q \in P$, generate rules below $Q(i,k)$.

(4) If $A \to \beta R \in P$, generate the rules below $R(j,k)$.

(5) Generate $A \to \beta R$ and the rules below $R(j,k)$.

(6) If $A \to QR \in P$, generate the rules below $Q(i,j)$ and $R(j,k)$.

Fig. 2. An Illustration of Rule Generation by Bridging Operations

1. Instead of the rule $A \to bc$, generate three rules $A \to BC$, $B \to b$, and $C \to c$.
2. Instead of the rule $A \to bC$ (or $A \to Bc$), generate two rules $A \to BC$ and $B \to b$ (or $A \to BC$ and $C \to c$, respectively).

Nonterminal symbols B and C are chosen from either previously used symbols or from new symbols as in the rule generation procedure.

4   Search for Rule Sets

Synapse has inputs of ordered sets S_P and S_N of positive and negative sample strings, respectively, and a set P_0 of initial rules for incremental learning of the grammars. The system searches for any set P of rules with $P_0 \subseteq P$ such that all the strings in S_P are derived from P but no string in S_N is derived from P. We use the following two search strategies for rule sets.

4.1   Global Search

Fig. 3 shows the top-level procedure for global search. The system controls the search by iterative deepening on the number of rules to be generated. First, the number of initial rules is assigned to the limit K of the number of rules. When the system fails to generate sufficient rules to parse the samples within this limit, it increases the limit by one and iterates the search. By this control, it is assured that the procedure finds a grammar with the minimum number of rules at the expense that the system repeats the same search each time the limit is increased.

Procedure *GlobalSearch*(S_P, S_N : ordered set of rules, P_0 : set of rules)
(S_P and S_N are sets of positive and negative sample strings, respectively, and P_0 is a set of optional initial rules.)

Step 1 (Initialize variables.)
  $P \leftarrow P_0$ (P is a global variable holding the set of rules).
  $K \leftarrow |P_0|$ (the limit of the number of rules for iterrative depening).

Step 2: For each $w \in S_P$, iterate the following operations 1 and 2.
  1. Call *RuleGeneration*(w, K).
  2. For each $v \in S_N$, test whether P derives v from S by parsing algorithm. If there is a string v derived from P, then terminate (Failure).
  If no set of rules is obtained, then add 1 to K and iterate Step 2.

Step 3: Output the result P, and terminate (Success).
  For finding multiple solutions, backtrack to the previous choice point.

Fig. 3. Top-Level Procedure for Global Search

It is obvious that the combination of the rule generation procedure and the global (or serial) search has correctness in the sense that every output rule set derives all positive sample strings, and none of negative samples. It is shown in [9] that the bridging rule generation also has the "completeness" for finding the minimum sets of rules in revised CNF for any given samples and sets of initial rules. This property does not hold for synthesizing grammars in extended CNF, because the rule generation procedure is restricted to produce rules of the form $A \rightarrow \beta$.

4.2 Serial Search

Fig. 3 shows the top-level procedure for serial search, in which the system generates additional rules for each positive sample by iterative deepening. After the system finds a rule set satisfying a positive sample and no negative samples, the process does not backtrack to redoing the search on the previous samples.

We can represent two search strategies by a search tree for a sequence $w_1, w_2, w_3, \cdots$ of positive samples such that:

1. The root node is labeled the initial rule set.
2. Each node at depth j is labeled a rule set R such that R is generated for strings $w_1, w_2, \cdots, w_j$, and hence R derives all these positive samples but no negative sample.

The global search scans the whole search tree to find the minimum set of rules by iterative deepening with the size of the set. The serial search finds the route in the search tree such that each branch of the route corresponds to the minimum increment of the number of rules. The cost of the serial search is the sum of costs of partial searches for finding the minimum rule set for each positive sample. In most cases, the computation time is much less than that by global search.

There are cases where the serial search process can find no rule set for a positive sample. This occurs when the process has generated a rule with the

---

Procedure *SerialSearch*(S_P, S_N : ordered set of rules, P_0 : set of rules)

(S_P and S_N are sets of positive and negative sample strings, respectively, and P_0 is a set of optional initial rules.)

Step 1: (Initialize variables.)

$P \leftarrow P_0$ (P is a global variable holding the set of rules).

$K \leftarrow |P|$ (a limit of the number of rules generated for one sample).

Step 2: ⌈Search for a rule set.⌋

For each string $w \in S_P$, iterate the following operations 1and 2. If no set of rules is obtained, then add 1 to K and iterate the operations.

  1. Call $P \leftarrow RuleGeneration(w, K)$.

  2. For each $v \in S_N$, test whether v is derived by P by parsing algorithm. If there is a string v derived from P, then terminate (Failure).

Step 3: Output the result P, and terminate (Success).

For finding multiple solutions, backtrack to the previous choice point.

Fig. 4. Top-Level Procedure for Serial Search

starting symbol S in its right hand side, and every generated rule set having this rule derives a negative sample. Therefore, we inhibit to generate any rule of the form either $X \rightarrow SY$ or $X \rightarrow YS$ in serial search, so that all the rules generated for a new positive sample can be independent from the rules for the previous samples. Note that this restriction on the form of rule sets, *non-recursion of the starting symbol*, does not affect generality for deriving CFLs.

5   Restriction on the Form of Rules or on Rule Sets

This section presents methods of finding the semi-optimum rule sets to reduce synthesis time. Each method considerably reduces synthesis time and slightly increases the number of rules from the minimum rule set search for most cases as shown in experimental results in the next section.

5.1   Rules with Non-minimum Nonterminal Symbols

For finding the minimum rule sets, it is necessary to minimize the nonterminal symbols that are included in the rules by operations 5, 6, and 7 in rule generation procedure. For searching the minimum rule set, the system tests whether it can use any existing nonterminal symbol before adding a new nonterminal symbol. The generation of rules with non-minimum nonterminal symbols omits this test and simply adds new symbols to the set of nonterminal symbols.

5.2   Restriction on the Form of Rules

There are cases where we improve the efficiency of the rule generation by restricting the forms of rules. The user can restrict the forms of rules and rule sets to be generated from the following list.

Indirect Recursion Rules are not of the form $X \rightarrow X\gamma$ or $X \rightarrow \beta X$.

Invertible The rule set does not contain two rules of the forms $X \rightarrow \beta\gamma$ and $Y \rightarrow \beta\gamma$ with $X \neq Y$, respectively.

Reset Free The rule set does not contain two rules of the forms either $A \rightarrow X\gamma$ and $A \rightarrow Y\gamma$ or $A \rightarrow \beta X$ and $A \rightarrow \beta Y$ with $X \neq Y$.

A rule set is *reversible*, if it is invertible and reset free. It is not difficult to prove that extended CNF with indirect recursion is a normal form. It is proved in [12] that reversible extended CNF is a normal form.

6   Synapse System and Performance Results

This section describes the practical system and shows experimental results obtained by Synapse Version 3, written in Prolog. We use a Xeon processor with 3.6 GHz clock and SWI-Prolog for Linux.

We check the correctness and ambiguity of the synthesized minimum rule sets by hand. For the other synthesized grammars, we only tested their correctness and ambiguity for a large number of samples. We use the number GR of all generated rules as an index of the size of the search tree, which does not directly depend on the number of samples and the processor environment as the computation time.

6.1   Using Synapse

We outline how to use Synapse for describing the real system as follows.

1. Input positive and negative samples and optional initial rules. For efficient synthesis, the positive samples are ordered by their lengths. The initial rules are either those of other grammars for incremental learning or simple supplement rules.
2. Select the form of rules to be generated from: revised CNF, extended CNF, and Chomsky normal form (CNF).
3. Set or select the following parameters.
   (a) An ambiguous grammar or an unambiguous grammar to be synthesized.
   (b) Select search strategy: global search or serial search.
   (c) Restriction of the forms of rules from the list in Section 5.2.
4. Start synthesis. Each time the system finds a new grammar, it outputs the rule set. The user can find another solution by redoing the search process.

Example: To learn a CFG for the set of strings over $\{a, b\}^+$ not of the form ww, we give Synapse the following samples.

Positive : $a, b, ab, ba, aaa, aab, aba, baa, bab, abb, bba, bbb, aaab, aaba, aabb, abaa,$
      $bbaa, abba, baba, bbba, aaaaa, \cdots.$

Negative : $aa, bb, aaaa, abab, baba, bbbb, aaaaaa, aabaab, abaaba, abbabb, baabaa,$
      $babbab, bbabba, bbbbbb, \cdots.$

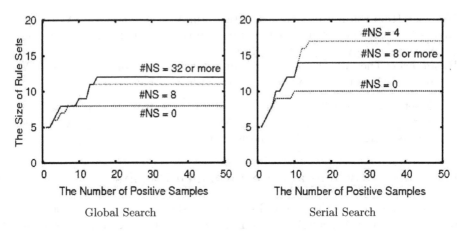

Fig. 5. Relations between the Sizes of Rule Sets and the Number of Positive Samples for Language (e) (#NS: the Number of Negative Samples)

By choosing CNF, an ambiguous grammar, all the restrictions on the form of rules and global search, Synapse outputs a grammar in CNF rules in Tables 1 (e) with 12 rules in approximately12 hours, after generating 1.4×10^7 rules ($GR = 1.4 \times 10^7$) in the search. At present, we have not obtained any reliable grammar for this language only from samples by serial search. If we give simple initial rules $C \to a$, $D \to b$, $E \to a|b$ to Synapse, it synthesizes the same rule set by global search in much shorter time. The system synthesizes a rule set with 9 rules in 7 second ($GR = 169$) by serial search. Fig. 5 shows that the relation

Table 1. Grammars Synthesized by Global Search

Language		Set of Rules
(a)	A	$S \to CD \mid SS,\ C \to a \mid CS,\ D \to b$
balanced parentheses	U	$S \to SE \mid CD,\ C \to a \mid CS,\ D \to b,\ E \to CD$
(b) palindromes $\{w \mid w = w^R\}$	A U	$S \to a \mid b \mid aa \mid bb \mid aP \mid bQ,\ P \to Sa,\ Q \to Sb$
(c) regular expression	A U	$S \to a \mid b \mid \epsilon \mid \emptyset \mid (P$ $P \to SQ,\ Q \to *) \mid +R \mid \cdot R \mid S)$
(d) twice as many a's as b's: $\{w \mid \#_a(w) = 2\#_b(w)\}$	A	$S \to aP \mid Pa \mid PR \mid SS,$ $P \to ab \mid ba \mid aQ \mid bR,\ Q \to Sb,\ R \to Sa,$
	U	$S \to CP \mid DQ \mid PC \mid QT,\ C \to a \mid RD,\ D \to b,$ $P \to CD \mid TC, Q \to CC,\ R \to CQ, T \to DS$
(e) not of the form ww: $\{ww \mid w \in \{a,b\}^+\}$	A	$S \to CD \mid DC \mid FE \mid GE,\ C \to a \mid FE,$ $D \to b \mid GE,\ E \to a \mid b,\ F \to EC,\ G \to ED$
(f) $\{a^i b^j c^k \mid i = j$ or $j = k\}$	A	$S \to aP \mid aQ,\ P \to bc \mid Pc \mid Uc,$ $Q \to aQ \mid aR \mid bT,\ R \to bc \mid bT,$ $T \to Rc,\ U \to Vb,\ V \to ab \mid aU$

A: ambiguous grammar in CNF.   U: unambiguous grammar in CNF.
w^R: the reversal of w. $\#_x(w)$: the number of x's in w.

Table 2. The Number of Rules (R), Computation Time in Second and the Numbers of All Generated Rules (GR) for Various Synthesis Methods for Languages in Table 1

		Global Search									Serial Search		
		Minimum set			Non-min. NT			Restricted			Restricted		
		R	Time	GR	R	Time	GR	R	Time	GR	R	Time	GR
(a)	A	4	0.07	32	4	0.05	13	5	0.16	47	7	0.05	16
	U	6	2.86	847	6	1.09	160	6	0.60	111	8	1.7	50
(b)	A	8	0.18	247	8	0.15	168	8	0.06	57	9	0.03	15
	U	8	0.19	247	8	0.13	168	8	0.07	57	8	0.08	36
(c)	A	10	210	2×10^4	10	3.5	417	10	3.24	368	14	0.24	19
	U	10	210	2×10^4	10	3.7	417	10	3.25	368	14	0.24	19
(d)	A	10	2×10^5	5×10^6	10	2200	7×10^4	10	619	2×10^4	15	0.38	15
	U*	10	3×10^4	5×10^5	10	1020	1×10^4	10	955	1×10^4	11	19	244
(e)	A*	8	1×10^4	9×10^5	8	2470	2×10^5	8	440	4×10^4	9	6.8	169
(f)	A	–	–	–	–	–	–	14	7×10^4	1×10^7	27	27	3×10^5

Minimum set: Search for rule sets with the minimum numbers of nonterminal symbols and without restrictions on the forms of rules.

Non-min. NT: No restriction on the number of nonterminal symbols.

Restricted: Restrictions on the forms of rules and no restriction on the number of nonterminal symbols.

(d)U* Initial rules $C \to a, D \to b$ are given (excluded from R).

(e)A* The following initial rules are given: $C \to a, D \to b, E \to a \mid b$.

between sizes of rule sets and the numbers of positive samples that are covered by the rule sets in learning this language. These plots suggest that approximately 16 positive samples and 32 or 8 negative samples are sufficient for obtaining this grammar by global search and serial search, respectively.

6.2 Performance Results

Tables 1 shows grammars synthesized by Synapse, and Table 2 the number of rules, computation time, and the number GR of generated rules for each of the generated grammars. Grammars (b), (c) and (e) are in CNF and the other grammars are in extended CNF. These grammars are solutions to exercise problems in the textbook by Hopcroft & Ullman [4]. Each of the grammars is the first result among multiple results. In global search, all the grammars are found with $R_{\max} = 2$, where parameter $R_{\max}$ is the limit of generated rules for one positive sample. By assigning this parameter, computation time and the value GR can be reduced by a factor of $1/3$ to $1/4$ as shown in [8].

We summarize the experimental results as follows:

- Both the synthesis time and the number GR by serial search are 10 to 10^4 times faster than those by global search. The rule sets obtained by serial search is generally one to three times larger than those by global search.

- By restricting the forms of rule sets, we can generally reduce computation time by a factor of 1/10 in both global and serial search. There are a few cases that the resulting rule sets have a few additional rules and both the computation time and the numbers GR increase as in (a) A.

- Compared with inductive CYK algorithm[8], the number GR by bridging rule generation is not specifically different from those by inductive CYK algorithm. Synthesis by bridging, however, is generally faster than that by inductive CYK algorithm that needs to repeat parsing in rule generation.

7 Concluding Remarks

In this paper, we described some novel methods and extensions for inferring CFG implemented in Synapse system, and showed some experimental results. The most important improvement from the previous system [8] is that more complex grammars are learned in shorter time. As a result, Synapse solved all the excise problems in the textbook by Hopcroft and Ullman [4]: the previous version could not synthesize an unambiguous CFG for languages (d) and an ambiguous CFG for (e).

The methods in the new version, including serial search and restriction on the form of rules, enable to find the semi-optimum rule sets. By this feature, Synapse can synthesize several semi-optimum grammars much faster than the previous version.

We are currently working on an extension of Synapse to synthesize definite clause grammars (DCGs), which are extended CFG represented by logic programs [2]. In DCG, nonterminal symbols can be extended to include terms with parameters of the form $A(P)$ or $A(P_1, P_2)$, where each of P, P_1, P_2 is a constant or a variable. Since we represent derivation trees by terms $\beta(i, j)$, which are of the same form in DCG, we can easily extend the rule generation for CNF to that for extended DCG rules with additional arguments.

Among future problems, the most important one is to analyze theoretical limitations, effectiveness and power of serial search. Another important subject is to apply our approaches to learning rules in functional logic programs and to syntactic pattern recognition based on synthesize the DCG rules.

Acknowledgements

The author would like to thank Akemi Hoshina, Yuudai Sugita, Keita Imada and Tomohiro Yamada for their help in writing and testing Synapse system. This work is partially supported by Research Institute for Technology of Tokyo Denki University, Q04J-08 and Q06J-06, and by the Ministry of Education, Science, Sports and Culture, Grant-in-Aid for Scientific Research, 16500090, 2004.

References

1. D. Angluin and M. Kharitonov, When and Won't Membership Queries Help?, *Jour. Computers and System Sciences* **50**, pp. 336-355, 1995.
2. I. Bratko, *PROLOG Programming for Artificial Intelligence, Third Edition*, Addison Wesley, 2000.
3. C. de la Higuera and J. Oncina, Inferring Deterministic Linear Langauges, *Computational Learning Theory; 15th Annual Conference on Computational Learning Theory (COLT 2002), LNCS 2375*, Springer-Verlag, pp. 185-200, 2002.
4. J. E. Hopcroft, and J. E. Ullman, *Introduction to Automata Theory, Languages, and Computation*, Addison-Wesley, 1979.
5. P. Langley and S. Stromsten, Learning Context-Free Grammars with a Simplicity Bias, *Machine Learning: ECML 2000, LNAI 1810*, Springer-Verlag, pp. 220-228, 2000.
6. K. Nakamura and Y. Ishiwata, Synthesizing context free grammars from sample strings based on inductive CYK algorithm, *Fifth International Colloquium on Grammatical Inference (ICGI 2000), LNAI 1891*, Springer-Verlag, pp. 186-195, 2000.
7. K. Nakamura, Incremental Learning of Context Free Grammars by Extended Inductive CYK Algorithm, *Workshop on Learning Context Free Grammars*, 2003.
8. K. Nakamura and M. Matsumoto, Incremental Learning of Context Free Grammars Based on Bottom-up Parsing and Search, *Pattern Recognition*, **38**, pp. 1384-1392, 2005.
9. K. Nakamura and A. Hoshina, Learning of Context Free Grammars by Parsing-Based Rule Generation and Rule Set Search (in Japanese), Trans. of JSAI, Vol. 21, pp. 371-379, 2006.
10. S. H. Nienhuys-Cheng and R. de Wolf, *Foundations of Inductive Logic Programming*, Springer, 1997.
11. L. Pitt and M. Warmuth, The Minimum Consistent DFA Problem Cannot be Approximated within any Polynomial, *Jour. of ACM* **40**, pp. 95-142, 1993.
12. Y. Sakakibara, Learning context-free grammars from positive structured examples, *Information and Computation* **97**, pp. 23- 60, 1992.
13. Y. Sakakibara, Recent advances of grammatical inference, *Theoretical Computer Science* **185**, pp. 15-45, 1997.
14. Y. Sakakibara, and H. Muramatsu, Learning of context-free grammars partially structured examples, *Fifth International Colloquium on Grammatical Inference (ICGI 2000), LNAI 1891*, Springer-Verlag, pp. 229-240, 2000.
15. T. Tanaka, Definite clause set grammars: A formalism for problem solving, *J. Logic Programming*, Vol. 10, No. 1, pp. 1-17, 1991.
16. M. Vervoort, *Emile 4.4.6 User Guide*, Universiteit van Amsterdam, 2002.

Variational Bayesian Grammar Induction for Natural Language

Kenichi Kurihara and Taisuke Sato

Tokyo Institute of Technology, Tokyo, Japan
{kurihara, sato}@mi.cs.titech.ac.jp

Abstract. This paper presents a new grammar induction algorithm for probabilistic context-free grammars (PCFGs). There is an approach to PCFG induction that is based on parameter estimation. Following this approach, we apply the variational Bayes to PCFGs. The variational Bayes (VB) is an approximation of Bayesian learning. It has been empirically shown that VB is less likely to cause overfitting. Moreover, the free energy of VB has been successfully used in model selection. Our algorithm can be seen as a generalization of PCFG induction algorithms proposed before. In the experiments, we empirically show that induced grammars achieve better parsing results than those of other PCFG induction algorithms. Based on the better parsing results, we give examples of recursive grammatical structures found by the proposed algorithm.

1 Introduction

Grammar induction is one of the most challenging tasks in natural language processing as Chomsky's "the poverty of the stimulus" says. Nonetheless, applications have already been proposed. For example, van Zaanen [18] applied grammar induction to build treebanks. Bockhorst and Craven [3] improved models of RNA sequences using grammar induction.

There is one practical approach to induce context-free grammars in natural language processing, which exploits parameter estimation of probabilistic context-free grammars (PCFGs) [13, 15, 4, 7]. Although this approach is not optimal, the empirical results showed good performance, e.g. over 90 % bracketing accuracy on the Wall Street Journal [15, 7]. They also utilize bracketed sentences. Brackets explicitly indicate the boundaries of constituents. One may criticize using brackets because making brackets have been expensive in terms of time and cost. However, unsupervised induction algorithms have been proposed to annotate brackets [8, 9].

This paper presents a variational Bayesian PCFG induction algorithm. Parameter-estimation-based induction has mainly two procedures. One is to estimate parameters, and the other is to choose a better grammatical structure based on a criterion. In previous work, parameter estimation is done with the Inside-Outside algorithm [2], which is an EM algorithm for PCFGs, and grammars are chosen by an approximate Bayesian posterior probability [16, 4]. Our algorithm can be seen as a Bayesian extension of parameter-estimation-based

Y. Sakakibara et al. (Eds.): ICGI 2006, LNAI 4201, pp. 84–96, 2006.

grammar induction. Moreover, our criterion to choose a grammar generalizes the approximate Bayesian posterior.

We experimentally show that our algorithm achieves better parsing results than other PCFG induction algorithms. One may be afraid that rule-based grammars do not parse some sentences due to the lack of rules. We propose an engineering approach to achieve 100% parsing coverage based on semi-supervised clustering that mixes labeled and unlabeled data [19]. As the better parsing results supports that induced grammars are well-organized, we give the examples of grammatically meaningful structures in induced grammars.

2   Parameter-Estimation-Based Grammar Induction

Since Lari and Young [11] empirically showed the possibility of statistical induction of PCFGs using the Inside-Outside algorithm [2], parameter-estimation-based grammar induction has received a great deal of attention. Largely speaking, there are two main issues. One is efficiency, and the other is a criterion to choose a grammatical structure.

In terms of efficiency, Pereira and Schabes [13] extended the Inside-Outside algorithm to take advantage of constituent bracketing information in a training corpus. Brackets help the algorithm improve parameter estimation and efficiency. While Pereira and Schabes [13] fixed the number of non-terminals, an incremental grammar induction algorithm has been proposed for more efficiency [7].

Grammar induction can be seen as a search problem whose search space is possible grammars. From this viewpoint, a criterion to choose a grammatical structure plays a critical role. Stolcke and Omohundro [16], Chen [4] use Bayesian posterior probabilities as a criterion where the posterior is approximated by Viterbi parses. This approximation is a special case of the variational Bayes.

Our algorithm exploits the variational Bayes. Therefore, our algorithm is a Bayesian extension of an efficient algorithm proposed by Hogenhout and Matsumoto [7] and the generalization of Bayesian induction studied by Stolcke and Omohundro [16], Chen [4].

3   Variational Bayesian Learning

The variational Bayes (VB) [1, 6] has succeeded in many applications [12, 17]. It is empirically shown that VB is less likely to cause overfitting than the EM algorithm, and the free energy calculated by VB can be exploited as a criterion of model selection[1].

---

[1] The minimum description length (MDL) and Bayesian information criterion (BIC) are also often used as criteria for model selection. However, they are not proper to non-identifiable probabilistic models, s.t. hidden Markov models, maximum entropy models, PCFGs, etc., due to their singular Fisher information matrices. Although VB is still an approximation of true Bayesian learning, its free energy is free from this problem.

Let $X = (x_1, ..., x_N)$, $Y = (y_1, ..., y_N)$ and $\boldsymbol{\theta}$ be observed data, hidden variables and the set of parameters, respectively. VB estimates the variational posterior distribution $q(\boldsymbol{\theta}, Y)$ which approximates the true posterior distribution $p(\boldsymbol{\theta}, Y|X)$ whereas the EM algorithm conducts the point estimation of parameters. The objective function of $q(\boldsymbol{\theta}, Y)$ is free energy $\mathcal{F}$, which is defined as an upper bound of a negative log likelihood,

$$-\log p(X) = -\log \sum_Y \int d\boldsymbol{\theta} \; q(\boldsymbol{\theta}, Y) \frac{p(X, \boldsymbol{\theta}, Y)}{q(\boldsymbol{\theta}, Y)}$$

$$\leq -\sum_Y \int d\boldsymbol{\theta} \; q(\boldsymbol{\theta}, Y) \log \frac{p(X, \boldsymbol{\theta}, Y)}{q(\boldsymbol{\theta}, Y)} \equiv \mathcal{F}(X). \tag{1}$$

It is easy to see that the difference between the free energy and the negative log marginal likelihood[2] is KL-divergence between the posterior $q(\boldsymbol{\theta}, Y)$ and the true posterior $p(\boldsymbol{\theta}, Y|X)$,

$$\mathcal{F}(X) + \log p(X) = \mathrm{KL}(q(\boldsymbol{\theta}, Y) \| p(\boldsymbol{\theta}, Y|X)). \tag{2}$$

Since minimizing the free energy leads to minimizing the distance between $q(\boldsymbol{\theta}, Y)$ and $p(\boldsymbol{\theta}, Y|X)$, the optimal $q(\boldsymbol{\theta}, Y)$ as an approximation of $p(\boldsymbol{\theta}, Y|X)$ is given at the minimum free energy.

Assuming a factorization, $q(\boldsymbol{\theta}, Y) = q(\boldsymbol{\theta})q(Y)$, we find the following equations by taking variation of the free energy with respect to $q(\boldsymbol{\theta}, Y)$ and setting to zero.

$$q(\boldsymbol{\theta}) \propto \exp \left[E[\log p(X, Y, \boldsymbol{\theta})]_{q(Y)} \right], \tag{3}$$

$$q(Y) \propto \exp \left[E[\log p(X, Y, \boldsymbol{\theta})]_{q(\boldsymbol{\theta})} \right], \tag{4}$$

where $E[f(x)]_{q(x)} = \int dx f(x)q(x)$. The optimal $q(\boldsymbol{\theta}, Y)$ is iteratively estimated by updating $q(\boldsymbol{\theta})$ and $q(Y)$ alternately. Note that if we give an constraints on, $q(\boldsymbol{\theta}) = \delta(\boldsymbol{\theta}, \boldsymbol{\theta}^*)$ where $\boldsymbol{\theta}^* = \arg\max_{\boldsymbol{\theta}} \exp \left[E[\log p(X, Y, \boldsymbol{\theta})]_{q(Y)} \right]$, the above algorithm will be the EM algorithm. Therefore, the EM algorithm is a special case of VB.

Next, we explain the important property of the free energy, capability of model selection. Let's assume that we have many models which can describe probabilistic events. What we want to do here is to choose the most likely model. In the Bayesian approach, people choose one which maximizes a marginal likelihood, $p(X)$. In VB, we choose one which minimizes the free energy, which is an upper bound of the negative log marginal likelihood, Eqn.1.

4   Proposed Algorithm

4.1   Variational Bayes for PCFGs

In our previous work, we proposed a VB algorithm for PCFGs, and empirically showed that VB is less likely to cause overfitting than the Inside-Outside

---

[2] When a probabilistic model gives event x with probability $p(x|\boldsymbol{\theta})$, the marginal likelihood is $p(x) = \int d\boldsymbol{\theta} p(x|\boldsymbol{\theta})p(\boldsymbol{\theta})$.

algorithm[10]. In this section, we briefly explain the VB for PCFGs, then derive the free energy as a criterion to search for a grammatical structure.

Let $G = (V_N, V_T, R, S, \boldsymbol{\theta})$ be a PCFG where V_N, V_T, R and $\boldsymbol{\theta}$ are the sets of non-terminals, terminals, derivation rules and parameters, respectively, and S denotes the start symbol. Assuming the prior of parameters to be a product of Dirichlet distributions, the learning algorithm estimates the hyperparameters of the posterior. Let $\boldsymbol{u} = \{u_r | r \in R\}$ be the hyperparameters of the prior. The hyperparameters of the posterior are the converged values of $\boldsymbol{u}^{(k)}$ $(k = 0, 1, ...)$ defined as,

$$\boldsymbol{u}^{(0)} = \boldsymbol{u} \tag{5}$$

$$u_r^{(k+1)} = u_r + \sum_{n=1}^{N} \sum_{r \in \Phi(x_n)} \frac{\prod_{r \in R} \pi^{(k)}(r)^{c(r;\boldsymbol{r})}}{\sum_{\boldsymbol{r}' \in \Phi(x_n)} \prod_{r \in R} \pi^{(k)}(r)^{c(r;\boldsymbol{r}')}} c(r; \boldsymbol{r}) \tag{6}$$

$$\pi^{(k)}(A \to \alpha) = \exp \left[\psi(u_{A \to \alpha}^{(k)}) - \psi\left(\sum_{\alpha; A \to \alpha \in R} u_{A \to \alpha}^{(k)} \right) \right], \tag{7}$$

where $\Phi(x_n)$ is the set of all the derivations of sentence x_n, $c(r; \boldsymbol{r})$ is the number of occurrences of derivation rule r in derivation $\boldsymbol{r}$ and $\psi(\cdot)$ is the digamma function[3]. The computational complexity of updating k is equal to that of one iteration of the Inside-Outside algorithm, which is $\mathcal{O}(N \max_n (|x_n|)^3)$ where $|x_n|$ is the length of sentence x_n.

As we discussed in section 3, the free energy can be a criterion for model selection. Here, we derive the free energy of PCFGs as a criterion to choose a grammar,

$$\mathcal{F}(X, G) = -\sum_{n=1}^{N} \log \left[\sum_{\boldsymbol{r} \in \Phi(x_n)} \prod_{r \in R} \pi(r)^{c(r;\boldsymbol{r})} \right] + \sum_{A \in V_N} \log \frac{\Gamma\left(\sum_{\alpha; A \to \alpha \in R} u_{A \to \alpha}^* \right)}{\Gamma\left(\sum_{\alpha; A \to \alpha \in R} u_{A \to \alpha} \right)}$$
$$- \sum_{r \in R} \log \frac{\Gamma(u_r^*)}{\Gamma(u_r)} + \sum_{A \in V_N} \sum_{\alpha; A \to \alpha \in R} (u_{A \to \alpha}^* - u_{A \to \alpha}) \log \pi(A \to \alpha), \tag{8}$$

where u_r and u_r^* are the hyperparameters of the prior and the posterior of rule r, respectively. Although the first term of Eqn.8 is the most expensive, it can be computed efficiently by dynamic programming just as the Inside-Outside algorithm. Therefore, the computational complexity of Eqn.8 is $\mathcal{O}(N \max_n (|x_n|)^3)$.

Note that the free energy is reduced to the approximate posterior which Stolcke and Omohundro [16] and Chen [4] used, provided that $q(\boldsymbol{\theta}) = \delta(\boldsymbol{\theta}, \boldsymbol{\theta}^*)$ where $\boldsymbol{\theta}^* = \arg\max_{\boldsymbol{\theta}} p(\boldsymbol{\theta}|X)$, and the Viterbi approximation is taken. Therefore, their approximate posterior is a special case of the free energy, Eqn.8.

In the following section, we will show three procedures to search for a more likely grammar in the sense of this free energy.

---

[3] The digamma function is defined as $\psi(x) = \frac{\partial}{\partial x} \log \Gamma(x)$.

$$\begin{Bmatrix} S \to A\ B \\ A \to A\ B \\ A \to a \\ B \to B\ B \\ B \to a \end{Bmatrix} \xrightarrow{\text{merging}} \begin{Bmatrix} S \to A\ A \\ A \to A\ A \\ A \to a \end{Bmatrix} \qquad \begin{Bmatrix} S \to A\ B \\ A \to A\ B \\ A \to a \\ B \to a \end{Bmatrix} \xrightarrow{\text{splitting}} \begin{Bmatrix} S \to A1\ B \\ S \to A2\ B \\ A1 \to A1\ B \\ A1 \to A2\ B \\ A1 \to a \\ A2 \to A1\ B \\ A2 \to A2\ B \\ A2 \to a \\ B \to a \end{Bmatrix}$$

Fig. 1. The examples of merging and splitting. The left figure is merging, and the right is splitting.

4.2   Grammar Induction Algorithm

Grammar induction can be seen as a search problem whose search space is possible grammars. Several heuristics to search for a grammar have been proposed [4, 7, 3].

Our grammar induction algorithm has three procedures to search for a better grammar, which are merging non-terminals, splitting a non-terminal and deletion of a derivation rule. Merging was studied in [16], and split was proposed in [7]. Every time applying one of these procedures, we calculate the free energy, then we accept the modified grammar if the free energy is decreased.

Merging non-terminals generalizes a grammar, and Splitting a non-terminal specializes a grammar. Figure.1 is an example. The left hand side figure shows merging non-terminal A and B to A, and the right hand side shows splitting non-terminal A into $A1$ and $A2$.

The number of pairs of non-terminals to be merged is $\frac{1}{2}(|V_N| - 1)|V_N|$. Since it is not tractable to try all the pairs, we restrict the number of candidates to be merged. The measure to choose candidates is the cosine between the parameter vectors of two non-terminals,

$$cos(A, B) = \frac{\hat{\boldsymbol{\theta}}_A^T \hat{\boldsymbol{\theta}}_B}{||\hat{\boldsymbol{\theta}}_A||\ ||\hat{\boldsymbol{\theta}}_B||}, \tag{9}$$

where $\hat{\boldsymbol{\theta}}_A$ is a parameter vector consisting of all available rules whose left hand side is A. Letting $\theta(A \to \alpha)$ be the parameter of rule $A \to \alpha$, $\hat{\boldsymbol{\theta}}_A$ becomes[4]

$$\hat{\boldsymbol{\theta}}_A = (\hat{\theta}(A \to \alpha), \hat{\theta}(A \to \beta), ...)^T \tag{10}$$

$$\hat{\theta}(A \to \alpha) = \begin{cases} \int d\boldsymbol{\theta}\ q(\boldsymbol{\theta})\theta(A \to \alpha) & \text{if } A \to \alpha \in R \\ 0 & \text{otherwise.} \end{cases} \tag{11}$$

---

[4] To evaluate the cosine of any two non-terminals, the dimensionality of $\hat{\boldsymbol{\theta}}_A$ must be the same for any non-terminal A. Therefore, $\hat{\boldsymbol{\theta}}_A$ consists of any possible rules in Chomsky normal form regardless of their existence in R. Therefore, the dimensionality of $\hat{\boldsymbol{\theta}}_A$ is $|V_T| + |V_N|^2$ for all A.

The larger $cos(A, B)$ suggests that the roles of non-terminals A and B are closer. We also restrict the number of candidates to be split based on $\#_{V_N}(\cdot)$,

$$\#_{V_N}(A) = \sum_{\alpha; A \to \alpha \in R} u^*_{A \to \alpha} - u_{A \to \alpha}. \tag{12}$$

Since $\#_{V_N}(A)$ is the expected number of occurrences of non-terminal A in observed sentences, non-terminal A which has large $\#_{V_N}(A)$ may have overloaded syntactic roles.

We make a grammar compact by deleting redundant derivation rules. The candidates to be deleted are chosen based on $\#_R(\cdot)$,

$$\#_R(r) = u^*_r - u_r. \tag{13}$$

The less $\#_R(r)$ is, the fewer derivation rule r is used.

The input of our algorithm is an initial grammar and hyperparameters of the prior, u. Although they are arbitrary, in the experiments, we use initial grammar $G = (V_N, V_T, R, S)$ where $V_N = \{S\}$, $V_T = \{$terminals in a training corpus$\}$ and $R = \{S \to SS\} \cup \{S \to a | a \in V_T\}$.

Finally, we summarize our grammar induction algorithm in Fig.2. C_{split} and C_{merge} in step 4 and 6 are the maximum number of trials of merging and splitting, respectively. Although the total computational complexity depends on the number of iteration, the complexity in one iteration is equal to $\mathcal{O}(N \max_n(|x_n|)^3)$ as we see in section 4.1.

---

1. Input: an initial grammar and the hyperparameters, u, of the prior.
2. Estimate hyperparameters u^* of posteriors.
3. Sort non-terminals in descending order of $\#_{V_N}(\cdot)$.
4. for i in $1...C_{\text{split}}$
   (a) Split the ith candidate.
   (b) Estimate hyperparameters u^* of posteriors.
   (c) Delete derivation rules while the free energy decreases.
   (d) If the free energy is smaller than that in step 4a, accept the grammar, and go to step 3.
5. Sort pairs of non-terminals in descending order of their cosines.
6. for i in $1...C_{\text{merge}}$
   (a) Merge the ith candidate.
   (b) Estimate hyperparameters u^* of posteriors.
   (c) Delete derivation rules while the free energy decreases.
   (d) If the free energy is smaller than that in step 6a, accept the grammar, and go to step 3.
7. Output: an induced grammar.

Fig. 2. Grammar Induction Algorithm

5   Experiments: Parsing Results

We conducted parsing experiments. First, we compared our algorithm with other grammar induction algorithms. We also conducted an experiment of semi-supervised induction, that achieved 100% parsing coverage.

In every experiment, the Wall Street Journal (WSJ) in Penn Treebank is used for training and test. Training and test corpora consist of part-of-speech (POS) tag sequences. We fix the hyperparameter of the prior, u_r, to 1.0 for all derivation rule $r \in R$. This hyperparameter is known as an uninformative prior.

Since our algorithm belongs to Bayesian learning, the most likely parse, r^*, is given by summing out parameters,

$$r^* = \arg \max_{r \in \Phi(x)} = \int d\boldsymbol{\theta}\ p(\boldsymbol{r}, x|\boldsymbol{\theta})q(\boldsymbol{\theta}|u^*). \qquad (14)$$

Note that it is impossible to apply Viterbi-style parsing to Eqn.14. We therefore exploit reranking [5]. First, 10 Viterbi parses with $\hat{\boldsymbol{\theta}}$ are collected, then the most likely derivation is chosen by calculating Eqn.14 of each derivation.

5.1   Comparison with Other Grammar Induction

We compared our algorithm with Schabes et al. [15] and Hogenhout and Matsumoto [7]. We followed their experimental setting. The training and test corpora are subsets of WSJ. The training corpus had 1,000 sentences of 0-15 words. Test were done on different sentence length, 0-10, 0-15, 10-19 and 20-30 words. Each test corpus had 250 sentences[5]. We conducted these experiments five times.

Table 1 compares the results. "Hogenhout & Matsumoto (15)" and "Hogenhout & Matsumoto (18)" are induced grammars which have 15 and 18 nonterminals, respectively. The results are taken from [7]. "Schabes et al.", "Right Linear" and "Treebank grammar" mean Schabes's grammar induction, a systematic right linear branching except for the last punctuation and a grammar extracted from tree labels in WSJ, respectively. These results are from Schabes et al. [15]. Bracketing accuracy in Table 1 is the ration of predicted brackets which is consistent with correct brackets [13].

As Table 1 shows, the proposed algorithm achieved the best score in every test corpus. The parsing coverage of our method was over 99% (see Table 2). Induced grammars had average 22.4 non-terminals and 509.8 derivation rules. The algorithm converged in less than one hour on Pentium 4 3.8 GHz (SuSE 10.0).

One possible reason why our parsing results were better than others might be because the number of terminals in our induced grammars was larger than

---

[5] Schabes et al. used 1042 sentences of 0-15 words for training, and 84 sentences for test. Hogenhout and Matsumoto used 1000 sentences for training and 100 sentences for test. Hogenhout and Matsumoto used 31 POS tags after merging some rare POS tags for larger parsing coverage while Penn Treebank has 46 POS tags. In experiment "Hogenhout & Matsumoto (15)" and "Hogenhout & Matsumoto (18)" in Table 1, the training corpus contained sentences of 0-15 and 0-20 words, respectively.

Table 1. Comparison of bracketing accuracies with other methods on various sentence lengths

	bracketing accuracy			
#words	0-10	0-15	10-19	20-30
proposed algorithm	98.1	95.9	93.7	89.4
Hogenhout & Matsumoto (15)	92.0	91.7	83.8	72.0
Hogenhout & Matsumoto (18)	94.1	91.5	86.9	81.8
Schabes et al.	94.4	90.2	82.5	71.5
Right Linear	76	70	63	50
Treebank grammar	46	31	25	N/A

that of others. The larger number of non-terminals could capture language more appropriately. Hogenhout and Matsumoto [7] fixed the number of non-terminals to 15 or 18. Although our algorithm stops when the free energy converged, their algorithm does not have any criteria to stop. Moreover, it is straightforward to combine our algorithm with search algorithms, e.g. beam search, but it is unclear for their algorithm due to lack of the criteria of model selection. Although we did not compare our free energy with an approximate Bayesian posterior [16, 4], it is well known that the free energy of VB is a tighter bound to the true posterior than their approximate posterior.

5.2   Semi-supervised Induction as Robust Grammar Induction

In machine learning, semi-supervised learning has received considerable attention. Semi-supervised clustering [19] in grammar induction is to combine a bracketed training corpus and an unbracketed test corpus. Since the proposed algorithm accepts unbracketed sentences also, such a combined corpus leads to 100% parsing coverage on a test corpus even when a training corpus does not have some terminals which occur in a test corpus. We conducted an experiment to show how semi-supervised induction works. We used the same training and test corpora as Section 5.1. Our semi-supervised induction has two steps. First, we run the proposed algorithm only on a training corpus, then we add the following derivation rules to make the induced grammar redundant,

$$\{S \to SS\} \cup \{S \to a | a \in \{\text{terminals in a test corpus}\}\}$$

where S is a start symbol. After that, we run the algorithm on training and test corpora. Table 2 shows the results. "failure" is the number of sentences which were not parsed by the induced grammar. In semi-supervised part, digits in parentheses show the results of the failed sentences in bracketed induction[6]. The digits in parentheses are comparable with the average of all. This demonstrates grammars learned by semi-supervised induction work well also on sentences failed before. Although semi-supervised induction does not improve zero

---

[6] The corpus of length 10-19 does not have parentheses because the coverage was originally 100%.

Table 2. Grammar Induction and Semi-Supervised Induction

	#words	0-10	0-15	10-19	20-30
proposed algorithm	0-CB	85.6	66.6	45.6	12.1
	BA	98.1	95.9	93.7	89.4
	coverage	99.8	99.4	100.0	99.6
	failure	3/1250	8/1250	0/1250	5/1250
proposed algorithm	0-CB	86.0	65.9	44.0	11.4
+ semi-supervised		(100)	(87.5)	N/A	(0.0)
	BA	98.2	95.8	93.6	89.6
		(100)	(98.1)	N/A	(79.5)
	coverage	100.0	100.0	100.0	100.0
	failure	0/1250	0/1250	0/1250	0/1250

crossing brackets (0-CB)[7] and bracketing accuracy (BA), this would be because failed sentences are few, i.e. 3, 8, 0 and 5 sentences in 0-10, 0-15, 10-19 and 20-30 words test corpora, respectively.

We have proposed an approach to combine training and test corpora. However, this might be untractable when test corpora are very large. On-line learning is another approach. It is straightforward to apply on-line learning based on the variational Bayes [14]. This would turn the proposed algorithm into an efficient incremental semi-supervised induction algorithm.

6   Discussion: Induced Grammars

So far, we have shown the parsing results of our grammar induction algorithm. However, we believe strongly that grammar induction is not only for obtaining a parser but also can be a tool for grammatical structure understanding.

Fig.3 is an illustrative example of a parse tree predicted by an induced grammar. Fig.4 lists a subset of the induced grammar used in Fig.3. In this example, non-terminal 15 derives "DT JJ* NN" where DT is determiner, JJ is adjective and NN is noun. Therefore, non-terminal 15 can be interpreted as a noun phrase (NP). We can also find that start symbol S derives the following grammatical structure (see Appendix A),

$$S \Rightarrow \underbrace{(PRP|DT\ JJ^*\ NN)}_{subject}\ \underbrace{(VBD|VBZ|VBP)}_{verb}\ \underbrace{DT\ JJ^*\ NN}_{noun\text{-}phrase}\ IN\ \underbrace{DT\ JJ^*\ NN}_{noun\text{-}phrase}.$$

where $(\cdot|\cdot)$, $*$, ? are the usual notations of regular expressions, PRP is personal pronoun, VBD is verb (past tense), VBZ is verb (third person singular present), VBP is verb (non-third person singular present) and IN is preposition or subordinating conjunction. Clearly, this structure captures typical English sentences.

---

[7] 0-CB is the ratio of sentences whose brackets are completely consistent with correct brackets.

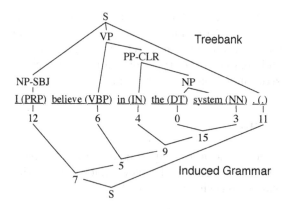

Fig. 3. A parse tree from Treebank and a parse tree predicted by an induced grammar

left hand side non-terminal	$\hat{\theta}$ derivation rule
15	0.28 15 → 0 3
0	0.62 0 → DT 0.11 0 → 0 10
10	0.47 10 → JJ
3	0.81 3 → NN

Fig. 4. The induced grammar in Fig.3. Using shown derivation rules, non-terminal 15 derives "DT JJ* NN", where DT is determiner, JJ is adjective and NN is noun.

The above discussion is based on selected examples, and nonsense structures can also be found due to redundant derivation rules. Actually, it is not trivial how to find meaningful grammatical structures. But, the parsing results support that induced grammars have meaningful structures.

7   Conclusion

We have proposed a variational Bayesian PCFG induction algorithm in the context of parameter-estimation-based grammar induction. Experimental results showed that the proposed algorithm induced more well-structured grammars in terms of parsing results than other PCFG induction algorithms. We also showed that induced PCFGs in fact had meaningful recursive structures.

As future work, we may need to exploit a dependency model to improve parsing results. Since our algorithm is greedy, we might combine our algorithm with a search algorithm such as beam search. Although we constrained ourselves to PCFGs, we should explore other types of grammars as well. Moreover, how to find meaningful structures from induced grammars remains to be investigated.

Acknowledgments

Special thanks to Dr. Kameya for helpful comments. This research was funded by the 21st Century COE Program "Framework for Systematization and Application of Large-scale Knowledge Resources."

Bibliography

[1] Hagai Attias. A variational Bayesian framework for graphical models. In *Advances in Neural Information Processing Systems*, volume 12, 2000.

[2] J. K. Baker. Trainable grammars for speech recognition. In D. H. Klatt and J. J. Wolf, editors, *Speech Communication Papers for the 97th Meeting of the Acoustical Society of America*, pages 547–550, 1979.

[3] Joseph Bockhorst and Mark Craven. Refining the structure of a stochastic context-free grammar. In *Proceedings of the 17th International Joint Conference on Artificial Intelligence*, 2001.

[4] Stanley F. Chen. Bayesian grammar induction for language modeling. In *Meeting of the Association for Computational Linguistics*, pages 228–235, 1995.

[5] Michael Collins. Discriminative reranking for natural language parsing. In *Proc. 17th International Conf. on Machine Learning*, pages 175–182, 2000.

[6] Zoubin Ghahramani and Matthew J. Beal. Variational inference for Bayesian mixtures of factor analysers. In *Advances in Neural Information Processing Systems*, volume 12, 2000.

[7] Wide R. Hogenhout and Yuji Matsumoto. A fast method for statistical grammar induction. *Natural Language Engineering*, 4(3):191–209, 1998.

[8] Dan Klein and Christopher D. Manning. A generative constituent-context model for improved grammar induction. In *Proceedings of the 40th Annual Meeting of the ACL*, 2002.

[9] Dan Klein and Christopher D. Manning. Corpus-based induction of syntactic structure: Models of dependency and constituency. In *Proceedings of the 42nd Annual Meeting of the ACL*, 2004.

[10] Kenichi Kurihara and Taisuke Sato. An application of the variational Bayesian approach to probabilistic context-free grammars, 2004. IJCNLP-04 Workshop beyond shallow analyses.

[11] Karim Lari and Steve Young. The estimation of stochastic context-free grammars using the inside-outside algorithm. *Computer Speech and Language*, 4:35–56, 1990.

[12] David J.C. MacKay. em ensemble learning for hidden markov models. Technical report, 1997.

[13] Fernando C. N. Pereira and Yves Schabes. Inside-outside reestimation from partially bracketed corpora. In *Meeting of the Association for Computational Linguistics*, pages 128–135, 1992.

[14] Masaaki Sato. Online model selection based on the variational bayes. In *Neural Computation*, volume 13, pages 1649–1681, 2001.

[15] Yves Schabes, Michal Roth, and Randy Osborne. Parsing the wall street journal with the inside-outside algorithm. In *ACL*, pages 341–347, 1993.

[16] Andreas Stolcke and Stephen Omohundro. Inducing probabilistic grammars by Bayesian model merging. In *International Conference on Grammatical Inference*, 1994.

[17] Naonori Ueda and Zoubin Ghahramani. Bayesian model search for mixture models based on optimizing variational bounds. *Neural Networks*, 15(10):1223–1241, 2002.

[18] Menno van Zaanen. Abl: Alighment-based learning. In *COLING*, volume 18, pages 961–967, 2000.

[19] Kiri Wagsta, Claire Cardie, Seth Rogers, and Stefan Schroedl. Constrained k-means clustering with background knowledge. In *Proceedings of 18th International Conference on Machine Learning*, pages 577–584, 2001.

Appendix

A   A Grammatical Structure in an Induced Grammar

Fig.5 lists a subset of the induced grammar used in Fig.3. These derivation rules leads a grammatical structure,

$$S \Rightarrow \underbrace{(\text{PRP}|\text{DT}\ \text{JJ}^*\ \text{NN})}_{\text{subject}}\ \underbrace{(\text{VBD}|\text{VBZ}|\text{VBP})}_{\text{verb}}\ \underbrace{\text{DT}\ \text{JJ}^*\ \text{NN}}_{\text{noun-phrase}}\ \text{IN}\ \underbrace{\text{DT}\ \text{JJ}^*\ \text{NN}}_{\text{noun-phrase}}\ .$$

$\hat{\theta}$	derivation rule
0.80	S → 7 11
0.64	7 → 12 5
0.23	12 → PRP
0.19	12 → 0 3
0.62	0 → DT
0.11	0 → 0 10
0.47	10 → JJ
0.81	3 → NN
0.79	5 → 6 9
0.30	6 → VBD
0.26	6 → VBZ
0.15	6 → VBP
0.26	9 → 8 1
0.24	8 → 0 3
0.48	1 → 4 15
0.55	4 → IN
0.28	15 → 0 3
0.85	11 → .

Fig. 5. A subset of the induced grammar in Fig.3

where PRP is personal noun, DT is determiner, JJ is adjective, NN is noun, VBD is verb (past tense), VBZ is verb (third person singular present), VBP is (non-third person singular present) and IN is preposition or subordinating conjunction. "DT JJ* NN" can be interpreted as a noun phrase. Therefore, (PRP|DT JJ* NN) is also a noun phrase. In this example, (PRP|DT JJ* NN) makes the subject of the sentence.

Stochastic Analysis of Lexical and Semantic Enhanced Structural Language Model

Shaojun Wang[1,2], Shaomin Wang[3], Li Cheng[4],
Russell Greiner[2], and Dale Schuurmans[2]

[1] Wright State University, USA
[2] University of Alberta, Canada
[3] Oracle, USA
[4] National ICT, Australia

Abstract. In this paper, we present a directed Markov random field model that integrates trigram models, structural language models (SLM) and probabilistic latent semantic analysis (PLSA) for the purpose of statistical language modeling. The SLM is essentially a generalization of shift-reduce probabilistic push-down automata thus more complex and powerful than probabilistic context free grammars (PCFGs). The added context-sensitiveness due to trigrams and PLSAs and violation of tree structure in the topology of the underlying random field model make the inference and parameter estimation problems plausibly intractable, however the analysis of the behavior of the lexical and semantic enhanced structural language model leads to a generalized inside-outside algorithm and thus to rigorous exact EM type re-estimation of the composite language model parameters.

Keywords: Language modeling, structural language model, trigram, probabilistic latent semantic analysis.

1 Introduction

Natural language perhaps is one of the most intriguing and complex stochastic processes (Chomsky 1956, Jelinek 1998). It was first studied by Shannon (1948) as a Markov chain model when he introduced information theory to illustrate many of its features. Since then various kinds of generative probabilistic language models have been proposed to capture different aspects of natural language regularity. The dominant motivation for language modeling has traditionally come from the field of speech recognition (Jelinek 1998), however statistical language models have recently become more widely used in many other application areas, such as information retrieval, machine translation, optical character recognition, spelling correction, document classification, and bioinformatics. The most recent advance is the work by Wang et al. (2005), where they have proposed a first generative probabilistic model of natural language, *a directed Markov random field model*, that combines trigram models, PCFGs and PLSAs (Hofmann 2001) and simultaneously exploits the relevant lexical, syntactic and

Y. Sakakibara et al. (Eds.): ICGI 2006, LNAI 4201, pp. 97–111, 2006.

semantic information of natural language with tractable parameter estimation algorithm.

Jelinek and Chelba (Chelba and Jelinek 2000, Jelinek 2004) have developed a structural language model that exploits syntactic structure incrementally while traversing the sentence from left to right, and used it to extract meaningful information from the word history, thus enabling the use of sentence level long range dependencies. SLM is essentially a generalization of shift-reduce probabilistic push-down automata and is non-context free (Jelinek 2004). A thorough comparative study between this model with PCFGs has been presented in (Abney et al. 1999). The probabilistic dependency structure in SLM is more complex than that in a PCFG. When SLM was originally introduced (Chelba and Jelinek 2000), it operated with the help of a set of stacks containing partial parses from which less probable sub-parse trees are discarded. The parameters were trained by a procedure based on n-best final parses. It has been shown that the use of SLM results in lower perplexities as well as lower error rates in speech recognition. When SLM is combined with trigram model with linear interpolation (Chelba and Jelinek 2000) or integrated with trigram model and semantic language model, which carry complementary dependency structure, under maximum entropy estimation paradigm (Khudanpur and Wu 2000) with SLM as a preprocessing tool to extract syntactic structure, almost additive results have been observed in perplexity or word error reductions. Later, Jelinek (2004) studied various stochastic properties of the SLM, in particular he generalized the CKY algorithm (Younger 1967) to obtain a chart which is able to directly compute the sentence probability thus making the stack unnecessary, moreover he derived a generalized inside-outside algorithm which leads to a rigorous EM type re-estimation for the SLM parameters.

Inspired by the works by Jelinek (2004) and Wang et al. (2005), we study the stochastic properties of a composite generative probabilistic language model which integrates trigram model, PLSA models with SLM. Similar as for PCFG (Jelinek et al. 1992) and SLM (Jelinek 2004), among the stochastic properties with which we study are the following ones:

– The probability of the generated sentence based on a generalization of the CKY algorithm.
– The probability of the next word given the sentence prefix.
– The probability of the most probable parse.
– Training algorithm for the statistical parameters of the composite language model.

The added context-sensitiveness due to trigrams and PLSAs and violation of tree structure in the topology of the underlying random field model make the inference and parameter estimation plausibly intractable, in the following we show that exact recursive algorithms do exist with the same order polynomial time complexity as in the SLM for the study of stochastic properties of the lexical and semantic enhanced SLM.

2 Jelinek and Chelba's Simplified Structural Language Model

In this section, we briefly describe the simplified structural language model (SSLM) which was introduced by Jelinek and Chelba (Chelba 1999, Chelba and Jelinek 2000, Jelinek and Chelba 1999, Jelinek 2004). SSLM is completely lexical, that is, phrases are annotated by headwords but not by non-terminals. As the operation of the SSLM proceeds, it generates a string of words, $w_0, w_1, \cdots, w_n, w_{n+1}$, where $\forall i = 1, \cdots, n, w_i \in \mathcal{V}, w_0 = < s >$, and $w_{n+1} = < /s >$, where $\mathcal{V}$ is the set of vocabulary, $< s >, < /s >$ are start and stop markers of the sentence, at the meantime, it also generates a parse consisting of a binary tree whose nodes are marked by *headwords* of phrases spanned by the subtree stemming from the leafs. The headword of a phrase can be any word belonging to the span of the phrase and the headword at the apex of the final tree is $< s >$. The SSLM operates from left to right, builds up the phrase structure in a bottom-up manner and it has two type of operations, *constructor* moves and *predictor* moves.

1. Constructor moves: The constructor looks at the pair of right most exposed headwords, h_{-2}, h_{-1} and takes an action $a \in \mathcal{A} = \{$adjoin **right**, adjoin **left**, **null**$\}$ with probability $\theta(a|h_{-2}h_{-1})$. The operations of these three actions are defined as the following:

- adjoin **right**: create an apex marked by the identity of h_{-1} and connect it by a leftward branch to its leftmost exposed headword h_{-2} and by a rightward branch to the exposed headword h_{-1}. Increase the indices of the current exposed headwords $h_{-3}, h_{-4}, \cdots$ by 1. These headwords together with h_{-1} become become the new set of exposed headwords.
- adjoin **left**: create an apex marked by the identity of h_{-2} and connect it by a leftward branch to its leftmost exposed headword h_{-2} and by a rightward branch to the exposed headword h_{-1}. Increase the indices of the new apex and those of the current exposed headwords $h_{-3}, h_{-4}, \cdots$ by 1. These headwords become become the new set of exposed headwords.
- **null**: leave headword indexing and current parse structure unchanged and pass control to the predictor.

If $a \in \{$adjoin **left**$\}$, adjoin **right**$\}$, the constructor stays in control and chooses the next action with probability $\theta(a|h_{-2}h_{-1})$. If $a = $ **null**, the constructor stops and the control is passed to the predictor. A **null** move ensures that the rightmost exposed headword will eventually be connected to the right and an **adjoin** move makes the right-most exposed headword being connected to the left.

2. Predictor moves: The predictor generates the next word w_i with probability $\theta(w_i|h_{-2}h_{-1}), w_i \in \mathcal{V} \cup < s >$. The indexes of the current headwords $h_{-1}, h_{-2}, \cdots$ are decreased by 1 and the newly generated word becomes the right most exposed headword. Control is then passed to the constructor.

As in (Wang et al. 2005), let X denote a set of random variables $(X_\tau)_{\tau \in \Gamma}$ taking values in a (discrete) probability spaces $(\mathcal{X}_\tau)_{\tau \in \Gamma}$ where Γ is a finite set of states. We define a (discrete) *directed Markov random field* to be a probability distribution $\mathcal{P}$ which admits a recursive factorization if there exist non-negative functions, $k^\tau(\cdot, \cdot), \tau \in \Gamma$ defined on $\mathcal{X}_\tau \times \mathcal{X}_{pa(\tau)}$, such that $\sum_{x_\tau} k^\tau(x_\tau, x_{pa(\tau)}) = 1$ and $\mathcal{P}$ has density $p(x) = \prod_{\tau \in \Gamma} k^\tau(x_\tau, x_{pa(\tau)})$

If the recursive factorization respects to a graph $\mathcal{G}$, then we have a Bayesian network (Lauritzen 1996). But broadly speaking, the recursive factorization can respect to a more complicated representation other than a graph which has a fixed set of nodes and edges.

All of the weighted grammars and automata can be described as directed Markov random fields, so is the (simplified) structural language model as developed by Jelinek and Chelba (Chelba and Jelinek 2000, Jelinek 2004).

3   Simplified Lexical and Semantic Enhanced Structural Language Model

We now describe the composite simplified structural language model enhanced by trigrams and PLSA models, which respectively encode the local lexical information of word co-occurrence and global-spanning semantic content at document level over the entire corpus.

When we combine trigram and PLSA models with SSLM to build a new generative language model, the constructor moves remain unchanged, the predictor however generates the next word w_i not only depending on the two left-most exposed headwords h_{-2}, h_{-1} but also the previous two words w_{i-2}, w_{i-1} as well as the current semantic content $g_i \in \mathcal{G}$ with probability $\theta(w_i | w_{i-2} w_{i-1} h_{-2} h_{-1} g_i)$. Figure 1 illustrates the structure of the simplified lexical and semantic enhanced structural language model.

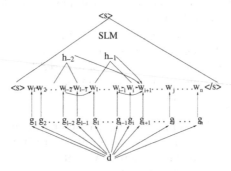

Fig. 1. Simplified lexical and semantic enhanced structural language model where the hidden information is the parse tree t and semantic content g

3.1   Computing the Probability of a Sentence

The inside probability $p_\theta(d, w_{i+1}^j, y[i, j] | w_i, x)$ of sentence W in document d is defined as the probability of the word subsequence $w_{i+1}^j = w_{i+1}, \cdots, w_j$ are generated and y becomes the headword of the phrase $w_i, \cdots, w_j$ given that x

is the last exposed headword preceding time i and the word w_i is generated. Figure 2 illustrates two situations on how the phrase $w_i, \cdots, w_j$ is generated.

The first way as illustrated in Figure 2 to generate $w_{i+1}, \cdots, w_j$ and create a phrase spanning $< i, j >$ whose headword is y, given that the headword of the preceding phrase is x and the word w_i is generated is the following: (i) a string $w_{i+1}, \cdots, w_l$ is generated, (ii) a phrase spanning $< i, l >$ is formed whose headword is y, (iii) the word w_{l+1} is generated from its preceding two words w_{l-1}, w_l and preceding two headwords x, y by averaging all possible semantic content g in document d, (iv) the string $w_{l+1}, \cdots, w_j$ is generated and the span $< l+1, j >$ forms a phrase whose headword is z, (v) finally, the two phrases are merged into one phrase with headword y via constructor move, adjoin left.

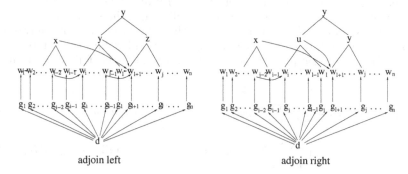

adjoin left   adjoin right

Fig. 2. Diagram illustrating inside probability recursions: adjoin left vs adjoin right

The second way as illustrated in Figure 2 to generate $w_{i+1}, \cdots, w_j$ and create a phrase spanning $< i, j >$ whose headword is y, given that the headword of the preceding phrase is x and the word w_i, is conceptually the same as the first situation with modular chance, that is, in (ii) a phrase spanning $< i, l >$ is formed with headword is u, then in (iii) the word w_{l+1} is generated from its preceding two words w_{l-1}, w_l and preceding two headwords x, u by averaging all possible semantic content g in document d, thus (iv) the string $w_{l+1}, \cdots, w_j$ is generated and the span $< l + 1, j >$ forms a phrase whose headword is y, (v) finally, the two phrases are merged into one phrase with headword y via constructor move, adjoin right.

Thus the inside probability $p_\theta(w_{i+1}^j, y[i, j] | w_i, x), \forall j > i, i = 0, 1, \cdots, n$ can be recursively computed by the following formula,

$$p_\theta(d, w_{i+1}^j, y[i,j] | w_i, x) = \sum_{l=i}^{j-1} \sum_z \Big(\sum_{g_{l+1} \in \mathcal{G}} \theta(w_{l+1} | x, y, w_{l-1}, w_l, g_{l+1}) \theta(\mathbf{null} | x, y) \quad (1)$$

$$\theta(g_{l+1} | d) \Big) p_\theta(d, w_{i+1}^l, y[i, j] | w_i, x) p_\theta(d, w_{l+2}^j, z[l + 1, j] | w_{l+1}, y) \theta(\mathbf{left} | y, z)$$

$$+ \sum_{l=i}^{j-1} \sum_z \Big(\sum_{g_{l+1} \in \mathcal{G}} \theta(w_{l+1} | x, u, w_{l-1}, w_l, g_{l+1}) \theta(\mathbf{null} | x, u)$$

$$\theta(g_{l+1} | d) \Big) p_\theta(d, w_{i+1}^l, u[i, j] | w_i, x) p_\theta(d, w_{l+2}^j, y[l + 1, j] | w_{l+1}, u) \theta(\mathbf{right} | u, y)$$

The boundary conditions for the above recursion are given as

$$p_\theta(d, w_{i+1}^i, y[i, i]|w_i, x) = p_\theta(d, h(w_i) = y|w, h_{-1}(T^{i-1}) = x) = 1 \quad \forall x \in W^{(i-1)}, y = w_i$$

and the probability of a sentence W in document d is given by

$$p_\theta(d, W) = p_\theta(d, w_2^{n+1}, </s> [1, n+1]|w_1, <s>) \left(\sum_{g_1 \in \mathcal{G}} \theta(w_1| <s> g_1)\theta(g_1|d) \right) \text{(2)}$$

3.2 Computing the Probability of Next Word Given the Sentence Prefix

In order to compute the left-to-right probability of a word given the sentence prefix, define $p_\theta(d, w_0^{i+1}, x)$ to be the probability that the sequence $w_0, w_1, \cdots,$ w_i, w_{i+1} in document d is generated such that the last exposed headword of the parse tree for the string $w_0, w_1, \cdots, w_i$ is x and define the set of words $W^{(i)} = \{w_0, w_1, \cdots, w_i\}$. Then $\forall x \in W^{(i)}$, we have the following recursive formula,

$$p_\theta(d, w_0^{l+1}, x) = \sum_{i=1}^{l} \sum_{y \in W^{(i-1)}} p_\theta(d, w_0^i, y)p_\theta(w_{i+1}^l, x[i, l]|w_i, y)$$

$$\left(\sum_{g_{l+1} \in \mathcal{G}} \theta(w_{l+1}|y, x, w_l, w_{l-1}, g_{l+1})\theta(\mathbf{null}|y, x)\theta(g_{l+1}|d) \right) \text{(3)}$$

with the initial conditions

$$p_\theta(d, w_0^1, x) = \begin{cases} \sum_{g_1 \in \mathcal{G}} \theta(w_1| <s> g_1)\theta(g_1|d) & \text{if } x = <s> \\ 0 & \text{otherwise} \end{cases}$$

Thus we have

$$p_\theta(d, w_0, w_1, \cdots, w_i, w_{i+1}) = \sum_{x \in W^{(i+1)}} p_\theta(d, w_0^{i+1}, x)$$

and

$$p_\theta(d, w_{i+1}|w_0, w_1, \cdots, w_i) = \frac{\sum_{x \in W^{(i+1)}} p_\theta(d, w_0^{i+1}, x)}{\sum_{x \in W^{(i+1)}} p_\theta(d, w_0^i, x)} \text{(4)}$$

3.3 Finding the Most Probable Parse

Denote $\hat{p}_\theta(w_{i+1}^j, y[i, j]|w_i, x)$ as the probability of the most probable sequence of moves that generate the words $w_{i+1}, \cdots, w_j$ with y being the headword of the phrase $w_i, w_{i+1}, \cdots, w_j$. Then finding the most probable parse can be recursively obtained by changing the sum sign in the inside probability computation into a max sign (Kschischang et al. 2001).

$$\hat{p}_\theta(d, w_{i+1}^j, y[i,j]||w_i, x) \tag{5}$$

$$= \max\left\{ \max_{l\in\{i,j-1\},z}\left[\left(\sum_{g_{l+1}\in\mathcal{G}} \theta(w_{l+1}|x,y,w_{l-1},w_l,g_{l+1})\right.\right.\right.$$

$$\theta(\mathbf{null}|x,y)\theta(g_{l+1}|d)\Big)\hat{p}_\theta(d,w_{i+1}^l,y[i,j]||w_i,x)\hat{p}_\theta(d,w_{l+2}^j,z[l+1,j]||w_{l+1},y)\theta(\mathbf{left}|y,z)\Big],$$

$$\max_{l\in\{i,j-1\},z}\left[\left(\sum_{g_{l+1}\in\mathcal{G}} \theta(w_{l+1}|x,u,w_{l-1},w_l,g_{l+1})\right.\right.$$

$$\theta(\mathbf{null}|x,u)\theta(g_{l+1}|d)\Big)\hat{p}_\theta(d,w_{i+1}^l,u[i,j]||w_i,x)\hat{p}_\theta(d,w_{l+2}^j,y[l+1,j]||w_{l+1},u)\theta(\mathbf{right}|u,y)\Big]\right\}$$

The boundary conditions for the above recursion are given as

$$\hat{p}_\theta(d,w_{i+1}^i,y[i,i]||w_i,x) = p_\theta(d,h(w_i)=y|w,h_{-1}(T^{i-1})=x)=1 \quad \forall x\in W^{(i-1)}, y=w_i$$

then the probability of most probable parse in sentence W in document d is given by

$$p_\theta(d,W,\hat{T}) = \hat{p}_\theta(d,w_2^{n+1},</s>[1,n+1]||w_1,<s>)\left(\sum_{g_1\in\mathcal{G}}\theta(w_1|<s>g_1)\theta(g_1|d)\right) \tag{6}$$

3.4   Training Algorithm for Simplified Lexical and Semantic Enhanced Structural Language Model

Without writing down explicit formula of likelihood function, Jelinek (2004) has derived an EM-type parameter estimation algorithm for SLM whose structure is considerably more complex than that of a probabilistic context free grammar, and it is a generalization of the inside-outside algorithm (Baker 1979). The derivation is conceptually based on relevant frequency counting for discrete data which is a common practice for estimating PCFGs (Lari and Young 1990). In this section, we derive parameter estimation algorithm for the composite simplified lexical and semantic enhanced structural language model from the general EM algorithm (Dempster et al. 1977). This leads to a further generalization of inside-outside algorithm proposed by Jelinek (2004).

Similar as in the composite trigram/PCFG/ PLSA model (Wang et al. 2005), the likelihood of the observed data $\mathcal{W}$ under this composite language model can be written as below:

$$\mathcal{L}(\mathcal{W},\theta) = \prod_{d\in\mathcal{D}}\left(\prod_l\left(\sum_{G_l}\left(\sum_T p_\theta(d,W_l,G_l,T)\right)\right)\right) \tag{7}$$

where

$$p_\theta(d,W_l,G_l,T) = \prod_{d\in\mathcal{D}}\left(\prod_l\left(\prod_{g\in\mathcal{G}}\theta(g|d)^{c(d,W_l,g)}\prod_{u,v,h_{-2},h_{-1}\in V,g\in\mathcal{G}}\right.\right.$$

$$\theta(w|uvh_{-2}h_{-1}g)^{c(uvwh_{-2}h_{-1}g;d,W_l,T)}\prod_{h_2,h_1\in V,a\in\mathcal{A}}\theta(a|h_{-2}h_{-1})^{c(h_{-2}h_{-1}a;d,W_l,T)}\Big)\Big)$$

where $p_\theta(d, W_l, G_l, T)$ is the probability of generating sentence W_l in document d with parse tree T and semantic content sequence G_l, $c(d, W_l, g)$ is the count of semantic content g in document d, $c(uvwh_{-2}h_{-1}g; d, W_l, T)$ is the count of trigrams uvw with w's two left most exposed headwords $h_{-2}h_{-1}$, parse tree T and semantic content g in sentence W_l of document d, and $c(h_{-2}h_{-1}a; d, W_l, T)$ is the count of constructor move a conditioning on $h_{-2}h_{-1}$ in sentence W_l of document d with parse tree T. The parameters $\theta(g|d), \theta(w|uvh_{-2}h_{-1}g), \theta(a|h_{-2}h_{-1})$ are normalized so that $\sum_{w \in V} \theta(w|uvh_{-2}h_{-1}g) = 1, \sum_{a \in \mathcal{A}} \theta(a|h_{-2}h_{-1}) = 1$ and $\sum_{g \in \mathcal{G}} \theta(g|d) = 1$.

Following Lafferty's (2000) derivation of the inside-outside formulas for updating the parameters of PCFGs and Wang et al.'s (2005) derivation of the generalized inside-outside formulas for updating the parameters of the composite trigram/PCFG/PLSA models from a general EM (Dempster et al. 1977) algorithm, we derive the generalized inside-outside algorithm for the simplified lexical and semantic enhanced structural language model.

To apply the EM algorithm, we consider the auxiliary function

$$Q(\theta', \theta) = \sum_d \sum_l \sum_{G_l} \sum_T p_\theta(G_l, T|d, W_l) \log \frac{p_{\theta'}(d, W_l, G_l, T)}{p_\theta(d, W_l, G_l, T)}$$

Because of the normalization constraints, the re-estimated parameters of the composite model are then the normalized conditional expected counts:

$$\theta'(a|h_{-2}h_{-1}) = \frac{\sum_{d \in \mathcal{D}} \sum_l \sum_{G_l} \sum_T p_\theta(G_l, T|d, W_l) c(h_{-2}h_{-1}a; d, W_l, T)}{\text{normalization over } a}$$

$$\theta'(w|uvh_{-2}h_{-1}g) = \frac{\sum_{d \in \mathcal{D}} \sum_l \sum_{G_l} \sum_T p_\theta(G_l, T|d, W_l) c(uvwh_{-2}h_{-1}g; d, W_l, T, g)}{\text{normalization over } w} \quad (8)$$

$$\theta'(g|d) = \frac{\sum_l \sum_{G_l} \sum_T p_\theta(G_l, T|d, W_l) c(d, W_l, g)}{\text{normalization over } g}$$

Thus we need to compute the conditional expected counts, the numerators of (8).

In general, the sum requires summing over an exponential number of parse trees due to combinatorial explosion of possible parse trees. However, just as with standard PCFGs (Lafferty 2000) and composite trigram/PCFG/PLSA model (Wang et al. 2005), it is easy to check that the following equations still hold

$$\sum_{G_l} \sum_T p_\theta(G_l, T|d, W_l) c(h_{-2}h_{-1}a; d, W_l, T) = \frac{\theta(a|h_{-2}h_{-1})}{p_\theta(d, W_l)} \frac{\partial p_\theta(d, W_l)}{\partial \theta(a|h_{-2}h_{-1})}, \quad (9)$$

$$\sum_{G_l} \sum_T p_\theta(G_l, T|d, W_l) c(uvwh_{-2}h_{-1}g; d, W_l, T, g) = \frac{\theta(w|uvh_{-2}h_{-1}g)}{p_\theta(d, W_l)} \frac{\partial p_\theta(d, W_l)}{\partial \theta(w|uvh_{-2}h_{-1}g)},$$

$$\sum_{G_l} \sum_T p_\theta(G_l, T|d, W_l) c(d, W_l, g) = \frac{\theta(g|d)}{p_\theta(d, W_l)} \frac{\partial p_\theta(d, W_l)}{\partial \theta(g|d)}$$

and it turns out that there is an efficient and exact way of computing the partial derivative on the right-hand side, *the generalized inside-outside algorithm*.

Now the central problem then becomes to recursively represent the probability of a sentence, W in a document, $p_\theta(d, W)$, in terms of its parameters. Following Jelinek's derivation for structural language model (Jelinek 2004), we first derive formulas for computing $p_\theta(d, W, x, y[i, j])$, the probability that W is produced by some tree T that has a phrase spanning $< i, j >$ whose headword is y and its immediately preceding exposed headword is x. More formally,

$$p_\theta(d, W, x, y[i, j]) \doteq p_\theta(d, w_0, w_1, \cdots, w_{n+1}, h_{-1}(w_0, \cdots, w_{i-1}) = x, h(w_i, \cdots, w_j) = y)$$
$$= p_\theta(d, w_0, w_1, \cdots, w_{n+1}, h_{-1}(w_0, \cdots, w_{i-1}) = x)$$
$$p_\theta(d, w_{i+1}, \cdots, w_j, h(w_i, \cdots, w_j) = y | w_i, h_{-1}(w_0, \cdots, w_{i-1}) = x)$$
$$p_\theta(d, w_{j+1}, \cdots, w_{n+1} | h_{-1}(w_0, \cdots, w_{i-1}) = x, h(w_i, \cdots, w_j) = y)$$

The middle term is an inside probability and can be recursively calculated. We need a way to compute the "outside probability" which is the product of the outer terms of the above equation,

$$p_\theta(d, w_0^i, w_{j+1}^{n+1}, x[i-1]; y[i, j]) \doteq p_\theta(d, w_0, w_1, \cdots, w_{n+1}, h_{-1}(w_0, \cdots, w_{i-1}) = x) \quad (10)$$
$$p_\theta(d, w_{j+1}, \cdots, w_{n+1} | h_{-1}(w_0, \cdots, w_{i-1}) = x, h(w_i, \cdots, w_j) = y)$$

We thus have

$$p_\theta(d, W) = \sum_{i,j} p_\theta(d, W, x, y[i, j])$$
$$= \sum_{i,j} p_\theta(d, w_0^i, w_{j+1}^{n+1}, x[i-1]; y[i, j]) p_\theta(d, w_{i+1}^j, y[i, j] | w_i, x) \quad (11)$$

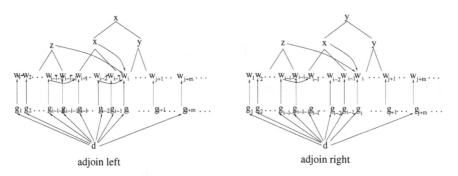

adjoin left   adjoin right

Fig. 3. Diagram illustrating outside probability recursions: first term in (11) is recursively computed with adjoin left and adjoin right being used respectively

Figures 3- 4 illustrate four cases that the outside probability $p_\theta(d, w_0^i, w_{j+1}^{n+1}, x[i-1]; y[i, j])$ can be recursively obtained by the inside and outside probabilities. In the first two cases, the first term in the definition of outside probability, $p_\theta(d, w_0, w_1, \cdots, w_{n+1}, h_{-1}(w_0, \cdots, w_{i-1}) = x)$ remains unchanged and it is the second term that is recursively represented by inside and outside probabilities,

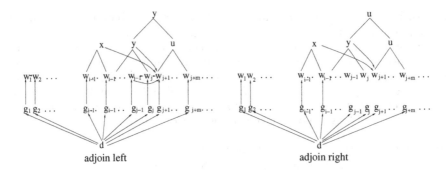

Fig. 4. Diagram illustrating outside probability recursions: second term in (11) is recursively computed with adjoin left and adjoin right being used respectively

and the difference between these two cases is on whether constructor move, adjoin left, or adjoin right is used. Similarly in the last two cases, the second term in the definition of outside probability, $p_\theta(d, w_{j+1}, \cdots, w_{n+1}|h_{-1}(w_0, \cdots, w_{i-1}) = x, h(w_i, \cdots, w_j) = y)$ remains unchanged and it is the first term that is recursively represented by inside and outside probabilities, and again the difference between these two cases is on whether constructor move, adjoin left, or adjoin right is used. This leads to the four double sums on the right-hand side of the following recursive formulas,

$$p_\theta(d, w_0^i, w_{j+1}^{n+1}, x[i-1]; y[i,j]) \tag{12}$$

$$=\sum_{k=1}^{i-1} \sum_{z \in W^{i-k-1}} \Big[p_\theta(d, w_0^{i-1}, w_{j+1}^{n+1}, z[i-k-1]; x[i-k,j]) p_\theta(d, w_{i-k-1}^{i-1}, x[i-k, i-1]|w_{i-1},z)$$

$$\Big(\sum_{g_i \in \mathcal{G}} \theta(w_i|z, x, w_{i-2}, w_{i-1}, g_i)\theta(\mathbf{null}|z, x)\theta(g_i|d) \Big) \theta(\mathbf{left}|x, y) \Big]$$

$$+\sum_{k=1}^{i-1} \sum_{z \in W^{i-k-1}} \Big[p_\theta(d, w_0^{i-1}, w_{j+1}^{n+1}, z[i-k-1]; y[i-k,j]) p_\theta(d, w_{i-k-1}^{i-1}, x[i-k, i-1]|w_{i-1},z)$$

$$\Big(\sum_{g_i \in \mathcal{G}} \theta(w_i|z, x, w_{i-2}, w_{i-1}, g_i)\theta(\mathbf{null}|z, x)\theta(g_i|d) \Big) \theta(\mathbf{right}|x, y) \Big]$$

$$+\sum_{m=i}^{n-j+1} \sum_{z \in W_{j+1}^{j+m}} \Big[p_\theta(d, w_0^i, w_{j+m+1}^{n+1}, x[i-1]; y[i, j+m]) p_\theta(d, w_{j+2}^{j+m}, u[j+1, j+m]|w_{j+1},y)$$

$$\Big(\sum_{g_{j+1} \in \mathcal{G}} \theta(w_{j+1}|x, y, w_{j-1}, w_j, g_{j+1})\theta(\mathbf{null}|x, y)\theta(g_{j+1}|d) \Big) \theta(\mathbf{left}|y, u) \Big]$$

$$+\sum_{m=i}^{n-j+1} \sum_{z \in W_{j+1}^{j+m}} \Big[p_\theta(d, w_0^i, w_{j+m+1}^{n+1}, x[i-1]; u[i, j+m]) p_\theta(d, w_{j+2}^{j+m}, u[j+1, j+m]|w_{j+1},y)$$

$$\Big(\sum_{g_{j+1} \in \mathcal{G}} \theta(w_{j+1}|x, y, w_{j-1}, w_j, g_{j+1})\theta(\mathbf{null}|x, y)\theta(g_{j+1}|d) \Big) \theta(\mathbf{right}|y, u) \Big]$$

with the boundary condition

$$p_\theta(d, w_0^1, w_{n+1}^{n+2}, x[0]; y[1, n+1]) = \begin{cases} \sum_{g_1 \in \mathcal{G}} \theta(w_1| < s > g_1)\theta(g_1|d) & \text{if } x =< s >, y =< /s > \\ 0 & \text{otherwise} \end{cases}$$

By (12), the outside probability can be recursively represented by a full set of model parameters. Thus by (11), calculating the derivative of the probability of a sentence W_l can be done recursively via calculating the derivative of outside probability. Then by (9), we have

$$\sum_{G_l} \sum_T p_\theta(G_l, T|d, W_l)c(h_{-2}h_{-1}a; d, W_l, T) = \sum_i \sum_j c_l(d, x, y, i, j, \mathbf{a}) \quad \forall\, a \in \mathcal{A},$$

$$\sum_{G_l} \sum_T p_\theta(G_l, T|d, W_l)c(uvwh_{-2}h_{-1}g; d, W_l, t, g) = \sum_i \sum_j c_l(d, x, y, i, j, \mathbf{null})$$

$$\delta(u = w_{j-1}, v = w_j, w = w_{j+1}),$$

$$\sum_{G_l} \sum_T p_\theta(G_l, T|d, W_l)c(d, W_l, g) = \sum_i \sum_j c_l(d, g, i, j)$$

where the quantities $c_l(d, x, y, i, j, \mathbf{a})$ and $c_l(d, g, i, j)$ are calculated by the following recursions,

$$c_l(d, x, y, i, j, a = \mathbf{left}) = \frac{1}{p_\theta(d, W_l)} p_\theta(d, w_{i+1}^j, y[i, j]|w_i, x)$$

$$\sum_z \sum_{k=1}^{i-1} \left[p_\theta(d, w_0^{i-1}, w_{j+1}^{n+1}, z[i-k-1]; x[i-k, j])p_\theta(d, w_{i-k-1}^{i-1}, x[i-k, i-1]|w_{i-1}, z) \right.$$

$$\left. \left(\sum_{g_i \in \mathcal{G}} \theta(w_i|z, x, w_{i-2}, w_{i-1}, g_i)\theta(\mathbf{null}|z, x)\theta(g_i|d) \right) \theta(\mathbf{left}|x, y) \right],$$

$$c_l(d, x, y, i, j, a = \mathbf{right})) = \frac{1}{p_\theta(d, W_l)} p_\theta(d, w_{i+1}^j, y[i, j]|w_i, x)$$

$$\sum_z \sum_{k=1}^{i-1} \left[p_\theta(d, w_0^{i-1}, w_{j+1}^{n+1}, z[i-k-1]; y[i-k, j])p_\theta(d, w_{i-k-1}^{i-1}, x[i-k, i-1]|w_{i-1}, z) \right.$$

$$\left. \left(\sum_{g_i \in \mathcal{G}} \theta(w_i|z, x, w_{i-2}, w_{i-1}, g_i)\theta(\mathbf{null}|z, x)\theta(g_i|d) \right) \theta(\mathbf{right}|x, y) \right],$$

$$c_l(d, x, y, i, j, a = \mathbf{null}) = \frac{1}{p_\theta(d, W_l)} p_\theta(d, w_{i+1}^j, y[i, j]|w_i, x)$$

$$\sum_u \sum_{m=i}^{n-j+1} \left[p_\theta(d, w_0^i, w_{j+m+1}^{n+1}, x[i-1]; y[i, j+m])p_\theta(w_{j+2}^{j+m}, u[j+1, j+m]|w_{j+1}, y) \right.$$

$$\left. \left(\sum_{g_{j+1} \in \mathcal{G}} \theta(w_{j+1}|x, y, w_{j-1}, w_j, g_{j+1})\theta(\mathbf{null}|x, y)\theta(g_{j+1}|d) \right) \theta(\mathbf{left}|y, u) \right]$$

$$+ \sum_u \sum_{m=i}^{n-j+1} \left[p_\theta(d, w_0^i, w_{j+m+1}^{n+1}, x[i-1]; u[i, j+m])p_\theta(d, w_{j+2}^{j+m}, u[j+1, j+m]|w_{j+1}, y) \right.$$

$$\left. \left(\sum_{g_{j+1} \in \mathcal{G}} \theta(w_{j+1}|x, y, w_{j-1}, w_j, g_{j+1})\theta(\mathbf{null}|x, y)\theta(g_{j+1}|d) \right) \theta(\mathbf{right}|y, u) \right],$$

$$c_l(d, g, i, j) = \frac{1}{p_\theta(d, W_l)} p_\theta(d, w_{i+1}^j, y[i, j]|w_i, x)$$

$$\sum_{u}\sum_{m=i}^{n-j+1}\left[p_\theta(d, w_0^i, w_{j+m+1}^{n+1}, x[i-1]; y[i, j+m])p_\theta(w_{j+2}^{j+m}, u[j+1, j+m]|w_{j+1}, y)\right.$$

$$\left.\left(\theta(w_{j+1}|x, y, w_{j-1}, w_j, g)\theta(\textbf{null}|x, y)\theta(g|d)\right)\theta(\textbf{left}|y, u)\right]$$

$$+\sum_{u}\sum_{m=i}^{n-j+1}\left[p_\theta(d, w_0^i, w_{j+m+1}^{n+1}, x[i-1]; u[i, j+m])p_\theta(d, w_{j+2}^{j+m}, u[j+1, j+m]|w_{j+1}, y)\right.$$

$$\left.\left(\theta(w_{j+1}|x, y, w_{j-1}, w_j, g)\theta(\textbf{null}|x, y)\theta(g|d)\right)\theta(\textbf{right}|y, u)\right],$$

In order to be consistent to the recursive formula for SSLM derived in (Jelinek 2004), we consider w_{j+1} to derive the formula for $c_l(d, g, i, j)$. An alternative formula exists if we consider w_i instead.

$$c_l(d, g, i, j) = \frac{1}{p_\theta(d, W_l)}p_\theta(d, w_{i+1}^j, y[i, j]|w_i, x)$$

$$\sum_{z}\sum_{k=1}^{i-1}\left[p_\theta(d, w_0^{i-1}, w_{j+1}^{n+1}, z[i-k-1]; x[i-k, j])p_\theta(d, w_{i-k-1}^{i-1}, x[i-k, i-1]|w_{i-1}, z)\right.$$

$$\left.\left(\theta(w_i|z, x, w_{i-2}, w_{i-1}, g)\theta(\textbf{null}|z, x)\theta(g|d)\right)\theta(\textbf{left}|x, y)\right]$$

$$+\sum_{z}\sum_{k=1}^{i-1}\left[p_\theta(d, w_0^{i-1}, w_{j+1}^{n+1}, z[i-k-1]; y[i-k, j])p_\theta(d, w_{i-k-1}^{i-1}, x[i-k, i-1]|w_{i-1}, z)\right.$$

$$\left.\left(\theta(w_i|z, x, w_{i-2}, w_{i-1}, g)\theta(\textbf{null}|z, x)\theta(g|d)\right)\theta(\textbf{right}|x, y)\right]$$

Then by (9), we get the re-estimates

$$\theta'(a|h_{-2} = x, h_{-1} = y) = \frac{\sum_{d}\sum_{l}\sum_{i}\sum_{j}c_l(d, x, y, i, j, a)}{\sum_{a'\in\mathcal{A}}\sum_{d}\sum_{l}\sum_{i}\sum_{j}c_l(d, x, y, i, j, a')}$$

$$\theta'(w|uvh_{-2} = x, h_{-1} = y) =$$

$$\frac{\sum_{d}\sum_{l}\sum_{i}\sum_{j}c_l(d, x, y, i, j, \textbf{null})\delta(u = w_{j-1}, v = w_j, w = w_{j+1})}{\sum_{w'\in\mathcal{V}}\sum_{d}\sum_{l}\sum_{i}\sum_{j}c_l(d, x, y, i, j, \textbf{null})\delta(u = w_{j-1}, v = w_j, w = w')}$$

$$\theta'(g|d) = \frac{\sum_{l}\sum_{i}\sum_{j}c_l(d, g, i, j)}{\sum_{g'\in\mathcal{G}}\sum_{l}\sum_{i}\sum_{j}c_l(d, g', i, j)}$$

4 Extension of Training to Complete Lexical and Semantic Enhanced Structural Language Models

We now extend our results to the complete structural language model which has more complex constructor than SSLM and an additional module, the **tagger**.

Each headword h is replaced by heads $\mathbf{h} = (h^1, h^2)$ where h^1 is a headword and h^2 is a tag or a non-terninal. The operation of complete lexical and semantic enhanced structural language model,

- Depending on the last two exposed heads $\mathbf{h}_{-2}, \mathbf{h}_{-1}$, the two preceding words w_{i-2}, w_{i-1} as well as current semantic node g_i, the predictor generates the next word w_i with probability $\theta(w_i|w_{i-2}w_{i-1}\mathbf{h}_{-2}\mathbf{h}_{-1}g_i)$.
- Depending on the last exposed head $\mathbf{h}_{-1}$ and current word w_i, the tagger tags w_i by a part of speech $f \in \mathcal{F}$ with probability $\theta(f|w_i\mathbf{h}_{-1})$, shifts heads left one position i.e., $\mathbf{h}'_{-i-1} = \mathbf{h}_{-i}, i = 1, \cdots$ and generates a new last exposed head, $\mathbf{h}'_{-1} = (h^1_{-1}, h^2_{-2}) = (w_i, f)$.
- The constructor operates with a probability $\theta(\mathbf{a}|\mathbf{h}_{-2}\mathbf{h}_{-1})$ where $\mathbf{a} \in \mathcal{A} = \{(\mathbf{right}||\gamma), (\mathbf{left}||\gamma), (\mathbf{up}||\gamma), \mathbf{null}\}$ where $\gamma \in \Gamma$, the set of non-terminal symbols.

The increased complexity of the complete lexical and semantic enhanced SLM mainly arises from the enlargement of headword vacabulary. The recursive formulas however can be updated with simple modular modifications.

5   Conclusions and Further Directions

We have shown how to integrate trigrams and PLSAs with the structural language model to build a composite generative probabilistic language model. The resulting composite language model has even more complex dependency structure but with more expressive power than the original SLM. We have studied its various stochastic properties and extended various recursive formulas with conceptually simple modular modifications, i.e., replacing $\theta(w_i|h_{-2}h_{-1})$ with $\sum_{g_i \in \mathcal{G}} \theta(w_i|w_{i-2}w_{i-1}h_{-2}h_{-1}g_i)\theta(g_i|d)$, while remaining the same order computational complexity. Even though the added context-sensitiveness due to trigrams and PLSAs and violation of tree structure in the topology of the underlying random field model make the inference and parameter estimation problems plausiblely intractable, these recursive formulas are nevertheless $exact$ to solve these problems for the lexical and semantic enhanced SLM. The main reason rendering this being true is that the computation of the probability of a sentence can be factorized into two parts where each part can be recursively calculated and no overlapping features exist when performing the computation recursively.

Statistical latural language processing is an empirical field, nevertheless some famous published papers in NLP only described the algorithms without any experimental justification for the usefullness. For example, James Baker's 4 pages paper (Baker 1979) showed the nowadays well known inside-outside algorithm with no empirical results. Similarly in Jelinek's paper (Jelinek 2004), there is no any experimental results too, mainly due to its $O(n^6)$ complexity where n is the length of a sentence. Our paper is in the same flavour of theirs, emphasizing algorithmic aspect. Similar as analyzed in (Jelinek 2004) for SLM, the complexity of the generalized inside-outside algorithm for the lexical and semantic enhanced SLM is in the same order as in SLM and is propotional to n^6.

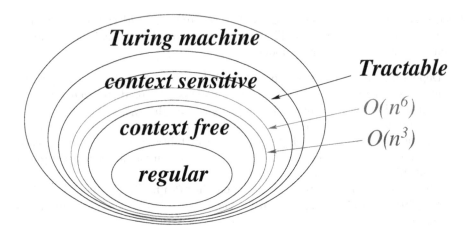

Fig. 5. In the Chormsky's hierarchy of grammars nested according to the increasing restrictions placed on the production rules in the grammar, there is a subclass of probabilistic context sensitive grammars which is tractable

Figure 5 illustrates the Chormsky's hierarchy of grammars in terms of computational complexity (Hopcroft and Ullman 1979) where there exist a tractable subclass of probabilistic context sensitive grammars with n^6 time complexity as well as a subclass of probabilistic context sensitive grammars with cubic time complexity. The n^6 order complexity makes all the algorithms developed in this work and in (Jelinek 2004) impractical. However various schemes as suggested in (Jelinek 2004) can be used to prune substantial fraction of entries from the charts by thresholding in the computation of inside and outside probabilities and limiting non-terminal productions. We plan to report experimental results by using these various techniques to approximately perform parameter estimations for the lexical and semantic enhanced SLM in the future.

References

1. S. Abney, D. McAllester, and F. Pereira. (1999). Relating probabilistic grammars and automata. *Proceedings of ACL*, 542-549.
2. J. Baker. (1979). Trainable grammars for speech recognition. *Proceedings of the 97th Meeting of the Acoustical Society of America*, 547-550.
3. C. Chelba. (1999). Exploiting syntactic structure for natural language modeling. *Ph.D. Dissertation*, Johns Hopkins University.
4. C. Chelba and F. Jelinek. (2000). Structured language modeling. *Computer Speech and Language*, 14(4):283-332.
5. N. Chomsky. (1956). Three models for the description of language. *IRE Transactions on Information Theory*, 2(3):113-24.
6. A. Dempster, N. Laird and D. Rubin. (1977). Maximum likelihood estimation from incomplete data via the EM algorithm. *Journal of Royal Statistical Society*, 39:1-38.

7. T. Hofmann. (2001). Unsupervised learning by probabilistic latent semantic analysis. *Machine Learning*, 42(1):177-196

8. J. Hopcroft and J. Ullman. (1979). *Introduction to Automata Theory, Languages and Computation*. Addison-Wesley.

9. F. Jelinek, J. Lafferty and R. Mercer. (1992). Basic methods of probabilistic context-free grammars. *Speech Recognition and Understanding: Recent Advances, Trends, and Applications*, P. Laface and R. De Mori, (Editors), 347-360, Springer-Verlag.

10. F. Jelinek. (1998). *Statistical Methods for Speech Recognition*. MIT Press.

11. F. Jelinek and C. Chelba. (1999). Putting language into language modeling. *Proceedings of the 6th EuroSpeech Communication and Technology*, 1-6.

12. F. Jelinek. (2004). Stochastic analysis of structured language modeling. *Mathematical Foundations of Speech and Language Processing*, M. Johnson, S. Khudanpur, M. Ostendorf and R. Rosenfeld (Editors), 37-72, Springer-Verlag.

13. S. Khudanpur and J. Wu. (2000). Maximum entropy techniques for exploiting syntactic, semantic and collocational dependencies in language modeling. *Computer Speech and Language*, 14(4):355-372.

14. F. Kschischang, B. Frey and H. Loeliger. (2001). Factor graphs and the sum-product algorithm *IEEE Transactions on Information Theory*, 47(2):498-519.

15. J. Lafferty. (2000). A derivation of the inside-outside algorithm from the EM algorithm. *IBM Research Report* 21636.

16. K. Lari and S. Young. (1990). The estimation of stochastic context-free grammars using the inside-outside algorithm. *Computer Speech and Language*, 4:35-56.

17. S. Lauritzen. (1996). *Graphical Models*. Oxford Press.

18. C. Shannon. (1948). A mathematical theory of communication. *Bell System Technical Journal*, 27(2):379-423.

19. S. Wang, S. Wang, R. Greiner, D. Schuurmans and L. Cheng. (2005). Exploiting syntactic, semantic and lexical regularities in language modeling via directed Markov random fields. *The 22nd International Conference on Machine Learning*, 953-960.

20. D. Younger. (1967). Recognition and parsing of context free languages in time N^3. *Information and Control*, 10:198-208.

Using Pseudo-stochastic Rational Languages in Probabilistic Grammatical Inference

Amaury Habrard, François Denis, and Yann Esposito

Laboratoire d'Informatique Fondamentale de Marseille (L.I.F.) UMR CNRS 6166
{habrard, fdenis, esposito}@cmi.univ-mrs.fr

Abstract. In probabilistic grammatical inference, a usual goal is to infer a good approximation of an unknown distribution P called a *stochastic language*. The estimate of P stands in some class of probabilistic models such as probabilistic automata (PA). In this paper, we focus on probabilistic models based on multiplicity automata (MA). The stochastic languages generated by MA are called *rational stochastic languages*; they strictly include stochastic languages generated by PA and admit a very concise canonical representation. Despite the fact that this class is not recursively enumerable, it is efficiently identifiable in the limit by using the algorithm DEES, introduced by the authors in a previous paper. However, the identification is not proper and before the convergence of the algorithm, DEES can produce MA that do not define stochastic languages. Nevertheless, it is possible to use these MA to define stochastic languages. We show that they belong to a broader class of rational series, that we call *pseudo-stochastic rational languages*. The aim of this paper is twofold. First we provide a theoretical study of pseudo-stochastic rational languages, the languages output by DEES, showing for example that this class is decidable within polynomial time. Second, we have carried out experiments to compare DEES to classical inference algorithms (ALERGIA and MDI). They show that DEES outperforms them in most cases.

Keywords: pseudo-stochastic rational languages, multiplicity automata, probabilistic grammatical inference.

1 Introduction

In probabilistic grammatical inference, we often consider stochastic languages which define distributions over Σ^*, the set of all the possible words over an alphabet Σ. In general, we consider an unknown distribution P and the goal is to find a good approximation given a finite sample of words independently drawn from P.

The class of probabilistic automata (PA) is often used for modeling such distributions. This class has the same expressiveness as Hidden Markov Models and is identifiable in the limit [4]. However, there exists no efficient algorithm for identifying PA. This can be explained by the fact that there exists no canonical representation of these automata which makes it difficult to correctly identify the structure of the target. One solution is to focus on subclasses of PA such as probabilistic deterministic automata [3, 10] but with an important lack of expressiveness. Another solution consists in considering the class of multiplicity automata (MA). These models admit a canonical representation which offers good opportunities from a machine learning point of view. MA define

Y. Sakakibara et al. (Eds.): ICGI 2006, LNAI 4201, pp. 112–124, 2006.

functions that compute rational series with values in $\mathbb{R}$ [5]. MA are a strict generalization of PA and the stochastic languages generated by PA are special cases of rational stochastic languages. Let us denote by $S_K^{rat}(\Sigma)$ the class of rational stochastic languages computed by MA with parameters in K where $K \in \{\mathbb{Q}, \mathbb{Q}^+, \mathbb{R}, \mathbb{R}^+\}$. With $K = \mathbb{Q}^+$ or $K = \mathbb{R}^+$, $S_K^{rat}(\Sigma)$ is exactly the class of stochastic languages generated by PA with parameters in K. But, when $K = \mathbb{Q}$ or $K = \mathbb{R}$, we obtain strictly greater classes. This provides several advantages: Elements of $S_K^{rat}(\Sigma)$ have a minimal normal representation, thus elements of $S_{K+}^{rat}(\Sigma)$ may have significantly smaller representation in $S_K^{rat}(\Sigma)$; parameters of these minimal representations are directly related to probabilities of some natural events of the form $u\Sigma^*$, which can be efficiently estimated from stochastic samples; lastly rational series over a field K form a vector space and efficient linear algebra techniques can be used to deal with rational stochastic languages.

However, the class $S_{\mathbb{Q}}^{rat}(\Sigma)$ presents a serious drawback: There exists no recursively enumerable subset class of MA which exactly generates it [4]. As a consequence, no proper identification algorithm can exist: indeed, applying a proper identification algorithm to an enumeration of samples of Σ^* would provide an enumeration of the class of rational stochastic languages over $\mathbb{Q}$. In spite of this result, there exists an efficient algorithm, DEES, which is able to identify $S_K^{rat}(\Sigma)$ in the limit. But before reaching the target, DEES can produce MA that do not define stochastic languages. However, it has been shown in [6] that with probability one, for any rational stochastic language p, if DEES is given as input a sufficiently large sample S drawn according to p, DEES outputs a rational series such that $\sum_{u \in \Sigma^*} r(u)$ converges absolutely to 1. Moreover, $\sum_{u \in \Sigma^*} |p(u) - r(u)|$ converges to 0 as the size of S increases. We show that these MA belong to a broader class of rational series, that we call *pseudo-stochastic rational languages*. A pseudo-stochastic rational language r has the property that $r(u\Sigma^*) = lim_{n \to \infty} r(u\Sigma^{\leq n})$ is defined for any word u and that $r(\Sigma^*) = 1$. A stochastic language p_r can be associated with r in such a way that $\sum_{u \in \Sigma^*} |p_r(u) - r(u)| = 2\sum_{r(u)<0} |r(u)|$ when the sum $\sum_{u \in \Sigma^*} r(u)$ is absolutely convergent. As a first consequence, $p_r = r$ when r is a stochastic language. As a second consequence, for any rational stochastic language p, if DEES is given as input increasing samples drawn according to p, DEES outputs pseudo-stochastic rational languages r such that $\sum_{u \in \Sigma^*} |p(u) - p_r(u)|$ converges to 0 as the size of S increases.

The aim of this paper is twofold: To provide a theoretical study of the class of pseudo-stochastic rational languages and a series of experiments to compare the performance of DEES to two classical inference algorithms: ALERGIA [3] and MDI [10]. We show that the class of pseudo-stochastic rational languages is decidable within polynomial time. We provide an algorithm that can be used to compute $p_r(u)$ from any MA that computes r. We also show how it is possible to simulate p_r using such an automaton. We show that there exist pseudo-stochastic rational languages r such that p_r is not rational. Finally, we show that it is undecidable whether two pseudo-stochastic rational languages define the same stochastic language. We have carried out many experiments which show that DEES outperforms ALERGIA and MDI in most cases. These results were expected since ALERGIA and MDI have not the same theoretical expressiveness and since DEES aims at producing a minimal representation of the target in the set of MA, which can be significantly smaller than the minimal equivalent PDA (if it exists).

The paper is organized as follows. In section 2, we introduce some background about multiplicity automata, rational series and stochastic languages and present the algorithm DEES. Section 3 deals with our study of pseudo-rational stochastic languages. Our experiments are detailed in Section 4.

2   Definitions and Notations

Rational Series, Multiplicity Automata and Stochastic Languages. Let Σ^* be the set of words on the finite alphabet Σ. A language is a subset of Σ^*. The empty word is denoted by ε and the length of a word u is denoted by $|u|$. For any integer k, let $\Sigma^k = \{u \in \Sigma^* : |u| = k\}$ and $\Sigma^{\leq k} = \{u \in \Sigma^* : |u| \leq k\}$. We denote by $<$ the length-lexicographic order on Σ^* and by $MinL$ the minimal element of a non empty language L according to this order. A subset S of Σ^* is *prefix-closed* if for any $u, v \in \Sigma^*$, $uv \in S \Rightarrow u \in S$. For any $S \subseteq \Sigma^*$, let $pref(S) = \{u \in \Sigma^* : \exists v \in \Sigma^*, uv \in S\}$ and $fact(S) = \{v \in \Sigma^* : \exists u, w \in \Sigma^*, uvw \in S\}$.

A *formal power series* is a mapping r of Σ^* into $\mathbb{R}$. The set of all formal power series is denoted by $\mathbb{R}\langle\langle\Sigma\rangle\rangle$. It is a vector space. For any series r and any word u, let us denote by $\dot{u}r$ the series defined by $\dot{u}r(w) = r(uw)$ for every word w. Let us denote by $supp(r)$ the *support* of r, i.e. the set $\{w \in \Sigma^* : r(w) \neq 0\}$.

A *stochastic language* is a formal series p which takes its values in $\mathbb{R}^+$ and such that $\sum_{w \in \Sigma^*} p(w) = 1$.

The set of all stochastic languages over Σ is denoted by $\mathcal{S}(\Sigma)$. For any language $L \subseteq \Sigma^*$ and any $p \in \mathcal{S}(\Sigma)$, let us denote $\sum_{w \in L} p(w)$ by $p(L)$. For any $p \in \mathcal{S}(\Sigma)$ and $u \in \Sigma$ such that $p(u\Sigma^*) \neq 0$, the *residual language* of p wrt u is the stochastic language defined by $u^{-1}p$ by $u^{-1}p(w) = \frac{p(uw)}{p(u\Sigma^*)}$. We denote by $res(p)$ the set $\{u \in \Sigma^* : p(u\Sigma^*) \neq 0\}$ and by $Res(p)$ the set $\{u^{-1}p : u \in res(p)\}$.

Let S be a sample over Σ^*, i.e. a multiset composed of words over Σ^*. We denote by p_S the empirical distribution over Σ^* associated with S. Let S be an infinite sample composed of words independently drawn according to a stochastic language p. We denote by S_n the sequence composed of the n first words of S.

We introduce now the notion of multiplicity automata (MA).

Let $K \in \{\mathbb{R}, \mathbb{Q}, \mathbb{R}^+, \mathbb{Q}^+\}$. A *$K$-multiplicity automaton (MA)* is a 5-tuple $\langle\Sigma, Q, \varphi, \iota, \tau\rangle$ where Q is a finite set of states, $\varphi : Q \times \Sigma \times Q \to K$ is the transition function, $\iota : Q \to K$ is the initialization function, $\tau : Q \to K$ is the termination function.

We extend the transition function φ to $Q \times \Sigma^* \times Q$ by $\varphi(q, wx, r) = \sum_{s \in Q} \varphi(q, w, s) \varphi(s, x, r)$ and $\varphi(q, \varepsilon, r) = 1$ if $q = r$ and 0 otherwise, for any $q, r \in Q$, $x \in \Sigma$ and $w \in \Sigma^*$. For any finite subset $L \subset \Sigma^*$ and any $R \subseteq Q$, define $\varphi(q, L, R) = \sum_{w \in L, r \in R} \varphi(q, w, r)$. We denote by $Q_I = \{q \in Q | \iota(q) \neq 0\}$ the set of *initial states* and by $Q_T = \{q \in Q | \tau(q) \neq 0\}$ the set of *terminal states*. A state $q \in Q$ is *accessible* (resp. *co-accessible*) if there exists $q_0 \in Q_I$ (resp. $q_t \in Q_T$) and $u \in \Sigma^*$ such that $\varphi(q_0, u, q) \neq 0$ (resp. $\varphi(q, u, q_t) \neq 0$). An MA is *trimmed* if all its states are accessible and co-accessible. From now, we only consider trimmed MA.

The *support* of an MA $A = \langle\Sigma, Q, \varphi, \iota, \tau\rangle$ is the *Non-deterministic Finite Automaton (NFA)* $\langle\Sigma, Q, Q_I, Q_T, \delta\rangle$ where $\delta(q, x) = \{q' \in Q | \varphi(q, x, q') \neq 0\}$.

The *spectral radius* of a square matrix M if the maximum magnitude of its eigen-values. Let $A = \langle \Sigma, Q = \{q_1, \ldots, q_n\}, \iota, \varphi, \tau \rangle$ be an MA. Let us denote by $\rho(A)$ be the spectral radius of the square matrix $[\varphi(q_i, \Sigma, q_j)]_{1 \leq i,j \leq n}$ ($\rho(A)$ does not depends on the order of the states). If $\rho(A) < 1$ then each sequence $r_{A,q}(\Sigma^{\leq n})$ converges to a number s_q and hence, $r(\Sigma^{\leq n})$ converges too [6]. Let us denote by $r(\Sigma^*)$ the limit of $r(\Sigma^{\leq n})$ when it exists. The numbers s_q are the unique solutions of the following linear system of equations (and therefore are computable within polynomial time):

$$s_q = r_{A,q} + \sum_{q' \in Q} \varphi(q, \Sigma, q')s_{q'} \text{ for } q \in Q.$$

It is decidable within polynomial time whether $\rho(A) < 1$ [2,7].

A *Probabilistic Automaton (PA)* is a trimmed MA $\langle \Sigma, Q, \varphi, \iota, \tau \rangle$ s.t. ι, φ and τ take their values in $[0, 1]$, s.t. $\sum_{q \in Q} \iota(q) = 1$ and for any state q, $\tau(q) + \varphi(q, \Sigma, Q) = 1$. A *Probabilistic Deterministic Automaton (PDA)* is a PA whose support is deterministic. It can be shown that Probabilistic Automata generate stochastic languages. Let us de-note by $\mathcal{S}_K^{PA}(\Sigma)$ (resp. $\mathcal{S}_K^{PDA}(\Sigma)$) the class of all stochastic languages which can be computed by a PA (resp. a PDA).

For any MA A, let r_A be the series defined by $r_A(w) = \sum_{q,r \in Q} \iota(q) \varphi(q, w, r)\tau(r)$. For any $q \in Q$, we define the series $r_{A,q}$ by $r_{A,q}(w) = \sum_{r \in Q} \varphi(q, w, r)\tau(r)$. An MA A is *reduced* if the set $\{r_{A,q} | q \in Q\}$ is linearly independent in the vector space $\mathbb{R}\langle\langle \Sigma \rangle\rangle$. An MA A is *prefix-closed* if its set of states Q is a prefix-closed subset of Σ^*, $Q_I = \{\varepsilon\}$ and $\forall u \in Q, \delta(\varepsilon, u) = \{u\}$ where δ is the transition function in the support of A.

Rational series have several characterization ([1, 9]). Here, we shall say that a for-mal power series over Σ is K-rational iff there exists a K-multiplicity automaton A such that $r = r_A$, where $K \in \{\mathbb{R}, \mathbb{R}^+, \mathbb{Q}, \mathbb{Q}^+\}$. Let us denote by $K^{rat}\langle\langle \Sigma \rangle\rangle$ the set of K-rational series over Σ and by $\mathcal{S}_K^{rat}(\Sigma) = K^{rat}\langle\langle \Sigma \rangle\rangle \cap \mathcal{S}(\Sigma)$, the set of *rational stochastic languages* over K. It can be shown that a series r is $\mathbb{R}$-rational iff the set $\{\dot{u}r | u \in \Sigma^*\}$ spans a finite dimensional vector subspace of $\mathbb{R}\langle\langle \Sigma \rangle\rangle$. As a corollary, a stochastic language p is $\mathbb{R}$-rational iff the set $Res(p)$ spans a finite di-mensional vector subspace $[Res(p)]$ of $\mathbb{R}\langle\langle \Sigma \rangle\rangle$. Rational stochastic languages have been studied in [5] from a language theoretical point of view. It is worth noting that $\mathcal{S}_{\mathbb{R}}^{PDA}(\Sigma) \subsetneq \mathcal{S}_{\mathbb{R}}^{PA}(\Sigma) = \mathcal{S}_{\mathbb{R}^+}^{rat}(\Sigma) \subsetneq \mathcal{S}_{\mathbb{R}}^{rat}(\Sigma)$. From now on, a rational stochastic language will always denote an $\mathbb{R}$-rational stochastic language. Rational stochastic lan-guages have a serious drawback. There exists no recursively enumerable subset of mul-tiplicity automata capable to generate them [4,5]. As a consequence, it is undecidable whether a given MA computes a stochastic language.

Every rational language is the support of a rational series but the converse is false: there exists rational series whose supports are not rational. For example, it can be shown that the complementary set of $\{a^n b^n | n \in \mathbb{N}\}$ in $\{a, b\}^*$ is the support of a rational series. However, a variant of Pumping Lemma holds for languages which are support of rational series. Let L be such a language. There exists an integer N such that for any word $w = uv \in L$ satisfying $|v| \geq N$, there exists v_1, v_2, v_3 such that $v = v_1v_2v_3$ and $L \cap uv_1v_2^*v_3$ is infinite [1]. Rational stochastic languages admit a canonical representation by reduced prefix-closed MA. Let p be a rational stochastic language and Q_p be the smallest basis of $[Res(p)]$ (for the order induced by $<$ on the finite subsets of Σ^*). Let $A = \langle \Sigma, Q_p, \varphi, \iota, \tau \rangle$ be the MA defined by: *(i)* $\iota(\varepsilon) = 1, \iota(u) = 0$ otherwise; $\tau(u) = u^{-1}p(\varepsilon)$, *(ii)* $\varphi(u, x, ux) = u^{-1}p(x\Sigma^*)$ if $u, ux \in Q_p$ and $x \in \Sigma$,

---

Input: a sample S **Output**: a prefix-closed reduced MA $A = \langle \Sigma, Q, \varphi, \iota, \tau \rangle$
$Q \leftarrow \{\varepsilon\}$; $\iota(\varepsilon) \leftarrow 1$; $\tau(\varepsilon) \leftarrow P_S(\varepsilon)$; $F \leftarrow \Sigma \cap pref(S)$ /*the frontier set*/;
while $F \neq \emptyset$ **do**

    $v \leftarrow MinF$ s.t. $v = u.x$ where $u \in \Sigma^*$ and $x \in \Sigma$; $F \leftarrow F \setminus \{v\}$;
    if $I(Q, v, S, |S|^{-1/3})$ has no solution **then**

        $Q \leftarrow Q \cup \{v\}$; $\iota(v) \leftarrow 0$; $\tau(v) \leftarrow P_S(v)/P_S(v\Sigma^*)$;
        $\varphi(u, x, v) \leftarrow P_S(v\Sigma^*)/P_S(u\Sigma^*)$; $F \leftarrow F \cup \{vx \in res(P_S)|x \in \Sigma\}\}$;

    else

        let $(\alpha_w)_{w \in Q}$ be a solution of $I(Q, v, S, |S|^{-1/3})$;
        foreach $w \in Q$ **do** $\varphi(u, x, w) \leftarrow \alpha_w P_S(v\Sigma^*)/P_S(u\Sigma^*)$;

Algorithm 1. Algorithm DEES

(iii) $\varphi(u, x, v) = \alpha_v u^{-1} p(x\Sigma^*)$ if $x \in \Sigma$, $ux \in (Q_p \Sigma \setminus Q_p) \cap res(p)$ and $(ux)^{-1}p = \sum_{v \in Q_p} \alpha_v v^{-1}p$. It can be shown that A is a reduced prefix-closed MA computing p and such that $\rho(A) < 1$. A is called the *canonical representation* of p. Note that the parameters of A correspond to natural components of the residual of p and can be estimated by using samples of p.

Inference of Rational Stochastic Languages. The algorithm DEES [6] is able to identify rational stochastic languages: with probability one, for every rational stochastic language p and every infinite sample S of p, there exists an integer N such that for every $n \geq N$, DEES(S_n) outputs the canonical representation A of p. Before its presentation, we introduce informally the basic idea of the algorithm. First, the goal is to find the structure of the automaton, *i.e.* the set of states Q_p smallest basis of $[Res(P)]$. The inference proceeds as follows: the algorithm begins by building a unique state which corresponds to the residual $\epsilon^{-1}p_S$. Each state of the automaton corresponds to some residual $u^{-1}p_s$ where u is the prefix of some examples in S. After having built a state corresponding to $u^{-1}p_s$, for any letter x, the algorithm studies the possibility of adding a new state corresponding to $(ux)^{-1}p_s$ or of creating transitions labeled by x that lead to the states already built in the automaton. A new state will be added to the automaton if the residual language corresponding to $(ux)^{-1}p_s$ cannot be approximated as a linear combination of the residual languages corresponding the states already built.

The pseudo-code of the algorithm is presented in Algorithm 1. In order to find a linear combination, DEES uses the following set of inequalities where S is a non empty finite sample of Σ^*, Q a prefix-closed subset of $pref(S)$, $v \in pref(S) \setminus Q$, and $\epsilon > 0$:

$$I(Q, v, S, \epsilon) = \{|v^{-1}P_S(w\Sigma^*) - \sum_{u \in Q} X_u u^{-1}P_S(w\Sigma^*)| \leq \epsilon | w \in fact(S)\} \cup \{\sum_{u \in Q} X_u = 1\}.$$

DEES runs in polynomial time in the size of S and identifies in the limit the structure of the canonical representation A of the target p. Once the correct structure of A is found, the algorithm computes estimates α_S of each parameter α of A such that $|\alpha - \alpha_S| = O(|S|^{-1/3})$. The output automaton A computes a rational series r_A such that $\sum_{w \in \Sigma^*} r_A(w)$ converges absolutely to 1. Moreover, it can be shown that r_A converges to the target p under the $D1$ distance (also called the $L1$ norm), stronger than distance

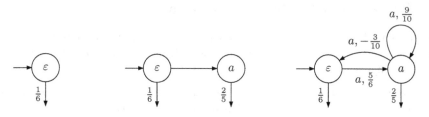

(a) Initialisation with ε.   (b) Creation of a new state.   (c) Final automaton.

Fig. 1. Illustration of the different steps of algorithm DEES

D_2 or D_∞: $\sum_{w \in \Sigma^*} |r_A(w) - p(w)|$ tends to 0 when the size of S tends to ∞. If the parameters of A are rational numbers, a variant of DEES can identify exactly the target [6].

We give now a simple example that illustrates DEES. Let us consider a sample $S = \{\varepsilon, a, aa, aaa\}$ such that $|\varepsilon| = 10$, $|a| = |aa| = 20$, $|aaa| = 10$. We have the following values for the empirical distribution: $P_S(\varepsilon) = P_S(aaa) = P_S(aaa\Sigma^*) = \frac{1}{6}$, $P_S(a) = P_S(aa) = \frac{1}{3}$, $P_S(a\Sigma^*) = \frac{5}{6}$, $P_S(aa\Sigma^*) = \frac{1}{2}$ and $P_S(aaaa\Sigma^*) = 0$, $\varepsilon = \frac{1}{(60)^{\frac{1}{3}}} \equiv$ 0.255. With the sample S, DEES will infer a multiplicity automaton in three steps:

1. We begin by constructing a state for ε (Figure 1(a)).
2. We examine $P_S(v\Sigma^*)$ with $v = \varepsilon a$ to decide if we need to add a new state for the string a. We obtain the following system which has in fact no solution and we create a new state as shown in Figure 1(b).

$$\left\{ \left| \frac{P_S(va\Sigma^*)}{P_S(v\Sigma^*)} - \frac{P_S(a\Sigma^*)}{P_S(\Sigma^*)} * X_\varepsilon \right| \leq b, \quad \left| \frac{P_S(vaa\Sigma^*)}{P_S(v\Sigma^*)} - \frac{P_S(aa\Sigma^*)}{P_S(\Sigma^*)} * X_\varepsilon \right| \leq b, \right.$$
$$\left. \left| \frac{P_S(vaaa\Sigma^*)}{P_S(v\Sigma^*)} - \frac{P_S(aaa\Sigma^*)}{P_S(\Sigma^*)} * X_\varepsilon \right| \leq b, \quad X_\varepsilon = 1 \right\}$$

3. We examine $P_S(v\Sigma^*)$ with $v = aa$ to decide if we need to create a new state for the string aa. We obtain the system below. It is easy to see that this system admits at least one solution $X_\varepsilon = -\frac{1}{2}$ and $X_a = \frac{3}{2}$. Then, we add two transitions to the automaton and we obtain the automaton of Figure 1(c) and the algorithm halts.

$$\left\{ \left| \frac{P_S(va\Sigma^*)}{P_S(v\Sigma^*)} - \frac{P_S(a\Sigma^*)}{P_S(\Sigma^*)} X_\varepsilon - \frac{P_S(aa\Sigma^*)}{P_S(a\Sigma^*)} X_a \right| \leq b, \left| \frac{P_S(vaa\Sigma^*)}{P_S(v\Sigma^*)} - \frac{P_S(aa\Sigma^*)}{P_S(\Sigma^*)} X_\varepsilon - \frac{P_S(aaa\Sigma^*)}{P_S(a\Sigma^*)} X_a \right| \leq b, \right.$$
$$\left. \left| \frac{P_S(vaaa\Sigma^*)}{P_S(v\Sigma^*)} - \frac{P_S(aaa\Sigma^*)}{P_S(\Sigma^*)} X_\varepsilon - \frac{P_S(aaa\Sigma^*)}{P_S(a\Sigma^*)} X_a \right| \leq b, \quad X_\varepsilon + X_a = 1 \right\}$$

Since no recursively enumerable subset of MA is capable to generate the set of rational stochastic languages, no identification algorithm can be proper. This remark applies to DEES. There is no guarantee at any step that the automaton A output by DEES computes a stochastic language. However, the rational series r computed by the MA output by DEES can be used to compute a stochastic language p_r that also converges to the target [6]. Moreover, they have several nice properties which make them close to stochastic languages: We call them pseudo-stochastic rational languages and we study their properties in the next Section.

3   Pseudo-stochastic Rational Languages

The canonical representation A of a rational stochastic language satisfies $\rho(A) < 1$ and $\sum_{w \in \Sigma^*} r_A(w) = 1$. We use this characteristic to define the notion of pseudo-stochastic rational language.

Definition 1. *We say that a rational series r is a* pseudo-stochastic language *if there exists an MA A which computes r and such that $\rho(A) < 1$ and if $r(\Sigma^*) = 1$.*

The condition $\rho(A) < 1$ implies that $r(\Sigma^*)$ is defined without ambiguity. A rational stochastic language is a pseudo-stochastic rational language but the converse is false.

Example. Let $A = \langle \Sigma, \{q_0\}, \varphi, \iota, \tau \rangle$ defined by $\Sigma = \{a, b\}$, $\iota(q_0) = \tau(q_0) = 1$, $\varphi(q_0, a, q_0) = 1$ and $\varphi(q_0, b, q_0) = -1$. We have $r_A(u) = (-1)^{|u|_b}$. Check that $\rho(A) = 0$ and $r_A(u\Sigma^*) = (-1)^{|u|_b}$ for every word u. Hence, r_A is a pseudo stochastic language.

As indicated in the previous section, any canonical representation A of a rational stochastic language satisfies $\rho(A) < 1$. In fact, the next Lemma shows that any reduced representation A of a pseudo-stochastic language satisfies $\rho(A) < 1$.

Lemma 1. *Let A be a reduced representation of a pseudo-stochastic language. Then, $\rho(A) < 1$.*

Proof. The proof is detailed in [8].

Proposition 1. *It is decidable within polynomial time whether a given MA computes a pseudo-stochastic language.*

Proof. Given an MA B, compute a reduced representation A of B, check whether $\rho(A) < 1$ and then, compute $r_A(\Sigma^*)$.   □

It has been shown in [6] that a stochastic language p_r can be associated with a pseudo-stochastic rational language r: the idea is to prune in Σ^* all subsets $u\Sigma^*$ such that $r(u\Sigma^*) \leq 0$ and to normalize in order to obtain a stochastic language. Let N be the smallest prefix-closed subset of Σ^* satisfying

$$\varepsilon \in N \text{ and } \forall u \in N, x \in \Sigma, ux \in N \text{ iff } r(ux\Sigma^*) > 0.$$

For every $u \in \Sigma^* \setminus N$, define $p_r(u) = 0$. For every $u \in N$, let $\lambda_u = Max(r(u), 0) + \sum_{x \in \Sigma} Max(r(ux\Sigma^*), 0)$. Then, define $p_r(u) = Max(r(u), 0)/\lambda_u$. It can be shown (see [6]) that $r(u) \leq 0 \Rightarrow p_r(u) = 0$ and $r(u) \geq 0 \Rightarrow r(u) \geq p_r(u)$.

The difference between r and p_r is simple to express when the sum $\sum_{u \in \Sigma^*} r(u)$ converges absolutely. Let $N_r = \sum_{r(u) \leq 0} |r(u)|$. We have $\sum_{w \in \Sigma^*} |r(u) - p_r(u)| = N_r + \sum_{r(u) > 0}(r(u) - p_r(u)) = 2N_r + \sum_{u \in \Sigma^*}(r(u) - p_r(u)) = 2N_r$. Note that when r is a stochastic language, $\sum_{u \in \Sigma^*} r(u)$ converges absolutely and $N_r = 0$. As a consequence, in that case, $p_r = r$. We give in Algorithm 2 an algorithm that computes $p_r(u)$ and $p_r(u\Sigma^*)$ for any word u from any MA that computes r. This algorithm is linear in the length of the input. It can be slightly modified to generate a word drawn according to p_r (see [8]).

The stochastic languages p_r associated with pseudo-stochastic rational languages r can be not rational.

Input: MA $A = \langle \Sigma, Q = \{q_1, \ldots, q_n\}, \varphi, \iota, \tau \rangle$ s.t. $\rho(A) < 1$ $r_A(\Sigma^*) = 1$, a word u

Output: $p_{r_A}(u), p_{r_A}(u\Sigma^*)$

for $i = 1, \ldots, n$ /* *this step is polynomial in* n *and is done once*/ **do**
  $\lfloor \quad s_i \leftarrow r_{A,q_i}(\Sigma^*); \qquad e_i \leftarrow \iota(q_i);$

$w \leftarrow \varepsilon; \qquad \lambda \leftarrow 1$ /* λ *is equal to* $p_{r_A}(w\Sigma^*)$*/ ;

repeat

  $\quad \mu \leftarrow \sum_{i=1}^{n} e_i \tau(q_i); \qquad S \leftarrow \{(w, Max(\mu, 0))\};$
  $\quad$ **for** $x \in \Sigma$ **do**
    $\quad \lfloor \quad \mu \leftarrow \sum_{i,j=1}^{n} e_i \varphi(q_i, x, q_j) s_j; \qquad S \leftarrow S \cup \{(wx, Max(\mu, 0))\};$
  $\quad \sigma \leftarrow \sum_{(v,\mu) \in S} \mu; \qquad S \leftarrow \{(x, \mu/\sigma) | (x, \mu) \in S\}$ /*normalization*/ ;
  $\quad$ **if** $w = u$ **then** $p_{r_A}(u) \leftarrow \lambda\mu$ /*where $(u, \mu) \in S$ and $\lambda = p_{r_A}(u\Sigma^*)$*/;
  $\quad$ **else**
    $\quad \lvert \quad$ Let $x \in \Sigma$ s.t. wx is a prefix of u and let μ s.t. $(wx, \mu) \in S$;
    $\quad \lvert \quad w \leftarrow wx; \qquad \lambda \leftarrow \lambda\mu; \qquad$ **for** $i = 1, \ldots, n$ **do** $e_i \leftarrow \sum_{j=1}^{n} e_j \varphi(q_j, x, q_i)$;
  $\quad$ **end**
until $w = u$;

Algorithm 2. Algorithm computing p_r

Proposition 2. *There exists pseudo-stochastic rational languages* r *such that* p_r *is not rational.*

Proof. Suppose that the parameters of the automaton A described on Figure 2 satisfy $\rho(\alpha + 1) + \tau_1 = 1$ and $\rho(\beta + 1) + \tau_2 = 1$ with $\alpha > \beta > 1$. Then the series r_{q_1} and r_{q_2} are rational stochastic languages and therefore, $r_A = 3r_{q_1}/2 - r_{q_2}/2$ is a rational series which satisfies $\sum_{u \in \Sigma^*} |r_A(u)| \leq 2$ and $\sum_{u \in \Sigma^*} r_A(u) = 1$. Let us show that p_{r_A} is not rational. For any $u \in \Sigma^*$, $r_A(u) = \frac{\rho^{|u|}}{2}(3\alpha^{|u|_a}\tau_1 - \beta^{|u|_b}\tau_2)$. For any integer n, there exists an integer m_n such that for any integer i, $r_A(a^n b^i) > 0$ iff $i \leq m_n$. Moreover, it is clear that m_n tends to infinity with m. Suppose now that p_{r_A} is rational and let L be its support. From the Pumping Lemma, there exists an integer N such that for any word $w = uv \in L$ satisfying $|v| \geq N$, there exists v_1, v_2, v_3 such that $v = v_1 v_2 v_3$ and $L \cap uv_1 v_2^* v_3$ is infinite. Let n be such that $m_n \geq N$ and let $u = a^n$ and $v = b^{m_n}$. Since $w = uv \in L$, $L \cap a^n b^*$ should be infinite, which is is false. Therefore, L is not the support of a rational language. $\qquad \square$

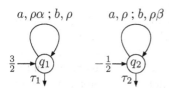

Fig. 2. An example of pseudo-stochastic rational languages which are not rational

Different rational series may yield the same pseudo-rational stochastic language. Is it decidable whether two pseudo-stochastic rational series define the same stochastic language? Unfortunately, the answer is no. The proof relies on the following result: it is undecidable whether a multiplicity automaton A over Σ satisfies $r_A(u) \leq 0$ for every $u \in \Sigma^*$ [9]. It is easy to show that this result still holds for the set of MA A which satisfy $|r_A(u)| \leq \lambda^{|u|}$, for any $\lambda > 0$.

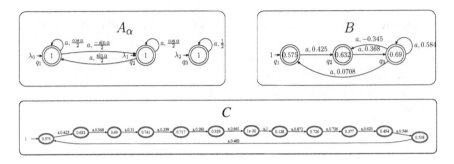

Fig. 3. A_α define stochastic language which can be represented by a PA with at least $2n$ states when $\alpha = \frac{\pi}{n}$. With $\lambda_0 = \lambda_2 = 1$ and $\lambda_1 = 0$, the MA $A_{\pi/6}$ defines a stochastic language P whose prefixed reduced representation is the MA B (with approximate values on transitions). In fact, P can be computed by a PDA and the smallest PA computing it is C.

Proposition 3. *It is undecidable whether two rational series define the same stochastic language.*

Proof. The proof is detailed in [8].

4   Experiments

In this section, we present a set of experiments allowing us to study the performance of the algorithm DEES for learning good stochastic language models. Hence, we will study the behavior of DEES with samples of distributions generated from PDA, PA and non rational stochastic language. We decide to compare DEES to the most well known probabilistic grammatical inference approaches: The algorithms *Alergia* [3] and *MDI* [10] that are able to identify PDAs. These algorithms can be tuned by a parameter, in the experiments we choose the best parameter which gives the best result on all the samples, but we didn't change the parameter according to the size of the sample in order to take into account the impact of the sample sizes.

In our experiments, we use two performance criteria. We measure the size of the inferred models by the number of states. Moreover, to evaluate the quality of the automata, we use the $D1$ norm[1] between two models A and A' defined by :
$$D1(A, A') = \sum_{u \in \Sigma^*} |P_A(u) - P_{A'}(u)|.$$
$D1$ norm is the strongest distance after Kullback Leibler. In practice, we use an approximation by considering a subset of Σ^* generated by A (A will be the target for us).

We carried out a first series of experiment where the target automaton can be represented by a PDA. We consider a stochastic language defined by the automaton on Figure 3. This stochastic language can be represented by a multiplicity automaton of three states and by an equivalent minimal PDA of twelve states [6] (Alergia and MDI can

---

[1] Note that we can't use the Kullback-Leibler measure because it is not robust with null probability strings which implies to smooth the learned models, and also because automata produced by DEES do not always define stochastic language, *i.e.* some strings may have a negative value.

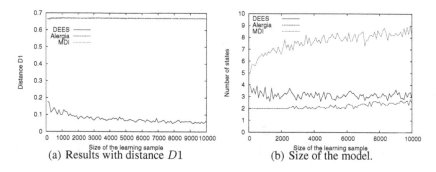

(a) Results with distance $D1$ (b) Size of the model.

Fig. 4. Results obtained with the prefix reduced multiplicity automaton of three states of Figure 3 admitting a representation with a PDA of twelve states

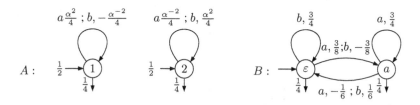

Fig. 5. Automaton A is a PA with non rational parameters in $\mathbb{R}^+$ ($\alpha = (\sqrt{5}+1)/2$). A can be represented by an MA B with rational parameters in $\mathbb{Q}$ [5]

then identify this automaton). To compare the performances of the three algorithms, we used the following experimental set up. From the target automaton, we generate samples from size 100 to 10000. Then, for each sample we learn an automaton with the three algorithms and compute the norm $D1$ between them and the target. We repeat this experimental setup 10 times and give the average results. Figure 4 reports the results obtained. If we consider the size of the learned models, DEES finds quickly the target automaton, while MDI only begins to tend to the target PDA after 10000 examples. The automata produced by Alergia are far from this target. This behavior can be explained by the fact that these two algorithms need significantly longer examples to find the correct target and thus larger samples, this is also amplified because there are more parameters to estimate. In practise we noticed that the correct structure can be found after more than 100000 examples. If we look at the distance $D1$, DEES outperforms MDI and Alergia (which have the same behavior) and begins to converge after 500 examples.

We carried out other series of experiments for evaluating DEES when the target belongs to the class of PA. First, we consider the simple automaton of Figure 5 which defines a stochastic language that can be represented by a PA with parameters in $\mathbb{R}^+$. We follow the same experimental setup as in the first experiment, the results are reported on Figure 6. According to our 2 performance criteria, DEES outperforms again Alergia and MDI. In fact, the target can not be modeled correctly by Alergia and MDI because it can not be represented by a PDA. This explains why these algorithms can't find a good model. For them, the best answer is to produce a unigram model. Alergia even

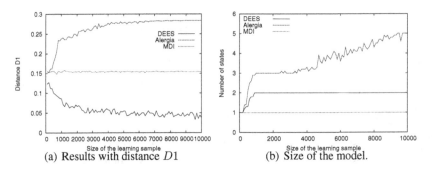

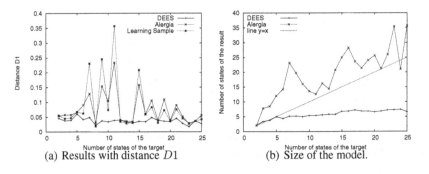

Fig. 6. Results obtained with the target automaton of Figure 5 admitting a representation in the class PA with non rational parameters

Fig. 7. Results obtained from a set of PA generated randomly

diverge at a given step (this behavior is due to its fusion criterion that becomes more restrictive with the increasing of the learning set) and MDI returns always the unigram. DEES finds the correct structure quickly and begins to converge after 1000 examples. This behavior confirms the fact DEES can produce better models with small samples because it constructs small representations. On the other hand, Alergia and MDI seem to need a huge number of examples to find a good approximation of the target, even when the target is relatively small.

We made another experiment in the class of PA. We study the behavior of DEES when the learning samples are generated from different targets randomly generated. For this experiment, we take an alphabet of three letters and we generate randomly some PA with a number of states from 2 to 25. The PA are generated in order to have a prefix representation which guarantees that all the states are reachable. The rest of the transitions and the values of the parameters are chosen randomly. Then, for each target, we generate 5 samples of size 300 times the number of states of the target. We made this choice because we think that for small targets the samples may be sufficient to find a good approximation, while for bigger targets there is a clear lack of examples. This last point allows us to see the behaviors of the algorithms with small amounts of data. We learn an automaton from each sample and compare it to the corresponding target. Note that we didn't use MDI in this experiment because this algorithm is extremely

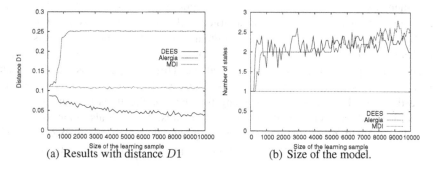

(a) Results with distance $D1$ (b) Size of the model.

Fig. 8. Results obtained with samples generated from a non rational stochastic language

hard to tune, which implies an important cost in time for finding a good parameter. The parameter of Alergia is fixed to a reasonable value kept for all the experiment. Results for Alergia and DEES are reported on Figure 7. We also add the empirical distance of the samples to the target automaton. If you consider the $D1$ norm, the performances of Alergia depend highly on the empirical distribution. Alergia infers models close, or better, than those produced by DEES only when the empirical distribution is already very good, thus when it is not necessary to learn. Moreover, Alergia has a greater variance which implies a weak robustness. On the other hand, DEES is always able to learn significantly small models almost always better, even with small samples.

Finally, we carried out a last experiment where the objective is to study the behavior of the three algorithms with samples generated from a non rational stochastic language. We consider, as a target, the stochastic language generated using the p_r algorithm from the automaton of Figure 2 (note that this automaton admits a prefix reduced representation of 2 states). We took $\rho = 3/10$, $\alpha = 3/2$ and $\beta = 5/4$. We follow the same experimental setup than the first experiment. Since we use rational representations, we measure the distance $D1$ from the automaton of Figure 2 using a sample generated by p_r (*i.e.* we measure the $D1$ only for strings with a strictly positive value). The results are presented on Figure 8. MDI and Alergia are clearly not able to build a good estimation of the target distribution and we see that their best answer is to produce a unigram. On the other hand, DEES is able to identify a structure close to the MA that was used for defining the distribution and produces good automata after 2000 examples. This means that DEES seems able to produce pseudo-stochastic rational languages which are closed to a non rational stochastic distribution.

5   Conclusion

In this paper, we studied the class of pseudo-stochastic rational languages (PSRL) that are stochastic languages defined by multiplicity automata which do not define stochastic languages but share some properties with them. We showed that it is possible to decide wether an MA defines a PSRL, but we can't decide wether two MA define the same PSRL. Moreover, it is possible to define a stochastic language from these MA but this language is not rational in general. Despite of these drawbacks, we showed experimentally that DEES produces MA computing pseudo-stochastic rational languages that provide good estimates of a target stochastic language. We recall here that DEES is able to output automata with a minimal number of parameters which is clearly an advantage from a machine learning standpoint, especially for dealing with small datasets. Moreover, our experiments showed that DEES outperforms standard probabilistic grammatical inference approaches. Thus, we think that the class of pseudo-stochastic rational languages is promising for many applications in grammatical inference. Beyond the fact to continue the study of this class, we also plan to consider methods that could infer a class of MA strictly greater than the class of PSRL. We also began to work on an adaptation of the approaches presented in this paper to trees.

References

1. J. Berstel and C. Reutenauer. *Les séries rationnelles et leurs langages*. Masson, 1984.
2. V.D. Blondel and J.N. Tsitsiklis. A survey of computational complexity results in systems and control. *Automatica*, 36(9):1249–1274, September 2000.
3. R.C. Carrasco and J. Oncina. Learning stochastic regular grammars by means of a state merging method. In *Proceedings of ICGI'94*, LNAI, pages 139–150. Springer, 1994.
4. F. Denis and Y. Esposito. Learning classes of probabilistic automata. In *Proceedings COLT'04*, volume 3120 of *LNCS*, pages 124–139. Springer, 2004.
5. F. Denis and Y. Esposito. Rational stochastic language. Technical report, LIF - Université de Provence, 2006. http://fr.arxiv.org/abs/cs.LG/0602093.
6. F. Denis, Y. Esposito, and A. Habrard. Learning rational stochastic languages. In *Proceedings of 19th Annual Conference on Learning Theory (COLT'06)*, 2006.
7. F.R. Gantmacher. *Théorie des matrices, tomes 1 et 2*. Dunod, 1966.
8. A. Habrard, F. Denis, and Y. Esposito. Using pseudo-stochastic rational languages in probabilistic grammatical inference. http://fr.arxiv.org/, 2006. Extended version.
9. A. Salomaa and M. Soittola. *Automata: Theoretic Aspects of Formal Power Series*. Springer-Verlag, 1978.
10. F. Thollard, P. Dupont, and C. de la Higuera. Probabilistic dfa inference using kullback–leibler divergence and minimality. In *Proceedings of ICML'00*, pages 975–982, June 2000.

Learning Analysis by Reduction from Positive Data[*]

František Mráz[1], Friedrich Otto[2], and Martin Plátek[1]

[1] Charles University, Faculty of Mathematics and Physics
Department of Computer Science, Malostranské nám. 25
118 00 PRAHA 1, Czech Republic
mraz@ksvi.ms.mff.cuni.cz, Martin.Platek@mff.cuni.cz
[2] Fachbereich Mathematik/Informatik, Universität Kassel
34109 Kassel, Germany
otto@theory.informatik.uni-kassel.de

Abstract. Analysis by reduction is a linguistically motivated method for checking correctness of a sentence. It can be modelled by restarting automata. In this paper we propose a method for learning restarting automata which are strictly locally testable (SLT-R-automata). The method is based on the concept of identification in the limit from positive examples only. Also we characterize the class of languages accepted by SLT-R-automata with respect to the Chomsky hierarchy.

1   Introduction

Analysis by reduction [7,8,12] consists in stepwise simplifications (reductions) of a given (lexically disambiguated) extended sentence until a correct simple sentence is obtained, which is then accepted, or until an error is found and the input is rejected. Each simplification replaces a short part of the sentence by an even shorter one. Analysis by reduction can be modelled by restarting automata, which have been studied for several years now [6,11]. However, only few tools have been developed so far that support the design of restarting automata. In this paper we propose a method for learning restarting automata (analysis by reduction) from positive examples. Obviously, each restarting automaton learnt can be used for language recognition. Thus, by learning a restarting automaton we implicitly learn the language accepted by it, but in addition, a restarting automaton (analysis by reduction) enables nice error localization in rejected words/sentences (see, e.g. [7]).

Several attempts for learning restarting automata by genetic algorithms have been made before [2,5]. The results are far from being applicable. Here we propose another method based on the concept of identification in the limit from

[*] F. Mráz and M. Plátek were partially supported by the Grant Agency of the Czech Republic under Grant-No. 201/04/2102 and by the program 'Information Society' under project 1ET100300517. F. Mráz was also supported by the Grant Agency of Charles University in Prague under Grant-No. 358/2006/A-INF/MFF.

Y. Sakakibara et al. (Eds.): ICGI 2006, LNAI 4201, pp. 125–136, 2006.

positive data. Our proposed method uses positive samples of simplifications (reductions) and positive samples of so-called simple words (sentences) of the language to be learnt. The new algorithm could substantially improve applicability
of restarting automata/analysis by reduction.

In this paper we describe the learning protocol for learning a subclass of
restarting automata called *strictly locally testable* restarting automata. Their
definition as well as the protocol for learning them is based on the notion of
strictly locally testable languages [9,14]. Further, we compare the class of languages learnable in this way to the classes of the Chomsky hierarchy.

2   Definitions and Notations

Throughout the paper we will use λ to denote the empty word. Further, $|w|$ will
denote the *length* of the word w, and by $\subset$ we denote the proper subset relation.

In order to define the analysis by reduction, we introduce syntactic reduction
systems.

Definition 1. *A syntactic reduction system is a tuple* $R = (\Sigma, \Gamma, \vdash_R, L_S)$,
where Σ *is a finite nonempty* input alphabet, Γ *is a finite nonempty* work-
ing alphabet *containing* Σ, $\vdash_R \subseteq \Gamma^* \times \Gamma^*$ *is a* reduction relation, *and* $L_S \subseteq \Gamma^*$
is a set of simple sentential forms. *Any string from* Γ^* *is called a* sentential
form. *The reflexive and transitive closure of* $\vdash_R$ *is denoted by* $\vdash_R^*$.

With each syntactic reduction system $R = (\Sigma, \Gamma, \vdash_R, L_S)$ *we associate the
following two languages:*

– *the* input language *of* R: $L(R)\ \ = \{\, u \in \Sigma^* \mid \exists\, v \in L_S : u \vdash_R^* v \,\}$,
– *the* characteristic language *of* R: $L_C(R) = \{\, u \in \Gamma^* \mid \exists\, v \in L_S : u \vdash_R^* v \,\}$.

Thus, a word $u \in \Sigma^*$ (a sentential form $u \in \Gamma^*$) belongs to the input language
(the characteristic language) of R if and only if u can be reduced to a simple
sentential form $v \in L_S$. Trivially, $L(R) = L_C(R) \cap \Sigma^*$.

Definition 2. *A syntactic reduction system* $R = (\Sigma, \Gamma, \vdash_R, L_S)$ *is called:*

– length-reducing *if, for each* $u, v \in \Gamma^*$, $u \vdash_R v$ *implies* $|u| > |v|$;
– locally reducing *if there exists a constant* $k > 0$ *such that, for each* $u, v \in \Gamma^*$,
  $u \vdash_R v$ *implies that there exist words* $u_1, u_2, x, y \in \Gamma^*$ *for which* $u = u_1 x u_2$
  and $v = u_1 y u_2$, *and* $|x| \le k$.

Syntactic reduction systems that are length-reducing and locally reducing are
a formalization of the analysis by reduction of the type we are interested in.
In the case of a natural language, the relation $\vdash_R$ corresponds to a stepwise
simplification of (extended) sentences, and L_S corresponds to (correct) simple
sentences. The analysis by reduction is nondeterministic in the sense that:

– one word (sentential form) can be reduced in several different ways to different sentential forms;

- for a word $u \in L(R)$ there can exist two or more simple sentential forms to which u can be reduced;
- even if $u \in L_C(R)$, there can exist a sentential form v such that $u \vdash_R^* v$, but $v \notin L_C(R)$.

The analysis by reduction has the so-called *error preserving property*:

$$\text{if } u \vdash_R^* v, \text{ and } u \notin L_C(R), \text{ then } v \notin L_C(R).$$

The analysis by reduction has been modelled by several types of restarting automata [11]. One of them is the RRWW-automaton [7]. Instead of its formal definition we will use its alternative representation adapted from [10].

Definition 3. *A restarting automaton is a system* $M = (\Sigma, \Gamma, I)$, *where* Σ *is an input alphabet,* Γ *is a working alphabet containing* Σ, *and* I *is a finite set of meta-instructions of the following two types:*

(1) A rewriting meta-instruction is of the form $(E_l, x \rightarrow y, E_r)$, *where* $x, y \in \Gamma^*$ *such that* $|x| > |y|$, *and* $E_l, E_r \subseteq \Gamma^*$ *are regular languages called* left *and* right *constraints.*

(2) An accepting *meta-instruction is of the form* (E, Accept), *where* $E \subseteq \Gamma^*$ *is a regular language.*

A restarting automaton $M = (\Sigma, \Gamma, I)$ *induces a length-reducing and locally reducing syntactic reduction system* $R(M) := (\Sigma, \Gamma, \vdash_M^c, S(M))$ *as follows:*

a) for each $u, v \in \Gamma^*$, $u \vdash_M^c v$ *if and only if there exist an instruction* $i = (E_l, x \rightarrow y, E_r)$ *in* I *and words* $u_1, u_2 \in \Gamma^*$ *such that* $u = u_1 x u_2$, $v = u_1 y u_2$, $u_1 \in E_l$, *and* $u_2 \in E_r$; *and*

b) $S(M) := \bigcup_{(E, \mathsf{Accept}) \in I} E$.

By $\vdash_M^{c*}$ we denote the reflexive and transitive closure of $\vdash_M^c$. Accordingly, the restarting automaton $M = (\Sigma, \Gamma, I)$ defines an *input language* $L(M)$ and a *characteristic language* $L_C(M)$:

- $L(M) = \{ w \in \Sigma^* \mid \exists z \in S(M) : w \vdash_M^{c*} z \}$, and
- $L_C(M) = \{ w \in \Gamma^* \mid \exists z \in S(M) : w \vdash_M^{c*} z \}$.

Thus, an input word (a sentential form) w is accepted by M if and only if w can be reduced to some simple sentential form $z \in S(M)$.

The problem of learning analysis by reduction/a restarting automaton consists in learning the reduction relation $\vdash_M^c$ and the set of simple sentential forms $S(M)$. For simplicity, we will suppose a helpful teacher, which splits the problem of learning a restarting automaton into learning individual meta-instructions. Even knowing that $ababab \vdash_M^c ababa$ by some meta-instruction, we do not know whether a subword ab was replaced by the empty word λ, or a subword ba was replaced by λ, or some aba was rewritten to a, or some other rewriting was applied. Therefore, we suppose an even more helpful teacher which marks the rewritten part of such a word. In this way we reduce the problem of learning one meta-instruction to the learning of regular languages of constraints in meta-instructions. For this we can use one of the oldest models for language learning — the identification in the limit [4].

For a language L, a *positive presentation* of L is an infinite sequence $\{w_i\}_{i=1}^\infty$ of words from L such that every $w \in L$ occurs at least once in the sequence. Let $\mathcal{M}$ be a class of automata, and let $\mathcal{A}$ be an algorithm which, on input $\{w_1, \ldots, w_i\}$ (for any $i \geq 1$), returns a conjecture automaton $M_i \in \mathcal{M}$. The algorithm $\mathcal{A}$ is said to *learn (or identify) a language L in the limit from positive data using $\mathcal{M}$* if, for any positive presentation of L, the infinite sequence of automata $\{M_i\}_{i=1}^\infty$ in $\mathcal{M}$ produced by $\mathcal{A}$ satisfies the property that there exists an automaton M in $\mathcal{M}$ such that $L(M) = L$, and for all sufficiently large i, M_i is identical to M. A class of languages $\mathcal{L}$ is *learnable in the limit from positive data* (using $\mathcal{M}$) if there exists an algorithm $\mathcal{A}$ that, for each $L \in \mathcal{L}$, learns L in the limit from positive data using $\mathcal{M}$.

Gold [4] showed that any class of languages containing all finite sets and at least one infinite set is not learnable in the limit from positive data only. This fact implies that even the class of regular languages is not learnable in the limit from positive data. One of the well-known language classes which are learnable in the limit from positive data are the strictly locally testable languages [9,14].

In the following we will use Reg, CFL, and CSL to denote the class of regular, context-free, and context-sensitive languages, respectively. Let $P_k(w)$ and $S_k(w)$ be the prefix and the suffix of a word w of length k, respectively. Further, let $I_k(w)$ be the set of all substrings of w of length k except the prefix and suffix of w of length k, that is,

$$I_k(w) = \{\, u \mid |u| = k \text{ and } w = xuy, \text{ for some nonempty words } x, y\,\}.$$

These are defined only for $|w| \geq k$. If $|w| = k$, then $P_k(w) = S_k(w) = w$, while $I_k(w)$ is empty, whenever $k \leq |w| \leq k + 1$. For example, $P_2(aababab) = aa$, $S_2(aababab) = ab$, and $I_2(aababab) = \{ab, ba\}$.

Definition 4. *Let k be a positive integer. A language $L \subseteq \Sigma^*$ is strictly k-testable if there exist finite sets $A, B, C \subseteq \Sigma^k$ such that, for all $w \in L$ satisfying $|w| \geq k$, we have*

$$w \in L \quad \text{if and only if} \quad P_k(w) \in A, \ S_k(w) \in B, \text{ and } I_k(w) \subseteq C.$$

In this case, (A, B, C) is called a triple *for L.*

We will say that L is strictly locally testable *if it is strictly k-testable for some $k > 0$.*

Note that the definition of 'strictly k-testable' says nothing about the strings of length $k - 1$ or less. Hence, L is strictly k-testable if and only if

$$L \cap \Sigma^k \Sigma^* = (A\Sigma^* \cap \Sigma^* B) - \Sigma^+ (\Sigma^k - C) \Sigma^+. \tag{1}$$

For example, the language $(a + b)^*$ is strictly 1-testable, as $(a + b)^+$ can be expressed in the form (1) by $(A, B, C) = (\{a, b\}, \{a, b\}, \{a, b\})$, and the language

$a(baa)^+$ is strictly 3-testable, as it can be expressed in the form (1) by the triple $(A, B, C) = (\{aba\}, \{baa\}, \{aba, baa, aab\})$.

We will denote the family of strictly k-testable languages by k-SLT and the class of strictly locally testable languages by SLT. It is easy to see that SLT $\subset$ Reg (for example, the regular language $(aa)^*$ is not strictly locally testable). It is also known that

$$k\text{-SLT} \subset (k+1)\text{-SLT}.$$

Let us briefly recall a learning algorithm for strictly k-testable languages from [13]. For a triple $S = (A, B, C)$, where $A, B, C \subseteq \Sigma^k$, we use the notation $L'(A, B, C)$ as a shorthand for the set $L'(A, B, C) := A \cap B \cap (\Sigma^k - C)$. First, we present a construction which, for a given triple $S = (A, B, C)$, where $A, B, C \subseteq \Sigma^k$, constructs a deterministic finite-state automaton (DFA) $M_S = (Q, \Sigma, \delta, q_0, F)$ such that $L(M_S) = (A\Sigma^* \cap \Sigma^* B) - \Sigma^+ (\Sigma^k - C)\Sigma^+$:

$$Q := \begin{cases} Q_I \cup \{\, [\widehat{x}] \mid x \in L'(A, B, C) \,\} & \text{if } L'(A, B, C) \neq \emptyset, \\ Q_I & \text{otherwise,} \end{cases}$$

where

$$Q_I := \{\, [\lambda], [a_1], [a_1 a_2], \ldots, [a_1 \ldots a_{k-1}] \mid a_1 \ldots a_k \in A, a_1, \ldots, a_k \in \Sigma \,\}$$
$$\cup \{\, [x] \mid x \in A \cup B \cup C \,\}.$$

Further,

$$q_0 := [\lambda],$$

$$F := \begin{cases} \{\, [\beta] \mid \beta \in B \,\} \cup \{\, [\widehat{x}] \mid x \in L'(A, B, C) \,\} & \text{if } L'(A, B, C) \neq \emptyset, \\ \{\, [\beta] \mid \beta \in B \,\} & \text{otherwise,} \end{cases}$$

and δ is defined as follows:

(i) for each $\alpha = a_1 \ldots a_k \in A$ ($a_1, \ldots, a_k \in \Sigma$):

$$\delta(q_0, a_1) := [a_1],$$
$$\delta([w_i], a_{i+1}) := [w_i a_{i+1}], \quad \text{where } w_i = a_1 \ldots a_i \ (1 \leq i \leq k-2),$$
$$\delta([w_{k-1}], a_k) := \begin{cases} [\widehat{\alpha}] & \text{if } \alpha \in B \cap (\Sigma^k - C), \\ [\alpha] & \text{otherwise,} \end{cases} \quad \text{where } w_{k-1} = a_1 \ldots a_{k-1};$$

(ii) for each $[ax], [xb] \in Q$ such that $|x| = k-1$, $ax \in A$, $xb \in B \cup C$:

$$\delta([\widehat{ax}], b) := [xb] \qquad \text{if } ax \in B \cap (\Sigma^k - C),$$
$$\delta([ax], b) := [xb] \qquad \text{otherwise;}$$

(iii) for each $[ax], [xb] \in Q$ such that $|x| = k-1$, $ax \in C$, $xb \in B \cup C$:

$$\delta([ax], b) := [xb].$$

We say that the constructed automaton M_S is *associated* to the triple $S = (A, B, C)$. The constructed DFA is in general not the minimal finite-state automaton recognizing $L = L(M_S)$.

Now we present the learning algorithm LA (adapted from [13]).

Input: an integer $k > 0$ and a positive presentation of a target strictly k-testable language U.

Output: a sequence of DFAs accepting strictly k-testable languages.

Procedure:

   initialize $E_0 := \emptyset$;

   let $S_{E_0} = (\emptyset, \emptyset, \emptyset)$ be the initial triple;

   construct DFA M_{E_0} accepting $E_0 (= \emptyset)$;

   repeat (forever)

      let $M_{E_i} = (Q_{E_i}, \Sigma, \delta_{E_i}, q_0, F_{E_i})$ be the current DFA;

      read the next positive example w_{i+1};

      if $w_{i+1} \in L(M_{E_i})$ **then**

         $E_{i+1} := E_i$;

         $M_{E_{i+1}} := M_{E_i}$;

      else

         $E_{i+1} := E_i \cup \{w_{i+1}\}$;

         construct the DFA $M_{E_{i+1}}$ associated with the triple

$$S_{E_{i+1}} = (A_{E_{i+1}}, B_{E_{i+1}}, C_{E_{i+1}}),$$

         where $A_{E_{i+1}} = A_{E_i} \cup P_k(w_{i+1})$,
                 $B_{E_{i+1}} = B_{E_i} \cup S_k(w_{i+1})$,
                 $C_{E_{i+1}} = C_{E_i} \cup I_k(w_{i+1})$.

   output M_{i+1}.

Yokomori and Kobayashi have shown that LA learns in the limit a DFA M_E such that $U = L(M_E)$.

Fact 5. [13] *Let* $M_{E_0}, M_{E_1}, \dots, M_{E_i}, \dots$ *be the sequence of DFAs produced by the above algorithm LA. Then*

1. *for each* $i \geq 0$, $L(M_{E_i}) \subseteq L(M_{E_{i+1}}) \subseteq U$, *and*
2. *there exists* $r > 0$ *such that, for each* $i \geq 0$, $M_{E_r} = M_{E_{r+i}}$, *and* $L(M_{E_r}) = U$.

We now define a restricted version of restarting automata, which use strictly k-testable languages only.

Definition 6. *Let* k *be a positive integer and* Γ *be an alphabet.*

- *We say that a rewriting meta-instruction* $(E_l, x \to y, E_r)$, *where* $E_l, E_r \subseteq \Gamma^*$ *and* $x, y \in \Gamma^*$, *is strictly* k-*testable, i f the languages* E_l, E_r *are strictly* k-*testable and* $k \geq |x| > |y|$.
- *We say that an accepting meta-instruction* (E, Accept), *where* $E \subseteq \Gamma^*$, *is strictly* k-*testable if* E *is strictly* k-*testable.*

- *We say that a restarting automaton M is strictly k-testable if all its meta-instructions are strictly k-testable.*
- *We say that a restarting automaton is strictly locally testable, if it is strictly k-testable for some $k \geq 1$.*

Let k-SLT-R denote the class of all strictly k-testable restarting automata, and let SLT-R denote the class of all strictly locally testable restarting automata. For any class of restarting automata $\mathcal{A}$, $\mathcal{L}(\mathcal{A})$ denotes the class of all input languages recognized by automata from $\mathcal{A}$.

Below we present an example of an SLT-R-automaton.

Example 1. Let $M = (\{a,b\}, \{a,b\}, I)$ be the restarting automaton defined by the following three meta-instructions:

$$1. \quad (a+b, \mathsf{Accept}),$$
$$2. \quad (a^*, aa \rightarrow b, b^*),$$
$$3. \quad (b^*, bb \rightarrow a, a^*).$$

This automaton accepts the language

$$L(M) = \{ a^{2i}b^j \mid i, j \geq 0, i+j = 2^n \text{ for some } n \geq 0 \} \cup \{ b^{2i}a^j \mid i, j \geq 0, i+j = 2^n \text{ for some } n \geq 0 \}.$$

It is easy to check that all the constraints in the above instructions are strictly 2-testable languages. Hence, M is a strictly 2-testable restarting automaton.

Example 2. To illustrate our approach we now consider the process of learning an unknown target language together with its analysis by reduction. Let us suppose that we know that the target language contains the words abc, $aabbc$, $aaabbbc$, $aabbbbd$, $abbd$, and that the following reductions (on words which need not belong to the target language) are possible (the rewritten subwords are underlined):

$$aaa\underline{ab}bbbc \vdash aaabbbc,$$
$$aa\underline{ab}bbbbbc \vdash aabbbbbc,$$
$$aaa\underline{ab}bbbbbd \vdash aaabbbbd,$$
$$aa\underline{ab}bbbbbd \vdash aabbbbd.$$

In this extremely simple example we can see that two types of rewritings $ab \rightarrow \lambda$ and $abb \rightarrow \lambda$ are used. We decide that we want to learn two meta-instructions. The first meta-instruction should enable the first two reductions, and the second meta-instruction should enable the remaining two reductions. In general, the partition of the set of sample reductions into groups which should be realized by different meta-instructions must be done by a helpful teacher.

The first meta-instruction will be of the form

$$(E_{L,1}, ab \rightarrow \lambda, E_{R,1}),$$

where the language $E_{L,1}$ contains the words aaa, aa, and the second language $E_{R,1}$ contains the words $bbbc, bbbbbc$. This meta-instruction can be learnt as a strictly k-testable meta-instruction, for $k \geq 2$, as the rewritten part is of length 2. Using the words aaa, aa as the first two positive examples for the strictly locally-testable language $E_{L,1}$, the algorithm LA with $k = 2$ produces the triple $(\{aa\}, \{aa\}, \{aa\})$. This triple represents the language aaa^*. Further, using $bbbc, bbbbbc$ as input for LA with $k = 2$, we get the triple $(\{bb\}, \{bc\}, \{bb\})$, which represents the language bbb^*c. Hence we get the first meta-instruction

$$\text{(a)} \qquad (aaa^*, ab \to \lambda, bbb^*c).$$

In an analogous way, the second rewriting meta-instruction can be learnt from the last two examples of reductions:

$$aaa\underline{abb}bbbbd \vdash aaabbbbd \qquad \text{and} \qquad aa\underline{abb}bbbbd \vdash aabbbbd.$$

The learnt strictly 3-testable meta-instruction (as there are 3 symbols deleted in one reduction) is

$$\text{(b)} \qquad (aaaa^*, abb \to \lambda, bbbb^*d).$$

Now we know that the meta-instruction (a) can describe reductions of words of length at least 7 and the meta-instruction (b) can describe reductions of words of length at least 10. Let us now suppose that we know all "short words" of the target language of length at most 7. Hence, we can use the set of words $S = \{abc, aabbc, aaabbbc, aabbbbd, abbd\}$ as an input for LA in order to learn the language of simple sentential forms. For each $k < 6$, the algorithm LA with input S learns also at least one word of length at most 7 which does not belong to S. For $k = 6$, LA learns the strictly 6-testable language $\{aabbbbd, aaabbbc\}$.

Thus, we have learnt a 6-SLT-R-automaton $M = (\{a, b, c, d\}, \{a, b, c, d\}, I)$ with three meta-instructions:

$$\text{(a) } (aaa^*, ab \to \lambda, bbb^*c),$$
$$\text{(b) } (aaaa^*, abb \to \lambda, bbbb^*d),$$
$$\text{(c) } (aaabbbc + aabbbbd, \text{Accept}).$$

M accepts the language $L = \{a^n b^n c \mid n \geq 3\} \cup \{a^n b^{2n} d \mid n \geq 2\}$. This is a fairly good approximation for the language $L_0 = \{a^n b^n c \mid n \geq 1\} \cup \{a^n b^{2n} d \mid n \geq 1\}$, which is known to be context-free but not deterministic context-free.

Actually we have learned analysis by reduction with two reduction rules and a single accepting rule:

(a) If a word is a sequence of a's followed by a sequence of b's finished by the letter c (of length at least 7), then it can be simplified by deleting the subword ab.

(b) If a word is a sequence of a's followed by a sequence of b's finished by the letter d (of length at least 10), then it can be simplified by deleting the subword abb.

(c) The words $aaabbbc$ and $aabbbbd$ belong to the language.

All SLT-R-automata can be learnt in the way proposed above. In the next section we will characterize the class of languages, which can be learnt in this way.

Note that according to [4] the class of strictly locally testable languages (SLT) as a whole is not learnable in the limit from only positive data. However, the inference algorithm can be used effectively to identify any language from this class in the limit through a complete (both positive and negative) presentation sequence of the language [3]. This can be accomplished by starting with $k = 2$ and using successive positive samples to infer progressively larger (less restricted) 2-SLT's until a negative sample, which is incompatible with the current language, appears. Then k is increased by one, and the process continues in the same way with the successive samples. Eventually, the correct value of k will be reached and then no other negative sample will ever be incompatible. The inferred language will then grow progressively with the successive positive samples until the target k-SLT is identified.

The above learning protocol can be used also for learning strictly locally testable rewriting meta-instructions, but it requires a helpful teacher as follows. Suppose a learner is being taught a rewriting meta-instruction of the form $(E_l, aba \rightarrow b, E_r)$. Knowing that aba cannot be rewritten into b in the word $aabaaaa$, it is possible that:

- either $a \notin E_l$ and $aaa \in E_r$, or
- $a \in E_l$ and $aaa \notin E_r$, or
- $a \notin E_l$ and $aaa \notin E_r$.

Hence, this information must be supplied by a teacher.

3   Characterization of the Class of SLT-R-Languages

SLT-R-automata are quite powerful. They can accept all growing context-sensitive languages (GCSL) as input languages. Growing context-sensitive languages are the languages generated by growing context-sensitive grammars. A Chomsky grammar $G = (V_N, V_T, S, P)$ with a set of nonterminals V_N, a set of terminals V_T, an initial nonterminal $S \in V_N$ and a set of rules P is *growing context-sensitive* if the start symbol S does not appear on the right-hand side of any production of G, and if $|\alpha| < |\beta|$ holds for all productions $(\alpha \rightarrow \beta) \in P$ satisfying $\alpha \neq S$.

Theorem 1. GCSL $\subset \mathcal{L}(\text{SLT-R}) \subseteq$ CSL.

Proof. Let $G = (V_N, V_T, S, P)$ be a growing context-sensitive grammar. We construct an SLT-R-automaton $M = (\Sigma, \Gamma, I)$ recognizing $L(M) = L(G)$. To this end we take $\Sigma := V_T$, $\Gamma := (V_N \smallsetminus \{S\}) \cup V_T$, and

$$I := \{(\{\beta \mid S \rightarrow \beta \in P\}, \text{Accept})\} \cup \{(\Gamma^*, \beta \rightarrow \alpha, \Gamma^*) \mid \alpha \neq S, \text{ and } \alpha \rightarrow \beta \in P\}.$$

Trivially, M works as an analytical version of the grammar G without the rules with the initial nonterminal S, but M directly accepts (without any reduction) all right-hand sides of productions with left-hand side S. Hence $L(M) = L(G)$. This implies that GCSL $\subseteq \mathcal{L}(\text{SLT-R})$.

Moreover, the language $L_{copy} = \{\, w\#w \mid w \in \{a, b\}^* \,\}$, which is not growing context-sensitive (see [1]), can be accepted by the following SLT-R-automaton $M_{copy} = (\Sigma, \Gamma, I_{copy})$, where $\Sigma = \{a, b, \#\}$, $\Gamma = \Sigma \cup \{A_{xy} \mid x, y \in \{a, b\}\}$, and I_{copy} consists of the following meta-instructions:

(1) $(xy(a + b)^*\#, xy \to A_{xy}, (a + b)^*)$,   for each $x, y \in \{a, b\}$;
(2) $(\lambda, xy \to A_{xy}, (a + b + \#A_{xy})^*)$,   for each $x, y \in \{a, b\}$;
(3) $(A_{xy}(a + b)^*\#, A_{xy} \to \lambda, (a + b)^*)$,   for each $x, y \in \{a, b\}$;
(4) $(\lambda, A_{xy} \to \lambda, (a + b + \#)^*)$,   for each $x, y \in \{a, b\}$;
(5) $(\# + a\#a + b\#b, \text{Accept})$.

Each meta-instruction of M_{copy} preserves the number of occurrences of the symbol $\#$ in the current word. All words accepted by M_{copy} using the single accepting meta-instruction (5) contain exactly one occurrence of $\#$. Hence, each word accepted by M_{copy} contains exactly one occurrence of $\#$. For an input word w of length at least 4 and of the form $(a + b)^*\#(a + b)^*$, the only applicable meta-instruction is a meta-instruction of form (1). In the resulting word, $\#$ is followed by the working symbol A_{xy}, where $x, y \in \{a, b\}$ are the first two symbols of the word. Such a word can be reduced only by a meta-instruction of form (2). Further, M_{copy} must use appropriate meta-instructions of forms (3) and (4). This is possible only if the word is of the form $w = xyu\#xyv$ for some $x, y \in \{a, b\}$, $u, v \in \{a, b\}^*$. After executing 4 meta-instructions, M_{copy} obtains the word $u\#v$. Now it is easy to see that M_{copy} accepts exactly the language L_{copy}. Moreover, all meta-instructions in I_{copy} are strictly 2-testable. Thus, GCSL $\subset \mathcal{L}(\text{SLT-R})$.

On the other hand, each restarting automaton can be simulated by a linear bounded automaton, from which it follows that $\mathcal{L}(\text{SLT-R}) \subseteq \text{CSL}$.   □

For a restarting automaton $M = (\Sigma, \Gamma, I)$, the symbols from $\Gamma - \Sigma$ are called *auxiliary symbols*. From a practical point of view, analysis by reduction without auxiliary symbols enables the most transparent analysis with the best error localization.

Theorem 2. *Each regular language can be accepted by an* SLT-R-*automaton without auxiliary symbols.*

Proof. For each regular language $L \subseteq \Sigma^*$, there exists a finite-state automaton A recognizing L. Let k denote the number of states of A. Reading a prefix of a word from Σ^* of length at least $k - 1$, the automaton A must pass some state at least two times. Hence, for each word z of length $k - 1$, there exist words $u, v, w \in \Sigma^*$ such that $z = uvw$, $v \neq \lambda$, and the automaton A is in the same state after reading both prefixes u and uv. Hence, for each word $x \in \Sigma^*$, we have $uvwx \in L$ if and only if $uwx \in L$. Hence, we can construct a $(k - 1)$-SLT-automaton $M = (\Sigma, \Sigma, I)$ accepting L in the following way. M will have one accepting meta-instruction

$$(L \cap \Sigma^{<k-1}, \text{Accept}),$$

which is $(k-1)$-SLT. For each $z \in \Sigma^{k-1}$, the automaton M will have a rewriting meta-instruction

$(\{\lambda\}, z \rightarrow uw, \Sigma^*)$, where $z = uvw$ and u, v, w are the words from above,

which is also $(k-1)$-SLT. It is easy to see that

- if $|x| < k-1$, then $x \in L$ if and only if $x \in L(M)$,
- if $|x| \geq k-1$, then there exists a word $x' \in \Sigma^*$, $|x'| < |x|$, such that $x \vdash_M^c x'$, and $x \in L$ if and only if $x' \in L$.

From this it follows that $L(M) = L$. $\qquad\qquad\square$

Note that the SLT-R-automaton M constructed in the above proof only uses a finite language in its single accepting meta-instruction, and that all its rewriting instruction enable only the language $\{\lambda\}$ in their left constraints.

The above theorem shows that $\mathsf{Reg} \subseteq \mathcal{L}(\mathsf{SLT\text{-}R})$. This inclusion is proper even if we consider SLT-R-automata without auxiliary symbols (or consider SLT-R-automata recognizing characteristic languages). Such automata can accept even some non-context-free languages (see the automaton M from Example 1). Theorem 1 implies that each context-free language can be accepted by an SLT-R-automaton. Unfortunately, restarting automata without auxiliary symbols cannot accept all context-free languages. In [7] it is shown that the context-free language

$$L = \{a^n b^n \mid n \geq 0\} \cup \{a^n b^m \mid m > 2n \geq 0\}$$

cannot be accepted by any restarting automaton without auxiliary symbols. Hence we obtain the following consequence.

Theorem 3. CFL $\subset \mathcal{L}(\mathsf{SLT\text{-}R})$, *but there exist context-free languages which cannot be accepted by any* SLT-R-*automaton without auxiliary symbols.*

4   Conclusions

There are many possible approaches for learning analysis by reduction/restarting automata. Our proposed method which reduces it to learning the corresponding set of meta-instructions has several advantages:

1. The whole task of learning a restarting automaton can be split into smaller tasks of learning one meta-instruction at a time. Learning several simpler meta-instructions should be computationally simpler than learning the whole language at once.
2. For learning different meta-instructions we can use different models and algorithms for learning regular languages.
3. The learning can be done in an incremental way. First we can learn some basic meta-instructions which define only a subset of the target language. Then we can continue to learn new meta-instructions to improve our approximation of the target language.

4. A rewriting meta-instruction of a restarting automaton M is called *correctness preserving* if, for each rewriting $u \vdash^c_M v$ according to this meta-instruction, it holds that $u \in L_C(M)$ iff $v \in L_C(M)$. If we succeed to learn correctness preserving meta-instructions, then it is possible to learn the target language in parallel. That is, two or more (correctness preserving) meta-instructions can be learned separately and finally put together in one automaton.

The proposed approach can use any known algorithm for learning regular languages. Accordingly, we plan to also consider other learning protocols like learning from positive and negative examples, learning using membership and equivalence queries, etc.

References

1. G. Buntrock and F. Otto. Growing context-sensitive languages and Church-Rosser languages. *Information and Computation*, 141:1–36, 1998.
2. J. Čejka. Learning correctness preserving reduction analysis. BSc. project, Faculty of Mathematics and Physics, Charles University, Prague, 2003. In Czech.
3. P. Garcia and E. Vidal. Inference of k-testable languages in the strict sense and application to syntactic pattern recognition. *IEEE Transactions on Pattern Analysis and Machine Intelligence*, 12:920–925, 1990.
4. E. M. Gold. Language identification in the limit. *Information and Control*, 10:447–474, 1967.
5. P. Hoffmann. Learning restarting automata by genetic algorithms. In M. Bieliková, ed., *SOFSEM 2002: Student research forum*, Milovy, Czech Republic, 15–20, 2002.
6. P. Jančar, F. Mráz, M. Plátek, and J. Vogel. Restarting automata. In H. Reichel, ed., *FCT'95, Proc.*, LNCS **965**, Springer, Berlin, 283–292, 1995.
7. P. Jančar, F. Mráz, M. Plátek, and J. Vogel. On monotonic automata with a restart operation. *Journal of Automata, Languages and Combinatorics*, 4:287–311, 1999.
8. M. Lopatková, M. Plátek, and V. Kuboň. Modeling syntax of free word-order languages: Dependency analysis by reduction. In V. Matoušek, P. Mautner and T. Pavelka, eds, *TSD 2005, Proc.*, LNCS **3658**, Springer, Berlin, 140–147, 2005.
9. R. McNaughton. Algebraic decision procedures for local testability. *Mathematical Systems Theory*, 8:60–76, 1974.
10. G. Niemann and F. Otto. On the power of RRWW-automata. In M. Ito, G. Păun, and S. Yu, eds., *Words, Semigroups, and Transductions*. World Scientific, Singapore, 341–355, 2001.
11. F. Otto. Restarting automata and their relation to the Chomsky hierarchy. In Z. Ésik and Z. Fülöp, eds., *DLT 2003, Proc.*, LNCS **2710**, Springer, Berlin, 55–74, 2003.
12. M. Plátek, M. Lopatková, and K. Oliva. Restarting automata: motivations and applications. In: M. Holzer (ed.), *Workshop 'Petrinetze' and 13. Theorietag 'Formale Sprachen und Automaten'*, Proc., Institut für Informatik, Technische Universität München, 90–96, 2003..
13. T. Yokomori, and S. Kobayashi. Learning local languages and their application to DNA sequence analysis. IEEE Trans. on Pattern Anal. and Machine Intell., 20:1067–1079, 1998.
14. Y. Zalcstein. Locally testable languages. *Journal of Computer and System Sciences*, 6:151–167, 1972.

Inferring Grammars for Mildly Context Sensitive Languages in Polynomial-Time

Tim Oates[1], Tom Armstrong[1], Leonor Becerra Bonache[2], and Mike Atamas[1]

[1] University of Maryland Baltimore County
Baltimore, MD 21250 USA
{oates, arm1, m39}@umbc.edu
[2] Rovira i Virgili University
Pl. Imperial Tarraco 1, 43005, Tarragona, Spain
leonor.becerra@estudiants.urv.es

Abstract. Natural languages contain regular, context-free, and context-sensitive syntactic constructions, yet none of these classes of formal languages can be identified in the limit from positive examples. Mildly context-sensitive languages are able to represent some context-sensitive constructions, those most common in natural languages, such as multiple agreement, crossed agreement, and duplication. These languages are attractive for natural language applications due to their expressiveness, and the fact that they are not fully context-sensitive should lead to computational advantages as well. We realize one such computational advantage by presenting the first polynomial-time algorithm for inferring Simple External Context Grammars, a class of mildly context-sensitive grammars, from positive examples.

1 Introduction

Despite the fact that every normal child masters his native language, the learning mechanisms that underly this distinctly human feat are poorly understood. The ease with which children learn language belies the underlying complexity of the task. They face a number of theoretical challenges, including apparently insufficient data from which to learn lexical semantics (Quine's "gavagai" problem [1]) or syntax (Chomsky's "argument from the poverty of the stimulus" [2]). For example, it is known that many classes or formal languages, such as regular and context-free, cannot be learned solely from positive examples, i.e., strings that are in the (regular or context-free) language to be learned [3]. This is problematic because children either do not receive negative examples (i.e., strings that are not in the language to be learned) or pay little attention when such examples are presented [4].

There are a few standard ways of avoiding these theoretical obstacles to learning syntax from positive examples. One is to assume the existence of information in addition to positive examples that comprise the training data. For example, most algorithms for learning context-free grammars from positive examples assume that each example is paired with its unlabeled derivation tree, which is the parse tree for the string from which the non-terminal labels on the interior nodes

Y. Sakakibara et al. (Eds.): ICGI 2006, LNAI 4201, pp. 137–147, 2006.

have been removed [5,6]. An alternative is to restrict the class of languages from which the language to be learned can be drawn. A variety of subsets of the set of all regular languages are known to be learnable from positive examples [7].

These approaches to learning the syntax of formal languages are problematic when applying the resulting algorithms to learning the syntax of natural languages. For example, the additional information assumed to exist may in fact not be available to children. For example, children clearly do not receive utterances paired with unlabeled derivation trees (though see [8] for a method for inferring these trees from the sensory context). Also, natural languages exhibit some syntactic constructions that are regular, some that are context-free, and some that are context-sensitive. Therefore, restricted classes of regular or context-free languages have insufficient expressiveness.

In this paper, we present a polynomial-time algorithm for learning Simple External Contextual ($\mathcal{SEC}_p$) languages from positive data. $\mathcal{SEC}_p$ languages are *mildly context sensitive*. That is, they can express the context-sensitive syntactic constructions that are most prevalent in natural languages, such as multiple agreement, crossed agreement, and duplication [9]. In addition, neither the regular languages nor the context-free languages are a proper subset of the $\mathcal{SEC}_p$ languages. That is, there exist regular and context-free languages for which no corresponding $\mathcal{SEC}_p$ language exists.

Because expressiveness and computational tractability are typically inversely related, the goal of most mildly context-sensitive languages is to provide sufficient context sensitivity for natural language applications while keeping open the possibility of polynomial-time algorithms for standard tasks such as parsing and grammar induction. Currently, the most efficient algorithm known for learning $\mathcal{SEC}_p$ languages from positive examples is exponential [10]. This paper presents the first polynomial-time algorithm for learning $\mathcal{SEC}_p$ languages from positive data, and proves its correctness, thereby realizing the computational advantages of the restricted expressiveness of $\mathcal{SEC}_p$ languages.

The remainder of this paper is organized as follows. Section 2 describes External Contextual grammars and Simple External Contextual grammars in more detail. Section 3 describes our algorithm for learning $\mathcal{SEC}_p$ grammars from positive data. Section 4 establishes various theorems about the correctness of the algorithm. Finally, Section 5 concludes and points to future work.

2   External Contextual Grammars

This section reviews Mildly Context-Sensitive grammars beginning with External Contextual ($\mathcal{EC}_p$) grammars and then a subset of them called Marcus Simple Many-Dimensional External Contextual ($\mathcal{SEC}_p$) grammars.

An $\mathcal{EC}_p$ grammar is a three-tuple $G = (\Sigma, A, N)$, Σ is the alphabet of G, A is a finite set of p-words over Σ called the *axioms* of G, and N is a finite set of productions. A production is a pair, (S, C) where S is a set of *selectors*, strings over Σ^*, and C is a p-context. The parameter $p \in \mathbb{N}$ specifies the dimensionality of the p-words and p-contexts.

A *p-word* x over Σ is a p-dimensional vector whose components are strings over Σ, i.e., $x = (x_1, x_2, ..., x_p)$, where $x_i \in \Sigma^*$. A *p-context* c over Σ is a p-dimensional vector whose components are contexts over Σ, i.e., $c = [c_1, c_2, ..., c_p]$ where $c_i = (u_i, v_i), u_i, v_i \in \Sigma^*$, $1 \leq i \leq p$. We denote vectors of words with parentheses, and vectors of contexts with square brackets. Strings in the language of the grammar are derived by *applying* contexts to the axioms and subsequent strings (wrapping elements of p-contexts around corresponding elements of p-words) if an element of the selector set matches a substring of the derivation (e.g. maximal matching) for the context. For the remainder of the paper, we consider languages with maximal matching selector sets containing Σ^*. The number of contexts applied in a derivation of a string is called the *depth* of the string.

Let $x = (x_1, x_2, ..., x_p)$ and $y = (y_1, y_2, ..., y_p)$ be two p-words over Σ. By definition, $x \Rightarrow_G y$ iff $y = (u_1 x_1 v_1, u_2 x_2 v_2, ..., u_p x_p v_p)$ for some p-context $c = [(u_1, v_1), (u_2, v_2), ..., (u_p, v_p)] \in C$.

The $\mathcal{EC}_p$ language family is superfinite (a language class is superfinite if it contains every finite language and at least one infinite language) and therefore is not learnable in the limit from positive data [3]. All finite languages can be represented in $\mathcal{EC}_p$ by a grammar consisting of a finite set of axioms and an empty set of productions. We restrict the class of languages to Simple External Contextual ($\mathcal{SEC}_p$) grammars where the axiom set contains a single p-word over Σ. $\mathcal{SEC}_p$ grammars are further specified by a parameter q, the degree of the grammar or the number of productions, and can be abbreviated by $\mathcal{SEC}_p^q$.

The $\mathcal{SEC}_p$ family spans multiple language classes in the Chomsky hierarchy (see figure 1). Both are strictly contained in the class of context-sensitive languages and are incomparable with the classes of context-free and regular languages. Yet they can express the context-sensitive syntactic constructions that are most prevalent in natural languages.

Consider the $\mathcal{SEC}_2^1$ grammar G, the three-tuple, $(\{a, b, c\}, \{(\lambda, \lambda)\}, \{(\{w | w \in \Sigma^*\}, [(a, b), (c, \lambda)])\})$. The derivation of the string $aabbcc$ is the application of the context twice to the axiom: $(\lambda, \lambda) \vdash (a\lambda b, c\lambda\lambda) \vdash (aa\lambda bb, cc\lambda\lambda\lambda)$. Finally the internal strings are concatenated resulting in $aabbcc$. Note that $L(G) = \{a^n b^n c^n \mid n \geq 0\}$.

3 Induction Algorithm

The input to our algorithm is a set of strings, S, in an $\mathcal{SEC}_p^q$ language where the dimensionality, p, and degree, q, are known. S must contain at least all strings in the language up to a depth d (the value of d is discussed later). The shortest string in S is the concatenation of the elements in the axiom. However, there are multiple possibilities for what the actual axiom is (depending on the dimensionality of the language). From the shortest string, a set of possible axioms, A, is generated. For example, if p=2 and the shortest string in S is aa, then the set of possible axioms is $\{(\lambda, aa), (a, a), (aa, \lambda)\}$.

Each subsequent string in S is derived beginning with the axiom and some number of context applications. For every $a_j \in A$, every further element of S

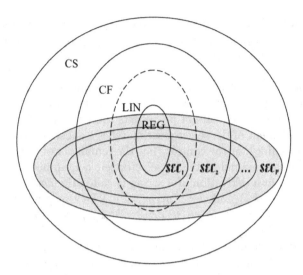

Fig. 1. The $\mathcal{SEC}_p$ family spans multiple language classes in the Chomsky hierarchy

is processed assuming that its derivation is of depth one (i.e. a set of candidate contexts can be generated by inferring contexts that derive a string from the axiom in one step) and the contexts stored in a set P. Next, all ways of choosing q elements from P are paired with the axiom to form grammars. Each candidate grammar, G', is used to derive all the strings in $L(G')$ up to depth d. If $L^d(G') \nsubseteq S$ or G' cannot parse all of the strings in $S - L^d(G')$, then G' is removed from the set of candidate grammars. Additional strings in the input set increase the number of candidate grammars, but will not exclude grammars. Later, we prove that if a grammar, G, generates only $L^d(G)$ in derivations up to depth d, then G generates $L(G)$.

Consider the following example, an input set $S = \{a, aaa, bab, ababa, baaab, aaaaa, bbabb\}$ for a language generated by an $\mathcal{SEC}_1^1$ grammar. The input is exhaustive up to depth 2. The shortest string in S is a and, because $p = 1$, (a) is the only possible axiom. Assuming that aaa was generated by a single application of a context to (a), the possible contexts that can generate the input set are $\{[(\lambda, aa)], [(a, a)], [(aa, \lambda)]\}$. This is done again for bab, resulting in $\{[(b, b)]\}$, and for the remainder of the strings in the input set. All of the possible pairs of contexts are then put in a set G. The only $g_i \in G$ that can generate S and only generate S is $\{[(a, a)], [(b, b)]\}$; the rest are discarded. In this example, there was only one possible axiom. If this language had been $\mathcal{SEC}_2^2$, then the possible axioms would have been $\{[(\lambda, a)], [(a, \lambda)]\}$. Unlike this example, input sets can be generated by several grammars, some of which have distinct axioms.

The running time of the algorithm (see figure 2) depends upon the dimensionality and degree of the grammar, the size of the axiom, and the maximum depth of the input set. Given the shortest string, the axiom, in the input set, there are $(|axiom| + 1)^{p-1}$ possible axioms (inserting p-1 separations into the shortest string). Given a string s_i, all of the possible contexts to

INFER-GRAMMAR($d, p, q, inputSet$)
```
 1   shortest ← FIND-SHORTEST(inputSet)
 2   axioms ← GENERATE-POSSIBLE-AXIOMS(p, shortest)
 3   finalGrammars ← {}
 4   result ← {}
 5
 6   for axiom ∈ axioms
 7   do possibleContexts ← {}
 8       for i ∈ inputSet
 9       do possibleContexts.push[GENERATE-POSSIBLE-CONTEXTS(i, axiom)]
10
11       possibleGrammars ← GENERATE-ALL-CONTEXT-COMBINATIONS(possibleContexts)
12       for j ∈ possibleGrammars
13       do if CAN-GENERATE-ALL-STRINGS(j, axiom)
14               then finalGrammars.push[{j, axiom}]
15
16   for k ∈ finalGrammars
17   do if GENERATES-EXACT-LIST(d, k, inputSet)
18           then result.push[k]
19   RETURN(result)
```

Fig. 2. Pseudocode of the inference algorithm

derive s_i with one application is at most $(|s| + 1)^{2p}$. Given the set of all contexts from above, we can pick all sets of contexts of size q, or $\binom{(|s|+1)^{2p}}{q}$. Given a candidate grammar, all of the strings that it generates up to a depth of d can be enumerated and compared to elements in the input set in at most $(\sum_{i=1}^{d} q^i) * |inputSet|$ steps. Therefore, the cost of the nested loop is bounded by $(\sum_{i=1}^{d} q^i) * |inputSet| * \binom{(|s|+1)^{2p}}{q} * (|axiom| + 1)^{p-1}$.

What we will next prove is that the size of the input set is finite and small (in some cases depth 3 suffices), and that with a small dimension, degree and axiom, the problem of inferring the grammar with our algorithm becomes tractable.

4 Proof of the Existence of a Characteristic Sample

We prove that a finite sample of the language, a characteristic sample, is sufficient to infer a grammar for the language. Let G and G' be minimal $\mathcal{SEC}_p$ grammars as follows:

G = (p, q, A, C_1, C_2, ..., C_q)
G' = (p', q', A', C_1', C_2', ..., C_q')

A is the axiom and C_i is a context. Assume that p = p' and q = q'. A grammar is minimal if there is no other grammar with smaller values of p or q with the same language.

For a vector of strings X, let CONCAT(X) equal the string obtained by concatenating all strings in X in the order in which they occur. We use the symbol / to denote application of a production. For example, C_i/A is the p-vector obtained by applying context C_i to axiom A. Let $L^d(G)$ be the set of strings in $L(G)$ that require d or fewer derivation steps. $L^0(G) = \{CONCAT(A)\}$. We want to prove the following theorem.

Theorem 1. *$L(G) = L(G')$ and $CONCAT(C_i/A) \neq CONCAT(C_j/A)$ for $i \neq j$ and $1 \leq i, j \leq q$ if and only if $L^d(G) = L^d(G')$ for an appropriately small d and minimal grammars, G and G'.*

We now prove a series of lemmas and theorems to this end.

Lemma 1. *If $L(G) = L(G')$ then $CONCAT(A) = CONCAT(A')$.*

Proof. Suppose $L(G) = L(G')$ but $CONCAT(A) \neq CONCAT(A')$. The shortest string in $L(G)$ is $CONCAT(A)$ because all other contexts, being non-empty, add characters when applied to the axiom. If $CONCAT(A) \neq CONCAT(A')$ then the shortest string in $L(G)$ is not equal to the shortest string in $L(G')$, which means that $L(G) \neq L(G')$. This is a contradiction, so $CONCAT(A)$ must equal $CONCAT(A')$. □

Lemma 2. *If $L(G) = L(G')$ and $CONCAT(C_i/A) \neq CONCAT(C_j/A)$ for $i \neq j$ and $1 \leq i, j \leq q$, then there is a bijective mapping (one-to-one and onto) f from contexts in G to contexts in G' such that $CONCAT(C_i/A) = CONCAT(C'_{f(i)}/A')$. That is, for each C_i in G there exists precisely one C'_j in G' such that $CONCAT(C_i/A) = CONCAT(C'_j/A')$, and for each C'_i in G' there exists precisely one C_j in G such that $CONCAT(C'_i/A') = CONCAT(C_j/A)$.*

Proof. Suppose that no bijective mapping, f, from contexts in G to contexts in G' such that $CONCAT(C_i/A) = CONCAT(C'_{f(i)}/A')$ exists. Without such a mapping, there is a string in $L(G)$ and $L(G')$, S, that is the least criminal, the shortest string violating this mapping. This string must have a derivation of depth one in G, else the mapping would hold. The derivation of S in G is $CONCAT(C_i/A)$ and in G' is $CONCAT(C'_l/.../C'_s/A')$. That is, the derivation of S in G requires one context whereas the derivation of S in G' requires at least two contexts. All contexts used in the derivation of S in G' are used to derive shorter strings contained in both $L(G)$ and $L(G')$ (e.g. $CONCAT(C'_l/A')=CONCAT(C_j/A)$ for some l and j). These depth one strings, shorter than S, form a bijective mapping, h, because they are not the least criminal string. The characters contributed by C_i are the same as $C'_l, ... ,C'_s$. Each of $C'_l, ... , C'_s$ map to a context in G that contribute the same characters, therefore $C_{h(l)}, ... , C_{h(s)}$ contribute the same characters as C_i. The string S is derived in G using either C_i or $C_{h(l)}, ... , C_{h(s)}$ thus making C_i superfluous and G non-minimal, a contradiction. □

Lemma 3. *If $L(G) = L(G')$ and $CONCAT(C_i/A) \neq CONCAT(C_j/A)$ for $i \neq j$ and $1 \leq i, j \leq q$, then strings in $L(G)$ and $L(G')$ have the same derivations up to renaming of contexts.*

Said differently, there is a bijective mapping (one-to-one and onto) f from contexts in G to contexts in G' such that if string S has derivation D in G then the derivation of S in G' can be obtained by applying the mapping to each context in D. That is, if the derivation of S in $L(G)$ is $C_i/C_j/.../C_k/A$ then the derivation of S in G' is $C'_{f(i)}/C'_{f(j)}/.../C'_{f(k)}/A'$

Proof. All derivations begin with the axiom A. Consider one-step derivations of the form C_i/A, which means context C_i is applied to axiom A. Let S_0 = CONCAT(A) and S_1 = CONCAT(C_i/A). The only difference between S_0 and S_1 is that S_1 contains, in addition to the characters in A, the characters in CONCAT(C_i) in the same linear order, though they may not be contiguous. No context other than C_i can add those characters in one step because CONCAT(C_i/A) $\neq$ CONCAT(C_j/A) for i $\neq$ j and $1 \leq$ i, j $\leq$ q.

By lemma 2, there must exist a context C'_j in G' such that CONCAT(C_i/A) = CONCAT(C'_j/A). For the sake of simplicity, we assume that context is C'_i. Because C_i is unique among the contexts in G, so must C'_i be among the contexts in G' (by lemma 2). Therefore, the only way to derive S_1 in G' is C'_i/A', and all strings in $L^1(G)$ have the same derivations in L(G') up to renaming of contexts.

Suppose, inductively, that this holds for derivations up to depth d. Let S_d be any string in L(G) that requires d derivations and let S_{d+1} be any string in L(G) derivable from S_d by applying one more context. By the induction assumption, the derivation of S_d is the same (up to renaming of contexts) in G and G'. Whatever context is added in G to S_d to obtain S_{d+1}, its analog in G' must be applied to derive S_{d+1} because no other context can add the required characters.   □

Theorem 2. *If $L(G) = L(G')$ and $CONCAT(C_i/A) \neq CONCAT(C_j/A)$ for i $\neq$ j and $1 \leq$ i, j $\leq$ q, then $L^d(G) = L^d(G')$ for any depth d.*

Proof. Suppose L(G) = L(G') but $L^d(G) \neq L^d(G)$ for some depth d. Let d be the smallest such depth for which this is the case. Then either there exists an S in $L^d(G)$ that requires d derivation steps that is not in $L^d(G')$, or vice versa. Without loss of generality, we focus on the former case. Because L(G) = L(G'), there must be some depth d' > d such that S is in $L^{d'}(G')$. However, by lemma 3, if there is a depth d derivation of S in G, there is a depth d derivation of S in G'. This is a contradiction, so $L^d(G) = L^d(G')$ for all depths d.   □

Theorem 3. *There exists a finite d, such that for all grammars G and G', if $L^d(G) = L^d(G')$ then $L(G) = L(G')$.*

Proof. Let the proposition P be equivalent to $L^d(G) = L^d(G')$ and let the proposition Q be equivalent to $L(G) = L(G')$. Then the theorem can be stated formally as

$$(\forall G)(\forall G')(\exists d)[P \rightarrow Q] \tag{1}$$

To prove that this is a tautology, it suffices to show that the negation of (1) is a contradiction. The negation can be written

$$(\exists G)(\exists G')(\forall d)[P \wedge \neg Q] \tag{2}$$

$$(\exists G)(\exists G')(\forall d)[(L^d(G) = L^d(G')) \wedge (L(G) \neq L(G'))] \tag{3}$$

The last equation states that there exist grammars G and G' such that at any finite depth the strings produced by either grammar are equal but the languages are not. With any finite language, this is clearly a contradiction. In an infinite language, the set of all possible depths in that language is clearly denumerable. The only restriction on d is that it belong to $\mathbb{N}$, making the set of all d countably infinite. For both the set of all d and the set of all possible depths, a bijection from $\mathbb{N}$ exists, so they must be of the same size. Thus, comparing the languages at all finite d is equivalent to comparing the whole language, making (3) a contradiction. Since the negation of (1) is a contradiction, (1) must be a tautology. Therefore, there exists a finite d such that for all grammars G and G', if $L^d(G) = L^d(G')$ then $L(G) = L(G')$.   □

Theorems 2 and 3 collectively prove Theorem 1. Theorem 1 and its proof establish that there exists a finite depth d such that the strings in $L^d(G)$ for any $\mathcal{SEC}_p^q$ grammar are a characteristic sample, i.e., they uniquely identify the language. In the complexity analysis of our learning algorithm, d is a constant, but as with any constant hidden inside $O()$ notation, if the constant is large it can make the algorithm practically infeasible. We now show that for $\mathcal{SEC}_1^1$ languages $d = 2$ suffices, and for $\mathcal{SEC}_1^q$ languages $d = 3$ suffices. We conjecture that $d = 3$ is sufficient for arbitrary p and q, and are working on the proof.

We begin with the following lemma:

Lemma 4. *Let $A, B \in \Sigma^+$. If $AB = BA$, then there exists $p \in \Sigma^+$ and integers $x, y > 0$ such that $A = p^x$ and $B = p^y$.*

Proof. Let $n = |A|$ and $m = |B|$. Let S_i denote the ith character in string S, where the index of the first character is 1, and $S_{i,j}$ denote the sub-string of S from characters i through j. Trivially, $AB_i = BA_i$ because $AB = BA$. That is, the ith character in the string AB must equal the ith character in the string BA. Also, $AB_i = BA_{(i+m) \bmod (n+m)}$ because regardless of whether A or B contributes the ith character in AB, that same character contributed by the same string occurs in position $(i + m) \bmod (n + m)$ in BA. From this we can conclude that $AB_i = BA_i = BA_{(i+km) \bmod (n+m)}$ for positive integers k. Therefore, for $g = GCD(n, m)$ every g^{th} character in AB is the same, and thus for $p = A_{1,g}$, $x = n/g$, and $y = m/g$ it is the case that $A = p^x$ and $B = p^y$.   □

The following two theorems say that the strings in $L^2(G)$ are a characteristic sample for SEC_1^1 grammars and that the strings in L^3 are a characteristic sample for SEC_q^1 grammars, respectively.

Theorem 4. *Let G and G' be minimal $\mathcal{SEC}_1^1$ grammars. It is the case that $L^2(G) = L^2(G')$ iff $L(G) = L(G')$.*

Proof. Let A and A' be the axioms of G and G', and let C and C' be the contexts of G and G'. Because the grammars are minimal, neither C nor C' can be (λ, λ). Therefore, the strings in $L^2(G)$ in increasing order of length are $\{A, C/A, C/C/A\}$, and likewise for $L^2(G') = \{A', C'/A', C'/C'/A'\}$. Clearly, if $L(G) = L(G')$ then $L^2(G) = L^2(G')$. It remains to show that if $L^2(G) = L^2(G')$ then $L(G) = L(G')$.

It follows from $L^2(G) = L^2(G')$ that $A = A'$ (otherwise the two shortest strings in the languages would differ) and $CONCAT(C/A) = CONCAT(C'/A')$

(otherwise there is no way for $C/A = C'/A'$). Henceforth, we will use A to refer to the axiom of either grammar.

Because $CONCAT(C/A) = CONCAT(C'/A')$, it must be the case that for some $X, Y, Z \in \Sigma^*$, with at least one in Σ^+, we can write $C = (XY, Z)$ and $C' = (X, YZ)$. If $C = C'$ then $Y = \lambda$ and the languages are equal. Consider the case where $Y \neq \lambda$. We need to establish that if this change impacts the generated language, this impact will be seen at or before depth 2. Note that any of X, Z, and A can be λ, so there are eight possible values for the depth 2 languages shown in table 1.

Table 1. Eight possible cases of assigning the empty string for L^2

EMPTY STRINGS	$L^2(G)$	$L^2(G')$
A, X, Z	$\{\lambda, Y, YY\}$	$\{\lambda, Y, YY\}$
A, X	$\{\lambda, YZ, YYZZ\}$	$\{\lambda, YZ, YZYZ\}$
A, Z	$\{\lambda, XY, XYXY\}$	$\{\lambda, XY, XXYY\}$
A	$\{\lambda, XYZ, XYXYZZ\}$	$\{\lambda, XYZ, XXYZYZ\}$
X, Z	$\{A, YA, YYA\}$	$\{A, AY, AYY\}$
X	$\{A, YAZ, YYAZZ\}$	$\{\lambda, AYZ, AYZYZ\}$
Z	$\{A, XYA, XYXYA\}$	$\{A, XAY, XXAYY\}$
	$\{A, XYAZ, XYXYAZZ\}$	$\{A, XAYZ, XXAYZYZ\}$

It is easy to show that for each of these cases, if $L^2(G) = L^2(G')$ then $L(G) = L(G')$. We demonstrate the line of reasoning with the most difficult case, which is the last in the table above and corresponds to the case in which none of A, X, or Z are empty. Note that $C/A = XYAZ$ and $C'/A' = XAYZ$. Because the depth 2 languages are the same, $XYAZ = XAYZ$. Stripping away the common prefix and suffix of these strings yields $YA = AY$ and, by Lemma 4 above, there exists some $p \in \Sigma^+$ such that $Y = p^n$ and $A = p^m$. Also, because $C/C/A = XYXYAZZ = XXAYZYZ = C'/C'/A'$, it is the case that $YXYAZ = XAYZY$, which can be rewritten as $p^n X p^n p^m Z = X p^m p^n Z p^n$. Clearly, it must be the case that $X = p^k$ and $Z = p^l$ for some integers $k, l > 0$. Therefore, d applications of context C to A yields the string $p^{m+d(n+k+l)}$, as do d applications of context C' to A. Therefore, $L(G) = L(G')$. Analogous reasoning yields the same result in the seven other cases in the table above.   □

Theorem 5. *Let G and G' be minimal $\mathcal{SEC}_q^1$ grammars such that for contexts in G it is the case that $CONCAT(C_i/A) \neq CONCAT(C_j/A)$ for $i \neq j$ and $1 \leq i, j \leq q$. It is the case that $L^3(G) = L^3(G')$ iff $L(G) = L(G')$.*

Proof. **(sketch)** This proof is similar to the proof of Lemma 4. Because the concatenation of the strings in the contexts of G differ, and because the languages of G and G' are the same up to depth 3, there is a bijective mapping between contexts in G and G', at least for derivations of strings up to depth 3. Suppose there is a context $C_i = (XY, Z)$ in G, which is mapped to context $C'_i = (X, YZ)$ in G'. We need to show that if the movement of Y from C to C' will impact the language, such impact will appear in L^3.

Let $C'_j = (U, V)$ be some other context in G'. This context may be unmodified from C_j in G, or the characters in UV may be split differently between the two halves of the context. In the latter case, Theorem 4 tells us that the subsets of $L(G)$ and $L(G')$ that involve only applications of C_j and C'_j are the same. Therefore, regardless of whether $C_j = C'_j$ or only $CONCAT(C_j/A) = CONCAT(C'_j/A')$, we will write the contents of C_j and C'_j as (U, V) because the exact distribution of characters in the contexts is immaterial to our purposes.

Because $L^3(G) = L^3(G')$, it is the case that $C_i/C_j/A = C'_i/C'_j/A'$, and therefore $XYUAVZ = XUAVYZ$. Stripping away the common prefix and suffix, we are left with $YUAV = UAVY$ and by Lemma 4 for some $p \in \Sigma^+$ it is the case that $Y = p^m$ and $UAV = p^n$. Because the length of p cannot be determined, it might be that $UVA = p$, with each of U, V, and A contributing part of p. However, because $C_i/C_j/C_j/A = C'_i/C'_j/C'_j/A'$, we know that $YUUAVV = UUAVVY$, which means that Y, U, A, and V all contain an integer number of occurrences of p. $\qquad\square$

5   Conclusion and Future Work

This paper presented the first polynomial-time algorithm for inferring $\mathcal{SEC}^q_p$ grammars from positive data. This class of mildly context-sensitive languages is important because it has just enough context sensitivity to express the most common context-sensitive constructions found in natural languages while keeping open the possibility of computational tractability. Theorem 1 established that a finite sample suffices to infer $\mathcal{SEC}^q_p$ grammars using our algorithm, and theorems 4 and 5 show that this sample is small when the axiom of the grammar to be learned contains a single string (i.e., p = 1).

Future work will proceed by removing some working assumptions such as a priori dimensionality and degree values. We want to extend our algorithm to any number of axioms and arbitrary selectors, thus learning external contextual grammars. As $\mathcal{EC}_p$ languages are superfinite, additional information is required to learn the grammars. We are interested in leveraging structural information and prior approaches to learning context-free grammars for $\mathcal{EC}_p$ grammar learning. Also, the ability of this formalism to describe non-context-free structures is particularly alluring for real world data applications (e.g. inference of grammars for natural language, user modeling).

References

1. Quine, W.V.O.: Word and object. MIT Press (1960)
2. Chomsky, N.: Reflections on Language. Pantheon (1975)
3. Gold, E.M.: Language identification in the limit. Information and Control **10** (1967) 447–474
4. Marcus, G.F.: Negative evidence in language acquisition. Cognition **46** (1993) 53–85
5. Makinen, E.: On the structural grammatical inference problem for some classes of context-free grammars. Information Processing Letters **42** (1992) 1–5

6. Oates, T., Desai, D., Bhat, V.: Learning k-reversible context-free grammars from positive structural examples. In: Proceedings of the Nineteenth International Conference on Machine Learning. (2002)

7. Makinen, E.: Inferring regular languages by merging nonterminals. TR A-19987-6, Department of Computer Science, University of Tampere (1997)

8. Oates, T., Armstrong, T., Harris, J., Nejman, M.: On the relationship between lexical semantics and syntax for the inference of context-free grammars. In: Proceedings of AAAI. (2004) 431–436

9. Kudlek, M., Martn-Vide, C., Mateescu, A., Mitrana, V.: Contexts and the concept of mild context-sensitivity. In: Linguistics and Philosophy 26. (2002) 703–725

10. Becerra-Bonache, L., Yokomori, T.: Learning mild context-sensitiveness: Toward understanding children's language learning. In: Proceedings of the 7th International Colloquium on Grammatical Inference. (2004) 53–64

Planar Languages and Learnability

Alexander Clark[1], Christophe Costa Florêncio[1],
Chris Watkins[1], and Mariette Serayet[2]

[1] Department of Computer Science, Royal Holloway,
University of London, Egham TW20 0EX, UK
alexc@cs.rhul.ac.uk, chris@cs.rhul.ac.uk, chrisw@cs.rhul.ac.uk
[2] Faculté des Sciences et Techniques, Département Informatique, 23,
Rue du Docteur Paul Michelon, 42023 Saint-Etienne Cedex 2, France
mariette.serayet@bvra.univ-st-etienne.fr

Abstract. Strings can be mapped into Hilbert spaces using feature maps such as the Parikh map. Languages can then be defined as the pre-image of hyperplanes in the feature space, rather than using grammars or automata. These are the *planar* languages. In this paper we show that using techniques from kernel-based learning, we can represent and efficiently learn, from positive data alone, various linguistically interesting context-sensitive languages. In particular we show that the cross-serial dependencies in Swiss German, that established the non-context-freeness of natural language, are learnable using a standard kernel. We demonstrate the polynomial-time identifiability in the limit of these classes, and discuss some language theoretic properties of these classes, and their relationship to the choice of kernel/feature map.

1 Introduction

Formal languages, whether used in linguistics or in computer science, have traditionally been represented either by grammars or by various simple machine formalisms. In linguistics context-free grammars have been widely used as a representative tool. With the discovery of demonstrably non-context-free phenomena in syntax, most famously in Swiss German ([Huy84, Shi85]), attention switched away from grammatical formalisms based on CFG, such as GPSG, to more powerful formalisms that were capable of modelling these phenomena: these are generally restricted to the mildly context-sensitive languages (see [JS96] for an overview).

From a linguistic point of view these formalisms have a number of desirable properties, but from a learnability point of view they are far too unrestricted. Even very simple classes of these formalisms, such as acyclic deterministic finite state automata, are already unlearnable when using modern characterisations of learnability, because intractable cryptographic problems can be embedded in the learning of these tasks.

Chomsky correctly identified accounting for the learnability of language as one of the principal challenges for linguistics. The Principles and Parameters approach is one solution to this problem: by specifying a class of languages

Y. Sakakibara et al. (Eds.): ICGI 2006, LNAI 4201, pp. 148–160, 2006.

parametrised by a small set of parameters the learnability problem can be simplified. Unfortunately problems of lexical acquisition, cross-language ambiguity and the intertwining of parameter settings meant that no satisfactory theory of parameter-based learning has ever been presented. In this paper, rather than taking an overexpressive class of representations and trying to make it learnable by imposing additional restrictions on it, we take an alternative route. We restrict ourselves to a class of representations that are inherently learnable from positive data alone. At this point the class has a limited range, yet it is capable of representing some classic examples of mildly context-sensitive languages.

We define the class of *planar* languages. These are languages that correspond to planes in a feature space. Using standard linear algebra techniques we are then able to learn the minimal plane that contains the data points from positive data alone. This does not restrict us to (semi)linear languages: the function that maps datapoints to feature vectors can, and generally will, do so in a non-linear fashion. This geometrical representation of languages allows us to apply the mature theory of linear algebra to the problems of grammatical inference.

We give a simple example before giving formal definitions. Consider the language L defined as the set of all strings containing equal numbers of as and bs. If we define a feature map from this set of strings to a plane, where the first coordinate is the number of as in the string and the second coordinate the number of bs, so that aab is mapped to the point $(2, 1)$ and so on, we see that all of the strings in the language will be mapped to points that lie on the line $x = y$, such as $(1, 1)$, $(2, 2)$ and so on. Additionally we can see that every string whose image lies on this line is also in the language. Thus L can be defined using a one-dimensional hyperplane in this feature space, and is thus a planar language.

Obviously the feature mapping limits the class of languages that can be defined, and with this trivial mapping, the Parikh map, only very few languages can be characterised. A major reason for this is that the feature mapping is not *injective*, i.e. there are pairs of distinct strings, such as ab and ba, that are mapped to the same point in the feature space, $(1, 1)$. In this paper we will use the implicit feature maps defined by string kernels ([Wat99]), in particular the gap-weighted kernel, that have the property of being injective for suitable choices of the kernel hyperparameters.

In the rest of this paper we discuss the properties of planar languages. After defining notation, we present simple examples of planar languages, as well as examples of languages that are not planar languages. We then discuss the closure properties of the class of planar languages, their relation to other well-studied classes, learnability properties, and conclude with some directions for future research. Our focus in this paper is on the learnability and language-theoretic issues, so we won't discuss the algorithmic/computational issues involved. We have implemented and tested thoroughly all of the results presented here, see [CCFWS06] for discussion.

2   Planar Languages

We will use the following definitions and notation. We have a finite non-empty set Σ, which we call the vocabulary. We consider the free monoid Σ^* with identity/empty string ε. A language L is a subset of Σ^*. We will write $a, b \ldots$ for elements of Σ^*. We write $|u|$ for the length of a string u, and we will write $|u|_v$ for the number of occurrences of v as a substring of u. We will also write $u[i]$ for the ith character of u, where $1 \leq i \leq |u|$. Sequences of indices are written $\mathbf{i}$, and $s(\mathbf{i})$ will denote the non-contiguous substring of s composed of the characters at the positions in s specified by $\mathbf{i}$.

We will consider feature maps ϕ from Σ^* into a possibly infinite dimensional Hilbert space H. For the purposes of this paper we can consider these to be real vector spaces, with the standard inner product which we will write as $\langle u, v \rangle$. When the dimension of the Hilbert space is very high it can be prohibitively expensive or impossible to calculate $\phi(x)$ directly. Accordingly for every ϕ we can define a kernel function from $\Sigma^* \times \Sigma^* \to R$, which is defined as $\kappa(u, v) = \langle \phi(u), \phi(v) \rangle$. Thus such feature spaces can still be used with many machine learning algorithms, since these are often based on the distance between points in a feature space. This approach is sometimes called the *kernel trick* and was first used in [ABR64], in the context of linear separators.

For the algorithms we discuss here it will be possible to compute $\kappa(u, v)$ in time polynomial in $|u|$ and $|v|$. Details of the dynamic programming techniques that make this possible can be found in [STC04]. It is possible to perform all of the calculations described here using only the kernel computations rather than working directly with the images of the strings in the Hilbert space.

2.1   Planarity

Given a particular kernel κ and associated feature map $\phi : \Sigma^* \to H$ we can give the following definition.

Definition 1. *A language $L \subseteq \Sigma^*$ is κ-planar if there is a finite set of strings $\{u_1, \ldots, u_n\}$ such that $L = \{w \in \Sigma^* \mid \exists \alpha_1 \ldots \alpha_i \in \mathbb{R} : \sum_i^n \alpha_i = 1 \wedge \sum_i^n \alpha_i \phi(u_i) = \phi(w)\}$.*

Given a κ-planar language L we can define the rank of L to be the cardinality of the smallest subset that defines the language. Note that this definition restricts planar languages to those of finite rank, and secondly that we restrict ourselves to affine combinations of strings u_i. This has the effect of slightly increasing the expressive power of the formalism, so that for example the languages do not necessarily contain the preimage of the origin, where it exists.

Definition 2. *For a language $L \subseteq \Sigma^*$, we define*

$$\mathrm{H}(L) = \{h \in H \mid \exists n > 0, w_1 \ldots w_n \in L, \alpha_1, \ldots \alpha_n \text{ such that}$$
$$\textstyle\sum_i \alpha_i = 1, \sum_i \alpha_i \phi(w_i) = h\}$$

where H is the feature space. Thus $\mathrm{H}(L)$ is the smallest hyperplane that contains the image of L.

For any finite set of strings $U = \{u_1, \ldots, u_n\}$ and a test string v, and any polynomially evaluable kernel κ with associated feature map ϕ, there is an algorithm for deciding whether $\phi(w) \in \mathrm{H}(u_1, \ldots, u_n)$, which runs in time polynomial in $n, |v|$ and $\sum_i |u_i|$. This algorithm, based on standard techniques, described in [STC04], involves computations only using the matrix of kernel values, and proceeds by normalising this matrix, which has the effect of translating the data in feature space so that the mean of the data lies in the origin, and performing an eigendecomposition of this matrix; it is then easy to project the test point v onto the perpendicular vectors to compute the distance in feature space of the point from the plane formed by U. Neglecting the issue of the numerical stability of these algorithms, which is beyond the scope of this paper, this distance will be zero if and only if $\phi(v)$ lies in the plane $H(L)$.

2.2 Kernels

We will now define the various kernels used in this paper. We will use the convention [STC04] that $\mathbf{i} = (i_1, \ldots, i_{|u|})$ ranges over the set of all strictly ordered tuples of indices. The following kernels are standard kernels in the literature.

Definition 3. *The* **All-k-Subsequences** *kernel.*
The feature space associated with the **All-k-Subsequences** *kernel is indexed by $I = \cup_{i=0}^{k} \Sigma^i$, with the embedding given by $\phi_u(s) = |\{\mathbf{i} : u = s(\mathbf{i})\}|, u \in I$.*

The Parikh kernel is simply the special case of **All-k-Subsequences** with $k = 1$.

Definition 4. *The* **p-Spectrum** *kernel.*
The feature space associated with the **p-Spectrum** *kernel is indexed by $I = \Sigma^p$, with the embedding given by $\phi_u^p(s) = |\{(v_1, v_2) : s = v_1 u v_2\}|, u \in \Sigma^p$. The associated kernel is defined as $\kappa_p(s, t) = \langle \phi^p(s), \phi^p(t) \rangle = \Sigma_{u \in \Sigma^p} \phi_u^p(s) \phi_u^p(t)$.*

We now define the schema kernel, which has not been discussed anywhere else before. We do not use it directly but just as a means to prove the injectivity of another kernel.

Definition 5. *Let $\Sigma' = \Sigma \cup \{?\}$. A schema is any sequence $\sigma \in \Sigma'^+$. A gapped schema is an element of $\Sigma \times \{?\}^* \times \Sigma$, or an element of Σ.*

Given a string u and a schema σ the count of the schema in a string is the number of times it matches exactly, where ? matches any symbol. More formally: $|\{i | \forall j = 1, \ldots |\sigma|, \sigma[i] =? \text{ or } \sigma[i] = u[i + j]\}|$.

Definition 6. *The* **gapSchemas** *kernel.*
*The gapped schema feature map (**gapSchemas**) maps strings to vectors, where each feature is indexed by a gapped schema, and the value of the feature is the count of the schema in the string. The gapped schema kernel is the kernel based on the gapped schema feature map.*

Example 7. The feature vector obtained from $\phi(abba)$ assigns 2 to features a and b, 1 to features $ab, ba, bb, a?b, b?a, a??a$, and 0 to all others.

Proposition 8. *The* **gapSchemas** *kernel is injective.*

Proof. By construction of the inverse function. Given an feature representation $h \in H$, and a $w \in \Sigma^*$ such that $\phi(w) = h$. Let l be the length of the longest schema with a non-zero value in h, which will be unique. Clearly $|w| = l$.

1. The first character of the string is the first character of the longest schema.
2. The nth character (for $n > 1$) contributes as first character to one of the schemas of length $l - n + 1$, but not to the schemas of length $l - n + 2$. So, let S_n be the multiset enumerating just all first characters of schemas of $l - n + 1$. Then the nth character is the only element of the set $S_n - S_{n-1}$. □

Definition 9. *The gap-weighted subsequences feature map (*gapWeighted*): All non-contiguous subsequences of length p where each occurrence is weighted exponentially by the number of gaps. This is adjusted by a hyperparameter λ. $\phi_u(s) = \sum_{i:u=s(i)} \lambda^{l(i)}$ where $|u| = p$. $l(i)$ is defined as $1 + i_{|i|} - i_1$.*
The gap-weighted subsequences feature kernel is the kernel based on the gap-weighted subsequences feature map.

Definition 10. *The   gap-weighted   subsequences   plus   feature   map (*gapWeighted+*): Combines* **gapWeighted** *and the Parikh kernel times λ.[1] We also define the associated kernel.*

Example 11. For $p = 2$:

$$\phi(bab) = \begin{pmatrix} a : \lambda \\ b : 2\lambda \\ aa : 0 \\ ab : \lambda^2 \\ ba : \lambda^2 \\ bb : \lambda^3 \end{pmatrix}$$

2.3   Injectivity of the gapWeighted+ Kernel

The proof of the following proposition makes use of the existence of transcendental numbers. A transcendental number is any complex number that is not algebraic, that is, not the solution of a non-zero polynomial equation with integer (or, equivalently, rational) coefficients; some standard examples are π and e. The intuition behind the proof is that there is a correspondence between gapped schemas and the complex polynomials obtained from the **gapWeighted+** kernel.

---

[1] We could use the standard Parikh kernel here, the λ factor is purely for technical reasons.

Proposition 12. *There exists an injective function f from* **gapSchemas** *feature representations to* **gapWeighted+** *feature representations, for p = 2.*

Proof. We write H_1 for the space of **gapSchemas** representations and ϕ_1 for the associated feature map, and H_2, ϕ_2 for the space of **gapWeighted+** feature representations, and its map. We define f as follows: $f_a(h) = \lambda h_a$, $f_{ab}(h) = h_{ab}\lambda^2 + h_{a?b}\lambda^3 + \ldots$.

By construction we can see that $\phi_2(w) = f(\phi_1(w))$. Suppose we have two elements h, h' of H_1, that lie in $\phi_1(\Sigma^*)$, such that $f(h) = f(h')$. This means that for every feature ab, we have $f_{ab}(h) = f_{ab}(h')$ and therefore $h_{ab}\lambda^2 + h_{a?b}\lambda^3 + \ldots = h'_{ab}\lambda^2 + h'_{a?b}\lambda^3 + \ldots$. This means that λ is the root of the polynomial $(h_{ab} - h'_{ab})\lambda^2 + (h_{a?b} - h'_{a?b})\lambda^3 + \cdots = 0$. Note that this is a polynomial since we will only have finitely many non-zero feature values for images of strings. Since λ is transcendental this means that all of the coefficients must be zero, i.e. $h_{ab} = h'_{ab}, h_{a?b} = h'_{a?b}, \ldots$. Therefore $h = h'$ and the map is injective. □

An algorithm implementing f^{-1} exists: from the **gapWeighted+** feature representation the length of the string, l, and thus of the longest schema, can be calculated. Consider the total sum of all the values from the **gapWeighted+** feature representation. We can simply enumerate all possible values for this sum; λ^2 for $l = 2$, $2\lambda^2 + \lambda^3$ for $l = 3$, $3\lambda^2 + 2\lambda^3 + \lambda^4$ for $l = 4$ etc, until we find one equal or very close to the total sum (note this is an increasing sequence, so termination is guaranteed).

Given the value of l and λ, the value v_i of every coordinate i of the **gapWeighted+** feature representation can be matched against an exhaustive list of all polynomials possible for a single coordinate: $c_1\lambda + c_2\lambda^2 + c_3\lambda^3 + \cdots + c_l\lambda^l$, where $0 \leq c_2 \leq \min(\text{floor}(v_i/\lambda), l - 1), 0 \leq c_3 \leq \min(\text{floor}(v_i/\lambda), l - 2), \ldots, 0 \leq c_l \leq \min(\text{floor}(v_i/\lambda), 1)$ (note that the length of this list is bounded by l). Each of these polynomials corresponds to one unique combination of schemas, and from the **gapSchemas** feature representation the string can easily be generated.

Proposition 13. *The* **gapWeighted+** *kernel is injective for any transcendental value for λ and p = 2.*

Proof. Since there exists an injective function f from **gapSchemas** feature representations to **gapWeighted+** feature representations, and since the composition of two injective functions is also injective, the **gapWeighted+** kernel is injective. □

Note that the choice of value for λ is crucial, and that when $\lambda \to 0$, for example, the **gapWeighted+** kernel is not injective. In this case the kernel behaves like the p-**Spectrum** kernel, which is not injective: for $p = 2$, $aaacaaa$ and $aacaaaa$ have the same image.

Note that the inclusion of the Parikh kernel in **gapWeighted+** is necessary only for dealing with languages containing strings of length 1. If we restrict the domain to a class of languages whose shortest strings are of length at least $l, l > 1$, then **gapWeighted** (and thus **gapWeighted+**) is injective for this domain for any $p \geq 2$.

3   Generative Capacity

Clearly the generative capacity of a given class of planar languages depends crucially on the kernel used. Consider the kernel $\kappa_L(u, v) = 1$ if $u, v \in L$ and 0 otherwise, for any language L: using this trivial kernel L is κ_L-planar. Similarly, planes in the feature space defined by the discrete kernel $\kappa(u, v) = 1$ if $u = v$ and 0 otherwise, are the images of the finite languages, where the rank is the cardinality of the language.

The class of **gapWeighted** planar languages contains quite expressive languages. It contains the copy language with disjoint alphabet: given an alphabet Σ split into two disjoint sets Σ_1, Σ_2, with a bijection f between them, it is defined as $\{uv | u \in \Sigma_1^*, v \in \Sigma_2^*, v[i] = f(u[i])\}$. For example, with $\Sigma = \{a, b\}$ and $\Sigma' = \{c, d\}$, $f(a) = c, f(b) = d$, $abacdc$ is grammatical. Informally, the plane corresponding to this language (given this kernel) is simply defined by $|s|_{ba} = 0$ (for all $b \in \Sigma2, a \in \Sigma_1$), $|s|_a = |s|_c, |s|_{ab} = |s|_{cd}$ for all $a, b \in \Sigma_1, c, d \in \Sigma_2$. This language is a direct model of the Swiss German crossing dependencies construction mentioned in the introduction, the u substring represents a list of noun phrases, the v part a list of verb phrases.

The language $a^n b^m c^n d^m$ is planar for **All-k-Subsequences**, $k = 2$. It can be expressed in linear constraints: $|u|_a = |u|_c, |u|_b = |u|_d, |u|_{ba} = |u|_{ca} \ldots = 0$. It's easy to see that the MIX language (all permutations of $a^n b^n c^n$ for all n) and dependent branches language ($a^n b^m c^m d^l e^l$, $n = m + l > 0$) can be expressed in similar fashion.

Some languages that can be easily expressed with linear constraints can be expressed in more conventional formalisms only with very large grammars. For example, [Asv06] shows that the size of context-free grammars in Chomksy normal form that generate finite languages containing all permutations of n different symbols grow by a function exponential in n.

3.1   Planar Languages and the Chomsky Hierarchy

Planar languages *cross-cut* the Chomsky Hierarchy. Exactly what subset of each degree of the hierarchy they include depends on the kernel used.

Example 14. The class of languages $\mathcal{L}_{All2}$, all languages planar in the feature space of the
All-k-Subsequences kernel with $k = 2$, contains:

1. Finite languages: both $\{a\}, \{a, ab\}$ are in L_{All2}, but $\{abba\}$ isn't. The string $abba$ maps to a point in feature space that $baab$ maps to as well, so $\{abba, baab\}$ *is* in $\mathcal{L}_{All2}$.
2. Regular languages: $\{a^*\}$ is in $\mathcal{L}_{All2}$, but not **Even**, the language containing all and only strings of even length.
3. Context-free languages: $a^n b^n$ is in $\mathcal{L}_{All2}$, but not the bracket language.
4. Mildly context-sensitive languages: $a^n b^n c^n$.
5. Non-mildly context-sensitive languages: $a^n b^n c^n d^n e^n$, but not a^{n^2}.

3.2   Relationship with k-testable Languages

The class of k-testable languages has been shown to be learnable, and have been applied in bioinformatics, see [YK98].

If κ_p is the p-**Spectrum** kernel, then the k-testable languages are κ_p-planar, which is obvious from the definitions. However, the converse does not hold, the language with equal numbers of as and bs is κ_1 planar but not locally testable.

4   Closure Properties of Planar Languages

Planar languages do not enjoy most of the well-known closure properties. It is easy to see that for example the class of Parikh-planar languages is not closed under concatenation: both a^* and b^* are Parikh-planar, but $\{a^*b^*\}$ isn't. Similarly they are not closed under union, or homomorphism. Two exceptions are the obvious property of being closed under reversal, and under intersection:

Proposition 15. *The intersection of two κ-planar languages is κ-planar.*

Proof. Suppose that L_1 and L_2 are κ-planar for some kernel κ. Consider $H(L_1 \cap L_2)$, the least plane that contains the image of the intersection of L_1 and L_2 (Recall Definition 2).

Suppose $w \in L_1$ and $w \in L_2$. Clearly $\phi(w) \in H(L_1 \cap L_2)$. Conversely suppose we have a w such that $\phi(w) \in H(L_1 \cap L_2)$. Now $H(L_1 \cap L_2) \subset H(L_1)$ so $\phi(w) \in H(L_1)$. Since L_1 is planar, $w \in L_1$. Similarly $w \in L_2$. So, $\phi(w) \in H(L_1 \cap L_2)$ if and only if $w \in L_1 \cap L_2$. Since L_1 and L_2 are planar, $H(L_1)$ has finite dimension, and thus so does $H(L_1 \cap L_2)$. Therefore $L_1 \cap L_2$ is planar.   □

Note also that the resulting hyperplane will be of lower dimensionality than the intersecting planes (and will have the same dimensionality only if these are identical).

5   Learnability

As was previously mentioned, the main motivation for studying κ-planar languages is their inherent learnability. There exists a simple and efficient algorithm to learn any of them from positive data: just use as the representation all linear combinations of the sample data, i.e. find the smallest hyperplane that contains all data points. We define a slightly modified algorithm SPAN(σ) that checks for any new data-point whether it is generated by the current hypothesis (this can easily be determined, since distance from the plane can be computed in polynomial time), and only changes its conjecture when necessary. The new conjecture will have the new data-point added to the base description. Algorithm 1 presents this more formally:

At any given point we have a set of strings that form a basis in feature space for the plane. These strings will be linearly independent: $|U|$ will be equal to the rank of $H(U)$. For any language L such that $H(L)$ has finite rank r, we can see

---

Algorithm 1. SPAN learning algorithm

Inputs: kernel κ, training data $S = \{w_1, \ldots w_l\}$
$U = \{\}$
for $i = 1$ to $i = l$ **do**
  if $\phi(w_i) \notin \mathrm{H}(U)$ **then**
    $U = U \cup \{w_i\}$
  end if
end for

---

that SPAN, will converge to a representation of the preimage of $H(L)$ after at most r mind changes.

The notion of learnability we will apply here is known as identification in the limit ([Gol67]). Within this framework, a class of languages is considered learnable if there exists a (computable) function over sequences of input data that converges on a correct hypothesis after a finite amount of data (assuming all data is presented eventually).

5.1 Resource-Based Constraints on Learners

Identification in the limit of a class guarantees the existence of learning algorithms for that class, but the learning problem is not necessarily tractable. Since we are interested in applications we need to specify further constraints on the learner. Ideally we would use some notion of polynomial identification in the limit. There are several around ([dlH95, Yok91] among others), but they are all of a somewhat ad-hoc nature. The latter is one of the more restrictive ones and thus suits our present purpose best. [Yok91] defines a class as *polynomial-time identifiable in the limit from positive data* if there exists a learning algorithm for that class such that both the number of explicit errors of prediction and the computation time it needs for any sequence of data are bounded by polynomials over the complexity of the representation (rank, in this case).

5.2 Behavioural Constraints on Learners

Identification in the limit provides criteria for the success of a learning process, but grants total freedom to learners prior to convergence. Generally speaking it's desirable to be able to impose additional constraints, to guarantee 'rational' behaviour of the learner. Formally this simply means choosing a subset of possible learners.

Many different constraints have been studied in the literature, we define the ones relevant to this discussion:

Definition 16. *Consistent learning*
A learning function φ is consistent *on $\mathcal{G}$ if for any $L \in \mathrm{L}(\mathcal{G})$ and for any finite sequence $\langle s_0, \ldots, s_i \rangle$ of elements of L, either $\varphi(\langle s_0, \ldots, s_i \rangle)$ is undefined or $\{s_0, \ldots, s_i\} \subseteq \mathrm{L}(\varphi(\langle s_0, \ldots, s_i \rangle))$.*

Definition 17. *(Strong) Monotonicity*
The learning function φ is monotone increasing *or* strong monotonic *if for all finite sequences $\langle s_0, \ldots, s_n \rangle$ and $\langle s_0, \ldots, s_{n+m} \rangle$, whenever $\varphi(\langle s_0, \ldots, s_n \rangle)$ and $\varphi(\langle s_0, \ldots, s_{n+m} \rangle)$ are defined, $\mathrm{L}(\varphi(\langle s_0, \ldots, s_n \rangle)) \subseteq \mathrm{L}(\varphi(\langle s_0, \ldots, s_{n+m} \rangle))$.*

Definition 18. *Incrementality*
The learning function φ is incremental *if there exists a computable function ψ such that*
$$\varphi(\langle s_0, \ldots, s_{n+1} \rangle) \simeq \psi(\varphi(\langle s_0, \ldots, s_n \rangle), s_{n+1}).$$

5.3   Learnability of Planar Languages

We are now in a position to demonstrate a strong learnability result for planar languages. Even under a combination of various constraints on the use of resources and on behaviour this class is learnable:

Theorem 19. *The class of κ-planar languages is identifiable in the limit, with polynomial size characteristic set, a polynomial number of mind changes, and polynomial computation, by a learner that is simultaneously consistent, monotone increasing and incremental.*

Proof. For any plane of rank r there is a set C of strings such that $|C| = r$ and for any enumeration e of C, $|\mathrm{SPAN}(e)| = r$ (trivial). It follows immediately that for any enumeration e of C, $\mathrm{SPAN}(e)$ defines a plane for L, and thus that C is a characteristic set for L.

Consider $C' = C \cup S$, where S is a finite subset of L. By definition of planar language and SPAN, S is in the language defined by plane $\mathrm{SPAN}(e)$, so for any enumeration e' of C', $\mathrm{SPAN}(e') = \mathrm{SPAN}(e)$, both define a plane for L.

Therefore the learning function based on SPAN will, after encountering all elements from a characteristic set C, hypothesise L and will not diverge from this hypothesis. This proves identifiability in the limit of the class of planar languages.

The characteristic set has a size[2] polynomial (in fact linear) in the rank of the target plane, the learner need only change its mind as many times as the size of the characteristic set, and SPAN can be implemented to run in polynomial time.

A learner for planar languages based on SPAN is consistent and monotone increasing by definition. Incrementality is trivial: the plane is defined in terms of the set of basis strings; this basis and the new data-point are enough to generate a new hypothesis.   □

5.4   Finite Elasticity

Learnability, and related properties like existence of a mind change bound, are largely determined by topological properties of the class under consideration.

---

[2] Here 'size' simply means cardinality of the set. It makes little sense to include the length of the strings in this definition, since the class includes for example the finite language with one element $a^{10^{100}}$.

One such property is the existence of an *infinite ascending chain* of languages. This means that for $L_0, L_1, \ldots, L_n, \ldots$ in that class, $L_0 \subset L_1 \subset \ldots \subset L_n \subset \ldots$. This implies the weaker property known as *infinite elasticity*:

Definition 20. *(In)finite elasticity[Wri89, MSW91]*
A class $\mathcal{L}$ of languages is said to have infinite elasticity *if there exists an infinite sequence $\langle s_n \rangle_{n \in \mathbb{N}}$ of sentences and an infinite sequence $\langle L_n \rangle_{n \in \mathbb{N}}$ of languages in $\mathcal{L}$ such that for all $n \in \mathbb{N}$, $s_n \notin L_n$, and $\{s_0, \ldots, s_n\} \subseteq L_{n+1}$.*

A class $\mathcal{L}$ of languages is said to have finite elasticity *if it does not have infinite elasticity.*

Finite elasticity is a sufficient condition for learnability under two conditions, as shown in [Wri89]:

Theorem 21. *(Wright)* *Let $\mathcal{G}$ be a class of grammars for a class of recursive languages, where $G \in \mathcal{G}$ is at least semi-decidable. If $\mathrm{L}(\mathcal{G})$ has finite elasticity, then $\mathcal{G}$ is identifiable in the limit.*

Thus one route to proving learnability of a class is demonstrating it has finite elasticity, which has the added benefit of allowing one to easily define a conservative learning algorithm. In this context this is not necessary, however we do get nice closure properties for free.

Proposition 22. *If the feature space defined by κ has finite dimension, then the class of κ-planar languages has finite elasticity.*

Proof. Suppose the class has infinite elasticity, with strings $s_1, \ldots$ and languages $L_1 \ldots$. If we define $S_n = H(\{s_0, \ldots, s_n\})$, then $S_{n-1} \subseteq L_n$, and $S_n \nsubseteq L_n$. Obviously, $S_0 \subset S_1 \ldots$, which constitutes an infinite ascending chain. Since S_n must be of greater rank than S_{n-1}, and every S_n is included in a language in the class, there can't be any bound on the rank of the planes for languages in the class. This is in contradiction with the hypothesis that the feature space has finite dimension.   □

This does not hold for all planar languages. Any class of planar languages that contains all finite languages (c.f. the kernel based on all substrings) has an infinite ascending chain. It *does* hold for **gapWeighted-** and **gapWeighted+** planar languages.

It is straightforward to establish the following corollary (see [Wri89]):

Corollary 23. *Any finite union of classes of κ-planar languages where κ is finite dimensional has finite elasticity.*

Thus planar languages can be generalised to larger classes of learnable languages. Unfortunately, the naive learning algorithms for these classes will run in exponential time.

6   Conclusion

There is very little work to which the current approach can be compared. [Sal05] presents some steps towards defining languages using constraints on subsequence counts. [Kon04] discusses an approach to embedding languages in a feature space, but using different techniques, and only modelling the locally testable languages.

Our approach has a number of limitations. First, while we can learn a number of simple languages, it is not clear that this approach will scale to learning much more complex languages. To get learnability for large scale problems, we will need to combine these techniques with other, perhaps more traditional, grammatical inference algorithms. Secondly, the size of the representations can be quite large, particularly if we use kernels that involve longer substrings; in the worst case this size can be $|\Sigma|^p$ where p is the length of the subsequences represented in the kernel. Finally, though the algorithms are polynomial, their naive application has a computational cost that is cubic in the number of examples. Thus it will be difficult to solve problems with more than several thousand examples on current workstations, without careful optimisations.

We have introduced the class of planar languages, an inherently learnable class of languages with high expressive power, defined in term of string kernels. This is the first application of this family of techniques to the problems of grammatical inference. This class contains interesting context-sensitive languages, including some classic examples from computational linguistics. We have carried out extensive experimental verification of the approach described here [CCFWS06] and have confirmed the practical efficiency of these techniques. These classes are defined in terms of planes in a feature space, which can be efficiently learned with standard machine learning techniques from positive data alone. The choice of kernel determines the expressive power and closure properties of the resulting class. Two kernels have been shown to be injective (depending on the choice of hyperparameters), a particular important property in the context of GI. We have also shown that for some kernels, planar languages have the desirable property of finite elasticity. This allows easy extension to richer classes of languages whilst retaining good learnability properties.

Planar languages are a novel approach to GI, and it seems we have only scratched the surface. An interesting topic for future research would be language classes defined using linear inequalities, which would correspond to half-spaces in the feature space. Such classes would allow the expression of natural language phenomena such as Chinese number words. Another direction would be the definition of new string kernels for specific purposes. The kernels we have considered are in most cases standard, well-studied kernels, so it is likely that new ones can be designed that are better suited for grammatical inference.

Acknowledgements

This work has benefitted from the support of the EU funded PASCAL Network of Excellence on Pattern Analysis, Statistical Modelling and Computational Learning.

References

[ABR64]   M. A. Aizerman, E. M. Braverman, and L. I. Rozonoer. Theoretical foundations of the potential function method in pattern recognition. *Automation and Remote Control*, 25:821–837, 1964.

[Asv06]   Peter R. J. Asveld. Generating all permutations by context-free grammars in Chomsky normal form. *Theoretical Computer Science (TCS)*, 354(1):118–130, 2006.

[CCFWS06]   Alexander Clark, Christophe Costa Florêncio and Chris Watkins. Languages as hyperplanes: grammatical inference with string kernels. In *ECML, 17th European Conference on Machine Learning*. Springer-Verlag, 2006.

[dlH95]   Colin de la Higuera. Characteristic sets for polynomial grammatical inference. In *Proceedings of the International Colloquium on Grammatical Inference ICGI-96*. Springer-Verlag, 1995.

[Gol67]   E. Mark Gold. Language identification in the limit. *Information and Control*, 10:447–474, 1967.

[Huy84]   Riny Huybregts. The weak inadequacy of context-free phrase structure grammars. In Ger J. de Haan, Mieke Trommelen, and Wim Zonneveld, editors, *Van Periferie naar Kern*. Foris, Dordrecht, 1984.

[JS96]   Aravind K. Joshi and Yves Schabes. Tree-adjoining grammars. In Grzegorz Rosenberg and Arto Salomaa, editors, *Handbook of Formal Languages*, volume 3, pages 69–123. Springer-Verlag, New York, 1996.

[Kon04]   Leonid Kontorovich. Learning linearly separable languages. Technical Report CMU-CALD-04-105, School of Computer Science, CMU, 2004.

[MSW91]   Tatsuya Motoki, Takeshi Shinohara, and Keith Wright. The correct definition of finite elasticity: Corrigendum to identification of unions. In *The Fourth Workshop on Computational Learning Theory*. San Mateo, Calif.: Morgan Kaufmann, 1991.

[Sal05]   Arto Salomaa. On languages defined by numerical parameters. Technical Report 663, Turku Centre for Computer Science, 2005.

[Shi85]   Stuart M. Shieber. Evidence against the context-freeness of natural language. *Linguistics and Philosophy*, 8:333–343, 1985.

[STC04]   John Shawe-Taylor and Nello Christianini. *Kernel Methods for Pattern Analysis*. Cambridge University Press, 2004.

[Wat99]   Chris Watkins. Dynamic alignment kernels. Technical Report CSD-TR-98-11, Department of Computer Science, Royal Holloway College, University of London, 1999.

[Wri89]   Keith Wright. Identification of unions of languages drawn from an identifiable class. In *The 1989 Workshop on Computational Learning Theory*, pages 328–333. San Mateo, Calif.: Morgan Kaufmann, 1989.

[YK98]   Takashi Yokomori and Satoshi Kobayashi. Learning local languages and their application to DNA sequence analysis. *IEEE Trans. Pattern Anal. Mach. Intell.*, 20(10):1067–1079, 1998.

[Yok91]   Takashi Yokomori. Polynomial-time learning of very simple grammars from positive data. In *Proceedings of the Fourth Annual Workshop on Computational Learning Theory*, pages 213–227, University of California, Santa Cruz, 5–7 August 1991. ACM Press.

A Unified Algorithm for Extending Classes of Languages Identifiable in the Limit from Positive Data⋆

Mitsuo Wakatsuki, Etsuji Tomita, and Go Yamada

Department of Information and Communication Engineering,
Faculty of Electro-Communications,
The University of Electro-Communications
Chofugaoka 1–5–1, Chofu, Tokyo 182-8585, Japan
{wakatuki, tomita}@ice.uec.ac.jp

Abstract. We are concerned with a *unified* algorithm for extending classes of languages identifiable in the limit from positive data. Let $\mathcal{L}$ be a class of languages to be based on and let $\mathcal{X}$ be a class of finite subsets of strings. The extended class of $\mathcal{L}$, denoted by $\mathcal{C}(\mathcal{L}, \mathcal{X})$, is defined by these $\mathcal{L}$ and $\mathcal{X}$. Here we give a sufficient condition for $\mathcal{C}(\mathcal{L}, \mathcal{X})$ to be identifiable in the limit from positive data and we present a unified identification algorithm for it. Furthermore, we show that some proper subclasses of $\mathcal{C}(\mathcal{L}, \mathcal{X})$ are polynomial time identifiable in the limit from positive data in the sense of Yokomori.

1 Introduction

In the study of inductive inference of formal languages, Gold [4] defined the notion of *identification in the limit* and showed that the class of languages containing all finite sets and one infinite set, which is called a *superfinite* class, is not identifiable in the limit from *positive data*. This means that even the class of regular languages is not identifiable in the limit from positive data. Angluin [1] has given several conditions for a class of languages to be identifiable in the limit from positive data, and she has presented some examples of identifiable classes. She has also proposed subclasses of regular languages called k-reversible languages for each $k \geq 0$, and has shown that these classes are identifiable in the limit from positive data, requiring a polynomial time for updating conjectures [2].

From the practical point of view, the inductive inference algorithm must have a good *time efficiency* in addition to running with only positive data. One may define the notion of *polynomial time identification in the limit* in various ways. Pitt [8] has proposed a reasonable definition for polynomial time identifiability in the limit. By making a slight modification of his definition, Yokomori [10] has proposed another definition for polynomial time identifiability in the

---

⋆ This work is supported in part by Grants-in-Aid for Scientific Research Nos. 13680435, 16300001 and 18500108 from the Ministry of Education, Culture, Sports, Science and Technology of Japan.

Y. Sakakibara et al. (Eds.): ICGI 2006, LNAI 4201, pp. 161–174, 2006.

limit from positive data, and he has proved that a class of languages accepted by strictly deterministic automata (SDAs) [9][10], which is a proper subclass of regular languages, is polynomial time identifiable in the limit from positive data.

An SDA is an extended deterministic finite automaton, which is intuitively a state transition graph in which the set X of labels for edges is a finite subset of strings over an alphabet Σ, that satisfies the following conditions: for any x in X, there uniquely exists an edge (a pair of states) whose label is x, and for any distinct labels x_1, x_2 in X, the first symbol of x_1 differs from that of x_2. This SDA can be also represented by a pair (M, φ) of a corresponding deterministic finite automaton M and a homomorphism $\varphi : \Sigma'^* \to \Sigma^*$ such that $X = \varphi(\Sigma')$ for some alphabet Σ', where the language accepted by M is in the class of Szilard languages of linear grammars [7]. That is, the class of languages accepted by SDAs is the extended class of Szilard languages of linear grammars. In a similar way to this, some kind of language classes can be extended.

In this paper, we are concerned with a unified algorithm for extending classes of languages identifiable in the limit from positive data. Let $\mathcal{L}$ be a class of languages over Σ' to be based on and $\mathcal{X}$ a class of finite subsets of strings over Σ, where there exists a morphism $\varphi : \Sigma'^* \to X^*$ for some $X \in \mathcal{X}$. The extended class of $\mathcal{L}$, denoted by $\mathcal{C}(\mathcal{L}, \mathcal{X})$, is defined by these $\mathcal{L}$ and $\mathcal{X}$. Kobayashi and Yokomori [6] proved that for each $k \geq 0$, a class $\mathcal{C}(\mathcal{R}ev_k, \mathcal{X}_0)$ of languages, where $\mathcal{R}ev_k$ is a class of k-reversible languages and $\mathcal{X}_0$ is a class of codes [3], is identifiable in the limit from positive data. However, they have not shown the identification algorithm for $\mathcal{C}(\mathcal{R}ev_k, \mathcal{X}_0)$, and it is still unknown whether the time complexity of the algorithm is polynomial in the sense of Yokomori [10]. Here we give a sufficient condition for $\mathcal{C}(\mathcal{L}, \mathcal{X})$ to be identifiable in the limit from positive data and present a unified identification algorithm for it. Furthermore, we show that some proper subclasses of $\mathcal{C}(\mathcal{R}ev_k, \mathcal{X}_0)$ are polynomial time identifiable in the limit from positive data.

2   Definitions

2.1   Basic Definitions and Notation

We assume that the reader is familiar with the basics of automata and formal language theory. For the definitions and notation not stated here, see, e.g., [5].

A *semigroup* consists of a set S with a binary associative operation defined on S. A *monoid* M is a semigroup which possesses a two-sided identity, where the identity element is denoted by ε_M or simply by ε. A *morphism* from a monoid M into a monoid N is a function $\varphi : M \to N$ which satisfies, for all $m_1, m_2 \in M$, $\varphi(m_1 m_2) = \varphi(m_1)\varphi(m_2)$, and furthermore $\varphi(\varepsilon_M) = \varepsilon_N$.

An *alphabet* Σ is a finite set of symbols. For any finite set S of finite-length strings over Σ, we denote by S^* (respectively, S^+) the set of all finite-length strings obtained by concatenating zero (one, resp.) or more elements of S, where the concatenation of strings u and v is simply denoted by uv. Note that the set S^* (respectively, S^+) is the submonoid (subsemigroup, resp.) generated by S.

In particular, Σ^* denotes the set of all finite-length strings over Σ. The string of length 0 (the empty string) is denoted by ε. We denote by $|w|$ the length of a string w and by $|S|$ the cardinality of a set S. A *language* over Σ is any subset L of Σ^*. For a string $w \in \Sigma^*$, alph(w) denotes the set of symbols appearing in w. For a language $L \subseteq \Sigma^*$, let alph(L) = $\cup_{w \in L}$alph(w).

2.2 Polynomial Time Identification in the Limit from Positive Data

In this paper, we adopt Yokomori's definition in [10] for the notion of polynomial time identification in the limit from positive data.

For any class of languages to be identified, let $\mathcal{R}$ be a *class of representations* for a class of languages. Instances of such representations are automata, grammars, and so on. Given an r in $\mathcal{R}$, $L(r)$ denotes the language represented by r. A *positive presentation* of $L(r)$ is any infinite sequence of data such that every $w \in L(r)$ occurs at least once in the sequence and no other string not in $L(r)$ appears in the sequence. Each element of $L(r)$ is called a *positive example* (or simply, *example*) of $L(r)$.

Let r be a representation in $\mathcal{R}$. An algorithm $\mathcal{A}$ is said to *identify r in the limit from positive data* iff $\mathcal{A}$ takes any positive presentation of $L(r)$ as an input, and outputs an infinite sequence of representations in $\mathcal{R}$ such that there exist r' in $\mathcal{R}$ and $j > 0$ so that for all $i \geq j$, the i-th conjecture (representation) r_i is identical to r' and $L(r') = L(r)$. A class $\mathcal{R}$ is *identifiable in the limit from positive data* iff there exists an algorithm $\mathcal{A}$ that, for any r in $\mathcal{R}$, identifies r in the limit from positive data.

Let $\mathcal{A}$ be an algorithm for identifying $\mathcal{R}$ in the limit from positive data. Suppose that after examining i examples, the algorithm $\mathcal{A}$ conjectures some r_i. We say that $\mathcal{A}$ makes an *implicit error of prediction* at step i if r_i is not consistent with the $(i+1)$-st example w_{i+1}, i.e., if $w_{i+1} \notin L(r_i)$.

Definition 1 (Yokomori [10], pp.157-158, Definition 2). *A class $\mathcal{R}$ is polynomial time identifiable in the limit from positive data iff there exists an algorithm $\mathcal{A}$ for identifying $\mathcal{R}$ in the limit from positive data with the property that there exist polynomials p and q such that for any n, for any r of size n, and for any positive presentation of $L(r)$, the time used by $\mathcal{A}$ between receiving the i-th example w_i and outputting the i-th conjecture r_i is at most $p(n, \sum_{j=1}^{i} |w_j|)$, and the number of implicit errors of prediction made by $\mathcal{A}$ is at most $q(n, l)$, where the size of r is the length of a description for r and $l = \text{Max}\{|w_j| \mid 1 \leq j \leq i\}$.*

3 Language Classes Extended by Using Codes

In this section, we introduce language classes extended by using codes.

Definition 2. *Let $w \in \Sigma^*$ and $X, Y \subseteq \Sigma^*$. Any sequence $(v_1, v_2, \ldots, v_n) \in (\Sigma^*)^n$ ($n \geq 0$) such that $w = v_1 v_2 \cdots v_n$ is called a* factorization *of w. Moreover, any sequence $(x_1, x_2, \ldots, x_n) \in X^n$ such that $w = x_1 x_2 \cdots x_n$ is called an X-factorization of w. If w has an X-factorization, i.e., $w \in X^*$, we say that X can* factorize w. Moreover, if any string in Y has an X-factorization, i.e., $Y \subseteq X^*$, we say that X can factorize Y.

Definition 3. A finite set X over Σ is said to be a finite factorizing set iff, for any x in X, $|x| \geq 1$ and $|x|$ is finite.

Example 1. Let $\Sigma_1 = \{y, o, u, f, e, l, v, r, h, a, p\}$, $w_1 = youfeelveryhappy(\in \Sigma_1^*)$, $X_1 = \{you, feel, very, happy\}(\subseteq \Sigma_1^*)$ and $Y_1 = \{youfeel(very)^i happy \mid i \geq 0\}(\subseteq \Sigma_1^*)$. A sequence $(you, feel, very, happy)$ is an X_1-factorization of w_1. Therefore, X_1 can factorize w_1. Also, X_1 can factorize Y_1. Moreover, X_1 is a finite factorizing set.

The next lemma follows from Definitions 2 and 3.

Lemma 1. Let $\mathcal{X}$ be a class of finite factorizing sets over Σ and $S \subseteq \Sigma^*$. For any $X \in \mathcal{X}$, it holds that X can factorize $S \cup \{\varepsilon\}$ iff X can factorize $S - \{\varepsilon\}$.

Proof. It can be proved by using the fact that X can factorize ε for any X. $\square$

Definition 4. A finite factorizing set X over Σ is said to be ambiguous iff there exists $w \in X^+$ which has at least two distinct X-factorizations. Otherwise, it is said to be unambiguous. Moreover, a class $\mathcal{X}$ of finite factorizing sets over Σ is said to be ambiguous iff there exists $X \in \mathcal{X}$ which is ambiguous. Otherwise, it is said to be unambiguous.

Example 2. Let $\Sigma_2 = \{b, e, g, i, n\}$ and $X_2 = \{be, beg, gin, in\}(\subseteq \Sigma_2^*)$. The finite factorizing set X_2 is ambiguous since there exists $w_2 = begin(\in X_2^+)$ which has two distinct X_2-factorizations, that is, (be, gin) and (beg, in). On the other hand, the finite factorizing set X_1 in Example 1 is unambiguous.

If a finite factorizing set X over Σ is unambiguous, X is also called a *code* ([3], p.38). Therefore, a class of unambiguous finite factorizing sets is a class of codes. Note that a code never contains the empty string ε. It is clear that any subset of a code is a code. In particular, the empty set $\emptyset$ is a code. For example, for any $k \geq 1$, Σ^k is a code over Σ.

For a string $w \in \Sigma^+$, firstchar(w) (respectively, lastchar(w)) denotes the first (last, resp.) symbol $(\in \Sigma)$ of w. For a set of strings $X \subseteq \Sigma^+$, let firstchar$(X) = \cup_{w \in X}$firstchar(w) and lastchar$(X) = \cup_{w \in X}$lastchar(w). Then, we define the following codes.

Definition 5. Let X be a code over Σ. X is called a strict prefix code (respectively, a strict suffix code) iff, for any pair of distinct elements $x_1, x_2 \in X$, it holds that firstchar$(x_1) \neq$ firstchar(x_2) (lastchar$(x_1) \neq$ lastchar(x_2), resp.).

Example 3. The set X_1 in Example 1 is a strict prefix code, but it is not a strict suffix code.

Let $\mathcal{SP}$, $\mathcal{SS}$ be the class of strict prefix codes, and that of strict suffix codes, respectively.

Definition 6. *Let $\mathcal{X}$ be a class of finite factorizing sets over Σ and $X \in \mathcal{X}$ a finite factorizing set that can factorize S for some nonempty subset S of Σ^*. X is said to be the* coarsest *finite factorizing set in $\mathcal{X}$ that can factorize S iff, for any $X' \in \mathcal{X}$ that can factorize S such that $X' \neq X$, it holds that $X'^* - X^* \neq \emptyset$.*

In general, for a given class $\mathcal{X}$ of finite factorizing sets over Σ and a given nonempty subset S of Σ^*, there exist *many* coarsest finite factorizing sets in $\mathcal{X}$ that can factorize S.

Example 4. Let $\Sigma_3 = \{a, b, c, d\}$ and $S_1 = \{a(bc)^i d \mid i \geq 1\}(\subseteq \Sigma_3^*)$. Let $\mathcal{X}_0$ be the class of codes over Σ_3. The sets $X_3 = \{abc, bc, d\}$, $X_4 = \{ab, cb, cd\}$ and $X_5 = \{a, bc, bcd\}$ are the coarsest codes in $\mathcal{X}_0$ that can factorize S_1.

For the class $\mathcal{SP}$ of strict prefix codes, the set X_3 is the coarsest code in $\mathcal{SP}$ that can factorize S_1. Similarly, for the class $\mathcal{SS}$ of strict suffix codes, the set X_5 is the coarsest code in $\mathcal{SS}$ that can factorize S_1.

For the class $\mathcal{SP}$ of strict prefix codes and the class $\mathcal{SS}$ of strict suffix codes, we have the following lemma from Definitions 4, 6 and 5.

Lemma 2. *For any nonempty subset S of Σ^*, there uniquely exists the coarsest code in the class $\mathcal{SP}$ (respectively, $\mathcal{SS}$) of strict prefix (suffix, resp.) codes over Σ that can factorize S.*

Proof. We shall show that, for any S, there uniquely exists the coarsest code in $\mathcal{SP}$ that can factorize S. For any S $(\subseteq \Sigma^*)$, there exists at least one coarsest code in $\mathcal{SP}$ since Σ is a code in $\mathcal{SP}$ that can factorize S.

Suppose for the sake of contradiction that there exist two distinct coarsest codes X_1, X_2 in $\mathcal{SP}$ that can factorize S. Since X_1 is the coarsest code that can factorize S and $X_1 \neq X_2$, it holds that $S \subseteq X_1^*$ and $X_2^* - X_1^* \neq \emptyset$ from Definition 6. Similarly, it holds that $S \subseteq X_2^*$ and $X_1^* - X_2^* \neq \emptyset$. Therefore, it holds that $S \subseteq X_1^* \cap X_2^* \subset X_1^*$ and $S \subseteq X_1^* \cap X_2^* \subset X_2^*$. In order to prove this lemma, it suffices to show that there exists a strict prefix code $X_3 \in \mathcal{SP}$ such that $X_3^* = X_1^* \cap X_2^*$. Note that, for any $x \in X_1^+ \cap X_2^+$, it holds that firstchar$(x) \in$ firstchar$(X_1^+ \cap X_2^+) =$ firstchar$(X_1) \cap$ firstchar(X_2).

For any $a \in$ firstchar$(X_1) \cap$ firstchar(X_2), there exists only one *shortest* string $z_a \in \Sigma^*$ such that $az_a \in X_1^+ \cap X_2^+$ since $X_1, X_2 \in \mathcal{SP}$. Let $X_3 = \{az_a \in X_1^+ \cap X_2^+ \mid a \in$ firstchar$(X_1) \cap$ firstchar$(X_2)\}$. Then, X_3 is a strict prefix code. Furthermore, it holds that $X_3^* = \{\varepsilon\} \cup X_3^+ \subseteq \{\varepsilon\} \cup [X_1^+ \cap X_2^+]^+ = \{\varepsilon\} \cup [X_1^+ \cap X_2^+] = X_1^* \cap X_2^*$.

Conversely, for any $x \in X_1^+ \cap X_2^+$, we can show that $x = v_1 v_2 \cdots v_n$, where $n \geq 1$, such that $v_i \in X_1^+ \cap X_2^+$ and, for any proper prefix v_i' of v_i, $v_i' \notin X_1^+ \cap X_2^+$ for $1 \leq i \leq n$. For each v_i, let $a_i =$ firstchar$(v_i) \in \Sigma$. Then, it holds that $v_i = a_i z_{a_i}$ for $1 \leq i \leq n$, where z_{a_i} is a *shortest* string such that $a_i z_{a_i} \in X_1^+ \cap X_2^+$ for each $a_i \in \Sigma$. Since $X_1, X_2 \in \mathcal{SP}$, it holds that $v_i \in X_3$ for $1 \leq i \leq n$. Then, it holds that $X_1^* \cap X_2^* = \{\varepsilon\} \cup [X_1^+ \cap X_2^+] \subseteq \{\varepsilon\} \cup X_3^+ = X_3^*$.

Therefore, it holds that $X_3^* = X_1^* \cap X_2^*$. Then, $X_3 \in \mathcal{SP}$ can factorize S. Thus, it holds that $X_3^* - X_1^* = \emptyset$ and $X_3^* - X_2^* = \emptyset$, which is a contradiction since X_1 and X_2 are the coarsest codes.

In a similar way to this, we can prove that, for any S, there uniquely exists the coarsest code in $\mathcal{SS}$ that can factorize S.   □

For a subclass $\mathcal{X}$ of codes over Σ, if, for any $S \subseteq \Sigma^*$, there uniquely exists the coarsest code in $\mathcal{X}$ that can factorize S, we have the following lemma.

Lemma 3. *Let $\mathcal{X}$ be a class of codes over Σ and S a nonempty subset of Σ^*. If, for any S, there uniquely exists the coarsest code X_S in $\mathcal{X}$ that can factorize S, then for any code $X \in \mathcal{X}$ that can factorize S, it holds that $(S \subseteq) X_S^* \subseteq X^*$.*

Proof. Suppose for the sake of contradiction that $X_S^* - Y^* \neq \emptyset$ for some code $Y \in \mathcal{X}$ that can factorize S. Since X_S is the unique coarsest code in $\mathcal{X}$ that can factorize S, Y is not the coarsest code in $\mathcal{X}$ that can factorize S. Therefore, there exists some code $Z \in \mathcal{X}$ that can factorize S such that $Z \neq Y$ and $Z^* - Y^* = \emptyset$ (i.e., $Z^* \subset Y^*$) from Definition 6. Let $Z_0 \in \mathcal{X}$ be a code that can factorize S such that $Z_0^* \subset Y^*$ and $Z'^* - Z_0^* \neq \emptyset$ for any code $Z' \in \mathcal{X}$ that can factorize S such that $Z'^* \subset Y^*$ and $Z' \neq Z_0$. Since $Z_0^* \subset Y^*$, it holds that $X_S^* - Z_0^* \neq \emptyset$ from the assumption that $X_S^* - Y^* \neq \emptyset$. Therefore, for any code $X \in \mathcal{X}$ that can factorize S such that $X \neq Z_0$, it holds that $X^* - Z_0^* \neq \emptyset$. Thus, $Z_0 \in \mathcal{X}$ is the coarsest code that can factorize S, which is a contradiction.   □

Berstel and Perrin [3] proved the following proposition and corollary from the definition of a code. They are useful for our later discussion.

Proposition 1 (Berstel and Perrin [3], p.38, Proposition 1.1). *If a subset X of Σ^* is a code, then any morphism $\varphi : \Sigma'^* \to \Sigma^*$ which induces a bijection of some alphabet Σ' onto X is injective. Conversely, if there exists an injective morphism $\varphi : \Sigma'^* \to \Sigma^*$ such that $X = \varphi(\Sigma')$, then X is a code.*

Corollary 1 (Berstel and Perrin [3], pp.39–40, Corollary 1.2). *Let $\varphi : \Sigma_1^* \to \Sigma_2^*$ be an injective morphism. If X is a code over Σ_1, then $\varphi(X)$ is a code over Σ_2. If Y is a code over Σ_2, then $\varphi^{-1}(Y)$ is a code over Σ_1.*

Such an injective morphism φ in Proposition 1 is called a *coding morphism* for X. In Corollary 1, if $Y = \varphi(X)$, then it holds that $\varphi^{-1}(\varphi(X)) = X$.

Let $\mathcal{L}$ be a class of some languages over Σ' and $\mathcal{X}$ a class of some finite factorizing sets over Σ. Now we define a new class of languages over Σ, denoted by $\mathcal{C}(\mathcal{L}, \mathcal{X})$, using these $\mathcal{L}$ and $\mathcal{X}$ as follows.

Definition 7. *A class of languages denoted by $\mathcal{C}(\mathcal{L}, \mathcal{X})$ over Σ is defined as the class obtained by the following procedure: (1) For every language $L \in \mathcal{L}$ over Σ', let $\Sigma_L' = \text{alph}(L) (\subseteq \Sigma')$. Note that Σ_L' is a code over Σ'. (2) For every finite factorizing set $X \in \mathcal{X}$ over Σ such that $|X| = |\Sigma_L'|$, define a bijection φ of Σ_L' onto X. (3) For each $L \in \mathcal{L}$ and $\varphi : \Sigma'^* \to \Sigma^*$ such that $X = \varphi(\Sigma_L')$, a language $\varphi(L) \in \mathcal{C}(\mathcal{L}, \mathcal{X})$ over Σ is defined as $\varphi(L) = \{\varphi(w) \in X^* \mid w \in L\}$.*

Example 5. Let $L_1 = \{abc^i d \mid i \geq 0\}$ in some language class $\mathcal{L}_1$, where $\Sigma_{L_1}' = \{a, b, c, d\}$. For the code $X_1 = \{you, feel, very, happy\} \in \mathcal{SP}$ in Example 1, define a bijection φ_1 of Σ_{L_1}' onto X_1 as follows: $\varphi_1(a) = you, \varphi_1(b) = feel, \varphi_1(c) =$

very, and $\varphi_1(d) = happy$. Then, a language $\varphi_1(L_1) \in \mathcal{C}(\mathcal{L}_1, \mathcal{SP})$ is $\{youfeel$ $(very)^i happy \mid i \geq 0\}$.

Let L_0 be a language over Σ and Y a code over Σ that can factorize L_0. That is, it holds that $L_0 \subseteq Y^* \subseteq \Sigma^*$. Let $\varphi : \Sigma'^* \to \Sigma^*$ be an injective morphism. Since Y is a code over Σ, it holds that $\varphi^{-1}(Y)$ is a code over Σ' from Corollary 1. Since Y can factorize L_0, it holds that $\varphi^{-1}(L_0) \subseteq \varphi^{-1}(Y^*) = [\varphi^{-1}(Y)]^* \subseteq \Sigma'^*$. Therefore, the code $\varphi^{-1}(Y)$ can factorize the language $\varphi^{-1}(L_0)$.

Definition 8. *Let $\mathcal{L}$ be a class of some languages over Σ and $\Sigma' \subseteq \Sigma$. We say that the class $\mathcal{L}$ is* closed under the inverse coding morphism *iff, for any $L \in \mathcal{L}$ and any code $X \subseteq \Sigma^*$ that can factorize L, it holds that $\varphi^{-1}(L) \in \mathcal{L}$, where $\varphi : \Sigma'^* \to \Sigma^*$ is a coding morphism such that $X = \varphi(\Sigma')$.*

Hereafter, we are only concerned with a class $\mathcal{C}(\mathcal{L}, \mathcal{X})$ of languages that satisfies the following conditions 1 and 2.

Condition 1. *The class $\mathcal{L}$ of languages satisfies the following conditions: (1) $\mathcal{L}$ is closed under the inverse coding morphism, and (2) $\mathcal{L}$ is identifiable in the limit from positive data.*

Condition 2. *The class $\mathcal{X}$ of finite factorizing sets over Σ satisfies the following conditions: (1) $\mathcal{X}$ is unambiguous. (That is, $\mathcal{X}$ is a class of codes.) (2) For any nonempty subset S of Σ^*, there uniquely exists the coarsest code X_S in $\mathcal{X}$ that can factorize S. (3) For any positive presentation of S such that $S \subseteq X^+$ for some $X \in \mathcal{X}$, there exists an algorithm for identifying the coarsest code $X_S \in \mathcal{X}$ that can factorize S in the limit. (This algorithm is called an identification algorithm for the coarsest code in $\mathcal{X}$ in the limit from positive data.)*

4   Identification Algorithm

Let $\mathcal{A}_\mathcal{L}$ be an identification algorithm in Condition 1 and $\mathcal{A}_\mathcal{X}$ an identification algorithm in Condition 2.

The flow of the algorithm $\mathcal{A}_\mathcal{L}$ can be written as follows, where the (black box) function $\mathrm{CONSTRUCT}(r', w')$ receives a positive example w' of the target language L' and a representation r' for a language in $\mathcal{L}$ as input, and outputs an updated representation for a language in $\mathcal{L}$ obtained by modifying r' from w'.

Identification Algorithm $\mathcal{A}_\mathcal{L}$
Input: a positive presentation $w'_1, w'_2, \ldots$ of a target language L' in $\mathcal{L}$
Output: a sequence of representations $r'_1, r'_2, \ldots$,
         where r'_i $(i \geq 1)$ is a representation for a language $L(r'_i)$ in $\mathcal{L}$
Procedure
begin
   $S'_0 := \emptyset; \quad \Sigma'_0 := \emptyset; \quad$ initialize r'_0 so that $L(r'_0) = \emptyset; \quad i := 1;$
   repeat (forever)
      read the next positive example w'_i;
      $S'_i := S'_{i-1} \cup \{w'_i\}; \quad \Sigma'_i := \Sigma'_{i-1} \cup \mathrm{alph}(w'_i);$

if $w_i' \in L(r_{i-1}')$ **then** $r_i' := r_{i-1}'$
else $r_i' := \text{CONSTRUCT}(r_{i-1}', w_i')$ **fi**
output r_i'; $i := i + 1$
end

Moreover, the flow of the algorithm $\mathcal{A}_{\mathcal{X}}$ can be written as follows, where the (black box) function $\text{UPDATE}(X', w')$ receives a positive example $w' \in X^+$ for the target code $X \in \mathcal{X}$ and a code $X' \in \mathcal{X}$ as input, and outputs the coarsest code in $\mathcal{X}$ that can factorize $X' \cup \{w'\}$.

Identification Algorithm $\mathcal{A}_{\mathcal{X}}$
Input: a positive presentation $w_1, w_2, \ldots$ of X^+,
       where $X \in \mathcal{X}$ is a target code such that $X = \varphi(\Sigma')$ for some Σ'
Output: a sequence of the coarsest codes $X_1, X_2, \ldots,$
       where X_i $(i \geq 1)$ can factorize $\{w_1, w_2, \ldots, w_i\}$
Procedure
begin
   $S_0 := \emptyset$; $\Sigma_0 := \emptyset$; $X_0 := \emptyset$; $i := 1$;
   repeat (forever)
     read the next positive example w_i;
     $S_i := S_{i-1} \cup \{w_i\}$; $\Sigma_i := \Sigma_{i-1} \cup \text{alph}(w_i)$;
     $X_i := \text{UPDATE}(X_{i-1}, w_i)$;
     output X_i; $i := i + 1$
end

Now we present a unified identification algorithm $\mathcal{A}_{\mathcal{C}(\mathcal{L},\mathcal{X})}$ for a class $\mathcal{C}(\mathcal{L}, \mathcal{X})$ of languages that satisfies Conditions 1 and 2. This algorithm is an extended version of the above algorithms $\mathcal{A}_{\mathcal{L}}$ and $\mathcal{A}_{\mathcal{X}}$. The algorithm $\mathcal{A}_{\mathcal{C}(\mathcal{L},\mathcal{X})}$ is given in the following.

Identification Algorithm $\mathcal{A}_{\mathcal{C}(\mathcal{L},\mathcal{X})}$
Input: a positive presentation $w_1, w_2, \ldots$ of a target language in $\mathcal{C}(\mathcal{L}, \mathcal{X})$
Output: a sequence of pairs $(r_1, X_1), (r_2, X_2), \ldots$ such that $\varphi_i(L(r_i)) \in$
       $\mathcal{C}(\mathcal{L}, \mathcal{X})(i \geq 1)$, where r_i is a representation for a language $L(r_i)$
       and X_i is a code such that $X_i = \varphi_i(\Sigma_i')$ for a coding morphism
       $\varphi_i : \Sigma_i'^* \to \Sigma^*$
Procedure
begin
   $S_0 := \emptyset$; $\Sigma_0 := \emptyset$; $S_0' := \emptyset$; $\Sigma_0' := \emptyset$; $X_0 := \emptyset$;
   initialize φ_0 so that $\varphi_0(\Sigma_0') = X_0$;   initialize r_0 so that $L(r_0) = \emptyset$;
   $i := 1$;   read the next positive example w_i;
   while $w_i = \varepsilon$ **do**
     $S_i := \{\varepsilon\}$; $\Sigma_i := \emptyset$; $S_i' := \{\varepsilon\}$; $\Sigma_i' := \emptyset$; $X_i := \emptyset$; $\varphi_i := \varphi_{i-1}$;
     if $L(r_{i-1}) = \{\varepsilon\}$ **then** $r_i := r_{i-1}$
     else $r_i := \text{CONSTRUCT}(r_{i-1}, \varepsilon)$ /* Call the function in $\mathcal{A}_{\mathcal{L}}$. */
     fi
     output (r_i, X_i) as a conjecture for a language $\{\varepsilon\}$;

$i := i + 1;$ read the next positive example w_i

od

repeat (forever)

   $S_i := S_{i-1} \cup \{w_i\};$ $\Sigma_i := \Sigma_{i-1} \cup \text{alph}(w_i);$

   if $w_i \neq \varepsilon$

   then $X_i := \text{UPDATE}(X_{i-1}, w_i)$ /* Call the function in $\mathcal{A}_{\mathcal{X}}$. */

   else $X_i := X_{i-1}$ **fi**

   if $X_i \neq X_{i-1}$ **then**

      let a set Σ_i' be given as $|\Sigma_i'| = |X_i|$, where $X_i \subset \Sigma_i'^*;$

      let φ_i be a bijection of Σ_i' onto $X_i;$

      $W := \varphi_i^{-1}(S_i);$ $S_0' := \emptyset;$ reset r_0' so that $L(r_0') = \emptyset;$ $j := 1;$

      repeat

         $w_j' := \varphi_i^{-1}(w_j);$ $W := W - \{w_j'\};$ $S_j' := S_{j-1}' \cup \{w_j'\};$

         if $w_j' \in L(r_{j-1}')$ **then** $r_j' := r_{j-1}'$

         else $r_j' := \text{CONSTRUCT}(r_{j-1}', w_j')$ /* Call the function in $\mathcal{A}_{\mathcal{L}}$. */

         fi

         $j := j + 1$

      until $W = \emptyset;$ /* When $i = j - 1$, it holds that $S_i' = \varphi_i^{-1}(S_i)$. */

      $r_i := r_i'$

   else

      $\Sigma_i' := \Sigma_{i-1}';$ $\varphi_i := \varphi_{i-1};$ $w_i' := \varphi_i^{-1}(w_i);$

      $S_i' := S_{i-1}' \cup \{w_i'\};$ /* It holds that $S_i' = \varphi_i^{-1}(S_i)$. */

      if $w_i' \in L(r_{i-1})$ **then** $r_i := r_{i-1}$

      else $r_i := \text{CONSTRUCT}(r_{i-1}, w_i')$ /* Call the function in $\mathcal{A}_{\mathcal{L}}$. */

      fi   **fi**

   output (r_i, X_i) as a conjecture for a language $\varphi_i(L(r_i));$

   $i := i + 1;$ read the next positive example w_i

end

From Definition 7, for any language $L \in \mathcal{C}(\mathcal{L}, \mathcal{X})$, we can show that $L = \varphi(L')$ for some $L' \in \mathcal{L}$ and some bijection φ of $\Sigma_{L'}'$ onto X, where $\Sigma_{L'}' = \text{alph}(L') \ (\subseteq \Sigma')$ and $X \in \mathcal{X}$. The algorithm $\mathcal{A}_{\mathcal{C}(\mathcal{L}, \mathcal{X})}$ outputs a sequence of pairs (r_i, X_i) $(i = 1, 2, \ldots)$ such that $L_i = \varphi_i(L(r_i)) \in \mathcal{C}(\mathcal{L}, \mathcal{X})$, where $L_i \supseteq S_i = \{w_1, w_2, \ldots, w_i\}$, $\Sigma_i' = \text{alph}(\varphi_i^{-1}(S_i))$ and $X_i = \varphi_i(\Sigma_i')$. Note that the algorithm $\mathcal{A}_{\mathcal{C}(\mathcal{L}, \mathcal{X})}$ needs only a positive presentation $w_1, w_2, \ldots$ of a target language $L \in \mathcal{C}(\mathcal{L}, \mathcal{X})$.

4.1   Correctness of the Identification Algorithm

In the case where the target language in $\mathcal{C}(\mathcal{L}, \mathcal{X})$ is $\{\varepsilon\}$, the algorithm $\mathcal{A}_{\mathcal{C}(\mathcal{L}, \mathcal{X})}$ outputs the conjecture (r, X) such that $L(r) = \{\varepsilon\}$ and $X = \emptyset$. Next we are concerned with a target language $L_* \in \mathcal{C}(\mathcal{L}, \mathcal{X})$ such that $L_* \neq \emptyset$ and $L_* \neq \{\varepsilon\}$. From Definition 7, a target language L_* can be denoted by $L_* = \varphi_*(L_*')$ for some $L_*' \in \mathcal{L}$ and some coding morphism $\varphi_* : \Sigma'^* \to \Sigma^*$ such that $X_* = \varphi_*(\Sigma_{L_*'})$ for some $X_* \in \mathcal{X}$ over Σ, where $\Sigma_{L_*'} = \text{alph}(L_*') \ (\subseteq \Sigma')$.

The next lemma derives from the algorithm $\mathcal{A}_{\mathcal{X}}$.

Lemma 4. *Suppose that $\varphi_*(L'_*) \neq \emptyset$ and $\varphi_*(L'_*) \neq \{\varepsilon\}$. For any positive presentation of $\varphi_*(L'_*) - \{\varepsilon\}$, the algorithm $\mathcal{A}_{\mathcal{X}}$ identifies the coarsest code $X_{\varphi_*(L'_*)} \in \mathcal{X}$ that can factorize $\varphi_*(L'_*)$ in the limit.*

Proof. Since $\varphi_*(L'_*) \neq \emptyset$ and $\varphi_*(L'_*) \neq \{\varepsilon\}$, $\varphi_*(L'_*) - \{\varepsilon\}$ is a nonempty set such that $\varphi_*(L'_*) - \{\varepsilon\} \subseteq X^+$ for some $X \in \mathcal{X}$. Then, since the class $\mathcal{X}$ of codes satisfies Condition 2, there uniquely exists the coarsest code $X_{\varphi_*(L'_*) - \{\varepsilon\}} \in \mathcal{X}$ that can factorize $\varphi_*(L'_*) - \{\varepsilon\}$. Also, for any positive presentation of $\varphi_*(L'_*) - \{\varepsilon\}$, $\mathcal{A}_{\mathcal{X}}$ identifies $X_{\varphi_*(L'_*) - \{\varepsilon\}}$ in the limit. Thus, from Lemma 1, $X_{\varphi_*(L'_*) - \{\varepsilon\}}$ is identical to the coarsest code $X_{\varphi_*(L'_*)}$ that can factorize $\varphi_*(L'_*)$. □

Lemma 4 assures that there exists a large enough number N_1 such that, for each $i \geq N_1$, X_i in the algorithm $\mathcal{A}_{\mathcal{C}(\mathcal{L}, \mathcal{X})}$ is identical to the coarsest code $X_{\varphi_*(L'_*)}$. Since Σ'_i and φ_i in $\mathcal{A}_{\mathcal{C}(\mathcal{L}, \mathcal{X})}$ are not updated any more for $i > N_1$, we may let $\Sigma' = \Sigma'_i$ and $\varphi' = \varphi_i$. Then, the followings hold.

(1) From the above assumption, $X_* \in \mathcal{X}$ can factorize $\varphi_*(L'_*)$. For any $X' \in \mathcal{X}$ that can factorize $\varphi_*(L'_*)$, it holds that $\varphi_*(L'_*) \subseteq (X_{\varphi_*(L'_*)})^* \subseteq X'^*$ for the coarsest code $X_{\varphi_*(L'_*)}$ from Lemma 3. Therefore, it holds that $\varphi_*(L'_*) \subseteq (X_{\varphi_*(L'_*)})^* \subseteq (X_*)^*$.

(2) φ' is a bijection of Σ' onto $X_{\varphi_*(L'_*)}$.

Furthermore, we may assume that $\Sigma' \subseteq \Sigma$. Then, the next key lemma holds.

Lemma 5. *The language $\varphi'^{-1}(\varphi_*(L'_*))$ is in $\mathcal{L}$.*

Proof. Since φ_* is a bijection of $\Sigma_{L'_*}$ onto X_* and X_* can factorize $X_{\varphi_*(L'_*)}$, it holds that $\varphi_*^{-1}(X_{\varphi_*(L'_*)}) \subseteq \varphi_*^{-1}((X_{\varphi_*(L'_*)})^*) \subseteq \varphi_*^{-1}((X_*)^*) = (\varphi_*^{-1}(X_*))^* = (\Sigma_{L'_*})^*$. Let $X' = \varphi_*^{-1}(X_{\varphi_*(L'_*)})$. Since $X_{\varphi_*(L'_*)}$ is the coarsest code that can factorize $\varphi_*(L'_*)$, it holds that X' is a code over $\Sigma_{L'_*}$ from Corollary 1 and that $L'_* = \varphi_*^{-1}(\varphi_*(L'_*)) \subseteq \varphi_*^{-1}((X_{\varphi_*(L'_*)})^*) = (\varphi_*^{-1}(X_{\varphi_*(L'_*)}))^* (= X'^*)$, i.e., X' can factorize L'_*.

In the algorithm $\mathcal{A}_{\mathcal{C}(\mathcal{L}, \mathcal{X})}$, it holds that $\varphi'^{-1}(\varphi_*(L'_*)) \subseteq \varphi'^{-1}((X_{\varphi_*(L'_*)})^*) = (\varphi'^{-1}(X_{\varphi_*(L'_*)}))^* = \Sigma'^*$ since $\varphi_*(L'_*) \subseteq (X_{\varphi_*(L'_*)})^*$ and $X_{\varphi_*(L'_*)} = \varphi'(\Sigma')$.

Let $\psi = \varphi_*^{-1} \circ \varphi'$. Then, it holds that $\psi(\Sigma') = \varphi_*^{-1} \circ \varphi'(\Sigma') = \varphi_*^{-1}(\varphi'(\Sigma')) = \varphi_*^{-1}(X_{\varphi_*(L'_*)}) = X'$.

Since $L'_* \in \mathcal{L}$, X' is a code that can factorize L'_* (i.e., $L'_* \subseteq X'^*$), and ψ is a bijection of Σ' onto X' (i.e., $X' = \psi(\Sigma')$), it holds that $\psi^{-1}(L'_*) \in \mathcal{L}$ from Condition 1. Therefore, we have that $\varphi'^{-1}(\varphi_*(L'_*)) = \varphi'^{-1} \circ \varphi_*(L'_*) = (\varphi_*^{-1} \circ \varphi')^{-1}(L'_*) = \psi^{-1}(L'_*) \in \mathcal{L}$. □

A sequence $\varphi'^{-1}(w_1), \varphi'^{-1}(w_2), \ldots$ is a positive presentation of $\varphi'^{-1}(\varphi_*(L'_*))$ corresponding to a positive presentation $w_1, w_2, \ldots$ of $\varphi_*(L'_*)$. Since $\varphi'^{-1}(\varphi_*(L'_*)) \in \mathcal{L}$ from Lemma 5, the algorithm $\mathcal{A}_{\mathcal{L}}$ identifies $\varphi'^{-1}(\varphi_*(L'_*))$ in the limit from positive data. That is, there exists a large enough number N_2 such that, for each $i \geq N_2$, r_i is identical to $\tilde{r}$ such that $L(\tilde{r}) = \varphi'^{-1}(\varphi_*(L'_*))$. Then, for each time where $i \geq N_2$, $\mathcal{A}_{\mathcal{C}(\mathcal{L}, \mathcal{X})}$ outputs a pair of $\tilde{r}$ and $X_{\varphi_*(L'_*)}$ such that $X_{\varphi_*(L'_*)} = \varphi'(\Sigma')$. Thus, we have that $\varphi'(L(\tilde{r})) = \varphi'(\varphi'^{-1}(\varphi_*(L'_*))) = \varphi_*(L'_*)$, where $\varphi_*(L'_*)$ is the target language. Then, we have the next theorem.

Theorem 1. *The class $\mathcal{C}(\mathcal{L}, \mathcal{X})$ of languages that satisfies Conditions 1 and 2 is identifiable in the limit from positive data.*

Note that Theorem 1 assures that there exists a large enough number N_2 such that, for each $i \geq N_2$, $\varphi_i(L(r_i)) = \varphi_*(L'_*)$, but it does not neccesarily hold that $L(r_i) = L'_*$, $\Sigma'_i = \Sigma_{L'_*}$ ($= \mathrm{alph}(L'_*)$), $X_i = X_*$ and $\varphi' = \varphi_*$.

4.2 Time Analysis of the Identification Algorithm

Suppose that a sequence $w_1, w_2, \ldots$ is a positive presentation of the target language in $\mathcal{C}(\mathcal{L}, \mathcal{X})$ that satisfies Conditions 1 and 2. Let $S_i = \{w_1, w_2, \ldots, w_i\}$ and $S'_i = \{\varphi'^{-1}(w_j) \mid w_j \in S_i - \{\varepsilon\}, 1 \leq j \leq i\}$ for each $i \geq 1$.

[**Time for Updating a Conjecture**] The time used by $\mathcal{A}_{\mathcal{C}(\mathcal{L}, \mathcal{X})}$ between receiving the i-th example w_i and outputting the i-th conjecture (r_i, X_i) for a language $\varphi_i(L(r_i))$, where $X_i = \varphi_i(\Sigma'_i)$ and $\Sigma'_i = \mathrm{alph}(S'_i)$, is mainly given by the total time for computing the following three procedures: (1) the function UPDATE(X_{i-1}, w_i), (2) the procedure computing the set S'_i, and (3) the functions CONSTRUCT(r'_{j-1}, S'_j) for all $1 \leq j \leq i$. The above procedures "(1)" and "(2)" depend on the properties of the class $\mathcal{X}$, while the procedure "(3)" depends on the properties of the class $\mathcal{L}$. The time for computing the procedure "(1)" corresponds to the time used by $\mathcal{A}_{\mathcal{X}}$ for updating a conjecture X_i. The time for computing the procedure "(2)" is equal to the time for computing X_i-factorizations of w_j for all j ($1 \leq j \leq i$). And then, the time for computing procedure "(3)" corresponds to the total time used by $\mathcal{A}_{\mathcal{L}}$ between receiving the first example $\varphi_1^{-1}(w_1)$ and outputting the i-th conjecture r'_i.

[**The Number of Implicit Errors**] In the learning process of $\mathcal{A}_{\mathcal{C}(\mathcal{L}, \mathcal{X})}$, whenever $X_i \neq X_{i-1}$, a set Σ'_i and a bijection φ_i are computed over again by using an updated code X_i. In this case, for each i, the number of updating conjectures r'_j ($1 \leq j \leq i$) in $\mathcal{A}_{\mathcal{C}(\mathcal{L}, \mathcal{X})}$ is bounded by the number of implicit errors of prediction made by $\mathcal{A}_{\mathcal{L}}$. Therefore, the number of implicit errors of prediction made by $\mathcal{A}_{\mathcal{C}(\mathcal{L}, \mathcal{X})}$ is bounded by the number of implicit errors of prediction made by $\mathcal{A}_{\mathcal{L}}$ multiplied by that of prediction made by $\mathcal{A}_{\mathcal{X}}$.

5 Examples of Applications

The identification algorithm $\mathcal{A}_{\mathcal{C}(\mathcal{L}, \mathcal{X})}$ is a unified algorithm for a class $\mathcal{C}(\mathcal{L}, \mathcal{X})$ of languages that satisfies Conditions 1 and 2. We shall show some examples of applying this algorithm to pairs of some class of languages and that of codes in the followings.

Let $M = (Q, \Sigma, \delta, q_0, F)$ be a *deterministic finite automaton* (DFA, for short), where Q is the finite set of *states*, Σ is the finite set of *input symbols*, $\delta : Q \times \Sigma \to Q$ is the *transition function*, q_0 ($\in Q$) is the *initial* state, and F ($\subseteq Q$) is the set of *final* states. A usual extension of a transition function δ to a function $\delta : Q \times \Sigma^* \to Q$ allows us to deal with transitions by strings. For a state $q \in Q$, let $L(q) = \{w \in \Sigma^* \mid \delta(q, w) \in F\}$. A language accepted by a DFA M, denoted by $L(M)$, is defined to be $L(q_0)$. A language is said to be *regular* iff it is accepted by a DFA.

A DFA M is said to be *minimal* iff, for any $q \in Q$, there exist $u \in \Sigma^*$ such that $\delta(q_0, u) = q$ and $v \in \Sigma^*$ such that $\delta(q, v) \in F$, and for any pair of distinct states $q_1, q_2 \in Q$, it holds that $L(q_1) \neq L(q_2)$. Note that, for any regular language L, there exists a minimal DFA M such that $L(M) = L$ [5].

For any nonnegative integer k, a string $u \in \Sigma^*$ is said to be a *k-leader* of a state $q \in Q$ of a DFA M iff $|u| = k$ and there exists a state $p \in Q$ such that $\delta(p, u) = q$.

Now we define the following languages.

Definition 9. *A DFA M is said to be a* restricted strictly deterministic automaton *(RSDA, for short) iff, for any $a \in \Sigma$, there exists at most one pair of states $(p, q) \in Q \times Q$ such that $\delta(p, a) = q$. The language accepted by an RSDA M is said to be a* restricted strictly regular language *(RSRL, for short).*

Definition 10. *Let k be a positive integer. A DFA M is said to be a k-definite DFA (k-DDFA, for short) iff, for any pair of distinct states q_1 and q_2 in Q, there exists no string that is a k-leader of both q_1 and q_2. The language accepted by a k-DDFA M is said to be a k-definite regular language (k-DRL, for short).*

Let $\mathcal{RSR}$, $\mathcal{DR}_k$, and $\mathcal{Rev}_k$ be the class of RSRLs, the class of k-DRLs for each $k \geq 1$, and the class of k-reversible languages [2] for each $k \geq 0$, respectively. From Definitions 9 and 10, we can show that for each $k \geq 1$, the following relationships hold: $\mathcal{RSR} \subset \mathcal{DR}_k \subset \mathcal{Rev}_k$. Therefore, these classes are identifiable in the limit from positive data. Furthermore, we can prove the following lemma.

Lemma 6. *All of the classes $\mathcal{RSR}$, $\mathcal{DR}_k$ for any $k \geq 1$, and $\mathcal{Rev}_k$ for any $k \geq 0$ are closed under the inverse coding morphism.*

Proof. We shall show that $\mathcal{RSR}$ is closed under the inverse coding morphism.

For any $L \in \mathcal{RSR}$, there exists an RSDA $M = (Q, \Sigma, \delta, q_0, F)$ such that $L(M) = L$. For any code $X \subseteq \Sigma^*$ that can factorize L, it holds that $L \subseteq X^*$. Let Σ' be an alphabet such that $X = \varphi(\Sigma')$ for some coding morphism $\varphi : \Sigma'^* \to \Sigma^*$. Then, it holds that $\varphi^{-1}(L) \subseteq \varphi^{-1}(X^*) = (\varphi^{-1}(X))^* = \Sigma'^*$. Therefore, there exists a minimal DFA $M' = (Q', \Sigma', \delta', q_0', F')$ such that $L(M') = \varphi^{-1}(L(M))$. Note that, for any $w \in \Sigma'^*$, it holds that $w \in L(M')$ iff $\varphi(w) \in L(M)$.

Suppose for the sake of contradiction that M' is not an RSDA. Then, for some $a \in \Sigma'$, M' has a pair of transition functions $\delta'(p_1, a) = q_1$ and $\delta'(p_2, a) = q_2$ such that $p_1 \neq p_2$ or $q_1 \neq q_2$. Since M' is minimal, it holds that $L(p_1) \neq L(p_2)$ or $L(q_1) \neq L(q_2)$. Let $u_1, u_2 \in \Sigma'^*$ be strings such that $\delta'(q_0', u_1) = p_1$ and $\delta'(q_0', u_2) = p_2$. And let $v_1, v_2 \in \Sigma'^*$ be strings such that $\delta'(q_1, v_1), \delta'(q_2, v_2) \in F'$. Then, it holds that $u_1 a v_1, u_2 a v_2 \in L(M')$. Therefore, in the RSDA M, it holds that $\varphi(u_1 a v_1), \varphi(u_2 a v_2) \in L(M)$. Then, there exist $r_1, r_2 \in Q$ such that $\delta(q_0, \varphi(u_1)) = r_1$ and $\delta(q_0, \varphi(u_2)) = r_2$. Furthermore, there exist $s_1, s_2 \in Q$ such that $\delta(r_1, \varphi(a)) = s_1$ and $\delta(r_2, \varphi(a)) = s_2$. Since $\varphi(a) \in X \subseteq \Sigma^+$ and M is an RSDA, it should hold that $r_1 = r_2$ and $s_1 = s_2$. Therefore, $\delta(q_0, \varphi(u_1)) = \delta(q_0, \varphi(u_2)) = r_1$ and $\delta(q_0, \varphi(u_1 a)) = \delta(q_0, \varphi(u_2 a)) = s_1$.

In the case where $p_1 \neq p_2$, by symmetry, we may assume that for some $z \in \Sigma'^*$, $z \in L(p_1)$ and $z \notin L(p_2)$. Then, it holds that $u_1 z \in L(M')$ and $u_2 z \notin L(M')$. Therefore, it holds that $\varphi(u_1 z) \in L(M)$ and $\varphi(u_2 z) \notin L(M)$. Since $\varphi(u_1 z) \in L(M)$ and $\delta(q_0, \varphi(u_1)) = \delta(q_0, \varphi(u_2))$, it holds that $\varphi(u_2 z) \in L(M)$. This is a contradiction.

In the case where $q_1 \neq q_2$, by symmetry, we may assume that for some $z \in \Sigma'^*$, $z \in L(q_1)$ and $z \notin L(q_2)$. Then, it holds that $u_1 a z \in L(M')$ and $u_2 a z \notin L(M')$. Therefore, it holds that $\varphi(u_1 a z) \in L(M)$ and $\varphi(u_2 a z) \notin L(M)$. Since $\varphi(u_1 a z) \in L(M)$ and $\delta(q_0, \varphi(u_1 a)) = \delta(q_0, \varphi(u_2 a))$, it holds that $\varphi(u_2 a z) \in L(M)$. This is a contradiction.

Therefore, M' is an RSDA. Thus, $\mathcal{RSR}$ is closed under the inverse coding morphism.

In a similar way to this, we can prove that all the classes $\mathcal{DR}_k$ for any $k \geq 1$ and $\mathcal{Rev}_k$ for any $k \geq 0$ are closed under the inverse coding morphism. □

Thus, all of the classes $\mathcal{RSR}$, $\mathcal{DR}_k$ for any $k \geq 1$, and $\mathcal{Rev}_k$ for any $k \geq 0$ satisfy Condition 1 from Lemma 6.

We can show that the class $C(\mathcal{RSR}, \mathcal{SP})$ of languages coincides with the class of strictly regular languages [10], where $\mathcal{SP}$ is the class of strict prefix codes. Also, since $\mathcal{RSR}$ coincides with the class of Szilard languages of linear grammars [7], the function CONSTRUCT(r'_{i-1}, w'_i) in $\mathcal{A}_{\mathcal{RSR}}$ can be written as almost the same procedure CONSTRUCT(Δ_i) in [10], p.166 except Σ'_i is used instead of T_i. When $\mathcal{A}_{\mathcal{RSR}}$ receives $w'_1, w'_2, \ldots, w'_i$ as input, the total time for updating conjectures of $\mathcal{A}_{\mathcal{RSR}}$ is bounded by $O(\sum_{j=1}^{i} |w'_j|)$. Furthermore, the number of implicit errors of prediction made by $\mathcal{A}_{\mathcal{RSR}}$ is bounded by $O(|\Sigma'|)$. In a similar way to this analysis, we can show that the total time for updating conjectures of $\mathcal{A}_{\mathcal{DR}_k}$ for each $k \geq 1$ is bounded by $O(\sum_{j=1}^{i} |w'_j|)$ and the number of implicit errors of prediction made by $\mathcal{A}_{\mathcal{DR}_k}$ is bounded by $O(|\Sigma'|^{k+1})$.

In the class $\mathcal{SP}$ of strict prefix codes over Σ, for any $S \subseteq \Sigma^*$, there uniquely exists the coarsest code in $\mathcal{SP}$ that can factorize S from Lemma 2. And then, the function UPDATE(X_{i-1}, w_i) in $\mathcal{A}_{\mathcal{SP}}$ is the same as the procedure UPDATE(T_{i-1}, w_i) in [10], p.164. In a similar way to [10], we can prove that this function outputs the coarsest code that can factorize $\{w_1, w_2, \ldots, w_i\}$. Therefore, the class $\mathcal{SP}$ satisfies Condition 2. Similarly, we can show that the class $\mathcal{SS}$ of strict suffix codes also satisfies Condition 2. When $\mathcal{A}_{\mathcal{SP}}$ (respectively, $\mathcal{A}_{\mathcal{SS}}$) receives $w_1, w_2, \ldots, w_i$ as input, the time used by $\mathcal{A}_{\mathcal{SP}}$ ($\mathcal{A}_{\mathcal{SS}}$, resp.) for updating conjectures is bounded by $O(|\Sigma| l^2)$, where $l = \text{Max}\{|w_1|, |w_2|, \ldots, |w_i|\}$. The number of implicit errors of prediction made by $\mathcal{A}_{\mathcal{SP}}$ ($\mathcal{A}_{\mathcal{SS}}$, resp.) is bounded by $O(|\Sigma| l)$.

Summarizing the above results, we have the next theorem.

Theorem 2. *The class $C(\mathcal{RSR}, \mathcal{SS})$ of languages, which is incomparable to the class $C(\mathcal{RSR}, \mathcal{SP})$, is polynomial time identifiable in the limit from positive data. For each $k \geq 1$, the class $C(\mathcal{DR}_k, \mathcal{SP})$ ($C(\mathcal{DR}_k, \mathcal{SS})$, respectively) of languages is polynomial time identifiable in the limit from positive data when we regard k to be a constant.*

6   Conclusions

We have been concerned with a *unified* algorithm for extending classes of languages identifiable in the limit from positive data. When the extended class $\mathcal{C}(\mathcal{L}, \mathcal{X})$ of languages satisfies Conditions 1 and 2, $\mathcal{C}(\mathcal{L}, \mathcal{X})$ is identifiable in the limit from positive data. Then, we have presented a *unified* identification algorithm $\mathcal{A}_{\mathcal{C}(\mathcal{L}, \mathcal{X})}$ for the class $\mathcal{C}(\mathcal{L}, \mathcal{X})$ of languages in question.

References

1. Angluin, D., *Inductive inference of formal languages from positive data*, Inform. and Control **45** (1980), 117-135.
2. Angluin, D., *Inference of reversible languages*, J. ACM **29** (1982), 741-765.
3. Berstel, J. and D. Perrin, "Theory of Codes", Academic Press, Inc., 1985.
4. Gold, E. M., *Language identification in the limit*, Inform. and Control **10** (1967), 447-474.
5. Harrison, M. A., "Introduction to Formal Language Theory", Addison-Wesley, Reading, Massachusetts, 1972.
6. Kobayashi, S. and T. Yokomori, *Identifiability of subspaces and homomorphic images of zero-reversible languages*, ALT'97, LNAI **1316** (1997), 48-61.
7. Mäkinen, E., *The grammatical inference problem for the Szilard languages of linear grammars*, Inform. Process. Lett. **36** (1990), 203-206.
8. Pitt, L., *Inductive inference, DFAs, and computational complexity*, Proc. 2nd Workshop on Analogical and Inductive Inference, LNAI **397** (1989), 18-44.
9. Tanida, N. and T. Yokomori, *Polynomial-time identification of strictly regular languages in the limit*, IEICE Trans. on Inform. and Systems **E75-D** (1992), 125-132.
10. Yokomori, T., *On polynomial-time learnability in the limit of strictly deterministic automata*, Machine Learning **19** (1995), 153-179.

Protein Motif Prediction by Grammatical Inference*

Piedachu Peris, Damián López, Marcelino Campos, and José M. Sempere

Departamento de Sistemas Informáticos y Computación.
Universidad Politécnica de Valencia.
Camino de Vera s/n
46071 Valencia (SPAIN)
{pperis, dlopez, mcampos, jsempere}@dsic.upv.es

Abstract. The rapid growth of protein sequence databases is exceeding the capacity of biochemically and structurally characterizing new proteins. Therefore, it is very important the development of tools to locate, within protein sequences, those subsequences with an associated function or specific feature. In our work, we propose a method to predict one of those functional motifs (coiled coil), related with protein interaction. Our approach uses even linear languages inference to obtain a transductor which will be used to label unknown sequences. The experiments carried out show that our method outperforms the results of previous approaches.

Keywords: Grammatical inference, bioinformatics, protein motif location.

1 Introduction

Processing of biological data is a key task in many applied fields. Recently, an explosion of papers apply Pattern Recognition techniques to bioinformatics tasks [1,2]. Formal Language Theory and Grammatical Inference (GI) are also playing an important role and it is expected that they could lead to good applied results [3,4]. Some works use GI techniques in order to address, among other tasks: secondary structure identification [5], protein motifs detection [6,7,8], optimal consensus sequence discovery [9,10] or gene prediction [11].

The selection of proteins with certain characteristics from genomic sequences is a central goal of computational biology. One aspect of this problem is to detect certain subsequences, known as domains or motifs, with some interesting functional features.

Coiled coil domains are of interest for molecular biologists studying a variety of processes such as protein transportation and interaction. It has been shown that coiled coil motif is implied in membrane fusion and the infection of cells by

---

* Work supported by the CICYT TIC2000-1153 and the Generalitat Valenciana GV06/068.

Y. Sakakibara et al. (Eds.): ICGI 2006, LNAI 4201, pp. 175–187, 2006.

viruses or parasites [12][13]. Predictions based on analysis of primary sequences suggest that approximately 2-3% of all protein residues form coiled coils [14].

The coiled coil motif consist of two α-helices wrapping around each other forming a supercoil. The sequences of coiled coils are made of seven-residue (amino acids) repeats which forms a pattern usually denoted $(abcdefg)_n$ where the position of each residue is noted from a to g. Within this pattern, called also heptad, generally an hydrophobic core occurs every four and then three residues apart, that is, at positions a and d. The interaction between two α-helices in a coiled coil involves these hydrophobic residues. The result is a highly versatile protein interaction mechanism (see Figure 1). Due to its simplicity and regularity, the coiled coil is one of the most extensively studied protein motifs.

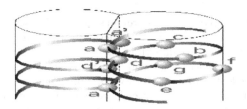

Fig. 1. A schematic coiled coil representation is shown. The relative position of amino acids in a characteristic coiled coil heptad repeat is marked with bullets. Residues at the a and d positions are predominantly hydrophobic. Due to the α-helical structure, residues at the a and d position are spatially close one each other. Both features (hydrophobicity and spatial arrangement), provide a versatile protein interaction mechanism.

Several programs for predicting coiled coil domains have been proposed. The most relevant to large-scale annotations are *coils* [15] (probably the most widely used), *paircoil* [16] and *multicoil* [14]. All these programs are based on the probability of appearance of every amino acid in each position of the characteristic heptad, extracted from known coiled coil motifs. Multicoil is the most specialized one, and aims to detect double or triple coiled coil domains. All of them are based on a *Position Specific Scoring Matrix* (PSSM) (also known as *Position Weighted Matrix*) approach [17]. This general scheme considers the probabilities of appearance of each possible residue in each position of the motif. These probabilities are obtained from sequences with confirmed motifs or considering multiple sequence alignments of functionally related sequences. This approach has also been widely used in gene-finding tasks.

The work by Lupas et al. [15] takes into account that even very short proteins have stable coiled coils containing four or five heptads, and analyzes the test sequences using a sliding window of 28 amino acids. A score for each amino acid in the sequence of the protein is obtained using the probabilities of the PSSM. Then, the score distributions for general globular proteins and coiled coil sequences are approximated with Gaussian curves used to obtain, for each amino acid of the protein, a probability of belonging to a coiled coil motif.

Although this approach is widely known by the biological community, it is known that the method leads to a significant number of *false positives*, some of them due to the continuous appearance of some frequent amino acids in coiled coil regions (for instance, $(Lys - Lys - Lys)_n$ scores highly though it is not a coiled coil). To solve this problem, Berger et al. [16] follow the same PSSM approach but taking into account the pairwise amino acid correlations in known coiled coils. The correlations and the size of the window used were empirically selected, and,

- the correlations between the pairs of amino acids placed in positions $(i, i + 1)$ and $(i, i + 4)$ were considered.
- the size of the sliding window was set to 30.

The authors claim that the approach is useful to discard false positives detected by the Lupas' approach. They carry out a wide experimentation to show the behaviour and present several examples of false positives detected.

Nevertheless, the problem of locating general coiled coil motifs still remains open. Several authors have noted several important coiled-proteins that are not detected when the previous methods are used (among others, fusion-membrane proteins of the human and simian inmunodeficiency virus or Ebola virus [18]). Thus, several other works propose solutions for more specific instances of the problem [19][18].

In our work, we use a grammatical approach to locate coiled coil motifs within protein sequences. Previous related works address the task of detecting protein structures: α-helix structures in protein sequences [20] or even the coiled coil motif [7,8].

We address the problem of predicting the coiled coil motifs of a given protein. Our approach considers the original sequence and an annotated reduced version which distinguish between coiled coil and non-coiled coil subsequences. This data is combined into an even linear structure and used to infer *Even Linear Languages* (ELL). The inferred languages are then used to build a transductor suitable to translate, that is, to distinguish coiled and non-coiled regions in problem sequences. The results of the experimentation carried out are compared with other existing approaches. Our work is organized as follows: Section 2 summarizes some definitions and the notation used; Section 3 explains our approach to the problem; Section 4 shows the experimental results and the indexes used to compare our results with previous ones; Finally, some conclusions and future lines of research end the paper.

2   Notation and Definitions

Let Σ be an alphabet and Σ^* the set of words over the alphabet. For any word $x \in \Sigma^*$ let x_i denote the i-th symbol of the sequence, let $|x|$ denote the length of the word and let x^r denote the reverse of x. Let also λ denote the empty word. A grammar is denoted by $G = (N, \Sigma, P, S)$ where N and Σ are the auxiliar and terminal alphabets, P is the set of productions and $S \in N$ is the initial symbol or axiom. The language generated by G is denoted by $L(G)$.

An *Even Linear Grammar (ELG)* is a context-free grammar [21] where the productions are of the forms:

$A \rightarrow xBy$ where $A, B \in N$, $x, y \in \Sigma^*$ and $|x| = |y|$
$A \rightarrow x$ where $A \in N$, $x \in \Sigma^*$

The class of Even linear Languages (ELL) is a subclass of the context free languages and includes properly the class of regular languages. Given an ELG, it is possible to obtain an equivalent one where the productions are of the form.

$A \rightarrow aBb$ where $A, B \in N$, $a, b \in \Sigma$
$A \rightarrow a$ where $A \in N$, $a \in \Sigma \cup \{\lambda\}$

The learning of ELL can be reduced to the inference of regular languages [22]. The general algorithm consists in transforming the training strings through a function $\sigma : \Sigma^* \rightarrow [\Sigma \times \Sigma]^* \cup [\Sigma]^*$ defined as follows:

$\sigma(\lambda) = \lambda$
$\sigma(a) = [a]$ where $a \in \Sigma$
$\sigma(axb) = [ab]\sigma(x)$ where $a, b \in \Sigma$ and $x \in \Sigma^*$

Once applied the function σ, it is possible to use any regular language inference algorithm to learn a language over the alphabet $[\Sigma \times \Sigma]^* \cup [\Sigma]^*$ and then transform the productions of the obtained regular grammar to undo the transformation σ as follows:

$\forall A \rightarrow [ab]B \in P$ add the production $A \rightarrow aBb$ to the ELG
$\forall A \rightarrow [a] \in P$ add the production $A \rightarrow a$ to the ELG
$\forall A \rightarrow \lambda \in P$ add all these productions to the ELG

Obviously, whenever the GI algorithm identifies a subclass of regular languages, then a subclass of ELL is obtained.

A *finite state transducer* is defined by a system $\tau = (Q, \Sigma, \Delta, q_0, Q_F, E)$ where: Q is a set of states, Σ and Δ are respectively the input and output alphabets, q_0 is the initial state, $Q_F \subseteq Q$ is the set of final states and $E \subseteq (Q \times \Sigma^* \times \Delta^* \times Q)$ is the set of transitions of the transducer. A successful path in a transducer is a sequence of transitions $(q_0, x_1, y_1, q_1), (q_1, x_2, y_2, q_2), \ldots, (q_{n-1}, x_n, y_n, q_n)$ where $q_n \in Q_F$ and for $1 \leq i \leq n$: $q_i \in Q$, $x_i \in \Sigma^*$ and $y_i \in \Delta^*$. Note that a path can be denoted as $(q_0, x_1 x_2 \ldots x_n, y_1 y_2 \ldots y_n, q_n)$ whenever the sequence of states are not of particular concern. A transduction is defined as a function $t : \Sigma^* \rightarrow \Delta^*$ where $t(x) = y$ if and only if there exist a successful path (q_0, x, y, q_n). We refer the interested reader to [23].

3   Grammatical Inference Approach to Coiled Coil Prediction

Several methods have been proposed to solve the coiled coil motif location task. The most widely known are the PSSM-based methods by Lupas and Berger

[15,16], but also Hidden Markov Models have been used [24] as well as Neural Networks approaches [25]. This motif occurs always on an underlying α-helix protein structure. It is important to note, on the one hand, that the detection of α-helix structure has been successfully addressed by GI methods [20], and in the other hand, the biological regularity of the coiled coil pattern (that is, the characteristic repeated heptad). This two facts support our GI approach to tackle this task.

In our work we address the protein motif location problem as a transduction problem. In such a way that, given an amino acid sequence, we propose a method to obtain a sequence with the same length which distinguishes between those amino acids within a motif and those that are not. The inference of transducers has been widely studied by the GI community, in our work, we take into account the special features of our problem to propose a method based on inference of ELL. Our approach firstly transforms the available data to obtain a training set with even linear structure. This set was used to infer an ELL. The transducer is obtained using the structure of the ELG inferred. To do so, note that, given a ELG $G = (N, \Sigma, P, S)$ that does not contain productions of the form $A \rightarrow a$, $a \in \Sigma$, it is possible to obtain a transducer $\tau = (N, \Sigma, \Sigma, S, Q_F, E)$ where:

$$Q_F = \{A \in N \ : \ (A \rightarrow \lambda) \in P\}$$
$$E = \{(A, a, b, B) \ : \ (A \rightarrow aBb) \in P\}$$

Example 1 shows how this transformation work.

Example 1 *Given the ELG $G = (N, \Sigma, P, S)$ with the productions:*

$$S \rightarrow aS0 \mid bB1$$
$$A \rightarrow aA1 \mid bS0$$
$$B \rightarrow aA1 \mid bB1 \mid \lambda$$

then, the transducer $\tau = (N, \Sigma, \Sigma, S, \{B\}, E)$ is obtained where:

$$E = \left\{ \begin{array}{l} (S, a, 0, S), \ (S, b, 1, B), \ (A, a, 1, A), \\ (A, b, 0, S), \ (B, a, 1, A), \ (B, b, 1, B) \end{array} \right\}$$

The resulting transducer is shown in Figure 2.

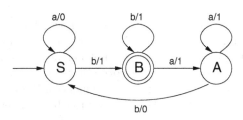

Fig. 2. A three states transducer example. A label x/y denotes that the transition symbol is x with output y. For instance, the transduction of *baabaab* is 1110001

□

As we stated before, the learning problem for ELL can be reduced to the problem of learning regular languages. In our work, in order to learn the ELL, we use an algorithm to infer *k-testable in the strict sense* (*k*-TSS) languages [26,27,5]. The class of *k*-TSS languages is contained into the regular languages class and it is characterized by the set of segments of length *k* that appear in the words of the language. The characteristic coiled coil heptad lead us to consider this algorithm as a first suitable candidate.

Our approach considered a set of protein sequences P with known coiled coil motifs and another set L of strings over $\Delta = \{c, n\}$ with, a labeled sequence l_x for each sequence x in P. The labeled sequence was obtained in such a way that distinguish between the amino acids corresponding to coiled and non-coiled regions. That is, given the string $x = x_1 x_2 \ldots x_n \in P$ and its corresponding labeled string $l_x = l_1 l_2 \ldots l_n \in L$, $l_i = c$ whenever x_i correspond to a coiled coil motif, otherwise $l_i = n$.

These sets were combined to obtain another set M with the strings $x l_x^r$. Note that the strings in this set have an even linear structure and even length. The set M was used to obtain a transducer by ELL inference. The general method is summarized in Algorithm 3.1.

Algorithm 3.1. Coiled coil Grammatical Inference approach.

Input:
  - A set P of amino acid sequences with known coiled coil motifs.
  - A set L of motif labeled sequences. Each string x in P has its corresponding string l_x in L.

Output:
  - A transducer to locate coiled coil motifs.

Method:
  - Combine the sets P and L to obtain the training set M with strings $x l_x^r$
  - Apply to the strings in M the transformation function σ
  - Apply a GI algorithm for (a subclass of) regular languages
  - Undo the transformation σ to obtain the ELG from the regular language
  - Return the transducer obtained from the ELG

EndMethod.

The returned transducer can be used to analyze problem sequences to obtain the corresponding transduction. Note that the transducer may be non-deterministic and the test sequences may not belong to the language accepted by the transducer. Therefore, an error-correcting parser (for instance Viterbi's algorithm) is necessary to analyze the test sequences. We used a standard configuration of Viterbi's algorithm when a GI approach is applied to pattern recognition tasks (i.e. [8]). We considered the number of times each transition of the transducer is used to probabilize it. The error-correcting analysis considered only low probability substitution errors for edit operations.

4   Experimental Results

In order to test our approach we considered two different datasets: The first one contains sequences extracted from SwissProt Database (release 40, April 2003) [28]. All the sequences selected contain a non-potential coiled coil annotation. Potential annotations are those based mainly on homology results. Potential motifs were not included in the database because the function of potential domains has not been yet assured. The resulting 350 sequences database has been previously used by [7,8]. The second coiled coil dataset was build by Delorenzi and Speed [24]. This dataset considered sequences of *Protein Data Bank* [29]. This database contains structural information of the tertiary structure of the proteins and it is more suitable to obtain confident information. From the information stored in the database, two sets were built: one with those coiled coil sequences with experimental confirmation (397 sequences), and another with sequences from which coiled coils motifs were eliminated (1525 sequences).

Protein sequences can be considered as strings in an 22 symbols alphabet (20 amino acids plus the glutamic and aspartic acids[1]). In order to reduce the alphabet size without loss of information, two different codifications were considered. The first one is due to Dayhoff and is based on some properties of the amino acids. This codification has been previously used in some GI papers [20,7,8]. Second codification used considers only two symbols which distinguish between hydrophobic and polar amino acids. This codification was used because this feature is key in the coiled coil motif. Figure shows the correspondence of each amino acid for both codifications.

amino acid	P/H	Dayhoff
C	p	a
R, H, K,	p	d
D, E	p	c
N, Q	p	c
B, Z	p	g
Y	p	f
G	p	b
S, T	p	b
A, P	h	b
F, W	h	f
L, V, M, I	h	e

Fig. 3. Amino acid codifications

Several measures are suitable to evaluate the results. Some of them are reviewed in [30] under a scope of gene-finding problems. Nevertheless, they are

---

[1] Some sequences also contain the symbol X. This happens whenever it is not clear which amino acids occupy a certain position. In this work, we did not consider such sequences (just one sequences in the first dataset and two sequences in the second).

suitable to be applied to motif location tasks. Among all the measures proposed, *Sensitivity* and *Specificity* are probably the most used. Sensitivity (Sn) measures the probability of predict those symbols inside a motif. Specificity (Sp) measures the probability of predicted segments to be actually motifs.

These measures are computed using the following partial results:

True Positives (TP): symbols of the sequence inside a motif that are correctly annotated.

True Negatives (TN): symbols of the sequence outside a motif that are correctly annotated.

False Positives (FP): symbols of the sequence outside a motif that are annotated as they were inside one.

False Negatives (FN): symbols of the sequence inside a motif that are not correctly annotated.

Using these measures, both Sn and Sp can be computed as follows:

$$Sn = \frac{TP}{TP + FN} \qquad Sp = \frac{TP}{TP + FP}$$

Note that neither Sn nor Sp alone constitute a good measure. The *Correlation Coefficient* (CC) is defined in order to use a single value that summarizes both results. It can be computed as follows:

$$CC = \frac{(TP \cdot TN) - (FN \cdot FP)}{\sqrt{(TP + FN) \cdot (TN + FP) \cdot (TP + FP) \cdot (TN + FN)}}$$

Although CC has some statistical properties [30] it has also an undesirable drawback. It is not defined when any factor of the root is zero. Some measures have been defined to overcome this inconvenient, we will use the *Approximate Correlation* (AC) which is defined as follows:

$$AC = \left\{ \frac{1}{4} \left[\frac{TP}{TP + FN} + \frac{TP}{TP + FP} + \frac{TN}{TN + FP} + \frac{TN}{TN + FN} \right] - 0.5 \right\} \cdot 2$$

In order to evaluate the results, it has to be noted that, for some samples, it was not possible to calculate Sp and CC, and therefore, these samples were not taken into account. The Approximate Correlation AC considers all samples, including those for which it was not possible to calculate CC or Sp. This can explain why in some cases the difference between AC and CC is relevant. This fact makes AC the most reliable measure in order to evaluate the global performance of our approach.

In order to test our approach, both datasets were processed using the same scheme. We considered several values of the GI algorithm k parameter, and performed a leaving-one-out experiment (all the sequences but one were used to infer the transducer and the remaining one to test the performance. This process is iterated to consider the whole dataset).

Our results are also compared with the output of coils and paircoil methods. Note that these methods are based on the physic-chemical properties of the coiled coil motif, therefore, no training is needed. Public versions of these programs are available at [31] and [32] respectively. Both approaches use a default probability threshold of 0.5. This threshold has to be reached to consider an amino acid as belonging to a coiled coil motif. Note that to lower this threshold implies an increasing of the sensibility and a decreasing of the specificity levels. In the same way, to higher the default parameter implies an increasing of the sensibility but a decreasing of the sensibility levels. We are interested in the general behaviour, therefore, we will consider the default threshold value.

The two symbols codification did not obtain significant results, thus, we will show only the best configuration performance for this codification. The results obtained by the subset of SwissProt database are shown in Table 1.

Table 1. Experimental results when the coiled subset of SwissProt was used. Note the improvement of the results obtained by our method. Although bigger k parameter values lead to higher sensitivity, best results are obtained by using $k = 8$.

Method		Sn	Sp	CC	AC
coils		0.4568	0.8022	0.4897	0.4155
paircoil		0.4996	0.8209	0.5676	0.4806
IGcoils (Dayhoff coding)	$k = 2$	0.7865	0.7226	0.6355	0.5480
	$k = 3$	0.8287	0.7610	0.6799	0.6365
	$k = 4$	0.8095	0.8491	0.7547	0.7164
	$k = 5$	0.7688	0.9563	0.8741	0.7728
	$k = 6$	0.8527	0.9804	0.9291	0.8638
	$k = 7$	0.9180	0.9701	0.9420	0.9085
	$k = 8$	0.9506	0.9673	0.9529	0.9338
	$k = 9$	0.9696	0.9614	0.9498	0.9428
	$k = 10$	0.9710	0.9624	0.9479	0.9457
IGcoils (P/H coding)	$k = 8$	0.6526	0.7887	0.6113	0.5174

The experimental results when the Delorenzi database was used are shown in Table 2. Note that in this experiment, the lower values of the inference parameter, the worse values of the sensitivity and specificity. Nevertheless, considering the correlation coefficient (or the approximate correlation as well), our approach improves the results.

One of the most important drawbacks of the Lupas' method is the number of false positives that it produces. Berger et al. considered this fact as their main motivation to develop their approach. In order to compare the performance of our method when non-coiled sequences are to be tested, we carried out the following experiment: two transducers were inferred, each one considering all the sequences of the two different datasets (i.e. the coiled coil SwissProt subset and the Delorenzi dataset). The sequences of the non-coiled dataset where

Table 2. Experimental results when the coiled Delorenzi's database was used. Best results were obtained for $k = 7$ and $k = 8$. This result is consistent with the heptad-based biological characterization of the motif.

Method		Sn	Sp	CC	AC
coils		0.6688	0.8552	0.6372	0.6222
paircoil		0.6511	0.8489	0.6693	0.5972
IGcoils (Dayhoff coding)	$k = 2$	0.6269	0.7420	0.6501	0.5058
	$k = 3$	0.6353	0.7616	0.6730	0.5342
	$k = 4$	0.6275	0.7778	0.6793	0.5654
	$k = 5$	0.5709	0.8249	0.6842	0.5729
	$k = 6$	0.5262	0.8730	0.7395	0.5692
	$k = 7$	0.5465	0.9212	0.8128	0.5952
	$k = 8$	0.6058	0.9002	0.8036	0.6356
IGcoils (P/H coding)	$k = 8$	0.4012	0.8001	0.6020	0.3883

Table 3. Experimental results when the non-coiled dataset was processed. Upper two rows show the percentage of symbols predicted inside a coiled coil motif (error rate). Lower rows show the number of sequences in the non-coiled dataset with any erroneous prediction. All this results were obtained with the Dayhoff coding.

		IGcoils			Coils	Paircoil
		$k = 6$	$k = 7$	$k = 8$		
% error rate	SwissProt dataset	0.0118	0.0175	0.0254	0.0058	0.0023
	Delorenzi dataset	0.0036	0.0030	0.0016		
# of erroneous sequences	SwissProt dataset	104	123	140	57	12
	Delorenzi dataset	26	18	12		

then independently tested considering this two transducers, and two measures were work out: the error percentage and the number of sequences with a motif predicted. Note that these sequences were processed to delete all the coiled coil motifs, therefore, all the coiled coil predictions are erroneous. The results obtained with the two symbols codification were not significant, therefore, we only show the results (summarized in table 3) obtained when the Dayhoff coding was used.

The results obtained by transducers inferred with the SwissProt dataset are not comparable to previous methods. Nevertheless, those transducers inferred using the Delorenzi dataset obtained better results than Lupas' and Berger's methods. It could be argued that some homology between the Delorenzi's coiled coil and non-coiled datasets somewhat biases the results, but this can be refused by noting that the datasets were built considering low homology between the sequences and that there are many more sequences in the non-coiled dataset than in the coiled one.

5   Conclusions and Future Work

This work addresses the task of protein motif prediction by applying GI techniques. Previous methods are based on the physical-chemical characterization of the motif. This allow to use a Position Weighted Matrices approach to predict new motifs. The results obtained lead us to conjecture that it is not necessary to biologically characterize a new motif in order to develop prediction tools. It is also to note that these results are feasible to be extended to other bioinformatic tasks.

In all cases, the results obtained with the Dayhoff coding were much better than those obtained with the two symbols codification. Therefore, in what follows we will refer only to Dayhoff codification.

The results obtained using the first corpus (coiled sequences from SwissProt) show that our method outperforms previous approaches. Nevertheless this results are somewhat misleading because the transducers inferred lead to a high number of false positives (both error rate and number of sequences with erroneous predictions) when non-coiled sequences are tested.

When the Delorenzi's dataset was considered, our approach gave better results to those obtained by previous methods. This is mainly due to an increase of the specificity levels. This fact is specially motivating in order to apply new prediction methods, because it is very important to reduce the number of false positives. The experiments involving non-coiled sequences confirmed the good performance of our approach, which obtains lower error rate with the same number of erroneous sequences.

Future lines of work should consider, the consideration of other inference algorithms. Specially interesting are the learning of synchronized and non-synchronized ELL [33]. Bigger datasets (modeling coiled coil motif or other biologically interesting motifs) should also be considered. The comparison between GI and NN or HMM approaches to protein motif location is left also as future work.

References

1. Editorial. The fundamental role of pattern recognition for gene-expresion/micro-array data in bioinformatics. *Pattern Recognition*, 38:2226–2228, 2005.
2. A.W-C. Liew, H. Yan, and M. Yang. Pattern recognition techniques for the emerging field of bioinformatics: A review. *Pattern Recognition*, 38:2055–2073, 2005.
3. D.B. Searls. The language of genes. *Nature*, 420:211–217, 2002.
4. Y. Sakakibara. Grammatical inference in bioinformatics. *IEEE Transactions on Pattern Analysis and Machine Intelligence*, 27(7):1051–1062, 2005.
5. T. Yokomori and S. Kobayashi. Learning local languages and their application to dna sequence analysis. *IEEE Transactions on Pattern Analysis and Machine Intelligence*, 20(10):1067–1079, 1998.
6. S. Arikawa, S. Kuhara, S. Miyano, A. Shinohara, and T. Shinohara. A learning algorithm for elementary formal systems and its experiments on identification of transmembrane domains. In *Proceedings of the 25th Hawaii Intl. Conf. on System Sciences*. IEEE, 1992. ISBN: 0-8186-2420-0.

7. D. Lopez, A. Cano, M. Vazquez de Parga, B. Calles, J.M. Sempere, T. Perez, J. Ruiz, and P. Garcia. Detection of functional motifs in biosequences: A grammatical inference approach. In *Proceedings of the 5th Annual Spanish Bioinformatics Conference*, pages 72–75. Univ. Politècnica de Catalunya, 2004. ISBN: 84-7653-863-4.

8. D. López, A. Cano, M. Vázquez de Parga, B. Calles, J. M. Sempere, T. Pérez, M. Campos, J. Ruiz, and P. García. Motif discovery by k-tss grammatical inference. In G. Paliouras C. de la Higuera, T. Oates and M. Van Zaanen, editors, *IJCAI-05 Workshop on Grammatical Inference Applications: Successes and Future Challenges*, 2005. Working Notes.

9. A. Brazma, I. Johansen, J. Vilo, and E. Ukkonen. Pattern discovery in biosequences. *LNAI*, 1433:257–270, 1998. 4th Intl. Colloquium, ICGI'98.

10. H. Arimura, A. Wataki, R. Fujino, and S. Arikawa. A fast algorithm for discovery optimal string patterns in large databases. *LNAI*, 1501:247–261, 1998. 9th Intl. Conference, ALT'98.

11. P. Peris, D. López, M. Campos, and J.M. Sempere. Gene-finding by grammatical inference. *(submitted manuscript)*.

12. J.J. Skehel and D.C. Wiley. Coiled coils in both intracellular vesicle and viral membrane fusion. *Cell*, 95:871–874, 1998.

13. D.C. Chan and P.S. Kim. Hiv entry and its inhibition. *Cell*, 93:681–684, 1998.

14. E. Wolf, P.S. Kim, and B. Berger. Multicoil: a program for predicting two- and three-stranded coiled coils. *Protein Science*, 6:1179–1189, 1997.

15. A. Lupas, M. Van Dyke, and J. Stock. Predicting coiled coild from protein sequences. *Science*, 252:1162–1164, 1991.

16. B. Berger, D.B. Wilson, E. Wolf, T. Tonchev, M. Milla, and P. S. Kim. Predicting coiled coils by use of pairwise residue correlation. *Proc. Natl. Acad. Sci.*, 92:8259–8263, 1995.

17. C. Mathé, M.F. Sagot, T. Schiex, and P. Rouzé. Current methods of gene prediction, their strengths and weakenesses. *Nucleic Acid Research*, 30(19):4103–4117, 2002.

18. M. Singh, B. Berger, and P.S. Kim. Learncoil-vmf: Computational evidence for coiled-coil-like motifs in many viral membrane fusion proteins. *J. Mol. Biol.*, 290:1031–1041, 1999.

19. M. Singh, B. Berger, P.S. Kim, J.M. Berger, and A.G. Cochran. Computational learning reveals coiled coil-like motifs in histidine kinase linker domains. *Proc. Natl. Acad. Sci.*, 95:2738–2743, 1998.

20. T. Yokomori, N. Ishida, and S. Kobayashi. Learning local languages and its application to protein α-chain identification. In *Proceedings of the Twenty-Seventh Annual Hawaii International Conference on System Sciences*, pages 113–122. IEEE, 1994.

21. J. Hopcroft and J. Ullman. *Introduction to Automata Theory, Languages and Computation*. Addison-Wesley Publishing Company, 1979.

22. J.M. Sempere and P. García. A characterization of even linear languages and its application to the learning problem. *LNAI*, 862:38–44, 1994.

23. J. Berstel. *Transductions and context-free languages*. Teubner Studienbücher, 1979.

24. M. Delorenzi and T. Speed. An hmm model for coiled-coil domains and a comparison with pssm-based predictions. *Bioinformatics*, 18(4):617–625, 2002.

25. M. Campos and D. López. Neural network approach to locate motifs in biosequences. 3773:214–221, 2005. 10th Iberoamerican Congress on Pattern Recognition, CIARP 2005.

26. T. Knuutila. *Advances in Structural and Syntactic Pattern Recognition: Proc. of the International Workshop*, chapter Inference of k-Testable Tree Languages, pages 109–120. World Scientific, 1992.

27. P. García.   Learning *k*-testable tree sets from positive data.   Technical Report DSIC/II/46/1993, Departamento de Sistemas Informáticos y Computación. Universidad Politécnica de Valencia, 1993.   Available on: `http://www.dsic.upv.es/users/tlcc/tlcc.html`.

28. Swiss-Prot groups at SIB and at EBI. Uniprot database (swissprot and trembl). http://www.expasy.ch/sprot/.

29. Protein data bank. http://www.rcsb.org/pdb/Welcome.do.

30. M. Burset and R. Guigó. Evaluation of gene structure prediction programs. *Genomics*, 34:353–367, 1996.

31. Source Code NCOILS, 1999. http://www.russell.embl.de/cgi-bin/coils-svr.pl.

32. PAIRCOIL   implementation   by   the   authors,   1995. http://theory.lcs.mit.edu/ bab/computing.

33. J.M. Sempere and P. García. Learning locally testable even linear languages form positive data. *LNAI*, 2484:225–236, 2002.

Grammatical Inference in Practice:
A Case Study in the Biomedical Domain

Sophia Katrenko and Pieter Adriaans

Human-Computer Studies Lab, University of Amsterdam
katrenko@science.uva.nl, pietera@science.uva.nl

Abstract. In this paper we discuss an approach to named entity recognition (NER) based on grammatical inference (GI). Previous GI approaches have aimed at constructing a grammar underlying a given text source. It has been noted that the rules produced by GI can also be interpreted semantically [16] where a non-terminal describes interchangeable elements which are the instances of the same concepts. Such an observation leads to the hypothesis that GI might be useful for finding concept instances in a text. Furthermore, it should also be possible to discover relations between concepts, or more precisely, the way such relations are expressed linguistically.

Throughout the paper, we propose a general framework for using GI for named entity recognition by discussing several possible approaches. In addition, we demonstrate that these methods successfully work on biomedical data using an existing GI tool.

1   Introduction

As any other domain, biomedicine can be characterized by a large amount of information presented by different means. These include collections of articles (such as Medline), databases of genes and other biomolecular data such as ontologies [2]. Considering the fact that such resources need to be updated often, their curation is a tedious task usually involving a human expert.

To facilitate this task, a solution is required that allows for semi-automatic knowledge acquisition. In this setting, an expert is presented only with the most relevant information to be preprocessed. Although there have been many approaches that focus on fully automatic knowledge acquisition via supervised machine learning, these methods require the availability of large collections of data already annotated by humans. Annotated resources are not always available for the domain in question, moreover it is often difficult to apply techniques used on a certain type of data to another domain. This poses the question, are there any alternatives that are based on unsupervised learning?

This paper describes a case study that aims at finding out how useful GI can be for semantic acquisition. At first sight grammatical inference appears to be a suitable candidate in the biomedical domain, for several reasons. Firstly, it has been shown that the output of GI is often semantically biased, specifically entities exemplifying the same semantic class are likely to be generated by the

Y. Sakakibara et al. (Eds.): ICGI 2006, LNAI 4201, pp. 188–200, 2006.

same non-terminal in the grammar. According to these assumptions, we expect proteins, disorders and any other biomedical entities to be clustered together. In addition GI can also be used in bootstrapping where new instances can be learned given some background knowledge.

In the biomedical domain, there are several tasks which may benefit from knowledge acquisition by grammatical inference. For instance, named entity recognition (e.g., identification of genes and proteins in a text), relation discovery (e.g., learning interactions among biomedical entities), and semi-automatic enrichment of existing ontologies and dictionaries. Unsupervised methods are known to provide relatively high precision but low recall. We aim to test how well GI may help during the process of constructing ontologies and semantic resources in a semi-automatic way, with a focus on precision.

The research questions of our study are as follows:

1. Does GI induce not only syntactic categories but semantic categories as well?
2. How granular will the acquired semantic information be? What factors affect the granularity?

This paper is organized as follows. We start with the discussion of relevant work and motivation for using grammatical inference to named entity recognition. We then describe our methodology and present some experiments.

2   Related Work

NER can also be considered as a concept instantiation or ontology population step. When building an ontology, there are several layers to be distinguished [5]. They are often referred to as meta-conceptual (defining top-level semantics), conceptual (reflecting concepts in a given domain) and instance layers. Hence, concept instantiation is a task of finding a set of all possible instances of a given concept. Named entities are usually discovered based on the contextual information in combination with some orthographic features.

The interdependency of syntax and semantics has been discussed by many researchers, which resulted in studies on how syntactic structure triggers semantic interpretation [6]. Syntactic information can be used for the relation discovery as well as for the named entity recognition. In the relation learning setting, many approaches rely on the predefined syntactic patterns, such as a triple $subj - verb - obj$. Here, a subject and an object refer to the arguments X and Y of a binary relation $rel(X, Y)$ expressed by a verb. Although such methods provide useful information, the desired relation can be expressed by other syntactic structures, which can be very much style dependent. For instance, the same relation can be expressed by $X - adjective - Y$ as in the phrase X-*dependent* Y. Clearly, when an expert or a user wishes to build a set of syntactic patterns to find all instances of a desired relation in a text, he needs to look up the entire text corpus. There is also no guarantee that the new unseen documents will necessarily contain the same patterns.

Having noticed that hand-written rules are accurate but fail to find all new instances in the unseen data, many researchers proposed using either methods which would combine different syntactic views (as in [12], [9]) or methods based on the frequent patterns in the syntactically analyzed data.

It has also been shown that the semantic roles are dependent on the syntactic functions. The correspondence of the dependency relations to the conceptual relations has been observed by [6], who made use of the dependency structures to perform semantic interpretation. They have explicitly defined the mappings from syntactic level onto conceptual level, such as *subject* → *agent*, *direct object* → *patient*, etc.

3   Motivation

In the machine learning practice, there are two major approaches to be distinguished. The first of them relies on the data sets annotated by humans (and hence, often referred to as a gold standard). Consequently, a machine learning method is trained on the annotated data and builds a model M.[1] This model can then be applied to the unseen data to measure how well M performs. The second approach aims at finding structure or relevant information in data without any information given a priori. Grammatical inference is usually placed among the unsupervised methods since its main goal is to induce a finite structural description corresponding to possibly infinite set of examples [1]. Although GI is naturally thought to be used for the learning a grammar of natural language, its applicability is much wider.

Over the past decades, there have been many approaches to grammar induction. Most of them have made use of an alignment of sentences, albeit done in different ways. *Emile* has been proposed in the early 90s. *Adios*[16] represents one of the most recent developments in the field. To our knowledge, not all of the developments in the field have been compared against each other. Two of the approaches, *Emile* and *ABL*, have been tested on the same corpora [19].

In most cases, grammar induction tools output terminals and non-terminals following the formal definition of a language. We argue that GI tools can be used for the named entity recognition (or more widely, concept instantiation) as well as for relation discovery. First of all, terminals can be interpreted as named entities. As grammar induction outputs clusters whose elements are interchangeable in a certain context, it leads to the assumption that such clusters may present domain-dependent information. Apart from analyzing terminals, it is also possible to evaluate production rules. Such rules are not restricted to the certain length (unless one defines it explicitly), moreover, they offer a certain amount of generality. This happens because of the initial goal behind the grammatical inference - it accounts for the grammar of a given language by suggesting the grammatical rules which, in turn, can be used for the generation of novel sentences.

One of the advantages of using GI for NER is an interpretability of the production rules. Contrary to many machine learning methods making use of the

---

[1] This holds for a model-driven setting. Another option is a data-driven approach.

fixed-size context, rules based on GI might provide some insights on what contexts are crucial for concept instantiation. These rules can be contrasted to the widely used Hearst patterns [7] which are hand-written and always rely on the expertise of a user. We aim at discovering such patterns in an unsupervised way.

Yet another advantage of GI lies in the possibility to find recursive rules. Production rules quite often include more than one concept instance, which makes it possible to use the rules in a recursive way. First, all rules involving a single concept instance are applied. After no such rule can be applied, the rules consisting of several concept instances are to be used. This step is especially important for the NER tasks, where each entity can have a complex structure spanning over several words.

The grammar inference has already been used for different tasks, including information extraction [4] and user navigation on the Web [8]. The main argument for applying GI to such tasks is its ability to model sequences. In particular, for the information extraction task, it has been shown that grammatical inference may increase precision of the extraction.

4   Methodology

One of the biggest challenges in the unsupervised learning is evaluation [14]. It has to be done either by expert, or by using existing resources (such as semantic networks or ontologies). An alternative way would be to use already labeled data to evaluate the output of the grammar induction tool. All three approaches to the evaluation have been widely used. The first of these approaches is popular, however due to its possible subjectivity this method is sometimes referred to as the *looks-good-to-me* method. The second method relies heavily upon existing resources and is more suited to measuring precision than recall.

Our approach is entirely unsupervised and can be thought of as clustering the concept instances.[2] In the real-world situation, the output of GI has to be verified and labeled by an expert. To ease the evaluation process, we decided to use the annotated corpora. As a result, our approach remains unsupervised (because GI is carried out on the raw unannotated data) but it is possible to evaluate the output automatically. Instead of asking an expert, we compare the GI output against the annotation already present in the data.

4.1   Named Entity Recognition by Clustering

To detect named entities, we evaluate terminals grouped into one cluster based on the interchangeability principle. In other words, these are the shortest production rules consisting of terminals only, such as $E \rightarrow MEK1$ and $E \rightarrow Stat5$. Here, the proteins $MEK1$ and $Stat5$ form a cluster. As discussed above, the evaluation of terminals can be performed in two ways. If one uses annotated corpora, each element of a cluster can be assigned a semantic label. A cluster of terminals is

---

[2] This method is in line with [13].

then assigned a label using voting. Alternatively, each cluster can be labeled by an expert.

Strategy: Named Entity Recognition by Clustering

1. Perform GI on an unannotated data set
2. Consider every cluster of terminals and assign semantic class labels to each of its elements
3. If there are any elements in the given semantic class C which have more than one distinct semantic label assigned, perform voting
4. Measure the quality of the assignment

In addition we might look for patterns which classify the unseen examples with respect to the defined named entity classes. If the instances of the semantic class **protein** occur in the production rule $P \rightarrow E\ expression$ (where E refers to the production rules above), it can be concluded that this production rule is a good pattern to identify protein names. The evaluation in the latter case is straightforward - the selected patterns are applied to a test data set and all predictions are evaluated according to a given annotation.

4.2   Bootstrapping

Bootstrapping is a process of learning the instances of the given semantic classes in the iterative fashion. Several approaches to bootstrapping have been proposed ([17], [18]). Bootsrapping generally works as follows: given a set of *seed words* and an unannotated corpus, all patterns including seeds are extracted. The most confident patterns are then used on the same corpus to extract new instances. The extracted instances are added to the pool of instances. The process is repeated iteratively. We present our algorithm for bootstrapping in Algorithm 1.

Our intuition behind combining GI with bootstrapping is the following. In each iteration of bootstrapping we find more instances of a certain semantic class C. If one substitutes all these instances by their semantic label in a text, he will likely reduce the entropy of a text and can possibly find more instances of the same type. Obviously, this will not lead to more instances of C within the same rule (pattern) Y, but it might help to find other patterns which due to the current parameters (e.g., generality factor) have not been found in the previous step. The reduction in entropy might be especially important for the statistically-based GI methods.

In general, there are several open issues in bootstrapping approach. These are a stopping criterion, selection of the instances to be added to the pool on each iteration step and selection of seeds (W). In the literature these issues have been tackled by proposing to start with the N most frequent words as seeds and to add instances based on the confidence score of a pattern they are induced with [17]. Although the selection of seeds seems to be natural, a confidence score of a pattern can be calculated in many different ways. Moreover, at a certain moment GI will converge to the syntactic clusters rather than semantic. We have decided

Algorithm 1. Bootstrapping

Require: C - a semantic class, *corpus*, *interaction*
N most frequent words $w_s, s = 1, ..., N$: $\forall w_s\ label(w_s) = C$, $W = \bigcup w_s$
1: $iter = 0$
2: replace all occurrences of $w_s \in W$ in *corpus*, store it as *corpus$_{iter}$*
3: $gi(corpus_{iter})$ { carry out GI on *corpus$_{iter}$* }
4: **for** each cluster of terminals $E_j, j = 1, \ldots, m$ **do**
5:    **if** $\exists\ e_i, i = 1, \ldots, k, e_i \in E_j \wedge label(e_i) = C$ **then**
6:       **if** *interaction* $== true$ **then**
7:          present E_j to an expert
8:       **else**
9:          add E_j to a pool: $Pool_C = \bigcup E_j$
10:       **end if**
11:    **end if**
12: **end for**
13: create *corpus$_{iter+1}$* by replacing all occurrences of $p_l, l = 1, \ldots k, p_l \in Pool_C$
   in *corpus$_{iter}$* by C
14: $iter = iter + 1$
15: Go to Step 3
16: **return** $Pool_C$ of instances of a semantic class C

---

to disregard the selection of patterns either by introducing a human interaction or by selecting all possible instances found on each step. In the experimental set-up we used a human interaction, which in our case was reduced to the selection of known instances from the annotated corpora.

5   Experiments

5.1   Pattern Acquisition in Adios

The grammatical inference tool we explore in this paper is Adios [16].[3] It is based on a statistical search for patterns in a given corpus using motif extraction (MEX) algorithm. According to the evaluation of this tool on several tasks, such as grammatical constituents, protein motif discovery ([11]) and others, Adios has provided accurate results. This supports our motivation to select it for the NER purposes.

Adios outputs equivalence classes $E_i, i = 1, \ldots, n$, whose elements are interchangeable and patterns $P_j, j = 1, \ldots, m$. A pattern is usually a linear sequence of elements (any combination of variable and terminals). In terms of grammar definition, a pattern corresponds to a production rule, while an equivalence class represents a subset of a set of terminals. For example, both $P \rightarrow germinal$ $centers$ and $P \rightarrow E\ expression$ are patterns. An equivalence class E in the latter pattern is the following: $E \rightarrow \{MEK1, Stat5\}$. Therefore, the pattern

---

[3] Adios stands for the Automatic Distillation of Structures, available from http://www.adios.tau.ac.il

can be expanded in two different ways, either as $P \rightarrow MEK1$ *expression* or as $P \rightarrow Stat5$ *expression*. In Section 4.1 we referred to equivalence classes as clusters of terminals.

This method allows recursion, i.e. that equivalence class can have both, other equivalence classes and patterns as its elements. On the other hand, a pattern can consist of either other patterns or equivalence classes. This type of recursion must be taken into account if one wishes to expand the existing equivalence classes or patterns.

Each pattern P_i is supplied by the occurrence number, significance score, generality factor and its length. These are four parameters which can be used for the pattern filtering by setting the thresholds for all of them. For more information on Adios algorithm, an interested reader is referred to [16].

For the experiments discussed below, we have used the following settings: a size of a context window - 4, a generalization factor η - 0.7.[4]

5.2   Data

For our experiments, we have chosen three different data sets to work on. All of them come from the biomedical field and has been used for the discovery of different biomedical entities in a text [10].

Each corpus has been considered based on the manner it has been collected and on the types of biomolecular entities it contains. Among all corpora, Epilepsy is the only one not labeled by a human expert. It has been gathered by querying Medline abstracts with *gene-name AND epilepsy*, where gene-name stands for a name of a gene causing epilepsy. Since this corpus has not been annotated, it is only assumed that it is relevant for a study of epilepsy. Contrary to Epilepsy, Almed and BioNLP have been annotated by the experts. In particular, Almed consists of the annotated proteins only (225 Medline abstracts). In addition to this corpus, we have chosen to use subset of Genia (BioNLP)[10] in order to study how well different semantic classes are separable from each other. For the BioNLP corpus we have 5 semantic classes, **protein**, **DNA**, **RNA**, **cell_type** and **cell_line**. It is also the largest corpus in this study, consisting of 2,000 Medline abstracts.

5.3   Qualitative Evaluation

Experiments on Almed corpus have shown that proteins are often grouped together. Besides clusters of proteins, other semantically related terms, such as cities (e.g., Lausanne, Tokyo, Manchester) are also grouped together. These results have been supported by analysis of Epilepsy corpus, namely, we have received clusters of genes. Apart from these biomolecular entities, we observed other equivalence classes which are relevant to the domain. For example, GI has discovered different types of disorders such as *episodic ataxia type I, episodic ataxia type II, cortical dysplasia* and others.

---

[4] Unless specified otherwise.

As we have used a subset of BioNLP in order to evaluate if GI can separate different biomolecular instances, we have inspected equivalence classes and patterns for this corpus. Although most equivalence classes mostly contain named entities annotated by human experts, it also turned out that it is sometimes difficult to distinguish between some semantic types of named entities. In other words, the named entity detection is very high, whereas the classification vary from one cluster to another. We inspected this corpus closer and discovered that it happens either because the instances are ambiguous, or due to some inconsistency in the annotation. This holds for such semantic classes, as **cell_line** and **cell_type** on the one hand, and **DNA** and **protein**, on the other. For instance, a phrase *HIV-1-infected cells* has received two different labels, **cell_line** and **cell_type**.

Table 1. Instances of **protein**, **DNA** and **RNA** from BioNLP corpus

protein	DNA	RNA
Jak3	AP3-L	ICAM-I mRNA
STAT1	WGATAR	p45 mRNA
STAT3	GASd/EBSd	CIITA mRNA
STAT5	L1	Rhom-2 mRNA
JAK1	L2	TCF-1 mRNA

Table 2. Instances of **cell_line** and **cell_type** from BioNLP corpus

cell_type	cell_line
monocyte lineage	UV-irradiated Jurkat cells
granulocyte-macrophage lineage	stimulated Jurkat cells
hematopoietic lineage	TNF-alpha-stimulated
adult lineage	Nef+ Jurkat cells
B-cell lineage	Stat6-expressing Jurkat cells

Some examples discovered on the BioNLP corpus are given in Table 1 and Table 2. We have also observed that there are found biomolecular instances of different length. Although initially we assumed that we are likely to find the shortest protein names, we have also discovered two, three and four elements long protein names. The longest protein name we found consists of 5 words and is *myeloid cell nuclear differentiation antigen*. The distribution of protein names for BioNLP corpus is shown on Fig. 1.

5.4   Quantitative Evaluation

NER by Clustering When carrying out the evaluation of GI output, we took into account both types of output, equivalence classes and patterns. Since many named entities in the biomedical domain consist of more than one word, we decided to evaluate patterns as well. We only consider cases where a pattern

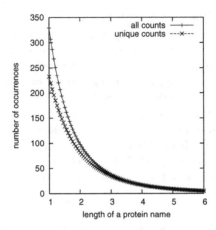

Fig. 1. Distribution of protein names (BioNLP)

represents an entire instance, as in $P=\{hematopoietic\ lineage\}$. For BioNLP corpus, the number of equivalence classes accompanied by the number of patterns and the number of acquired instances (true positives - TP) is given in Table 3.

Table 3. Number of equivalence classes and patterns for BioNLP

sem. class	#eq. class	#patterns	#TP
protein	55	18	476
DNA	13	1	176
RNA	1	-	8
cell_type	11	1	93
cell_line	5	3	127

We have calculated precision using the micro- and macro-average measures. We define macro-averaged precision as a percentage of correctly identified instances of a given semantic class X in a cluster j, $j = 1,\ldots n$ with average over all clusters. In contrast to this, micro-averaged precision is measured as a number of all correctly classified instances of a semantic class X, divided by the number all instances assigned X.

In terms of true positives (TP) and false positives (FP), macro-average precision P_{mc} for n equivalence classes is defined as follows:

$$P_{mc} = \frac{1}{n} \sum_{i=1}^{n} \frac{TP_i}{TP_i + FP_i}$$

Micro-average P_{mr} is calculated as

$$P_{mr} = \frac{\sum_{i=1}^{n} TP_i}{\sum_{i=1}^{n} TP_i + FP_i}$$

Divergence between two measures is caused by the different size of clusters. Precision for BioNLP data is shown on Fig. 2.[5] As one may notice, semantic class **DNA** has a high micro- and macro-averaged precision. Although precision for **RNA** is also high, we have found only one cluster **RNA**. Micro-averaged precision for Almed corpus is equal to 66.67%, macro-averaging results in 70.29%.

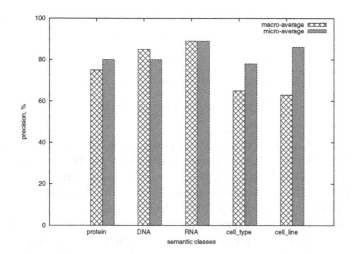

Fig. 2. Precision (BioNLP)

Since *Adios* also offers additional information on generality of the patterns, it is of a certain interest to analyze clusters not only based on the precision but on the generality and length of the patterns which extract the elements of a certain cluster. For instance, we expect a short pattern with a low generality score to produce a noisy cluster, whereas a longer pattern with higher generalization score can extract more precise information. We evaluated clusters from BioNLP corpus and proved our intuition. Equivalence classes being part of a pattern with domain-dependent words (such as *factor*) are more precise in comparison to the clusters induced by the patterns with the closed-class words (determiners, conjunctions, and others).

NER by Bootstrapping. We conducted several experiments with bootstrapping on Almed corpus. The experiments supported our intuition that adding known proteins to the protein pool enabled more proteins to be found in subsequent iterations. We found that the performance of bootsrapping varies significantly depending upon the seeds selected. For instance, by selecting the five most frequent protein names as seeds ($N = 5$, null iteration), we obtain more than 60 new protein names already in the first iteration (Fig. 3). As expected, we also observed a decrease in the entropy after each of the earlier iterations.

---

[5] When calculating precision of equivalence classes, all patterns which have been assigned a corresponding semantic class label were left out.

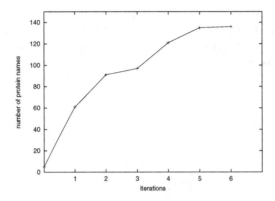

Fig. 3. Bootstrapping on AImed

The bootstrapping process is finished either when an equivalence class containing a given semantic class converged syntactically (so there are no instances
to be added to a pool) or when there are no instances of a given semantic class
in the output of GI. The first option can be carried out (semi-)automatically,
whereas in the second case an expert is confronted with all equivalence classes in
a corpus. Figure 3 presents results using the first approach. However, the second
method is also useful, especially in the cases when instances of the same semantic class occur in different contexts and are therefore not clustered together. We
have also tested the second method. After the 6th iteration (no new instances
added to a pool), we inspected the output of grammatical inference and have
lowered a generalization factor η to 0.6 and added about 180 proteins more to
a pool. Nevertheless, bootstrapping can be applied to find more named entities
without changing GI parameters. Initial clustering on Almed results in 116 proteins, bootstrapping, however, increases this number. Although the main focus
of this study is precision, we note that by using bootstrapping approach the
expected recall on Almed data set gets higher in each iteration.

6   Conclusion

The experiments we have conducted on the different sets have provided an evidence that GI can be used for the knowledge acquisition. Both research questions
we have formulated can be answered positively. Not only grammar induction allows for accurate detection of named entities in a domain-dependent text (in our
case, in the biomedical domain), it is also able to distinguish between different
subclasses of a given semantic class. Based on our quantitative and qualitative
evaluation of clustering, we conclude that GI can assist an expert when creating
ontologies. We also proposed bootstrapping approach as a step towards boosting
coverage and recall.

In the future research, we plan to investigate the bootstrapping method
on other data sets and to compare our results against other bootstrapping

methods[17], [18]. We have already mentioned that most grammar induction tools have their own parameters, such as a generalization factor or a significance score, which can be used as criteria for the rule set selection. For the future research, we plan to test different settings and to explore which parameters are of the most importance. We believe that such parameters can also be used to define the threshold or a stopping criterion for bootstrapping.

As we show in this paper, grammatical inference can be used for the concept instantiation and relation learning providing useful cues for performing such tasks. This technique can also be used in conjunction with other techniques. The famous claim in the machine learning field is that no method can perform better than others on all unseen data sets. This leads to investigation of the ensemble methods ([3], [15]), which would allow to combine different machine learning methods. As the results have shown, the meta-learning constitutes an attractive option. We plan to use the methods presented in this paper as one of the weak classifiers and to combine them with other known ML methods.

Acknowledgments. The authors thank their colleagues from the Human-Computer Studies Lab and Adaptive Information Disclosure project, in particular Edgar Meij (UvA), Willem van Hage (VUA), and Maarten van Someren (HCSL). We are also grateful to the anonymous reviewers for their helpful comments. Special thanks to Zach Solan who made his tool *Adios* freely available. This work is part of the Virtual Lab e-Science project (www.vl-e.org).

References

1. Adriaans, P., and Zaanen, van M.: Computational Grammar Induction for Linguists. Grammars **7**, (2004) 57–68
2. Craven, M., and Kumlien, J.: Constructing Biological Knowledge Bases by Extracting Information from Text Sources. In Proceedings of the 7th International Conference on Intelligent Systems for Molecular Biology (ISMB-99), 1999
3. Dietteriech, T. G.: Ensemble Methods in Machine Learning. Lecture Notes in Computer Science, **1857**, (2000) 1–15
4. Freitag, D.: Using Grammatical Inference to Improve Precision in Information Extraction. Workshop on Grammatical Inference, Automata Induction, and Language Acquisition (ICML'97), Nashville, (1997)
5. Hachey, B., and Grover, C. et al.: Use of Ontologies for Cross-lingual Information Management in the Web. In Proceedings of the Ontologies and Information Extraction International Workshop (EUROLAN 2003), Bucarest, Romania, July 28 - August 8, (2003)
6. Hahn, U. and Romacker, M.: An Integrated Model of Semantic and Conceptual Interpretation from Dependency Structures. In Proceedings of the 18th Conference on Computational Linguistics, Saarbrücken, Germany, (2000) 271–277
7. Hearst, Marti A.: Automatic Acquisition of Hyponyms from Large Text Corpora. In Proceedings of the 14th International Conference on Computational Linguistics, Nantes, France, (1992)
8. Karampatziakis, N., Paliouras, G., Pierrakos, D. and Stamatopoulos, P.: Navigation pattern discovery using grammatical inference. In ICGI'2004, (2004)

9. Katrenko, S. and Adriaans, P. W.: Learning Relations from Biomedical Corpora Using Dependency Tree Levels. In Benelearn'2006, (2006)
10. Kim, J.-D. et al.: Introduction to the Bio-Entity Recognition Task at JNLPBA. In JNLPBA'2004, (2004)
11. Kunik, V., Solan, Z., Edelman, S., Ruppin, E., and Horn, D.: Motif Extraction and Protein Classification. In CSB, (2005)
12. Pradhan, S., Haciouglu, K., Ward, W., Martin, J. H., and Jurafsky, D.: Semantic Role Chunking Combining Complementary Syntactic Views. In Proceedings of the 9th Conference on Natural Language Learning (CONNL 2005), Ann Arbor, MI, (2005)
13. Reinberger, M.-L., Spyns, P., Pretorius, A.J., and Daelemans, W.: Automatic initiation of an ontology. In Proceedings of ODBase'04, (2004) 600–617
14. Roberts, A., and Atwell, E.: The Use of Corpora for Automatic Evaluation of Grammar Inference Systems. In Proceedings of of the Corpus Linguistics 2003 Conference, (2003)
15. Sigletos, G., Paliouras, G., Spyropoulos, C. D., Hatzopoulos, M.: Voting and Stacked Generalization. In JMLR, (2005) 1751–1782
16. Solan, Z., Ruppin, E., and Horn, D., and Edelman, S.: Automatic acquisition and efficient representation of syntactic structures. In NIPS, (2002)
17. Thelen, M. and Riloff, E.: A Bootstrapping Method for Learning Semantic Lexicons using Extraction Pattern Contexts. In Proceedings of the 2002 Conference on Empirical Methods in Natural Language Processing (EMNLP), (2002)
18. Valarakos, Alexandros G., Paliouras G., Karkaletsis V., and Vouros G. A.: Enhancing Ontological Knowledge Through Ontology Population and Enrichment, In Proceedings of the 14th International Conference Engineering Knowledge in the Age of the Semantic Web, Whittlebury Hall, UK, (2004)
19. Zaanen, van M. and Adriaans, P.: Alignment-Based Learning versus EMILE: A Comparison, In Proceedings of the Belgian-Dutch Conference on Artificial Intelligence (BNAIC), Amsterdam, the Netherlands, (2001), 315-322

Inferring Grammar Rules of Programming Language Dialects

Alpana Dubey, Pankaj Jalote, and Sanjeev Kumar Aggarwal

Dept of Computer Science and Engineering,
Indian Institute of Technology,
Kanpur - 208016. India
{alpanad, jalote, ska}@iitk.ac.in

Abstract. In this paper we address the problem of grammatical inference in the programming language domain. The grammar of a programming language is an important asset because it is used in developing many software engineering tools. Sometimes, grammars of languages are not available and have to be inferred from the source code; especially in the case of programming language dialects. We propose an approach for inferring the grammar of a programming language when an incomplete grammar along with a set of correct programs is given as input. The approach infers a set of grammar rules such that the addition of these rules makes the initial grammar complete. A grammar is complete if it parses all the input programs successfully. We also proposes a rule evaluation order, i.e. an order in which the rules are evaluated for correctness. A set of rules are correct if their addition makes the grammar complete. Experiments show that the proposed rule evaluation order improves the process of grammar inference.

Keywords: Programming language grammars, Dialects, Minimum Description Length Principle.

1 Introduction

Grammar of a programming language is an important asset because it is used in developing software analysis and modification tools. For automatically generating such tools one must have the underlying grammar of the programming language. Grammar can be extracted from many resources like compiler source codes, grammar specification files and reference manuals. Sometimes these resources are not available, particularly when programs are written in some dialect of a standard programming language. For example, C* is a data parallel dialect of C which was developed by Thinking Machines Corp for Connection Machine (CM2 and CM5) SIMD processors. Since Thinking Machines Corp no longer exists, it is very hard to find out the compiler source code or the reference manual for C*. The only thing which is available are programs written in C* and the executable of C* compiler. In some cases resources are available but they are not complete. For example, Lämmel et al [14] have discussed the problem of incomplete reference manuals they faced while recovering COBOL grammar

Y. Sakakibara et al. (Eds.): ICGI 2006, LNAI 4201, pp. 201–213, 2006.

from the reference manual of IBM COBOL. In above cases the only information available is the source code (i.e. programs) and an incomplete grammar. Since programming language grammars can be expressed with a context free grammars (CFG)[1], we focus on the problem of CFG inference in this paper.

Theoretical results on the problem of CFG inference are negative. For example, Gold's theory says [9] that no language in the Chomsky hierarchy can be learned / inferred exactly in the finite time from positive samples (set of valid sentences) alone. Although context free languages (CFL) can be learned from positive and negative samples [10] but they cannot be learned in polynomial time because the class of regular languages, which is a subset of CFL, is not learnable in polynomial time [3]. Only deterministic finite automata (DFA) are learnable in polynomial time if they have access to an oracle which can answer membership query (whether the string proposed by the learner falls in the unknown language?) and equivalence query (whether the learned grammar is equivalent to the unknown grammar?). Therefore, the problem of CFG inference suffers from the performance problem as discussed in [5].

In spite of above results, a large body of work on CFG inference exists in the natural language processing (NLP) and theoretical domain [1], [6], [16], [17], [19], [20]. The techniques proposed in theoretical domain address the problem of inferring small subclasses of CFL and programming languages do not fall in those classes because programming languages are usually LR; Koshiba et. al. [13] have shown that a subclass of LR language, called LR even linear language, cannot be learned from positive samples alone. Only a few techniques, available in the literature, address the problem of grammar extraction/inference in the programming language domain [4], [5], [7], [12], [14], [18]. Some of these techniques are heuristic techniques which do not guarantee the correctness. A deterministic technique proposed in [8] infers keyword based grammar rules, e.g. rule corresponding to keywords *while*, *for* etc.; it infers only those rules whose right hand side (RHS) starts with a keyword.

In this paper we address the problem of inferring a grammar of a dialect when a set of valid programs written in the dialect and the grammar of the standard language are given as input. The missing rules in the initial grammar contain new keywords or new operators. This assumption is based on the study of PL dialects. We found that the main extensions in PL dialect are keyword based statements and new expressions. For example, C* contains additional statements with keywords *where*, *with* etc. and supports vector operations with new operators.

As the existing approach [8] can not infer the grammar rules in which a new terminal occurs in the middle of the RHS[2]; it can not infer grammar rules involving new operators as operators usually occur in the middle of the RHS of the rule, e.g. *expression* + *expression*. We present a generalized approach for inferring the missing grammar rules where a new terminal (operator or keyword)

---

[1] Although there are few constructs which are context sensitive but those are expressed by associating translation rules with CFG rules.

[2] A new terminal is a generic term used to denote new keywords, new operators etc.

can occur in the middle of the RHS. Since, the exact learning of CFG is not possible from a set of valid sentences, we address the following problem [9]: Given an incomplete grammar G and a set of valid programs $\mathbb{P}$, infer a grammar G' which is complete w.r.t. $\mathbb{P}$. Grammar G' is complete w.r.t. $\mathbb{P}$ if $\mathbb{P} \subseteq L(G')$.

An approach for inferring a grammar is to iteratively build a set of possible rules from $\mathbb{P}$ and then evaluate the correctness of those rules. A set of rules $\mathbb{GR}$ is correct w.r.t. $\mathbb{P}$ and an initial grammar $G = (N, T, P, S)$, if the modified grammar $G' = (N, T, P \cup \mathbb{GR}, S)$ is complete w.r.t. $\mathbb{P}$. The main problems faced by such technique, which for example has been employed in [8], is that it is not efficient as the search space of possible rules is very large. This is because grammars of programming languages are large (typically 200-400 productions). An incorrect choice of a grammar rule may severely hamper the performance of the approach as it has to backtrack and select another rule. Therefore, a bias towards correct rule is very important for good performance.

We propose a rule evaluation order which is closely based on the principle of minimum description length (MDL). The MDL principle is a well established concept in the machine learning literature; it says that the best hypothesis for a given set of data is the one which can represent the data most compactly. In our problem scenario we check the completeness of those grammars first which compactly represent $\mathbb{P}$. We associate a weight with each rule to capture the notion of compactness. The weight of rule closely follows the MDL principle. We check the correctness of those rules first which have more weight. Results show that using proposed rule evaluation order, a complete grammar can be inferred with fewer number of trials. Langley et al [15], [11] have studied the effect of MDL based approach on the grammar inference process, but their results are based on the artificial subsets of English grammar (i.e. in the NLP domain). Their approach starts with a set of a very specific grammar and uses the MDL criterion to generalize it; hence they explore the best grammar in the space of complete grammars whereas this paper focuses on inferring a complete grammar.

The rest of the paper is organized as follows. Section 2 briefly discusses the technique proposed in [8]. Section 3 discusses our approach. Section 4 proposes a rule evaluation order and investigates its effect on the grammar inference process. Section 5 discusses the results and concludes the paper. Standard notations are used for representing various terms related to the context free grammar [2]. Terms production and rule are used interchangeably throughout the paper.

2   Background

In this section we briefly present the technique proposed in [8]. We use it to explain and demonstrate our approach. The technique in [8] starts with a set of programs $\mathbb{P}$ and an incomplete grammar $G = (N, T, P, S)$[3]. The approach infers keyword based rules; it is based on three main assumptions: (1) Statements corresponding to each new keyword can be expressed by exactly one grammar rule.

---

[3] Terms related to the context free grammar are borrowed from [2].

For example, syntax of the statement corresponding to keyword *while* is expressible with one rule, i.e. *statement → while (expression) statement*. Therefore,
if T_{new} is the set of new keywords then $|T_{new}|$ rules are needed to make the
initial grammar complete. (2) The set T_{new} is known beforehand; i.e. the lexical analyzer does not recognize a new keyword as an existing terminal or as an
unknown terminal. (3) The right hand side (RHS) of missing rules start with a
new keyword. That is, missing rules are of the form $A → K\alpha$, where $A \in N$,
$\alpha \in (N \cup T)^*$ and $K \in T_{new}$.

The technique is an iterative one which involves backtracking. In each iteration
a set of possible rules corresponding to a new keyword is built and one among
them is added to G. Once a rule corresponding to each new keyword is added to
G (i.e. after $|T_{new}|$ iterations), the modified G is checked for the completeness
w.r.t. $\mathbb{P}$. If the modified G is incomplete then the algorithm backtracks and
selects another rule. A set of possible rules corresponding to a keyword K is
computed in three steps: (1) LHSs gathering phase: gathers possible left hand
sides (LHSs) of the rule, (2) RHSs gathering phase: gathers possible right hand
sides (RHSs) of the rule and (3) Rule building phase: uses the set of possible
LHSs and possible RHSs to build a set of possible rules. We demonstrate steps
(1) and (2) with an example as follows:

Suppose, we are given an incomplete ANSI C grammar in which a grammar
rule corresponding to keyword *while* (i.e. $T_{new} = \{while\}$) is missing and a
program shown in figure 1(a) is given as input; i.e. a single rule is sufficient for
completing the grammar. For gathering possible LHSs, an LR parser [2] is generated from the given incomplete grammar. The input program is parsed with the
parser. The parser will get stuck at the first occurrence of keyword *while* which
is shown as *error point* in figure 1(a). The set of possible LHSs of the rule, corresponding to keyword *while*, is computed from the LR-itemsets corresponding
to the top of the LR-parser stack. If itemset at the top of stack contains an item
of form $[A → \alpha \bullet B \beta]$ then B is collected in the possible LHSs set. A reduce
operation is invoked for all the items of form $[A → \alpha \bullet]$. This reduce operation
is called *"forced reduction"* because reduction is performed without looking at
the next token. If multiple reductions are possible on the top of the stack then a
separate copy of the stack is made for each possible reduction and reduction is
performed on that copy. The forced reduction is performed as long as the top of
the stack has at least one possible reduction or it becomes empty. For example,
in figure 1(b) top state has LR-item $[statement → expression\ SEMICOL \bullet]^4$,
therefore forced reduction will be performed. After the forced reduction top state
contains LR-item $[statement → statement\_list \bullet statement]$. Hence, nonterminal *statement* is added in the possible LHSs set.

For building the set of possible RHSs, the approach starts from the last occurrence of the keyword *while* (shown in figure 1(a)) and considers each succeeding
terminal as a possible end point of the substring derived from the missing rule. For

---

[4] In real C grammar the number of possible LHSs, possible RHSs and LR-items in each
itemset is very large. Above example shows only few of them to make the illustration
simple.

each substring, a set of symbol strings which can derive it is built; all the symbol strings are added in the set of possible RHSs. For example, substring *while* ($x >$ 10) can be derived from symbol strings *while* (*conditional_expression*), *while* (*expression*) and *while* (*id* $> NUM$), hence these symbol strings are added in the possible RHSs set. The set of possible RHSs and possible rules are shown in figure 1(b). Each rule in the set of possible rules is evaluated for the correctness; if the rule is correct then approach returns that rule else it checks another rule. A set of possible correct rules is shown in figure 1(b); the approach returns the first correct rule it encounters.

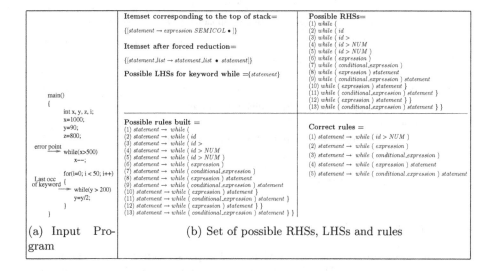

(a) Input Program

(b) Set of possible RHSs, LHSs and rules

Fig. 1. Process of inferring correct grammar rules

3   Our Approach

In this section we discuss an approach which infers missing rules of form $A \rightarrow \alpha K \beta$; here α and β can be empty strings and K is a new terminal which can be either a new keyword or a new operator. The overall approach is shown in figure 2 which, like the previous approach (section 2), is an iterative approach with backtracking. In each iteration a set of possible rules corresponding to a new terminal is built and one among them is added in the grammar. The set of possible LHSs, RHSs and rules corresponding to a new terminal K are represented as $\mathbb{L}_K$, $\mathbb{R}_K$ and PR_K respectively. We discuss the LHSs and the RHSs building phases in the detail. We explain the approach when an incomplete ANSI C grammar is given as input in which a rule corresponding to operator $>$ is missing. Extension of the approach for inferring multiple missing rules is discussed later. The terms "new terminal" and "new keyword" are used interchangeably as our focus is to infer not only the grammar rules corresponding to new keywords but also the rules which involve new operators. An input program is represented as $w_{1,n}$

where n is the number of terminals in the program. w_i denotes i^{th} terminal of the program and $w_{i,j}$ denotes the portion of the program which starts at index i and ends at index j.

Function INFER_RULES(P, G, T$_{new}$)   ▷ T_{new} is a set of new terminals

1. **while** T_{new} is not empty **do**

2.   Select a new terminal $K \in T_{new}$, remove K from T_{new}

3.   Build a set of possible LHSs corresponding to K and collect in $\mathbb{L}_K$

4.   Build a set of possible RHSs corresponding to K and collect in $\mathbb{R}_K$

5.   Build a set of possible rules PR_K orresponding to K using $\mathbb{L}_K$ and $\mathbb{R}_K$

6.   Select a rule $r_i \in PR_K$ and add in G

7. **if** G parses all the programs in $\mathbb{P}$

8.   Output all rules added in different iterations

9. **else**

10.   Backtrack to previous iteration and try another rule

Fig. 2. Overall rule inference process

3.1   LHSs Generation Phase

First, the input program is parsed with the LR parser generated by the incomplete ANSI C grammar. We call this parser the approximate parser. Unlike the previous approach, possible LHSs in our approach are gathered from each configuration the approximate parser passes[5]. I.e. at each step, the top itemset of the parser stack is checked; if it contains an item of type $[A \rightarrow \alpha \bullet B \ \beta]$, then B is added in the set of possible LHSs. Once the parser reaches to the error state, forced reduction is performed to collect the remaining possible LHSs. The idea behind collecting possible LHSs from each configuration the parser passes is as follows:

Suppose a program shown in figure 3(a) is given as input. The first occurrence of the new terminal, $>$, is shown in the figure 3(a); Suppose this is f^{th} token. Substrings covered by the first and the last occurrences of the missing rule, corresponding to $>$, are shown by shaded regions in the figure 3(a). If the substring covered by the first occurrence of the missing rule starts from the mth token ($m \leq f$), then a complete parser (i.e. a parser generated from a complete ANSI C grammar) will start recognizing the substring covered by the missing rule from m^{th} token. Since the value of m is not known, each index i ($1 \leq i \leq f$) is considered as a possible starting point of the substring covered by the missing

---

[5] In the previous approach, possible LHSs are gathered from the parser once it reaches the error state.

rule. Therefore, possible LHSs are gathered from each configuration the approximate parser passes while parsing the input program. Figure 3(b) shows the set of possible LHSs gathered from the program. We are not showing all possible LHSs and each top itemset of the parser stack to make the illustration simple[6].

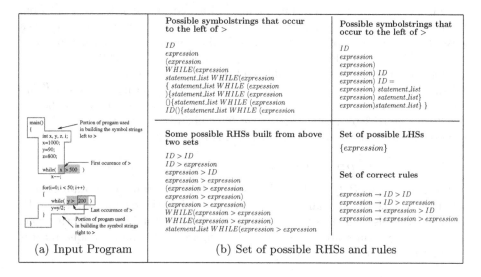

(a) Input Program   (b) Set of possible RHSs and rules

Fig. 3. Process of inferring correct grammar rules

3.2 RHSs Gathering Phase

Since the RHS of the missing rule is of the form $\alpha\ K\ \beta$ (α and β can be empty strings and K is a new terminal), we divide the possible RHS in two parts: (1) Part which occurs to the left of the new terminal, i.e. α. (2) Part which occurs to the right of the new terminal, i.e. β. A set of possible αs, denoted as $\mathbb{R}_K^L$, and a set of possible βs, denoted as $\mathbb{R}_K^R$, are used for building $\mathbb{R}_K$. For building $\mathbb{R}_K^L$ and $\mathbb{R}_K^R$ the input program (suppose w) is first parsed with the incomplete grammar using the CYK parser. Suppose, f and l are the indices of the first and the last occurrences of K. For building $\mathbb{R}_K^L$, we consider each index i ($1 \le i < f$) as a possible starting point of the substring derived by the missing rule and symbol strings which can derive substring $w_{i,f-1}$ are added in the $\mathbb{R}_K^L$. Similarly, for building $\mathbb{R}_K^R$, each index j ($l < j \le n$) is considered as a possible end point of the substring derived by the last occurrence of the missing rule and symbol strings that can derive substring $w_{l+1,j}$ are added in the set $\mathbb{R}_K^R$. The set of symbol strings that can derive a substring $w_{p,q}$ (for $0 < p \le q \le n$) is built by using the table generated from the CYK parser[7]. Set $\mathbb{R}_K$ is built by

---

[6] These sets are a very large for a real programming language grammar.

[7] CYK parser builds a table, called CYK table, while parsing the program; where each cell $C(m,n)$ contains all the nonterminals that derive substring $w_{m,n}$.

concatenating the symbol strings taken from $\mathbb{R}_K^L$ and $\mathbb{R}_K^R$ as follows:

$$\mathbb{R}_K = \{\alpha \, K \, \beta \mid \forall \alpha \in \mathbb{R}_K^L \ \& \ \forall \beta \in \mathbb{R}_K^R\}$$

Note: Sets $\mathbb{R}_K^L$ and $\mathbb{R}_K^R$ both additionally contain empty string ϵ. This is for considering those cases when the RHS of missing rule is either of form $K\alpha$ or of form αK.

Consider the program shown in the figure 3(a). For building $\mathbb{R}_>^L$ we start from the beginning of the program (i.e. *main*) and consider each terminal onwards as a possible starting point of the substring derived by the missing rule corresponding to $>$. Similarly for building $\mathbb{R}_>^R$, we start from the terminal '200' and consider each terminal onwards as a possible end point of the substring derived by the missing rule. The portions of the program used in computing $\mathbb{R}_>^L$ and $\mathbb{R}_>^R$ are shown in figure 3(a) by boxed regions. Sets $\mathbb{R}_>^L$ and $\mathbb{R}_>^R$ are shown in the figure 3(b). Figure 3(b) also shows the set $\mathbb{R}_>$ built from these two sets. The set of possible rules corresponding to $>$, $PR_>$, is built using $\mathbb{L}_>$ and $\mathbb{R}_>$ as follows:

$$PR_> = \{A \to \alpha : \forall A \in \mathbb{L}_> \ \& \ \forall B \in \mathbb{R}_>\}$$

Each rule r_i, in $PR_>$ is checked to see whether the grammar obtained after adding r_i is able to parse all the programs; if yes then the technique returns the grammar rule else rollbacks the changes in the grammar and checks another rule. A set of correct rules are also shown in the figure 3(b). The technique returns the first correct rule it encounters.

3.3 Extracting Multiple Missing Rules

In the case of multiple missing rules, the approach iteratively builds a set of possible rules corresponding to each new terminal and adds them in the grammar. A set of possible rules (PR_K) corresponding to a new terminal K is built as follows: Programs where K is the first new terminal are used for computing the set $\mathbb{L}_K$. The set $\mathbb{R}_K$ is computed in two parts as discussed previously: (1) computation of the set $\mathbb{R}_K^L$ is done from those programs where K is the first new terminal and (2) computation of the set $\mathbb{R}_K^R$ is done from those programs where K is the last new terminal. The method for computing $\mathbb{L}_K$, $\mathbb{R}_K^R$, $\mathbb{R}_K^L$, $\mathbb{R}_K$ and PR_K is the same as discussed in the previous section. The above method for building possible rules requires that there is at-least one program where K is the first new terminal and at-least one program where K is the last new terminal. Hence, the approach in each iteration selects (figure 3, line 2) a new terminal which fulfills the above condition. Once a rule corresponding to K is added in G, K no longer remains a new terminal. Therefore, other new terminals will occupy the position of the first and the last new terminals in those programs where K is the first and the last new terminal.

4   A Criterion for Rule Evaluation Order

The approach given in [8] and the approach we discussed in the previous section both result in a large number of possible rules. For example, while experimenting with different PL grammars, *viz*, C, Java, Matlab, Cobol, we found that the number of possible rules corresponding to different keywords was of the order of $10^5 - 10^6$. For example while experimenting with the C grammar, where a rule corresponding to keyword *case* was missing, the number of possible rules was 1.2×10^5. Even after reducing the number of possible rules by the unit production optimization[8] [8] it was of order 400. Therefore, a selection of incorrect rule is very costly for the performance of the algorithm. In this section, we investigate a rule evaluation order for improving the process of grammar inference. We associate a weight with each rule (in PR) to represent the above notion.

Definition 1. *Weight of a rule $A \rightarrow \beta$ w.r.t. $\mathbb{P}$ is:*

$$weight_{\mathbb{P}}(A \rightarrow \beta) = \frac{coverage_{\mathbb{P}}(\beta)}{|\beta|} \qquad (1)$$

Where $coverage_{\mathbb{P}}(A \rightarrow \beta)$ is coverage of the rule w.r.t. $\mathbb{P}$. Coverage depends upon the largest substring $A \rightarrow \beta$ derives in each program of $\mathbb{P}$.

Definition 2. *Coverage of a rule $A \rightarrow \beta$ w.r.t. $\mathbb{P}$ is:*

$$coverage_{\mathbb{P}}(A \rightarrow \beta) = \sum_{w \in \mathbb{P}} (coverage_w(A \rightarrow \beta)) \qquad (2)$$

where

$$coverage_w(A \rightarrow \beta) = \frac{1}{|w|} \ max\{k - i + 1 | \beta \overset{*}{\Rightarrow} w_{i,k} \ \forall i, k, \ 1 \le i \le k \le |w|\} \ (3)$$

Proposed weight criterion is used for ordering the rules while evaluating their correctness. Our hypothesis is that rules with higher weights are generally correct rules. Hence, we evaluate the correctness of each rule in the non-increasing order of weights to improve the process of grammar inference. The above rule ordering criterion is closely based on the principle of Minimum Description Length (MDL). The MDL principle says that the best hypothesis for a given set of data is the one which describes the data most compactly. A hypothesis compactly represents the data if the size of the hypothesis and the description of the data in that hypothesis both are small. Here rules with higher weights are those which have smaller number of symbols and derive larger substring in each program, therefore the criterion closely (not exactly) follows the MDL principle. Since we do not consider the representation of whole program using the grammar, the weight does not exactly follows the MDL principle.

Example 1. Consider the input program shown in figure 1(a) and possible rule *statement* $\rightarrow$ *while* (*expression*) shown in figure 1(b). Substrings derived by this

---

[8] Given two possible rules $A \rightarrow X_1 X_2$ and $A \rightarrow Y_1 Y_2$; if $X_1 \rightarrow Y_1$ and $X_2 \rightarrow Y_2$, then unit production optimization adds the rule $A \rightarrow X_1 X_2$ only in the set of possible rules because the incorrectness of $A \rightarrow X_1 X_2$ implies the incorrectness of $A \rightarrow Y_1 Y_2$.

rule are *while* ($x > 500$) and *while* ($y > 200$). The total number of tokens in program is 62, hence coverage of *statement* → *while* (*expression*) is 6/62 = 0.09. Coverage and weights of few possible rules, taken from figure 1(b), are shown in figure 4. Rules *statement* → *while* (*expression*) *statement* and *statement* → *while* (*conditional_expression*) *statement* have the highest weight, hence their correctness is checked first. Since both rules are correct, the approach will return any of these rules.

(1) *statement* → *while* (	*coverage* = 0.03, *weight* = 0.01
(2) *statement* → *while* (*id*	*coverage* = 0.05, *weight* = 0.01
(3) *statement* → *while* (*id* >	*coverage* = 0.06, *weight* = 0.01
(4) *statement* → *while* (*id* > *NUM*	*coverage* = 0.08, *weight* = 0.01
(5) *statement* → *while* (*id* > *NUM*)	*coverage* = 0.09, *weight* = 0.01
(6) *statement* → *while* (*expression*)	*coverage* = 0.09, *weight* = 0.02
(7) *statement* → *while* (*conditional_expression*)	*coverage* = 0.09, *weight* = 0.02
(8) *statement* → *while* (*expression*) *statement*	*coverage* = 0.19, *weight* = 0.038
(9) *statement* → *while* (*conditional_expression*) *statement*	*coverage* = 0.19, *weight* = 0.038
(10) *statement* → *while* (*expression*) *statement* }	*coverage* = 0.21, *weight* = 0.035

Fig. 4. Weight and coverage of different rules of figure 1(b)

4.1 Experiments

To evaluate the hypothesis that rules with higher weights are usually correct rules, a set of experiments were conducted on different programming language grammars, *viz.*, C, Java, Matlab and Cobol. We removed rules corresponding to different keywords and operators from their grammars and built a set of possible rules from input programs using the proposed technique[9]. Possible rules were checked for their correctness in the non-increasing order of weights. We checked for the number of times the highest weight rule was the correct rule. In order to increase the number of test cases, experiments were done considering one input program, two input programs and more than one input programs.

Table 1 summarizes all the results. Table 1 shows that out of 355 test runs, 67.89% times rules with the highest weight are correct and 28.17% times the rules with the second highest weight are correct. Only in 3.94% cases rules which have weights lesser than the second highest weight are correct.

Table 1 also compares the actual time taken by the unoptimized approach (the approach proposed in [8])[10] and the time taken by the approach which uses the rule ordering optimization. It is evident from the table that the time taken by rule ordering optimization is either comparable or less than that taken by the unoptimized approach.

Table 3 shows the results of the experiments in which multiple missing rules are inferred from a set of programs. In order to study the proposed rule evaluation criterion, we counted the number of times the algorithm unsuccessfully checked the completeness of a grammar and later backtracked to select another rule. We can observe that with the proposed rule evaluation order, we reach a complete

---

[9] A set of programs and grammars on which the experiments are done can be found on http://www.cse.iitk.ac.in/users/alpanad/grammars.

[10] Experiments are done on Pentium 4 2.4 GHz processor with 512 MB RAM.

Table 1. Experiment on MDL based rule evaluation order and its comparison with the time taken by unoptimized approach (times are in seconds)

Language	Constructs	No of test cases	#times highest rank rule is correct	#times second highest is rule is correct	Others	Time with-out opti-mization	Time with optimiza-tion	Avg size of progs
Java	case, switch, enum, while, for	82	69	9	4	616	525	66
C	case, switch, break, while, for	104	91	10	3	20781	1454	100
Matlab	case, for, switch, otherwise	108	27	77	4	267	249	38
Cobol	read, perform, move	20	14	4	2	266	250	64

Table 2. Examples of inferred rules

Language	New terminal	Rule with the highest weight
Matlab	/.	$expression \rightarrow index\_expression\_list$ /. $array\_list$
Matlab	.^	$expression \rightarrow index\_expression\_list$.^ $array\_list$
Matlab	otherwise	$stmt \rightarrow OTHERWISE\ expr\_stmt$
Java	case	$LocalVarDeclOrStmt \rightarrow CASE\ CondiExpr\ COLON\ LocalVarDeclAndStmt$
C	case	$select\_stmt \rightarrow CASE\ cond\_expr\ COLON\ stmt\_list$
Cobol	move	$clause \rightarrow MOVE\ file\_name\_string\ loop\_condition\_part2$

grammar in the first trial in most of the cases. Table 2 shows few examples of the rules returned by the approach in some of the experiments.

4.2 Discussion

We observe from the experiments that the proposed weight criterion helps in directing the search of correct rules. Only in 3.94% cases inference process has checked those rules which have weights lesser than the second highest weight. Therefore, using the proposed rule evaluation order we can infer correct grammar rules quickly. Although, proposed weight metric ensures to get correct grammar rules quickly, it does not talk about the goodness of the inferred grammar rule. For example, rules *statement* → *while (expression) statement* and

Table 3. Experiments on multiple rules inference

Language	Constructs	No of Pro-grams	Avg size of a prog	No of tri-als	Actual time
	for, while	2	33	1	1.5 min
Matlab	for, switch, case, otherwise, while	5	29	13	19.5 min
	switch, case, otherwise	3	27	1	2.2 min
	try, catch	4	98	1	14.9 min
Java	if, while	3	37	4	6.7 min
	switch, case, enum	7	61	1	17.6 min
	switch, case, try, catch, enum	7	61	1	24.23 min
	switch, case	1	16	1	3sec
C	switch, case, break	1	16	1	7.3secs
	switch, case, break, default, while, for	1	16	1	14.1secs
Cobol	read, perform, move	3	56	1	1.3min

statement → *while* (*conditional_expression*) *statement* in figure 1(b) both have same weight. Therefore, we face the problem of selecting a good rule from these two rules.

5   Conclusions

This paper proposes an approach for inferring grammar rules from a set of programs. This paper also investigates a rule evaluation order to direct the search process of correct rules in the set of possible rules. The approach and the MDL based criterion are validated by removing rules corresponding to different keywords and operators in four programming languages. Although the weight criterion improves the process of grammar inference, in many instances there can be more than one correct rule with the same weight. As a future work, we plan to investigate the goodness criteria of correct rules for addressing the problem of selecting a good grammar rule from a set of correct rules.

References

1. Pieter W Adriaans. *Language Learning for Categorial Perspective*. PhD thesis, University of Amsterdam, Amsterdam, Netherlands, November 1992.
2. Alfred V. Aho, Ravi Sethi, and Jeffrey D. Ullman. *Compilers Principles, Techniques, and Tools*. Pearson Education (Singapore) Pte. Ltd., 2002.
3. Dana Angluin. Learning regular sets from queries and counterexamples. *Inf. Comput.*, 75(2):87–106, 1987.
4. Matej Crepinsek, Marjan Mernik, Faizan Javed, Barrett R. Bryant, and Alan Sprague. Extracting grammar from programs: evolutionary approach. *SIGPLAN Not.*, 40(4):39–46, 2005.
5. Matej Crepinsek, Marjan Mernik, and Viljem Zumer. Extracting grammar from programs: brute force approach. *SIGPLAN Not.*, 40(4):29–38, 2005.
6. Colin de la Higuera. A bibliographical study of grammatical inference. *Pattern Recognition*, 38:1332–1348, 2005.
7. Alpana Dubey, Sanjeev K. Aggarwal, and Pankaj Jalote. A technique for extracting keyword based rules from a set of programs. In *CSMR '05: Proceedings of the Ninth European Conference on Software Maintenance and Reengineering (CSMR'05)*, pages 217–225, Manchester, UK, 2005. IEEE Computer Society.
8. Alpana Dubey, Pankaj Jalote, and Sanjeev K. Aggarwal. A deterministic technique for extracting keyword based grammar rules from programs. In *Proceedings of 21st Annual ACM Symposium on Applied Computing, PL track*, pages 1631–1632, Dijon, France, April 2006. ACM SIGAPP.
9. E. Mark Gold. Language identification in the limit. *Information and Control*, 10(5):447–474, 1967.
10. E. Mark Gold. Complexity of automaton identification from given data. *Information and Control*, 37(3):302–320, 1978.
11. Peter Grünwald. A minimum description length approach to grammar inference. In *Connectionist, Statistical, and Symbolic Approaches to Learning for Natural Language Processing*, pages 203–216, London, UK, 1996. Springer-Verlag.

12. Rahul Jain, Sanjeev Kumar Aggarwal, Pankaj Jalote, and Shiladitya Biswas. An interactive method for extracting grammar from programs. *Softw. Pract. Exper.*, 34(5):433–447, 2004.
13. Takeshi Koshiba, Erkki Makinen, and Yuji Takada. Learning deterministic even linear languages from positive examples. *Theor. Comput. Sci.*, 185(1):63–79, 1997.
14. R. Lämmel and C. Verhoef. Semi-automatic Grammar Recovery. *Software— Practice & Experience*, 31(15):1395–1438, December 2001.
15. Pat Langley and Sean Stromsten. Learning context-free grammars with a simplicity bias. In *ECML '00: Proceedings of the 11th European Conference on Machine Learning*, pages 220–228, London, UK, 2000. Springer-Verlag.
16. Steve Lawrence, C. Lee Giles, and Sandiway Fong. Natural language grammatical inference with recurrent neural networks. *IEEE Transactions on Knowledge and Data Engineering*, 12(1):126–140, 2000.
17. Lillian Lee. Learning of context-free languages: A survey of the literature. Technical Report TR-12-96, Harvard University, 1996. URL: ftp://deas-ftp.harvard.edu/techreports/tr-12-96.ps.gz.
18. Marjan Mernik, Goran Gerlic, Viljem Zumer, and Barrett Bryant. Can a parser be generated from examples? In *Proceedings of 18th ACM symposium on applied computing*, pages 1063–1067. ACM Press, 2003.
19. Rajesh Parekh and Vasant Honovar. *Grammar Inference, Automata Induction, and Language Acquision*, chapter Invited chapter. Dale, Moisl and Somers (Ed). New York: Marcel Dekker, 2000.
20. Menno van Zaanen. ABL: Alignment-based learning. In *COLING 2000 - Proceedings of the 18th International Conference on Computational Linguistics*, pages 961–967, Saarbrücken, Germany, Aug 2000.

The Tenjinno Machine Translation Competition

Bradford Starkie[1], Menno van Zaanen[2], and Dominique Estival[3]

[1] Starkie Enterprises Pty. Ltd.,
52 Boisdale Street, Surrey Hills (Melbourne), Victoria 3127 Australia
bstarkie@starkieenterprises.com
http://www.bradstarkie.id.au
[2] Macquarie University,
North Ryde (Sydney), NSW 2109 Australia
menno@ics.mq.edu.au
http://www.ics.mq.edu.au/ menno
[3] Appen Pty. Ltd.,
Level 6, North Tower 1, Railway Street, Chatswood (Sydney), NSW 2067 Australia
destival@appen.com.au
http://www.ics.mq.edu.au/ destival

Abstract. This paper describes the Tenjinno Machine Translation Competition held as part of the International Colloquium on Grammatical Inference 2006. The competition aimed to promote the development of new and better practical grammatical inference algorithms used in machine translation. Tenjinno focuses on formal models used in machine translation. We discuss design issues and decisions made when creating the competition. For the purpose of setting the competition tasks, a measure of the complexity of learning a transducer was developed. This measure has enabled us to compare the competition tasks to other published results, and it can be seen that the problems solved in the competition were of a greater complexity and were solved with lower word error rates than other published results. In addition the complexity measures and benchmark problems can be used to track the progress of the state-of-the-art into the future.

1 Introduction

This paper describes the Tenjinno machine translation competition, held in conjunction with the eighth International Colloquium on Grammatical Inference (ICGI 2006). The competition aimed to measure and improve upon the current state-of-the-art in grammatical inference. Tenjinno was the successor to the earlier Abbadingo [1], Gowachin and Omphalos [2, 3] competitions.

At the ICGI 2004 it was decided that it would be desirable to have a competition task that more closely resembles a real world application compared to earlier competitions; hence the task of machine translation was chosen. However, although described as a machine translation competition, Tenjinno was in fact a transducer inference competition. Machine translation has obvious applications in the translation of human languages, but the problem of translation is more general and has applications beyond natural language. For instance,

Y. Sakakibara et al. (Eds.): ICGI 2006, LNAI 4201, pp. 214–226, 2006.

it is a cornerstone of genomics that the translation of DNA into living things is a predominately deterministic process. For this reason, we invited submission from practitioners from all areas of computer science including machine learning, natural language processing, formal languages, machine translation and bioinformatics.

The competition differed from other machine translation competitions such as the DARPA machine translation competitions [4] in the following important ways:

- The languages were artificial and were derived from formal models.
- We expected that competitors would infer the model used to derive the data exactly and the metric used to measure the winner reflected this expectation.

In Section 2, we present the task we chose for the competition and describe the two formalisms that were used. In Section 3, we describe how the competition was set up and explain the measure used to estimate the current state-of-the art, and we also explain the name Tenjinno. In Section 4, we describe the results of the competition.

2 Task Description

Essentially, we generated several automatic machine translation systems that were based on finite state transducers and syntax directed translation schemata. Using these formal models, we generated sentences in the source language and corresponding translations in the target language. This generated data, containing both source and target sentences aligned on a sentence by sentence basis, was provided to the competitors who used these sentences to train their translation systems.

Test data, containing only source sentences, was also provided. The task for the competitors was to generate the corresponding target sentences. The translated sentences could then be submitted to the competition Oracle, which determined whether or not the problem had been solved.

There were four problems proposed on the web site and these were ranked according to the difficulty of the translation process. At the close of the competition, the competitor who had solved the highest-ranking problem would be declared the winner of the competition overall. The two lowest ranking problems were to translate sentences produced from Finite State Transducers (FSTs), while the higher ranking problems were to translate sentences produced from Syntax Directed Translation Schema (SDTS).

Finite State Transducers (FST) were chosen as one of the formalisms for the Tenjinno competition mainly because there has been a history of research into the inference of FSTs published at previous ICGIs. The SDTS formalism was chosen because, unlike FSTs, SDTSs are expressive enough to define the reordering of constituents when translating from one language to another.

Reordering of constituents is a common task when translating between natural languages and its formalisation is an important issue for Machine Translation.

For instance, it is often necessary to translate from Subject Verb Object (SVO) languages into Subject Object Verb (SOV) languages, with arbitrarily large constituents as either subjects or objects. However, the inference of SDTSs has not been well researched yet and it was hoped that the Tenjinno competition would spur interest into this field.

In the Tenjinno competition, some of the transducers were deterministic and some were non-deterministic, and labelled as such. The problems labelled non-deterministic were ranked higher (i.e. more difficult) than those labelled deterministic. This distinction was made because it has been shown in previous competitions [2, 3] that the inference of non-deterministic grammars is a more difficult task.

Where the transducers were non-deterministic, they can be shown to be unambiguous. This was a deliberate design choice of the competition, due the fact that the number of translations for a sentence can quickly become significantly large when the transducer is ambiguous.

2.1   Finite State Transducers

A Finite State Transducer (FST) is a formalism that can translate strings to strings directly using a finite state machine.

An FST (which can also be seen as a regular syntax-directed translation scheme) [5] T is a tuple $\langle N, \Sigma, \Delta, R, I \rangle$ where N is a finite set of non-terminal symbols or states, I is the initial state, Σ is a finite set of input terminal symbols and Δ is a finite set of output terminals.

R is the set of rules which can take one of the two following forms:

- $A \rightarrow aB, wB$ for $A, B \in N, a \in \Sigma, w \in \Delta^*$ or
- $A \rightarrow a, w$ for $a \in \Sigma, w \in \Delta^*$.

The right-hand side of rules are separated into two parts by a comma. Each of the parts represents information about a language; the source language first, followed by the target language. Table 1 gives an example of a finite state transducer.

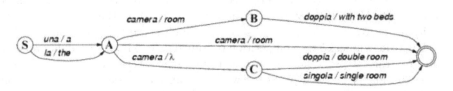

Fig. 1. The Finite State Transducer of Table 1 shown diagrammatically

An input string "x" can be mapped to the output string "y" denoted (x, y) if there is a translation from $(S, S) \Rightarrow (x_1 A_1, y_1 A_1) \Rightarrow (x_1 x_2 A_2, y_1 y_2 A_2) \Rightarrow \cdots \Rightarrow (x, y)$ where $\Rightarrow$ denotes the application of a rule.

If there is a translation from (S, S) to (x, y), (x, y) is known as a translation pair. For instance, given the FST shown in Table 1, (una camera doppia, a double

Table 1. A non-deterministic Finite State Transducer

$S \rightarrow$una A, a A
$S \rightarrow$la A, the A
$A \rightarrow$camera B, room B
$A \rightarrow$camera, room
$A \rightarrow$camera C, C
$B \rightarrow$doppia, with two beds
$C \rightarrow$doppia, double room
$C \rightarrow$singola, single room

room) can be shown to be a translation pair as follows: $(S, S) \Rightarrow (\text{una}A, \text{a}A) \Rightarrow$ (una camera$C$, aC) $\Rightarrow$ (una camera doppia, a double room).

We say that a finite transducer is deterministic if, for each rule of the form $A \rightarrow aB, wB$ where a $\in \Sigma \cup \{\epsilon\}$, w $\in \Delta^*$ and $B \in N \cup \{\epsilon\}$, there does not exist any other rule of the form $A \rightarrow aC, hC$ where $C \in N \cup \{\epsilon\}$ and h $\in \Delta^*$. Although every language that is accepted by a non-deterministic finite-state automaton is also accepted by a deterministic finite-state automaton, there exist non-deterministic finite-state transducers for which there is no equivalent deterministic finite-state transducer [6].

2.2 Syntax Directed Translation Schema

A Syntax-Directed Translation Schema (SDTS) is a transducer in which both the input and output languages are described using a context-free grammar, and there is a one to one mapping between parse trees in the input language and parse trees in the output language, and similarly a one to one mapping between parse trees in the output language and parse trees in the input language.

An SDTS [7] T is a tuple $\langle N, \Sigma, \Delta, R, I \rangle$ where N is a finite set of non-terminal symbols or states, I is the initial state, Σ is a finite set of input terminal symbols and Δ is a finite set of output terminals.

R is the set of rules which can take on the form $A \rightarrow$ a, b where a $\in (N \cup \Sigma)^*$ and b $\in (N \cup \Delta)^*$ and the non-terminals in "a" are a permutation of the non-terminals in "b". If a non-terminal B appears more than once in "a" or "b" then we use superscripts to indicate the association, for example, in the rule $A \rightarrow B^{(1)}CB^{(2)}, B^{(2)}B^{(1)}C$. This association is an intimate part of the rule.

Table 2 gives an example of a syntax directed translation schema.

From Table 2, it can be seen that $(0\ 0\ 1\ 1\ 1, \text{b b b a a})$ is a translation pair as follows:

Table 2. A simple Syntax-Directed Translation Schema

$S \rightarrow 0AS, SA\text{a}$
$A \rightarrow 0SA, AS\text{a}$
$S \rightarrow 1, \text{b}$
$A \rightarrow 1, \text{b}$

$(S, S) \Rightarrow (0AS, SAa) \Rightarrow (0\ 0SAS, SASa\ a) \Rightarrow (0\ 0\ 1AS, SAb\ a\ a) \Rightarrow$
$\Rightarrow (0\ 0\ 1\ 1S, Sb\ b\ b\ a\ a) \Rightarrow (0\ 0\ 1\ 1\ 1, b\ b\ b\ a\ a)$.

Note that in this example, the input sequence is always leftmost expanded, but the output sequence is not.

It can be seen that finite state transducers are a sub-class of simple syntax-directed translation schemata [8]. It can also be seen that input and output languages defined by a FST must be regular, but in the case of SDTSs the input and output languages can be context-free and not regular. This enables SDTSs to translate individual words in an input text according to long range dependencies between words in the input text, whereas such dependencies cannot be represented using a FST. For example, consider the SDTS shown in Table 3. In this example, whether or not the word "b" is translated into an "f" or a "g" depends upon whether or not either an "a" or a "c" was presented earlier in the input text. Here, $(S, S) \Rightarrow^* (a\ c\ d\ b, j\ f)$ and $(S, S) \Rightarrow^* (c\ c\ d\ b, j\ g)$.

Table 3. An SDTS that is not a FST

$$S \rightarrow aSb, Sf$$
$$S \rightarrow a\ b, f$$
$$S \rightarrow cSb, Sg$$
$$S \rightarrow c\ b, g$$
$$S \rightarrow aSd, Sh$$
$$S \rightarrow a\ d, h$$
$$S \rightarrow cSd, Sj$$
$$S \rightarrow c\ d, j$$

3   Competition Philosophy

In this section, we describe the underlying philosophy we followed while designing the Tenjinno competition and define the requirements of the competition. We also discuss how we ranked the competition problems and explain the measure we used to estimate the current state-of-the-art. Finally, we explain how Tenjinno, the name of the competition, was derived.

3.1   Requirements

The target transducers and the training and testing examples were created with the following objectives in mind:

1. The learning task should be sufficiently difficult. Specifically, the problems should be just outside of the current state-of-the-art, but not so difficult that it is unlikely that a winner would be found.
2. It should be provable either that the training sentences are sufficient to identify the target transducer or that it is at least possible to give an estimation of the probability of the training sentences being sufficient.

To determine whether or not requirement 1 was met, a measure of the complexity of the learning task was derived, similar to that used for the Omphalos Competition [2, 3]. The measure was derived by creating a model of the learning task based upon a brute force search. In this model, the learner is presented with an infinite stream of translation pair sets, where each set consists of a string in the input language and all translations of that sentence. After each presentation the learner constructs a set of hypothetical SDTS each of the form $\langle N, \Sigma, \Delta, R, I \rangle$ where Σ is the set of input terminal symbols observed in the translation pair sets and Δ is the set of output terminals observed in the translation pair sets, and no rule in R is longer than the length of any sequence observed in the translation pair sets. The brute force learner initially assumes that $|N| = 1$ and constructs all possible SDTSs. The learner then discards all SDTSs that are inconsistent with the observed translation pair sets. If no SDTS remains in the hypothesis set, then the number of non-terminals is increased and the process is repeated until at least one SDTS consistent with the observed translation pair sets is found.

This process can be shown to terminate because, for any given number of non-terminals, there are a finite number of possible SDTSs and it is known that there exists at least one SDTS that is consistent with the observed translation pair sets (i.e. the SDTS used to generate the translation pair sets). When there are more than one candidate SDTS, the learner selects one according to any linear ordering where one SDTS is considered more favourable than another if it contains fewer non-terminals and shorter rules.

It can be seen that for any SDTS, when the set of observation pairs used to train the model includes at least one translation pair generated for each of the rules, it causes the learning algorithm to construct a set of hypothesis SDTSs that includes the target SDTS. If a selected hypothesis is inconsistent with the target SDTS, then at some finite point in time a translation pair set will be presented to the learner that causes the learner to discard the incorrect hypothesis.

Therefore, provided enough translation pairs are presented to this algorithm (and an infinite amount of memory and computing time is available), this algorithm will always identify the target SDTS. The size of the hypothesis space that needs to be created by such a learning algorithm forms the basis of the complexity measure. This model is also used to determine whether the training data is sufficient to enable competitors to identify the target transducer. An upper bound on the number of samples required is derived using PAC learning theory [9], but it was decided to construct significantly smaller test sets than is suggested using the PAC learning equations, based upon the knowledge that the upper bounds indicated from the PAC learning equations assume that all hypotheses in the hypothesis space are mutually exclusive, which is not the case for the brute force algorithm.

3.2   The Ranking of the Competition Problems

The Tenjinno competition adopted a linear ordering for the competition problems based upon the formalism used, the complexity of the problems, and whether or not the formal model from which the data was derived is deterministic.

It is well understood that the class of transducers that can be described using FSTs is a proper subset of the class of transducers that can be described using SDTSs [7]. Similarly, it is well known that the class of transducers that can be described using deterministic FSTs is a subset of the class of transducers that can be described using non-deterministic FSTs. The class of transducers that can be described using deterministic SDTSs is also a subset of the class of transducers that can be described using non-deterministic SDTSs [6].

Since solving the problem generated from a non-deterministic model is considered to be more difficult, if both problems for one class of transducers were solved, the competitor who had solved the non-deterministic problem would be declared the winner.

In addition, a complexity measure for each learning task was constructed to enable a comparison between the competition problems and problems with well known benchmark corpora. During the life of the competition, the organisers reserved the right to add easier problems or more difficult problems problems, as indicated by the complexity measure.

Table 4 describes the equations used to measure the complexity of the competition problems. Different measures are used for the different classes of problems.

Because the FST equation is the simpler of the two, we will describe how it was derived but leave it to the reader to determine why the SDTS equation describes the number of possible SDTS, given the input parameters.

The complexity measure for the FST tasks describes an upper bound on the number of possible FSTs that could be constructed given a finite set of input symbols, output symbols and non-terminals of size σ, δ and n respectively, where there are at most L non-terminal and output symbols on the right hand side of the longest rule.

Firstly it can be seen that if, given the input parameters, there are R possible rules, then the number of possible FSTs is 2^R. This is because, in any given FST, each possible rule can either be present or not. Therefore the exponent of the complexity measure describes the number of possible rules. Each rule has one non-terminal on the left hand side which can take on n different values, and one input symbol from the input language on the right hand side which can take on one of σ different values, hence the exponent begins with $n \times \sigma$. The right hand side can have either 0 or 1 non-terminals. We consider both cases by adding both possibilities using the summation $\sum_{j=0}^{1}$ where j describes the number of non-terminals. There are n choices of non-terminals hence there are n^j possible ways of selecting j non-terminals. Note that when there are 0 non-terminals $n^j = 1$. If the right hand side has j non-terminals there can be up to $k = L - j$ terminal symbols on the right hand side. There are δ choices of output terminals, and these terminals can be repeated. Therefore there are δ^k ways of selecting them. Note that L defines the maximum length of a right-hand side; there can be less than L symbols. We can consider all possibilities using the summation $\sum_{k=0}^{L-j} \delta^k$. Hence the number of possible FSTs given the input parameters is $2^{n \times \sigma \times \sum_{j=0}^{1}(n^j \times \sum_{k=0}^{L-j} \delta^k)}$.

Similarly, the complexity measure for the SDTS tasks describes an upper bound on the number of possible SDTSs that could be constructed given a finite set of input symbols, output symbols and non-terminals of size σ, δ and n respectively, where there are at most L symbols on the right hand side of the longest rule. Specifically the number of non-terminals symbols and output symbols on any given rule is less than L, and the number of non-terminals symbols and input symbols on any given rule is less than L.

Table 4. Formalisms with their complexity measures

Formalism	Complexity Measure
SDTS	$2^{n \times \sum_{i=0}^{L}(\sum_{j=0}^{i}\binom{n+j-1}{j} \times \binom{\sigma+i-j-1}{i-j} \times i! \times \sum_{k=j}^{L}(\binom{\delta+k-j-1}{k-j} \times k!)))}$
FST	$2^{n \times \sigma \times \sum_{j=0}^{L}(n^{j} \times \sum_{k=0}^{L-j} \delta^{k})}$

where

n=the number of non-terminals
σ=the size of the input lexicon
δ=the size of the output lexicon
L=the length of the longest rule

Construction of Non-deterministic Transducers. The finite state transducer (FST) of problem 2 can be shown to be non-deterministic but unambiguous. Firstly, the transducer is non-deterministic because it has non-deterministic state transitions such as $S \rightarrow \text{a b } cX, cX$ and $S \rightarrow \text{a b } cZ, bZ$. However the correct state transition can always be determined by looking at most three characters ahead; that is, the underlying context-free backbone is $LL(3)$, which implies that the underlying grammar is unambiguous.

The syntax directed translation schema (SDTS) of problem 4 was constructed as follows. First a randomly generated $LR(1)$ grammar was constructed. Because this grammar was $LR(1)$, it was known to be unambiguous. This grammar included center recursion to ensure that it was not regular. A construct of the form $a^n b^m$ where $n, m > 1$ and $m \neq n$ was then added to one of the non-terminals. This was known to be unambiguous because it was the union of two disjoint $LR(1)$ grammars. The SDTS was constructed in such a way that the mapping from input symbols to output symbols depends upon whether $m > n$ or $n < m$. Any parser that can parse these sentence needs to determine whether $m > n$ or $n > m$ before deciding which rule to apply. This requires an arbitrary amount of lookahead, and thus this transducer is non-deterministic and cannot be represented by a deterministic SDTS.

3.3 Estimating the Current State-of-the-Art

To ensure that the competition problems where just beyond the state-of-the-art, the proceedings of recent conferences were examined to identify the performance of different inference techniques on some corpora commonly used for the inference of machine translation systems. The complexities of the problems in the Tenjinno competition were then set to be an order of magnitude larger than these problems. In addition, the complexities of the problems were set to be large enough that they could not be solved using a brute force search in the time in which the competition was open (i.e. there are approximately 1.57×10^{13} microseconds in a six month period).

Table 5 contains a list of some corpora commonly used for the inference of machine translation systems. This data is derived from Casacuberta [5], Amengual et al. [10], Matusov et al. [11]. Some of the earlier experiments listed here are described in Vidal and Casacuberta [12] as being indicative of the state-of-the-art. Conveniently the documents from which this table has been compiled describe experiments in which n-gram finite state transducers were inferred from the given corpora. In addition, the corpora were described in sufficient detail in those papers to allow for easy comparison between the complexity of the learning tasks and the word error rates obtained.

Although there is yet to be a published technique that can achieve a 0% word error rate on any of these corpora, it should be noted that these corpora are natural language corpora, which are unlikely to be defined using finite state transducers. Therefore, we would expect that the word error rates obtained using the techniques described in the papers on data defined using finite state transducers would be better than that listed in Table 5.

It seemed appropriate to begin with competition tasks that were of a slightly greater complexity to those listed in this table. When calculating the complexity of the underlying models we used the somewhat arbitrary assumption that it is possible to learn the structure of the underlying models from the training examples without n-gram smoothing, that is whether or not the probability of each possible transition is either zero or non-zero. Therefore we have estimated the number of non-terminals to be either one quarter of the number of words in the training examples, or the number of possible states in the given n-gram $\{(d+1)^{n-1}\}$ whichever is smallest.

We have also included a column which gives an estimate of the complexity of an SDTS that might be used to describe the target language. The SDTS measure is estimated using the given vocabularies and assuming that the target SDTS could be described using a similar number of non-terminals to the number of Penn Treebank tags. Specifically, we selected the number of non-terminals to be 36 and have arbitrarily selected the length of the longest rule to be 7.

Most of the corpora in Table 5 [5, 10, 11] have large vocabularies. Some other commonly used corpora, such as the Canadian Hansard, are used because of the close alignment between word orders in the source and target languages (e.g. French and English). However, as was mentioned earlier, word reordering is of crucial importance in translation between natural languages and it is one of the difficult problems for machine translation. For this reason, although the problems in the Tenjinno competition have a complexity similar to those listed in Table 5, the Tenjinno problems have smaller vocabularies and derive more of their complexity from non-monotonic alignment.

Using the results of Table 5 the complexities of the Tenjinno competition problems were selected to be just outside of the complexities listed in Table 6.

Table 5. Properties of commonly used corpora for the inference of machine translation systems

Corpus	Translation pair	Source lexicon	Target lexicon	Word error rate
EuTrans-0	Spanish →English	683	514	0.74%
EuTrans-I	Spanish →English	686	513	9.7%
EuTrans-II	Italian →English	2,459	1,712	28.3%
Verbmobil	German→English	7,939	4,672	36.2%
Basic Travel Corpus	Chinese →English	7,643	6,982	48%

Table 6. Estimated complexity of commonly used corpora for the inference of machine translation systems

Corpus	$\log_2$ of FSM complexity	$\log_2$ of SDTS complexity
EuTrans-0	1.89×10^{19}(7 class n-gram)	2.30×10^{37}
EuTrans-I	2.14×10^{22}(4-gram)	3.45×10^{39}
EuTrans-II	3.16×10^{24}(4-gram)	6.87×10^{46}
Verbmobil	3.89×10^{28}(4-gram)	6.91×10^{48}
Basic Travel Corpus	3.99×10^{28}(4-gram)	8.56×10^{50}

3.4   The Name Tenjinno

Since the conference was held in Japan, the ICGI competition committee decided to have a Japanese inspired name for the ICGI 2006 competition and that ideally the name should be related to language and learning. Using these requirements, we decided to use the Japanese name "Tenjin" as the basis for the name of the competition. Tenjin is the Shinto kami of scholarship, the deified Sugawara no Michizane.

Tenjin is a word that appeared frequently on the Internet at the time of the competition (645,000 hits on Google, measured before the start of the competition) and therefore we have added the Japanese particle "no" to the end of the word, so that it became the "Tenjin no" competition, or loosely Tenjin's competition. Although "no" should be a separate word, by conjugating it with Tenjin (i.e. Tenjinno), we created something more unique. For instance at the time of the competition, "Tenjin no" returned 97,000 hits, "Tenjin-no" 1,060 hits, but "Tenjinno" returned only 12 hits, and the website of the Tenjinno competition was the highest ranked result.

4   Participation and Results

The Tenjinno Competition started on 3rd January 2006. The website (http://www.ics.mq.edu.au/~tenjinno/) had been made available a few days before, but the oracle came online on 3rd January. In total, while the competition was open, the website received 2,550 visits. The datasets were downloaded by users from 63 different sites. Overall, users from 200 sites have accessed the website.

Table 7 lists the competition problems, along with their complexities and the status of each problem i.e. whether or not the problem was solved. The problems are listed in order of increasing difficulty. The winner of the competition overall was the competitor that solved the highest ranking problem according to this table.

Table 7. Properties of the problems of Tenjinno

Problem	Formalism	$\log_2$ Complexity	Status
1	Deterministic FST	7.27×10^{31}	Solved
2	Non Deterministic Unambiguous FST	7.27×10^{31}	Unsolved
3	Deterministic SDTS	7.24×10^{34}	Unsolved
4	Non Deterministic Unambiguous SDTS	8.28×10^{34}	Unsolved

Problem 1 was solved on 6th April 2006 by Alexander Clark (Royal Holloway University of London), who was also the winner of the Omphalos competition [2]. At the closing of the competition on 1st July 2006 the remaining problems (2, 3, and 4) were unsolved and thus Alexander Clark was declared the winner overall.

Table 8. Important dates for the Tenjinno competition

Date	Event
31 December 2005	Competition details available on the website
1 January 2006	Competition begins
1 July 2006	Competition closes
2 July 2006	Competition winner announced
September 2006	Tenjinno session at ICGI-2006

5   Conclusions

In contrast to previous ICGI competitions the problems in the Tenjinno competition mirrored a real world task. Set in the context of machine translation, the task was to learn a translation between sentences in two paired artificial languages. This task is interesting from a formal perspective, where one may try different approaches, for example learning grammars for both languages and finding a mapping between them or learning one grammar and tree operations on the resulting derivation. It is also interesting from an application perspective, because machine translation has always been an important research topic in natural language processing and machine translation applications have become more successful recently and gained more visibility.

For the purpose of setting the competition tasks, extensions to the complexity measure used in the Omphalos competition were used and are described in this paper. These measures have enabled us to compare the competition problems with other published results in the field of machine translation. Using this measure, we can see that the problems solved in the competition were of a greater complexity and were solved with lower word error rates than other published results. One reason for this is undoubtedly because, unlike real world tasks, it is known that the training and test data are derived from formal models similar to those learnt by the grammatical inference software. Despite this, we believe that the competition has played a role in focusing research onto an important area of grammatical inference. In addition the complexity measures and benchmark problems can be used to track the progress of the state-of-the-art into the future.

Bibliography

[1] Kevin J. Lang, Barak A. Pearlmutter, and Rodney A. Price. Results of the Abbadingo One DFA learning competition and a new evidence-driven state merging algorithm. In V. Honavar and G. Slutzki, editors, *Proceedings of the Fourth International Conference on Grammar Inference*, volume 1433 of *Lecture Notes in AI*, pages 1–12, Berlin Heidelberg, Germany, 1998. Springer-Verlag.

[2] Bradford Starkie, François Coste, and Menno van Zaanen. The Omphalos context-free grammar learning competition. In Paliouras and Sakakibara [13], pages 16–27.

[3] Bradford Starkie, François Coste, and Menno van Zaanen. Progressing the state-of-the-art in grammatical inference by competition. *AI Communications*, 18(2): 93–115, 2005.

[4] National Institute of Standards and Technology. The 2006 nist machine translation evaluation plan (mt06), 2006. URL http://www.nist.gov/speech/tests/mt/doc/mt06_evalplan.v4.pdf

[5] F. Casacuberta. Inference of finite-state transducers by using regular grammars and morphisms. In Arlindo L. Oliveira, editor, *Grammatical Inference: Algorithms and Applications (ICGI); Lisbon, Portugal*, volume 1891 of *Lecture Notes in AI*, pages 1–14, Berlin Heidelberg, Germany, September 11–13 2000. Springer-Verlag.

[6] E. Gurari. *An Introduction to the Theory of Computation*. Computer Science Press, Rockville:MD, USA, 1989.

[7] A.V. Aho and J.D. Ullman. *The theory of parsing, translation, and compiling*. Prentice Hall, Englewood Cliffs:NJ, USA, 1972.

[8] K.S. Fu. *Syntactic pattern recognition and applications*. Advances in computing science and technology series. Prentice Hall, Englewood Cliffs:NJ, USA, 1982.

[9] L. G. Valiant. A theory of the learnable. *Communications of the Association for Computing Machinery*, 27(11):1134–1142, 1984.

[10] J.C. Amengual, A. Castaño, A. Castellanos, V.M. Jiménez, D. Llorens, A. Marzal, F. Prat, J.M. Vilar, J.M. Benedi, F. Casacuberta, M. Pastor, and E. Vidal. The eutrans-i spoken language translation system. *Machine Translation*, 15(1):75–103, 2000.

[11] E. Matusov, S. Kanthak, and H. Ney. Efficient statistical machine translation with constrained reordering. In *European Association for Machine Translation (EAMT) 10th Annual Conference; Budapest, Hungary*, pages 181–188, 2005.

[12] E. Vidal and F. Casacuberta. Learning finite-state models for machine translation. In Paliouras and Sakakibara [13], pages 3–15.

[13] Georgios Paliouras and Yasubumi Sakakibara, editors. *Grammatical Inference: Algorithms and Applications: Seventh International Colloquium, (ICGI); Athens, Greece*, volume 3264 of *Lecture Notes in AI*, Berlin Heidelberg, Germany, October 11–13 2004. Springer-Verlag.

Large Scale Inference of Deterministic Transductions: Tenjinno Problem 1

Alexander Clark

Department of Computer Science, Royal Holloway, University of London,
Egham, Surrey TW20 0EX

Abstract. We discuss the problem of large scale grammatical inference in the context of the Tenjinno competition, with reference to the inference of deterministic finite state transducers, and discuss the design of the algorithms and the design and implementation of the program that solved the first problem. Though the OSTIA algorithm has good asymptotic guarantees for this class of problems, the amount of data required is prohibitive. We therefore developed a new strategy for inferring large scale transducers that is more adapted for large random instances of the type in question, which involved combining traditional state merging algorithms for inference of finite state automata with EM based alignment algorithms and state splitting algorithms.

1 Introduction

The Tenjinno competition [14] is a grammatical inference competition where the problem tasks, though from synthetic data, are designed to approximate the problem of machine translation. The problem consists of inferring a transduction from one symbol sequence (the input sequence) to another symbol sequence (the output sequence). Once inferred the transduction must be applied to some new input data to generate a predicted output sequence. These sequences are then submitted to a web-based oracle. If all of the output sequences are exactly correct then the oracle will say so; otherwise, the oracle merely states that the data is incorrect. No other feedback is given. The problems were generated according to some random process which was unspecified.

The first problem, which we study here, is a deterministic sequential transducer. The key factor here is simply the size of the problem; the input alphabet size was 1001, and the output alphabet was 1000. The problem clearly had many thousands of states, and the amount of training data was 100,000 pairs, with 10,000 test strings. Thus the problem is very substantial; indeed of the same size as real world problems in machine translation, though current SMT systems train on many millions or even billions of sentences.

The outline of our approach is as follows. We started by discarding the output data and considering the input data alone. This will be a regular language, and given the parameters of the problem, the distinguishability of the underlying deterministic finite state automaton would be high. We accordingly constructed the prefix tree acceptor for the data, creating an automaton with over 1,000,000

Y. Sakakibara et al. (Eds.): ICGI 2006, LNAI 4201, pp. 227–239, 2006.

states and then used a state merging algorithm, with appropriate optimisations, to construct a more compact automaton with less than 20,000 states. We then used a novel alignment algorithm based on the Expectation-Maximization algorithm to attach an output string to each transition, which also identified some errors (incorrectly merged states) which were then split, and the aligment corrected, until we had a correctly aligned transducer with 20,000 states that generated the training data correctly. Using the information now from the outputs on the transition, we could merge the automaton more freely. A final phase used the test data itself, to merge states to increase the coverage to include all of the test data.

In the rest of the paper, we start by defining our notation, Section 2, and then describe approaches to the inference of finite state models both for languages and for transductions, Section 3. We then discuss the Tenjinno problem, Section 4 and then present the algorithm that we developed to solve the problem Section 5. We discuss the alignment algorithm in Section 7 in some detail, and finish with some remarks about the competition design and the issues about applying theoretical algorithms to large scale problems.

2   Notation

We are interested in transductions between finite strings. We have a finite input alphabet Σ, and a finite output alphabet Ξ. We write Σ^* for the free monoid generated by Σ and Ξ^* similarly. We write λ for the empty string in both monoids, since this will not be confusing. We write $|u|$ for the length of a string, and uv, or occasionally $u + v$ for the concatenation of elements of Σ^* . We will use letters a, b for elements of Σ and also for elements of Σ^* of length 1. We write $u \sqsubseteq v$ if u is a contiguous subsequence (factor) of v , i.e. $\exists, l, r \in \Sigma^*$ s.t. $lur = v$. For a string u we will write u_i for the ith letter in the string, i.e. $u = u_1 u_2 \ldots u_{|u|}$ we will write $u[i : j]$ for the substring $u_{i+1} \ldots u_j$, so $u[i : i] = \lambda$, $u[0 : |u|] = u$.

A transduction is a subset T of $\Sigma^* \times \Xi^*$. Here we are interested in transductions that are deterministic and unambiguous. A transduction T is unambiguous if $(u, v) \in T, (u, v') \in T$ implies $v = v'$.

The transductions in the Tenjinno competition are of various formal types, problem 1 being a deterministic finite state transducer.

A deterministic finite state automaton A is a tuple $\langle Q, \Sigma, q_0, q_f, \tau \rangle$, where

- Q is a finite set of states,
- Σ is the alphabet, a finite set of symbols,
- $q_0 \in Q$ is the single initial state,
- $q_f \notin Q$ is the final state,
- $\tau : Q \times \Sigma \to Q \cup \{q_f\}$ is a partial function that defines the transitions.

We extend the transition function τ to Σ^* in the normal way. This automaton then defines a language $L(A) = \{u \in \Sigma^* | \tau(q_0, u) = q_f\}$. The definition we use here means that the language is prefix free: i.e. if $u \in L(A)$ and $uv \in L(A)$ then $v = \lambda$.

A key idea here is that of the signature of a state. The signature of a state $q \in Q$ is defined as $\text{sig}(q) = \{\sigma \in \Sigma | \exists q' \in Q : \tau(q, \sigma) = q'\}$ - i.e. the set of letters that label transitions out of the state q.

A deterministic finite state transducer T is a DFA together with an output alphabet Ξ and a function $\gamma : Q \times \Sigma \to \Xi^*$ where the domain of γ is the same as the domain of τ. We extend γ to Σ^*, and then this transducer defines a partial function $\phi_T : \Sigma^* \mapsto \Xi^*$ where $\phi(u) = v$ if and only if $\tau(q_0, u) = q_f$ and $\gamma(q_0, u) = v$.

The inference problem is to infer a transducer T, given a set of pairs of strings from $\Sigma^* \times \Xi^*$ which we will write $X = (u_1, v_1), \ldots (u_n, v_n)$, Then given some new input data $Y = x_1, \ldots x_{n'}$ we predict values of $\phi_T(x_i')$ which are then compared to an oracle. No feedback is given except when there is an exact match.

3   Inference of Finite State Models

There are basically two methods of learning finite state automata. The first, which learns DFAs uses a state merging algorithm starting from a prefix tree acceptor [3,6]. This can be proven to be correct under various assumptions. The second, which can learn some non-deterministic finite state automata, uses a randomly initialised Hidden Markov Model, together with an iterative statistical optimisation algorithm to find a local optimum – normally the Expectation Maximisation (EM) algorithm [7,2] is used because of its simplicity, elegance, and rapid convergence, but other methods of non-convex optimisation can be used, or gradient ascent. These optimisation problems are in general hard to solve exactly ([1]), and these algorithms will only find a local optimum rather than the global one.

Analogously with these two methods, there are two standard algorithms for learning finite state transducers. The first, OSTIA, [12] essentially uses a state merging algorithm on the transducer, together with an algorithm for shifting the outputs to an appropriate spot. While it is provably correct in the identification in the limit framework, it is not necessarily going to produce satisfactory results on smaller data sets. The second method, analogous to the use of HMMs, uses stochastic finite state transducers, also sometimes known as Pair Hidden Markov Models [8], with again a training algorithm based on the EM algorithm. This has been demonstrated to be effective for learning some simple transductions [4].

4   Problem Analysis

Problem 1 appeared to have been generated randomly. Accordingly we would expect the out-degrees of the states to be distributed binomially. As a first step we examined the histogram of signatures of the prefix tree acceptor which is shown in Table 1.

There are in principle three sources of information: the input language (the domain of the transduction), the output language, and the relationship between

Table 1. Signature histograms. This shows the numbers of different signatures of various sizes, of the various automata produced. For each automaton, we give the total number of distinct signatures of a given size n, and the total number of states with signatures of that size. We give the results for three automata: the initial prefix tree acceptor, the automaton formed after merging, and the final correct one. Note for the PTA, that there is only one empty signature, and we have exactly 95000 states with this – one for each training string. There are 1001 different signatures of size 1: one for each letter in the input alphabet.

$|\text{sig}(q)|$	PTA		Merged		Final	
	n	N	n	N	n	N
0	1	95000	1	6520	1	1
1	1001	860039	841	2090	5	5
2	15920	41278	894	942	23	23
3	7580	12756	2059	2362	1923	1923
4	4764	6259	3906	3907	3904	3904
5	1955	2250	2089	2089	2089	2090
6	77	84	81	81	81	81
7	2	2	4	4	4	4
8	0	0	0	0	0	0
total	31300	1017668	9875	17995	8030	8031

the two of them. The large input alphabet means that the occurrence of a transition gives a huge amount of information, and allows us to identify pairs of states in the prefix tree that were generated by the same state in the transducer. Thus given that there is a very easily detectable structure in the input language, and that the inference of deterministic finite state languages is now a mature field, it seems appropriate to start by trying to find a compact DFA that generates the input language. The input and output languages are both regular but very different in structure. For example, the input language has 4 symbols that can appear as the first symbol in a word, whereas the output language has 922 (out of a possible 1000!). The reason for this enormous difference is that the output language is not "deterministic" – if we consider the generative process, there will be numerous transitions that only generate the empty string – thus the transitions between the states are not detectable from the symbols. Accordingly, learning the output language requires very different techniques from learning the input language, and after a few preliminary experiments, we decided to focus on learning the input language. However, given the large size of the problems, and the limited amount of data, we could not merge states only when we were very sure that they were equivalent, and thus it was inevitable that some errors would occur in the learning of the automaton. When learning an automaton from positive data only, it is very difficult to detect over-generalisation. When learning a transducer, the situation is very much easier: the output strings give you a great deal of information as to which transitions are being taken. Obviously in this case, we have some problems because so many of the transitions output the empty string: but enough of the states generate proper output strings, that we can detect problems.

Existing algorithms are not suitable for this approach: non-deterministic learning algorithms require a global optimisation that is quadratic in the number of states, which is not feasible on this scale of problem, and the OSTIA algorithm is sensitive to the order in which states are merged, and in this case we need to merge where the data permits, rather than in a fixed order.

5   Algorithm

We now describe the algorithm we applied to this problem.

- We shuffled the data set randomly and split the data into a training set of 95,000 pairs, and a validation set of 5,000 pairs, which we used to detect bugs and errors.
- We then removed the output data.
- On this input data we then constructed the prefix tree acceptor, and then ran a very efficient, aggressive state merging algorithm based on the signatures of the states, until we had an automaton, shown as Merged in Table 1.
- We then used an EM based alignment algorithm, with initialisation based on co-occurrence statistics. This is described in Section 7 below. This algorithm was also used to split states that had erroneously been merged earlier. This produces a small automaton that correctly models the training data.
- Using the additional information given by the output labels, we continued merging, but using a similarity measure that was sensitive to possible misalignments of the outputs.
- The final phase used the input strings from the test data to drive the state merging algorithm, until all of the test data was accepted by the transducer.

We will now describe the various phases of the algorithm in more detail.

6   Initial Merging

The initial merging algorithm followed standard techniques for DFA inference. We computed the prefix tree acceptor, and then merged states that were similar according to a variety of similarity measures, and then recursively determinised the results. Given the large size of the automata, with over 10^6 states, the similarity measures were selected based on the ease with which efficient indices could be constructed.

After looking at the PTA signature histogram in Table 1 we decided to start by merging states that shared 3 elements of their signature. To do this we created an index that stored for every 3-tuple of input symbols the set of states whose signatures are a superset of that tuple.

$$T(\sigma_1, \sigma_2, \sigma_3) = \{q \in Q : \{\sigma_1, \sigma_2, \sigma_3\} \subseteq sig(q)\} \tag{1}$$

Then for every tuple above a threshold, we merge all of those states. We use two heuristics to control rampant overgeneralisation. First we assumed an upper bound on the cardinality of the signatures – if we have a state with more than 8 outgoing states then we assume this is an error, and secondly we have to maintain the prefix-free property. If that is violated then we *know* we have an error. In that case, we undo the merge, and continue. This reduces the automaton size to about $500,000$ states. We then switch to looking at merging states whose signatures share only two symbols using classes of the form:

$$P(\sigma_1, \sigma_2) = \{q \in Q : \{\sigma_1, \sigma_2\} \subseteq sig(q)\} \tag{2}$$

together with a measure of similarity based on the recursive computation of similarity.

Finally we resorted to merging states with signature of width 1. We looked for states that had not been merged; i.e. states that generate only a single string. For a state q such that $|\{w|\tau(q,w) = q_f\}| = 1$, and such that if $\tau(q',a) = q$ then $|sig(q')| > 1$, we iterate along the unique path of states from q, and stop when we can find another state q'' such that $\tau(q'',w) = q_f$, and such that $|w| > k$ for some fixed threshold k. If there is such a state, then we merge q and q'. This helps only marginally with the coverage of the automaton, but it is very important with the alignment algorithm, since it forces the output strings away from the ends of the strings.

6.1   Similarity Computation

We compute a recursive similarity measure between the nodes, based on the number of symbols that they overlap with.

$$\begin{aligned}
s_1(q,q') &= 1 \text{ if } q = q' \\
&= -\infty \text{ if only one of } q, q' \text{ is } q_f \\
&= |sig(q) \cap sig(q')| \text{ otherwise}
\end{aligned} \tag{3}$$

$$s_n(q,q') = \sum_{a \in sig(q) \cap sig(q')} (1 + s_{n-1}(\tau(q,a), \tau(q',a))) \tag{4}$$

When we merge states such that $s_1(q,q') = 2$ we also require that $s_2(q,q')$ is larger than some threshold: we manually tweaked these thresholds at each iteration to get good performance. The definition in line 2 of Equation 3 has the effect of enforcing the prefix-free property: if we merged an accepting state with a non-accepting one, this would violate this property.

7   EM Based Alignment Algorithm

We now consider the alignment algorithm. We are given a DFA, and a set of training pairs, and we wish to attach to each transition of the DFA an element of Ξ^* such that the resulting transducer will model the training transduction correctly. Note first of all that this involves solving a set of word equations. Let $v_{q,a}$ be the output attached to the transition from q labelled with the letter a.

If we translate the input data into the sequence of transitions generated, e.g $u = u_1 u_2 \ldots u_l$, this will produce the output v. This is an equation $v_{\delta(q_0, \lambda), u_1} + v_{\delta(q_0, u_1), u_2} + \cdots v_{\delta(q_0, u_1 \ldots u_{l-1}), u_l} = v$. We will have one of these equations for each training pair (so 100,000 equations) and one variable for each transition. We only align when the number of transitions is much less (say 20,000) than the number of equations. If the structure of the automaton is correct, we can simply solve these equations, by mapping them into linear equation(s), for example, using a Parikh map [13], or simply having variables representing the length of each string and using standard techniques for solving very large sparse linear systems. However in most cases, we will have made an error somewhere, and thus there will not be an exact solution. On the other hand, large parts of the automaton may be correct and thus will have solutions. We solve this by considering a relaxation of the problem. We associate with each transition not a unique output, but a probability distribution over a set of strings. We then adjust the parameters of the distributions to maximise the probability of the observed outputs. If the automaton is correct, then we hope to converge on a solution which will give every output string a probability of one, given the input string – i.e. all of the distributions will eventually converge to putting all of the probability mass on a single string. If the automaton has been merged incorrectly, then there will be transitions which cannot be assigned a single string consistently, and at convergence the distribution for that transition will generate more than one string (the support of the distribution will have cardinality greater than one). We then use this as a diagnostic test for splitting states of the automata.

The output distribution is a multinomial distribution over a set of strings. For every transition $t = (q, \sigma, q')$, we define a finite set of strings $O_t \subset \Xi^*$, where $O_t = \{o_1, \ldots o_n\}$. We then define a multinomial distribution over this set using a set of parameters $\alpha_1, \ldots \alpha_n$ where each α_i is the probability that this transition will generate the corresponding string o_i, and $\sum_i \alpha_i = 1$.

Given a maximum length L for the output strings, for a string $v \in \Xi^*$ define the set of all substrings of v of length at most L by $Sub_L(v) = \{w : |w| \leq L \wedge w \sqsubseteq v\}$.

For a transition $t = (q, a)$ we can define the set of all training pairs such that this transition is taken.

$$C_{q,a} = \{(u, v) \in X | \exists l, r \in \Sigma^*, u = lar \wedge \tau(q_0, l) = q\} \tag{5}$$

$$O_{q,a} = \bigcap_{(u,v) \in C_{q,a}} Sub_L(v) \tag{6}$$

Intuitively this is the set of all substrings that occur in every output string associated with this transition. Note that $\lambda \in O_{q,a}$, so the cardinality is always at least 1. Thus we know that, if the structure of the automaton is correct, the true output associated with that transition will be in the set $O_{q,a}$. Note the relationship to the insights of [15].

Given this set, we initialise the probabilities with the following computation where $\alpha(q, a, w)$ is the parameter for the transition (q, a) labelled with $w \in \Xi^*$, where Z is a normalisation constant.

$$\alpha(q, a, w) = \frac{1}{Z} \left(\frac{|\{(u, v) \in X \,|\, w \sqsubseteq v\}|}{|C_{q,a}|} + \epsilon \right) \tag{7}$$

We add a small random fluctuation ϵ to break symmetry.

Computational note. Calculating this efficiently requires computing a suffix array for the set of strings $v_1, \ldots v_n$, and then for each transition (q, a) computing a bit vector representation of the set of $C_{q,a}$; given these two data structures we can then compute all of the α parameters rapidly.

We can illustrate this with a simple example: the string **zs bq** occurs 23 times in the output strings of the training data. In each of these 23 cases the symbol **hgc** occurs in the input strings. Thus *a priori* it is quite likely that the transition generating **hgc** might be generating the string **zs bq**. Accordingly we would give this one a high probability.

7.1   Iterative Optimisation

For each transition we have a multinomial distribution over a finite subset of $\varXi^*$. We will write these as $P(v|(q, a))$ Given an input string u, the probability of the transducer generating v is given by the sum over all possible alignments between the input and output strings. We write $l = |u|$ and $m = |v|$, and take the alignment variable at the beginning and end to be fixed, $i_0 = 0$ and $i_l = m$.

$$P(v|u) = \sum_{i_0=0}^{0} \sum_{i_1=i_0}^{m} \sum_{i_2=i_1}^{m} \cdots \sum_{i_l=m}^{m} \prod_j P(v[i_{j-1} : i_j]|(\tau(q_0, u[0 : j]), u_j)) \tag{8}$$

The calculation of this sum with exponentially many terms can be performed efficiently using modifications of standard dynamic programming techniques, which we outline below.

We now want to maximise the following expression for the log likelihood.

$$\mathcal{L} = \sum_{i=1}^{n} \log P(v_i | u_i) \tag{9}$$

We do this using the EM algorithm. We compute the expected number of times that each string is generated by the transition and then normalise. This requires a two-dimensional DP trellis as is used for IOHMMs or PHMMs [10]. Since the recursions used are non-standard, because the state is fixed we give them here. We compute the forward and backward probabilities for a pair of strings $u_1 \ldots u_m \to v_1 \ldots v_n$ as follows.

$$f(0, 0) = \qquad\qquad\qquad 1$$
$$f(0, j) = \qquad\qquad\qquad 0 \text{ if } j > 0$$
$$f(i, j) = \textstyle\sum_{k=0}^{j} f(i - 1, k) \alpha(\tau(q_0, u[0 : i - 1]), u_i, v[k : j]) \text{ if } i > 0$$

$$b(l, m) = \qquad\qquad\qquad 1$$
$$b(l, j) = \qquad\qquad\qquad 0 \text{ if } j < m$$
$$b(i, j) = \sum_{k=j}^{l} b(i+1, k)\alpha(\tau(q_0, u[0:i]), u_i, v[j:k]) \text{ if } i < l$$

Given these forward and backward probabilities we can compute the expectation of a particular output being produced, given a particular pair at a particular point where $\tau(q_0, u[0:i]) = q$, $a = u[i:i+1]$ and where $w = v[j:k]$:

$$P((q, a) \to w | u \to v) = \frac{f(i, j)\alpha(q, a, w)b(i+1, k)}{P(v|u)} \tag{10}$$

This is the E-step; the M step just sets the values of α and normalises. This is computationally quite intensive, requiring over an hour of computation and 2 Gigabytes of memory. We run this algorithm to convergence. Ideally this would converge to a log likelihood of 0, which would indicated that every transition was deterministically assigned a particular output.

However, at convergence the log likelihood is -700 (for 95,000 strings). Thus though the vast majority of transitions were unambiguously assigned an output string, there were 11 transitions that did not converge to unambiguous distributions. This was because there were two strings (or sets of strings) that needed to have different outputs. An advantage of this algorithm is that we can identify the exact location of the errors, and thus it is possible to split those states, so that we can have a unique output for every transition.

7.2   Splitting Erroneous States

The alignment algorithm above will not always produce a solution – for example if we merge the whole automaton much too aggressively then all of the transitions might only be able to output λ. In that case this approach would not work, and one would have to relax the requirement that all of the output strings lie in the intersection defined above.

We can now identify problematic states in the transducer. Given a transition (q, a) that we cannot assign an output string to deterministically, we take two pairs of training strings (u_1, v_1) and (u_2, v_2) such that the Viterbi output for that transition (i.e. the one generated by the single most likely alignment) is different. Thus we will have two pairs in the training set $(m_1 a r_1, s_1 w_1 t_1)$ and $(m_2 a r_2, s_2 w_2 t_2)$ such that $\tau(q_0, m_1) = \tau(q_0, m_2) = q$ and such that we want the transition to generate w_1 in the first case and w_2 in the second case. To do this we need to split states so that $\tau(q_0, m_1) \neq \tau(q_0, m_2)$.

We find the smallest i such that $m_1 = j_1 k_1$, $m_2 = j_2 k_2$, $|k_1| = |k_2| = i$, and $\tau(q_0, j_1) \neq \tau(q_0, j_2)$. We then split all of the i states $\tau(q_0, m_1[0 : |j_1| + 1])$ to $\tau(q_0, m_1[0 : |j_1| + i]) = \tau(q_0, m_1)$.

To split a state q, we take the set of all transitions that end in q, $I_q = \{(q', a) | \tau(q', a) = q\}$, and for each element of I_q we create a separate state $q_{(q,a)}$. We then change every transition in I_q so that $\tau(q', a) = q_{(q,a)}$. The outgoing transitions of all of the new states are identical to that of q. The end result of these manipulations is that the two transitions can now be assigned the correct outputs.

At this point we have a smallish automaton that correctly transduces the training data, partially transduces the validation set, and has low coverage on the test data. Our goal now is to merge, while maintaining the transduction on the training set, until we cover the test set.

8   Merge/Split Algorithm

A transducer is onward if for every state, $(|\{(q', a)|\tau(q', a) = q\}| = 1)$ the outgoing transitions do not have a nonzero common output prefix. We define the output prefix of a state q to be the longest common prefix of all outputs generated starting from that state, i.e. the longest common prefix of the set of strings $\{v \in \Xi^* | \exists u \in \Sigma^*, \text{ s.t. } \tau(q, u) = q_f \wedge \gamma(q, u) = v\}$. It is simple to make a transducer onward, by identifying states which only have one incoming transition, and moving all non trivial output prefixes onto them. In our case we only considered states with in-degree one. More formally given a state q with only one incoming transition (q', a) such that $\tau(q', a) = q$, and such that there is a non empty string $u \in \Xi^+$ for all letters $b \in \Sigma$, such that $\tau(q, b)$ is defined, $\exists v \in \Xi^*$ such that $\gamma(q, b) = uv$.

We then use a state merging algorithm that uses the additional information from the output symbols.

When we merge incompatible arcs we push the residue onto arcs, just as is done in the OSTIA algorithm. This fails if we hit an incoming arc, or if we hit the edge. The latter is fatal, but with the other we can again split nodes. This happened 5 times. When we merge two states q, q' which both have a transition a, such that $\gamma(q, a) = uv$ and $\gamma(q', a) = uv'$ where v and v' start with different letters, and if the two states $\tau(q, a), \tau(q', a)$ have no other incoming arcs, we can then push the residues v and v' onto the outgoing arcs of the states $\tau(q, a), \tau(q', a)$, which will then give the two transitions the same output strings $\gamma(q, a) = \gamma(q', a) = u$, so that they can be merged. If however, there are other transitions into the same state say $\tau(p, b) = \tau(q, a)$, we can't do this. In this case we can split this node $\tau(p, b)$ into different ones, so that there is only one incoming transition into each node, and they can be pushed succesfully.

9   Final Phase

At this point the transducer was still not accepting all of the test input strings. Accordingly we used the test input data itself to drive the merging algorithm. For each string x_i in the test data that is not accepted by the transducer, we identified the longest prefix of x_i that was accepted. Take the longest l_i such that $x_i = l_i a r_i$, where $l_i, r_i \in \Sigma^*, a \in \Sigma$, such that $\tau(q_0, l_i) = q$. There is by construction no transition (q, a). We thus define $\text{sig}^+(q) = \text{sig}(q) \cup \{a\}$, using our knowledge of the test data to augment the information available. We then search for a state in the automaton with a signature that includes this one. Since $|\text{sig}^+(q)| \geq 2$, in each case we found a state that included this. In a couple of cases, there was more than one such state, in which case we selected the one with largest count. At the end of this process, we had constructed an automaton that correctly modelled the training data and accepted the test strings. The final signature histogram is shown in Table 1, which shows the expected binomial distribution.

10   Implementation

The programs written for this project were all implemented in Java, based on an existing code base. We experimented with a number of other techniques beyond those described here. We started by writing an exploratory data analysis tool, that allowed us to examine parts of the transducers being generated, starting with the onward sequential transducer constructed directly from the training data. We extended this to a simple command line interpreter, that allowed validation, storing of intermediate results, and other related computations. Since the data sets were large, the time for loading and storing the data sets and the large automata/transducers generated in the early phases of the algorithm was very substantial. Important productivity gains were achieved by keeping the data sets resident in memory.

The efficient implementation of the algorithms described in this paper required the use of a number of specialised algorithms. We focussed on applying algorithms with good theoretical efficiency rather than on constant factor optimisations. The transitions between states were represented, given the large alphabet size, using a sorted linked lists. Merging between states was performed using a union-find algorithm. Since we would sometimes make mistakes in the merging, by trying to merge incompatible nodes, we made this non-destructive, using a graph unification based algorithm originally developed for unification based parsing [9], that uses generational dereferencing. This allowed "undo" operations, when merging operations had undesirable consequences, without the prohibitive expense of copying entire transducers. Since all of the output strings are substrings of the output strings of the training data, we represented these lazily, without copying. This meant that taking substrings was a constant time/space operation, which gives an important efficiency gain – as used in algorithms for linear time construction of suffix trees [11]. These were implemented as immutable value classes. We also used suffix arrays extensively – we constructed these naively, rather than from suffix trees, but given the comparatively short length of the strings, this was efficient enough.

11   Discussion

First, in many respects learning a transducer is easier than learning an automaton; the output strings allow one to identify overgeneralisation during the state merging process. Thus we can say that large random instances of deterministic sequential transducers can be efficiently learned. Again the presence of a large alphabet turns out to be a great help for solving large grammatical inference problems [5].

Competitions of this sort are undoubtedly a good way of pushing forward the state of the art. The real question then is as to what direction the state of the art should be pushed in. The two elements of this competition were first of all the requirement for exact identification, which is perhaps misconceived, since it rules out the sort of approximation techniques that will be useful in dealing with real world problems. The large size of the problems is very useful – first of all it rules out manual or semi-manual approaches. Indeed when developing the algorithms here, the automata are so large that actually inspecting them is out of the question or even misleading. One is forced to look at the automata through statistical summaries of particular properties, such as the signature histograms shown above. The large size of the problems means that the context free inference problems are extremely computationally intensive. A lot of the algorithms that might work, such as inversion transduction grammars [16,17] have prohibitively high, albeit polynomial, complexity.

The exercise was ultimately succesful. A number of lessons can be drawn from this exercise. First, large random instances can be solved accurately from small amounts of data. The number of states in the final automaton was over 5,000, and the number of string pairs in the training data was only 100,000. So the amount of data is less than quadratic. An important issue is that inevitably errors will occur. Mechanisms should be put in place for detecting and correcting errors.

Finally, very large scale state merging algorithms are practical using efficient data structures and indices. In our case, the use of a customised index, which was carefully tuned, allowed a state merging algorithm to run on a PTA with over a million states, very rapidly on a standard workstation. However in real world applications, random instances are less interesting. Naturally occurring instances tend not to have such clean properties (but then we do not have to get the problem exactly right). In particular, finite-state approximations to machine translation tasks will tend to have multiple states that are very similar, and thus will require a more refined approach.

There are a number of ways in which this work could be improved. Firstly, it would clearly be preferrable to combine the alignment and state merging phases; one way of doing this would be to annotate each transition with some vector of posterior probabilities, and incorporate this into the similarity computation.

Acknowledgements

I would like to thank the organisers of the Tenjinno competition.

References

1. N. Abe and M. K. Warmuth. On the computational complexity of approximating distributions by probabilistic automata. *Machine Learning*, 9:205–260, 1992.
2. L. E. Baum and T. Petrie. Statistical inference for probabilistic functions of finite state markov chains. *Annals of Mathematical Statistics*, 37:1559–1663, 1966.
3. R. C. Carrasco and J. Oncina. Learning stochastic regular grammars by means of a state merging method. In R. C. Carrasco and J. Oncina, editors, *Grammatical Inference and Applications, ICGI-94*, number 862 in LNAI, pages 139–152, Berlin, Heidelberg, 1994. Springer Verlag.

4. Alexander Clark. Memory-based learning of morphology with stochastic transducers. In *Proceedings of the 40th Annual Meeting of the Association for Computational Linguistics (ACL)*, pages 513–520, 2002.

5. Alexander Clark. Learning deterministic context free grammars in the Omphalos competition. *Machine Learning*, 2006. to appear.

6. Alexander Clark and Franck Thollard. Partially distribution-free learning of regular languages from positive samples. In *Proceedings of COLING*, Geneva, Switzerland, 2004.

7. A. P. Dempster, N. M. Laird, and D. B. Rubin. Maximum likelihood from incomplete data via the EM algorithm. *Journal of the Royal Statistical Society Series B*, 39:1–38, 1977.

8. R. Durbin, S. Eddy, A. Krogh, and G. Mitchison. *Biological Sequence Analysis: Probabilistic Models of proteins and nucleic acids*. Cambridge University Press, 1998.

9. Martin C. Emele. Unification with lazy non-redundant copying. In *Meeting of the Association for Computational Linguistics*, pages 323–330, 1991.

10. F.Casacuberta. Probabilistic estimation of stochastic regular syntax-directed translation schemes. In R.Moreno, editor, *VI Spanish Symposium on Pattern Recognition and Image Analysis*, pages 201–297. AERFAI, 1995.

11. Dan Gusfield. *Algorithms on Strings, Trees and Sequences: Computer Science and Computational Biology*. Cambridge University Press, 1997.

12. J. Oncina, P. García, and E. Vidal. Learning subsequential transducers for pattern recognition interpretation tasks. *IEEE Transactions on Pattern Analysis and Machine Intelligence*, 15:448–458, 1993.

13. R. J. Parikh. On context-free languages. *Journal of the ACM*, 13(4):570–581, 1966.

14. Brad Starkie, Menno van Zaanen, and Dominique Estival. Tenjinno machine translation competition. http://www.ics.mq.edu.au/~tenjinno/, 2006.

15. J. M. Vilar. Improve the learning of subsequential transducers by using alignments and dictionaries. In *Proceedings of ICGI*, pages 298–311, 2000.

16. Dekai Wu. Stochastic inversion transduction grammars, with application to segmentation, bracketing, and alignment of parallel corpora. In *IJCAI-95*, pages 1328–1335, Montreal, August 1995.

17. Hao Zhang and Daniel Gildea. Stochastic lexicalized inversion transduction grammar for alignment. In *Proceedings of the 43rd Annual Conference of the Association for Computational Linguistics (ACL-05)*, 2005.

A Discriminative Model of Stochastic Edit Distance in the Form of a Conditional Transducer*

Marc Bernard, Jean-Christophe Janodet, and Marc Sebban

EURISE, Université Jean Monnet de Saint-Etienne,
23, rue Paul Michelon, 42023 Saint-Etienne, France
{marc.bernard, janodet, marc.sebban}@univ-st-etienne.fr

Abstract. Many real-world applications such as spell-checking or DNA analysis use the Levenshtein edit-distance to compute similarities between strings. In practice, the costs of the primitive edit operations (insertion, deletion and substitution of symbols) are generally hand-tuned. In this paper, we propose an algorithm to learn these costs. The underlying model is a probabilitic transducer, computed by using grammatical inference techniques, that allows us to learn both the structure and the probabilities of the model. Beyond the fact that the learned transducers are neither deterministic nor stochastic in the standard terminology, they are conditional, thus independant from the distributions of the input strings. Finally, we show through experiments that our method allows us to design cost functions that depend on the string context where the edit operations are used. In other words, we get kinds of *context-sensitive* edit distances.

Keywords: Edit Distance, Stochastic Transducers, Discriminative Models, Grammatical Inference.

1 Introduction

Real world applications such as spell checking, speech recognition, DNA analysis or plagiarism detection often use the Levenshtein distance, the so-called Edit Distance (ED) [12], to compute similarities of string pairs. The common feature of ED-based methods is that they are static, in the sense of using *a priori* fixed costs for the primitive edit operations (insertion, deletion, substitution), that leaves little room for adaptation to the string context. Nevertheless, in many real domains, the level of an edit cost should be able to depend not only on the pair of symbols handled but also on the context where the operation occurs. For instance, in computational biology, a given edit operation involving the same two symbols can highly depend on its location in the DNA sequence.

---

* This work was supported in part by the IST Programme of the European Community, under the PASCAL Network of Excellence, IST-2002-506778. This publication only reflects the authors' views.

Y. Sakakibara et al. (Eds.): ICGI 2006, LNAI 4201, pp. 240–252, 2006.

One solution would consist in manually assigning costs to edit operations that reflect the likelihood of the corresponding transformations. But the setting up of this strategy is difficult and seems to be not realistic overall for applications with a low level of expertise. Some recent work tried to overcome the previously mentioned drawbacks by automatically learning the primitive edit costs, rather than hand-tuning them for each domain. Several probabilistic models have been proposed to learn a *stochastic* ED in the form of stochastic transducers [9,1,8], conditional random fields (CRF) [7], or pair-Hidden Markov Models (pair-HMM) [5]. These models provide a probability distribution over the edit operations and thus over the string pairs. The stochastic ED between two sequences can then be computed from the negative logarithm of the probability of the string pair.

Although these methods have provided some significant improvements on pattern recognition tasks in comparison with the classic non-learned ED, they share at least one of the following two drawbacks (sometimes both). The first one is a *statistical bias* of the inferred model. Actually, the majority of these approaches aim at learning a *generative* model rather than a *discriminative* classifier [2]. In other words, they learn a joint probability distribution $p(x, y)$ over the string pairs (x, y), so the resulting conditional density $p(y|x)$, required in classification tasks, is a biased classifier that depends on the input distribution $p(x)$. A solution, as proposed in [7,8], consists in directly learning a conditional distribution, called a *discriminative* classifier.

The second drawback is a *limitation on the expressive power* of the model. Actually, the structure of the learned model (*i.e.* the number of states in the transducer or in the CRF or in the pair-HMM) is always *a priori* fixed in the proposed approaches. The goal is to learn the parameters (the edit costs) assuming that the fixed structure is able to capture the most important configurations which can arise from the alignment of two sequences. Since determining such a structure depends on the domain, this often constitutes a tricky task that can result in a bad adaptation of the model to the string context.

In this paper, we propose to take into account both these problems, by learning not only the structure but also the parameters of a so-called *conditional edit transducer*. The motivations that justify the learning of such a transducer are the following. First, we think that an efficient way to model a stochastic ED actually consists in viewing it as a stochastic transduction between the input X and output Y alphabets [8,9]. In other words, it means that the relation constituted by a set of (*input,output*) strings can be compiled in the form of a 2-tape automaton, called a *stochastic finite-state transducer*. The interpretation of the ED as a stochastic transduction naturally leads to two possible string distances [9]: the first one describes the most likely transduction between the two strings, while the second is defined by aggregating all transductions between them. In this paper, we focus on the first stochastic distance, a so-called *Viterbi Edit Distance* [9]. We motivate this choice by the fact that we will use an adaptation of the well-known Viterbi algorithm for learning the structure **and** the parameters of the *conditional edit transducer*.

Actually, stochastic transducers suffer from the lack of training algorithms [6] which generally only learn the parameters of an imposed structure, using the Expectation Maximization algorithm (EM) [4]. We claim in this paper that this drawback can be efficiently overcome using grammatical inference algorithms, that constitutes the second motivation of our work. Basically, a transduction between two strings $x \in X^*$ and $y \in Y^*$, in the specific domain of the ED, can be rewritten using an adapted Viterbi algorithm in the form of an optimal sequence of edit operations $z = z_1...z_n, z_i \in (X \cup \{\lambda\}) \times (Y \cup \{\lambda\}) \setminus \{(\lambda, \lambda)\}$ (where λ is the empty string). Thus, we can exploit grammatical inference algorithms for learning over this new alphabet the structure of the model (and its parameters) in the form of a probabilistic finite state automaton.

The rest of this paper is organized as follows. After some notations and definitions in Section 2 and 3, we propose an adaptive approach for learning a conditional edit transducer. This learning requires to find an optimal alignment of string pairs in the form of a set of edit operations (Section 4). From this new set of sequences built on the alphabet of edit operations, we infer a probabilistic automaton with ALERGIA [3]. To learn a discriminative model, the automaton is corrected to satisfy constraints of conditional distribution (Section 5). The conditional edit transducer is then deduced from the automaton by splitting each transition according to the input and output alphabets. In Section 6, we carry out several series of experiments showing the behavior of our learned ED in a comparative study.

2   On Edit Distances

An *alphabet* X is a finite nonempty set of symbols called *letters*. A *string* x over X is a finite sequence $x = a_1 a_2 \dots a_n$ of letters. Let $|x|$ denote the length of x, λ the empty string and X^* the set of all strings. In the sequel, we will use two (non necessarily) distinct alphabets X and Y whose respective strings will generally be indicated by $x = a_1 a_2 \dots a_n$ and $y = b_1 b_2 \dots b_m$, for sake of simplicity.

Let us recall that the *edit distance* is the smallest number of substitutions, insertions and deletions required to transform a string x into another y. More formally, let $E_s = X \times Y$ be the set of *substitutions*, $E_i = \{\lambda\} \times Y$ the set of *insertions*, $E_d = X \times \{\lambda\}$ the set of *deletions* and $Z = E_s \cup E_i \cup E_d$ the set of all edit operations: $Z = (X \cup \{\lambda\}) \times (Y \cup \{\lambda\}) \setminus \{(\lambda, \lambda)\}$. An element $(a, b) \in Z$ will be denoted $(a : b)$. Let $c : Z \to \mathbb{R}^+$ be a fixed *primitive cost function* that assigns a non negative weight to each edit operation. The *edit distance* $d(x, y)$ between two strings $x \in X^*$ and $y \in Y^*$ is recursively defined as follows:

$$d(x, y) = \min \begin{cases} 0 & \text{if } x = \lambda \text{ and } y = \lambda \\ c(a : b) + d(x', y') & \text{if } x = ax' \text{ and } y = by' \\ c(a : \lambda) + d(x', y) & \text{if } x = ax' \\ c(\lambda : b) + d(x, y') & \text{if } y = by'. \end{cases}$$

The edit distance can also be defined through the notion of alignment. Given two strings $x \in X^*$ and $y \in Y^*$, an *alignment* between x and y is a sequence of edit operations, thus a string $z = (u_1 : v_1) \ldots (u_p : v_p) \in Z^*$, such that (1) $u_i \in X \cup \{\lambda\}$ and $v_i \in Y \cup \{\lambda\}$ and $(u_i : v_i) \neq (\lambda : \lambda)$ for all $i \in 1..p$ and (2) $x = u_1 u_2 \ldots u_p$ and $y = v_1 v_2 \ldots v_p$. Let $L(x, y)$ denote the set of all alignments between x and y. Computing $d(x, y)$ consists in exhibiting an alignment of minimum cost between x and y: $d(x, y) = \min_{\{z \in L(x,y) : z = z_1 \ldots z_p\}} c(z_1) + \cdots + c(z_p)$. For instance, assuming that $X = Y = \{a, b\}$ and $c(a_i : b_j) = 1$ if $a_i \neq b_j$ and 0 otherwise, we get $d(aba, bab) = 2$ with $(a : \lambda)(b : b)(a : a)(\lambda : b)$ or $(\lambda : b)(a : a)(b : b)(a : \lambda)$ as minimal alignments.

Notice that both $d(x, y)$ and the alignments of minimum cost between x and y can be computed in $\mathcal{O}(|x| \cdot |y|)$ time using dynamic programming techniques [12]. However, faced with practical situations, the problem is generally not to efficiently compute the edit distance itself but rather to find a relevant primitive cost function able to capture the most important configurations which can arise from the alignments of two sequences. As we said in introduction, imposing a unique cost for a substitution of two letters, whatever they are, and not taking into account the location where this edit operation occurs in the alignment (that we call the string context), is not relevant for dealing with complex problems. We propose in the following to learn a suited probabilistic model, called a *conditional edit-transducer*, to take into account this string context.

3   On Conditional Edit-Transducers

Roughly speaking, a standard transducer is a finite state machine that takes strings from an input alphabet X and rewrites them into strings of an output alphabet Y. In the context of edit distance, every alignment between $x \in X^*$ and $y \in Y^*$ can be viewed as a rewrite derivation of x into y using the edit operations. So a finite state machine that would achieve this transduction is a special transducer, called an *edit transducer*, whose transitions are labelled from the unique alphabet Z of edit operations.

Definition 1. *A finite-state edit-transducer (FSET) is a 5-tuple $\mathcal{A} = \langle Q, Z, i, F, T \rangle$ such that Q is a finite set of states, $Z = (X \cup \{\lambda\}) \times (Y \cup \{\lambda\}) \setminus \{(\lambda, \lambda)\}$ the alphabet of edit operations, $i \in Q$ the initial state and $F : Q \to [0, 1]$ (resp., $T : Q \times Z \times Q \to [0, 1]$) a function that assigns a weight to every state (resp., transition). We also assume the following Determinism Condition: $\forall p \in Q, \forall (a : b) \in Z$, $\mathrm{Card}(\{q : T(p, (a : b), q) > 0\}) \leq 1$.*

A state is *final* iff $F(p) > 0$. Moreover, we will never consider the transitions $(p, (a : b), q)$ whose weights $T(p, (a : b), q)$ are null since they are not useful from a computational point of view. Indeed, computing the weight of an alignment $z = z_1 \ldots z_n \in Z^*$ w.r.t. a FSET $\mathcal{A} = \langle Q, Z, i, F, T \rangle$, denoted $P(z|\mathcal{A})$, consists in finding a sequence of transitions $(i, z_1, p_1)(p_1, z_2, p_2) \ldots (p_{n-1}, z_n, p_n)$ that starts from the initial state and is labeled with the letters of z. Due to the Determinism Condition, at most one such a path exists in $\mathcal{A}$ and then, the weight is: $P(z|\mathcal{A}) = T(i, z_1, p_1) \times T(p_1, z_2, p_2) \times \cdots \times T(p_{n-1}, z_n, p_n) \times F(p_n)$.

Since we aim here at learning a discriminative model, let us now define a *conditional* FSET:

Definition 2. *A conditional finite-state edit-transducer (*CFSET*) is a* FSET $C = \langle Q, Z, i, F, T \rangle$, *whose transitions are written* $(b|a)$ *rather than* $(a : b) \in Z$, *such that,* $\forall p \in Q, \forall a \in X$,

$$F(p) + \sum_{b \in Y, q \in Q} T(p, (b|\lambda), q) = 1, \quad (1)$$

$$\sum_{b \in Y, q \in Q} T(p, (b|a), q) + \sum_{q \in Q} T(p, (\lambda|a), q) + \sum_{b \in Y, q \in Q} T(p, (b|\lambda), q) = 1. \quad (2)$$

An example of CFSET is given in Fig.1(a). Basically, a CFSET C *is not* a DPFA [11] over Z^* since $F(p) + \sum_{(b|a) \in Z, q \in Q} T(p, (b|a), q) \neq 1$ in general. However, by using Constraints (1) and (2), we can show that for every fixed input string $x \in X^*$, $P(y|C, x) = \sum_{z \in L(x,y)} P(z|C)$ defines a distribution over Y^*: $\sum_{y \in Y^*} P(y|C, x) = 1$, that is the reason why we speak of *conditional* FSETs. A formal proof of this property, in the case of a CFSET *with only one state*, can be found in [8]. Below, we just give a hint of the general case on an example.

Let us fix $x = aa$ and consider the CFSET C of Fig.1(a). C can be used to produce strings of Y^* incrementally by following its transitions while consuming the letters of x. For instance, starting from the initial state 1, there are 3 cases: Either, one can produce a b (with a probability of 0.3) from nothing (insertion) by following the transition $(1, (b|\lambda), 2)$, and must then produce a string from state 2, by remembering that no letter of x was consumed. Or, one can make a substitution of an a by a b (with a probability of 0.5), by following the transition $(1, (b|a), 1)$, and must then produce a string from state 1, by remembering that one a of x was consumed, so that only one a remains in the input. Or, one can delete an a (with a probability of 0.2) in the input without producing anything (deletion), by following the transition $(1, (\lambda|a), 1)$, and must then produce a string from state 1 and only one a in input. When all the letters of the input string are consumed, no more substitution or deletion can be done, whatever the state. So one can only make last insertions before stopping. For instance, directed by $x = aa$ and C, the string $bbbb$ can be produced by the following path: $(1, (b|a), 1)(1, (b|\lambda), 2)(2, (b|a), 1)(1, (b|\lambda), 2)$.

More generally, we can build the automaton P that generates all the strings of Y^* following the transitions of C while consuming the letters of x (see Fig.1(b)). The states are pairs of the form $\langle k, \alpha \rangle$ where $k \in \{1, 2\}$ is a state of C and α is a prefix of $x = aa$ corresponding to the beginning of x that is already consumed, *i.e.*, $\alpha \in \{\lambda, a, aa\}$. The initial state is $\langle 1, \lambda \rangle$ since 1 is the initial state of C and no letter of x is initially read. A state $\langle k, \alpha \rangle$ is final iff (1) k is a final state in C and (2) all the letters of x have been consumed: $\alpha = x = aa$. The transitions are of the form $(\langle k, \alpha \rangle, (b_j|a_i), \langle l, \beta \rangle)$ and they appear iff (1) $(k, (b_j|a_i), l)$ is a transition in C and (2) $\beta = \alpha.a_i$, that is to say, $\beta = \alpha$ in the case of a insertion $(b_j|a_i) = (b|\lambda)$ and $\beta = \alpha.a$ in the case of a deletion $(b_j|a_i) = (\lambda|a)$ or a substitution $(b_j|a_i) = (b|a)$. Finally, the transitions and the final states come with the probabilities that are assigned by C.

It is now clear that if we want P to generate a distribution over Y^*, then P must be a PFA [11], *i.e.*, for every state, the probability of the outgoing transitions

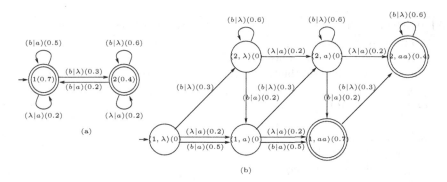

Fig. 1. (a) The CFSET $\mathcal{C}$. (b) The probabilistic automaton $\mathcal{P}$ modeling the distribution over Y^* conditionally to $\mathcal{C}$ and the input string $x = aa$.

plus the probability of this state to be final must be 1. This is exactly the statements of Constraints (1) and (2). Indeed, Constraint (1) concerns the case where all the letters in the input string x are consumed, thus tackles the final states of $\mathcal{P}$; the generation of the output string can only be done by using insertions, before stopping. Constraint (2) concerns the case where not all the letters in the input string x are consumed yet, thus tackles the non final states of $\mathcal{P}$; all the edit operations can be used to generate the output string, but this generation is forbidden to stop (since some letters of x remains to be consumed). Hence, Constraints (1) and (2) insure that for every fixed input string x, the construction of $\mathcal{P}$ yields a PFA, that brings: $\sum_{y \in Y^*} P(y|\mathcal{C}, x) = 1$.

At last but not least, by using the same terminology as that of [9], two edit distances can be defined from every CFSET $\mathcal{C}$, the *stochastic edit distance*: $d_{\mathcal{C}}^s(y|x) = -\log P(y|\mathcal{C}, x) = -\log \left(\sum_{z \in L(x,y)} P(z|\mathcal{C}) \right)$ and the *Viterbi edit distance*: $d_{\mathcal{C}}^v(y|x) = -\log \left(\max_{z \in L(x,y)} P(z|\mathcal{C}) \right)$. We will only consider the latter in the rest of the paper. Indeed, on the one hand, we propose in Section 4 an efficient algorithm that allows us to compute the Viterbi edit distance. On the other hand, we will need this algorithm to develop, in Section 5, a method to learn the structure and the parameters of a CFSET that maximizes the likelihood of a learning sample. So studying only the Viterbi edit distance allows us to kill two birds with one stone.

4   Computing the Viterbi Edit Distance from a CFSET

Given two strings $x \in X^*$ and $y \in Y^*$, a CFSET provides several possible alignments between x and y. For instance, if we consider that of Fig.1(a), then the strings $x = aa$ and $y = bbb$ may be aligned by $z_1 = (b|a)(b|a)(b|\lambda)$ or $z_2 = (b|\lambda)(b|a)(b|\lambda)(\lambda|a)$. Nevertheless, as $P(z_1|\mathcal{C}) = 0.5 \times 0.5 \times 0.3 \times 0.4 = 0.03$ and $P(z_2|\mathcal{C}) = 0.3 \times 0.2 \times 0.3 \times 0.2 \times 0.4 = 0.00144$, we deduce that z_1 may be the optimal alignment between x and y, unless there exists another alignment of higher probability, that is not the case of z_2.

Algorithm 1. Probability of an optimal alignment between x and y

---

Input: Two strings $x = a_1 \ldots a_n \in X^*$ and $y = b_1 \ldots b_m \in Y^*$ and a CFSET
$\quad\quad \mathcal{C} = \langle Q, Z, 1, F, T \rangle$ whose states are $Q = \{1, \ldots, |Q|\}$ and 1 is initial.
Output: Maximum probability of every alignment between x and y w.r.t. $\mathcal{C}$.
$M[0][0][1] \leftarrow 1$;
for $s = 2$ **to** $|Q|$ **do**
$\quad \lfloor \quad M[0][0][s] \leftarrow 0$;

for $i = 1$ **to** n **do**
$\quad |$ **for** $s = 1$ **to** $|Q|$ **do**
$\quad | \quad \lfloor \quad M[i][0][s] \leftarrow \max_{t \in Q} M[i-1][0][t] \times T(t, (\lambda|a_i), s)$;

for $j = 1$ **to** m **do**
$\quad |$ **for** $s = 1$ **to** $|Q|$ **do**
$\quad | \quad \lfloor \quad M[0][j][s] \leftarrow \max_{t \in Q} M[0][j-1][t] \times T(t, (b_j|\lambda), s)$;

for $i = 1$ **to** n **do**
$\quad |$ **for** $j = 1$ **to** m **do**
$\quad | \quad |$ **for** $s = 1$ **to** $|Q|$ **do**
$\quad | \quad | \quad | \quad m_{deletion} \leftarrow \max_{t \in Q} M[i-1][j][t] \times T(t, (\lambda|a_i), s)$;
$\quad | \quad | \quad | \quad m_{insertion} \leftarrow \max_{t \in Q} M[i][j-1][t] \times T(t, (b_j|\lambda), s)$;
$\quad | \quad | \quad | \quad m_{substitution} \leftarrow \max_{t \in Q} M[i-1][j-1][t] \times T(t, (b_j|a_i), s)$;
$\quad | \quad | \quad \lfloor \quad M[i][j][s] \leftarrow \max(m_{deletion}, m_{insertion}, m_{substitution})$;

return $\max_{s \in Q} M[n][m][s] \times F(s)$

Algo.1 allows us to compute the probability of an optimal alignment between two strings $x = a_1 \ldots a_n$ and $y = b_1 \ldots b_m$ w.r.t. a CFSET $\mathcal{C} = \langle Q, Z, 1, F, T \rangle$ by dynamic programming. It uses a 3-dimension matrix M to store the probabilities according to (1) input and output strings (that is similar to the standard edit distance) and (2) the state in progress (that is new). More precisely, M's dimensions are $(0..|x|) \times (0..|y|) \times (1..|Q|)$ and $M[i][j][s]$ contains the probability of an optimal alignment, that reaches the state s, between the prefix $a_1 \ldots a_i$ of x and the prefix $b_1 \ldots b_j$ of y.

In Fig.2, we show an example of execution when $x = aa$ and $y = bbb$ and the CFSET $\mathcal{C}$ is that of Fig.1(a). Our algorithm fills up M, cell after cell. Let us focus on the computation of $M[2][1][1]$ (whose result, 0.1, is underlined in Fig.2). This cell must contain the maximum probability, according to $\mathcal{C}$, to reach state 1 after having consumed aa in input and produced b in output. Several possibilities can lead to this situation. (1) One can reach state 1 by making a deletion of an a in input, starting from a cell, in state 1 or 2, where a had been consumed in input and b produced in output, thus from the cells $M[1][1][1]$ or $M[1][1][2]$. By Algo.1, we get:

$$m_{deletion} = \max_{t \in Q} M[1][1][t] \times T(t, (\lambda|a), 1) = 0.1$$

(2) One can reach state 1 by making an insertion of a b in output, starting from a cell where aa had been consumed in input and no b produced in output, thus

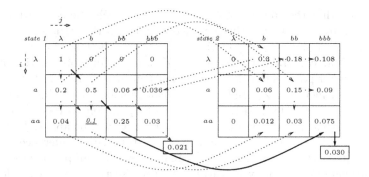

Fig. 2. Computation of $d^v_{\mathcal{C}}(y|x)$ when $x = aa$, $y = bbb$ w.r.t. the CFSET $\mathcal{C}$ of Fig.1(a). Each cell $M[i][j][s]$ contains the probability of an optimal alignment, that reaches the state s, between the prefix $a_1 \ldots a_i$ of x and the prefix $b_1 \ldots b_j$ of y. The arrows are useful to re-construct all the possible alignments between x and y. Both cells out of the arrays contain the probabilities of such alignments. As $0.030 > 0.021$, we deduce that $d^v_{\mathcal{C}}(bbb|aa) = -\log 0.03 \simeq 1.52$ thanks to the optimal alignment $(b|a)(b|a)(b|\lambda)$.

from the cells $M[2][0][1]$ or $M[2][0][2]$. By Algo.1, we get:

$$m_{insertion} = \max_{t \in Q} M[2][0][t] \times T(t, (b|\lambda), 1) = 0.$$

(3) One can reach state 1 by making the substitution of a b by an a, starting from a cell where a had been consumed in input and λ produced in output, thus from the cells $M[1][0][1]$ and $M[1][0][2]$. By Algo.1, we get:

$$m_{substitution} = \max_{t \in Q} M[1][0][t] \times T(t, (b|a), 1) = 0.1$$

Therefore, $M[2][1][1] = 0.1$. Moreover, this score is achieved after either a deletion $(\lambda|a)$ from $M[1][1][1]$ or a substitution $(b|a)$ from $M[1][0][0]$, what we indicate in Fig.2 with the dotted arrows that point to the cell $M[2][1][1]$.

At the end of the loops, all the letters of x are consumed and all those of y are produced. So Algo.1 returns:

$$\max_{s \in Q} M[2][3][s] \times F(s) = \max(M[2][3][1] \times F(1), M[2][3][2] \times F(2)) = 0.03.$$

So $d^v_{\mathcal{C}}(bbb|aa) = -\log 0.03 \simeq 1.52$. Moreover, since we have stored the best edit operations in M, we deduce that only one alignment is optimal: $(b|a)(b|a)(b|\lambda)$.

5   Learning an Optimal CFEST

The second task we have to tackle concerns the learning of the CFSET. As we said in introduction, stochastic transducers suffer from the lack of learning algorithm. The main reason comes from the fact that stochastic transducers are not deterministic with respect to the input strings. We are going to show in this section that the specific context of learning stochastic edit distance leaves room for learning not only the parameters but also the structure of a CFSET. The strategy of our iterative algorithm is based on the following remarks.

By Def.2, an edit transducer over $X^* \times Y^*$ is a kind of probabilistic automaton over Z^*. So our point is that learning a CFSET ultimately returns to the problem of learning a PFA over Z^*. Indeed, if we can replace each string pair (x, y) of the learning sample by a sequence z of edit operations corresponding to the most probable alignment between x and y, then we will be able to learn a DPFA modeling the Viterbi edit distance with usual grammatical inference algorithms (such as ALERGIA [3] or MDI [10]). Fortunately, Algo.1 can provide us with such optimal alignments. However, learning a probabilistic model in the form of a DPFA from the alignments will provide us with a *generative* model, that is to say, a joint distribution over $X^* \times Y^*$. In order to learn a *discriminative* model, we have to re-normalize the current distribution at each iteration.

Algorithm 2. Learning the optimal CFSET

Input: A sample $LS = \{(x_k, y_k) : x_k \in X^*, y_k \in Y^*, k \in 1..n\}$ of string pairs.
Output: A CFSET $\mathcal{C}$.
$\mathcal{C} \leftarrow$ a random CFSET;
repeat
  | let z_k be the most probable alignment of x_k and y_k w.r.t. $\mathcal{C}$ for all $k \in 1..n$;
  | $\mathcal{A} \leftarrow$ ALERGIA($\{z_1, \ldots, z_n\}$);
  | $\mathcal{C} \leftarrow$ NORMALIZATION($\mathcal{A}, \{\gamma(p, z, q) : p, q \in Q, z \in Z \cup \{(\lambda : \lambda)\}\}$);
until $\left(\sum_{k=1}^{n} d_{\mathcal{C}}^v(y_k | x_k)\right)$ does not decrease anymore;
return $\mathcal{A}$;

The pseudo-code of our learning algorithm is presented in Algo.2. We initialize our model to a random CFSET. Then, we run the following iterative estimation procedure. We use Algo.1 and the current CFSET for assigning the most probable alignment z_k to each string pair $(x_k, y_k) \in LS$. Then, we run ALERGIA for learning a DPFA over Z^*. Once the learning is achieved, we re-normalize the joint distribution described by this generative model to fulfill Constraints (1) and (2) of Def.2 and get a CFSET. The algorithm loops until the Viterbi edit distances computed on the learning sample does not decrease (significantly) anymore. This stopping criterium is equivalent to maximize the likelihood $\left(\prod_{k=1}^{n} P(y_k | \mathcal{C}, x_k)\right)$ over LS, due to the definition of the distance.

To achieve the normalization, we must know the number of times each transition (p, z, q) of the DPFA $\mathcal{A}$ has been used by the learning sequences. These values, that are denoted $\gamma(p, z, q)$, are either directly returned by the inference algorithm (that is the case of ALERGIA), or must be computed by parsing again the learning sample. By convention, $\gamma(p, (\lambda : \lambda), p)$ denotes the number of times the parsing of any learning string ends in the state p. Once the frequencies $\gamma(p, z, q)$ are known, we can re-normalize each probability $T(p, z, q)$ of $\mathcal{A}$ that is the aim of Algo.3.

Algorithm 3. Normalization fulfilling Constraints (1) and (2)

Input: A DPFA $\mathcal{A} = \langle Q, Z, i, F, T \rangle$ with the set of frequencies $\gamma(p, z, q)$.

Output: The corresponding CFSET after normalization.

for each $p \in Q$ **do**

$\quad N_p \leftarrow \sum_{q \in Q} \sum_{z \in Z \cup \{(\lambda : \lambda)\}} \gamma(p, z, q);$

$\quad N_p(\lambda) \leftarrow \sum_{q \in Q} \sum_{b_j \in Y} \gamma(p, (\lambda : b_j), q);$

$\quad N_p(a_i) \leftarrow \sum_{q \in Q} \sum_{b_j \in Y \cup \{\lambda\}} \gamma(p, (a_i : b_j), q), \forall a_i \in X;$

$\quad \delta_p \leftarrow 1 - (N_p(\lambda)/N_p);$

$\quad$ **for** all $a_i \in X, b_j \in Y, q \in Q$ **do**

$\quad\quad T(p, (b_j | \lambda), q) \leftarrow \gamma(p, (\lambda : b_j), q)/N_p;$

$\quad\quad T(p, (\lambda | a_i), q) \leftarrow \gamma(p, (a_i : \lambda), q) \times \delta_p / N_p(a_i);$

$\quad\quad T(p, (b_j | a_i), q) \leftarrow \gamma(p, (a_i : b_j), q) \times \delta_p / N_p(a_i);$

$\quad F(p) \leftarrow \delta_p;$

return $\mathcal{A}$;

It is easy to check that this algorithm is sound: it suffices to verify that Constraints (1) and (2) are satisfied by all the states after normalization. This proof is presented in detail in [8] in the case of a CFSET with only state. It basically also applies to the case of several states since only local information to the states has to be considered, and no information concerning the relations between the states. Notice also that this normalization was proved to be optimal in the framework of an EM procedure [8].

6   Experiments

6.1   Application in Pattern Recognition on the NIST Database

To assess the performance of our algorithm on a pattern recognition task, we run it on the real world problem of handwritten digit classification. To achieve this task, we used a subset of the well-known NIST Database of the National Institute of Standards and Technology. The digits of this database are described in the form of 128×128 bitmap images written by 100 different writers. In our experimental setup, for simplifying our process, we reduced the size of the bitmaps to 16×16 images.

Then, we used a growing number of these digits as learning sample LS, and we kept 1,000 digits in a test sample TS. Since stochastic transducers handle strings, we encoded each digit in an octal form, according to a feature extraction strategy consisting in using Freeman codes for transforming the original vector in an octal string. Fig.3 describes the strategy from a sample of the class "9".

For learning our CFSET, we need a learning set of string pairs. We follow the strategy proposed in [9] consisting in building pairs of "similar" strings that describe the possible distortions between instances of each class $(0 \ldots 9)$. It is possible to automatically build such pairs of (input,output) strings, where an input is a learning string of LS, and the output is a prototype of the input.

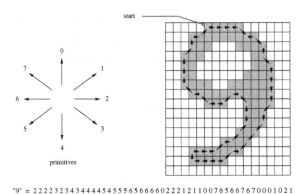

"9" = 2222323434444545556566660222121100765667670001021

Fig. 3. Example of string coding character. Starting from the next found pixel (scanning the digit left-to-right from the top), the coding algorithm builds a string with absolute direction of the next pixel in the border.

To achieve this task, we used as prototype the corresponding 1-nearest-neighbor in LS (using the classic edit distance with the same edit cost for an insertion, deletion or a substitution) of each input.

Note that we could have used other ways to construct string pairs. A solution would be to generate all pairs in the same class. Beyond large complexity costs, this strategy would not be relevant in such a digit recognition task. Actually, the classes of digits are intrinsically multimodal. For example, a zero can be written either with an open loop or a closed one. In this case, the string that represents an "open" zero cannot be considered as a distortion of a "closed" zero, but rather as a different manner (a sort of sub-class) to design this digit. Therefore, a nearest-neighbor based strategy seems to be much more relevant.

We aim at showing with this series of experiments that learning the primitive edit costs of an edit distance in the form of a CFSET is more relevant than imposing these costs in advance. Thus, we will compare our approach with the classic edit distance. The experimental setup is the following: (1) Each set i of digits ($i = 0, .., 9$) is divided in 2 parts: a learning set LS_i and a test set TS_i. (2) From each LS_i, we build a set of string pairs PS_i in the form of $(x, NN(x))$, $\forall x \in LS_i$, where $NN(x) = \text{argmin}_{y \in LS_i - \{x\}} d(x, y)$ (d is the classic edit distance). (3) We learn a CFSET $\mathcal{C}$ from $\bigcup_i PS_i$ with our approach. (4) We classify each test digit $x' \in \bigcup_i TS_i$ by (a) the class i of the learning string $y \in \bigcup_i LS_i$ minimizing $d_{\mathcal{C}}^v(y|x')$ and (b) the class i of its nearest-neighbor $NN(x') \in \bigcup_i LS_i$.

Using the previous experimental setup, we can then compare the two approaches under exactly the same conditions. In order to assess each algorithm in different configurations, the number of learning strings varied from 50 (5 for each class of digits) to 500 (50 for each class), with a step of 50 strings per class. The test accuracy was computed with a test set containing always 1,000 strings (*i.e.* $|\bigcup_i TS_i| = 1,000$). The chart of Fig.4(a) shows the results of our experiments on the NIST database. As already shown in [8], learning an ED in the form of a *conditional* edit transducer is clearly relevant to achieve a pattern recognition task. Whatever the size of the learning set, the error rate obtained using a classic edit distance is always higher than that obtained by using a CFSET. Note that even if theoretically, we expect the two methods to converge to the same rate when $|LS| \to \infty$, it means that our method needs less learning examples to reach the same error rate.

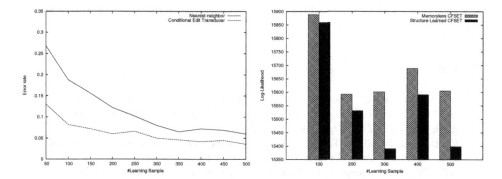

Fig. 4. 4(a)Results on the NIST database. 4(b) Comparison between memoryless CF-SETs and CFSETs whose structure was learned.

6.2   Results on an Artificial Database

In this second series of experiments, we aim at showing the advantage of learning the parameters *and the structure* of a conditional tranducer with respect to other approaches that fix the structure. To this purpose, we focus on the algorithm by Oncina and Sebban that learns conditional memoryless edit-tranducers, that is to say, CFSETs with only one state. We use a random FSET with 5 states whose input and output alphabets are $X = Y = \{a, b, c, d\}$. Thus, every state has 24 outgoing transitions, labeled by the edit operations in $Z = (X \cup \{\lambda\}) \times (Y \cup \{\lambda\}) \setminus \{(\lambda, \lambda)\}$. Then we use this FSET to generate 1,000 strings over Z^*, that allow us to deduce 1000 string pairs over $X^* \times Y^*$. Half of them are used by both the algorithms to learn: the learning sample varies from 100 to 500 strings, with a step of 100 strings. The 500 other strings constitute the test set (TS). In order to measure the performance of both methods, we compute $\sum_{(x,y) \in TS} d_C^v(y|x)$. The less this measure is, the best the CFSET is.

Fig.4(b) shows our results. From this histogram, we observe that a memoryless CFSET is systematically less powerfull than a CFSET whose structure was learned. Notice that the best results were obtained with 300 and 500 learning examples by transducers that had exactly 5 states, so that were relatively close to the target generating model. This result confirms that our method is able to capture the sensitivity of the edit costs to the string context, that is obviously not the case of a memoryless transducer with fixed costs.

7   Conclusion

In this paper, we propose a new algorithm to learn the cost function of a stochastic edit distance. Our method relies on conditional edit transducers whose parameters *and* structure are learned, thanks to grammatical inference techniques. Those transducers inherit all the advantages of conditional models described by Oncina and Sebban in [8]. Moreover, our experiments show that learning the structure allows us to overcome the memoryless transducers, since many-states transducers model complex edit cost functions that take into account the string-context where they are used.

References

1. M. Bilenko and R. Mooney. Adaptive duplicate detection using learnable string similarity measures. In *Proc. of the 9th Int. Conf. on Knowledge Discovery and Data Mining (KDD'03)*, pages 39–48, 2003.
2. G. Bouchard and B. Triggs. The tradeoff between generative and discriminative classifiers. In J. Antoch, editor, *Proc. in Computational Statistics (COMPSTAT'04), 16th Symp. of IASC*, volume 16, Prague, 2004. Physica-Verlag.
3. R. C. Carrasco and J. Oncina. Learning stochastic regular grammars by means of a state merging method. In *Proc. of 1st Int. Colloquium in Grammatical Inference (ICGI'94)*, pages 139–150. LNAI 862, 1994.
4. A. Dempster, M. Laird, and D. Rubin. Maximun likelihood from incomplete data via the em algorithm. *Journal of the Royal Statistical Society*, B(39):1–38, 1977.
5. R. Durbin, S.R. Eddy, A. Krogh, and G. Mitchison. *Biological sequence analysis*. Cambridge University Press, 1998.
6. J. Eisner. Parameter estimation for probabilistic finite-state transducers. In *Proceedings of the 40th Annual Meeting of the Association for Computational Linguistics*, pages 1–8, Philadelphia, July 2002.
7. A. McCallum, K. Bellare, and P. Pereira. A conditional random field for discriminatively-trained finite-state string edit distance. In *Proc. 21th Annual Conference on Uncertainty in Artificial Intelligence (UAI'05)*, pages 388–400, Arlington, Virginia, 2005. AUAI Press.
8. J. Oncina and M. Sebban. Learning stochastic edit distance: application in handwritten character recognition. *Journal of Pattern Recognition*, to appear, 2006.
9. E. S. Ristad and P. N. Yianilos. Learning string-edit distance. *IEEE Trans. on Pattern Analysis and Machine Intelligence*, 20(5):522–532, 1998.
10. F. Thollard, P. Dupont, and C. de la Higuera. Probabilistic DFA inference using kullback-leibler divergence and minimality. In *Proc. 17th Int. Conf. on Machine Learning (ICML'00)*, pages 975–982. Morgan Kaufmann, San Francisco, CA, 2000.
11. E. Vidal, F. Thollard, C. de la Higuera, F. Casacuberta, and R. C. Carrasco. Probabilistic finite-state machines. *IEEE Trans. in Pattern Analysis and Machine Intelligence*, 27(7):1013–1039, 2005.
12. R. A. Wagner and M. J. Fischer. The string-to-string correction problem. *Journal of the ACM*, 21(1):168–173, 1974.

Learning n-Ary Node Selecting Tree Transducers from Completely Annotated Examples

A. Lemay[1], J. Niehren[2], and R. Gilleron[1]

Mostrare project of INRIA Futurs, LIFL, Lille France
[1] University of Lille 3
[2] INRIA Futurs

Abstract. We present the first algorithm for learning n-ary node selection queries in trees from completely annotated examples by methods of grammatical inference. We propose to represent n-ary queries by deterministic n-ary node selecting tree transducers (n-NSTTs). These are tree automata that capture the class of monadic second-order definable n-ary queries. We show that n-NSTT defined polynomially bounded n-ary queries can be learned from polynomial time and data. An application in Web information extraction yields encouraging results.

1 Introduction

The problem of selecting nodes in trees is the most basic and fundamental querying problem in the context of XML [8,14,12]. In this paper, we propose a new machine learning algorithm based on grammatical inference for learning n-ary node selection queries. We will illustrate its interest in an application to wrapper induction for Web information extraction [10,4,13,18].

We consider finite rooted directed sibling-ordered unranked trees $t \in T_\Sigma$ with nodes labeled in a fixed signature Σ. An n-ary query in such trees [14,9,15] is a function q that maps trees $t \in T_\Sigma$ to sets of n-tuples of nodes $q(t) \subseteq \mathtt{nodes}(t)^n$. *Boolean queries* are 0-ary queries and can be identified with tree languages[1]. Monadic queries where $n = 1$ select nodes in trees. Binary queries where $n = 2$ select pairs of nodes in trees, and so on. The most natural way to represent n-ary queries is *monadic second-order logic (MSO)*, i.e. by MSO-formulas with n free variables. MSO-defined queries are *regular*, i.e. definable by tree automata over $\Sigma \times \mathtt{Bool}^n$, and vice versa. This follows from Thatcher and Wright's theorem in the case of ranked trees [19] and carries over to unranked trees.

We investigate learning algorithms for MSO-definable n-ary queries. The input is a set of completely annotated examples for the target query q. These are pairs $(t, q(t))$ for some tree $t \in T_\Sigma$. Completely annotated examples contain positive information on all tuples in $q(t)$, and negative information on all others. In the Boolean case, they coincide with the positive and negative examples for tree languages, i.e. whether a tree belongs to the language or not.

---

[1] This is well-known in database theory. A tree t belongs to the language defined by a Boolean query q if and only if the empty 0-tuple () belongs to $q(t)$.

Y. Sakakibara et al. (Eds.): ICGI 2006, LNAI 4201, pp. 253–267, 2006.

All learnability results depend on how n-ary queries are represented. The following properties are wishful in general, and in particular for applications to Web information extraction.

Learnability. For all n-ary queries q a representative can be learned from polynomial time and data in form of completely annotated examples.

Expressiveness. All n-ary MSO-definable queries can be represented.

Efficiency. Given a representation of an n-ary query q and a tree t the set $q(t)$ can be enumerated efficiently.

For $n = 0$ all three conditions can be satisfied when representing tree languages by bottom-up deterministic tree automata. Completely annotated examples then coincide with positive and negative examples. Learning algorithms for deterministic tree automata from positive and negative examples (RPNI) have been studied in [5].

For $n = 1$, these properties have been shown recently [1,2] when representing monadic queries by deterministic *node selecting tree transducer* (NSTTs). These are *functional* tree automata over $\Sigma \times$ Bool, which define relabeling functions from trees over Σ to trees over Bool. Selected nodes are relabeled to true, all others to false. A learning algorithm from polynomial time and date can be obtained by adapting RPNI to deterministic NSTTs while taking functionality into account, for the treatment of negative information. MSO completeness for deterministic NSTTs can still be inferred from Thatcher and Wright's theorem, despite of the restriction to functionality. Efficient query answering is possible in linear time by a two phases algorithm.

For $n > 1$, the question is still open whether there exists a representation formalism for n-ary queries that satisfies the above three properties. A number of principle problems arise. The most disturbing fact is that functional tree automata over $\Sigma \times$ Bool^n are not sufficiently expressive for $n > 1$. They can only define finite unions of Cartesian closed n-ary queries as shown in [15]. These are clearly insufficient in theory and practice.

Furthermore, the number of n-tuples in $q(t) \subseteq$ nodes$(t)^n$ may become exponential for unbounded n so that efficient enumeration becomes an issue for $n > 1$. Completely annotated examples for q may thus become huge. This should not happen in practice of information extraction. In theory, we will restrict ourselves to queries where the number of answers is polynomially bounded in the size of the tree. Our learning algorithms will have to use compact representations for huge sets of negative examples, i.e., complements nodes$(t)^n - q(t)$.

In this article, we propose to represent n-ary queries in Σ-trees by deterministic tree automata over $\Sigma \times$ Bool^n that recognize canonical languages, where every accepted tree corresponds to precisely one n-tuple. We call tree automata with canonical languages *n-ary node selection tree transducer (n-NSTTs)*.

All tree automata obtained from MSO formula have canonical languages as long as all free variables are first-order. However, most NSTTs are *not* 1-NSTTs and vice versa. Despite of this, both classes of automata have the same expressiveness – they can both represent all monadic MSO definable queries, but differently.

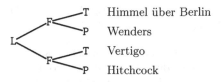

Himmel über Berlin

Wenders

Vertigo

Hitchcock

Fig. 1. The binary tree `two-films` with some data content

We show how to learn deterministic n-NSTTs from completely annotated examples. Our algorithm satisfies the learning model from polynomial time and data, under the assumption that the number of answers to queries is polynomially bounded in the size of the tree. The main problem is to represent the possibly exponential amount of negative information contained in a set of completely annotated examples in a compact manner. In the monadic case, this could be solved by the functionality requirement on NSTTs which is no more available for n-NSTTs. We also show that answers of n-ary queries represented by deterministic n-NSTTs can be enumerated efficiently.

We have implemented our algorithm and started applying it to Web information extraction. We assume highly structured Web pages generated by some database. First experiments yield encouraging results for the n-ary case, that let us hope for competitive systems by future work.

2   N-Ary Node Selecting Tree Transducer

We introduce n-NSTTs for binary trees. Unranked trees will be considered in Section 6. The principal difference between 1-NSTTs as presented here and NSTTs from [1] is essential to generalize smoothly from monadic to n-ary queries.

Let $\mathbb{N} = 1, 2, , \ldots$ be the natural numbers without 0 and $\mathsf{Bool} = \{0, 1\}$ the Booleans. We denote the cardinality of a set A by $|A|$. Given a finite set Σ of *node labels*, a finite directed sibling-ordered *binary tree* $t \in T_\Sigma$ is either a label $a \in \Sigma$ or a triple $a(t_1, t_2)$ consisting of a label $a \in \Sigma$ and two binary trees $t_1, t_2 \in T_\Sigma$. Fig. 1, for instance, contains the binary tree `two-films` $= \mathsf{L}(\mathsf{F}(\mathsf{T}, \mathsf{P}), \mathsf{F}(\mathsf{T}, \mathsf{P}))$ where $\Sigma = \{\mathsf{L}, \mathsf{F}, \mathsf{T}, \mathsf{P}\}$. This tree represents a list (L) of two films (F) each having a title (T) and a producer (P). Rather than putting data content into tree labels, we assume an external mapping from nodes to data values. Note that nodes may carry the same label while containing different data. For instance, both films have different producers and titles. This works as long as we carefully distinguish different nodes with the same label.

We identify node of trees with their relative address from the root. The node 2·1, for instance, is the first child of the second child of the root. In the example in Fig. 1, this is the T node containing *Vertigo*. We write $t(v)$ for the label of some $v \in \mathsf{nodes}(t)$, for instance: `two-films`$(2 \cdot 1) = \mathsf{T}$. We denote by $\mathsf{nodes}(t) \subseteq \mathbb{N}^*$ the set of nodes of a tree t. We say that two trees have *the same shape* if they have the same sets of nodes. We write $\mathsf{size}(t)$ for $|\mathsf{nodes}(t)|$.

Definition 1. *An* n-ary query *in trees over Σ is a function q from trees $t \in T_\Sigma$ to sets of n-tuples of nodes $q(t) \subseteq \mathtt{nodes}(t)^n$.*

Let the binary query `title-producer-pairs` ask for all pairs of titles and producers in trees that encode lists of films. From the tree `two-films`, this query selects the following node pairs: `title-producer-pairs(two-films)` $= \{(1{\cdot}1, 1{\cdot}2), (2{\cdot}1, 2{\cdot}2)\}$

The usual idea how to represent n-ary queries by tree automata stems from early work on `MSO` [19]. It consists in identifying n-ary queries over Σ with tree languages over $\Sigma \times \mathsf{Bool}^n$. These can then be recognized by a tree automaton. There are several possibilities in doing so, which differ in how many n-tuples may be encoded by Boolean annotations at the same tree. For $n = 2$ for instance, consider $\mathsf{L}_{00}(\mathsf{F}_{00}(\mathsf{T}_{10}, \mathsf{P}_{01}), \mathsf{F}_{00}(\mathsf{T}_{10}, \mathsf{P}_{01}))$. This tree is annotated by pairs of Booleans that represent 4 pairs of nodes: $\{(1{\cdot}1, 1{\cdot}2), (2{\cdot}1, 2{\cdot}2), (1{\cdot}1, 2{\cdot}2), (2{\cdot}1, 1{\cdot}2)\}$. The third and fourth pair may be unwanted since they mix up the titles and producers. We cannot annotate, however, only the first two pairs to the same copy of tree `two-films`, we need two independent copies: $\mathsf{L}_{00}(\mathsf{F}_{00}(\mathsf{T}_{10}, \mathsf{P}_{01}), \mathsf{F}_{00}(\mathsf{T}_{00}, \mathsf{P}_{00}))$ and $\mathsf{L}_{00}(\mathsf{F}_{00}(\mathsf{T}_{00}, \mathsf{P}_{00}), \mathsf{F}_{00}(\mathsf{T}_{10}, \mathsf{P}_{01}))$. This contrasts strongly with the monadic case, where one can always annotate all tuples in $q(t)$ to a unique copy of t. Such compact annotations lead to functional tree languages, as recognized by the NSTTs in [1].

In the n-ary case, however, several copies of t need to be annotated, one for each of its n-tuples. We call trees over $\Sigma \times \mathsf{Bool}^n$ *tuple trees* if they are annotated by a single n-tuple. Every tree over $\Sigma \times \mathsf{Bool}^n$ can be decomposed in a unique manner into two trees of the same shape, a tree $t \in T_\Sigma$ and its Boolean annotation $\beta \in T_{\mathsf{Bool}^n}$. We write $t \times \beta$ for the unique tree in $\Sigma \times \mathsf{Bool}^n$ that can be decomposed into t and β. Given a n-tuple α and $1 \le i \le n$ let $\Pi_i(\alpha)$ be the i-th component of α. If $t \times \beta$ is a tuple tree then β corresponds to a unique n-tuple $\boldsymbol{\beta} \in \mathtt{nodes}(t)^n$ such that:

$$\forall v \in \mathtt{nodes}(t) \ \forall 1 \le i \le n : \ \Pi_i(\beta(v)) = 1 \text{ iff } \Pi_i(\boldsymbol{\beta}) = v$$

We call tree languages over $\Sigma \times \mathsf{Bool}^n$ *canonical* if all trees contained are tuple trees. Clearly, every n-ary query q over Σ is represented by exactly one canonical language.

We will use tree automata to represent canonical languages, so we recall their definition. A *tree automaton* A over Σ is a triple that consists of three finite sets $\mathtt{states}(A)$, $\mathtt{final}(A) \subseteq \mathtt{states}(A)$, and $\mathtt{rules}(A)$, so that all rules are or the form $a \to q$ or $a(q_1, q_2) \to q$ where $a \in \Sigma$ and $q, q_1, q_2 \in \mathtt{states}(A)$. A *run* of a tree automaton A on a tree t is a function $r : \mathtt{nodes}(A) \to \mathtt{states}(A)$ so that all states that r assigns to nodes of t are justified by some rule of A. A run r of A on t is *successful* if it maps the root of t to a final state of A, i.e. $r(\varepsilon) \in \mathtt{final}(A)$. We write $\mathtt{succ\_runs}_A(t)$ for the set of successful runs by A on t. The *language* $L(A)$ is the set of all trees $t \in T_\Sigma$ that permit a successful run by A. The size measure for automata in this paper counts states and rules: $\mathtt{size}(A) = |\mathtt{rules}(A)| + |\mathtt{states}(A)|$. We call a tree automaton *trimmed* if all of its states are used in some successful run.

Definition 2. *An* n-ary node selecting tree transducer (n-NSTT) *over* Σ *is a tree automaton over* $\Sigma \times \text{Bool}^n$ *that recognizes a canonical language.*

An n-NSTT A over Σ *represents* the n-ary query q_A in trees $t \in T_\Sigma$ such that:

$$q_A(t) = \{\boldsymbol{\beta} \in \text{nodes}(t)^n \mid t \times \boldsymbol{\beta} \in L(A)\}$$

In other words, a query q is represented by all n-NSTTs that recognize the language of all tuple trees for q. All such n-NSTTs are *equivalent* in that they recognize the same language. Thatcher and Wright's theorem [19] states that n-NSTTs capture the class of MSO-definable n-ary queries. Thus, 1-NSTT $\neq$ NSTT even though both of them capture monadic MSO-definable queries.

3   Membership Testing to the Class of n-NSTTs

We present an efficient algorithm for testing whether a tree automaton is an n-NSTT. The results on types obtained on the way will help avoiding such tests during query induction in Section 5.

An n-*type* $\boldsymbol{b}$ is an n-tuple of non-negative integers, that is $\boldsymbol{b} \in (\mathbb{N} \cup \{0\})^n$. All bit vectors in Bool^n are n-types. The *type of a tree* $\beta \in T_{\text{Bool}^n}$ is the n-type obtained by summing up all labels of nodes in β.

$$\text{T}(\beta) = \sum_{v \in \text{nodes}(\beta)} \beta(v)$$

Note that $t \times \beta$ is a tuple tree if and only if $\text{T}(\beta) = (1, \ldots, 1) = 1^n$. Let A be a tree automaton over $\Sigma \times \text{Bool}^n$. To every $q \in \text{states}(A)$, we assign a set $\text{T}(q)$ of n-types by the following inference rules:

$$\frac{(a, \boldsymbol{b}) \to q \in \text{rules}(A)}{\boldsymbol{b} \in \text{T}(q)} \quad \frac{(a, \boldsymbol{b})(q_1, q_2) \to q \in \text{rules}(A) \quad \boldsymbol{b}_1 \in \text{T}(q_1) \quad \boldsymbol{b}_2 \in \text{T}(q_2)}{\boldsymbol{b} + \boldsymbol{b}_1 + \boldsymbol{b}_2 \in \text{T}(q)}$$

Lemma 1. *If r is a run of A on $t \times \beta$ then $\text{T}(\beta) \in \text{T}(r(\varepsilon))$.*

Lemma 2. *For all $q \in \text{states}(A)$ and $\boldsymbol{b} \in \text{T}(q)$ there exists a tree $t \times \beta$ over $\Sigma \times \text{Bool}^n$ and a run r of A on this tree such that $q = r(\varepsilon)$ and $\text{T}(\beta) = \boldsymbol{b}$.*

Lemma 3. *If A is a trimmed n-NSTT then $\text{T}(q) \subseteq \text{Bool}^n$ is a singleton.*

Proof. To see that $\text{T}(q) \neq \emptyset$, note that we assume A to be trimmed. Thus there exists a tree $t \times \beta$ and a run r on that tree such that $r(\varepsilon) = q$. By Lemma 1 it follows that $\text{T}(\beta) \in \text{T}(q)$. To see that $\text{T}(q) \in \text{Bool}^n$, let $\boldsymbol{b} \in \text{T}(q)$. By Lemma 2 there exists a tree $t \times \beta$ over $\Sigma \times \text{Bool}^n$ and a run r of A on this tree such that $q = r(\varepsilon)$ and $\text{T}(\beta) = \boldsymbol{b}$. Since A is trimmed there exists a tree in $\tilde{t} \times \tilde{\beta} \in L(A)$ that contains $t \times \beta$ as a subtree. Hence: $\boldsymbol{b} = \text{T}(\beta) \leq \text{T}(\tilde{\beta}) = 1^n$. It remains to show that $\text{T}(q)$ is a singleton, so let us assume that $\boldsymbol{b}' \in \text{T}(q)$ too. By Lemma 2 there exists a second tree $t' \times \beta'$ over $\Sigma \times \text{Bool}^n$ and a run r' of A on this tree such that $q = r'(\varepsilon)$ and $\text{T}(\beta') = \boldsymbol{b}'$. Let $\tilde{t}' \times \tilde{\beta}'$ be the tree obtained by replacing one occurrence of $t \times \beta$ in $\tilde{t} \times \tilde{\beta}$ by $t' \times \beta'$. Note that $\tilde{t}' \times \tilde{\beta}' \in L(A)$, hence

$T(\beta') = 1^n$. Let V be the set of nodes of $\tilde{t} \times \tilde{\beta}$ that have not been affected by the substitution.

$$1^n = T(\tilde{\beta}) = T(\beta) + \sum_{v \in V} \tilde{\beta}(v)$$
$$1^n = T(\tilde{\beta}') = T(\beta') + \sum_{v \in V} \tilde{\beta}'(v)$$

Since $\tilde{\beta}(v) = \tilde{\beta}'(v)$ for all $v \in V$, $T(\beta) = T(\beta')$ so that $b = b'$.

Lemma 4. *A trimmed automaton A over $\Sigma \times \text{Bool}^n$ is an n-NSTT iff $T(q) = \{1^n\}$ for all $q \in final(A)$.*

Proof. let A be a trimmed n-NSTT and let $q \in final(A)$. Since A is trimmed there exists a tree $t \times \beta$ and a run r on that tree such that $r(\varepsilon) = q$. Thus $t \times \beta \in L(A)$ so that $T(\beta) = 1^n$. By Lemma 1, it follows that $1^n \in T(q)$. This set is a singleton by Lemma 3 so that $T(q) = \{1^n\}$. For the converse, it follows from Lemma 1, that all $t \times \beta \in L(A)$ satisfy $T(\beta) = 1^n$ so that they are tuple trees.

Proposition 1. *Whether a tree automaton A over $\Sigma \times \text{Bool}^n$ is an n-NSTT can be decided in polynomial time $O(size(A) \times n)$. If so, all types in $\{T(q) \mid q \in states(A)\}$ can be computed in the same time.*

Proof. Lemma 4 gives us a way to check whether a tree automaton is an n-NSTT. In the first step, we trim the automaton without changing its language. This requires linear time $O(size(A) \times n)$. We then compute all values $T(q)$ by saturation with respect to the defining rules. We exit saturation immediately, if it tries to add a second element to some type set, or if it tries to add a non-Boolean n-type. If this happens then we return false, which is justified by Lemma 3. Note that all positions in rules will be touched at most once and all type sets at most twice. Hence, saturation can be implemented in time $O(size(A) \times n)$. If saturation succeeds then we apply the third step. All types have been computed successfully now. We check for all $q \in final(A)$ whether $T(q) = \{1^n\}$. If so we return true otherwise false, which is licenced by Lemma 4. This can be done in time $O(size(A) \times n)$ too.

4   Efficient Answer Enumeration

We develop an efficient algorithm for enumerating the answers of an n-NSTT defined query on a given input tree. The insights gained will again be used in our learning algorithm.

Given an n-NSTT A and a tree t the problem is to compute all β such that $t \times \beta \in L(A)$. The first step to do is to project A to a tree automaton over Σ that we denote by $\pi(A)$. This automaton satisfies $states(\pi(A)) = states(A)$ and $final(\pi(A)) = final(A)$. Its rules are inferred by the following two schemata where $a \in \Sigma$ and $b \in \text{Bool}^n$:

$$\frac{(a, b)(q_1, q_2) \to q \in \text{rules}(A)}{a(q_1, q_2) \to q \in \text{rules}(\pi(A))} \qquad \frac{(a, b) \to q \in \text{rules}(A)}{a \to q \in \text{rules}(\pi(A))}$$

Given an trimmed n-NSTT A, let $\mathrm{T}_A : \mathtt{states}(A) \to \mathsf{Bool}^n$ be the function that maps states of A to their unique n-type according to Lemma 3. The following lemma permits to type rules of projections of n-NSTTs.

Lemma 5. *For all trimmed n-NSTTs A, labels $a \in \Sigma$, and $q, q_1, q_2 \in \mathtt{states}(A)$:*

$$a \to q \in \mathit{rules}(\pi(A)) \quad \text{iff} \quad (a, \mathrm{T}_A(q)) \to q \in \mathit{rules}(A)$$
$$a(q_1, q_2) \to q \in \mathit{rules}(\pi(A)) \quad \text{iff} \quad (a, \boldsymbol{b})(q_1, q_2) \to q \in \mathit{rules}(A)$$
$$\text{where } \boldsymbol{b} = \mathrm{T}_A(q) - \mathrm{T}_A(q_1) - \mathrm{T}_A(q_2)$$

Proof. The implications from the right to the left are obvious from the definition of the rules of $\pi(A)$. For the converse there are two cases. First, assume $a \to q \in \mathtt{rules}(\pi(A))$. By definition of $\pi(A)$ there exists $\boldsymbol{b} \in \mathsf{Bool}^n$ such that $(a, \boldsymbol{b}) \to q \in \mathtt{rules}(\pi(A))$. Lemma 1 shows that $\boldsymbol{b} = \mathrm{T}_A(q)$. Second, assume $a(q_1, q_2) \to q \in \mathtt{rules}(\pi(A))$. By definition of $\pi(A)$ there exists $\boldsymbol{b} \in \mathsf{Bool}^n$ such that $(a, \boldsymbol{b})(q_1, q_2) \to q \in \mathtt{rules}(A)$. Since A is trimmed, there exist a tree $t_1 \times \beta_1$ and $t_2 \times \beta_2$ over $\Sigma \times \mathsf{Bool}$ that can be evaluated by A into states q_1 and q_2 respectively. Thus, the tree $(a, \boldsymbol{b})(t_1 \times \beta_1, t_2 \times \beta_2)$ can be evaluated to q by A. Lemma 1 shows that $\boldsymbol{b} + \mathrm{T}_A(q_1) + \mathrm{T}_A(q_2) = \mathrm{T}_A(q)$. Hence, $\boldsymbol{b} = \mathrm{T}_A(q) - \mathrm{T}_A(q_1) - \mathrm{T}_A(q_2)$.

For every tree run r of a trimmed tree automaton A over $\Sigma \times \mathsf{Bool}^n$ on some tree with node v we define a function mapping nodes to n-types.

$$\mathrm{T}_A^r(v) = \begin{cases} \mathrm{T}_A(r(v)) & \text{if } v \text{ is a leaf} \\ \mathrm{T}_A(r(v)) - \mathrm{T}_A^r(r(v{\cdot}1)) - \mathrm{T}_A^r(r(v{\cdot}2)) & \text{else} \end{cases}$$

Note that T_A^r can be identified with the unique $\beta \in T_{\mathsf{Bool}^n}$ such that $\beta(v) = \mathrm{T}_A^r(v)$ for all nodes v.

Lemma 6. *For all trimmed n-NSTTs A, $t \in T_\Sigma$, and $r : \mathtt{nodes}(t) \to \mathtt{states}(A)$:*

$$r \in \mathsf{succ\_runs}_{\pi(A)}(t) \quad \text{iff} \quad r \in \mathsf{succ\_runs}_A(t \times \mathrm{T}_A^r)$$

Proof. Straightforward from Lemma 5 by induction on trees t.

Recall that a tree automaton is unambiguous, if no tree permits more than one successful run. All deterministic tree automata are unambiguous.

Proposition 2. *Let A be a trimmed unambiguous n-NSTT. For all trees $t \in T_\Sigma$, the function mapping $r \in \mathsf{succ\_runs}_{\pi(A)}(t)$ to Boolean annotations T_A^r in T_{Bool^n} is a bijection with range $\{\beta \mid t \times \beta \in L(A)\}$.*

Proof. First note that the function always maps to $\{\beta \mid t \times \beta \in L(A)\}$. This follows from Lemma 6. If $r \in \mathsf{succ\_runs}_{\pi(A)}(t)$ then $r \in \mathsf{succ\_runs}_A(t \times \mathrm{T}_A^r)$ so that $t \times \mathrm{T}_A^r \in L(A)$. Second, we show that the function is onto. To see this, we show by induction on t that if r is a run of A on $t \times \beta$ then $\beta = \mathrm{T}_A^r$. Let β such that $t \times \beta \in L(A)$. Thus, there exists $r \in \mathsf{succ\_runs}_A(t \times \beta)$ so that $\beta = \mathrm{T}_A^r$. By Lemma 6, it also holds that $r \in \mathsf{succ\_runs}_{\pi(A)}(t)$ so that T_A^r is a value taken by the function. Third, we have to show that the function is one-to-one. Let $r_1, r_2 \in \mathsf{succ\_runs}_{\pi(A)}(t)$ such that $\mathrm{T}_A^{r_1} = \mathrm{T}_A^{r_2}$. By Lemma 6 it holds that $r_i \in \mathsf{succ\_runs}_A(t \times \mathrm{T}_A^{r_i})$ for both $i = 1, 2$. Hence, r_1, r_2 are successful runs of A on the same tree, so they are equal by unambiguity of A.

Theorem 1. *For every unambiguous n-NSTT A, we can compute an algorithm in time $O(size(A) \times n)$ that enumerates $q_A(t)$ with delay $O(size(A) \times size(t) \times n)$ per n-tuple.*

Hence, one can compute the answer set $q_A(t)$ for unambiguous n-NSTTs A on trees t in time $O((|q_A(t)| + 1) \times size(A) \times size(t) \times n)$.

Proof. In order to enumerate the answer set $q_A(t)$ of an n-NSTTs A it is sufficient to enumerate the set $\{\beta \mid t \times \beta \in L(A)\}$ since every β can be transformed in linear time into a unique n-tuple $\boldsymbol{\beta}$ by definition of n-NSTTs. This set is in bijection to the set of successful runs of $\pi(A)$ on t by Proposition 2. Given an unambiguous n-NSTT A, we trim A, compute its projection $\pi(A)$ and types T_A in time $O(size(A) \times n)$. Given a tree $t \in T_\Sigma$ the algorithm proceeds as follows. It enumerates $r \in \text{succ\_runs}_A(t)$ with delay $O(size(A) \times size(t) \times n)$ per run and return all n-tuples of nodes corresponding to some Boolean annotation T_A^r.

5   Learning Model and Algorithm

The learning model for words languages from polynomial time and data with positive and negative examples [7,6] can be adapted to tree languages.

Definition 3. *Tree languages over a fixed set Σ represented tree automata in some class C are called* identifiable from polynomial time and data *if there exist two polynomials p_1 and p_2 and an algorithm* learner *such that:*

- *for all input samples $S \subseteq T_\Sigma \times$ Bool, learner(S) returns a tree automaton $A \in C$ in time $O(p_1(|S|))$, that is consistent with S in that for all $t \times b \in S$: $t \in L(A)$ iff $b = 1$;*
- *for all tree automata $A \in C$ there exists a so called characteristic sample* char(A) *of cardinality less than $p_2(size(A))$ such that, for all input samples $S \supseteq$ char(A), learner(S) returns a tree automaton $A' \in C$ equivalent to A.*

In contrast to the case of words, the learning model for trees bounds the *cardinality* of the characteristic sample, not its size. This relaxation may be acceptable as long as one is only interested in the existence of a polynomial time learner. If C is the class of deterministic tree automata, the learner can be defined by the RPNI algorithm in [17].

The model for learning tree languages is only partially adapted to queries. The question is which examples to use for n-ary queries. Let q be an *n*-ary query. A *completely annotated example for q* for q is a pair $(t, q(t))$ where $t \in T_\Sigma$. We call t called CARRIER of $(t, q(t))$. For a set S of completely annotated examples for q, we denote by CARRIER(S) the set of supports. A completely annotated example $(t, q(t))$ defines $|q(t)|$ positive examples, i.e. a positive example $(t \times \beta, 1)$ for each tuple tree $t \times \beta$ with β in $q(t)$. It also defines implicit negative examples, i.e. trees $(t \times \beta, 0)$ with β not in $q(t)$ for all t in CARRIER(S).

The cardinality of a completely annotated example $(t, q(t))$ is $q(t) + 1$. The size of a completely annotated example $(t, q(t))$ is $size(t) + |q(t)| \times n$. A sample is a set of completely annotated examples for a target query q, its cardinality is the sum of the cardinalities of all completely annotated examples in S, its size is the sum of sizes of all completely annotated examples in S. A tree automaton A over $\Sigma \times \text{Bool}^n$ is *consistent with a sample* S if every tree $t \times \beta$ with $(t, q(t))$ in S and $\beta \in q(t)$ is in $L(A)$ and if there is no tree $t \times \beta$ in $L(A)$ such that $(t, q(t))$ is in S and β is not in $q(t)$.

The model for learning queries is defined w.r.t. a query representation formalism. Two query representations are said to be equivalent if they represent the same query. This leads us to the following definition:

Definition 4. *n-ary queries represented by a query representation formalism $\mathcal{R}$ are said to be* identifiable from polynomial time and data *from completely annotated examples if there exist two polynomials p_1 and p_2 and an algorithm* learner *such that:*

- *for all input samples S of completely annotated n-ary examples* learner(S) *returns a representation $A \in \mathcal{R}$ in time $O(p_1(|S|))$ that is consistent with S;*
- *for all query representations $A \in \mathcal{R}$ there exists a so called characteristic sample* char(A) *for A of cardinality less than $p_2(|A|)$ such that, for all input sample $S \supseteq$ char(A),* learner(S) *returns a query representation $A' \in \mathcal{R}$ equivalent to A.*

Let us recall that, for a tree t and an n-ary query q, the number of selected n-tuples in $q(t)$ is at most $\texttt{size}(t)^n$. Therefore, if we consider a target query $q_{n,t}$ that extract all n-tuples of a tree t and no tuple for every other tree, the characteristic sample should contain the completely annotated example $(t, q_{n,t}(t))$ whose cardinality is $\texttt{size}(t) + \texttt{size}(t)^n \times n$. This holds for arbitrary query representation formalisms. In order to avoid this blow-up, we restrict ourselves to queries that selects a polynomially bounded number of n-tuples per tree: an n-ary query q over Σ-trees is said to be *polynomially bounded* if there is a polynomial p such that for each trees $t \in T_\Sigma$, $|q(t)| < p(\texttt{size}(t))$.

Theorem 2. *Polynomially bounded n-ary queries represented by deterministic n-NSTTs are identifiable from polynomial time and data from completely annotated examples.*

Before defining the learning algorithm we recall the basics of the RPNI algorithm for trees. RPNI inputs a sample of positive and negative examples. It first computes an initial deterministic tree automaton which recognizes exactly the set of positive examples in the sample. It then merges states as long as possible while verifying consistency (no negative example in the sample is recognized) and preserving determinism. The order of state fusions matters.

Merging works as follows: Let A be the initial automaton. We consider a partition π of $\texttt{states}(A)$. The equivalence class of q in that partition is denoted by $\pi(q)$. The quotions of A with respect to π is denoted by A/π. It is the automaton which satisfies $\texttt{states}(A/\pi) = \pi$ and $\texttt{final}(A) = \{p \in \pi \mid \pi \cap \texttt{final}(A) \neq \emptyset\}$. The rules of A are defined such that $(a, b) \to q \in \texttt{rules}(A) \Rightarrow (a, b) \to \pi(q) \in$

$\text{rules}(A/\pi)$ and $(f, \boldsymbol{b})(q_1, q_2) \to q \in \text{rules}(A), \Rightarrow (f, \boldsymbol{b})(\pi(q_1), \pi(q_2)) \to \pi(q) \in \text{rules}(A/\pi)$. State merging is performed by a function $\text{merge}(A, \pi, q_i, q_j)$ that outputs a partition π' such that $\pi'(q_i) = \pi'(q_j)$ and other elements of π are preserved. Function $\text{det-merge}(A, \pi, q_i, q_j)$ first merges q_i and q_j and then performs further merges such that the resulting automaton becomes deterministic.

The learning algorithm learner for n-ary queries represented by deterministic n-NSTTs is set to be $\text{RPNI}_{n-\text{NSTT}}$. It is given in Figure 2. It uses the same schema than the RPNI algorithm for tree languages, but with the following features:

- the positive examples are tuple trees $t \times \beta$ for every $t \in \text{CARRIER}(S)$ such that $q(t) \neq \emptyset$ and $\beta \in q(t)$;
- not all deterministic tree automata over $\Sigma \times \text{Bool}^n$ are deterministic n-NSTTs, therefore after every merge we have to check whether the resulting automaton is an n-NSTT, this is done using the T function (see Proposition 1). Note that, as one never merges states of different type, we denote, for a partition π of $\text{states}(A)$ considered by the algorithm and for a set of states $p \in \pi$, $\text{T}(p)$ as the type of its states;
- we do not have negative examples, but the hypothesis of completely annotated examples as input allows to define implicit negative examples: $t \times \beta$ such that $(t, q(t)) \in S$ and $\beta \notin q(t)$. As there is a bijection between runs on Σ-trees and answers of a query (see lemma 6), verifying whether an implicit negative example is recognized or not is the same as verifying that the number of runs on the support of the input sample does not grow. This replaces the usual consistency check of RPNI-like algorithms.
- Also, note that RPNI requires an order on states. In the initial automaton, each state can be associated to the single tree that it recognizes; states are then ordered following a fixed order on those trees.

The initial n-NSTT A is consistent with the input sample S because it recognizes exactly the set S^+ of tuple trees constructed from S. Let us suppose that, at every call to det-merge, the n-NSTT A/π is consistent with S. The automaton A/π' satisfies $L(A) \subseteq L(A/\pi')$. To check whether A/π is consistent with S, it is sufficient to test whether there is no new tree $t \times \beta$ in $L(A')$ with $t \in \text{CARRIER}(S)$. From lemma 6, this is equivalent to check whether, for every tree t in $\text{CARRIER}(S)$, the number of successful runs of the projected automaton $\pi(A)$ is equal to $|q(t)|$. Counting the number of successful runs on an input tree can be done in $O(\text{size}(S))$. Note that we do not consider the size of A' because it is lower than the size of A, and the size of A is linear in the size of S.

Also, we compute the T function described in section 3 on A. As A is an $n - \text{NSTT}$, condition of lemma 4 is satisfied for A. It is easy to verify that those conditions are also satisfied for A/π if and only if there do not exist two states of different types in the same element of π. This is guaranteed by the fact we never merge states of different types.

Thus $\text{RPNI}_{n-\text{NSTT}}$ computes in polynomial time, for every input sample S, an n-NSTT consistent with S. To end the proof of Theorem 2, it remains to prove the second item of Definition 4, i.e. we must define characteristic samples

---

$\text{RPNI}_{n-\text{NSTT}}$

Input: a sample S of completely annotated examples
    compute $S^+ = \{t \times \beta \mid t \in \text{CARRIER}(S), \beta \in q(t)\}$
    let A be the minimal deterministic n-NSTT such that $L(A) = S^+$
    Compute T and order states of A from q_i to q_n
    let $m = \Sigma_{t \in \text{CARRIER}(S)} |q(t)|$
    let π be the trivial partition of $\mathbf{states}(A)$
    For $i = 0$ **to** $|\mathbf{states}(A)|$ **do**
        let q be the state with the smallest index in $\pi(q_i)$
        If $q_i = q$ **then** % q_i has not been merged
            For $j = 0$ **to** $i - 1$ **do**
                If $\text{T}(q_i) = \text{T}(q_j)$ **then**
                    $\pi' \leftarrow \text{det-merge}(A, \pi, q_i, q_j)$
                    let m' be the number of runs of A/π' on $\text{CARRIER}(S)$
                    % test consistency with negative information
                    If $m = m'$ **then** $\pi \leftarrow \pi'$ and **Exit Inner Loop**
Output : A/π

Fig. 2. The learning algorithm learner for n-ary queries represented by deterministic n-NSTTs

for n-ary queries represented by deterministic n-NSTTs, and we must prove the convergence property of $\text{RPNI}_{n-\text{NSTT}}$ w.r.t. characteristic samples.

Tree languages represented by deterministic automata are identifiable from polynomial time and data [17]. Thus n-ary queries, considered as tree languages over $\Sigma \times \text{Bool}^n$, represented by deterministic n-NSTTs are identifiable from polynomial time and data. But, recall that this result is true in the learning model from positive and negative examples. Let learner$'$ = RPNI be the learning algorithm for tree languages represented by deterministic tree automata and char$'$ be the function computing the characteristic sample associated with a deterministic tree automaton. Let A be a deterministic n-NSTT, char$'(A)$ is the characteristic sample for A which is the representation of a tree language of $\Sigma \times \text{Bool}^n$-trees. We define the characteristic sample char(A) for A which is the representation of an n-ary query by:

$$\text{char}(A) = \{(t, q(t)) \mid (t \times \beta, b) \in \text{char}'(A)\}$$

We show that the cardinality of char(A) is polynomial. As tree languages represented by deterministic tree automata are learnable from polynomial time and data, there is a polynomial p_2' such that the cardinality of char$'(A)$ is less than $p_2'(s)$. Consequently, the number of trees t such that there exists an example $(t \times \beta, b) \in \text{char}'(A)$ is less than $p_2'(s)$. Therefore, $\text{CARRIER}(S)$ has cardinality less than $p_2'(s)$. As we consider polynomially bounded queries, the cardinality of every completely annotated example is polynomial. Thus there is a polynomial p_2 such that the cardinality of char(A) is less than $p_2(S)$.

Let learner be set to $\text{RPNI}_{n-\text{NSTT}}$. We have shown that, for every sample S, $\text{RPNI}_{n-\text{NSTT}}$ outputs in polynomial time an n-NSTT consistent with S. It remains to show that if $\text{char}(A) \subseteq S$ then $\text{RPNI}_{n-\text{NSTT}}$ with input S outputs an n-NSTT, denoted by $\text{RPNI}_{n-\text{NSTT}}(S)$, equivalent to A.

Let A be the target n-NSTT, let S be a sample that contains $\text{char}(A)$, we define the sample S' of positive and negative examples by:

$$S' = \{(t \times \beta, 1) \mid t \in \text{CARRIER}(S), \beta \in q(t)\} \cup \{(t \times \beta, 0) \mid t \in \text{CARRIER}(S), \beta \notin q(t)\}$$

By definition of $\text{char}(A)$ and of S', we have $\text{char}'(A) \subseteq S'$. Then, RPNI with input S' outputs a deterministic automaton $\text{RPNI}(S') = A'$ such that $L(A') = L(A)$.

It remains to show that $\text{RPNI}_{n-\text{NSTT}}(S) = \text{RPNI}(S')$. First, verifying that the number of runs on $\text{CARRIER}(S)$ does not grow is equivalent to the consistency test done by RPNI w.r.t. S' (as said above). Second, if $\text{char}(A) \subseteq S$, and consequently $\text{char}'(A) \subseteq S'$, $\text{RPNI}(S') = A'$ is an n-NSTT because $L(A') = L(A)$ is canonical. Therefore, under the hypothesis that $\text{char}(A) \subseteq S$, at every step of $\text{RPNI}_{n-\text{NSTT}}$, the current deterministic automaton is an n-NSTT. This is because otherwise a tree which is not a tuple tree would be accepted (the sequence of languages is increasing according to inclusion because states are merged). Thus, under the hypothesis that $\text{char}(A) \subseteq S$, merged states will always be of the same type. Thus, $\text{RPNI}_{n-\text{NSTT}}(S) = \text{RPNI}(S')$.

6   n-NSTTs for Unranked Trees

HTML or XML documents parse into unranked trees where every node may have a list of children of unbounded length, not only two. The notion of n-ary queries carries over literally.

As an example, consider the unranked tree film-list in Fig. 3. This tree represents a list (L) of three films (F), two of which are directed by Hitchcock (H) and one by Wenders (W). The letter (T) represents the title of the film. The binary query hitchcock asks for pairs of directors and title in films by Hitchcock. From film-list, this query selects the following pairs of nodes: hitchcock(film-list) = $\{(1 \cdot 2, 1 \cdot 1), (3 \cdot 2, 3 \cdot 1)\}$. The tree in Fig. 3 is annotated by the first pair $(1 \cdot 2, 1 \cdot 1)$.

For extending n-NSTTs to unranked trees, we only need a notion of tree automata for unranked trees. It must come with a good notion of bottom-up determinism, for which the Myhill-Nerode theorem holds. This needs some care [11]. We solve this problem as in [1] by using stepwise tree automata [3]. These have the further advantage that they can be identified with standard tree automata operating on binary encodings of unranked trees, so that all our learning algorithms carry over.

An example of stepwise tree automaton inferred by our learning algorithm is given Fig. 3. This automaton has been inferred from completely annotated example for query hitchcock, and recognizes that query, at least for documents of the correct type.

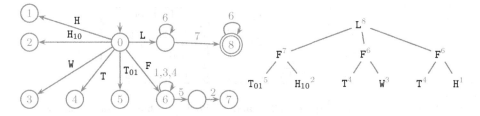

Fig. 3. A stepwise tree automaton inferred by our algorithm $\text{RPNI}_{2\text{-NSTT}}$ (left); the tree film-list annotated by a successful run; state 8 is obtained by evaluating the word $L \cdot 7 \cdot 6 \cdot 6$. Bit vectors 00 are ignored, so we write L instead of L_{00}

# Ex.	Okra						Bigbook					
	$\text{RPNI}_{\text{NSTT}}$			$\text{RPNI}_{1\text{-NSTT}}$			$\text{RPNI}_{\text{NSTT}}$			$\text{RPNI}_{1\text{-NSTT}}$		
	F-meas.	Init.	infer.	F-meas.	Init.	infer.	F-meas.	Init.	infer.	F-meas.	Init.	infer.
1	100 %	72	24	97.1 %	624	30	68.4 %	162	37	89.4 %	485	29
2	100 %	82	24	98.3 %	547	28	91.3 %	172	42	98.6 %	877	29
3	100 %	85	24	94.3 %	1045	31	100 %	179	48	100 %	1226	30

Fig. 4. Learning monadic queries by RPNI for either NSTTs [2] or 1-NSTTs as proposed here: F-measure, sizes of initial and inferred automata

7   Application to Web Information Extraction

We have implemented our learning algorithm and started applying it to Web information extraction tasks. We have added a single heuristic proposed in [6], which consists in typing states, so that only trees compatible with HTML syntax are recognized. Textual values and attributes are ignored.

In the case of monadic queries, we compare our algorithm $\text{RPNI}_{1\text{-NSTT}}$ with $\text{RPNI}_{\text{NSTT}}$ from [2]. We use the RISE benchmark: www.isi.edu/info-agents/RISE. Results are averaged over 30 experiments. They are presented in Fig. 4. Our algorithm achieves a little worse on the Okra benchmark, because this benchmark contains pages with a single element to be extracted. On Bigbook, however, $\text{RPNI}_{1\text{-NSTT}}$ performs better than $\text{RPNI}_{\text{NSTT}}$. It is interesting to observe that our technique produce bigger initial automata (because of canonicity, we have one input tree per tuple), but output automata are roughly of the same size for the two systems. These experiments show that induction of NSTTs and 1-NSTTs yield similarly good performance while using different representation schemas.

For n-ary queries, we run $\text{RPNI}_{n-\text{NSTT}}$ on the benchmarks Bigbook and Okra. The results are promising. We also use the Datafoot benchmark available at www.grappa.univ-lille3.fr/~marty/corpus.html. It contains different documents with various structures: lists, tables, rotated tables, cross-tables among others. We learn from only one completely annotated Web document. "Success" means that we achieve 100% F-measure on other web pages. Experimental

	Okra			Bigbook		
# Examples	F-meas.	Init.	Infer.	F-meas.	Init.	Infer.
1	90.4 %	469	31	89.9 %	505	33
2	97.6 %	781	31	95.2 %	891	33
3	99.4 %	1171	32	100 %	1342	34

Fig. 5. Results of RPNI$_{2\text{-NSTT}}$ on Okra and Bigbook benchmarks on a binary task: extraction of (name, mail) on Okra and (name, address) on Bigbook

Dataset	Succ. ?	Description	Dataset	Succ. ?	Description
L0	YES	table with tuples in rows	L5	YES	fake list (sequence of EM)
L1	NO	table with tuples in columns	L6	NO	fake list 2 (sequence of SPAN)
L2	YES	2 column table w/ separator	L7	YES	list of descriptions (DD/DT tag)
L3	YES	nested lists	L8	YES	description and list of SPAN
L4	YES	lists without separator	L9	YES	list of tables, one element factorized

Fig. 6. RPNI$_{2\text{-NSTT}}$ on Web pages with various structures from the Datafoot benchmark

results are given in Fig. 6. They are generally very positive. Limitation arise only in the case of non regular queries (L1), or when the tree structure alone is not sufficiently informative (L6). These limitations are to be expected of course.

Future Work

Completely annotated examples are not realistic in practice of information extraction. As in the monadic case, we will have to introduce intelligent tree pruning techniques in order to cut of irrelevant parts of documents. This is needed to deal with partially annotated documents, in order to reduce the annotation effort and to improve the quality of inferred queries. It is fundamental to interactive learning of n-ary queries.

References

1. J. Carme, R. Gilleron, A. Lemay, and J. Niehren. Interactive learning of node selecting tree transducer. *Machine Learning*, 2006.
2. J. Carme, A. Lemay, and J. Niehren. Learning node selecting tree transducer from completely annotated examples. In *ICGI*, vol. 3264 of *LNAI*, p. 91–102. 2004.
3. J. Carme, J. Niehren, and M. Tommasi. Querying unranked trees with stepwise tree automata. In *RTA*, vol. 3091 of *LNCS*, p. 105 – 118. 2004.
4. B. Chidlovskii. Wrapping web information providers by transducer induction. In *ECML*, vol. 2167 of *LNAI*, p. 61 – 73, 2001.
5. A. Corbí, J. Oncina, and P. García. Learning regular languages from a complete sample by error correcting techniques. *IEE*, p. 4/1–4/7, 1993.
6. C. de la Higuera. Characteristic sets for polynomial grammatical inference. *Machine Learning*, 27:125–137, 1997.

7. E.M. Gold. Complexity of automaton identification from given data. *Inf. Cont,* 37:302–320, 1978.
8. G. Gottlob and C. Koch. Monadic queries over tree-structured data. In *17th Annual IEEE Symposium on Logic in Computer Science,* p. 189–202, 2002.
9. H. Hosoya and B. Pierce. Regular expression pattern matching for XML. *Journal of Functional Programming,* 6(13):961–1004, 2003.
10. N. Kushmerick. Wrapper induction: Efficiency and expressiveness. *Artificial Intelligence,* 118(1-2):15–68, 2000.
11. W. Martens and J. Niehren. On the minimization of XML schemas and tree automata for unranked trees. *Journal of Computer and System Science,* 2006.
12. Gerome Miklau and Dan Suciu. Containment and equivalence for a fragment of xpath. *Journal of the ACM,* 51(1):2–45, 2004.
13. I. Muslea, S. Minton, and C. Knoblock. Active learning with strong and weak views: a case study on wrapper induction. In *IJCAI 2003,* p. 415–420, 2003.
14. F. Neven and J. Van Den Bussche. Expressiveness of structured document query languages based on attribute grammars. *Journal of the ACM,* 49(1):56–100, 2002.
15. J. Niehren, Laurent Planque, J.M. Talbot, and S. Tison. N-ary queries by tree automata. In *DBPL,* vol. 3774 of *LNCS,* p. 217–231. 2005.
16. J. Oncina and P. Garcia. Inferring regular languages in polynomial update time. In *Pattern Recognition and Image Analysis,* p. 49–61, 1992.
17. J. Oncina and P. García. Inference of recognizable tree sets. Tech. report, Universidad de Alicante, 1993. DSIC-II/47/93.
18. S. Raeymaekers, M. Bruynooghe, and J. Van den Bussche. Learning (k,l)-contextual tree languages for information extraction. In *ECML,* vol. 3720 of *LNAI,* p. 305–316, 2005.
19. J. W. Thatcher and J. B. Wright. Generalized finite automata with an application to a decision problem of second-order logic. *Math. System Theory,* 2:57–82, 1968.

Learning Multiplicity Tree Automata[*,**]

Amaury Habrard[1] and Jose Oncina[2,***]

[1] LIF – Université de Provence
39, rue Frédéric Joliot Curie – 13453 Marseille cedex 13 – France
`amaury.habrard@lif.univ-mrs.fr`
[2] Dep. de Lenguajes y Sistemas Informático
Universidad de Alicante E-03071 Alicante – Spain
`oncina@dlsi.ua.es`

Abstract. In this paper, we present a theoretical approach for the problem of learning multiplicity tree automata. These automata allows one to define functions which compute a number for each tree. They can be seen as a strict generalization of stochastic tree automata since they allow to define functions over any field K. A multiplicity automaton admits a support which is a non deterministic automaton. From a grammatical inference point of view, this paper presents a contribution which is original due to the combination of two important aspects. This is the first time, as far as we now, that a learning method focuses on non deterministic tree automata which computes functions over a field. The algorithm proposed in this paper stands in Angluin's exact model where a learner is allowed to use membership and equivalence queries. We show that this algorithm is polynomial in time in function of the size of the representation.

Keywords: multiplicity tree automata, recognizable tree series, learning from equivalence and membership queries.

1 Introduction

Trees are natural candidates for modeling a hierarchy in data, and for example they are particularly relevant to model a web page. Recently, due to the potential applications in the web, a lot of machine learning approaches devoted to trees have been proposed. From a grammatical inference standpoint, the natural objects for dealing with tree-structured data are tree automata and tree languages [1,2]. These objects are natural extensions of finite automata on strings, except that the alphabet is constituted of functional symbols representing labels of tree nodes. Several learning algorithms has been proposed in the literature for learning tree automata. Among them we can cite those of Knuutila *et al.*[3], Garcia *et al.*[4]

---

[*] This work was supported in part by the IST Programme of the European Community, under the PASCAL Network of Excellence, IST-2002-506778. This publication only reflects the authors' views.
[**] This work is part of the ARA marmota french projet.
[***] This work was done when the second author was visiting the LIF Marseille.

Y. Sakakibara et al. (Eds.): ICGI 2006, LNAI 4201, pp. 268–280, 2006.

and Kosala *et al.*[5] for dealing with an unranked alphabet. Besombes *et al.* [6] have studied the learning of regular tree languages using positive examples and membership queries. Carme *et al.* [7] have proposed to learn specific tree transducers for information extraction applications. In the probabilistic case, we can cite Carrasco *et al.* [8] and Rico *et al.* [9]. An important remark has to be made here: In general, these approaches have focused on learning deterministic models which may imply the construction of models with a high complexity.

In this paper, we propose to study the learnability of multiplicity tree automata. Informally, a multiplicity tree automaton defines a function allowing one to associate to any tree a value in a field K (for example $\mathbb{R}$ or $\mathbb{Q}$). We call such an automaton a K-multiplicity tree automaton. For example, stochastic tree automata are then particular cases of multiplicity automata where $K = [0, 1]$. However, multiplicity automata do not compute stochastic distribution in general. For example, you can define multiplicity tree automata that represent a function which computes the number of occurrences of a given symbol in a tree. There exists a notion of support for a multiplicity automaton which corresponds to a non deterministic finite tree automaton. This non determinism characterize a greater expressiveness than deterministic models. Another crucial point has to be made here. For defining a multiplicity automaton, we define functions which compute the value of a subtree when a transition is applied to analyse the subtree. In the case of a multiplicity automaton these functions are *multilinear* (*e.g.* for symbol of arity p we define a $p-$linear function) and offer a good expressiveness for defining the global function computed by a multiplicity automaton. In fact, the function computed by multiplicity automata are usually referred as recognizable formal power series on trees [10,11].

Hence, this article combines two main improvements for learning tree automata. The method we present allows us to learn tree automata with a non deterministic support that compute functions from a set of trees to a field K. This is, as far as we know, the first time that a learning method is proposed for multiplicity tree automata. We think that this research direction can be very promising due to the potential applications notably in information extraction from the web.

In the case of strings, some learning methods of multiplicity automata have already been published: [12]. But, there exists no similar work for trees. The adaptation to trees is not trivial since the use of multilinear mappings for transitions are a real improvement in comparison with the string case.

We propose a learning algorithm for multiplicity tree automata which stands in Angluin's *exact learning model* [13]. In this framework, the learning algorithm is allowed to ask queries to an oracle. The algorithm can ask equivalence queries to know if he found the correct hypothesis. In the opposite case, a counterexample is returned by the oracle. Membership queries are also available to have information about one example. The algorithm we present runs in polynomial time in the size of the target and needs a number of queries also polynomial in the size of the target. This algorithm exploits a result showing that the number of states of a minimal multiplicity tree automaton is exactly the rank (which is finite) of the Hankel matrix of the power tree series it represents. The underlying principle of our approach is to find a hierarchical basis which allows to generate all the element of the target multiplicity automaton. This basis is then used for building the tree automaton which is minimal since a basis is a minimal representation by definition.

The paper is organised as follows. In Section 2, we introduce some background about recognizable formal tree series and multiplicity automata. The Hankel Matrix associated to a recognizable series is defined in Section 3. In this section, we also characterize recognizable tree series in terms of the dimension of their associated Hankel Matrix. The learning algorithm is presented in Section 4.

2   Background

To begin with, we introduce the alphabet for defining trees and the concept of free magma which is an equivalent to the free monoid Σ^* over strings.

Following [10], Let F be a finite set of function symbols, that is a ranked alphabet $F = F_0 \cup F_1 \cup \cdots \cup F_p$. The elements in F_p are the function symbols of *arity* p. We denote by $M(F)$ the free magma generated by F. The elements in $M(F)$ are called *trees*. If t is a tree and $t \notin F_0$ then there exists an integer $p \geq 0$, a symbol function $f \in F_p$, and trees $t_1, \ldots, t_p$ such that $t = f(t_1, \ldots, t_p)$.

Definition 1. *Let K be a commutative field. A* formal power tree series (TS) *on $M(F)$ with coefficients in K is a mapping*

$$S : M(F) \to K$$

The set of all TS on $M(F)$ with coefficients in K is denoted by $K\{\{F\}\}$.

2.1   Recognizable Formal Power Tree Series (RTS)

Let V be a finite dimensional vector space over the field K, let $dim(V)$ be the dimension of V and let $x \in V$, we denote by $[x]_i$ the ith coordinate of the vector x. In the following, the vector V will represent intermediate values used in a non deterministic analysis of a tree by a multiplicity automaton. Each dimension of V will correspond to the result associated to a state of the multiplicity tree automaton.

We denote by $\mathcal{L}(V^p; V)$ the set of p-linear mappings from V^p to V. Let $\mathcal{L} = \cup_{p \geq 0} \mathcal{L}(V^p; V)$. The vector space V is an $\mathcal{L}$-magma with $\mathcal{L}(V^p; V)$ as the function set with arity p. Thus any mapping $\mu : F \to \mathcal{L}$ which maps F_p into $\mathcal{L}(V^p; V)$ converts V into an F-magma.

Intuitively, μ will correspond to a transition in the automaton that defines the next states used during the analysis of a tree.

Definition 2. *A* linear representation *of the free magma $M(F)$ is a couple (V, μ), where V is a finite dimensional vector space over K, and where $\mu : F \to \mathcal{L}$ maps F_p into $\mathcal{L}(V^p; V)$ for each $p \geq 0$.*

Thus for each $f \in F_p$, $\mu(f) : V^p \to V$ is p-linear, and since $M(F)$ is free, μ extends uniquely to a morphism $\mu : M(F) \to V$ by the formula

$$\mu(f(t_1, \ldots, t_p)) = \mu(f)(\mu(t_1), \ldots, \mu(t_p)). \tag{1}$$

Definition 3. *let S be a TS on $M(F)$, then S is a recognizable TS (RTS) if there exists a triple (V, μ, λ), where (V, μ) is a linear representation of $M(F)$, and $\lambda : V \to K$ is a linear form, such that $S(t) = \lambda(\mu(t))$ for all t in $M(F)$.*

(V, μ, λ) is called a *Multiplicity Tree Automaton* (MTA) and we say that (V, μ, λ) is a representation of S. Intuitively, if we try to make the link between these automata and classical automata in language theory, the states of a multiplicity automaton correspond to a basis of V. The transitions are defined by μ and the final states by λ. According to this definition, multiplicity tree automata can be seen as an extension of bottom-up tree automata.

In order to illustrate these objects, we provide an example introduced in [10]. We consider a recognizable tree series S (*i.e.* a multiplicity tree automaton) computing the number of occurrences of a symbol f in a tree.

We define a MTA (V, λ, μ) where $V = \mathbb{Q}^2$ and (e_1, e_2) a canonical basis of V (*i.e.* $e_1 = (1, 0)$ and $e_2 = (1, 0)$). We define μ and λ such that:

$$\forall g \in F_q, g \neq f : \mu(g)(e_{i_1}, \ldots, e_{i_q}) = \begin{cases} e_1 \text{ if } e_{i_1} = \cdots = e_{i_q} = e_1 \\ e_2 \text{ if there exists exactly one } e_{i_j} \text{ s.t. } e_{i_j} = e_2 \\ 0 \text{ otherwise} \end{cases}$$

$$f \in F_p : \mu(f)(e_{i_1}, \ldots, e_{i_p}) = \begin{cases} e_1 + e_2 \text{ if } e_{i_1} = \cdots = e_{i_p} = e_1 \\ e_2 \text{ if there exists exactly one } e_{i_j} \text{ s.t. } e_{i_j} = e_2 \\ 0 \text{ otherwise} \end{cases}$$

$$\forall a \in F_0 : \mu(a) = \begin{cases} e_1 \text{ if } a \neq f \\ e_1 + e_2 \text{ if } a = f \in F_0 \\ 0 \text{ otherwise} \end{cases}$$

Finally $\lambda(e_1) = 0$ and $\lambda(e_2) = 1$.

It can be shown that $\mu(t) = e_1 + S(t)e_2$, then $\lambda(\mu(t)) = S(t)$. Let's see an example of a computation of $S(t)$. Consider $t = f(a, g(f(a, a)))$ over the ranked alphabet $F_0 = \{a\}$, $F_1 = \{g(\cdot)\}$ $F_2 = \{'f(\cdot, \cdot)'\}$.

$$\begin{aligned}
\mu(f(a, g(f(a, a)))) &= \mu(f)(\mu(a), \mu(g(f(a, a)))) \\
&= \mu(f)(e_1, \mu(g)(\mu(f(a, a)))) \\
&= \mu(f)(e_1, \mu(g)(\mu(f)(\mu(a), \mu(a)))) \\
&= \mu(f)(e_1, \mu(g)(\mu(f)(e_1, e_1))) \\
&= \mu(f)(e_1, \mu(g)(e_1 + e_2)) \\
&= \mu(f)(e_1, \mu(g)(e_1)) + \mu(f)(e_1, \mu(g)(e_2)) \\
&= \mu(f)(e_1, \mu(g)(e_1)) + \mu(f)(e_1, \mu(g)(e_2)) \\
&= \mu(f)(e_1, e_1) + \mu(f)(e_1, e_2) = e_1 + e_2 + e_2 = e_1 + 2e_2
\end{aligned}$$

Hence $\lambda(\mu(t)) = 2$.

2.2 Contexts

We introduce contexts which allow us to define an equivalent notion of concatenation for trees. Let $ be a zero arity function symbol not in F_0, a context is an element of the free-magma $M(F \cup \{\$\})$ such that the symbol $ appears exactly one time. We denote by $M(\$, F)$ such set.

Let $c \neq \$$ be a context, then, there exists two integers p and n ($n \leq p$), a symbol function $f \in F_p$, trees $t_1, \ldots, t_{p-1}$ and a context c' such that $c = f(t_1, \ldots, t_{n-1}, c', t_n, \ldots, t_{p-1})$. Let t be a tree and let c be a context, $t \cdot c$ denotes the tree obtained by substituting the symbol $ in the context c by the tree t.

The μ function can be extended to work over contexts ($\mu : M(\$, F) \to \mathcal{L}(V; V)$) recursively on the following way:

$$\mu(\$)(x) = x$$
$$\mu(f(t_1, \ldots, t_{n-1}, c, t_n, \ldots, t_p))(x) = \mu(f)(\mu(t_1), \ldots, \mu(t_{n-1}), \mu(c)(x), \mu(t_n), \ldots, \mu(t_p))$$

It is easy to see that $\mu(t \cdot c) = \mu(c)(\mu(t))$. Let t be a tree we define $\mathrm{Suf}(t) = \{c' : \exists t', t' \cdot c = t\}$.

2.3 Multilinear Functions

Let $V = K^d$, let $f : V^p \to V$ be a p-linear function, such that $f(x_1, \ldots x_p) = y$ then f can be expressed as:

$$[y]_i = \sum_{\substack{1 \leq j_i \leq d \\ i=1,\ldots,p}} f_{i,j_1,\ldots,j_p} [x_1]_{j_1} \ldots [x_p]_{j_p} \tag{2}$$

where $f_{i,j_1,\ldots,j_p}$ are the d^{p+1} parameters that define the function f. Note that in order to fully specify an MTA (V, μ, λ) ($V = K^r$), we need:

- d parameters to specify λ
- $\sum_{i:|F_i| \neq 0} |F_i| d^{i+1}$ parameters to specify the multilinear functions.

Let (V, μ, λ) a MTA, as $\lambda : V \to K$ is a linear function it can be represented as a vector ($\lambda = (\lambda_1, \ldots, \lambda_d)$).

In the same way, when applied over contexts, μ gives a linear function over vectors in V ($\mu : M(\$, F) \to \mathcal{L}(V; V)$), this linear function can be represented as a $d \times d$ matrix. For example, Using this notation, the equation $\lambda(\mu(t \cdot c)) = \lambda(\mu(c)(\mu(t)))$ can be written clearly as $\mu(t \cdot c)\lambda = \mu(t)\mu(c)\lambda$.

3 Hankel Matrix and Recognizable Tree Series

3.1 The Hankel Matrix

Informally, the Hankel Matrix of a TS S is an infinite matrix that represents all the possible values for S. The rows of the matrix are indexed by trees and the columns by contexts. A value in this matrix corresponds to the value in the series S for the tree built by the concatenation of the tree on the row and the context on the column. An example is drawn on Figure 1.

Definition 4. *The* Hankel matrix *(HM) of a TS $S \in K\{\{F\}\}$ (HM(S)) is an infinite matrix $H : M(F) \times M(\$, F) \to K$ such that $H_{t,c} = S(t \cdot c)$ $\forall t \in M(F), c \in M(\$, F)$.*

	$\$$	$f(\$, a)$	$f(\$, b)$	$f(a, \$)$	$\cdots$
a	$S(a)$	$S(f(a,a))$	$S(f(a,b))$	$S(f(a,a))$	$\cdots$
b	$S(b)$	$S(f(b,a))$	$S(f(b,b))$	$S(f(a,b))$	$\cdots$
$f(a,a)$	$S(f(a,a))$	$S(f(f(a,a),a))$	$S(f(f(a,a),b))$	$S(f(a,f(a,a)))$	$\cdots$
$\vdots$	$\vdots$	$\vdots$	$\vdots$	$\vdots$	$\ddots$

Fig. 1. An example of the Hankel Matrix of a tree series S

Let t be a tree, a row of the Hankel Matrix is defined by H_t, then $H_t(c) = H_{t,c}$.

Lemma 1. *Let (V, μ, λ) an MTA of a TS $S \in K\{\{F\}\}$, let H the Hankel Matrix of S, then $rank(H) \le dim(V)$.*

Proof. Let $d = dim(V)$, define a $\infty \times d$ matrix R such that $R(t, i) = [\mu(t)]_i$ and define a $d \times \infty$ matrix C such that $C(i, c) = [\mu(c)\lambda]_i$. Clearly, $H = RC$, but as $rank(C) \le d$ and $rank(R) \le d$, then $rank(H) \le d$. $\qquad \square$

3.2 Recognizable Tree Series

We are going to show that a TS is recognizable if an only if its HM has a finite rank. For this purpose, we will introduce the notion of hierarchical generator and show that this generator allows us to generate all the entries of the HM.

Definition 5. *Let H be an HM, we say that $B = \{e_1, \ldots, e_d\}$ is a* hierarchical generator *(HG) in H if*

1. *each $e_i \in B$ is* linearly independent *(LI) of the rest ($\nexists \alpha_j \in K : H_{e_i} = \sum_{1 \le j \le d, \, i \ne j} \alpha_i H_{e_j}$)*
2. *$\forall e_i = f(e_{i_1}, \ldots, e_{i_p}) \in B$ then $e_{i_j} \in B$, $j = 1, \ldots, p$.*
3. *There is no tree $t = f(e_{i_1}, \ldots, e_{i_p})$, $t \notin B$, $e_{i_j} \in B, j = 1, \ldots, d$, such that t is LI of B.*

Given any HM H, note that the previous definition does not imply that any HG for H should be a basis for the HM. A HG can be easily extracted from an HM following Algorithm 1 HG. In order to eliminate any ambiguity, we should fix an arbitrary order on trees, any order can be chosen.

Algorithm 2 describes the algorithm MTAB to extract an MTA from an HM. Although in the present version it works on infinite HM (then it is not really an algorithm) we are going to use it later with finite size portions of the HM.

Algorithm HG(H)

input: Hankel matrix H
output: a hierarchical generator B

1. initialize $B = \{\}$, $i = 1$
2. search for the smaller tree $e_i = f(e_{i_1}, \ldots, e_{i_p})$ such that $e_{i_j} \in B$, $j = 1, \ldots, p$ and H_{e_i} is not a linear combination of $\{H_{e_1}, \ldots, H_{e_{i-1}}\}$.
3. if not found then halt.
   if found then add it to B and increment i.
4. go to 2

Algo. 1. Algorithm HG to obtain a Hierarchical Generator from a Hankel Matrix

Algorithm MTAB(H)

input: a Hankel matrix H
output: a representation (V, μ, λ)

1. Obtain a hierarchical generator $e_1, \ldots, e_d$ from H.
2. Set $dim(V) = d$.
3. Set $\lambda_i = H(e_i)$, $i = 1, \ldots, d$
4. $\forall p, \forall f \in F_p, \forall i_1, \ldots, i_p, 1 \leq i_j \leq d$, let α_i such that: $H_{f(e_{i_1}, \ldots, e_{i_p})} = \sum_{i=1}^{r} \alpha_i H_{e_i}$. Then fix $f_{i, i_1, \ldots, i_p} = \alpha_i$.

Algo. 2. Algorithm MTAB that builds representation from a Hankel Matrix

Now we present a series of lemma necessary to show that the multiplicity automaton extracted by algorithm MTAB represents the TS defined by its HM. Let δ_{ij} representing a function that returns always 0 except when $i = j$ it returns 1.

Lemma 2. *Let H be the Hankel matrix of a RTS $S \in \{\{K\}\}$. Let $(V, \mu, \lambda) =$* MTAB(H)*, then*

$$[\mu(e_i)]_j = \delta_{ij}.$$

Proof. Note that as e_i are elements of the generator and let $e_i = f(e_{i_1}, \ldots, e_{i_p})$, using the algorithm, $f_{k, i_1, \ldots, i_p} = \delta_{ik}$.

We prove the result by induction in the height of the trees in the generator. Let $e_i \in F_0$, then $p = 0$ and $f_k = \delta_{ik}$, in such case, $[\mu(e_i)]_j = f_j = \delta_{ij}$ as required. Now let $e_i = f(e_{i_1}, \ldots, e_{i_p})$ and suppose, by induction, that $[\mu(e_{i_j})]_k = \delta_{i_j k}$, $j = 1, \ldots, p$. Then,

$$
\begin{aligned}
[\mu(e_i)]_j &= [\mu(f(e_{i_1}, \ldots, e_{i_p}))]_j \\
&= [\mu(f)(\mu(e_{i_1}), \ldots, \mu(e_{i_p}))]_j && \text{by Equation 1} \\
&= \sum_{j_1} f_{j, j_1, \ldots, j_p} [\mu(e_{i_1})]_{j_1} \ldots [\mu(e_{i_p})]_{j_p} && \mu(f) \text{ is a multilinear function} \\
&= \sum_{j_1} f_{j, j_1, \ldots, j_p} \delta_{i_1 j_1} \ldots \delta_{i_p j_p} && \text{induction step}
\end{aligned}
$$

$$= f_{j,i_1,\dots,i_p} = \delta_{ij} \quad \text{by Algorithm MTAB} \qquad \qquad \square$$

Note that as a consequence of the Lemma 2, $\mu(e_i)\lambda = H(e_i), i = 1,\dots,r$.

Lemma 3. *Let H be the HM of a RTS $S \in \{\{K\}\}$. Let $(V,\mu,\lambda) = \text{MTAB}(H)$. Let $B = \{e_1,\dots,e_d\} = \text{HG}(H)$. then,*

$$\mu(f(e_{j_1},\dots,e_{j_p})) = \sum_{j=1}^{r} f_{j,j_1,\dots,j_p}\mu(e_j). \qquad (3)$$

Proof.

$$
\begin{aligned}
\left[\mu(f(e_{j_1},\dots,e_{j_p}))\right]_i &= \left[(\mu f)(\mu(e_{j_1}),\dots \mu(e_{j_p}))\right]_i && \text{by Equation 1}\\
&= \sum_{1\le k_i\le p} f_{i,k_1,\dots,k_p}[\mu(e_{j_1})_{k_1}]\dots[\mu(e_{j_p})_{k_p}] && \text{by Equation 2}\\
&= \sum_{1\le k_i\le p} f_{i,k_1,\dots,k_p}\delta_{j_1,k_1}\dots\delta_{j_p,k_p} && \text{by Lemma 2}\\
&= f_{i,j_1,\dots,j_p}\\
&= \left[\sum_{j=1}^{r} f_{j,j_1,\dots,j_p}\delta_{ij}\right]_i = \left[\sum_{j=1}^{r} f_{j,j_1,\dots,j_p}\mu(e_j)\right]_i && \text{by Lemma 2} \quad\square
\end{aligned}
$$

Lemma 4. *Let H be the HM of a RTS $S \in \{\{K\}\}$. Let $(V,\mu,\lambda) = \text{MTAB}(H)$. Let $B = \{e_1,\dots,e_d\} = \text{HG}(H)$. Then, for all context c*
$$H_{e_i}(c) = \mu(e_i)\mu(c)\lambda.$$

Proof. By induction, the base case ($c = \$$) is evident since $\mu(e_i)\lambda = H_{e_i}(\$)$. Let us show that $H_{f(e_{j_1},\dots,e_{j_p})}(c) = \mu(f(e_{j_1},\dots,e_{j_p})\cdot c)\lambda$.

$$
\begin{aligned}
H_{f(e_{j_1},\dots,e_{j_p})}(c) &= \sum_{j=1}^{d} f_{j,j_1,\dots,j_p}H_{e_j}(c) && \text{by algorithm MTAB}\\
&= \sum_{j=1}^{d} f_{j,j_1,\dots,j_p}\mu(e_j)\mu(c)\lambda && \text{by induction step}\\
&= \mu(f(e_{j_1},\dots,e_{j_p}))\mu(c)\lambda && \text{by Lemma 3}\\
&= \mu(f(e_{j_1},\dots,e_{j_p})\cdot c)\lambda && \qquad\square
\end{aligned}
$$

Theorem 1. *Let H be the HM of a RTS $S \in \{\{K\}\}$. Let $(V,\mu,\lambda) = \text{MTAB}(H)$. Then, $S(t) = \mu(t)\lambda$.*

Proof. Let $B = \{e_1,\dots,e_d\} = \text{HG}(H)$. Note that for $f \in F_0$

$$
\begin{aligned}
H_f(c) &= \sum_{i=1}^{d} f_i H_{e_i}(c) && \text{by Algorithm MTAB}\\
&= \sum_{i=1}^{d} f_i \mu(e_i)\mu(c)\lambda && \text{by Lemma 4}
\end{aligned}
$$

$$= \sum_{i=1}^{d} f_i \sum_{j=1}^{d} [\mu(e_i)]_j \, [\mu(c)\lambda]_j$$

$$= \sum_{i=1}^{d} f_i \sum_{j=1}^{d} \delta_{ij} \, [\mu(c)\lambda]_j \qquad\qquad \text{by Lemma 2}$$

$$= \sum_{i=1}^{d} f_i \, [\mu(c)\lambda]_i$$

$$= \sum_{i=1}^{d} \mu(f)_i \, [\mu(c)\lambda]_i \qquad\qquad \text{by Equation 2}$$

$$= \mu(f)\mu(c)\lambda = \mu(f \cdot c)\lambda$$

And we have what we wanted because for any tree t, it exists an $f \in F_0$ and a context c such that $t = a \cdot c$. Then, $S(t) = H_f(c) = \mu(f \cdot c)\lambda = \mu(t)\lambda$. □

Corollary 1. *Let H be the Hankel Matrix of a RTS $S \in \{\{K\}\}$. Then, the MTA (V, μ, λ) that represents S with a smaller $dim(V)$ satisfies that $rank(H) = dim(V)$.*

Proof. By Lemma 1 we have that $rank(H) \leq dim(V)$, and by Theorem 1 we have shown that, using algorithm MTAB, we can build a representation (V, μ, λ) consistent with H such that $dim(V) \leq rank(H)$. □

Corollary 2. *Let H be the HM of a RTS $S \in \{\{K\}\}$, HG(H) is a basis, i.e. HG(H) can generate all the Hankel Matrix H.*

Corollary 3. *Let H be the Hankel Matrix of a RTS $S \in \{\{K\}\}$. The MTA $(V, \mu, \lambda) = $ MTAB(H) is the representation of S that minimizes $dim(V)$.*

4   Inference Algorithm

The learning model we use is the exact learning model of Angluin [13]. Let f be a target function. At each step of the inference procedure, the learning algorithm can propose an hypothesis function h by making an equivalence query (EQ) to an oracle. This oracle answers YES if h is equivalent to f on all input assignments. In this case the target is identified, the learning algorithm succeeds and halts. Otherwise, the answer to the equivalence query is NO and the algorithm receives a counterexample, that is an assignment z such that $f(z) \neq h(z)$. Moreover, the learning algorithm is also allowed to query an oracle for the value of the function f on a particular assignment z by making a membership query (MQ) on z. The response to such a query is the value $f(z)$. We say that the learner identifies a class of functions $\mathcal{F}$, if, for every function $f \in \mathcal{F}$, the learner outputs an hypothesis h that is equivalent to f and does so in polynomial time in the "size" of a shortest representation of f and the length of the longest counterexample.

To begin with, we define an experimental table which corresponds to a submatrix of the Hankel Matrix of a the target series S.

Algorithm `close`(M)

input: an ET $M = (T, C, \hat{H})$
output: a closed ET M

1. Let $B \leftarrow \text{HG}(M)$
2. if $\exists p, \exists f \in F_p, \exists e_{i_1}, \ldots, e_{i_p} \in B$
   $f(e_{i_1}, \ldots, e_{i_p}) \notin T$
   then $T \leftarrow T \cup f(e_{i_1}, \ldots, e_{i_p})$
   else halt
3. go to 1

Algo. 3. Algorithm `close` allowing to close a table

Algorithm `consistent`(M)

input: an experiment table
   $M = (T, C, \hat{H})$
output: a consistent table M

1. $M \leftarrow \text{close}(M)$
2. if exists $t \in T, c \in C : \hat{H}_{t,c} \neq \mu(t \cdot c)\lambda$
   then $C \leftarrow C \cup \text{Suf}(t \cdot c)$
   else halt
3. make membership queries to fill $\hat{H}$
4. go to 1

Algo. 4. Algorithm `consistent` allowing to keep a table consistent

Definition 6. *An* experiment table *(ET) is a 3-tuple* $(T, C, \hat{H})$ *such that:* T *is a set of trees,* C *is a set of contexts,* $\hat{H} : T \times C \to K$ *a submatrix of an HM.*

In the following, we will maintain this table filled such that $\hat{H}_{t,c} = S(t \cdot c)$.

Next definition will allows us to apply algorithm MTAB to any Experiment Table.

Definition 7. *Let* $M = (T, C, \hat{H})$ *be an ET and let* $B = \text{HG}(\hat{H})$. *M is closed if* $\forall p, \forall f \in F_p, \forall e_{i_1}, \ldots, e_{i_p} \in B, f(e_{i_1}, \ldots, e_{i_p}) \in T$

Algorithm 3 `close` is able to close any ET. Note that any call to `close` will include all the symbols in F_0.

The following definition will ensure that any extracted MTA by MTAB is consistent with the data in the Experiment Table.

Definition 8. *Let* $M = (T, C, \hat{H})$ *be a closed ET, let* $(V, \mu, \lambda) = \text{MTAB}(M)$. *An ET is consistent if* $\forall t \in T, \forall c \in C, \mu(t \cdot c)\lambda = \hat{H}_{t,c}$.

Definition 9. *A set of contexts* C *is suffix complete if* $\forall c \in C, \forall c_1, c_2 : c_1 \cdot c_2 = c$ *then* $c_2 \in C$.

Lemma 5. *Let* $M = (T, C, \hat{H})$ *be a closed ET such that* C *is suffix complete and let* $(V, \mu, \lambda) = \text{MTAB}(M)$. *For any tree* $t = f \cdot c : f \in F_0, c \in C$, *then* $\mu(f \cdot c)\lambda = \hat{H}_{f,c}$.

Proof. Sketch. A similar technique used in the proof of Theorem 1 allows to prove the result. Note that since some proofs of lemmas needed to show Theorem 1 use induction over trees and contexts, C should be suffix complete in order to guarantee its correctness. □

Lemma 6. *Let* $M = (C, T, \hat{H})$ *be a closed table with* C *suffix complete and let* $(V, \mu, \lambda) = \text{MTAB}(M)$. *Consider* $t \in T$ *and* $c \in C$ *such that* $\mu(t \cdot c)\lambda \neq \hat{H}_{t,c}$, *we can decompose* $t \cdot c = f \cdot c'$ *where* $f \in F_0$. *Let* $M' = (T', C', \hat{H}') = \text{closed}((T, C \cup \text{Suf}(f \cdot c'), \hat{H}))$; *then* $\mu'(f \cdot c')\lambda = \hat{H}'_{f,c'}$. *Moreover,* $rank(\hat{H}') > rank(\hat{H})$.

Algorithm LearnMTA(EQ, MS)

input: an equivalence oracle EQ
input: a membership oracle MS
output: a MTA A

1. Initialize: $T = \{\}$, $C = \{\}$, $A =$ an empty MTA, $M = (T, C, \hat{H})$ an empty ET.
2. Ask an equivalence query $EQ(A)$.
   If the answer is YES then halt with output A.
   Otherwise the answer is NO and z is a counterexample.
3. Add Suf(z) to C.
4. $M \leftarrow$ consistent(M)
5. $A \leftarrow$ MTAB(M)
6. go to 2

Algo. 5. inference algorithm LearnMTA

Proof. Sketch. A direct application of Lemma 5 ensures that $\mu'(f \cdot c')\lambda = \hat{H}'_{f,c'}$.

On the other hand, all the trees of the HG(M) are linearly independent. By adding new contexts in C, those trees remain linearly independent and then they will be a part of HG.

Let $A =$ MTAB(M) and $A' =$ MTAB(M'). Clearly all the trees in HG(M) are also in HG(M') but new trees should appear in HG(M'), otherwise, by construction, $A = A'$ and this is impossible because $\mu(f \cdot c')\lambda \neq \mu'(f \cdot c')\lambda$.

Thus, $rank(\hat{H}') > rank(\hat{H})$. $\qquad \square$

Theorem 2. *Let MQ and EQ respectively membership and equivalence oracles of a RTS S with an associated Hankel matrix H. Let $r = rank(H)$ LearnMTA(MQ, EQ) returns the minimal representation compatible with the target in polynomial time making at most r equivalence queries and $|A|m$ membership queries, where m is the length of the longest counterexample returned by the Equivalence Queries.*

Proof. In the same way as Lemma 6, it can be shown that the counterexample acts in a similar way as when a non consistency is found in the ET. In any case, after the **consistent** call (after step 4 of LearnMTA) a new MTA compatible with all the data in the ET is obtained. As shown in Lemma 6, the hierarchical generator HG of this MTA has strictly more trees than the previous one. As the number of trees in HG can not be bigger than the rank of the HM for the target MTA, then the process should finish and gives the correct hypothesis.

Now, looking at the time complexity, since all the steps of the algorithm can be done in polynomial time with respect to the size of the target MTA (linear independence of a set of vector, Algorithms HG, MTAB, close and consistent), it is evident that algorithm LearnMTA runs in polynomial time.

With respect to the queries, it is easy to see that the number of Equivalence Queries can no be larger than r (at most one for each tree added to HG).

Moreover, note that the all the results of the membership queries are stored in the equivalence table or were used to calculate the λ vector (of size r). It is easy to see that $|T| = \sum_{i:F_i \neq 0} |F_i| r^i$ and that $|C| \leq r.m$ since for a tree t we can define no more than $|t|$ contexts. Reminding that $|A| = \sum_{i:F_i \neq 0} |F_i| r^{i+1} + r$ then, the number of Membership Queries is lower that $|T||C| + r \leq |A| m$.   □

5   Conclusion

In this paper we proposed a learning algorithm for identifying multiplicity tree automata that define functions associating a number to any tree. We showed that the size of a minimal multiplicity tree automaton is function of the finite rank of its Hankel matrix. Our algorithm is able to identify the minimal automata in polynomial time in the exact learning model of Angluin. The originality of our approach is to find a hierarchical basis that permits to generate all the elements of the target series.

We think that multiplicity tree automata can offer a wide range of potential applications, especially for extraction information from the web. We showed that this class of automata is identifiable and our perspective is to find efficient approaches in other learning paradigms. We have begin to study a possible extension of the approach presented in [14,15], which allows to learn stochastic languages on strings represented by multiplicity automata, to trees.

References

1. Gécseg, F., Steinby, M.: Tree Automata. Akadémiai Kiadó, Budapest (1984)
2. Comon, H., Dauchet, M., Gilleron, R., Jacquemard, F., Lugiez, D., Tison, S., Tommasi, M.: Tree Automata Techniques and Applications . Available from: http://www.grappa.univ-lille3.fr/tata (1997)
3. Knuutila, T., Steinby, M.: Inference of tree languages from a finite sample: an algebraic approach. Theoretical Computer Science 129(2) (1994) 337–367
4. Garcia, P., Oncina, J.: Inference of recognizable tree sets. Research Report DSIC - II/47/93, Universidad Politécnica de Valencia (1993)
5. Kosala, R., Bruynooghe, M., den Bussche, J.V., Blockeel, H.: Information extraction from web documents based on local unranked tree automaton inference. In: Proceedings of IJCAI 2003. (2003) 403–408
6. Besombes, J., Marion, J.: Learning tree languages from positive examples and membership queries. In: Proceedings of ALT'04, Springer (2004) 440–453
7. Carme, J., Gilleron, R., Lemay, A., Niehren, J.: Interactive learning of node selecting tree transducer. Machine Learning (2006) to appear.
8. Carrasco, R., Oncina, J., Calera-Rubio, J.: Stochastic inference of regular tree languages. Machine Learning 44(1/2) (2001) 185–197
9. Rico-Juan, J., Calera, J., Carrasco, R.: Probabilistic k-testable tree-languages. In: Proceedings of ICGI 2000. Volume 1891 of LNCS., Springer (2000) 221–228
10. Berstel, J., Reutenauer, C.: Recognizable formal power series on trees. Theoretical Computer Science 18 (1982) 115–148
11. Esik, Z., Kuich, W.: Formal tree series. Journal of Automata Languages and Combinatorics 8(2) (2003) 219–285
12. Beimel, A., Bergadano, F., Bshouty, N., Kushilevitz, E., Varricchio, S.: Learning functions represented as multiplicity automata. Journal of the ACM 47(3) (2000) 506–530

13. Angluin, D.: Learning regular sets from queries and counterexamples. Information and Computation **75**(2) (1987) 87–106
14. Denis, F., Esposito, Y., Habrard, A.: Learning rational stochastic languages. In: Proceedings of COLT'06. (2006) to appear.
15. Denis, F., Esposito, Y.: Rational stochastic language. Technical report, LIF - Université de Provence (2006)

Learning DFA from Correction and Equivalence Queries[*]

Leonor Becerra-Bonache[1], Adrian Horia Dediu[1,2], and Cristina Tîrnăucă[1]

[1] Research Group on Mathematical Linguistics
Rovira i Virgili University
Pl. Imperial Tárraco 1, 43005 Tarragona, Spain
[2] Faculty of Engineering in Foreign Languages
University "Politehnica" of Bucharest
Splaiul Unirii 313, 060042 Bucharest, Romania
{leonor.becerra, adrianhoria.dediu, cristina.bibire}@estudiants.urv.es
http://www.grlmc.com

Abstract. In active learning, membership queries and equivalence queries have established themselves as the standard combination to be used. However, they are quite "unnatural" for real learning environments (membership queries are oversimplified and equivalence queries do not have a correspondence in a real life setting). Based on several linguistic arguments that support the presence of corrections in children's language acquisition, we propose another kind of query called correction query. We provide an algorithm that learns DFA using correction and equivalence queries in polynomial time. Despite the fact that the worst case complexity of our algorithm is not better than Angluin's algorithm, we show through a large number of experiments that the average number of queries is considerably reduced by using correction queries.

Keywords: Active learning, learning DFA, membership query, equivalence query, correction query.

1 Introduction

A general theory regarding human learning mechanisms that underlie natural language acquisition is still missing. Several questions arise from the beginning, among others: how are children able to learn languages so fluently and effortlessly, without explicit instruction? To what kind of data are they exposed to?

There is no doubt that children learn a language in part by hearing sentences of that language. However, there is an aspect of the child's linguistic environment which has been subject of a long debate and which is still an important research topic for both linguists and formal language theoreticians. While it is accepted that positive data are available to the child, the availability of another kind of data has been widely argued.

[*] This work was possible thanks to the FPU Fellowships AP2001-1880, AP2004-6968 from the Spanish Ministry of Education and Science and to the grant 2002CAJAL-BURV4, provided by the University Rovira i Virgili.

Y. Sakakibara et al. (Eds.): ICGI 2006, LNAI 4201, pp. 281–292, 2006.

Taking into account that children do not receive only passive information and they interact with their environment, we consider that active learning might be useful to model several aspects of children's language acquisition.

In active learning, the learner is allowed to ask queries to the teacher. Membership queries (MQs) and equivalence queries (EQs) have established themselves as the standard combination to be used. They were introduced by Angluin in [1]. She proved that DFA can be inferred in polynomial time from this type of queries (this algorithm is known as L^*). However, they are quite "unnatural" for real learning environments. For instance, when the learner asks about a word in the language, the teacher's answer *yes/no* is oversimplified.

As there is a growing evidence that corrections are available to children [2,3], we believe that they can play a complementary role in language learning, although the main source of information received during the learning process is positive data. Therefore, we propose another kind of query called correction query (CQ).

What should a good correction be like? It could be defined by some function that given any string associates some string in the language. This function might be deterministic or stochastic. In order to simplify the problem, we are going to consider in this paper a deterministic correction, which consists of the smallest string (in lex-length order) that attached to the end of the requested string will give us a string in the language.

Considering the simplicity of DFA and their adequacy for various applications of natural language processing (although regular languages have limited expressiveness), we consider that a starting point could be to apply corrections to learn DFA. We design an algorithm called *Learning from Corrections Algorithm* (*LCA*), which is able to infer a minimal complete DFA using CQs and EQs.

Although in the worst case our algorithm works as Angluin's algorithm, we show that in general *LCA* performs better. Therefore, we can see not only that it is possible to learn DFA from corrections, but also that the number of queries between the learner and the teacher until the discovering of the language is reduced considerably. Moreover, there are some classes of languages for which the number of EQs is reduced to only one (in this case, the conjectured DFA is equivalent to the target one) and therefore, we can consider that EQs are not necessary at all for these classes.

This paper is organized as follows. Formal preliminaries and several basic remarks are presented in Section 2. In Section 3 we describe the observation table as the main data structure of the algorithm, we give a proof for the correctness of our algorithm and we present the algorithm along with the time analysis. Section 4 contains a running example and Section 5 presents some comparative results with Angluin's algorithm, both theoretical and experimental. In Section 6 we present several concluding remarks.

2   Preliminaries

In this paper we follow standard definitions and notations in formal language theory. Supplementary information for this domain can be found in [4,5].

Let Σ be a finite set of symbols called the alphabet and let Σ^* be the set of strings over Σ. A *language* L over Σ is a subset of Σ^*. The elements of L are called *words* or *strings*. Let α, β, γ be strings in Σ^* and $|\alpha|$ be the length of the string α. λ is a special string called the *empty* string and has length 0. Given a string $\alpha = \beta\gamma$, β is the *prefix* of α and γ is the *suffix* of α.

A *deterministic finite automata* (DFA) is a 5-tuple $A = (Q, \Sigma, \delta, q_0, F)$ where Q is the (finite) set of states, Σ is a finite alphabet, $q_0 \in Q$ is the initial state, $F \subseteq Q$ is the set of final states and δ is a partial function that maps $Q \times \Sigma$ to Q. This function can be extended to words by writing $\delta(q, \lambda) = q$ and $\delta(q, s \cdot a) = \delta(\delta(q, s), a), \forall q \in Q, \forall s \in \Sigma^*, \forall a \in \Sigma$. A string s is accepted by A if $\delta(q_0, s) \in F$. The set of strings accepted by A is denoted by $L(A)$ and is called a *regular language*.

We say that a DFA $A = (Q, \Sigma, \delta, q_0, F)$ is *complete* if for all q in Q and a in Σ, $\delta(q, a)$ is defined (that is δ is a total function). For any DFA A, there exists a minimum state DFA A', such that $L(A) = L(A')$. Without loss of generality, we assume that the target DFA which is to be learned is a minimal complete DFA.

A state q is called a *live state* if there exist strings α and β such that $\delta(q_0, \alpha) = q$ and $\delta(q, \beta) \in F$. The set of all the live states is called the *liveSet(A)*. A state that is not in the *liveSet* is called a *dead state*. The set of all dead states is called the *deadSet(A)*. Note that for a minimal DFA A, *deadSet(A)* has at most one element.

For a string $\alpha \in \Sigma^*$, we denote the left quotient of L by α by $L_\alpha = \{\beta | \alpha\beta \in L\} = \{\beta | \delta(q_0, \alpha\beta) \in F\}$, where $A = (Q, \Sigma, q_0, \delta, F)$ is any automaton accepting the language L.

In a standard query learning algorithm, the learner interacts with a *teacher* that knows the *target language* (a regular language L over a known alphabet) and is assumed to answer correctly. The goal of the algorithm is to come up with a DFA accepting L. The teacher has to answer two types of queries: MQs - the learner asks if a string α is in L, and the teacher answers "yes" or "no"; EQs - the learner makes a conjecture of the DFA; the teacher answers "yes" if the learner automaton is isomorphic with the target automaton and "no" otherwise; if the answer is "no" a string α in the symmetric difference of $L(A)$ and L is returned (the *counter example*). See [1,6] for detailed explanations of the model.

We are going to propose another type of query called CQ. It is an extension of the MQ; the difference consists in the type of answer that we receive from the teacher. Instead of a yes/no answer, a string called the *correctingString* is returned to the learner.

The *correctingString* of α with respect to L is the minimum word (in lex-length order, denoted by $\preceq$) of the set L_α. In the case that $L_\alpha = \emptyset$ we set the *correctingString* of α w.r.t. L to φ, where φ is a symbol which does not belong to the alphabet Σ. With these considerations, for the sake of simplicity in notations, we use C instead of *correctingString*. Hence, C is a function from Σ^* to $\Sigma^* \cup \varphi$. Note that $C(\alpha) = \lambda$ if and only if $\alpha \in L$.

Remark 1. If α, β, γ are strings in Σ^* such that $C(\alpha) = \beta \cdot \gamma$ then $C(\alpha \cdot \beta) = \gamma$.

Remark 2. For any $\alpha, \beta \in \Sigma^*$, if $L_\alpha = \emptyset$ then $L_{\alpha \cdot \beta} = \emptyset$.

Remark 3. For any $\alpha \in \Sigma^*$, the following results hold:

1. If $C(\alpha) \neq \varphi$ then $C(\alpha \cdot C(\alpha)) = \lambda$.
2. If $C(\alpha) = \varphi$ then $\forall \beta \in \Sigma^*$, $C(\alpha\beta) = \varphi$.

3   Learning from Corrections Algorithm (*LCA*)

We describe the learning algorithm LCA and show that it efficiently learns an initially unknown regular set from an adequate teacher. Let L be the unknown regular set and let Σ be the alphabet of L.

3.1   Observation Tables

The information we have at each step of the algorithm is organized into an *observation table* consisting of: a nonempty finite prefix-closed set S of strings, a nonempty finite suffix-closed set E of strings, and the restriction of the mapping C to the set $((S \cup S\Sigma) \cdot E)$. The observation table will be denoted (S, E, C).

An observation table can be visualized as a two-dimensional array with rows labelled by elements of $S \cup S\Sigma$ and columns labelled by elements of E with the entry for row s and column e equal to $C(s \cdot e)$. If s is an element of $(S \cup S\Sigma)$ then $row(s)$ denotes the finite function from E to $\Sigma^* \cup \{\varphi\}$ defined by $row(s)(e) = C(s \cdot e)$. By $rows(S)$ we understand the set $\{row(s) \mid s \in S\}$.

The algorithm LCA uses the observation table to build a DFA. Rows labelled by the elements of S are the candidates for states of the automaton being constructed, and columns labelled by the elements of E correspond to distinguishing experiments for these states. Rows labelled by elements of $S\Sigma$ are used to construct the transition function.

Closed, consistent observation tables. An observation table is called *closed* if for every s in $(S\Sigma - S)$ there exists an s' in S such that $row(s) = row(s')$. An observation table is called *consistent* if for any s_1, s_2 in S such that $row(s_1) = row(s_2)$, we have $row(s_1 \cdot a) = row(s_2 \cdot a), \forall a \in \Sigma$.

If (S, E, C) is a closed, consistent observation table, we define a corresponding automaton $A(S, E, C) = (Q, \Sigma, \delta, q_0, F)$, where Q, q_0, F and δ are defined as follows:

$Q = \{row(s) \mid s \in S\}$
$q_0 = row(\lambda)$
$F = \{row(s) \mid s \in S \text{ and } C(s) = \lambda\}$
$\delta(row(s), a) = row(s \cdot a)$

One can see that this automaton is well defined and that $deadSet(A) = \{row(s) \mid s \in S \text{ and } C(s) = \varphi\}$ (from Remark 3 we know that $C(s) = \varphi \Rightarrow C(s \cdot a) = \varphi, \forall a \in \Sigma$).

Definition 1. *Assume that (S, E, C) is a closed and consistent observation table. We say that the automaton $A = (Q, \Sigma, \delta, q_0, F)$ is consistent with the function C if for every s in $S \cup S\Sigma$ and e in E, the following statements hold:*

1. $C(s \cdot e) = \varphi \Leftrightarrow \delta(q_0, s \cdot e) \in deadSet(A)$,
2. $C(s \cdot e) = t \Leftrightarrow (\delta(q_0, s \cdot e \cdot t) \in F$ and $\forall t' \in \Sigma^* \ (\delta(q_0, s \cdot e \cdot t') \in F \Rightarrow t \preceq t'))$.

The important fact about the automaton $A(S, E, C)$ is the following.

Theorem 1. *If (S, E, C) is a closed and consistent observation table, then the automaton $A(S, E, C)$ is consistent with the finite function C. Any other automaton consistent with C but inequivalent to $A(S, E, C)$ must have more states.*

The theorem follows from the following sequence of straightforward lemmas.

Lemma 1. *Assume that (S, E, C) is a closed and consistent observation table. For the automaton $A(S, E, C)$ and for every s in $S \cup S\Sigma$, $\delta(q_0, s) = row(s)$.*

Lemma 2. *If (S, E, C) is a closed and consistent observation table and the automaton $A(S, E, C)$ is $(Q, \Sigma, \delta, q_0, F)$, then for each s in $S \cup S\Sigma$ and all $e \in E$, there exists s' in S such that $\delta(q_0, s \cdot e) = \delta(q_0, s')$ and $C(s \cdot e) = C(s')$.*

Lemma 3. *Assume that (S, E, C) is a closed and consistent observation table. Then the automaton $A = A(S, E, C)$ is consistent with the function C.*

Lemma 4. *Assume that (S, E, C) is a closed, consistent observation table. Suppose the automaton $A(S, E, C)$ has n states. If $A' = (Q', \Sigma, \delta', q_0', F')$ is any automaton consistent with C that has n or fewer states, then A' is isomorphic with $A(S, E, C)$.*

Now, the proof of Theorem 1 follows, since Lemma 3 shows that $A(S, E, C)$ is consistent with C, and Lemma 4 shows that any other automaton consistent with C is either isomorphic to $A(S, E, C)$ or contains at least one more state. Thus, $A(S, E, C)$ is the unique smallest automaton consistent with C.

3.2   The Learner *LCA*

The learner algorithm uses as its main data structure the observation table that we described in the previous subsection. Initially $S = E = \lambda$. To determine C, *LCA* asks CQs for λ and each a in Σ. This initial observation table may or may not be closed and consistent.

The main loop of *LCA* tests the current observation table (S, E, C) in order to see if it is closed and consistent. If (S, E, C) is not closed, then *LCA* adds a new string to S and updates the table asking CQs for missing elements. If (S, E, C) is not consistent, then *LCA* adds a new string to E and updates the table using CQs for missing elements.

When the learner's automaton is closed and consistent the learner asks an EQ. The teacher's answers can be "yes" (in which case the algorithm terminates with the output $A(S, E, C)$) or "no" (in which case a counterexample is provided, all its prefixes are added to S and the table is updated using CQs).

Correctness of LCA. If the teacher answers always correctly then if *LCA* ever terminates its output is clearly the target one. Recall that the teacher's last answer to an *EQ* before halting is *yes*.

Algorithm 1. Learning from Corrections algorithm

1: Initialize S and E with λ
2: Ask correction queries for λ and each $a \in \Sigma$
3: Construct the initial observation table (S, E, C)
4: **repeat**
5:    **while** (S, E, C) is not closed or not consistent **do**
6:       **if** (S, E, C) is not closed **then**
7:          find s in S and a in Σ such that $row(s \cdot a) \notin rows(S)$
8:          add $s \cdot a$ to S
9:          extend C to $(S \cup S\Sigma)E$ using CQs
10:      **end if**
11:      **if** (S, E, C) is not consistent **then**
12:         find $s_1, s_2 \in S$, $a \in \Sigma$ and $e \in E$ such that $row(s_1) = row(s_2)$ and $C(s_1 \cdot a \cdot e) \neq C(s_2 \cdot a \cdot e)$
13:         add $a \cdot e$ to E
14:         extend C to $(S \cup S\Sigma)E$ using CQs
15:      **end if**
16:   **end while**
17:   Construct the conjecture $A(S, E, C)$
18:   **if** the teacher replies with a counter example s **then**
19:      add s and all its prefixes to S;
20:      extend C to $(S \cup S\Sigma)E$ using CQs;
21:   **end if**
22: **until** the teacher replies *yes* to the conjecture
23: Halt and output $A(S, E, C)$

Termination of LCA. To see that LCA terminates, notice that the injectivity of function ϕ defined on Lemma 4 implies that for any closed and consistent observation table (S, E, C), if n denotes the number of different values of $row(s)$ for s in S then any automaton consistent with C must have at least n states. The proof follows the lines of Angluin's paper [1].

Time analysis of LCA. The time complexity of LCA is polynomial in n and m (n is the number of states in the minimum automaton accepting L and m is the maximum length of any counterexample string presented by the teacher). For the details of the proof, the reader is referred to [1].

4   Running Example

In order to simplify the automata description we introduced the *linear transition table* that is a normal transition table with all the lines written on the same row.

We explain how our algorithm runs by tracing the evolution of the observation table for a language over the alphabet $\Sigma = \{0, 1\}$, $L = (0 + 110)^+$. We can see a minimal automaton associated with the mentioned language in Figure 1.

We observe that the linear transition table for this automaton is (q_1, q_2, q_1, q_2, q_3, q_4, q_3, q_3, q_1, q_3) and the set of final states is $F = \{q_1\}$.

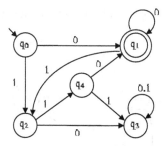

Fig. 1. Minimal automaton associated with the language $L = (0 + 110)^+$

Initially the learner starts with $S = \{\lambda\}, E = \{\lambda\}$ and the observation table described as Table 1.

Table 1.

T_1	λ
λ	0
0	$\lambda^{(\lambda,\lambda)}$
1	10

We can observe that the information for the string 0 and the experiment λ is known from the corresponding query for λ, since $C(\lambda) = 0$ implies $C(0) = \lambda$.

The table is not closed because $row(0)$ and $row(1)$ do not belong to $rows(S)$. We add the strings 0 and 1 to S and we extend the table using CQs. The observation table is still not closed since $row(10)$ does not belong to $rows(S)$. The algorithm adds the string 10 to S. We can notice that the corrections for the strings 100 and 101 are already known, since $C(10) = \varphi$ implies $C(100) = C(101) = \varphi$. The current observation table is represented in Table 2.

Table 2.

T_2	λ	State
λ	0	q_0
0	$\lambda^{(\lambda,\lambda)}$	$q_1 \in F$
1	10	q_2
10	φ	q_3
00	λ	$q_1 \in F$
01	10	q_2
11	$0^{(1,\lambda)}$	q_0
100	$\varphi^{(10,\lambda)}$	q_3
101	$\varphi^{(10,\lambda)}$	q_3

In this moment, we can see that the observation table is closed and consistent and it follows an EQ. The conjectured automaton has the linear transition table $(q_1, q_2, q_1, q_2, q_3, q_0, q_3, q_3)$ and the set of final states $F = \{q_1\}$ and the representation given in Figure 2.

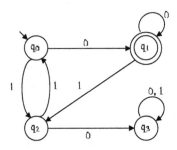

Fig. 2. The automaton associated with Table 2

This is not the target automaton and hence the teacher answers with a counter example. Suppose that the counter example returned is the string 11110. The algorithm adds this string and all its prefixes to S and updates the table. The current observation table is not consistent, since $row(\lambda)$ equals $row(11)$ but $C(\lambda \cdot 1 \cdot \lambda) \neq C(11 \cdot 1 \cdot \lambda)$. The algorithm adds the string 1 to E.

As we can see, the current observation table (Table 3) is closed and consistent and the conjectured automaton is isomorphic with the target one, so the teacher's answer to the EQ is positive. We notice that during the whole algorithm's execution, the learner asked only two EQs (the last one was successful) and eight CQs.

Table 3.

T_3	λ	1	State
λ	0	$10^{(1,\lambda)}$	q_0
0	$\lambda^{(\lambda,\lambda)}$	$10^{(01,\lambda)}$	$q_1 \in F$
1	10	$0^{(1,\lambda)}$	q_2
10	φ	$\varphi^{(10,\lambda)}$	q_3
11	$0^{(1,\lambda)}$	$\varphi^{(111,\lambda)}$	q_4
111	φ	$\varphi^{(111,\lambda)}$	q_3
1111	$\varphi^{(111,\lambda)}$	$\varphi^{(111,\lambda)}$	q_3
11110	$\varphi^{(111,\lambda)}$	$\varphi^{(111,\lambda)}$	q_3
00	λ	10	$q_1 \in F$
01	10	$0^{(01,\lambda)}$	q_2
100	$\varphi^{(10,\lambda)}$	$\varphi^{(10,\lambda)}$	q_3
101	$\varphi^{(10,\lambda)}$	$\varphi^{(10,\lambda)}$	q_3
110	$\lambda^{(1,\lambda)}$	10	$q_1 \in F$
1110	$\varphi^{(111,\lambda)}$	$\varphi^{(111,\lambda)}$	q_3
11111	$\varphi^{(111,\lambda)}$	$\varphi^{(111,\lambda)}$	q_3
111100	$\varphi^{(111,\lambda)}$	$\varphi^{(111,\lambda)}$	q_3
111101	$\varphi^{(111,\lambda)}$	$\varphi^{(111,\lambda)}$	q_3

5   Comparative Results

In this section we present some theoretical and practical results. We prove that there exist classes of languages for which the number of queries needed to learn is lower for our algorithm. Using running tests we also show that in practice our algorithm uses less queries.

5.1   Theoretical Results

We believe that in most of the cases LCA performs not worst that L^* and that there are several subclasses of regular languages for which our algorithm needs smaller number of queries. In the sequel we present one of such subclasses.

Without loss of generality, the teacher is supposed to return the shortest counterexample. Let L be the target language and m the size of the minimal complete DFA accepting L.

Definition 2. By $MQ_L(m)$ $(CQ_L(m))$ we denote the number of different words submitted by the learner L^* (LCA) to the teacher in order to identify L.

Theorem 2. There exists an infinite class of languages which require a polynomial number of MQs but a linear number of CQs in order to be identified.

Let us consider $\mathcal{S}_\Sigma$ the class of singletons over Σ, that is the languages which contain only one string. The theorem follows from the following two lemmas.

Lemma 5. For any fixed alphabet Σ of length k and any language L in $\mathcal{S}_\Sigma$ the number of MQs needed by L^* in order to identify L is:

$$MQ_L(m) = 2(k-1)m^2 - (4k-7)m + 2k - 5 . \tag{1}$$

Lemma 6. For any fixed alphabet Σ of length k and any language L in $\mathcal{S}_\Sigma$ the number of CQs needed by LCA in order to identify L is:

$$CQ_L(m) = (k-1)(m-1) + 2 . \tag{2}$$

and the number of EQs is only one.

Corollary 1. For the one letter alphabet, the class $\mathcal{S}_\Sigma$ needs a linear number of MQs and a constant number of CQs. More precisely, given the language L, L^* asks a total number of $3m - 3$ MQs (where m is the size of its minimal DFA), meanwhile LCA asks only 2 CQs.

5.2   Practical Results

Due to the coding of the states and to the embedded information within the teacher's answers, our practical results reflect the improvement brought by our algorithm.

We tested L^* and LCA on an randomly generated set of 209 DFA, all of them on a two letter alphabet. To be able to visualize the comparison between the efficiency of the two algorithms, we used the average value of the number of queries for automata with the same number of states. For that purpose, we needed a test set with equally distributed number of states (more precisely, we randomly generated 11 automata having 2, 3,... up to 20 states).

In order to generate the DFA test set, we used the public package from http://www.research.att.com/sw/tools/fsm/ having the documentation available in [7].

To generate random automata, we considered a maximum number of states of 20 for our examples. Without loss of generality, the initial state is always the state 0. Then we generate complete transition tables having the destination states generated randomly between 0 and the maximum number of states. For the number of final states, we generated a random number between 0 and the maximum number of states -1. Then, we generated again randomly the final states (without repeating twice the same state).

After minimizing, we checked the newly found DFA for non-equivalence with the already generated automata. In case of equivalence, we generated new automata. Finally, we checked for completeness and then we loaded the automata in our programs.

We generated two graphics for the results obtained with the two letters alphabet. The first one, represented in Figure 3, contains the average values for the number of EQs asked by L^* and LCA respectively, the average being computed for automata having the same number of states.

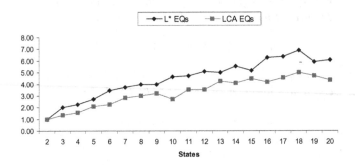

Fig. 3. EQs average values for automata with the same number of states;

The second graphic, represented in Figure 4, contains the average values obtained for the number of MQs and CQs, respectively, for automata with the same number of states.

We also run tests on different size alphabets. The results obtained strengthen our belief that the improvements of our algorithm are not limited to some small class of languages.

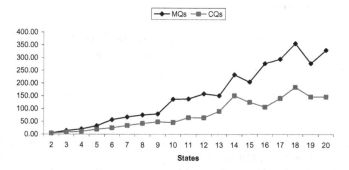

Fig. 4. MQs and CQs, average values for automata with the same number of states

6   Concluding Remarks

We propose a new paradigm for the computational learning theory, namely learning from corrections. Our algorithm based on Angluin's L^* learning algorithm for regular languages uses an observation table with *correcting strings* instead of 0s and 1s. In our running examples, generally, the number of EQs are less or equal than in Angluin's ones and the number of CQs is significantly smaller than the number of MQs.

The empirical results show that in most of the cases the number of queries used by LCA is smaller. We believe that this is related to the injectivity property: a language is injective if any two non equivalent strings (using the standard Myhill-Nerode equivalence) have different corrections. One can see that the rare cases in which our algorithm performs worse, compared to L^*, is when this injectivity property is far from being satisfied. On the other hand, when this property is fulfilled, EQs are no longer needed.

Among the improvements previously discussed, we would like to mention here the adequacy of CQs in a real learning process. They reflect in a more accurate manner the process of children's language acquisition. We are aware that this kind of formalism is for an ideal teacher who knows everything and always gives the correct answers and for practical applications our working hypothesis should be adjusted.

Since there is no correspondence of an EQ in a real situation (a child will never ask to the adult if her grammar is the correct one), as a future work we would like to extend our results on singleton languages to a bigger class and hence to enlarge the class of languages learnable from only CQs. Moreover, we will try to find subsets of regular languages for which LCA performs always better than L^* and to identify a necessary and sufficient condition for a class of languages to be faster learnable using our algorithm. We will also like to extend this result to Context Free and Mildly Context Sensitive Languages, which are considered more appropriate to model some aspects of natural language acquisition (probably another type of correction would be needed).

Acknowledgements

Special thanks to professors Victor Mitrana, Colin de la Higuera and Dana Angluin for valuable advices and a careful review. Also many thanks to anonymous reviewers for their remarks and suggestions.

References

1. Angluin, D.: Learning regular sets from queries and counterexamples. Information and Computation **75**(2) (1987) 87–106
2. Becerra-Bonache, L.: On the Learnability of Mildly Context-Sensitive Languages using Positive Data and Correction Queries. Doctoral thesis, Rovira i Virgili University (2006)
3. Becerra-Bonache, L., Yokomori, T.: Learning mild context-sensitiveness: Toward understanding children's language learning. In: Proceedings of the 7th International Colloquium on Grammatical Inference. (2004) 53–64
4. Hopcroft, J.E., Motwani, R., Ullman, J.D.: Introduction to Automata Theory, Languages and Computation. Addison-Wesley (2001)
5. Yu, S.: Finite automata. In Martin-Vide, C., Mitrana, V., Paun, G., eds.: Formal Languages and Applications. Studies in Fuzzyness and Soft Computing 148. Springer, Berlin (2004) 55–85 ISBN 3-540-20907-7.
6. Angluin, D.: Queries and concept learning. Machine Learning **2**(4) (1988) 319–342
7. Mohri, M., Pereira, F.C.N., Riley, M.: A rational design for a weighted finite-state transducer library. In: WIA '97: Revised Papers from the Second International Workshop on Implementing Automata, London, UK, Springer-Verlag (1998) 144–158

Using MDL for Grammar Induction

Pieter Adriaans and Ceriel Jacobs

Department of Computer Science,
University of Amsterdam,
Kruislaan 419, 1098VA Amsterdam, The Netherlands
Department of Computer Science,
Vrije Universiteit Amsterdam,
De Boelelaan 1081a,
1081HV Amsterdam, The Netherlands
pietera@science.uva.nl, ceriel@cs.vu.nl
http://www.uva.nl

Abstract. In this paper we study the application of the Minimum Description Length principle (or two-part-code optimization) to grammar induction in the light of recent developments in Kolmogorov complexity theory. We focus on issues that are important for construction of effective compression algorithms. We define an independent measure for the quality of a theory given a data set: the *randomness deficiency*. This is a measure of how typical the data set is for the theory. It can not be computed, but it can in many relevant cases be approximated. An optimal theory has minimal randomness deficiency. Using results from [4] and [2] we show that:

- Shorter code not necessarily leads to better theories. We prove that, in DFA induction, already as a result of a single deterministic merge of two nodes, divergence of randomness deficiency and MDL code can occur.
- Contrary to what is suggested by the results of [6] there is no fundamental difference between positive and negative data from an MDL perspective.
- MDL is extremely sensitive to the correct calculation of code length: model code and data-to-model code.

These results show why the applications of MDL to grammar induction so far have been disappointing. We show how the theoretical results can be deployed to create an effective algorithm for DFA induction. However, we believe that, since MDL is a global optimization criterion, MDL based solutions will in many cases be less effective in problem domains where local optimization criteria can be easily calculated. The algorithms were tested on the Abbadingo problems ([10]). The code was in Java, using the Satin ([17]) divide-and-conquer system that runs on top of the Ibis ([18]) Grid programming environment.

1 Introduction: MDL and Grammar Induction

In the domain of machine learning pure applications of MDL are rare, mainly because of the difficulties one encounters trying to define an adequate model

Y. Sakakibara et al. (Eds.): ICGI 2006, LNAI 4201, pp. 293–306, 2006.

code and data-to-model code. The field of grammar induction studies a whole class of algorithms that aims at constructing a grammar by means of incremental compression of the data set represented as a digraph. This digraph can be seen as the maximal theory equivalent with the data set. Every word in the data set is represented as a path in the digraph with the symbols either on the edges or on the nodes. The learning process takes the form of a guided incremental compression of the data set by means of merging or clustering of the nodes in the graph. None of these algorithms makes an explicit estimate of the MDL code. Instead they use heuristics to guide the model reduction. After a certain time a proposal for a grammar can be constructed from the current state of the compressed graph. Examples of such algorithms are SP ([15], [14]), EMILE ([8] [9]), ABL ([11]), ADIOS ([12]) and a number of DFA induction algorithms, specifically evidence driven state merging (EDSM), ([10], [16]). In this paper we present a sound theoretical basis to analyze the performance and idiosyncrasies of these algorithms in an MDL context.

2   MDL as Two-Part Code Optimization

We give the traditional formulation of MDL:

Definition 1. The Minimum Description Length principle: *The best theory to explain a set of data is the one which minimizes the sum of*

- *the length, in bits, of the description of the theory and*
- *the length, in bits, of the data when encoded with the help of the theory*

Let $M \in \mathcal{M}$ be a model in a class of models $\mathcal{M}$, and let D be a data set. The **prior probability** of a hypothesis or model M is $P(M)$. Probability of the data D is $P(D)$. **Posterior probability** of the model given the data is:

$$P(M|D) = \frac{P(M)P(D|M)}{P(D)}$$

The following derivation ([1]) illustrates the well known equivalence between MDL and the selection of the Maximum A posteriori hypothesis in the context of Shannon's information theory. Selecting the **Maximum A Posteriori hypothesis(MAP)**:

$$M_{MAP} \equiv argmax_{M \in \mathcal{M}} P(M|D)$$

$$= argmax_{M \in \mathcal{M}} (P(M)P(D|M))/P(D)$$

(since D is constant)

$$\equiv argmax_{M \in \mathcal{M}} (P(M)P(D|M))$$

$$\equiv argmax_{M \in \mathcal{M}} \log P(M) + \log P(D|M)$$

$$\equiv argmin_{M \in \mathcal{M}} - \log P(M) - \log P(D|M)$$

where according to Shannon $-\log P(M)$ is the length of the optimal *model-code* in bits and $-\log P(D|M)$ is the length of the optimal *data-to-mode-code* in bits. Ergo:

$$M_{MAP} \equiv M_{MDL}$$

The formula $argmin_{M \in \mathcal{M}} - \log P(M) - \log P(D|M)$ indicates that a model that generates an optimal data compression (i.e. the shortest code) is also the best model. This is true even if $\mathcal{M}$ does not contain the original intended model as was proved by [4].[1] It also suggests that compression algorithms can be used to approximate an optimal solution in terms of successive steps of incremental compression of the data set D. This is *not* true as was shown by [2]. Yet this illicit use of the principle of MDL is common practice.

In order to understand these results better we must answer two questions 1) What do we mean by the length of optimal or shortest code and 2) what is an independent measure of the quality of a model M given a data set D? The respective answers to these questions are *prefix-free Kolomogorov complexity* and *randomness deficiency*.

2.1   Kolmogorov Complexity

Let $x, y, z \in \mathcal{N}$, where $\mathcal{N}$ denotes the natural numbers and we identify $\mathcal{N}$ and $\{0, 1\}^*$ according to the correspondence

$$(0, \epsilon), (1, 0), (2, 1), (3, 00), (4, 01), \ldots$$

Here ϵ denotes the *empty word*. The *length* $|x|$ of x is the number of bits in the binary string x, not to be confused with the *cardinality* $|S|$ of a finite set S. For example, $|010| = 3$ and $|\epsilon| = 0$, while $|\{0, 1\}^n| = 2^n$ and $|\emptyset| = 0$. The emphasis is on binary sequences only for convenience; observations in any alphabet can be encoded in a 'theory neutral' way. Below we will use the natural numbers and the binary strings interchangeably. In the rest of the paper we will interpret the set of models $\mathcal{M}$ in the following way:

Definition 2. *Given the correspondence between natural numbers and binary strings $\mathcal{M}$ consists of an enumeration of all possible self-delimiting programs for a preselected arbitrary universal Turing machine U. Let x be an arbitrary bit string. The shortest program that produces x on U is $x^* = argmin_{M \in \mathcal{M}}(U(M) = x)$ and the Kolmogorov complexity of x is $K(x) = |x^*|$. The conditional Kolmogorov complexity of a string x given a string y is $K(x|y)$, this can be interpreted as the length of a program for x given input y. A string is defined to be random if $K(x) \geq |x|$.*

This makes $\mathcal{M}$ one of the most general model classes with a number of very desirable properties: it is universal since all possible programs are enumerated, because the programs are self-delimiting we can concatenate programs at will,

---

[1] This does *not* imply that MDL is always a good criterion for algorithmic approximation [5].

in order to create complex objects out of simple ones we can define an a-priori complexity and probability for binary strings. There are also some less desirable properties: $K(x)$ cannot be computed (but it can be approximated) and $K(x)$ is asymptotic, i.e. since it is defined relative to an arbitrary Turing machine U it makes less sense for objects of a size that is close to the size of the definition of U. Details can be checked in [3]. We have:

$$argmin_{M \in \mathcal{M}} - \log P(M) - \log P(D|M) =$$

$$argmin_{M \in \mathcal{M}} K(M) + K(D|M) = M_{MDL} \qquad (1)$$

Under this interpretation of $\mathcal{M}$ the length of the optimal code for an object is equivalent to its Kolmogorov complexity.

2.2   Randomness Deficiency

It is important to note that objects that are non-random are very rare. To make this more specific: in the limit the density of compressible strings x in the set $\{0,1\}^{\leq k}$ for which we have $K(x) < |x|$ is zero. The overwhelming majority of strings is random. In different words: an element is *typical* for a data set if and only if it is *random* in this data set. In yet different words: if it has maximal entropy in the data set. This insight allows us to formulate a theory independent measure for the quality of models: *randomness deficiency*.

We start by giving some estimates for upper-bounds of conditional complexity. Let $x \in M$ be a string in a finite model M then

$$K(x|M) \leq \log |M| + O(1) \qquad (2)$$

i.e. if we know the set M then we only have to specify an index of size $\log |M|$ to identify x in M. The factor $O(1)$ is needed for additional 'syntactic sugar' to reconstruct x from M and the index. Its importance is thus limited. Let $D \subseteq M$ be a subset of a finite model M. We specify $d = |D|$ and $m = |M|$. Now we have:

$$K(D|M,d) \leq \log \binom{m}{d} + O(1) \qquad (3)$$

Here the term $\binom{m}{d}$ specifies the size of the class of possible selections of d elements out of a set of m elements. The term $\log \binom{m}{d}$ gives the length of an index for this set. If we know M and d then this index allows us to reconstruct D.

A crucial insight is that the inequalities 2 and 3 become 'close' to equalities when respectively x and D are *typical* for M, i.e. when they are random in M. This typicality can be interpreted as a measure for the goodness of fit of the model M. A model M for a data set D is optimal if D is random in M, i.e. the randomness deficiency of D in M is minimal. The following definitions formulate this intuition. The *randomness deficiency* of D in M is defined by:

$$\delta(D|M,d) = \log \binom{m}{d} - K(D|M,d), \qquad (4)$$

for $D \subseteq M$, and ∞ otherwise. If the randomness deficiency is close to 0, then there are no simple special properties that single D out from the majority of data samples to be drawn from M.

The *minimal randomness deficiency* function is

$$\beta_D(\alpha) = \min_M \{\delta(D|M) : M \supseteq D, \ K(M) \leq \alpha\}, \tag{5}$$

If the randomness deficiency is minimal then the data set is typical for the theory and with high probability future data sets will share the same characteristics, i.e. minimal randomness deficiency is also a good measure for the future performance of models. For a formal proof of this intuition, see [4].

Learning as Incremental Compression. We now turn our attention to incremental compression. Equation 1 gives the length of the optimal *two-part-code*. The length of the two-part-code of an intermediate model M_i is given by:

$$\Lambda(M_i, d) = \log \binom{m_i}{d} + K(M_i, d) \geq K(D) - O(1) \tag{6}$$

[2] have shown that the randomness deficiency not necessarily decreases with the length of the MDL code, i.e. shorter code does not always give smaller randomness deficiency, e.g. a better theory.

3   Using MDL for DFA Induction

In the rest of this paper we will study these theoretical results in the practical context of DFA induction. We will follow the presentation in [13]. Below we show that the model improvement between two consecutive compression states during the execution of a DFA learning algorithm in general can not be computed.

We start with some relevant observations. We will restrict ourselves to languages in $\{0, 1\}^*$. The class of DFA is equivalent to the class of regular languages. We call the set of positive examples D^+ and the set of negative examples D^-. The complement of a regular language is a regular language. Consequently the task of finding an optimal model given D^+ is symmetric to the task of finding an optimal model given D^-. The task of finding the minimum DFA consistent with a set of positive and negative examples is *decidable*. We can enumerate all DFA's according to their size and test them on the data set. Yet this minimum DFA cannot be approximated within polynomial time ([7]).

The task of finding the smallest DFA consistent with a set of positive examples is trivial. This is the universal DFA. Yet the universal DFA will in most cases have a poor generalization error. MDL is a possible candidate for a solution here. Suppose that we have a finite positive data set representing an infinite regular language. The task is then to find a DFA with minimum expected generalization error over the set of the set of infinite regular languages consistent with D^+. MDL identifies such a DFA. Yet, if our results above are relevant, MDL will not help us to *construct* such a DFA in terms of a process of incremental compression or expansion.

Intuitively the MDL code would not give any guidance for compression (or expansion) of a theory if we could show that the randomness deficiency behaves independently of the MDL code: i.e the randomness deficiency could either grow or shrink with a reduction of the length of the MDL code. Below we will show that this is possible for any algorithm that merges or splits states in a DFA. The crucial insight is that when we merge two states (i.e. reduce the complexity of the model) the resulting index set for the data (i.e. the data-to-model code) in general becomes more complex, but also can be more simple. The effects are non-computable. This implies that MDL in the case of DFA is not a good guide when compressing or expanding theories. Before we prove this we give some definitions.

Definition 3. *A partition π of a set X is a set of nonempty subsets of X such that every element x in X is in exactly one of these subsets. $B(x, \pi) \subseteq X$ indicates the subset of the partition π of which x is an element.*

Definition 4. *Let $A = (Q, \Sigma, \delta, q_0, F)$ be a DFA, the quotient automaton $A/\pi = (Q', \Sigma, \delta', B(q_0, \pi), F')$ derived from A on the basis of a partition π of Q is defined as follows:*

- $Q' = Q/\pi = \{B(q, \pi)|q \in Q\}$,
- $F' = \{B \in Q'|B \cap F \neq \emptyset\}$,
- $\delta' : (Q' \times \Sigma) \to 2^{Q'} : \forall B, B' \in Q', \forall a \in \Sigma, B' \in \delta'(B, a)$ *iff* $\exists q, q' \in Q, q \in B, q' \in B'$ *and* $q' \in \delta(q, a)$.

We say that the states in Q that belong to the same block B are merged.

We give without proof:

Lemma 1. *If an automaton A/π_j is derived from an automaton A/π_i by means of a partition then $L(A/\pi_i) \subseteq L(A/\pi_j)$.*

The relevance of these definitions for grammar induction lies in the fact that we can increase or decrease the generality of the automaton and the associated language inclusion hierarchies by means of splitting and merging states.

Definition 5. *Let A be a DFA. An index set for A is a set that associates a unique natural number with each string that is accepted by A. The index set relative to certain data set $D \subseteq L(A)$ is $I_D = \{i|i \in \mathbf{N}, L(A)(i) \in D\}$. The initial segment associated with an index set D and $L(A)$ is the set $I_{\leq D} = \{i|i \in \mathbf{N}, \exists j \in I_D : j \geq i\}$, i.e. the set of all natural numbers that are smaller than or equal to an index in I_D. The maximal entropy of I_D in $I_{\leq D}$ is $\log \binom{|I_{\leq D}|}{|I_D|}$, where $|I_{\leq D}|$ is a measure for the total number of sentences in the language up to the sentence in D with the highest index and $|I_D|$ is the size of D.*

The notion of an initial segment is introduced to make the argument work for infinite languages. We have $K(D|A) \leq K(I_D) + O(1) \leq \log \binom{|I_{\leq D}|}{|I_D|} + O(1)$. Suppose that f is an accepting state of a DFA A, with index set I and that $D \subseteq L(A)$.

Definition 6. *The maximal state entropy of f given D is $I_{\leq D, f} = \log \left(\frac{|I_{\leq D, f}|}{|I_{D, f}|} \right)$, where $I_{\leq D, f}$ and $I_{D, f}$ identify those indexes that are associated with strings that are accepted in f.*

Note that there are data sets of low complexity for which the strict inequality $K(I_D | I_{\leq D}) < \sum_{f \in F} \log \left(\frac{|I_{\leq D, f}|}{|I_{D, f}|} \right) < \log \left(\frac{|I_{\leq D}|}{|I_D|} \right)$ holds. Yet for these data sets the individual state entropies might be still high, since any set of low complexity can be split into two sets of high complexity. For such data sets in general the data-to-model code will be optimized when states are merged. On the other hand if $K(I_D | I_{\leq D})$ is 'close' to $\log \left(\frac{|I_{\leq D}|}{|I_D|} \right)$ splitting of states is a better strategy.

According to our definition above M_0 is not worse than M_1 (as an explanation for D), in symbols: $M_0 \leq M_1$, if

- $\delta(D | M_0, d) \leq \delta(D | M_1, d)$; and
- $\Lambda(M_0, d) \leq \Lambda(M_1, d)$.

We will call these conditions the *MDL-step-conditions*. We have to remember that $\delta(D | M, d) = \log \binom{m}{d} - K(D | M, d)$ is the *randomness deficiency* and $\Lambda(M) = \log \binom{m}{d} + K(M, d) \geq K(D) - O(1)$ is the *total length of two-part code*, or MDL code, of D with help of model M and d. The step from M_1 to M_0 would violate the MDL-step-conditions if:

$$K(D | M_0, d) - K(D | M_1, d) < \log \binom{m_0}{d} - \log \binom{m_1}{d} \leq K(M_1, d) - K(M_0, d) \quad (7)$$

The following theorem states that these violations occur:

Theorem 1. *There are combinations of DFA's and data sets D, A/π_0 and A/π_1 such that $D \subseteq L(A/\pi_0) = L(A/\pi_1)$ and $A/\pi_1 = (A/\pi_0)/\pi_{step}$ that violate the MDL-step-conditions. The characteristics of these violations can not be computed. The δ function can fluctuate arbitrarily in a band-width of $\pm K(\pi_{step}) + O(1)$.*

Proof: Take an arbitrary DFA B. Construct two new DFA's A/π_0 and A/π_1 along the following lines: A/π_0 contains two copies of B, B_1 and B_0, the start state q_0 of A/π_0 has two outgoing transitions, one labelled 1 to the start state of B_1 and one labelled 0 to the start state of B_0. The language recognized by A/π_0 is $(0 + L(B)) \cup (1 + L(B))$. A/π_1 contains only one copy of B, the start state q_0 of A/π_1 has two outgoing transitions labelled 1 and 0 to the start state of B. The language recognized by A/π_1 is $\{0, 1\} + L(B)$. It is easy to verify that $\{0, 1\} + L(B) = (0 + L(B)) \cup (1 + L(B))$, thus $L(A/\pi_0) = L(A/\pi_1)$. Also there is a partition π_{step} such that $A/\pi_1 = (A/\pi_0)/\pi_{step}$: we simply merge B_1 and B_0 in A/π_0 to get A/π_1.

Take the terms of the inequality 7. Independent of any data set $\log \binom{m_0}{d} - \log \binom{m_1}{d} = 0$ since $L(A/\pi_0) = L(A/\pi_1)$. Furthermore there will be cases for which $K(A/\pi_0, d) > K(A/\pi_1, d)$, since $K(A/\pi_0)$ has strictly more states even if we correct for the redundancy of having two copies of B, and there is no definition of

Kolmogorov complexity that systematically defines higher complexity for DFA's with fewer states.

What we have to show is that, in these cases, there are data sets D for which the term $K(D|M_0,d) - K(D|M_1,d)$ can take any value (within a certain bandwidth). Let I_0 and I_1 be index sets associated with respectively A/π_0 and A/π_1. Note that I_0 and I_1 are not independent. Given I_0, A/π_0 and $(A/\pi_0)/\pi_{step}$ we can reconstruct I_1. Therefore $K(I_1|A/\pi_0, I_0) \leq K(\pi_{step}) + O(1)$, i.e. the maximal difference in complexity between I_0 and I_1 given A/π_0 is $K(\pi_{step})$, the complexity of the transformation between the two DFA's. This distance is symmetric within $O(1)$. This limits the bandwidth of the expression $K(D \mid M_0,d) - K(D|M_1,d)$.

Now select an accepting state $f_{1,\{0,1\}}$ in A/π_1 that is the result of merging two corresponding accepting states $f_{0,\{0\}}$ and $f_{0,\{1\}}$ in A/π_0. The related index sets are $I_{0,D,f_{0,\{0\}}}$, $I_{0,D,f_{0,\{1\}}}$ and $I_{1,D,f_{1,\{0,1\}}}$. The maximal state entropy for $f_{0,\{0\}}$ is given by

$$\log \left(\frac{|I_{0,\leq D,f_{0,\{0\}}}|}{|I_{0,D,f_{0,\{0\}}}|} \right)$$

similarly for $f_{0,\{1\}}$ and $f_{1,\{0,1\}}$. If these index sets are random then we have

$$K(I_{0,D,f_{0,\{0\}}}) + K(I_{0,D,f_{0,\{1\}}}) < K(I_{1,D,f_{1,\{0,1\}}})$$

since

$$\log \left(\frac{|I_{0,\leq D,f_{0,\{0\}}}|}{|I_{0,D,f_{0,\{0\}}}|} \right) + \log \left(\frac{|I_{0,\leq D,f_{0,\{1\}}}|}{|I_{0,D,f_{0,\{1\}}}|} \right) < \log \left(\frac{|I_{1,\leq D,f_{1,\{0,1\}}}|}{|I_{1,D,f_{0,\{0,1\}}}|} \right) =$$

$$\log \left(\frac{|I_{0,\leq D,f_{0,\{0\}}}| + |I_{0,\leq D,f_{0,\{1\}}}|}{|I_{0,D,f_{0,\{0\}}}| + |I_{0,D,f_{0,\{1\}}}|} \right)$$

In this case we do not benefit from merging states. Note that we are completely free to select D in such a way that any binary partition of indexes from $I_{1,D,f_{1,\{0,1\}}}$ into corresponding indexes in $I_{0,D,f_{0,\{0\}}}$ and $I_{0,D,f_{0,\{1\}}}$ is realized. In particular we can select a partition that is random in $I_{0,D,f_{0,\{0\}}}$ and $I_{0,D,f_{0,\{1\}}}$ and highly non-random in $I_{1,D,f_{1,\{0,1\}}}$. In this case we have:

$$K(I_{0,D,f_{0,\{0\}}}) + K(I_{0,D,f_{0,\{1\}}}) > K(I_{1,D,f_{1,\{0,1\}}})$$

Here we *do* benefit from merging states. Note that a corresponding argument holds for all triples $f'_{1,\{0,1\}}$, $f'_{0,\{0\}}$ and $f'_{0,\{1\}}$. By selecting appropriate data sets we can create arbitrary fluctuations in the difference of the conditional complexity of the index sets $I_{0,D}$ and $I_{1,D}$ of M_o and M_1. Since $K(D|M_0,d) = K(I_{0,D}|M_0,d) + O(1)$ and $K(D|M_1,d) = K(I_{1,D}|M_1,d) + O(1)$ we can give the expression

$$K(D|M_0,d) - K(D|M_1,d)$$

any value in the bandwidth $\pm K(\pi_{step})$. Note that we can define partitions of any complexity so that the value of $K(\pi_{step})$ can be arbitrary large and that the fluctuations cannot be computed because they are based on the conditional Kolmogorov complexity of the index sets.

End of proof.

Corollary 1. *Given a sample D of a regular language and an arbitrary DFA_D consistent with D, the optimal DFA_{opt} for D can not be approximated by means of expanding or compressing states in DFA_D. This holds if $D = D^+$, $D = D^-$ and if $D = D^+ \cup D^-$.*

Proof: Case: $D = D^+$, is immediately implied by theorem 1. Case: $D = D^-$, is implied by the previous case and the fact that the complement of a regular language is a regular language. The optimal automaton for the negative cases is the same as the one for the positive cases, with the accepting and non-accepting states exchanged, i.e. we try to construct an automaton with exactly the same structure. Case: $D = D^+ \cup D^-$, is implied by the previous two cases and the fact that in the proof of theorem 1 the languages accepted by M_0 and M_1 are the same. The positive randomness deficiency can fluctuate independent of the influence of the negative examples. If the randomness deficiency in relation to the positive examples fluctuates, then the randomness deficiency with respect to the negative examples will also fluctuate, i.e. the total randomness deficiency will fluctuate.

End of proof.

Discussion. It is worth noting that, given the results of [7] it was not to be expected that there would exist an algorithm that finds the DFA with minimal generalization error on the basis of D^+ in polynomial time. Under the condition that D^+ is dense enough and given the results above, the *optimal* DFA in terms of MDL will with high probability also be the *minimal* DFA consistent with D^+ and an arbitrary D^-. If we could find the optimal MDL DFA in polynomial time then we could simply focus on D^+, ignoring D^-, in order to find the minimal DFA consistent with D^+ and D^-. This would contradict the result of [7]. Note also that the task of finding a *minimal* automaton consistent with $D = D^+ \cup D^-$ is in many cases much simpler than the task of finding the automaton with *optimal randomness deficiency*, e.g. take the random case where there is only one negative example.

Following [6] it is generally thought that a combination of positive and negative examples gives a better chance of learning a language than positive examples alone. Corollary 1 shows that this is only the case in the limit when we can enumerate all solutions. Additional negative examples in general do not help us more than additional positive examples when we want to *construct* better solutions out of bad ones given a finite set D.

4   Implementing a Correct MDL Measure for DFA Induction

Theorem 1 implies that MDL in general will not be a reliable guide for the compression of a DFA. Yet there exist many DFA induction algorithms that use compression. In a lot of empirical cases this approach seems to work. The results presented above suggest that it is possible to use MDL directly as an empirical guidance for the merging of states in DFA induction. They also imply that we can use the same MDL measure both on positive and on complete data sets. The MDL data-to-model code formula below shows that this is indeed the case.

Suppose A is a DFA suggested as an explanation for a data set D. A has i accepting states and j non-accepting states. Since we use both positive and negative examples A must be functionally complete (i.e. have an outgoing arrow for each element of the lexicon from each state). Suppose l is the maximal length of a string in the Dataset D. D^+ is the set of positive examples, D^- the set of negative examples. d^+ is the number of positive examples, d^- the number of negative examples. There are $2^{l+1} - 1$ binary strings with length $\leq l$. Call this set N, n^+ is the number of strings accepted by A, n^- is the number of strings not accepted by A. A partitions N in two sets: N^+ and N^-. N^+ is partitioned in i subsets by the i accepting states of A and N^- is partitioned in j subsets by the j non-accepting states of A. The correct data-to-model code is:

$$\log(\prod_i \binom{n_i^+}{d_i^+} \times \prod_j \binom{n_j^-}{d_j^-}) = \sum_i (\log \binom{n_i^+}{d_i^+}) + \sum_j (\log \binom{n_j^-}{d_j^-}) \qquad (8)$$

One can read this as follows. The formula specifies an index for the data set D given the data set N. There are i pieces of code for the positive states, and j pieces of code for the negative states. If there are states that do not generate elements for D then their contribution to the length of the code is 0. When applying this formula to DFA induction one must estimate the values using the Stirling formula or an integral over $\log n!$[2]. Remember that from an MDL perspective we are only interested in the length of the index, not its specific value. The beautiful thing is that this index can always be used: for positive examples, for complete examples and even for only negative examples.

5   Some Experiments

We have developed a framework for experimenting with various search heuristics. The framework is built around the blue-fringe algorithm, which works as follows:[3] We start with the prefix tree acceptor, derived from the sample. The root is colored red, its children are colored blue, all other nodes are white. Then, we apply the following actions:

- As long as there are blue states that cannot be merged with any red node, we promote the shallowest of these states to red, and color its children blue.
- We compute the score for merging all blue/red pairs (see below for an explanation of 'score').

---

[2] The formula $\log \binom{n}{k}$ can be approximated by: $\log \binom{n}{k} \approx \int_{n-k}^{n} \log x \, dx - \int_{1}^{k} \log x \, dx$, which is easy to compute. Already for $k = 65$ the error is less than 1% and rapidly decreasing.

[3] For details, see: ([10], [16]).

– We merge the best scoring blue/red pair and color all children of red nodes that are not red themselves blue.

We repeat these steps until no merges are possible.

The score for merging a red/blue pair is the search heuristic. When using evidence driven state merging (EDSM) ([10], [16]), the score consists of the number of matching state labels of merged states, the higher the better.

We have used several variants of MDL for the search heuristic. As MDL is the sum of two parts, we describe these parts in detail below.

5.1   MDL Scoring

For an approximation of $K(M)$, the model code, we used the following reasoning: suppose a DFA A has n states, the alphabet Σ has $|\Sigma|$ symbols, and A is functionally complete. Then, there are $n \times |\Sigma|$ state transitions, each with n possible destinations. This gives $n^{n \times |\Sigma|}$ possibilities. Furthermore, each state is either accepting or non-accepting. This gives 2^n possibilities. Thus, assuming that state 1 always is the start state, in total there are $2^n \times n^{n \times |\Sigma|}$ possible functionally complete DFA's with n states. However, there is a lot of redundancy here, for each permutation of states $2...n$ there is an equivalent DFA. Thus, the length of an index identifying a specific DFA is $\log(2^n \times n^{n \times |\Sigma|}/(n-1)!) = n + n \times |\Sigma| \times \log(n) - \log((n-1)!)$.

We have experimented with several variations of data-to-model ($K(D|M, d)$) codes:

1. Simple MDL with only positives. This version uses $\log \binom{m^+}{d^+}$.
2. Simple MDL with positives and negatives. This version uses $\log \binom{m^+}{d^+} + \log \binom{m^-}{d^-}$.
3. Simple MDL with positives and complement. This version uses $\log \binom{m^+}{d^+} + \log \binom{(2^{l+1}-1-m^+)}{d^-}$.
4. MDL as in equation 8, with only positives.
5. MDL as in equation 8.

Note that there is no difference between MDL as in equation 8 with negatives or complement.

We have tried all of the above variants on the problem set of the Abbadingo DFA inference competition ([10]). All variants are able to solve problems A, B, C, D, and R. In addition, all variants except for variant 1 can solve problem 1. Variant 4 can also solve problem 2. In comparison, EDSM can solve all these problems, and also problems 3, 4, 6, and S. So, indeed, it seems that MDL is not a very reliable guide for the compression of a DFA. At least, EDSM is better.

But EDSM, on its own, fails too on some problems. To solve some of these problems, we have extended our framework allowing it to search a (small) part of the decision tree. The search is to a certain depth, and at each depth only the most promising candidates are maintained in a list. Initially, we place the prefix tree acceptor in the list. Then, for every candidate in the list, for all its red/blue merge candidates, apply the merge and then use the heuristic to compress the DFA until no further merges are possible. Determine the score of the resulting DFA (for EDSM, this is the number of states, for MDL, this is its MDL). We store the DFA from the list, the first merge, and the resulting score in a result list. When all candidates for the list are tried, the result list is sorted according to the score, and only the most promising candidates are kept. For these candidates, we apply its first merge, and store the result in the list for the next depth.

As this process becomes quite compute-intensive, even for moderate values of maximum search depth and list length, we have written this application in Java, using the Satin ([17]) divide-and-conquer system that runs on top of the Ibis ([18]) Grid programming environment. Abbadingo problem 7 was solved using a search depth of 5, a list length of 256, and EDSM as the search heuristic. We did not find a solution when using MDL as the search heuristic. The MDL search heuristic sometimes seems to indicate choices, much deeper in the decision tree, that don't lead to an optimal DFA. In fact, this is the reason why problem 3 is not solved with the MDL heuristic and why problem 2 is only solved by one of the MDL variants: the first 15 or so decisions are decisions that the EDSM heuristic also indicates (albeit in a different order), but then a decision is made that makes a solution impossible. The MDL values of the solutions found with EDSM are lower than the ones found by means of the MDL heuristic, so MDL as a measure is good, but MDL as guidance is not. This suggests that we could use EDSM as the search strategy and MDL as a judge of the result. Indeed, Abbadingo problem 7 was solved with the same depth and list parameters as by using the number of states as a judge of the result. The significance of this is that using the number of states as a judge of the result is not an option when there are only positive examples.

6   Conclusions and Further Work

We have studied MDL in terms of two-part code optimization and randomness deficiency. In this framework we showed that 1) Shorter code not necessarily leads to better theories, e.g. the randomness deficiency does not decrease mono-tonically with the MDL code, 2) contrary to what is suggested by the results of [6] there is no fundamental difference between positive and negative data from an MDL perspective, 3) MDL is extremely sensitive to the correct calculation of code length. We have proved that already as a result of a single merge the divergence of randomness deficiency and MDL code can occur. Using these ideas we have implemented a MDL variant of the EDSM algorithm ([10]). The results show that although MDL works well as a global optimization criterion, it falls short of the performance of algorithms that evaluate local features of the problem space. MDL can be described as a global strategy for featureless learning.

Suggestions for further work are: the extension of these ideas to more complex language classes, the implementation of a better estimate of the model code, the development of strategies for hybrid MDL learning (MDL applied to local representations of the problem space to bypass local optima) and a more efficient implementation of the algorithm on the grid.

Acknowledgments. This project is supported by a BSIK grant from the Dutch Ministry of Education, Culture and Science (OC&W) and is part of the ICT innovation program of the Ministry of Economic Affairs (EZ).

References

1. Mitchell T. M., , Machine Learning, McGraw-Hill, New York, (1997)
2. Adriaans P., Vitányi P.M.B., The power and perils of MDL, Human Computer Studies Lab, Universiteit van Amsterdam,(2005)
3. Li M., Vitányi P.M.B. An Introduction to Kolmogorov Complexity and Its Applications, 2nd ed., Springer-Verlag, New York, (1997)
4. Vereshchagin N.K., Vitányi P.M.B., Kolmogorov's structure functions and model selection, IEEE Trans. Information Theory, vol. 50, nr. 12, 3265–3290, (2004)
5. P.D. Grünwald P.D. and Langford J., Suboptimal behaviour of Bayes and MDL in classification under misspecification, COLT 2004
6. Gold, E. Mark, Language Identification in the Limit, Information and Control, vol. 10, nr. 5, 447–474, (1967)
7. Pitt L., Warmuth M. K., The Minimum Consistent DFA Problem Cannot be Approximated within any Polynomial, Journal of the ACM, vol. 40, nr. 1, 95–142, (1993)
8. Adriaans P., Vervoort M., The EMILE 4.1 grammar induction toolbox, in Grammatical Inference: Algorithms and Applications; 6th International Colloquium, ICGI 2002, P. Adriaans and H. Fernau and M. van Zaanen eds., LNCS/LNAI 2484, 293–295, (2002)
9. Vervoort M., Games, walks and Grammars, Thesis University of Amsterdam, (2000)
10. Lang K. J., Pearlmutter B. A., Price R. A. , Results of the Abbadingo One DFA learning competition and a new evidence-driven state merging algorithm, in Grammatical Inference: Algorithms and Applications; 6th International Colloquium, ICGI 2002, P. Adriaans and H. Fernau and M. van Zaanen eds., LNCS/LNAI 2484, 1–12, (2002)
11. van Zaanen M., Adriaans P., Alignment-Based Learning versus EMILE: A Comparison, in Proceedings of the Belgian-Dutch Conference on Artificial Intelligence (BNAIC); Amsterdam, the Netherlands, 315–322, (2001)
12. Solan Z., Horn D., Ruppin E., Edelman S., Unsupervised learning of natural languages, PNAS, vol. 102, nr. 33, 11629-11634, (2005)
13. Curnéjols A., Miclet L., Apprentissage artificiel, concepts et algorithmes, Eyrolles, (2003)
14. Wolff J.G., Computing As Compression: An Overview of the SP Theory and System, New Generation Comput., vol. 13, nr. 2, 187–214, (1995)
15. Wolff, J. G., Information Compression by Multiple Alignment, Unification and Search as a Unifying Principle in Computing and Cognition, Journal of Artificial Intelligence Research, vol. 19, nr. 3, 193–230, (2003)
16. Proceedings of the Workshop and Tutorial on Learning Context-Free Grammars held at the 14th European Conference on Machine Learning (ECML) and the 7th European Conference on Principles and Practice of Knowledge Discovery in Databases (PKDD); Dubrovnik, Croatia, de la Higuera, Colin and Adriaans, Pieter and van Zaanen, Menno and Oncina, Jose (eds.), (2003)

17. van Nieuwpoort R. V., Maassen J. Kielmann T., Bal H. E., Satin: Simple and Efficient Java-based Grid Programming, Scalable Computing: Practice and Experience, vol. 6, nr. 3, 19–32, (2005)

18. van Nieuwpoort R. V., Maassen J., Wrzesinska G., Hofman R., Jacobs C., Kielmann T. Bal H. E., Ibis: a Flexible and Efficient Java based Grid Programming Environment, Concurrency and Computation: Practice and Experience, vol. 17, nr. 7-8, 1079–1107, (2005)

Characteristic Sets for Inferring the Unions of the Tree Pattern Languages by the Most Fitting Hypotheses

Yen Kaow Ng[1] and Takeshi Shinohara[2]

[1] Kyushu Institute of Technology
Graduate School of Computer Science and Systems, Iizuka, 820, Japan
kalngyk@daisy.ai.kyutech.ac.jp
[2] Kyushu Institute of Technology
Department of Artificial Intelligence, Iizuka, 820, Japan
shino@ai.kyutech.ac.jp

Abstract. A tree pattern p is a first-order term in formal logic, and the language of p is the set of all the tree patterns obtainable by replacing each variable in p with a tree pattern containing no variables. We consider the inductive inference of the unions of these languages from positive examples using strategies that guarantee some forms of minimality during the learning process. By a result in our earlier work, the existence of a characteristic set for each language in a class $\mathcal{L}$ (within $\mathcal{L}$) implies that $\mathcal{L}$ can be identified in the limit by a learner that simply conjectures a hypothesis containing the examples, that is minimal in the number of elements of up to an appropriate size. Furthermore, if there is a size ℓ such that each candidate hypothesis has a characteristic set (within the languages in $\mathcal{L}$ that intersects non-emptily with the examples) that consists only of elements of up to size ℓ, then the hypotheses containing the least number of elements of up to size ℓ are at the same time minimal with respect to inclusion. In this paper we show how to determine such a size ℓ for the unions of the tree pattern languages, and hence allowing us to learn the class using hypotheses that fulfill the two mentioned notions of minimality.

1 Introduction

In this paper we consider the *characteristic sets* [2] for the unions of the languages generated by the *(ordered, ranked and finite) tree patterns* [15]. A tree pattern is a first-order term in formal logic. Intuitively a tree pattern can be understood as a tree structure with leaves labeled with constant symbols or variables. The variables may be replaced with other tree patterns. A tree pattern is said to be *ground* if it contains no variable. The language of a tree pattern p are all the ground tree patterns obtainable by substituting variables in p with ground tree patterns. A *characteristic set S of a language L within a class $\mathcal{L}$* is a finite set of elements in L such that if any language in $\mathcal{L}$ includes S, then it must also include L.

Y. Sakakibara et al. (Eds.): ICGI 2006, LNAI 4201, pp. 307–319, 2006.

Let $\mathcal{L}^k$ denote the class of unions of up to k tree pattern languages. We are interested in the characteristic sets of $\mathcal{L}^k$, for within the two classes $\mathcal{L}^k$ and $\mathcal{L}_T^k$. We now describe $\mathcal{L}_T^k$. For any given set T of ground tree patterns let $\mathcal{L}_T$ denote the class of tree pattern languages that intersect non-emptily with T. $\mathcal{L}_T^k$ is then, the class of unions of up to k languages from $\mathcal{L}_T$. We show in this paper how to compute, given a language $L \in \mathcal{L}^k$ and a class $\mathcal{L}'$ chosen from one of the following:

1. $\mathcal{L}^k$ where k is less than the alphabet size, and
2. $\mathcal{L}_T^k$ where k is independent of the alphabet size

a length ℓ_T, such that there is a characteristic set for L, consisting only of trees of up to the size ℓ_T, within $\mathcal{L}'$. The choice of $\mathcal{L}_T^k$ is due to an earlier result, which shall become clear later.

The present study is motivated by an interest to inductively infer, from positive examples [9], the unions of the tree pattern languages, using hypotheses that are minimal in some sense. In using such hypotheses, we are attempting to overcome the problem of over-generalization due to lack of negative examples. The learning of the class of the tree pattern languages is interesting since the tree patterns can also be thought of as abstractions of hierarchically structured data such as XML documents [10], which are becoming increasingly popular for use on the internet as well as for biological applications. Since the tree patterns are first-order terms in logic programs, this study can also be considered a first step towards the inductive inference of logic programs (e.g. Prolog programs) from positive data.

It has been previously shown that the unions of the tree pattern languages can be inferred efficiently when the number of languages allowed in a union is less than the alphabet size [4,7,6]. In this work we do not address the issue of efficiency in the learning process — our primary interest is to obtain hypotheses that possess some forms of minimality. In a previous work [13], we found that any class of languages $\mathcal{L} = \{L_i \mid i \in N^+\}$ where each language in the class has a characteristic set within the class, can be identified in the limit by the following learner `infer`, which basically outputs a hypothesis that contains the fewest elements of sizes up to the length of the input sequence. In the following, the learner is given as input the sequence σ.

`infer`(σ):
    If $|\sigma| = 0$, let $H = \emptyset$. (Initial hypothesis)
    If H is not among the languages containing all examples in σ with the
        fewest elements of sizes up to $|\sigma|$, find the language from among these
        minimal languages with the smallest index and set H to it.
    Note that the smallest index is used here to simplify convergence.
    Conjecture H.

The use of such minimal hypotheses is beneficial for the following reasons: (1) this reduces learning into a problem of counting the elements of the candidate hypotheses of up to some length (which is often computable), and (2) some works have suggested that such hypotheses may be desirable in some applications [8,12,14]. Note that `infer` is computable for the class of unions of tree pattern languages.

The previous work also showed that, if there exists a size ℓ such that, for every language L that is consistent with the input, there is a characteristic set of L (within $\mathcal{L}_T^k$) consisting only of elements of up to the size ℓ, then all the hypotheses containing the input that has the least number of elements of up to the size ℓ are also minimal with respect to inclusion (we restate this in Theorem 2). That is, we can obtain hypotheses that possess both of these notions of minimality. Note that hypotheses that are minimal with respect to inclusion possess a few interesting qualities [1], and may also help in the analysis of convergence of the learning process (via the characteristic sets).

This paper is structured as follows. In Section 2 we formally define the terminology and concepts needed for subsequent discussions. We define the two notions of minimality which we are interested in, and give earlier results on these notions of minimality. The motivation for our choice of classes that the characteristic sets are with respect to will become clear from this result. Section 3 discusses the existence of these characteristic sets. In Section 4 we show a sufficient size bound to the characteristic sets of the unions of the tree pattern languages, when the number of languages allowed in a union is less than the alphabet size. This restriction on the bound of the number of unions is the same as that in [4]. Finally, in Section 5, we study the characteristic sets with this restriction on the alphabet size removed.

2   Preliminaries

We follow mainly the definitions in [3]. The symbols N and N^+ denote the set of natural numbers and the set of positive integers respectively. $\emptyset$, $\in$, $\subset$, $\subseteq$ respectively denote empty set, element of, proper subset, subset. $\max(.)$, $\min(.)$ denote maximum and minimum of a set, where by convention $\max(\emptyset) = 0$ and $\min(\emptyset) = \infty$. Cardinality of a set S is written $card(S)$. $A - B$ denotes the set $\{x \mid x \in A \text{ and } x \notin B\}$. The symbol Σ denotes a finite alphabet, where each element of Σ is called a *function* and associated with a non-negative integer called an *arity*. A function with arity 0 is also called a *constant*. We assume that Σ contains at least one constant. Let $V = \{x_1, x_2, \ldots\}$ be a countable set of symbols disjoint from Σ. Each element in V is called a *variable*.

2.1   Tree Patterns

A *tree pattern* p over Σ is an expression defined recursively as follows: (1) a constant $f \in \Sigma$, or a variable $x \in V$ is a tree pattern; (2) For a function f with arity n, where $n \geq 1$, and tree patterns $t_1, \ldots, t_n$, $f(t_1, \ldots, t_n)$ is a tree pattern. The function f or variable x in (1) and (2) is the *root symbol* of p. We consider tree patterns to be defined from left to right, that is, in $f(t_1, \ldots, t_n)$ of (2), t_i is defined before t_j if $i < j$. A tree pattern t *occurs* in a tree pattern p just in case t is used in the recursive definition of p. We call each such occurrence of t a *node of p* (or simply *a node*). We say that a node u is the *i-th child* (or simply *a child*) of a node v of the term $f(t_1, \ldots, t_n)$, just in case u occurs as t_i $(1 \leq i \leq n)$ in v.

A tree pattern is said to be *ground* if it contains no variable. Let TP denote the set of all tree patterns and let TP_Σ denote the set of all ground tree patterns. The *size of a tree pattern p*, denoted by $\|p\|$, is the number of nodes in p (Note: this definition differs from that in [3]).

Given a tree pattern p and a node v in p, the *position of v*, written $\mathrm{pos}(v)$, is a string of natural numbers recursively defined as follows:

$$\mathrm{pos}(v) = \begin{cases} \epsilon \text{ (empty string)} & \text{if the node } v \text{ is } p \text{ itself.} \\ \mathrm{pos}(v')i & \text{if } v \text{ is the } i\text{-th child of the node } v' \text{ in } p. \\ \text{undefined} & \text{otherwise.} \end{cases}$$

We say that a function symbol c *occurs at a position ε in p* just in case $\mathrm{pos}(v) = \varepsilon$ for some node v in p and c is the root symbol of v. Likewise a tree pattern t *occurs at a position ε in p* just in case $\mathrm{pos}(v) = \varepsilon$ and v is an occurrence of t. The *height* of a tree pattern t, $|t|$, is $\max(\{|\mathrm{pos}(v)| \mid v \text{ is a node in } t\})$, where $|\mathrm{pos}(v)|$ is the length of the string $\mathrm{pos}(v)$. We say that a node v is *at depth h* just in case $|\mathrm{pos}(v)| = h$.

Finally, we let $\langle n \rangle_\Sigma$ denote the smallest size s such that there are n elements of the same height in $\{t \in TP_\Sigma \mid \|t\| \leq s\}$, if such elements exist.

Example 1. *Let $\Sigma = \{a, f\}$ where a is a constant and f is of arity 2. Consider $\langle 7 \rangle_\Sigma$. Let $p = f(f(f(a, a), x_1), f(x_2, x_3))$ (see below).*

By replacing either a or $f(a, a)$ in each of the variables in p (hence the maximum size of these tree patterns is 15), we can verify that there are at least 7 tree patterns (8 for this case) of equal height (that is, 3) in TP_Σ. Hence $\langle 7 \rangle_\Sigma \leq 15$.

The following Proposition states that such n ground tree patterns of equal height exist under very trivial conditions.

Proposition 1. *If Σ consists of at least one function of arity ≥ 2, then for all n, there exists n elements of the same height in TP_Σ.*

2.2   Languages of the Tree Patterns

A *substitution* is a finite set of the form $\{y_1/t_1, \ldots, y_n/t_n\}$, where each y_i is a distinct variable in V, and each t_i is a tree pattern different from y_i. An *instance* of a tree pattern p by a substitution $\theta = \{y_1/t_1, \ldots, y_n/t_n\}$, written $p\theta$, is the tree pattern obtained by simultaneously replacing each occurrence of the variable y_i with the term $t_i (1 \leq i \leq n)$. We write $p \preceq q$ iff $p = q\theta$ for some substitution θ.

We write $p \prec q$ just in case $p \preceq q$ but not $q \preceq p$. Given two sets of tree patterns P and Q, we write $P \sqsubseteq Q$ iff for each $p \in P$, $p \preceq q$ for some $q \in Q$. $P \sqsubset Q$ just in case $P \sqsubseteq Q$ but not $Q \sqsubseteq P$.

The language of a tree pattern p, written $L(p)$, is the set $L(p) = \{w \in TP_\Sigma \mid w \preceq p\}$. For a set $P \subseteq TP$, $L(P) = \bigcup_{p \in P} L(p)$ and $\mathcal{L}(P) = \{L(p) \mid p \in P\}$. For any class $\mathcal{L}$ of languages, $\mathcal{L}^k$ denotes the class $\{\bigcup_{L \in \mathcal{L}'} L \mid \mathcal{L}' \subseteq \mathcal{L} \wedge card(\mathcal{L}') \leq k\}$, while $\mathcal{L}^*$ denotes the class $\{\bigcup_{L \in \mathcal{L}'} L \mid \mathcal{L}' \subseteq \mathcal{L} \wedge card(\mathcal{L}') < \infty\}$.

Definition 1 (Characteristic sets [2]). *A characteristic set for a language L within a class $\mathcal{L}$ is a finite set S_L such that for each $L' \in \mathcal{L}$, $S_L \subseteq L' \Rightarrow L \subseteq L'$.*

Definition 2 (S_n). *For any $p \in TP$, we denote by $S_n(p)$ the set of all the elements of $L(p)$ obtainable by replacing variables in p with ground tree patterns of sizes up to n.*

2.3   The MINL and FC Notions of Minimality

We now describe two problems of finding, given a finite non-empty set $S \subseteq TP_\Sigma$, a language $L \in \mathcal{L}(TP)^k$ containing S that fulfills some notions of minimality. Earlier studies [1,17,5,13] have shown that solutions from either one these problems allow us to inductively infer any class of languages where each language in the class has a characteristic set within the class.

Definition 3. *Given a finite non-empty set $S \subset TP_\Sigma$ and $k \in N^+$,*
(1) The problem $\mathbf{MINL}(\mathcal{L}(TP), S, k)$ is to find a set of at most k tree patterns $P \subseteq TP$ such that $S \subseteq L(P)$ and there are no other set of up to k patterns $P' \subseteq TP$ where $S \subseteq L(P')$ such that $L(P') \subset L(P)$.
(2) The problem $\mathbf{FC}(\mathcal{L}(TP), S, k, \ell)$ is to find, among every set P of up to k tree patterns in $\{p \in TP \mid L(p) \cap S \neq \emptyset\}$ where $S \subseteq L(P)$, for one that minimizes $card(\bigcup_{p \in P}\{t \in L(p) \mid \|t\| \leq \ell\})$.
(3) $\mathcal{MINL}(\mathcal{L}(TP), S, k) = \{P \subseteq TP \mid P$ is a solution for $\mathbf{MINL}(\mathcal{L}(TP), S, k)\}$.
(4) $\mathcal{FC}(\mathcal{L}(TP), S, k, \ell) = \{P \subseteq TP \mid P$ is a solution for $\mathbf{FC}(\mathcal{L}(TP), S, k, \ell)\}$.

The following result shows that it is possible to find an element of $\mathcal{FC}$ that is at the same time an element of $\mathcal{MINL}$. This result gives us the main motivation for the present study.

Theorem 2 (Theorem 3 in [13]). *Given a finite non-empty $S \subseteq TP_\Sigma$ and $k \in N^+$. Let $\mathcal{C} = \{L \in \mathcal{L}(TP) \mid L \cap S \neq \emptyset\}$. If there exists $\ell \in N$ such that every language $L \in \mathcal{C}^k$ has a characteristic set S_L of elements of size not larger than ℓ within $\mathcal{C}^k$, then $\mathcal{FC}(\mathcal{L}(TP), S, k, \ell) \subseteq \mathcal{MINL}(\mathcal{L}(TP), S, k)$.*

Hence it suffices that we determine ℓ, a sufficient size for the elements of the characteristic sets for languages in $\mathcal{L}(TP)^k$, in order to obtain hypotheses that possess the minimality of both **FC** and **MINL**. Note that in Theorem 2, the characteristic sets required is only for within the class $\{L(p) \in \mathcal{L}(TP) \mid L(p) \cap S \neq \emptyset\}^k$. This class is considered in Section 5. We first examine the existence of these characteristic sets.

3 Existence of Characteristic Sets for Unions of Languages in $\mathcal{L}(TP)$

The following result, that shows that a characteristic set exists for every $L \in \mathcal{L}(TP)^k$ within $\mathcal{L}(TP)^k$, follows from Theorem 8 in [18] and a result discovered independently by Sato (Theorem 2.24 in [16]), Kobayashi and Yokomori (Proposition 7 in [11]).

Theorem 3 ([18] and [16,11]). *For every $k \in N^+$, every language $L \in \mathcal{L}(TP)^k$ has a characteristic set within $\mathcal{L}(TP)^k$.*

By Theorem 3 and Theorem 2 in [13], the class $\mathcal{L}(TP)^k$ can be inferred by a learner that bases its conjecture completely on a computation of **FC**.

Regrettably, Theorem 3 does not hold in the case of unbounded unions. To see this, let p be a tree pattern with at least one variable, and let S be any finite subset of $L(p)$. Now S itself is a union of $card(S)$ tree pattern languages (each of a single ground tree pattern), and hence not a characteristic set for $L(p)$. One might ask if the same problem would persist if we remove the ground tree pattern languages from the class, that is, consider instead the class $\mathcal{L}(TP-TP_\Sigma)$. However, a simple analysis shows that if Σ contains any function of arity ≥ 2, then the case is no different from that which allows ground tree pattern languages. For example, let f be a function of arity 2, let $p = f(x_1, x_2)$ and let $TP' = \{f(x_1, t) \mid t \in TP_\Sigma\}$. Then every language $L \in \mathcal{L}(TP')^*$ has $L \subset L(p)$, and for every $S \subseteq L(p)$, there is a language in $\mathcal{L}(TP')^*$ which includes S. (In fact, this shows that $\mathcal{L}(TP - TP_\Sigma)^*$ is not inferable from positive examples.) Conversely, if every function in Σ is of arity ≤ 1, then trivial characteristic sets exist for languages in $\mathcal{L}(TP - TP_\Sigma)^*$.

Lemma 1. *If Σ consists only of functions of arities ≤ 1, then for any finite $P \subseteq TP - TP_\Sigma$, $S_1(P)$ is a characteristic set for $L(P)$ within $\mathcal{L}(TP - TP_\Sigma)^*$.*

Proposition 4. *A characteristic set exists for every language in $\mathcal{L}(TP-TP_\Sigma)^*$ if and only if every function in Σ is of arity ≤ 1.*

4 Characteristic Sets Within Unions of Less Than $card(\Sigma)$ Languages

We first consider intuitively the task of finding, for any two given tree patterns p and q, an element in $L(p) - L(q)$. In the following example, any tree pattern obtained from p by replacing x_1 with a function other than f cannot be refined from q. While the same cannot be done for $L(p) - L(q')$, we note that it can be done if x_1 in q' is first replaced with $f(a, a)$, replicating the functions in p.

Out of this consideration, we make the following definition. For any $p, q \in TP$, q is said to *dutifully extend* p just in case if we take each of the variable occurrences in p to be mutually independent, then p refines to q. More intuitively, q dutifully extends p just in case if a function c occurs at position ε in p, c also occurs at position ε in q. In the example below, q dutifully extends p but q' and q'' do not. Note that $q \preceq p \Rightarrow q$ dutifully extends p.

We now attempt to find a most general refinement of a tree pattern q that dutifully extends a tree pattern p. Consider the following method, the output of which we denote by $\text{mge}\{q \supseteq p\}$.

dutifully_extend_p
1. Set $\text{mge}\{q \supseteq p\}$ to q.
2. If there is any function in $\text{mge}\{q \supseteq p\}$ that conflicts with functions in p, output "failure".
3. While there exists a function node, v say, in p where no corresponding function occurs at $\text{pos}(v)$ in $\text{mge}\{q \supseteq p\}$.
   3.1 Find a variable node u in $\text{mge}\{q \supseteq p\}$ at some prefixes of $\text{pos}(v)$. If no such variable node exists in $\text{mge}\{q \supseteq p\}$, output "failure".
   3.2 Let t be the tree pattern at $\text{pos}(u)$ in p. Replace each variable occurrence in t with a distinct variable not in $\text{mge}\{q \supseteq p\}$ and let t' denote the resultant tree pattern.
   3.3 Let x be the root symbol of u. Substitute each occurrence of x in $\text{mge}\{q \supseteq p\}$ with t'. If this results in any function in $\text{mge}\{q \supseteq p\}$ to conflict with functions in p, output "failure".
4. Output $\text{mge}\{q \supseteq p\}$.

It is clear that (1) $\text{mge}\{q \supseteq p\} \preceq q$, and (2) $\text{mge}\{q \supseteq p\}$ dutifully extends p. Intuitively, the method preserves the generality of $\text{mge}\{q \supseteq p\}$, by making only the necessary refinements to q to dutifully extend p (in steps 3.2~3.3). From this, we can verify that $L(p) \cap L(q) \subseteq \text{mge}\{q \supseteq p\}$. It can also be shown that (1) there exists exactly one such $\text{mge}\{q \supseteq p\}$, unique to renaming of variables, and (2) if the method outputs "failure", then no refinement of q dutifully extends p. Since $\text{mge}\{q \supseteq p\}$ agrees with p in both structure and functions, any discrepencies between $\text{mge}\{q \supseteq p\}$ and p can involve only variables in p.

We now find a sufficient size to the elements of the characteristic sets for the unions of the tree pattern languages, when the number of languages allowed in a union is less than the alphabet size.

Lemma 5. Let $p \in TP$ and $Q \subseteq TP$ be where $card(Q) < card(\Sigma)$. If $\{p\} \not\subseteq Q$ then there exists a ground tree pattern $t \in L(p) - L(Q)$ of size $(1 + \alpha)\|p\|$, where α is the largest arity of the functions in Σ.

Proof. Without loss of generality we assume that for each $q \in Q$, either q duti-fully extends p, or there exists some $q' \preceq q$ that dutifully extends p, since other-wise $L(p) \cap L(q) = \emptyset$. Let $Q' = \{\text{mge}\{q \supseteq p\} \mid q \in Q\}$. Note that $card(Q') < k$ and $L(p) \cap L(Q) = L(p) \cap L(Q')$. We now show that any such $q' \in Q'$ must be of one of two possible forms. Since q' dutifully extends p, $\|q'\| \geq \|p\|$. Now since for every $q \in Q$, $p \npreceq q$, one of the following cases must apply for $q' \in Q'$:

(C1) A variable x occurs in p at a position where a function c occurs in q'. In this case we say that x and c witnesses that q' fulfills (C1).

(C2) A variable x occurs in p at a position where a variable y occurs in q', however y also occurs in q' at a position where a variable $x' \neq x$ occurs in p. In this case we say that x witnesses that q' fulfills (C2). In the following example, the left-most occurrence of x_1 in p witnesses that q' fulfills (C2).

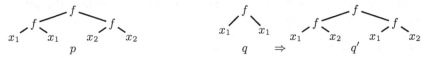

This is how we construct a ground tree pattern that cannot be refined from the tree patterns that fulfill (C1). Let variable x in p (with some $c \in \Sigma$) witness that the tree patterns $Q^x \subseteq Q'$ fulfill (C1), and let $\Sigma^x \subseteq \Sigma$ be such that for each $q' \in Q^x$, there exists $c \in \Sigma^x$ that witnesses that q' fulfills (C1) as witnessed by x and c. Clearly, no $q' \in Q^x$ refines to the tree pattern obtained by replacing every occurrence of x in p with a symbol in $\Sigma - \Sigma^x$. For the tree patterns fulfilling (C2) we do the following. Let X be a collection of the variables occurring in p such that for each q' that fulfills (C2), there is a variable in X that witnesses it. If we replace each of the variables in X with a distinct function, and all other variables that occur in p but is not in X with yet another distinct function, then all the q' fulfilling (C2) cannot refine to the resultant tree pattern. The following algorithm *find_t* does exactly these.

We first construct a basic set of ground tree patterns of at most height 1, for use in *find_t*. Let a be an arbitrary constant in Σ. For each function $f \in \Sigma$, let $f_a = f$ if f is a constant, otherwise f_a is tree pattern with root symbol f and the constant a as children. We let $\Lambda_a = \{f_a \mid f \in \Sigma\}$. It is clear that $card(\Lambda_a) = card(\Sigma)$.

find_t
1. Let $C = \Sigma$.
2. For each $q' \in Q'$, find a variable x in p that witnesses that q' fulfills (C1). Let X be the set of all such x found.
3. While Q' is not empty,
   3.1 For each $x \in X$, let Q^x be the set of all $q' \in Q'$ with a function occurring at some position where x occurs at in p.
   3.2 For each $q' \in Q^x$ find one function c which occurs at a position where x occurs at in p. Let C' be the collection of all such c found.
   3.3 Replace x with an element $f_a \in \Lambda_a$ where $f \in C - C'$ (this is possible because $card(C') \leq card(Q') < card(C)$), and remove f from C.
   3.4 Remove Q^x from Q'.

4. Let Q'' be the set of all q' that fulfills (C2) but not (C1).
5. For each $q' \in Q''$, find a variable x in p that witnesses that q' fulfills (C2).
   Let X be the set of all such x found.
   5.1 If $x \in X$ has not already been replaced, replace x with an element
       $f_a \in \Lambda_a$ where $f \in C$, and remove f from C.
6. Replace all remaining variables in p with an element $f_a \in \Lambda_a$ where $f \in C$.
   (Note that at most $card(Q') < card(\Sigma)$ elements have been removed from C
   prior to this step.)
7. Let t be the resultant pattern. Output t.

Since there are at most $\|p\|$ variable occurrences in p, the total number of
terms added to p in $find\_t$ is at most $\alpha\|p\|$. Since $t \not\preceq q'$ for any $q' \in Q'$,
$t \notin L(q')$ for each $q' \in Q'$. Clearly, $t \in L(p)$ by the substitutions done in $find\_t$,
but since $t \notin L(Q')$, $t \notin L(Q)$.   ∎

Theorem 6. *Let α be the largest arity of the functions in Σ and let $k <$
$card(\Sigma)$. For every collection of less than k tree patterns $P, Q \subseteq TP$, the following three statements are equivalent:*
(i) $S_\alpha(P) \subseteq L(Q)$, (ii) $P \sqsubseteq Q$, (iii) $L(P) \subseteq L(Q)$.

Proof. (ii)$\Rightarrow$(iii) by definition. (iii)$\Rightarrow$(i) is immediate. (i)$\Rightarrow$(ii) by Lemma 5.   ∎

The equivalence of (i) and (iii) says that for any set of less than k tree patterns
$P \subseteq TP$, $S_\alpha(P)$ is a characteristic set of $L(P)$ within $\mathcal{L}(TP)^k$.

Theorem 7. *Let α be the largest arity of the functions in Σ. For every finite,
non-empty $S \subseteq TP_\Sigma$ and $k < card(\Sigma)$, $\mathcal{FC}(\mathcal{L}(TP), S, k, \max(\{(1 + \alpha)\|t\| \mid t \in$
$S\})) \subseteq \mathcal{MINL}(\mathcal{L}(TP), S, k)$.*

5   Characteristic Sets Within $\{L \in \mathcal{L}(TP) \mid L \cap S \neq \emptyset\}^k$

We now remove the alphabet size restriction placed on the number of unions
allowed, and find, for any tree pattern language L, a sufficient size for constructing a characteristic set of L of only elements of up to that size, within
$\{L \in \mathcal{L}(TP) \mid L \cap S \neq \emptyset\}^k$, with the condition that there there is at least a
function of arity ≥ 2 in Σ.

A node u in q *exceeds* a node v in p just in case $pos(v)$ is a prefix of $pos(u)$.
u *properly exceeds* v just in case u exceeds v but v does not exceed u. A tree
pattern p *exceeds* a tree pattern q just in case no leaf node in p is properly
exceeded by some node in q.

Example 2. *Let $\Sigma = \{a, f, g\}$ where a is a constant, f is of arity 2, and g is
of arity 3. Let $p = f(f(a, a), x_1)$ and $q = g(x_1, a, f(x_2, x_3))$. Then, p exceeds q.*

Note that the notion of "exceed" is much easier to fulfill than the notion of "dutifully extend". For any p and q where p exceeds q, $p \not\preceq q$ implies certain relationship between p and mge$\{q \supseteq p\}$, which we will demonstrate in Lemma 9.

Lemma 8. *Let $p, q \in TP$ be such that no node in q properly exceeds any node of a variable in p, then $L(p) \cap L(q) \neq \emptyset \Rightarrow p$ exceeds q.*

Proof. If any node in q properly exceeds any node of a constant, then clearly $L(q) \cap L(p) = \emptyset$. Hence $L(q) \cap L(p) \neq \emptyset \Rightarrow$ no node q exceeds node of constants or variables in $p \Rightarrow p$ exceeds q. ∎

Lemma 9. *Suppose Σ contains at least one function of arity ≥ 2. Let $p \in TP$ and finite set $Q \subseteq TP$ be such that (1) no node in any $q \in Q$ properly exceeds any node of a variable in p, and (2) $\{p\} \not\sqsubseteq Q$, then there exists $w \in S_d(p) - L(Q)$, where $d = \langle \|p\| + card(Q) \rangle_\Sigma$.*

Proof. By Lemma 8, without loss of generality we assume p exceeds each $q \in Q$. Let $Q' = \{mge\{q \supseteq p\} \mid q \in Q\}$. It is clear that $L(p) \cap L(Q') = \emptyset \Rightarrow L(p) \cap L(Q) = \emptyset$.

We will now show that any $q' \in Q'$ must be of one of a few forms, which will allow us to construct a $w \in L(p) - \bigcup_{q' \in Q'} L(q')$. Since p exceeds q and $p \not\preceq q$, one of the following cases must apply for $q' = mge\{q \supseteq p\}$:

(C1) A variable x in p occurs at a position where a ground tree pattern t is found in q'. The following example shows how such a q' comes to be. Let $T_Q \subseteq TP_\Sigma$ be such that for each $q' \in Q'$ where (C1) is true, there is a $t \in T_Q$ which witnesses this.

(C2) A variable x in p occurs at a position where at the same position in q' we find a variable which has another occurrence at a position which is not occupied by x in p, as demonstrated in the following example with the variable x_2 in p.

(C3) A variable x in p occurs at a position where in q' we find a variable which has another occurrence at a node extending a variable leaf in p, as in the following example with the variable x_1 in p.

Suppose there are n distinct variables in p. Let $T \subseteq TP_\Sigma$ be a set of n tree patterns not in T_Q, each of the same height (this is possible by Proposition 1). Hence such T consists of trees of up to size $\langle n + card(Q) \rangle_\Sigma$. Since there are at most $\|p\|$ variables in p, each $t \in T$ is of size at most $\langle \|p\| + card(Q) \rangle_\Sigma$.

Let w be a tree obtained by replacing each distinct variable in p with a different tree in T. We claim that $w \not\preceq q'$. The case of (C1) is evident from that the variable corresponding to some $t \in T_Q$ is replaced with a $t' \notin T_Q$. The case of (C2) is evident from that every variable in p has been replaced with a different tree pattern. The case of (C3) is from that w is structurally impossible for q' to refine to, as observed by the height of the tree patterns required in variable substitutions. Hence no q' refines to w. Since $w \notin L(q')$ for all $q' \in Q'$, we have $w \notin L(Q') \Rightarrow w \notin L(Q)$.   ∎

The next Theorem uses Lemma 9 to show how to find, given any $p \in TP$ and $Q \subseteq TP$ where $L(p) - L(Q) \neq \emptyset$, a finite set $S \subseteq L(p)$ where $S \not\subseteq L(Q)$.

Theorem 10. *Suppose Σ contains at least one function of arity ≥ 2, and let α be the largest arity of the functions in Σ. Given finite, non-empty $S \subseteq TP_\Sigma$, $p \in TP$ and finite set $Q \subseteq \{t \in TP \mid L(t) \cap S \neq \emptyset\}$. Let $h = \max(\{|s| \mid s \in S\})$. Then either $L(p) \subseteq L(Q)$, or there exists $w \in S_{\langle \|p\|(1+\alpha^h)+card(Q) \rangle_\Sigma}(p) - L(Q)$.*

Proof. Let Λ be the set of all constants, and tree patterns of height 1 with only variables as children. For any pattern p, let $\Theta(p)$ denote the set of all the unique tree patterns $\{p\theta \mid \theta \text{ is a substitution that maps each variable in } p \text{ with a } t \in \Lambda\}$. One can show that:

- (A) $L(p) = L(\Theta(p))$.

and verify that:

- (B) For any tree pattern t let minvardepth$(t) = \min(\{|pos(x)| \mid x \text{ is a vari-}$ able node in $t\})$, then for all tree pattern $p' \in \Theta(p)$, minvardepth$(p') =$ minvardepth$(p) + 1$. That is, intuitively, the depth of each variable node increments by 1.

Consider the following computation which, given a tree pattern p and a set of tree patterns Q, decides if $L(p) \subseteq L(Q)$.

stage 0:
Let $G_0 = \{p\}$. Go to stage 1.

stage l:
If there exists some ground tree pattern in G_{l-1} not refinable from some $q \in Q$, output false.
Remove from G_{l-1} the patterns that can be refined from some $q \in Q$.
If $G_{l-1} = \emptyset$, output true.
Let $G_l = \bigcup_{p' \in G_{l-1}} \Theta(p')$, and go to stage $l + 1$.

It is clear that if the computation halts at any stage and outputs false, $L(p) \not\subseteq L(Q)$. By Condition (A), if the computation halts at any stage and outputs true, $L(p) \subseteq L(Q)$. Note that:

- (C) At each level l, each variable in every tree pattern $p' \in G_l$ is at depth at least l (by Condition (B)).

Assume that the computation continues pass stage h. By Condition (C), at stage h, every pattern in G_h has variables at depth $\geq h$ (that is, exactly h in the case that minvardepth$(p) = 0$). On the other hand, for each $q \in Q$, $L(q) \cap S \neq \emptyset$ $\Rightarrow$ no node in q can be at a depth larger than h. Hence every variable node for any $p' \in G_h$ must exceed its corresponding node in any $q \in Q$ (if such corresponding nodes exist), and fulfills condition (1) of Lemma 9.

Let $p' \in G_h$ such that $\{p'\} \not\sqsubseteq Q$ (such p' exists by our assumption that the computation passes stage h). By Lemma 9, there exists $w \in S_d(p') - L(q)$ where $d = \langle \|p'\| + card(Q) \rangle_\Sigma$. Since there are at most $\|p\|$ variables in p, $\|p'\|$ is at most $\|p\|(1 + \alpha^h)$. ∎

Corollary 1. *Suppose Σ contains at least one function of arity ≥ 2, and let α be the largest arity of the functions in Σ. Given finite non-empty $S \subseteq TP_\Sigma$, $k \in N^+$ and $p \in TP$. Let $h = \max(\{|s| \mid s \in S\})$. Then $S_{\langle \|p\|(1+\alpha^h)+k \rangle_\Sigma}(p)$ is a characteristic set for $L(p)$ within $\{L \in \mathcal{L}(TP) \mid L \cap S \neq \emptyset\}^k$.*

This gives us our main result.

Theorem 11. *Suppose Σ contains at least one function of arity ≥ 2. Given finite non-empty $S \subseteq TP_\Sigma$ and $k \in N^+$. Let $h = \max(\{|t| \mid t \in S\})$, $s = \max(\{\|t\| \mid t \in S\})$, and let α be the largest arity of the functions in Σ. Then $\mathcal{FC}(\mathcal{L}(TP), S, k, s(1+d)) \subseteq \mathcal{MINL}(\mathcal{L}(TP), S, k)$ where $d = \langle s(1+\alpha^h) + k \rangle_\Sigma$.*

6   Conclusions

We have seen how hypotheses fulfilling both the **MINL** and **FC** criteria of minimality can be obtained for the bounded unions of the tree pattern languages. It remains to be seen whether such hypotheses can be obtained efficiently. One of the ways to achieve this is to generate a set of candidate (unions of) tree patterns (note that such a candidate set is finite since for any finite set of examples, there are only finitely many tree pattern languages that intersect non-emptily with it), and then count the number of elements in these languages of up to the size required in Theorem 7 (or 11, if the number of unions is less than the alphabet size). Such countings, if computable efficiently, will help in the search for the minimal hypotheses discussed.

Acknowledgements. The authors would like to thank the anonymous referees for corrections and valuable comments, and Prof. Kouichi Hirata for many involved discussions. Yen Kaow Ng is supported by the Japanese Government Scholarship of the Ministry of Education, Science, Sports, Culture and Technology of Japan.

References

1. D. Angluin. Inductive inference of formal languages from positive data. *Information and Control*, 45:117–135, 1980.
2. D. Angluin. Inference of reversible languages. *J. of the ACM*, 29:741–765, 1982.
3. H. Arimura, H. Ishizaka, and T. Shinohara. Learning unions of tree patterns using queries. *Theoretical Computer Science*, 185(1):47–62, 1997.
4. H. Arimura, T. Shinohara, and S. Otsuki. A polynomial time algorithm for finding finite unions of tree pattern languages. In *Proc. of Nonmonotonic and Inductive Logic, Second Int. Workshop*, volume 659 of *LNAI*, pages 118–131. Springer-Verlag, 1991.
5. H. Arimura, T. Shinohara, and S. Otsuki. Polynomial time inference of unions of two tree pattern languages. *IEICE Transactions on Information and Systems*, E75-D(7):426–434, 1992.
6. H. Arimura, T. Shinohara, and S. Otsuki. Finding minimal generalizations for unions of pattern languages and its application to inductive inference from positive data. In *Proc. of STACS 94, 11th Annual Symposium on Theoretical Aspects of Computer Science*, volume 775 of *LNCS*, pages 649–660. Springer-Verlag, 1994.
7. H. Arimura, T. Shinohara, S. Otsuki, and H. Ishizaka. A generalization of the least general generalization. *Machine Intelligence 13*, 13:59–85, 1994.
8. C. Chan, M. Garofalakis, and R. Rastogi. RE-tree: an efficient index structure for regular expressions. *The VLDB Journal*, 12(2):102–119, 2003.
9. E. M. Gold. Language identification in the limit. *Information and Control*, 10:447–474, 1967.
10. W3C XML Core Working Group. Extensible Markup Language (XML) 1.0 (Third Edition). W3C Recommendation, 2004.
11. S. Kobayashi and T. Yokomori. Identifiability of subspaces and homomorphic images of zero-reversible languages. In *Proc. of Algorithmic Learning Theory, 8th Int. Conf., ALT'97*, volume 1316 of *LNAI*, pages 48–61. Springer-Verlag, 1997.
12. Y. K. Ng, H. Ono, and T. Shinohara. Measuring over-generalization in the minimal multiple generalizations of biosequences. In *Proc. of Discovery Science, 8th Int. Conf., DS 2005*, volume 3735 of *LNAI*, pages 176–188. Springer-Verlag, 2005.
13. Y. K. Ng and T. Shinohara. Inferring unions of the pattern languages by the most fitting covers. In *Proc. of Algorithmic Learning Theory, 16th Int. Conf., ALT 2005*, volume 3734 of *LNAI*, pages 269–282. Springer-Verlag, 2005.
14. Y. K. Ng and T. Shinohara. Finding consensus patterns in very scarce biosequence samples from their minimal multiple generalizations. In *Proc. of Advances in Knowledge Discovery and Data Mining, 10th Pacific-Asia Conf., PAKDD 2006*, volume 3918 of *LNAI*, pages 540–545. Springer-Verlag, 2006.
15. G.D. Plotkin. A note on inductive generalization. In *Machine Intelligence*, volume 5, pages 153–163. Edinburgh University Press, 1970.
16. M. Sato. Inductive inference of formal languages. *Bulletin of Informatics and Cybernetics*, 27(1):85–106, 1995.
17. T. Shinohara. Polynomial time inference of extended regular pattern languages. In *RIMS Symposia on Software Science and Engineering, Kyoto, Japan*, volume 147 of *LNCS*, pages 115–127. Springer-Verlag, 1982.
18. K. Wright. Identification of unions of languages drawn from an identifiable class. In *Proc. of the Second Annual Workshop on Computational Learning Theory*, pages 328–333. Morgan Kaufmann, 1989.

Learning Deterministic DEC Grammars Is Learning Rational Numbers

Pieter Adriaans

Department of Computer Science,
University of Amsterdam,
Kruislaan 419, 1098VA Amsterdam
pietera@science.uva.nl
http://www.uva.nl

Abstract. Below I show that the class of strings that can be learned by a deterministic DEC grammar is exactly the class of rational numbers between 0 and 1. I call this the class of semi-periodic or rational strings. Dynamically Expanding Context (Dec) grammars were introduced by Kohonen in order to model speech signals ([8]). They can be learned in quadratic time in the size of the grammar. They have been used successfully in the automatic generation and analysis of music ([7], [5], [6]).

1 DEC Grammars

Kohonen [8] originally developed the idea of Dynamically Expanding Context (DEC) grammars. DEC grammars are interesting because they are very easy to learn (polynomial complexity) and they have interesting potential applications. They have been applied successfully to, among other things, musical composition ([7], [6]). Adriaans en van Dungen [5] have developed an implementation of k-DEC grammars that can be used for real time online learning[1]. k-DEC grammars are powerful enough to produce a subjectively acceptable representation of the aspects of the style of a composer like Bach. Yet, it is not even clear whether DEC grammars in their pure deterministic form are grammars in the proper sense of the word, since each grammar only recognizes one infinite string. In this context the DEC languages are much more restricted than the so-called ω-languages that have been studied by various authors ([4], [3], [2], [1]). The basic idea behind DEC-grammars is the notion that the occurrence of a symbol in a string is determined by its predecessors. A DEC-grammar consists of rules that determine which symbol can occur in which context. A context is a string of symbols that precedes a symbol. A rule of a DEC-grammar has the following form:

$$X \Rightarrow y$$

Here X is a context, y is a symbol. These rules can be used to generate a string of symbols: in context X write symbol y. We will study a limited set of languages

---

[1] Musical compositions and improvisations made with the Instant Composer Tool (ICT), based on DEC grammars, created by Adriaans and Van Dungen can be downloaded http://www.pieter-adriaans.com/music.html

Y. Sakakibara et al. (Eds.): ICGI 2006, LNAI 4201, pp. 320–326, 2006.

generated by deterministic DEC-grammars. These grammars generate finite or infinite strings. Use S for a start symbol. The infinite string:

$$Sababababababab\ldots$$

is described by the DEC-grammar:

$$S \Rightarrow a,\ a \Rightarrow b,\ b \Rightarrow a$$

The string:

$$Sabdbebab$$

is described by the DEC-grammar:

$$S \Rightarrow a,\ a \Rightarrow b,\ ab \Rightarrow d,\ d \Rightarrow b,\ db \Rightarrow e,\ e \Rightarrow b,\ eb \Rightarrow a$$

If we use this grammar to generate a string starting from the symbol S we get:

$$Sabdbebabdbebabdbebabdbebabdbebabdbebabdbeb\ldots$$

The algorithm to learn a DEC-grammar (i.e. to find a DEC-Grammar which describes a particular string) is very simple. Say you want to find a DEC-Grammar for the string $Sabae$. You start to read the first symbol of the string, and you form the rule: $S \Rightarrow a$. Then you read the next symbol (which is b) and you form the rule: $a \Rightarrow b$ You proceed along these lines, generating rules, until you obtain the grammar:

$$S \Rightarrow a,\ a \Rightarrow b,\ b \Rightarrow a,\ a \Rightarrow e$$

This grammar is not deterministic anymore, because there are two possible successors of a, namely b and e. In order to repair this you update the rules in the grammar that violate the deterministic structure by expanding their context as necessary: $(a \Rightarrow b)$ is replaced by $(Sa \Rightarrow b)$ and $(a \Rightarrow e)$ is replaced by $(ba \Rightarrow e)$. The final grammar becomes:

$$S \Rightarrow a,\ Sa \Rightarrow b,\ b \Rightarrow a\ ba \Rightarrow e$$

This grammar only generates a finite string, because there is no rule of the form $\ldots e \Rightarrow \ldots$. From these examples it is clear that DEC grammars do not always distinguish between finite and infinite strings. In order to avoid problems with finite strings I will in the rest of the paper only deal with infinite strings. Finite strings can be modelled using a special blank symbol $-$. The string $Sabae$ then becomes $Sabae - - - \ldots$ and the corresponding grammar is:

$$S \Rightarrow a,\ Sa \Rightarrow b,\ b \Rightarrow a\ ba \Rightarrow e\ e \Rightarrow -,\ - \Rightarrow -$$

1.1 Numbers and Strings

Intuitively an infinite string with a finite DEC grammar must have a repeating pattern. To formalize this intuition we turn our attention to number theory. We use the standard number classes:

Definition 1. N (Z+) *is the set of natural numbers* $1, 2, 3 \ldots$
Z *the set of whole numbers or integers* $\ldots - 3, -2, -1, 0, 1, 2, 3 \ldots$.
Q *the set of rational numbers (expressible as p/q where p and q are integers)*,
R *the set of real numbers. An algebraic number is expressible as the root of a polynomial with integer coefficients. Non-algebraic numbers are transcendental.*

We need corresponding notions for strings. Let A be a finite alphabet. We define:

- A^*: the set of all finite strings consisting of elements of A.
- A^k: the set of all strings of length k consisting of elements of A.
- $A^{<k}$: the set of all strings of length less than k consisting of elements of A.
- A^∞: the set of all infinite strings consisting of elements of A.
- $[0, 1) \subset \mathbf{R}$ The interval between 0 (included) and 1 (not included).

Important are the set of binary strings $\{0, 1\}^*$ and the set of decimal strings $\{0, 1, 2, 3, 4, 5, 6, 7, 8, 9\}^*$.

Fact 1. *There is a one to one correspondence between elements of A^∞ and $[0, 1) \subset \mathbf{R}$. Each element of A^∞ corresponds with a unique fraction in a number system with base (radix) A.*[2]

Take the set of decimal fractions x such that $0 \leq x < 1$ and the associated set of strings $\{0, 1, 2, 3, 4, 5, 6, 7, 8, 9\}^\infty$. There are *terminating decimals* like $5/8 = 0.625$ and *non-terminating decimals* like $1/3 = 0.333 \ldots$ With each terminating decimal I will associate an infinite string with a tail of zero's: like $5/8 = 0.625000$ The non-terminating decimals can be periodic, i.e. $2/7 = 285714 \ldots$ where the block of digits 285714 repeats itself indefinitely.

We will call a decimal fraction $0.n$ semi-periodic if it is either finite or periodic with an initial arbitrary segment.

Theorem 2. $0.n$ *is a semi-periodic decimal fraction if and only if $0.n$ is rational.*

Proof: (*If*) We first take the simple periodic case. Suppose $0.n$ is a periodic decimal with a repeating block d with length $|d| = l$. In this case $0.n = d/(10^l - 1)$ which is a rational number. The semi-periodic case follows from the fact that **Q** is closed for addition and subtraction.
(*Only if*) Suppose $0.n$ is rational. We have $p/q = 0.n$. Consider the standard division algorithm. A division by q will have at most $q - 1$ rest values. Dividing by q therefore is either terminating or has a repeating block of at most $q - 1$ digits, i.e. it is semi-periodic.

Definition 2. *Suppose $0.n$ is a semi-periodic decimal fraction. The string n in $\{0, 1, 2, 3, 4, 5, 6, 7, 8, 9\}^\infty$, with possibly an infinite tail of zero's, is called a semi-periodic or rational string.*

Definition 3. *A deterministic connected DEC grammar is a triple $< \Sigma, P, S >$ where:*

---

[2] Strictly spoken the one to one correspondence is between representations of elements of A^∞ and $[0, 1) \subset \mathbf{R}$. Note that $0.9999... = 1.0$.

- Σ is a finite set of terminals.
- $S \in \mathbf{N}$ is a start symbol.
- P is a finite set consisting of the initial rule $S \Rightarrow \xi$ and a finite set of concatenation rules of the form $\eta \Rightarrow \xi$, where $\xi \in \Sigma$ and $\eta \in \Sigma^*$.

If we have a string $\delta \bullet \eta$ then the rule $\eta \Rightarrow \xi$ allows us to create $\delta \bullet \eta \bullet \xi$ ($\delta \in \Sigma^*$). The rules $\eta \Rightarrow \xi$ are deterministic, connected and minimal.

- Deterministic: no η is a prefix of any other η' nor identical.
- Connected: for each finite s string that can be constructed from the start symbol there is a rule $\eta \Rightarrow \eta \bullet \xi$ such that η is a postfix of s.
- Minimal: there are no superfluous rules.

Each DEC grammar generates a unique infinite string from the initial symbol. Let $\bullet$ be a concatenation operator and let S_i ($i \in \mathcal{N}$) be the finite string $S \bullet s_1 \bullet \ldots \bullet si$.

An algorithm for learning deterministic DEC grammars

```
Start
    Input: An infinite string s = S • s₁ • s₂ • s₃ • ...
    P =: {S ⇒ S • s₁}
    c =: 1
    Loop
        s = S_{c-1} • s_c • s_{c+1} • ... (S_{c-1} possibly empty)
        P' =: P ∪ {s_c ⇒ s_{c+1}}
        P =: make-deterministic(P', S_{c+1})
        c =: c + 1
    EndLoop
End

make-deterministic(P, S_c)
    If
        There are two rules η ⇒ ξ and η' ⇒ ξ' such that
        either η' = η or η' is a proper prefix of η.
    then
        Do
        If
            η' is a proper prefix of η
        then
            P=: expand-context(P, S_c, η' ⇒ ξ')
        If
            η' = η
        then
            P=: expand-context(P, S_c, η' ⇒ ξ')
            P=: expand-context(P, S_c, η ⇒ ξ)
        Od
    else
```

```
    Do nothing
```

expand-context$(P, S_c, \eta \Rightarrow \xi)$

```
    Do
        S_c = S_i • s_{i+1} • η • ξ • δ
        (ξ and s_{i+1} in Σ, S_i and δ in Σ* and possibly empty)
        P' =: (P − (η ⇒ ξ)) ∪ (s_{i+1} • η ⇒ ξ)
        make-deterministic(P', S_c)
    Od
```

Definition 4. *An infinite string s can be learned by a deterministic DEC grammar if there is a constant c such that after scanning s_c the rule set P stabilizes, i.e. P has a finite set of rules with finite heads.*

Theorem 3. *A string can be learned by a deterministic DEC grammar if and only if it is semi-periodic.*

Proof: (*If*) Suppose a string s is deterministic DEC learnable. Since the rules in P in the limit are finite deterministic and connected there must be a point in s where the rules start to loop, i.e. s must be semi-periodic.
(*Only if*) Suppose s is semi-periodic with an indefinitely repeating block d after some s_c for a constant c. Take $k = 2c$. Run k loops of the learning algorithm. Suppose that in the k-th loop we construct a rule $\eta \Rightarrow sk$.
Case 1) $|\eta| \leq c$. In this case η is a suffix of the periodic part of Sk. Therefore it will not be updated in consecutive loops.
Case 2) $|\eta| > c$. Here η consists of three parts $\eta = si • \mu • \nu$. ($\mu, \nu \in \Sigma^*$, $si \in \Sigma$) such that ν lies in the periodic part of Sk and μ in the non-periodic part. By its construction P will also contain a second rule $sj • \mu • \nu \Rightarrow sl$ ($sk \neq sl$, $si \neq sj$). This is a contradiction since $si • \mu • \nu$ is a suffix of $Sk - 1$ that is longer than $|Sk|/2$. So after k loops only rules with heads in the periodic part of the string will be created. The number of prefix free rules of this form that can exist is d. Therefore P will stabilize after at most k loops.

Lemma 1. *Suppose s is semi-periodic with an indefinitely repeating block d after some s_c for a constant c. An upperbound for the complexity of learning a DEC grammar for s is $O(c'k^2)$ where c' is constant and $k = 2c$.*

The proof of this lemma is immediate clear from the proof of theorem 3 and the observation that the algorithm has to scan a prefix of a length of maximally k of the string s at each pass of the central loop.

Lemma 2. *An infinite string is deterministic DEC learnable if and only if there exists a rational number that describes that string.*

This last lemma, that is a direct consequence of theorem 3, is a beautiful example of learning by compression. Each deterministic DEC grammar can be described by a rational number in a number system with the lexicon as its base.

To show that there are strings with short descriptions that are non periodic one only has to consider irrational numbers. The decimal expansion of the square root of 2 will be non-periodic. This holds in general for the class of so-called algebraic numbers: numbers that can be expressed as the root of a polynomial with integer coefficients. In this case $x^2 - 2 = 0$. The decimal expansions of transcendental numbers like e and π are also non-periodic but they have no algebraic definition.

1.2   Conclusion and Further Work

I have shown that DEC grammars can be learned easily in quadratic time and I have shown that the class of strings that can be learned in this way is equal to the class of rational numbers between 0 and 1. I believe that DEC grammars are interesting because they represent one of the simplest string analysis methods that I know. Further work would involve a deeper analysis of the possibilities to model musical styles. Another line of research would be aiming at a better understanding of the relation between various ω-languages and variants of DEC grammars. A specific deterministic DEC grammar only recognizes one infinite string. The whole class of strings that is recognized by the whole class of deterministic DEC grammars is exactly $\mathbf{Q}+$. The concept of DEC grammars might be weakened in various way in order to make the recognition of richer language classes possible. All these definitions focus on the structure of the rule set P:

Definition 5. *A non-deterministic DEC grammar is a DEC grammar in which the rule set P is non-deterministic, i.e. P is a finite set consisting of the initial rule $S \Rightarrow \xi$ and a finite set of concatenation rules of the form $\eta \Rightarrow \xi$, where $\xi \in \Sigma$ and $\eta \in \Sigma^*$, and where we can have two rules $\eta \Rightarrow \xi$ and $\eta \Rightarrow \xi'$ such that $\xi \neq \xi'$*
A stochastic DEC grammar is a tuple $< \Sigma, P, \mathcal{P}, S >$ such that $< \Sigma, P, S >$ is a non-deterministic DEC grammar and $\mathcal{P}$ is a probability distribution over P.
A k-DEC grammar is a non-deterministic DEC grammar for which the rules in P of the form $\eta \Rightarrow \xi$ satisfy $|\eta| \leq k$, i.e. the expansion of the contexts is limited to a ceiling k.

A detailed analysis of how these variants of DEC grammars behave in Büchi automata would be useful.

Acknowledgments. This project is supported by a BSIK grant from the Dutch Ministry of Education, Culture and Science (OC&W) and is part of the ICT innovation program of the Ministry of Economic Affairs (EZ).

References

1. de La Higuera C. and Janodet J. C., Inference of W-languages from prefixes, Theoretical Computer Science, vol. 313, 2, (2004), 295–312
2. Thomas, D. G., Humrosia Begam M., Subramanian K. G., Gnanasekaran S., Learning of Regular Bi-omega Languages, ICGI '02: Proceedings of the 6th International Colloquium on Grammatical Inference, (2002), 283–292

3. Thomas W., Automata on infinite objects, Handbook of theoretical computer science (vol. B): formal models and semantics, (1990), 133–191, MIT Press, Cambridge, MA, USA

4. Staiger L., ω-languages, Handbook of formal languages, vol. 3: beyond words, (1997), 339–387, Springer-Verlag New York, Inc., New York, NY, USA

5. Adriaans P., van Dungen M., A method for automatically controlling electronic musical devices by mean of real-time construction and search of a multi-level data structure, European Patent no. 1.062 656, United States Patent 6313390, (2001)

6. Kohonen T., Method for controlling an electronic musical device by utilizing search arguments and rules to generate digital code sequences, United States Patent 5418323, (1995)

7. Kohonen T., Laine P., Tiits K., Torkkola K., A Nonheuristic Automatic Composing Method, Music and Connectionism, MIT press, Peter M. Todd, D. Gareth Loy (eds.), (1991), 229–242

8. T. Kohonen, Dynamically Expanding Context, with application to the correction of symbol strings in the recognition of continuous speech, Proceedings of the 8th International Conference on Pattern Recognition (8th ICPR), Paris France, (1986), 1148–1151

Iso-array Acceptors and Learning

T. Kalyani[1], V.R. Dare[2], D.G. Thomas[2], and T. Robinson[2]

[1] Dept. of Mathematics, St. Joseph's College of Engineering, Chennai - 119, India
dgthomasmcc@yahoo.com
[2] Dept. of Mathematics, Madras Christian College, Tambaram, Chennai - 59, India
kalphd02@yahoo.com

Abstract. The notions of iso-arrays, iso-pictures, local iso-picture languages and recognizable iso-picture languages have been introduced and studied in [6]. In [6] we have provided an algorithm to learn local iso-picture languages through identification in the limit using positive data. In this paper, we construct a two-dimensional on-line tessellation automaton to recognize iso-picture languages and present an algorithm to learn recognizable iso-picture languages from positive data and restricted subset queries.

Keywords: Learning, iso-picture languages, recognizable iso-picture languages, two-dimensional on-line tessellation automaton.

1   Introduction

The first attempt at formalizing the concept of finite state recognizability for two-dimensional languages can be attributed to Blum and Hewitt who in [3] introduced the notion of a four way automaton moving on a two-dimensional tape as the natural extension of a one-dimensional two-way finite automaton. Since this work, several papers have been devoted to the study of the families of picture languages recognized by four-way automata and several other models of machines that read two dimensional tapes have been defined [4].

On the other hand, machine learning has been of great interest and much study has centered around the inductive inference of finite automata recognizing linear strings [1,2,5,7,9]. In [8], learning of certain classes of two-dimensional picture languages is considered.

Iso-arrays are made up of isosceles right angled triangles and an iso-picture is a picture formed by catenating iso-arrays of same size. We introduced the notion of iso-arrays, iso-pictures and iso-picture languages in [6]. A motivation for this study is that one can generate some interesting iso-picture languages which cannot be generated by earlier models available in the literature. In particular iso-picture languages include more picture languages like hexagonal picture languages, rectangular picture languages, languages of rhombuses and triangles. One application of the study of iso-picture languages is its use in the generation of interesting kolam patterns. Another application of this study lies in the area of tiling rectangular plane.

Y. Sakakibara et al. (Eds.): ICGI 2006, LNAI 4201, pp. 327–339, 2006.

In this paper we develop a recognizing device called two-dimensional on-line tessellation automaton to recognize iso-picture languages and provide examples. We have an interesting result that the class of all iso-picture languages recognized by two-dimensional on-line tessellation automata is exactly the family of iso-picture languages recognizable by iso-triangular tiling systems. We present a polynomial time algorithm that learns the class of recognizable iso-picture languages from positive data with restricted subset queries. Our approach is similar to the one that is proposed in [9].

2   Preliminaries

In this section we recall the notions of iso-pictures, iso-picture languages and iso-triangular tiling systems proposed in [6].

Let $\Sigma = \{$ $a_1\!\!\triangle\! a_3 \atop a_2$, $b_2\!\!\triangledown\! b_1 \atop b_3$, $c_3\!\!\triangleright\! c_2 \atop c_1$, $d_1\!\!\triangleleft\! d_2 \atop d_3$ $\}$ be a finite set of labeled isosceles right angled triangular tiles of dimensions $\frac{1}{\sqrt{2}}, \frac{1}{\sqrt{2}}$ and 1 unit, obtained by intersecting a unit square by its diagonals.

Definition 1. *Consider a tile $T \in \{A, B, C, D\}$. The left neighbour of T is the tile that occurs to the left side of T. This is denoted by $N(l, T)$. The left up neighbour of T is the tile that occurs to the left side of T and above it. This is denoted by $N(l_u, T)$. Similarly $N(l_d, T)$, $N(r, T)$, $N(r_u, T)$, $N(r_d, T)$, $N(u, T)$ and $N(d, T)$ are respectively the left down, right, right up, right down, up and down neighbours of T. It is possible that T does not have all the eight neighbours. The eight directions are indicated in the following diagram. Suppose $T = A$.*

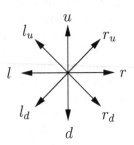

Then $N(r, A) = B$, $N(r_u, A) = C$, $N(r_d, A) = \phi$, $N(l, A) = B$,
$N(l_u, A) = D$, $N(l_d, A) = \phi$, $N(u, A) = \phi$, $N(d, A) = B$.
In a similar manner the neighbours of the tiles B, C and D can be defined.

Definition 2. *An iso-array of size $m(m \geq 1)$ is an isosceles right-angled triangular arrangement of elements of Σ, whose equal sides are denoted as S_1 and S_3 and the unequal side as S_2. It consists of m tiles along the side S_2 and it contains m^2 gluable elements of Σ. Iso-arrays can be classified as U-iso-array, D-iso-array, R-iso-array and L-iso-array, if tiles A, B, D and C are used in side S_2 respectively.*

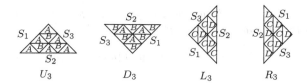

Fig. 1.

For example the U-iso-array of size 3 (U_3), D-iso-array of size 3 (D_3), L-iso-array of size 3 (L_3) and R-iso-array of size 3 (R_3) are shown in Fig. 1.

Iso-arrays of same size can be catenated using the following catenation operations. *Horizontal catenation* $\ominus$ is defined between U and D iso-arrays of same size. *Right catenation* $\oslash$ is defined between any two gluable iso-arrays of same size. This catenation includes the following:
(a) $D \oslash U$ (b) $U \oslash R$ (c) $D \oslash L$ (d) $R \oslash L$.
In a similar way vertical $\oslash$ and left $\oslash$ catenations can be defined.

Definition 3. *Let Σ be a finite alphabet of iso-triangular tiles. An iso-picture of size $(n, m), n, m \geq 1$ over Σ is a picture formed by catenating n-iso-arrays of size m. The number of tiles in any iso-picture of size (n, m) is nm^2.*

An element of an iso-picture p of size (n, m) is represented as $p(i, j, k)$, where i is the ith iso-array of the picture and j is the jth row of the ith iso-array and k is the kth element of jth row of the ith iso-array, where $i = 1, 2, \ldots, n$, $j = 1, 2, \ldots, m$ and $k = 1, 2, \ldots, 2j-1$. The set of all iso-pictures over the alphabet Σ is denoted by Σ_I^{**}. An iso-picture language L over Σ is a subset of Σ_I^{**}.

Definition 4. *Let p be an iso-picture of size (n, m). We denote by $B_{n', m'}(p)$, the set of all sub iso-pictures of p of size (n', m'), where $n' \leq n, m' \leq m$. $\hat{p}$ is an iso-picture obtained by surrounding p with a special boundary symbols*

 $\notin \Sigma$.

Definition 5. *An iso-picture language $L \subseteq \Sigma_I^{**}$ is called local if there exists a*

finite set θ of iso-arrays of size 2 over $\Sigma \cup \{$ $\}$ such that $L = \{p \in \Sigma_I^{**} / B_{1,2}(\hat{p}) \subseteq \theta\}$ and is denoted by $L(\theta)$.
The family of local iso-picture languages will be denoted by $ILOC$.
The iso-picture language of parallelograms over the tiles A, B is local and the iso-picture language of rhombuses over the tiles A, B is non local.

Definition 6. *Let $p \in \Sigma_I^{**}$ be an iso-picture. Let Σ and Γ be two finite alphabets and $\pi : \Gamma \to \Sigma$ be a mapping which we call, a projection. The projection by mapping π of picture p is the picture $p' \in \Sigma_I^{**}$ such that $p'(i, j, k) = \pi(p(i, j, k))$ for all $1 \leq i \leq n, 1 \leq j \leq m, 1 \leq k \leq 2j - 1$, where (n, m) is the size of the iso-picture. In this case $p' = \pi(p)$.*

Definition 7. *Let $L \subset \Gamma_I^{**}$ be an iso-picture language. The projection by mapping π of L is the language $L' = \{p'/p' = \pi(p) \forall p \in L\} \subseteq \Sigma_I^{**}$.*

We will denote by $\pi(L)$ the projection by mapping π of an iso picture language L.

Definition 8. *Let Σ be a finite alphabet. An iso-picture language $L \subseteq \Sigma_I^{**}$ is called recognizable if there exists a local iso-picture language L' over an alphabet Γ and a mapping $\pi : \Gamma \to \Sigma$ such that $L = \pi(L')$.*

The family of all recognizable iso-picture languages will be denoted by $IREC$.

Definition 9. *An iso-triangular tiling system IT is a 4-tuple $(\Sigma, \Gamma, \pi, \theta)$ where Σ and Γ are two finite sets of symbols, $\pi : \Gamma \to \Sigma$ is a projection and θ is a set of iso-arrays of size 2 over the alphabet $\Gamma \cup \{\triangle^{\#A}, \triangledown^{\#B}\}$.*

Definition 10. *An iso-picture language $L \subseteq \Sigma_I^{**}$ is tiling recognizable if there exists an iso-triangular tiling system $IT = (\Sigma, \Gamma, \pi, \theta)$ such that $L = \pi(L'(\theta))$, where $L'(\theta)$ is a local iso-picture language. We write $L = L(IT)$, and we say that L is the language recognized by IT. We denote by $\mathcal{L}(ITS)$ the family of all iso-picture languages recognizable by iso-triangular tiling systems.*

It is easy to see that $IREC$ is exactly the family of iso-picture languages tiling recognizable by iso-triangular tiling systems ($\mathcal{L}(ITS)$). i.e., $IREC = \mathcal{L}(ITS)$.

Example 1.

Let $\theta = \{$  $\}$

Then $L' = L'(\theta)$ is the local iso-picture language of rhombuses, where the diagonals are represented by the tiles $\triangle^{A2}$ and $\triangledown^{B2}$ and the tiles in the remaining positions are represented by tiles $\triangle^{A1}$ and $\triangledown^{B1}$, a member of which is shown in Fig. 2.

Applying the projection $\pi(A1) = \pi(A2) = A$ and $\pi(B1) = \pi(B2) = B$, we get $L = \pi(L')$. Therefore L, the language of rhombuses over the iso-triangular tiles A and B is a recognizable iso-picture language.

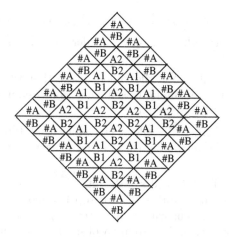

Fig. 2.

3   Automata for Iso-picture Languages

We define a two-dimensional on-line tessellation automaton referred to as $IPOTA$, to accept iso-picture languages. For simplicity we restrict the alphabet to have two tiles. This study can be extended for the alphabet having four tiles.

Definition 11. *A non-deterministic (deterministic) two-dimensional on-line tessellation automaton (IPOTA) is $\mathcal{A} = (\Sigma, Q, I, F, \delta)$ where Σ is an input alphabet {* $a_1\!\!\triangle\!a_3^{a_2}, \, b_3\!\!\overset{b_2}{\triangledown}\!b_1$ *}, Q is a finite set of states, $I \subseteq Q$ is the set of initial states, $F \subseteq Q$ is the set of final states and $\delta : Q \times Q \times \Sigma \to 2^Q$ ($\delta : Q \times Q \times \Sigma \to Q$) is the transition function.*

A run of $\mathcal{A}$ on an iso-picture $p \in \Sigma_I^{**}$ consists of associating a state from the set Q to each position (i, j, k) of p, such state is given by the transition function δ and depends on the states already associated.

A computation by a two-dimensional on-line tessellation automaton ($IPOTA$) on an iso-picture p of size (n, m), where $p_{ijk} \in \Sigma$, for $i = 1, 2, \ldots, n, j = 1, 2, \ldots, m, k = 1, 2, \ldots, 2j - 1$, and $\triangle\!{}_{\#A}, \, \overset{\#B}{\triangledown}$ are symbols not in Σ is given by the following algorithm.

Algorithm : Computation of a two-dimensional on-line tessellation automaton ($IPOTA$) to accept an iso-picture p of size (n, m).
Procedure :

1. At time $t = 0$, an initial state $q_0 \in I$ is associated with all the positions of $\hat{p}$ holding $\triangle\!{}_{\#A}, \, \overset{\#B}{\triangledown}$.

2. Scan p to get the left most vertex of p. It can be incident with either $\triangle^A$ tile or ∇^B tile or both tiles. Now consider the following: Suppose the left most vertex of p is

   (a) incident with only $\triangle^A$ tile. Then, name that tile as p_{111} and assign $i = 1$. Name the remaining tiles in that iso-array of size m according to their positions. Go to step 3.

   (b) incident with only ∇^B tile. Then name that tile as p_{111} and assign $i = 1$. Name the remaining tiles in that iso-array of size m according to their positions.

   (c) incident with both the tiles $\triangle^A$ and ∇^B. In this case scan p to get either the top most vertex of p or top left most vertex of p and then name the tile incident with that vertex as p_{111} and assign $i = 1$. Name the remaining tiles in that iso-array of size m according to their positions.

3. Scan p to get $N(r, p_{im1})$
   Repeat

   > If $N(r, p_{im1}) = \nabla^B$ then
   > (i) $i = i + 1$
   > (ii) name ∇^B as p_{i11} and then name the remaining tiles in that iso-array of size m according to their positions.
   > scan p to get $N(u, p_{i11})$
   >
   > If $N(u, p_{i11}) = \triangle^{\#A}$, Go to step 4
   > else if $N(u, p_{i11}) = \triangle^A$ then
   > (i) $i = i + 1$
   > (ii) name $\triangle^A$ as p_{i11} and then name the remaining tiles in that iso-array of size m according to their positions.
   > scan p to get $N(r, p_{im1})$

   Until $(N(r, p_{im1}) = \nabla^{\#B})$

4. If $N(r, p_{im1}) = \nabla^{\#B}$ then $j = i$

   If $N(u, p_{i11}) = \triangle^{\#A}$ then $j = i - 1$
   At time $t = 1$ states are associated simultaneously with positions holding
   $p_{111}, p_{121}, \ldots, p_{1m1}, p_{311}, p_{321}, \ldots, p_{3m1}, \ldots, p_{j11}, p_{j21}, \ldots, p_{jm1}$.
   The transition function δ is defined as
   $\delta(q_0, q_0, p_{lk1}) = s_{lk1}, l = 1, 3, \ldots, j, k = 1, 2, \ldots, m$.

   We view $\delta(q_0, q_0, p_{lk1}) = s_{lk1}$ as $\overset{q_0}{\underset{q_0 \quad p_{lk1}}{\bowtie}}$.

   At time $t = 2$ states are associated simultaneously with positions holding
   $p_{112}, p_{122}, \ldots, p_{1(m-1)2}, p_{211}, p_{312}, p_{322}, \ldots, p_{3(m-1)2}, p_{411}, \ldots, p_{j12}, p_{j22}, \ldots, p_{j(m-1)2}$.
   The transition function δ is defined as
   (i) $\delta(s_{lk1}, s_{l(k+1)1}, p_{lk2}) = s_{lk2}, l = 1, 3, \ldots, j, k = 1, 2, \ldots, m - 1$.

(i) $\delta(s_{(l-1)m1}, s_{(l+1)11}, p_{l11}) = s_{l11}, l = 2, 4, \ldots, j.$

We view $\delta(s_{lk1}, s_{l(k+1)1}, p_{lk2}) = s_{lk2}$ as [iso-array tile diagram with $s_{l(k+1)1}$, p_{lk2}, s_{lk1}] .

Similarly the transition functions can be defined at times $t = 3, 4, 5, \ldots, 2m$ according to the positions of the iso-arrays.

5. If $N(r, p_{im1}) = $ [▽ #B] then

   begin

   > $j = i - 1,$
   >
   > ⊛ scan p to get $N(r, p_{jm1})$
   >
   > If $N(r, p_{jm1}) = $ [△ #A], Go to ⊛⊛
   >
   > else if $N(r, p_{jm1}) = $ [△ A] then
   >
   > (i) $i = i + 1$
   >
   > (ii) name [△ A] as p_{i11} and then name the remaining tiles in that iso-array of size m according to their positions.
   >
   > scan p to get $N(d, p_{i11})$
   >
   > If $N(d, p_{i11}) = $ [▽ #B] , Go to ⊛⊛
   >
   > else if $N(d, p_{i11}) = $ [▽ B] then
   >
   > (i) $i = i + 1$
   >
   > (ii) name [▽ B] as p_{i11} and then name the remaining tiles in that iso-array of size m according to their positions.
   >
   > ⊛⊛ $j = j - 2$, if $j = 0$ Go to 7
   >
   > Go to ⊛

6. If $N(u, p_{i11}) = $ [△ #A] then

   > $j = i.$ Go to ⊛ of 5

7. At times $t = 2m + 1, 2m + 2, \ldots, 4m$, the transition functions can be defined according to the positions of the iso-arrays.

8. This process continues (3 to 7) till a state is associated to position $(n, m, 1)$. Similar procedure can be given for the other two cases (b and c) of 2.

A two-dimensional on-line tessellation automaton $IPOTA$ recognizes an iso-picture p if there exists a run of $\mathcal{A}$ on $\hat{p}$ such that the state associated to position $(n, m, 1)$ is a final state. The set of all iso-pictures recognised by $\mathcal{A}$ is denoted by $L(\mathcal{A})$. Let $\mathcal{L}(IPOTA)$ be the set of iso-picture languages recognized by $IPOTAs$. Given an iso-picture p of size (n, m) the run of $IPOTA$ on $\hat{p}$ takes nm^2 units of time.

As an example of $IPOTA$ a computation by a two-dimensional $IPOTA$ on iso-picture language of rhombuses p of size $(2, m)$ where $p_{ijk} \in \Sigma$ and [△ #A], [▽ #B] are symbols not in Σ is done as follows:

1. At time $t = 0$, an initial state $q_0 \in I$ is associated with all the positions of $\hat{p}$ (shown in Fig. 3) holding [△ #A] and [▽ #B] .

$$\hat{p} =$$

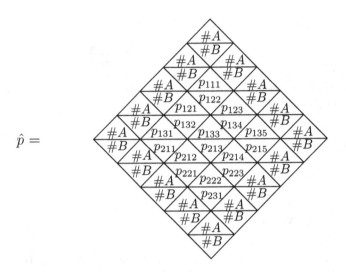

Fig. 3.

2. Scan p to get the left most vertex of p. It is incident with both the tiles and . In this case scan p to get the top most vertex of p name the tile incident with that vertex as p_{111}, $i = 1$, name the remaining tiles in that iso-array of size m according to their positions.

3. Scan p to get the down neighbour of p_{1m1}. If $N(d, p_{1m1}) =$, then $i = i+1$, name as p_{i11}, name the remaining tiles in that iso-array of size m according to their positions.

4. At time $t = 1$, states are associated simultaneously with positions holding $p_{111}, p_{121}, \ldots, p_{1m1}$. States $s_{1j1}, j = 1, \ldots, m$ from $\delta(q_0, q_0, p_{1j1})$ are associated with positions $p_{1j1}, j = 1, 2, \ldots, m$.

5. At time $t = 2$, states are associated simultaneously with positions $(1, 2, 2)$, $(1, 3, 2), \ldots, (1, m, 2), (2, 1, 1)$ respectively holding $p_{122}, p_{132}, \ldots, p_{1m2}, p_{211}$. State associated with the position p_{1j2} is an element of $\delta(s_{1j1}, s_{1(j-1)1}, p_{1j2})$, $j = 2, \ldots, m$. State associated with the position p_{211} is an element of $\delta(q_0, s_{1m1}, p_{211})$. We then proceed to the next diagonal.

6. (a) The state associated with each position $(1, j, k)$ where $k \neq 2j - 1$ by the transition function δ, depends on the states already associated with the positions $(1, j, k - 1), (1, j - 1, k - 1)$ and the symbol p_{1jk}.

   (b) The state associated with each position $(1, j, 2j - 1)$ by the transition function δ, depends on the state already associated with the position $(1, j, 2j - 2)$ and the position holding boundary symbol $\#$.

   Let $s_{1jk}, j = 1, 2, \ldots, m, k = 1, 2, \ldots, 2j - 1$ be the state associated with the position $(1, j, k)$ where the entry is p_{1jk}.

7. (a) The state associated with each position $(2, 1, k), k = 1, 2, \ldots, 2m - 1$, by the transition function δ, depends on the states already associated with the positions $(2, 1, k - 1), (1, m, k)$ and the symbol p_{21k}.

(b) The state associated with each position $(2, j, k)$, $j = 2, \ldots, m$, $k = 2, \ldots, 2j - 1$ by the transition function δ depends on the states already associated with the positions $(2, j, k-1), (2, j-1, k+1)$ and the symbol p_{2jk}.

(c) The state associated with each position $(2, j, 1), j = 2, \ldots, m$ by the transition function δ depends on the state already associated with the positions $(2, j-1, 2)$ and the position holding the boundary symbol $\#$.

This process continues till a state is associated to position $(2, m, 1)$. An $IPOTA$ recognizes an iso-picture p if there exists a run of $\mathcal{A}$ on $\hat{p}$ such that the state associated to position $(2, m, 1)$ is a final state.

Example 2. A two-dimensional on-line tessellation automaton to recognize the local iso-picture language $L(\theta)$ shown in Example 1 is given by:
$\mathcal{A}_1 = (\Sigma, Q, \{q_0\}, F, \delta)$
where $\Sigma = \{\triangle^{A_1}, \triangle^{A_2}, \triangledown^{B_1}, \triangledown^{B_2}\}$
$Q = \{q_0, q_1, q_2, q_3, q_4\}$, $F = \{q_4\}$ and
$\delta(q_0, q_0, A_2) = q_2$; $\delta(q_3, q_0, A_2) = q_2$ $\delta(q_0, q_0, A_1) = q_1$; $\delta(q_3, q_0, A_1) = q_1$
$\delta(q_1, q_2, B_2) = q_4$; $\delta(q_4, q_0, A_1) = q_1$ $\delta(q_1, q_1, B_1) = q_3$; $\delta(q_3, q_4, A_2) = q_2$
$\delta(q_2, q_1, B_1) = q_3$; $\delta(q_3, q_3, A_1) = q_1$ $\delta(q_0, q_2, B_2) = q_4$; $\delta(q_3, q_3, A_2) = q_2$
$\delta(q_3, q_4, A_1) = q_1$; $\delta(q_4, q_3, A_1) = q_1$ $\delta(q_0, q_1, B_1) = q_3$.

Example 3. A two-dimensional on-line tessellation automaton to accept the recognizable iso-picture language of rhombuses over two letters $\triangle^{A}$ and $\triangledown^{B}$ is given by:
$\mathcal{A}_2 = (\Sigma, Q, \{q_0\}, F, \delta)$
where $\Sigma = \{\triangle^{A}, \triangledown^{B}\}$, $Q = \{q_0, q_1, q_2, q_3\}$, $F = \{q_2\}$ and
$\delta(q_0, q_0, A) = q_1$ $\delta(q_1, q_1, B) = q_2$ $\delta(q_0, q_1, B) = q_2$ $\delta(q_2, q_0, A) = q_3$
$\delta(q_2, q_2, A) = q_3$ $\delta(q_3, q_3, B) = q_2$ $\delta(q_0, q_3, B) = q_2$.

4   Results

In this section, we show that $\mathcal{L}(IPOTA) = \mathcal{L}(ITS)$. To prove this, we have the following lemmas.

Lemma 1. *If an iso-picture language is recognized by an $IPOTA$, then it is recognized by a finite iso-triangular tiling system. i.e., $\mathcal{L}(IPOTA) \subseteq \mathcal{L}(ITS)$.*

Proof. Let $L \in \Sigma_I^{**}$ be a language recognized by a two-dimensional on-line tessellation automaton $\mathcal{A} = (\Sigma, Q, I, F, \delta)$. We have to show that there exists an iso-triangular tiling system IT that recognizes L.

Let $IT = (\Sigma, \Gamma, \theta, \pi)$ be an iso-triangular tiling system such that

$$\Gamma = (\Sigma \cup \{\#\}) \times Q. \quad \theta = \bigcup_{i=1}^{18} \theta_i$$

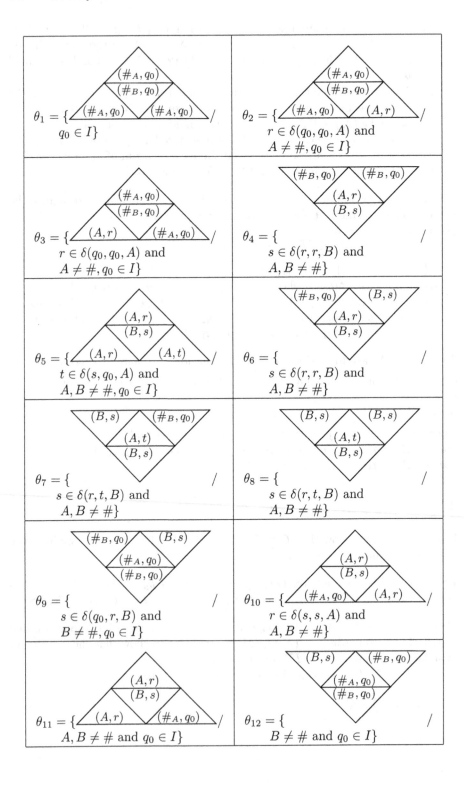

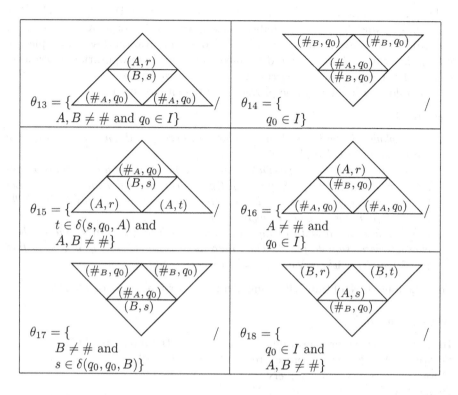

$\pi : \Sigma \cup \{\#\} \times Q \to \Sigma$ is such that $\pi(a, q) = a$, $\forall\, a \in \Sigma \cup \{\#\}, q \in Q$.

We notice that the set θ is defined in a way that a picture p' of the underlying local iso-picture language of $L(IT)$ describes exactly a run of $IPOTA$ $\mathcal{A}$ on $p = \pi(p')$. Then it is easy to verify that $L(A) = L(IT)$.

Lemma 2. *If an iso-picture language is recognizable by a finite iso-triangular tiling system then it is recognizable by a two-dimensional on-line tessellation automaton i.e., $\mathcal{L}(ITS) \subseteq \mathcal{L}(IPOTA)$.*

Proof. Let $L \subseteq \Sigma_I^{**}$ be a language recognized by the iso-triangular tiling system $(\Sigma, \Gamma, \theta, \pi)$ and L' is the underlying local language represented by the set of tiles θ. i.e., $\pi(L') = L$. It suffices to show that there exists an $IPOTA$ recognizing $L' \subseteq \Sigma_I^{**}$.

Lemma 3. *If L is a local iso-picture language, then it is recognizable by an $IPOTA$. i.e., $ILOC \subseteq \mathcal{L}(IPOTA)$.*

The proof of this lemma is omitted.

5   Learning of Recognizable Iso-picture Languages

In [6] we have provided an algorithm to learn local iso-picture languages through identification in the limit using positive data. In this section, we present an algorithm to learn recognizable iso-picture languages.

Let $\mathcal{A} = (\Sigma, Q, \{q_0\}, F, \delta)$ be an $IPOTA$ such that $L(\mathcal{A}) = L \in IREC$. Let $\Gamma = \Sigma \times Q$ and h_1, h_2 be alphabetic mappings on Γ given by $h_1(a, q) = a$, $h_2(a, q) = q$. An iso-picture p over Γ is called a computation description picture if $h_2(p)$ is a run of $\mathcal{A}$ on $h_1(p)$ and is called an accepting computation description picture if $h_2(p)$ is an accepting run. i.e., $\mathcal{A}$ recognizes $h_1(p)$.

The following lemma can be proved as in the case of strings.

Lemma 4.

1. The alphabet Γ contains $O(mn)$ elements where n is the number of states of the minimal $IPOTA$ $\mathcal{A}_L$ for L and $m = |\Sigma|$.
2. For $p \in L$, let $d(p)$ be an iso-picture over Γ representing an accepting computation description for p. $X(p) = h_2(d(p))$ is called a valid picture for p. Let $Val(p) = \{X(p)/X(p)$ is a valid picture for $p\}$. Then $|Val(p)| = O(n^{V(p)})$ where $V(p)$ is the product measure of p.
3. Let S be a local iso-picture language over Q such that $L = h(S)$ and R_S be a characteristic sample for S. Then there is a finite subset S_L of L such that $R_S \subseteq Val(S_L)$, where $Val(S_L) = \{Val(p)/p \in S(L)\}$.

From Lemma 4 we obtain a learning algorithm for languages of $IREC$.

Algorithm $IREC$

Input: A positive presentation of L, $n = |Q|$ for the minimal $IPOTA$ for L.
Output: A sequence of conjectures of the form $h(L(\theta))$.
Query: Restricted subset query.
Procedure:
    Initialize E_0 to ϕ
    Construct the initial $\theta_0 = \phi$
    Repeat (for ever)
        Let θ_i be the current conjecture
        read the next positive example p
        compute $Val(p) = \{\alpha_1, \alpha_2, \ldots, \alpha_t\}$
        for each j scan α_j to compute $\theta_{ij} = B_{1,2}(\hat{\alpha}_j)$
        ask if $h(L(\theta_{ij})) \subset L$ or not
        $Val(p) = Val(p) - \{\alpha_j/$ the answer is no$\}$
        $E_{i+1} = E_i \cup Val(p)$
        $\theta_{i+1} = \theta_i \cup \{B_{1,2}(\hat{\alpha})/\alpha \in Val(p)\}$
        Output θ_{i+1} as new conjecture.

Lemma 5. Let n be the number of states of the minimal $IPOTA$ accepting the recognizable iso-picture language L. After almost $t(n)$ subset queries, the algorithm $IREC$ produces a conjecture θ_i such that E_i includes a characteristic sample for a local iso-picture language U such that $L = h(U)$ where $t(n)$ is a polynomial in n, which depends on U.

This is a consequence of Lemma 4 and the fact that the maximum size for pictures in L is bounded by a polynomial in n. Summarizing, we obtain the following theorem.

Theorem 1. *Given an unknown recognizable iso-picture language L, the algorithm $IREC$ efficiently learns in the limit from positive data and restricted subset queries, a finite subset θ of $(\Sigma \cup \{\#\})^{1 \times 2}$ such that $L = h(L(\theta))$.*

Conclusion

In this paper, we developed a recognizing device called two-dimensional on-line tessellation automaton to recognize iso-picture languages. We have that the class of all iso-picture languages recognized by two-dimensional on-line tessellation automata is exactly the family of iso-picture languages recognizable by iso-triangular tiling systems (IT). We present an algorithm that learns the class of recognizable iso-picture languages from positive data with restricted subset queries.

References

1. D. Angluin, Inductive inference of formal languages from positive data, Information and Control, 45, 117-135, 1980.
2. D. Angluin, Learning regular sets from queries and counter examples, Inform. Comput, 75, 87-106, 1987.
3. M. Blum and C. Hewitt, Automata on a 2-dimensional tape, IEEE Symposium on switching and automata theory, 155-160 (1967).
4. D. Giammarresi and A. Restivo, Two-dimensional finite state recognizability, Fundamenta Informatica, 25(3,4), 399-422, (1996).
5. E.M. Gold, Language identification in the limit, Information and Control, 10, 447-474, 1967.
6. T. Kalyani, V.R. Dare and D.G. Thomas, Local and Recognizable iso Picture languages, Lecture Notes in Computer Science, 3316, (2004), 738-743.
7. Y. Sakakibara, Recent advances of grammatical inference, Theoretical Computer Science, 185, 15-45, (1997).
8. R. Siromoney, Lisa Mathew, K.G. Subramanian and V.R. Dare, Learning of Recognizable Picture Languages, International Journal of Pattern Recognition and Artificial Intelligence, 8, 627-639 (1994).
9. T. Yokomori, Learning local languages from positive data, In Proceedings of Fujitsu IIAS - SIS Workshop on Computational Learning Theory '89, 1-16, Numazu, 1989.

A Merging States Algorithm for Inference of *RFSAs**

Gloria Alvarez[1], Pedro García[2], and José Ruiz[2]

[1] Pontificia Universidad Javeriana - Seccional Cali. Colombia
[2] Universidad Politécnica de Valencia. Spain - DSIC
{galvarez@dsic, pgarcia, jruiz}.upv.es

Abstract. The aim of this paper is to present *MRIA*, a new merging states algorithm for inference of Residual Finite State Automata.

1 Introduction

We propose a non deterministic extension of *RPNI* algorithm, that will be called *MRIA* (**M**erging states **R**esidual finite state automata **I**nference **A**lgorithm). It extends *RPNI* finding inclusion relations among the residuals of the positive sample and merging states when it is possible or just keeping the transitions obtained from the inclusions.

MRIA outputs a *NFA* and converges to a *Residual Finite State Automaton* (*RFSA*) that recognizes the target language and which has the same number of states as the minimal *DFA* for that language. A postprocess can be done to the output automaton in order to obtain a *RFSA* of size between the canonical *RFSA* and the minimal *DFA* for the target language.

Definitions concerning Formal Languages can be found in [2]. Previous work related to *RFSAs* can be found in [1].

2 The *MRIA* Algorithm

Algorithm *MRIA* is a merging states algorithm that on input of a complete sample, outputs a non-deterministic finite state automaton which is consistent with the input.

The algorithm begins building the prefix tree acceptor of the positive sample, whose states are lexicographically ordered ($\ll$). It consists of two loops, the outer one takes care of the first state (q) that is being compared whereas the inner analyzes the states p such that $p \ll q$ in turn.

First it checks if p is *smaller* than q (that is, if the automaton that results of adding to the current one every transition of the form (q', a, q) for every existing transition of the form (q', a, p) does not recognize a negative sample. If q is an initial state, p is also added to I). If the answer is positive it keeps

---

* Work partially supported by Spanish CICYT under TIC2003-09319-C03-02 and Spanish GVA under GV06/068.

Y. Sakakibara et al. (Eds.): ICGI 2006, LNAI 4201, pp. 340–341, 2006.

the transitions resulting from this fact and if q has not been previously merged to a state previous to p, the comparison is checked in the other way. If both comparisons result positive, the states are merged. Two facts make this merging of states differ from the classical merging done by *RPNI*:

– The merges are not propagated to keep the automaton deterministic.
– A copy of state q is kept until the relations between q and all the previous states have been determined.

At the end of every inner loop, if the state q has not been merged with any previous one, a new hypothesis is emitted. This hypothesis is an automaton whose states are those previous to q and the transitions related to them.

Note that a state is only deleted when it has been compared with the rest of the previous ones. Otherwise, some transitions could not be obtained. That is the use of the boolean variable in the algorithm.

The complexity of the proposed algorithm is $O(n^3)$, being n the sum of the lengths of the input sample.

3   Example

Let $D_+ = \{\varepsilon, 00, 10, 11, 010\}$ and $D_- = \{0, 1, 01, 001\}$. The sequence of hypothesis emitted by *MRIA* and the output of *DeLeTe2* and *RPNI* under the same input are depicted in Fig. 1.

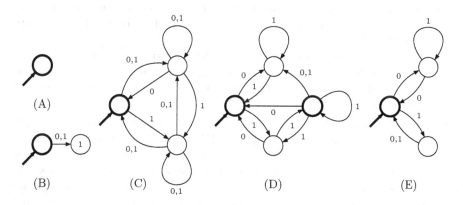

Fig. 1. A,B and C: Sequence of hypothesis emitted by *MRIA* algorithm. D and E hypothesis emitted by *DeLeTe2* and *RPNI* with the same input.

References

1. Denis, F. Lemay, A. and Terlutte, A. *Learning regular languages using RFSAs*. Theoretical Computer Science 313(2), pp 267-294 (2004).
2. Hopcroft, J. and Ullman, J. *Introduction to Automata Theory, Languages and Computation*. Addison-Wesley (1979).

Query-Based Learning of XPath Expressions*

Julien Carme, Michal Ceresna, and Max Goebel

Database and Artificial Intelligence Group,
Vienna University of Technology, Austria
{carme, ceresna, goebel}@dbai.tuwien.ac.at

Abstract. This work analyzes the application of active learning using example-based queries to the problem of constructing an XPath expression from visual interaction with an human user.

Keywords: XML, tree structured data, query based learning, XPath.

1 Introduction

XML is a widely used format for storing and publishing structured data. Formally, XML and also HTML documents are ordered and unranked trees with nodes labeled from an infinite alphabet Σ.

XPath [2] is a navigation language for XML documents, and it is an integral part of many other XML-related technologies. The XPath language consists of expressions whose formal grammar is defined in [2]. Let $p(t)$ denote the set of nodes of tree t navigated to via expression p, and let $p^?$ be the target XPath expression that should be learned.

Our aim is to build an algorithm where XPath expressions are constructed from interaction with a human user. That is, the user acts as an oracle for the learning algorithm. Therefore, we require that the queries can be easily answered in a visual manner.

Let us examine visualization of the most studied query types, the membership and equivalence queries. When applied to XML trees, an equivalence query is a question of the form $\forall t \in T_\Sigma \ : \ p(t) = p^?(t)$. Answers are either "yes" or "no", where for the latter we also return those nodes in the tree that witness the inequality as counterexamples. As is illustrated in Figure 1a, equivalence queries have a natural visualization. To answer them, the user simply marks missing or unwanted nodes inside of the currently rendered document. In practice, the universal quantification from the query is answered by testing the hypothesis on other XML documents given by the user.

Unfortunately, membership queries do not have a natural visualization. This is due to the fact that the trees $t \in T_\Sigma$ are chosen by the learning algorithm as part of the query itself, and existing algorithms generally construct these trees as a combination of sub-trees from previous examples. Such artificial trees are not

---

* This work was supported by the Austrian Science Fund under project No. L47-N04 and REWERSE, Network of Excellence, 6th European Framework Program.

Y. Sakakibara et al. (Eds.): ICGI 2006, LNAI 4201, pp. 342–343, 2006.

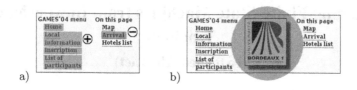

Fig. 1. Visualization of equivalence and membership queries

valid against the document schema or cannot be rendered, however. Moreover, the resulting document trees are confusing for the human user, resulting in an increase of the ratio of incorrect answers. Figure 1b illustrates an unnatural visualization, where the learning algorithm tries to insert an image.

2   Non-learnability Using Equivalence Queries

A learning algorithm using only equivalence queries would be an elegant solution for our application, circumventing difficulties with the visualization of other types of queries. However, using Angluin's definition of approximate fingerprints [1], we show non-learnability for several XPath fragments using only equivalence queries.

Theorem 1. *The XPath fragment with wild-card node matching (∗), child and descendant-or-self axes (/,//) has the approximate fingerprints.*

3   Conclusion

Our results show that many well studied types of queries such as membership, subset or superset queries are hard to use due to difficulties with their visualization. We show that equivalence queries—despite of having a natural visualization—are not strong enough to yield polynomial learnability results even for simple fragments.

References

1. Dana Angluin. Negative results for equivalence queries. *Machine Learning*, 5(2):121–150, 1990.
2. W3C Consortium. XML Path Language (XPath), 1999. Published on http://www.w3.org/TR/xpath/.

Learning Finite-State Machines from Inexperienced Teachers
(Extended Abstract)

Olga Grinchtein[1,*] and Martin Leucker[2]

[1] Department of Computer Systems, Uppsala University, Sweden
[2] Institut für Informatik, TU München, Germany

The general goal of query-based learning algorithms for finite-state machines is to identify a *machine*, usually of *minimum* size, that *agrees* with an *a priori* fixed (class of)
machines. For this, *queries* on how the underlying system behaves may be issued.

A popular setup is that of Angluin's L^* algorithm[Ang87], here adapted to the case of
finite-state machines, in which a minimal deterministic finite-state machine for a regular
language is learned based on so-called *membership* and *equivalence queries*. Using a
pictorial language, we have a *learner* whose job is to come up with the automaton to
learn, a *teacher* who may answer the output for a given input string as well an *oracle*
answering whether the automaton $\mathcal{H}$ currently proposed by the learner is correct or not.
This setting is depicted in Figure 1(a) (though assume that the *don't know* is not there).

In Angluin's setting, a teacher will always answer with the correct output symbol. In
many application scenarios, however, parts of the machine to learn are not completely
specified or not observable. Then, queries may be answered inconclusively, by *don't
know*, also denoted by ?.

In the full version of this paper [GL06], we study a learning algorithm (and variants
thereof), called ABSAT, ABSATI, and ABSATI2, that are designed to work with such
an *inexperienced* teacher. The oracle, however, does not change its functionality in the
setting discussed here (see Figure 1(a), the *don't know* is new).

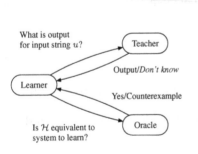

	bica	ABSAT	ABSATI	ABSATI2
	time	time	time	time
fo.70	n.a.	39.50	38.57	38.69
th.55	188.87	0.45	0.43	0.43
vmebus.master.m	59.93	1627.37	693.44	93.01
ifsm2	14.08	34.82	34.36	30.78
pe-send-ifc.fc	2.33	6.93	2.75	2.07
pe-send-ifc.fc.m	0.85	6.93	2.75	1.07
rubin1200	10.24	10.28	10.26	10.02
rubin2250	64.78	64.69	64.74	63.29
vbe4a	1.94	4.31	1.86	1.56
ex2	0.78	0.78	0.76	4.67

(a) L^* versus ABSAT   (b) Running times compared

Fig. 1. The setup for the learning algorithms and their performance

* Part of the work has been done during the author's stay at TU München supported by the
C F Liljewalchs fellowship, Uppsala University.

Y. Sakakibara et al. (Eds.): ICGI 2006, LNAI 4201, pp. 344–345, 2006.

In general, two types of learning algorithms for FSMs can be distinguished, so-called *online* and *offline* algorithms. Online algorithms, such as Angluin's L^* algorithm, query strings to the teacher. Offline algorithms get a fixed set of examples and no further queries are allowed before computing a minimal FSM conforming to the examples. Typical algorithms of this type are based on a characterization in terms of a constraint satisfaction problem (CSP) over the natural numbers due to Biermann [BF72].

Faced with an inexperienced teacher, we cannot rely completely on Angluin's algorithm. We therefore define an algorithm that is a combination of an online algorithm and an offline algorithm and is based on [OS98]. Similar to Angluin's algorithm, we round off the information on the automaton in question by asking queries. As queries can be answered by *?*, we may not be able to complete the information as in Angluin's setting to compute an FSM directly. For this, we use Biermann's approach for obtaining an FSM based on the enriched information. Our combination is conservative in the sense that in case all queries are answered by either *yes* or *no*, we obtain the same efficiency as for Angluin's algorithm. Furthermore, the encoding in terms of CSP is optimized based on the information collected in Angluin's algorithm.

While in [OS01] an efficient implementation for solving the resulting CSP problem is explained, we give an encoding as a SAT problem featuring a simple yet—as the examples show—very efficient inference algorithm by employing powerful SAT solvers.

Actually, our approach is quite similar to the one proposed in [OS98] and [OS01]. The main difference are that we use SAT solvers for solving the corresponding CSP problem (which gives algorithm ABSAT) and that we additionally propose incremental consistency checks (ABSATi) and an incremental construction of the CSP problem (ABSATi2), which both improves the overall efficiency.

To validate our approach in practice, we have employed our techniques to the problem of reducing incompletely specified finite-state machines. We have implemented our extensions within the C++ program called BICA, used in [OS98] and have reexamined BICA as well as our three versions on the same set of examples studied in [OS98] (see Figure 1(b)).

The overall conclusion is that although the behavior of a SAT solver is not completely predictable, our algorithms ABSATi and ABSATi2 are, for many examples, competitive alternatives to BICA, which especially work on examples that are too complex for BICA.

References

[Ang87] Dana Angluin. Learning regular sets from queries and counterexamples. *Information and Computation*, 75:87–106, 1987.

[BF72] A. W. Biermann and J. A. Feldman. On the synthesis of finite-state machines from samples of their behaviour. *IEEE Transactions on Computers*, 21:592–597, 1972.

[GL06] Olga Grinchtein and Martin Leucker. Learning finite-state machines from inexperienced teachers. Technical Report TUM-I0613, TU München, 2006.

[OS98] A. L. Oliveira and J. P. M. Silva. Efficient search techniques for the inference of minimum size finite automata. In *String processing and information retrieval*, 1998.

[OS01] Arlindo L. Oliveira and João P. Marques Silva. Efficient algorithms for the inference of minimum size dfas. *Machine Learning*, 44(1/2):93–119, 2001.

Suprasymbolic Grammar Induction by Recurrent Self-Organizing Maps[*]

Fuminori Mizushima[1] and Takashi Toyoshima[1,2]

[1] Dept. Brain Science and Engineering
[2] Dept. Human Sciences
Kyushu Institute of Technology
2-4 Hibikino, Wakamatsu, Kitakyushu, Fukuoka 808-0196 Japan
mizushima-fuminori@edu.brain.kyutech.ac.jp, toyo@brain.kyutech.ac.jp

Abstract. A preliminary experimental result is reported on language identification tasks by Recurrent Self-Organization Maps (RSOM) with a context map layer, using English part-of-speech strings of variable length. With subsymbolic processing, RSOM suprasymbolically sublimed syntactic rules into a topological configuration.

1 Introduction

We experimented on language identification tasks by a Self-Organizing Map, equipped with recurrent connections from a context map layer (RSOM). We trained RSOM with strings of category symbols of English sentences. Then, we tested with novel strings of various lengths with possible recursions. RSOM was able to identify, with an average of more than 90% accuracy, grammatical strings and ungrammatical strings of random sequences of category symbols.

2 Architecture and Algorithm of RSOM

RSOM we have designed is shown in Fig.1. The competition layer L and the context layer M are both two-dimensional planes of 15×15 square units.

An input string $\boldsymbol{x}_i = \left[\boldsymbol{x}_{i,1}, \boldsymbol{x}_{i,2}, \boldsymbol{x}_{i,3}, \cdots, \boldsymbol{x}_{i,j}\right]$ is fed to the input layer, one symbol by one symbol, where $\boldsymbol{x}_{i,j}$ is a category symbol of k-dimensional vector, 3-dimentional, encoded in 3-bit vector, in this study. For training and testing, grammatical strings are generated with an elementary set of context-free rewriting rules for English sentences, with category symbols, N (nouns), V (verbs), A (adjectives/adverbs), P (preposition), C (complementizers), D (determiners), I (inflections), and a period mark.

The weights $\boldsymbol{W}^{in}_{L_{u,v}}$ between an input symbol $\boldsymbol{x}_{i,j}$ and all the units on L, and the weights $\boldsymbol{W}^{con}_{L_{u,v}}$ between all the units on L and the context vectors $\boldsymbol{C} = [\boldsymbol{C}_{M_{1,1}}, \boldsymbol{C}_{M_{1,2}}, \cdots, \boldsymbol{C}_{M_{u,v}}]$ of all the units on M, jointly determine the

[*] The research reported here is partially supported by a 21st COE Program (#J19), granted to Kyushu Institute of Technology, by MEXT, Japan. The standard disclaimers apply.

Y. Sakakibara et al. (Eds.): ICGI 2006, LNAI 4201, pp. 346–348, 2006.
© Springer-Verlag Berlin Heidelberg 2006

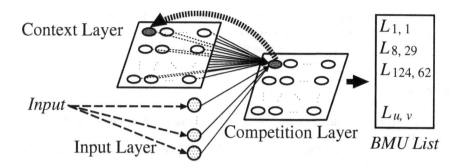

Fig. 1. A schematic RSOM architecture

Best Matching Unit (BMU) on L. The BMU $L^*_{u,v}$ at the state s will be the competition unit with the smallest sum of the Euclidean distances between the input vector $x_{i,j}$ and the weight $W^{in}_{L_{u,v}}$, and between C and the weights $W^{con}_{L_{u,v}}$, each of which is depreciated by the apportion rates γ and $(1 - \gamma)$, respectively, (1). The apportion ratio of γ to $(1 - \gamma)$ fixes the relative importance between the input and the context knowledge attained up to s, in determining $L^*_{u,v}$.

Once $L^*_{u,v}$ has been determined for an input $x_{i,j}$ at s, its weights and the weights of its neighboring units are updated toward the input vector and C. Then, C is attenuated by the rate β, and a dividend of the input vector at the rate of $(1 - \beta)$ is added to the context unit $M^*_{u,v}$, at the same coordinates as $L^*_{u,v}$, in accord with (2). This process is repeated for each category symbol, one by one. When an entire input string $x_i = [x_{i,1}, x_{i,2}, x_{i,3}, ..., x_{i,j}]$ is fed, all the weights are adjusted and the context layer M is flushed.

$$L^*_{u,v} = \arg \min_{L_{u,v}} \{\gamma \|x_{i,j} - W^{in}_{L_{u,v}}(s)\| + (1 - \gamma)\|C(s - 1) - W^{con}_{L_{u,v}}(s)\|\} . \quad (1)$$

$$\begin{cases} C_{M^*_{u,v}}(s) = \beta \times C_{M^*_{u,v}}(s - 1) + (1 - \beta) \times x_{i,j}(s) . \\ C_{M_{u,v}}(s) = \beta \times C_{M_{u,v}}(s - 1) . \end{cases} \quad (2)$$

Then, the next string is fed, one symbol by one symbol. When RSOM is trained with all the training strings, the next training cycle begins. The order of strings are randomized each cycle. After 100 training cycles are finished, all the weights are frozen, and all the training strings are fed one final time, determining BMUs for each symbol, without updating any weights. Instead, the system records the coordinates u, v of the BMUs for each symbol on the BMU List.

In simulation, if all the BMUs of a test string are on the BMU List, we judged the string as grammatical, while if any of the BMUs, even one, of a test string is not on the BMU List, the string is judged ungrammatical. With these criteria, we trained RSOM with 1,000 grammatical strings, and tested with 20,000 novel grammatical strings and 20,000 strings of random sequence of symbols, both of variable lengths. 10,000 of each were longer than the longest trainning string.

The result was that 98.73% of grammatical strings were judged correctly, and 86.43% of strings of random sequence of symbols were correctly judged ungramatical. That is, 92.58% accuracy on average.

References

[Gol67] Gold, E. M.: Language Identification in the Limit. Information and Control
         10 (1967) 447-474.
[Koh95] Kohonen, T.: Self-Organizing Maps. Springer-Verlag, Berlin Heidelberg New
         York (1995)

Graph-Based Structural Data Mining in Cognitive Pattern Interpretation*

Lidia Ogiela[1], Ryszard Tadeusiewicz[2], and Marek R. Ogiela[2]

[1] AGH University of Science and Technology, Faculty of Management,
Al. Mickiewicza 30, PL-30-059 Kraków, Poland
logiela@agh.edu.pl
[2] AGH University of Science and Technology, Institute of Automatics
{rtad, mogiela}@agh.edu.pl

Abstract. In this paper we will present opportunities for applying graph based linguistic formalisms for computer automatic understanding of meaning of wrist medical images. Thanks to the proposed method we can understand the merit content of the image even if the form of the image is very different from any known pattern. It seems that in the near future such technique may become one of the effective tools for semantic interpreting, and computer perception of visual medical data.

1 Introduction

In the paper we try to solve the automatic interpretation problem for selected class of medical images by application of linguistic approach using special kind picture description languages. A possibility to conduct such an analysis will be presented on the examples of analysis of patterns received during the examinations of wrist bones (fig. 1). Before coming to the interpretation of the changes it is necessary to preserve the sequence of operations like segmentation, skeletonization, and bone labelling [1,2]. The graphs obtained as a results are the starting point in the classification of morphological features by using graph grammars.

2 Picture Grammar Analysis

An example of understanding the morphological lesions of the shape with the use the graph grammars will be presented on analysis of the correctness between individual wrist bones on palm images. An intelligent interpretation of the analysed cases can enable the identification of additional wrist bones. It may also point to lack or lesions in the shape of bones as well as their synostoses with other wrist parts. An expansive graph grammar G_{exp} allowing describes the wrist bones is defined as presented on figure 1. The possibilities of describing image cases showing additional bones or showing synostoses can be recognised with the

---

* This work was supported by the AGH University of Science and Technology under Grant No. 10.10.120.39.

Y. Sakakibara et al. (Eds.): ICGI 2006, LNAI 4201, pp. 349–350, 2006.

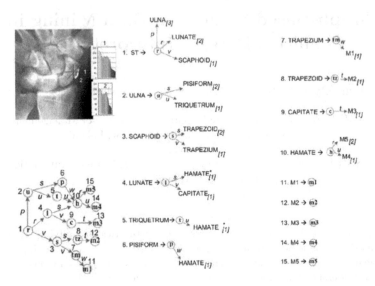

Fig. 1. Analysed image of the wrist bones with grammar describing of the correct build of wrist

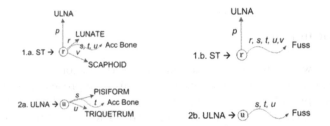

Fig. 2. Production sets describing: **A)** additional bones. **B)** Bone defects caused by bone joints or by bone dislocation.

use of additional rules specified on figure 2. As a result of structural analysis it is possible to describe pathogenesis of the deformations. Recognition was carried out on the basis of a set containing a few dozens images, and the efficiency of analysis exceeded the threshold of 90%.

References

1. Burgener, F. A., Kormano, M.: Bone and Joint Disorders. Thieme Stuttgart (1997)
2. Tadeusiewicz, R., Ogiela, M. R.: Medical Image Understanding Technology. Springer Berling-Heildelberg (2004)

Constructing Song Syntax
by Automata Induction

Kazutoshi Sasahara[1], Yasuki Kakishita[2], Tetsuro Nishino[2],
Miki Takahasi[1], and Kazuo Okanoya[1]

[1] Laboratory for Biolinguistics, RIKEN Brain Science Institute (BSI),
2-1 Hirosawa, Wako-shi, Saitama 351-0198, Japan
[2] Department of Information and Communication Engineering, Graduate School of
Electro-Communications, The University of Electro-Communications,
1-5-1 Chofugaoka, Chofu-shi, Tokyo 182-8585, Japan
sasahara@brain.riken.jp

We propose a new methodology for ethology in terms of automata induction. Recent studies on Bengalese finch reported unique features of its songs. As opposed to most other songbirds, the songs of the Bengalese finch are neither monotonous nor random; they can be represented by a finite automaton, which we call song syntax [3]. Juvenile finches learn songs from their fathers during a critical period. The song learning has a similarity to the grammatical inference from positive samples, which is known as Angluin's algorithm [1]. This is an induction algorithm for inferring certain subclasses of regular languages, which are known as k-reversible languages, from positive samples, where $k = 0, 1, 2, \ldots$. A regular language is k-reversible under the following condition: whenever two prefixes whose last k words match have a tail in common, then these prefixes have all tails in common. For each k, Angluin's algorithm provides a finite automaton that accepts the smallest k-reversible language, including the given finite positive sample within polynomial time.

In the previous studies, the songs were analyzed using the N-gram model, which does not ensure the uniqueness of the resulting automata from the given samples; therefore, appropriate N must be selected for each sample. In contrast, Angluin's algorithm provides a finite automaton accepting the unique (smallest) reversible language from a given song data; we can compare song syntaxes in different birds. The song syntaxes in two ways are dipicted in Fig.1.

To apply Angluin's algorithm to real song data, we introduce the following preprocessings:

- **Construct song units:** On the basis of acoustical properties, recorded songs (WAV format) converted to texts, which are delimited into song units at initial patterns (e.g. "ab" in Fig.1).
- **Reduction:** For the simplest description of song syntax, repeated song notes are reduced, incrementing the unit length of reduction, with the maximum limit of half the length of a song unit (e.g. abaaababb...→ababab...→ab...).
- **Denoising:** When constructing prefix-tree automata from song units, we calculate the transition probabilities of song notes at the branching points and eliminate transitions that are bellow a certain threshold (C_{cut}).

Y. Sakakibara et al. (Eds.): ICGI 2006, LNAI 4201, pp. 351–353, 2006.

- **Constrain k-reversibility:** Starting from $k = 0$, increase k, when the constructed song syntax still has backward transitions or self-loops [2].

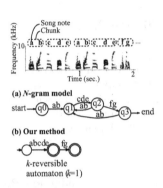

Fig. 1. The song syntaxes of Bengalese finch in two different ways. The letter string represents courtship song of a male Bengalese finch. (a) is constructed using N-gram model, and (b) is constructed using our method (1-reversible automaton).

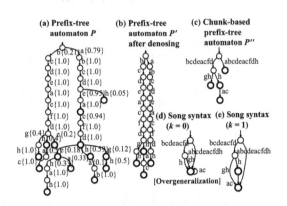

Fig. 2. Constructing song syntax. (a) Prefix-tree automaton P constructed from song units S'' (b) Prefix-tree automaton P' after denoising using $C_{cut} = 0.2$ (c) Chunk-based prefix-tree automaton P'' (d) Song syntax with $k = 0$ (e) Song syntax with $k = 1$ (see the text for detail).

In light of these procedures, we propose the constructing method of song syntax, where input is a song sample with bout S and output is a k-reversible automaton A that accepts S:

1. Construct a song unit sample S' from S.
2. Reduce repeated song notes in S' and include the result in S''.
3. Construct a prefix-tree automaton P from S'' (see Fig.2(a)).
4. Remove the transitions below cut-off level C_{cut} in P and include the result in P' (see Fig.2(b)).
5. Construct a chunk-based prefix-tree automaton P'' from P' (see Fig.2(c)).
6. Let $k = 0$.
7. Continue to merge states B_1 and B_2 where any of the following is true:
   - B_1 and B_2 have a common k-leader and the both are final states.
   - B_1 and B_2 have a common k-leader and transitions to B_3 with a common input (chunk).
   - There is a transition with a common input (chunk) to B_1 and B_2 from B_3.
8. Set the result in A'. If A' has repeated structures, then repeat step 7 with $k = k + 1$; otherwise, $A = A'$ (see Fig.2(d) and (e)).

Using the proposed method, we analyzed the songs of 10 Bengalese finches. As a result, we confirmed that our method could provide suitable song syntaxes for comparison between fathers and offsprings, and that song syntaxes could be represented as reversible automata with lower k-reversibility. Although the available data was not enough this time, the preliminary results indicated that our methodolgy is useful in ethology.

References

1. D. Angluin. Inference of Reversible Languages. *Journal of the Association for Computing Machinery*, 29(3):741–765, 1982.
2. R. C. Berwick and S. F. Pilato. Learning Syntax by Automata Induction. *Machine Learning*, 2(1):9–38, 1987.
3. K. Okanoya. Song Syntax in Bengalese Finches: Proximate and Ultimate Analyses. *Advances in the Study of Behavior*, 34:297–346, 2004.

Learning Reversible Languages with Terminal Distinguishability[*]

José M. Sempere

Departamento de Sistemas Informáticos y Computación
Universidad Politécnica de Valencia (Spain)
jsempere@dsic.upv.es
http://www.dsic.upv.es/users/tlcc/tlcc.html

Abstract. k-reversible languages are regular ones that offer interesting properties under the point of view of identification of formal languages in the limit. Different methods have been proposed to identify k-reversible languages in the limit from positive samples. Non-regular language classes have been reduced to regular reversible languages in order to solve their associated learning problems. In this work, we present a hierarchy of reversible languages which can be characterized by some properties related to the set of terminal segments of the automata (*terminal distinguishability*). Terminal distinguishability is a property that has been previously used to characterize other language families which can be identified in the limit from positive data. In the present work we combine reversibility and terminal distinguishability in order to define a new hierarchy of regular languages which is highly related to the k-reversible hierarchy. We will provide an efficient method to identify any given language in the hierarchy from only positive examples.

Definitions

Σ denotes an alphabet, Σ^* the infinite set of strings defined by Σ, Σ^l denotes the set of strings with length l. The reverse of any string u will be denoted by u^{inv}, and the set of segments of u with length k will be denoted by $seg(u, k)$. Given a finite automaton A, we denote the reverse automaton of A by A^{inv}. Given a finite automaton $A = (Q, \Sigma, \delta, I, F)$ and $q \in Q$, and given an integer value $k \geq 0$, we will say that $u \in \Sigma^k$, is a k-follower (k-leader) of q if $\delta(q, u) \neq \oslash$ (resp. $\delta^{inv}(q, u^{inv}) \neq \oslash$). A finite automaton A is *deterministic with lookahead* k if and only if for every three states q_1, q_2 and q_3, if $q_1, q_2 \in \delta(q_3, a)$, or $q_1, q_2 \in I$, then there is no common k-follower of q_1 and q_2.

k-reversible Languages with r-terminal Distinguishability: The $\mathcal{REV}(k, r)$ Class

Definition 1. *Let $A = (Q, \Sigma, \delta, I, F)$ be a finite automaton, and let k, r be integer values with $0 < r \leq k$. We will say that A is deterministic with lookahead*

---

[*] Work supported by the Spanish CICYT under contract TIC2003-09319-C03-02 and the Generalitat Valenciana GV06/068.

Y. Sakakibara et al. (Eds.): ICGI 2006, LNAI 4201, pp. 354–355, 2006.

k and r-terminal distinguishability iff for every three states q_1, q_2 and q_3, if $q_1, q_2 \in \delta(q_3, a)$, or $q_1, q_2 \in I$, then at least one of the following conditions holds:

1. *$\exists v_1 \in \Sigma^k$ being a k-follower of q_1 such that for all $v_2 \in \Sigma^k$ being a k-follower of q_2 $seg(v_1, r) \neq seg(v_2, r)$.*
2. *$\exists v_2 \in \Sigma^k$ being a k-follower of q_2 such that for all $v_1 \in \Sigma^k$ being a k-follower of q_1 $seg(v_2, r) \neq seg(v_1, r)$.*

Definition 2. *We will say that a finite automaton A is k-reversible with r-terminal distinguishability iff A is deterministic and A^{inv} is deterministic with lookahead k and r-terminal distinguishability.*

A language L is k-reversible with r-terminal distinguishability, with $0 < r \leq k$, if there exists a k-reversible finite automaton with r-terminal distinguishability A such that $L(A) = L$. We will denote the family of k-reversible languages with r-terminal distinguishability by $\mathcal{REV}(k, r)$. Observe that there exists narrow relation between the class $\mathcal{REV}(k)$ in Angluin's work [An82] and the class $\mathcal{REV}(k, r)$. The relationship between different language classes is showed through the following results.

Lemma 1. *For any $k > 0$, $\mathcal{REV}(k) \subsetneq \mathcal{REV}(k, k)$.*

Lemma 2. *For every integer values k and r such that $1 \leq r < k$, $\mathcal{REV}(k, r) \subset \mathcal{REV}(k, r + 1)$.*

Identifying $\mathcal{REV}(k, r)$ Languages in the Limit

In order to identify any $\mathcal{REV}(k, r)$ language in the limit we propose a modification of Angluin's algorithm [An82]. Observe that Angluin proposes the merging of two states (*blocks*) due to the following two criteria:

1. The two states produce non determinism
2. The two states have at least one transition with the same symbol to the same state and they have a common k-leader.

Here we propose an additional criterion which can be enunciated as follows: Two states (*blocks*) are merged if they have at least one transition with the same symbol to the same state and the conditions of definition 1 do not hold. The modified algorithm obtains the smallest language L such that L is in $\mathcal{REV}(k, r)$ and L contains the sample given as input. The proof follows from Angluin's work [An82]. The complexity of the modified algorithm is still polynomial, in fact $\mathcal{O}(C(k, r) \cdot n^3)$, where $C(k, r)$ is a constant that depends on the number of k-leaders of every state and the number of r segments.

Reference

[An82] D. Angluin. *Inference of Reversible Languages*. Journal of the Association for Computing Machinery. Vol 29 No 3, pp 741-765. July 1982.

Grammatical Inference for Syntax-Based Statistical Machine Translation

Menno van Zaanen[1] and Jeroen Geertzen[2]

[1] Division of Information and Communication Sciences
Department of Computing
Macquarie University
2109 Sydney, NSW, Australia
menno@ics.mq.edu.au
[2] Language and Information Science
Tilburg University
Tilburg, The Netherlands
j.geertzen@uvt.nl

Abstract. In this article we present a syntax-based translation system, called TABL (Translation using Alignment-Based Learning). It translates natural language sentences by mapping grammar rules (which are induced by the Alignment-Based Learning grammatical inference framework) of the source language to those of the target language. By parsing a sentence in the source language, the grammar rules in the derivation are translated using the mapping and subsequently, a derivation in the target language is generated. The initial results are encouraging, illustrating that this is a valid machine translation approach.

1 Introduction

Recently, there has been an increased interest in Statistical Machine Translation (SMT) [1]. SMT systems can be built using plain text only, which cuts down the development time of new MT systems immensely.

Some approaches that combine statistical learning with structured data by aligning syntax trees in two languages have been proposed previously [2, 3]. Here, we propose to use the Alignment-Based Learning framework [4] to generate these tree structures automatically.

For this task, the tree structures generated by ABL do not need to be linguistically correct. ABL only has to learn how words and phrases in one language (the source language) translate to words or phrases in another language (the target language).

2 Translation Using Alignment-Based Learning

Translation using Alignment-Based Learning (TABL) automatically learns a machine translation system from a sentence aligned bi-lingual corpus. ABL is applied to sentences in the source language and their translation in the target

Y. Sakakibara et al. (Eds.): ICGI 2006, LNAI 4201, pp. 356–357, 2006.

language. This structural information is used to analyse new source sentences and to generate translations.

TABL consists of two phases, the *training phase* and the *translation phase*. During the training phase ABL is applied to plain text translations in both the source and target language, creating a bracketed version of this data. Next, probabilistic context-free grammar (PCFG) rules are extracted [4, p. 53]. Grammar rules found in the derivations of both languages are stored, mapping each of the rules from the source language to the relevant (induced) rules in the target language. A concurrence score is also stored with each mapped rule.

During the translation phase, TABL parses a new source sentence using the PCFG of the source language. Next, using the mapping, the grammar rules of the derivation tree are mapped to those of the target language and a derivation in the target language is created. The yield of this derivation is the translation.

3   Results

To investigate how well this approach to machine translation really works, we applied TABL to different aligned corpora. Our test corpus showed over 80% correct translations, but about 50% of the sentences were not translated at all.

The reason why some sentences are not translated is that the target derivation is created by mapping from the source derivation. If the target derivation needs a different number of grammar rules, it cannot currently be generated.

4   Conclusion

In this article, we introduced TABL, a structure-based machine translation system, which demonstrates a novel application of the Alignment-Based Learning grammatical inference framework. Plain text collections that are aligned on sentence level are analysed, which results in grammars that show regularities in both languages. These regularities are then related between the languages. The resulting mapping illustrates how parts of sentences in the source language can be translated into equivalent parts in the target language.

Bibliography

[1] P. F. Brown, S.A. Della Pietra, V.J. Della Pietra, and R.L. Mercer. The mathematics of statistical machine translation: Parameter estimation. *Computational Linguistics*, 19:263–312, 1993.

[2] I. Dan Melamed. Statistical machine translation by parsing. In *42th Annual Meeting of the Association for Computational Linguistics; Barcelona, Spain*, 2004.

[3] Katharina Probst. *Automatically Induced Syntactic Transfer Rules for Machine Translation under a Very Limited Data Scenario*. PhD thesis, Carnegie Mellon University, Pittsburgh:PA, USA, 2005.

[4] Menno van Zaanen. *Bootstrapping Structure into Language: Alignment-Based Learning*. PhD thesis, University of Leeds, Leeds, UK, January 2002.

Author Index

Lecture Notes in Artificial Intelligence (LNAI)